The Contemporary Coast Salish:
Essays by Bruce Granville Miller

Edited by Bruce Granville Miller and Darby C. Stapp

Memoir 12

Journal of Northwest Anthropology

Richland, WA

2016

JOURNAL OF NORTHWEST ANTHROPOLOGY

FORMERLY NORTHWEST ANTHROPOLOGICAL RESEARCH NOTES

EDITORS

Darby C. Stapp
Richland, WA

Deward E. Walker, Jr.
University of Colorado

ASSOCIATE EDITORS

C. Melvin Aikens (University of Oregon), Haruo Aoki (University of California), Virginia Beavert (Yakama Nation), Don E. Dumond (University of Oregon), Don D. Fowler (University of Nevada), Raymond D. Fogelson (University of Chicago), Rodney Frey (University of Idaho), Ronald Halfmoon (Lapwai), Tom F. S. McFeat (University of Toronto), and Jay Miller (Lushootseed Research).

Julia G. Longenecker Operations Manager
Kara N. Powers Editorial Assistant
Heather Hansen Production Assistant

Composed by Northwest Anthropology LLC, Richland, WA; Printed by Create Space, On Demand Publishing LLC. Missing issue claim limit 18 months. For back issues and catalogue of prices contact Coyote Press, P O Box 3377, Salinas, CA 93912. <http://www.californiaprehistory.com>.

POLICY

Journal of Northwest Anthropology, published semiannually by Northwest Anthropology LLC in Richland, Washington, is a refereed journal and welcomes contributions of professional quality dealing with anthropological research in northwestern North America. Regular issues are published semiannually with additional memoirs issued as funds are available. Theoretical and interpretive studies and bibliographic works are preferred, although highly descriptive studies will be considered if they are theoretically significant. The primary criterion guiding selection of papers will be how much new research they can be expected to stimulate or facilitate.

SUBSCRIPTIONS

The subscription price is $45.00 U.S. per annum for individuals and small firms, payable in advance, $75.00 for institutional subscriptions, and $30.00 for students with proof of student status. Remittance should be made payable to *Northwest Anthropology LLC.* Subscriptions, manuscripts, change of address, and all other correspondence should be addressed to:

Darby C. Stapp
Journal of Northwest Anthropology
P.O. Box 1721
Richland, WA 99352-1721

telephone (509) 554-0441
e-mail dstapp@pocketinet.com
website www.northwestanthropology.com

MANUSCRIPTS

Manuscripts can be submitted in an electronic file in Microsoft Word sent via e-mail or on a CD to the Richland, WA, office. An abstract must accompany each manuscript. Questions of reference and style can be answered by referring to the style guide found on the website or to *Journal of Northwest Anthropology*, 47(1):109–118. Other problems of style can be normally solved through reference to *The Manual of Style,* University of Chicago Press. All illustrative materials (drawings, maps, diagrams, charts, and plates) will be designated "Figures" in a single, numbered series and will not exceed 6 x 9 inches. All tabular material will be part of a separately numbered series of "Tables." Authors will receive one free reprint of articles, memoirs, or full-issue monographs. Additional reprints may be produced by the author; however, they must be exact duplicates of the original and are not to be sold for profit.

Contents

Figures

Tables

Foreword

Injustice. Among the many things that trigger Bruce Miller's scholarly passion, this is without question the most salient. Let me illustrate. During one of the many fieldtrips we have taken together over the past quarter century, one incident stands out as a key to understanding the forces that drive the contributions of this book. One day, not long after the searing events of 9/11/2001 we were driving south from Vancouver, B.C. to visit with Bruce's friends, the leaders and community members of the Upper Skagit Tribe based in Sedro-Woolley, Washington. It is not a long drive—normally only about two hours, including the time it takes to cross the international border separating the U.S. and Canada. Bruce was driving, and I was the lone passenger. Since he made the trip often, he had a special NEXUS Pass that allowed easy transit for pre-approved commuters. I, on the other hand, had to exit the car and walk through the regular customs and immigration booth before rejoining Bruce and his car on the other side of the border. After clearing customs I proceeded to the lot where the car was parked, but there was no sign of Bruce. I waited patiently, and after what seemed like a very long time Bruce finally emerged with an angry scowl. He recounted that when asked if he had anything to declare he said "nothing"—just our lunches for the day. The officer asked to inspect our luggage and found my lunch bag containing a sandwich and an apple. This triggered the officer to ask Bruce to park the car and go inside for further inspection and questioning. It turned out that under the terms of the NEXUS pass system, pass holders were prohibited from bringing produce of any kind across the border into the U.S. and if they contravened this prohibition they could forfeit their Pass. Apparently, the border official decided to exercise his authority as an officer of the federal government to suspend Bruce Miller's NEXUS pass.

I felt awful to be the cause of this loss of privilege—a loss caused by my own ignorance and carelessness. If I had simply taken my lunch bag with me, I thought, none of this would have happened. I could easily have tossed the apple in the bin full of contraband and prohibited items and, then, no harm done. Bruce had a different view. During the remainder of our drive south to the Upper Skagit, he told me of many such incidents—and much more serious ones—that have characterized the experiences that many Coast Salish people from both sides of the border; encounters in their dealings with federal, state, and provincial authorities. Many of these stories lie at the heart of this book and they bring into sharp relief the enduring legacy of state power and legal systems and their role in negatively impacting the lives and livelihoods of generations of Coast Salish peoples. Chapter 18, The 'Really Real' Border and the Divided Salish Community, addresses how this arbitrary placement of an international border resulting from nineteenth-century colonial practices and intrusions continues to disrupt the relations among Coast Salish community and family members who happen to reside on different sides of this international boundary. Genuine injustices regularly erupt from this state power system and impact the personal, economic and spiritual lives of Coast Salish families. Coast Salish elders, dancers, and healers regularly have to cross the International border and bring with them materials that are essential to their ceremonial practices, including dance regalia, drums made from animal skins, and sometimes special foods. Some of these items are spiritually harmful and should never be shown to uninitiated members of the group or to strangers. This makes it very difficult at times for Coast Salish people to travel across the border because, even though protocols are in place, some officials on either side of the border have at times not known or have ignored them. Such incidents are much more serious than having one's apple confiscated or losing the NEXUS Pass privilege.

This selection of chapters spanning almost three decades of scholarship and representing an unusually productive career of research and writing is breathtaking in it scope and significance. The publisher is to be congratulated for bringing these chapters, published in a wide range of venues, all together in one place. This new and timely compendium will come to represent one of the finest examples of what has come to be known as "engaged ethnography"—an academic practice with real-world implications and outcomes. At its heart, Bruce Miller's work never shirks from addressing themes of inequality and injustice. We see this exemplified in the ways that power is wielded, whether social, political, economic or spiritual—both within Coast Salish communities and organizations and in their relations with the settler communities and organizations. This is not simply descriptive "objective" social science. As Bruce lays out in example after example, this work—this engaged anthropology—directly impacts court decisions and rulings, economic opportunities, and peoples' daily lives. Bruce Miller and his many students and colleagues through their ongoing work show that an anthropological approach can help to provide tools to both understand the historical roots of social injustices and to contribute to their resolution. That much of this work plays out in courts of law within the rigors of the justice systems in both Canada and the U.S. requires a scrupulous attention to detail and evidence. Many of the chapters in this volume show how this works in individual legal cases, whether dealing with fishing and hunting rights, movements across the international border, land claims cases, protection of spiritual locations and archaeological and historic places, gender discrimination, or arbitrary attacks against Indigenous people for simply trying to go shopping in their local Mall. Miller shows that ethnographies and oral histories, past and present, are increasingly used in legal cases, and they may be used in unpredictable ways—both in favor of and against the interests of Coast Salish peoples. This, he argues, means that we must be always aware that our work as anthropologists is never neutral and detached. This is true in the Coast Salish worlds and it is true in much of the rest of the world as well. This is one of the ways that Miller's work shows how Coast Salish anthropology can no longer be considered peripheral or somehow out of the mainstream as it was thought to be during much of the twentieth century. Instead, it is through the ongoing efforts of Miller and the many Coast Salish researchers—both Indigenous and non-Indigenous—that this region is retaking a central place in anthropological theory and practice.

It has been a privilege to witness, firsthand, the passion for justice that underlies Bruce's work. By reading these chapters, one cannot help but come away with a sense of the dynamic engagement that Miller's anthropology represents. I caution the reader, however, that if you should ever have occasion to travel with him across an international boundary—be sure to leave your contraband fruit and vegetables behind.

Michael Blake
Professor of Anthropology
University of British Columbia
Vancouver, BC
January 12, 2016

Preface

The *Journal of Northwest Anthropology* (JONA) is pleased to present *Memoir 12, The Contemporary Coast Salish: Essays by Bruce Granville Miller*. This publication represents a quarter century of research on the native people of the Pacific Northwest by Dr. Miller, currently a Professor of Anthropology at the University of British Columbia (UBC). Nineteen essays previously published in books or professional journals between 1989 and 2014 were selected for inclusion in this collection, supplemented by four new essays, section introductions, and a postscript. The previously published materials have been reproduced in their entirety, though changes in format and style have been made for consistency and readability; footnotes and endnotes have been converted to in-text citations where possible. Canadian spellings have been retained and Coast Salish spellings have been used as originally published.

Bruce Miller first came to the Pacific Northwest in 1976. His first involvement with the local Native population dates to his years in Tacoma, Washington, where he organized a public debate with the Puyallup Tribe, the City of Tacoma, and the Steilacoom Tribe over the very contentious issue of who owned the Port of Tacoma; the court eventually ruled in favor of the Puyallup. His interest in the Coast Salish dates to his years in Bellingham, Washington, where he had moved to pursue a Master's Degree in Anthropology at Western Washington University. Moving on to Arizona State University to pursue his doctorate, he completed his dissertation in 1989 entitled "A Sociocultural Explanation of the Election of Women to Tribal Office: The Upper Skagit Case." Dr. Miller returned to the Northwest in 1990, joining the UBC Faculty as an Assistant Professor of Anthropology. Focusing on topics such as gender, law, and relations with mainstream culture, Dr. Miller has contributed much to our knowledge of Northwest Indian peoples and the cultural dynamics that have aided and hindered their twentieth-century success.

The *Journal of Northwest Anthropology Memoir Series* strives to publish substantive anthropological material that will benefit the peoples of the Pacific Northwest. Among the works we seek are compilations of research generated by senior scholars and practitioners. The concept here is simple: allow the scholar to 1) select a sample of his or her publications for reprinting in the *Memoir*, 2) provide the context that led to publication, and 3) reflect on the impact that the publication has had on colleagues and the communities with whom they worked. The value and convenience of making a collection of publications available in one place is obvious; but more important to all of us is the power of reflection that emerges from such an effort. Our senior colleagues have spent a lifetime researching and applying their anthropological methods and theories. We provide a forum for them to reflect on their life's work and explain how their contributions relate to contemporary issues.

The Contemporary Coast Salish: Essays from Bruce Granville Miller represents our fourth publication of this genre. The tradition began with *Memoir 6, It's About Them, It's About Us, Its About You: A Decade of Papers from the Confederated Tribes of the Umatilla Indian Reservation (CTUIR) Cultural Resource Protection Program (CRPP)* (2002). This collection included the presentations and publications produced by the CTUIR CRPP between 1988 and 1998. Not only did the *Memoir* put the materials in one place at one time—most had never been published in any forum—but it also provided the program developers, Jeff Van Pelt and Michael S. Burney, time to reflect on the development of tribal resource protection in general—and the CRPP in particular—and share those thoughts with our readers. The formula was then followed with *Memoir 8, Rescues, Rants, and Researches: A Re-View of the Writings of Jay Miller* (2014), and *Memoir 10, Tribal Trio of the Northwest Coast* by Kenneth D. Tollefson (2015).

Other Memoirs in the series follow a different model, but are similar in their reflexive and comprehensive nature. *Memoir 7, A Festschrift in Honor of Max G. Pavesic*, edited by Kenneth C. Reid and Jerry R. Galm, is a collection of articles prepared by former students and colleagues of this well-known Idaho archaeologist. *Memoir 8, Sol Tax and Action Anthropology in 2012: The Final Word?* provided a contemporary review and assessment of action anthropology by various colleagues and admirers of Dr. Sol Tax; Dr. Tax had organized an important tribal fishing and hunting rights symposium at the 1972 American Anthropological Association (Walker 1968) and has also influenced a number of Pacific Northwest anthropologists, practicing and academic, thus explaining the relevance to Northwest anthropology. *Memoir 11, An Ethnographic Assessment of Some Cultural Landscapes in Southern Idaho and Wyoming*, by Deward E. Walker, Jr., Pamela Graves, Joe Ben Walker, and Dan Hutchison, provides a comprehensive discussion of the importance of cultural landscapes—a topic of increasing interest in cultural resource management today—along with detailed descriptions and color photographs of 35 landscapes of interest to the Shoshone, Paiute, and Bannock of the Duck Valley Indian Reservation.

With 2016 marking the 50th year of publication for the *Journal of Northwest Anthropology* (known as *Northwest Anthropological Research Notes* from 1967 to 1998), now is a good time to seek out future *Memoirs*. We encourage our readers to contact us to explore potential topics for *Memoirs* and to suggest this venue to their colleagues.

We have organized *The Contemporary Coast Salish: Essays by Bruce Granville Miller* into the following nine sections.

- Part I. Introduction
- Part II. Social Organization/Corporate Groups/Social Network
- Part III. Coast Salish Law
- Part IV. Gender and Political Life
- Part V. Coast Salish Relations with the Mainstream
- Part VI. The Border
- Part VII. Political Recognition
- Part VIII. Evidence Rules and Oral History
- Postscript.

An appendix is included that includes writings and presentations from Dr. Miller's career.

Several people were involved in the production of this *Memoir*. Kara Powers assisted with the book and cover design and overall quality control. Heather Hansen and Alexandra Martin assisted with conversion of the published material into word documents and proofing. David Payson conducted a technical editorial review.

Appreciation is expressed to the following publishers and journals for permission to republish the material: AltaMira Press*, American Behavioral Scientist, American Indian Culture and Research Journal*, *American Indian Quarterly, BC Studies, Ethnology, Pacific Northwest Quarterly,* University of Nebraska Press, UBC Law Review, *American Indian Quarterly*, University of British Columbia Press, and *Wicazo Sa Review*.

Darby C. Stapp
Co-Editor, *Journal of Northwest Anthropology Memoir Series*
Richland, Washington
January 2016

Part I
Introduction

In these essays I address crucial issues facing contemporary Coast Salish people and communities. Building on my own fieldwork, on the salvage ethnography of an earlier generation, and the work of present-day anthropologists, archaeologists, and historians, I describe current-day tribes and bands as composed of family corporate groups and detail their role in the transformations of gender and political systems. I examine tribal codes and courts, historical concepts and practices of justice, and the relations between the mainstream populations of British Columbia and Washington state and the Coast Salish themselves, including the circumstances of non-recognized tribes among the Coast Salish and world wide, the efforts to use oral traditions and the language of sacredness in court, and in media reporting. Engaging theories of borderlands and globalization, I write that studies of Coast Salish are constrained by the international border as are the people themselves, especially post September 11, 2001.

Figure 1. Bruce Miller making a presentation in 2009 on Aboriginal places in the Skagit Valley, Washington.

1

Currents in Coast Salish Research*

Early anthropologists, including those working on the West Coast with the Coast Salish (Figure 2), faced with the vast, complex array of Indigenous peoples of North America, developed concepts that enabled them to simplify the data, carry out analysis, and draw conclusions. These concepts, including the "culture area," the "watershed," and "seasonal rounds," have been fruitful and widely used, particularly in the early- and mid-twentieth century "recipe book" ethnographies of Coast Salish and other Northwest Coast peoples, which reported on categories such as life cycle, economic life, and spiritual life. But the concepts are also limiting because Coast Salish people have always travelled over mountain passes to work and live with relatives among the Interior Salish. Economic activity has always occurred outside of the patterned seasonal rounds, and beyond the watersheds where villages were located. This is not news to anthropologists, many of whom have pointed out the limitations, but the requirements of litigation have pushed anthropologists to introduce this point into their work and to rely less on—and even reject—the generalizations these concepts introduce. A recent outpouring of autobiographies and biographies (for example Harriette Dover Shelton's work, *Tulalip: From My Heart, An Autobiographical Account of a Reservation Community*) reinforces this point by showing the interactions of Coast Salish peoples across international borders, out of watersheds, beyond culture areas, and into real life (Shelton 2013).

Nevertheless, there is a long and successful history of ethnographic research among the Coast Salish peoples of the state of Washington and the province of British Columbia recently carried out by Wayne Suttles, William Elmendorf, Sally Snyder, Pam Amoss, Jay Miller, and others. These scholars built on the earlier work of Franz Boas and his students, including T. T. Waterman, and a number of ethnographically inclined amateurs. These anthropologists worked for decades with Coast Salish people, listening closely, and began to establish new, more analytically powerful ways of understanding the Indigenous peoples of the region. Suttles (1960) notably pioneered ecological anthropology and conducted detailed research concerning the economic activities of those he worked with, starting in the 1940s. Suttles carried on with his work for several decades, and reconstructed the lives of the ancestors of the Coast Salish. He and Elmendorf added the idea of social networks to their analyses, a theme picked up later by myself and by Jay Miller. The social network approach is considered in Part 1, Social Organization.

But there are some startling gaps. I experienced an epiphany when the Archaeological Society of British Columbia asked me to speak to them about sacred sites, a subject on which I had recently testified in court and written about in an academic journal. I scoured the notable ethnographic texts to see what had been written and found virtually nothing. I was certain that Coast Salish people had pointed out to the anthropologists the particular, exact locations of spiritual battles between shamans and transformers, for example. But these data were obscured by the anthropological interest in producing generalized notions, as in, "the Coast Salish do such and so." The particulars, however, are in the anthropologists' unpublished fieldnotes, in great detail. I borrowed a title from the linguist Dell Hymes and titled the talk "In Vain I Tried to Tell You," thinking of the Coast Salish peoples' efforts to communicate that their understandings of the

*Authored by Bruce Granville Miller in 2015.

landscape were of the ontologically distinct kind, rather than of the western scientific notion of laws. More recently the literature has shifted to foregrounding this perspective, for example Crisca Bierwert's *Brushed with Cedar* (1999). Past generations of scholars were certainly aware of Aboriginal perspectives but were obligated to write for publication within the traditions of their day.

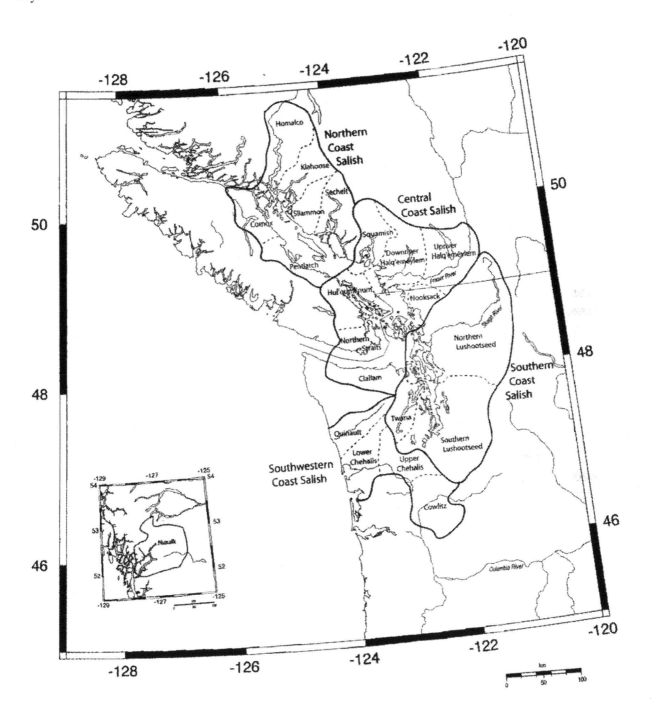

Figure 2. Map of the Northwest Coast of North America showing the major Coast Salish regions. (Map Credit: Bill Angelbeck).

Approaches today emphasize putting the Coast Salish into history, a trend perhaps best exemplified by Sasha Harmon's book *Indians in the Making: Ethnic Relations and Indian Identities around Puget Sound* (1998), a work that has inspired other historians, and anthropologists, by the effort to show how identity has been continually changing and adapting and responsive to shifts in public policy. In brief, we can now say, building on and moving beyond salvage ethnography, that Coast Salish society is emergent and historically contingent, just like everywhere else on the planet.

Although I have followed in the tradition of grounded fieldwork with Coast Salish people, my aim in my own work since the 1970s has not been primarily to reconstruct life in the contact period of the nineteenth century. Instead, I've applied these understandings to issues faced by and identified by Coast Salish people and communities in the contemporary period. Anthropology has now largely shifted from salvaging knowledge of earlier periods to the current day and I am not alone in this work. Others working with contemporary Coast Salish peoples within this perspective include Dan Boxberger, Crisca Bierwert, Brian Thom, Bill Angelbeck, and yet more. Keith Carlson and Paige Raibmon have added a new wrinkle to the work of historians by working intensively with oral historians of Coast Salish communities. They are among a new generation of historians trained to do this, in contrast to the generation before them, people such as Arthur Ray, who learned on the job.

Boxberger (2007) has pointed out that the anthropology of the Coast Salish has always been engaged with legal issues, and this remains true today. These legal problems include treaty-linked claims to land and resources in the U.S. as well as claims undertaken for rights and title in Canada. But the contemporary anthropology also aims to understand more broadly the rearrangement of relations with the mainstream population and the establishment of self-governance and sovereignty, arguably the dominant issue of the last several decades. The essays in this volume, particularly Part III, Coast Salish Law and Part V, Relations with the Mainstream, document the continual insistence by Coast Salish people on the use of their own laws and justice practices, even within the jurisdiction of the nation-state.

Because the social networks of the Coast Salish span the international border, and run all through the Salish Sea, with participants in marriages, winter ceremonials, and many other activities from both sides, two issues arise. First, my work considers Coast Salish in both countries and I suggest that the partitioning into two has been a problem, especially during the period of "small society" studies of the mid-twentieth century. Second, I examine the impact of the post-9/11 "hardened" international border on the lives of Coast Salish people. Here newer literatures on borders and border societies and on the transformations of the nation-state in a period of globalization, with the rapid flow of information and people, provide insights into how to approach these questions. A careful look at how Coast Salish respond shows both efforts at managing the problems of heightened surveillance by the nation-states and a disruptive fracturing. Several essays in Part VI, Borders, develop these points.

The fact that Coast Salish people live on both sides of the border creates a useful research tool that enables the identification of controllable variables. Despite many commonalities, such as the devastating effects of epidemics, communities have differences in contact history and the public policy directed towards them. I have used this variability to study the transformations of gender roles including the rise of Coast Salish women in tribal politics, which has occurred differently in the two countries. Initially I came to Puget Sound intending to study ethnicity and Coast Salish community life, perhaps along the lines of Natalie Robert's engaging study of the Swinomish community and the Skagit Valley, a 1975 dissertation at the University of Washington, but I found something else that interested me. Women were running the various tribal offices I visited and I wondered why and where the men were. This led to a study of tribal politics and gender centered on the Upper Skagit tribe, which I later expanded to include Coast Salish more broadly. Essays on these issues are included in Part IV, Gender and Political Life.

Theories of Social Organization

Here, with the help of the pioneering but obscure 1976 work of a University of Victoria faculty member, Kathleen Mooney (later Berthiaume), I began to understand how families groups were composed, progressed through a life cycle and eventually expired, and were then either reformed by a new generation of leadership (commonly siblings) or collapsed, with members re-affiliating with other families or departing the community. Elder members of the Upper Skagit community told me early in my dissertation work that there of "the four families of the tribe," as did younger members. But the lists of these families (these are commonly called by a last name even though not all members were so named) were not the same. This was, I determined, because both groups were identifying the large families of the social field of their youth.

Through interviews I found that the current family groupings, although created in the idiom of kinship, were not all co-resident and did not include all kin. But the families nevertheless supported one another in tribal elections, at fish camps, in gathering resources for ritual life such as naming ceremonies, and in competition with other families. For these reasons, I have referred to these groups as corporate families. Previous Coast Salish literature had emphasized lineal descent instead of how the contemporary working groups were actually composed. I now describe Coast Salish bands/tribes as collections of competing corporate family groups, which unite when faced with an external threat, following the lead of the old-fashioned British structural-functionalist anthropology of Evans-Pritchard (1940) and segmentary lineage systems. Nevertheless, the model shows its utility in understanding tribal/band elections.

In an early publication, my student Jen Pylypa and I pointed out that there are health implications for this form of social organization (Miller and Pylpa 1995). I had interviewed and become aware of several important tribal leaders who were without care in their old age because their own corporate group had collapsed, or rather exploded like a super-nova event, leaving them without help. This is predictable within the model of corporate group life-cycling I developed, a point that service providers could make use of. Tribal elections, too, could be explained with this model.

Those families at the largest point of expansion during the life-cycle were able to elect their members to tribal office. Smaller families could not and instead frequently supported what I called "technocrat" female candidates, those who linked families to the outside world of schools, hospitals, and banks, from their own or other small families. At this point I gathered the electoral results for Coast Salish bands in Canada and tribes in the U.S. and found that female electoral success is strongly correlated with size of band, size of average income, and the existence of large male income such as through fishing (Miller 1992). I was not yet aware that this trend towards the increasing participation of women in local level politics was a worldwide development. All of the essays in this *Memoir* reflect the significance of the family "corporate groups" that compose the contemporary Coast Salish nations.

I have tried to consider with archaeological colleagues what the time depth of this form of social organization might be, a question still unanswered. Recent literature has been critical of the over-reliance in archaeology of ethnographic models, and I agree with this critique (for example Grier 2007). But I also argue for the converse; that thinking through broader time scales might be useful in writing about contemporary communities. What do we know archaeologically that might reframe our thinking about today? With colleagues Bob Mierendorf, Bill Angelbeck, and Molly Malone we began to address this issue in preparing an historic atlas for the Upper Skagit community. We organized panels for the Northwest Anthropological Conference in 2014 and 2015 to present some of our ideas.

In the Upper Skagit Atlas (in press) I write,

> Among these themes is the tension between aggregation and disaggregation—that is, the people, longhouses and villages centralizing and dispersing. Another theme is the tension between egalitarian values and practices and social hierarchy. Related to these two themes is the movement between the presence of formal political positions, such as chiefly status, that could be passed down to children or laterally to brothers or other relatives, and the long-term resistance to any form of political authority. (Miller, in press)

The Upper Skagit, we argue, have engaged in creative tension around these points for a long time, well predating contact and visible in both archaeological data and in contemporary tribal electoral results. Part II, Social Organization is composed of essays on these issues. Essays in Part IV, Gender and Political Life, are also concerned with social organization.

Cultural Difference

In working with Coast Salish communities on contemporary issues, I have been repeatedly struck by the continuing importance of culture and cultural difference. Anthropology has engaged in an extensive critique of the concept of culture, with many arguing that it should be jettisoned altogether and others pointing to what they regard as exoticizing the "other." Culture, we now understand, is contested and not uniform in a society. The critiques are from both materialists and post-modern sources. Eric Wolf, for example, wrote,

> Concepts like 'nation,' 'society,' and 'culture' name bits and threatened to turn names into things. Only by understanding these names as bundles of relationships, and by placing them back into the field from which they were abstracted, can we hope to avoid misleading inferences and increase our share of understanding. (Wolf 1982:3)

But despite the critiques, I believe that members of Coast Salish communities continue to have distinctive understandings of the world, different from those of the mainstream, even while clearly understanding the non-Indigenous world (Figure 3).

In recent decades Coast Salish people have foregrounded the distinctions between themselves and the mainstream in making the case for the need for their own free-standing legal systems (which exist among Coast Salish in the U.S. but not in Canada), for their own health services and their own child welfare organizations, schools, and other forms of institutional self-governance. In responding to the contemporary period of "apology," I wrote that the Coast Salish already have their own practices of apology and the government or the churches in apologizing for the grievances of colonial domination ought to find out what these are to avoid making an already bad situation worse (Miller 2006; this essay is included in Part III). These are cultural differences. Coast Salish concepts of law and justice, as I point out in *The Problem of Justice* (Miller 2001), are not the same as the common law system, although they can co-exist, have important parallels and can be partially integrated into Canadian and American law (as noted in my 2011 book, *Oral History on Trial: Recognizing Aboriginal Narratives in the Courts*). Coast Salish culture must be

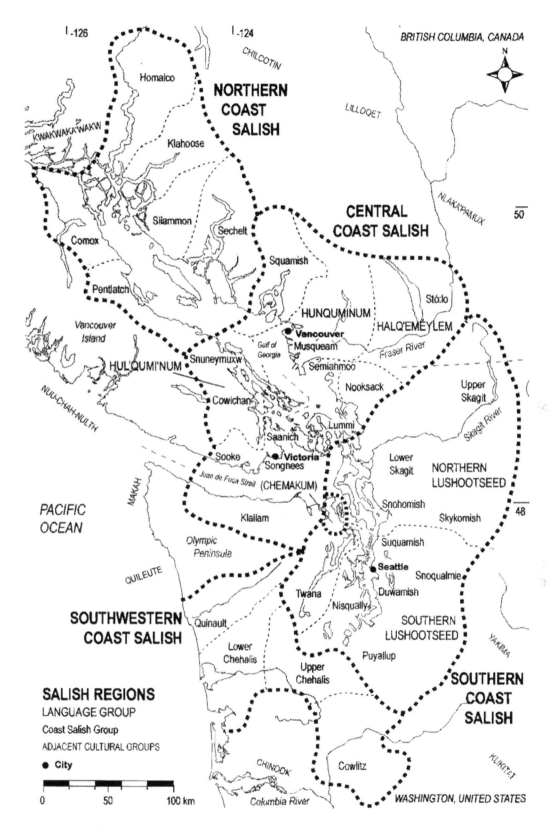

Figure 3. Coast Salish languages and the locations of contemporary tribes/bands. (Map Credit: Bill Angelbeck).

understood historically, and is changing and dynamic, but there are also threads running through it of great antiquity. My UBC colleague Michael Kew and I wrote a book chapter, "Locating Aboriginal Governments in the Political Landscape," in which we describe how cultural differences influence political processes, sometimes a point of confusion for mainstream bureaucrats and politicians (Kew and Miller 1999). Other essays in Part V, Relations with the Mainstream, point to how Coast Salish strategically manage these difficult relations in court, in the media, in politics, and other sites, and the forms of pressure they face. Part III, Coast Salish Law, includes essays about historic legal systems and the difficulties of translating them into the present-day.

The Violence and Exclusion of Contact and Beyond

My work with communities and with ethnohistoric research has led me to believe that Coast Salish histories with non-Indigenous peoples, the Americans, British, and Canadians, and even among themselves post-contact, have been far more violent than commonly understood or the descriptive ethnographies would suggest. Bill Angelbeck and Eric McLay have shown the military force of the Coast Salish in their studies of the Battle of Maple Bay (2011). I have also found this through my work with the Lamalchi descendant community (known as the Hwlitsum, with whom I have done oral history work over the last decade), who opposed the British Navy, driving gunboats from their bay in a battle in 1863. But even less well understood is the extent to which Coast Salish peoples have been displaced, segregated, and made the object of pioneer self-glorification by implications that Indigenous people stand in the way of a new society built around the values of progress and hard work. The settler population restricted the movement of Coast Salish peoples by controlling them on reserves/reservations, pushed them off settlements to create national forests and parks, took over resource stations, and regulated their movements in cities. These practices have not ceased.

Regarding this later point, I came to understand the critical importance of these efforts at control through my work in the B.C. Human Rights Tribunal, particularly in the case of *Radek v Henderson et al.* Gladys Radek, while not Coast Salish (she is Tsimshian), lived in Coast Salish territory in Native Housing in downtown Vancouver. There she observed Native people (to use a common Canadian phrasing) being pushed around and mistreated in a mall and she brought this issue to the tribunal. Her lawyer hired me and I attempted to explain to the tribunal the historic grievances suffered by Coast Salish and other Indigenous peoples of the territory, and how this relates to today (Miller 2003).

In brief, Radek and other Indigenous peoples were sometimes physically restrained from walking in a public mall, with security personnel even following them into bathrooms, demanding to see their money, or forcing them to walk across the street. The guards were trained to remove "suspicious" people. I pointed out that since these guards were raised in an environment in which negative stereotypes of Native people predominated, Native people would be differentially regarded as "suspicious" and removed.

In the twenty-first century, then, Indigenous people of Vancouver, in some situations, could not enter public places. This is nothing new, as sociologist Renisa Mawani (2010) has pointed out. Later I gave testimony in *Pivot v Downtown Ambassadors* regarding the efforts of a quasi-police group, the "Ambassadors," and the implications of their demands that Aboriginal street people move along so that tourists might not see them. Pivot Legal Society, which brought this case, lost, but won on appeal to the Supreme Court of British Columbia.

In her *Reasons for Judgment* in the case of *Vancouver Area Drug Users v. British Columbia Human Rights Tribunal* (May 10, 2015), Supreme Court justice Madame Justice Sharma ruled that the Downtown "Ambassadors" Program, which operated in the Downtown Eastside, differentially discriminated against homeless Aboriginal people. She rejected the judgment in the Human Rights Tribunal that there was "insufficient evidence to prove a *prima facie* case of discrimination because there was no evidence of a nexus between any adverse impact on homeless people and the race, colour, ancestry, mental or physical condition of anyone." Instead, she relied on my testimony showing this nexus through stereotyping by the "Ambassadors" in the absence of statistical evidence, testimony by Aboriginal people, or the intention to discriminate. In my expert report and direct testimony, I analyzed the instructions given the Ambassadors and their reports of interactions with homeless people. Justice Sharma wrote, paragraph 104, "The bottom line of Dr. Miller's evidence is that the behaviours on which the Program focused are behaviours that co-exist with members of the Class." She referred the Tribunal back to the approach to determining discrimination I took in *Radek v Henderson*, the earlier Human Rights Tribunal decision. This is now the law of British Columbia.

My approach to testimony in *Radek* was founded on spending time in Coast Salish communities. This included including eight summers in residence in Stó:lō territory residing in the Richard Malloway longhouse with the UBC ethnographic field school founded by Julie Cruikshank and myself, and a year of work as an Early Childhood Educator at Upper Skagit, talking with band members, and listening to their conversations. I learned of the continuous oppressive practices of surveillance of the Coast Salish by police, social workers, and others of the group of officials, the disciplinary powers that Foucault (1977) writes operate at the capillaries. I later spoke to a group of senior administrators at UBC, the university where I am employed, and explained that Coast Salish and other First Nations students find the campus of UBC to be unwelcoming and foreign to them, which is a form of racial segregation. They were surprised to hear that. Anthropologists, historians, legal scholars, and sociologists, among other academics, are beginning to understand the significance of these forms of malign surveillance and rejection of Aboriginal peoples and it is worth underscoring its role in the history of contact.

At present I am conducting a study of the B.C. Human Rights Tribunal to try to understand if it has efficacy for Indigenous people or might be better regarded as an institution that is too bureaucratic, legalistic, and time and money-consuming to be meaningful. Preliminarily, after examining all of the cases in which the tribunal has rendered judgments and pulling out those involving Aboriginal people, I believe that the tribunal is largely irrelevant, except that transformative cases such as *Radek* have occurred.

Boxberger (1989), employing a core/periphery model derived from world systems theory, made a convincing and powerful case for exclusion in documenting how the Lummi fishermen were incorporated into the salmon fishery when the non-Native population was unavailable, such as during World War II, and excluded when it became possible and convenient. We need, as scholars of the Coast Salish, to work at all scales and registers, to do more of this sort of work in all domains—in fisheries, in city downtowns, in hospitals (where First Nations people commonly encounter racism), in universities, and elsewhere. We are long past and far away from salvage anthropology, but we still need that early work to understand the perspective of today's people, including those facing oppressive surveillance and exclusion.

Understanding the Contact Period and Implications for the Present

The anthropologist Gerald Sider recently published *Skin to Skin: Death and Life for Inuit and Innu* (2014), which concerns Inuit and Innu Indigenous peoples of Canada. He argues that what we know ethnographically as their traditional cultures and which was documented in the mode of salvage anthropology, were, in reality, adaptations to the semi-starvation and starvation brought on by the policies and practices of the Canadian state, the Hudson's Bay Company, and the Mennonite missionaries. These groups, Sider writes, used the withholding of food to control populations. There is new academic interest in starvation in residential schools, in communities, and elsewhere. This practice of starvation and food-withholding certainly occurred among the Coast Salish, for example, in the concentration camps established during the so-called Treaty Wars of the 1850s and in residential schools. The Coast Salish men, arrested for illegal fishing and hunting in the period from the 1930s until the Boldt decision in the 1970s restored fishing rights, were themselves facing food shortages derived from the loss of access to their historic economic practices.

Relatedly, Wilson Duff (1964) made a start at understanding the role of epidemic disease in eroding Coast Salish peoples' control of their own lands. An important journal article by Guilmet et al. (1991) followed up some years later. This is not to suggest that the task of anthropology is to document disaster, but that we can recalibrate our understanding and make clearer the distance tribal communities have traveled in their efforts to reestablish their sovereignty.

In brief, in the anthropological study of the place of Coast Salish people in the contemporary world, I suggest, we should ground our work in the lives of people and the community and in understanding and accounting for the forces of segregation, discrimination, and oppression that Coast Salish people have experienced. Too many times in giving testimony in human rights tribunals and courts, I have encountered "experts" for the state or Crown who have never been in a Coast Salish community, know little or nothing of their historic experience, and believe they can provide relevant testimony simply from what they have read. In one instance, the expert for the state of Washington derived his testimony solely from reading the *Handbook of North American Indians,* Volume 7, *Northwest Coast.* He was not even the worst.

In a landmark Canadian case called *Delgamuukw*, 1997, the appeals court judge concluded that oral history should have the "same footing" as written history. This distinctive, landmark ruling was met by an effort by the Crown (the Canadian federal Department of Justice) to hire an expert who contrived a way to make oral history virtually useless in court and succeed in more than a dozen cases across Canada. He argued such things as this: tribal oral historians who read the anthropology and history of their community are not necessarily the recipients of an unbroken generation-to-generation transmission of oral traditional materials and are therefore contaminated and can either not be accepted as oral historians or their testimony given significant weight. Further, oral traditions once committed to paper are like any other document, amenable to standard historiographic methods and can be understood without the context of Indigenous understandings of their own oral materials. It seems to me particularly malicious, as a matter of national practice, to systematically dispossess Indigenous nations and later hire experts to render grotesque, uninformed misrepresentations of their histories and lives in a period when these nations can finally attempt to reclaim their rights and title.

I wrote to the court about various misreadings of the literature undertaken by this "expert" and pointed to real examples of tribal oral historians to help the court understand how oral historians work. I profiled Sonny McHalsie (Naxaxalhts'i), the Stó:lō oral historian, for this purpose. I told McHalsie about the issue of contamination raised by the Crown expert and asked his reaction to such a proposition. McHalsie responded by saying that when he reads what Wilson Duff (or some other anthropologist or historian) wrote based on an interview with an elder, he was trying to figure out what the elder actually said rather than what the academic wrote. In short, McHalsie, far from being seduced by the anthropology or history of the Stó:lō (virtually all of which he has read), and reliant on that work, forms his oral histories from what his elders have told him. All of this is discussed in my book, *Oral History on Trial* (Miller 2011).

Early anthropologists and the subsequent generation of Suttles and others, in particular Sally Snyder (1964), did a magnificent job of recording oral histories, which are of tremendous use to communities now in litigation and engaged in re-embracing their own traditions. Molly Malone (2013) pointed out that although there are few oral historians today who can give long and complete narratives, mythology, and family histories are still told in various forms and in various ways. Although partial, they still convey meaning, and as Vi Hilbert pointed out, are there when people are ready to embrace them. Part VIII, Evidence Rules and Oral History, takes up the problem of orality and literacy in a essay arguing that the Vancouver Island "Douglas Treaties" of the 1850s are themselves oral histories.

Positive Science and Experience-Near Anthropology

There is an important place for what might be called positivist social science in working with Coast Salish people and in anthropology. I hope that my studies of gender and tribal/band elections in Part IV make that point. But there is also a place for a different sort of scholarship, one in which rationality is not central. Rather, *experience-near* anthropology, too, has a role. This is research that builds on other senses, what the historian of religion Karen Armstrong (2010) refers to as mythos, which, she says, has been paired with logos, as fundamental human forms of understanding. Stated differently, this is when the single-minded pursuit of data is momentarily set aside "and the opportunity to enter deeply into the world of our hosts was embraced . . . this led to insights and knowledge that redefined the relationship with our hosts, deepened our ability to interact with them in more meaningful ways, and opened the door to epistemological and ontological issues that begged to be addressed" (Goulet and Miller 2007:1).

One tribal cultural advisor of my acquaintance told me that he came to distrust an anthropologist who informed him he was an atheist. This meant, the advisor believes, that this anthropologist could not comprehend Coast Salish spiritual concepts and practices, absent any experience with spiritual life. I am not sure if this is true, and it violates something of the underlying anthropological premise of commensurability, but I believe that it is true that rational thought is far from the totality of the human ability to learn and experience. What if we took Coast Salish epistemology seriously rather than explaining it away with functionalist arguments? This is not to argue for a literalist understanding of cosmology (to take an example from Christianity, that God created the earth in six days). Rather, it is to understand that historically, and to a good extent today, Coast Salish culture was permeated with the spiritual concerns and their universe full of spirit beings who intersected with humans. From the moment of birth until long past death, Coast Salish practices are informed by this perspective. Even today, we cannot quite get it right without grasping that. I do not think this *experience-near* approach is incompatible with foregrounding the devastation of colonization. Rather, the two can work together. We can use our empathetic insights to grasp the meaning of the material and the political.

Further, we might more forcefully use our understandings of the Coast Salish to comment on the pressing issues facing Indigenous peoples around the world. In my work with non-recognized bands of Coast Salish in both the U.S. and in Canada, I came to realize that the discourses surrounding identity and recognition, and the processes for gaining recognition by the state, were largely misguided, but in quite different ways. In *Invisible Indigenes* (Miller 2004) I used what I had learned in these two countries to examine what was happening globally. In brief, in an era of rising Indigenous populations and in enhanced resource extraction in the marginal areas into which Indigenous peoples have been pushed historically, states have found it convenient to reduce the number of Indigenous peoples. They have done this by "erasure by accountants," to borrow a phrase. This has happened all over the globe in different ways. Indigenous communities in Taiwan and Brazil (these are two I am aware of) have benefited by knowing how this works elsewhere and in preparing to defend themselves from the loss of their land and their community itself. Chapter 22 in Part VII considers federal recognition.

Our times, today and for the last few decades, have been shaped by the reemergence of Coast Salish self-governance. When I began my work with the communities, none, or virtually none of the present tribal centers and the programs housed in them had yet been built. Programs of the repatriation of ancestors from museums and academic collections to Coast Salish communities are happening now, in our time. All of this makes it enormously interesting to live and work in the Coast Salish world. It is an important time today and the grounded perspective and methods of anthropology enable us to make the kinds of contributions few other disciplines attempt. One can only wonder what the next fifty years will bring.

References Cited

Angelbeck, Bill and Eric McLay. 2011. The Battle at Maple Bay: The Dynamics of Coast Salish Political Organization through Oral Histories. *Ethnohistory*, 58(3):359–392.

Armstrong, Karen. 2010. *The Case for God*. New York: Anchor Books.

Bierwert, Crisca. 1999. *Brushed* by *Cedar, Living by the River: Coast Salish Figures of Power*. Tucson: University of Arizona Press.

Boxberger, Daniel L. 1989. *To Fish in Common: The Ethnohistory of Lummi Indian Salmon Fishing*. Lincoln: University of Nebraska Press.

——— 2007. The Not So Common. In *"Be of Good Mind": Essays on the Coast Salish*, edited by Bruce Miller, pp. 55–81. Vancouver B.C.: UBC Press.

Duff, Wilson. 1964. The Indian History of British Columbia, Vol. 1: The Impact of the White Man. *Anthropology in British Columbia Memoirs*, 5. Victoria: University of British Columbia Museum.

Evans-Pritchard, E. E. 1940. *The Nuer*. Oxford: Clarendon Press.

Foucault, Michel. 1977. *Discipline and Punish: The Birth of the Prison*. New York: Pantheon Books.

Goulet, Jean-Guy and Bruce Granville Miller, editors. 2007. *Extraordinary Anthropology: Transformations in the Field*. Lincoln: University of Nebraska Press.

Grier, Colin. 2007. Consuming the Recent for Constructing the Ancient: The Role of Ethnography in Coast Salish Archaeological Interpretation. In *"Be of Good Mind": Essays on the Coast Salish*, edited by Bruce Miller, pp. 284–307. Vancouver B.C.: UBC Press.

Guilmet, George M., Robert T. Boyd, David L. Whited, and Nile Thompson. 1991. The Legacy of Introduced Disease: the Southern Coast Salish. *American Indian Culture and Research Journal*, 15:1–32.

Harmon, Alexandra. 1998. *Indians in the Making: Ethnic Relations and Indian Identities around Puget Sound*. Berkeley: University of California Press.

Kew, J. E. Michael and Bruce G. Miller. 1999. Locating Aboriginal Governments in the Political Landscape. In *Seeking Sustainability in the Lower Fraser Basin,* edited by Michael Healey, 47–63. Vancouver: Institute for Resources and the Environment, Westwater Research.

Malone, Molly. 2013. Where the Water Meets the Land: Between Culture and History in Upper Skagit Aboriginal Territory. Ph.D. dissertation, Department of Anthropology, University of British Columbia.

Mawani, Renisa. 2010. *Colonial Proximities: Crossracial Encounters and Juridical Truths in British Columbia, 1871–1921*. Vancouver, B.C.: UBC Press.

Miller, Bruce Granville. 1992. Women and Politics: Comparative Evidence from the Northwest Coast. *Ethnology*, 31(4):367–383.

———— 2001. *The Problem of Justice: Tradition and Law in the Coast Salish World.* Lincoln: University of Nebraska Press.

———— 2003. Report to the B.C. Human Rights Tribunal Regarding *Radek v Henderson*, July 20.

———— 2004. *Invisible Indigenes: The Politics of Non-Recognition.* Lincoln: University of Nebraska Press.

———— 2006. Bringing Culture In: Community Responses to Apology, Reconciliation, and Reparations. *American Indian Culture and Research Journal*, 30(4):1–17.

———— 2011. *Oral History on Trial: Recognizing Aboriginal Narratives in the Courts.* Vancouver: UBC Press.

Miller, Bruce Granville, Bill Angelbeck, Molly Malone, Robert Mierendorf, Jan Perrier. (in press). *Upper Skagit Historical Atlas.* Sedro-Woolley, Washington: Upper Skagit Tribe.

Miller, Bruce G., and Jen Pylypa. 1995. The Dilemma of Mental Health Paraprofessionals at Home. *American Indian and Alaska Native Mental Health: The Journal of the National Center*, 6(2):13–33.

Mooney, Kathleen. 1976. Social Distance and Exchange: The Coast Salish Case. *Ethnology,* 15(4):323–346.

Roberts, Natalie A. 1975. A History of the Swinomish Tribal Community. Ph.D. dissertation, Department of Anthropology, University of Washington.

Shelton, Harriette Dover with Darleen Fitzpatrick, editor. 2013. *Tulalip: From My Heart, An Autobiographical Account of a Reservation Community.* Seattle: University of Washington Press.

Sider, Gerald. 2014. *Skin* for *Skin: Death and Life for Inuit and Innu.* Chapel Hill, NC: Duke University Press.

14

Snyder, Sally. 1964. Skagit Society and its Existential Basis: An Ethnofolkloristic Reconstruction. Ph.D. dissertation, Department of Anthropology, University of Washington

Suttles, Wayne. 1960. Affinal Ties, Subsistence, and Prestige Among the Coast Salish. *American Anthropologist,* 62(2):296–305.

——— editor. 1990. *Handbook of North American Indians.* Vol. 7, *Northwest Coast.* Washington, D.C.: Smithsonian Institution.

Wolf, Eric 1982. *Europe and the People without History.* London: University of California Press.

Cases Cited

Reasons for Judgment. *Delgamuukw v British Columbia* [1997] 3 S.C.R. 1010

Reasons for Decision. *Radek v. Henderson Development (Canada) and Securiguard Services (No. 3),* 2005 BCHRT 302.

Reasons for Judgment. *Vancouver Area Drug Users v. British Columbia Human Rights Tribunal,* 2015 BCSC 534.

Part II
Theories of Social Organization

These essays present a theory of social organization that foregrounds the creation of working groups of related peoples, which I call corporate family groups. My claim is that contemporary state-recognized bands and tribes are composed of these competing corporate groups. These groups of relatives support each other in spiritual life (such as entry into the winter ceremonial, naming, and memorials), and support members for tribal political office. They convey information internally. But they are not clans and are temporal with predictable life cycles, with implications for politics, health, and other domains. The first entry, Chapter 2, is the Introduction to my edited volume, *"Be of Good Mind": Essays on the Coast Salish*, which contains, in part, a discussion of the corporate group and the social networks that contain them. The second, Chapter 3, is also from a book, *Seeking Sustainability in the Lower Fraser Basin: Issues and Choices*, edited by Michael Healey; my colleague Michael Kew and I write about how outside institutions, including governments, might respectfully engage with Coast Salish political leaders, who are themselves acting within the family system. Chapter 4, *Creating Chiefdoms: The Puget Sound Case*, a journal article written by myself and Daniel Boxberger, takes up issues of social organization in the mid-nineteenth century, at the time of the Treaty of Point Elliott. This was a period of rapid change in life in Puget Sound, with the consolidation of villages and the creation of chiefdoms in some instances. Boxberger and I were concerned that theories of Coast Salish social organization of the period carefully reflected Aboriginal life on the ground because these anthropological theories created standards that would have to be met in legal processes, including federal recognition. Inadequate theories would create standards of evidence that could not be satisfied. Social organization, we wrote, must be put into history and understood as dynamic and changing.

Taken together, these chapters argue for a Coast Salish version of social organization that is grounded in the corporate family and in place (and in spiritual life), but flexible enough to address changing conditions. I build on several levels of analysis, from family cycling to regional networks. Historically, Coast Salish people have been able to act collectively to repulse raiders, such as in the Battle of Maple Bay, but without regional formal political or legal authorities or structures.

Journal of Northwest Anthropology, Memoir 12:16–38 (2016)

2

Introduction to *"Be of Good Mind": Essays on the Coast Salish**

Why a Coast Salish Volume?

The late 1980s and early 1990s was a watershed period in the study of the peoples and communities of western Washington and British Columbia, who, following the name of the language family to which they belong, are known collectively as the Coast Salish.[1] During that period, Wayne Suttles' (1987) *Coast Salish Essays* was published, and in 1990 his edited *Handbook of North American Indians,* Volume 7, *Northwest Coast,* appeared in print. As subsequent chapters show, Suttles has been enormously influential, and while he later published additional materials, including a massive grammar of the Musqueam language in 2004, the *Essays* and the *Handbook* are the high-water mark of his approach. Suttles' dissertation work, which he conducted in the 1940s, and his later publications reveal his interest in the anthropological "four-fields" approach (ethnology, linguistics, archaeology, and, with less emphasis, physical anthropology). The preface to his dissertation makes clear how he would go about understanding Coast Salish society:

> In the summer of 1946 when the Anthropology Department of the University of Washington began archaeological work in the San Juan Islands, I spent a few days trying to get what ethnographic information I could from Indians living in and around the islands, information which would be of use to archaeologists. At the time my purpose was merely to determine who occupied the islands in most recent times and to get the location of village and camp sites. But as this work progressed, I came to realize the necessity for getting as full an account as possible of the specific activities that went on at each place. My interest extended first to subsistence and then to the relation of economy to the whole culture of the peoples of the area. (Suttles 1951:i)

His dissertation project led Suttles to pioneer in the emerging field of cultural ecology (described by David Schaepe in Chapter 8 [Miller 2007]), but he retained a broad, holistic frame of reference, and his *Essays* reveals an interest in religion, art, adaptation to contact, and comparative studies of Northwest Coast peoples, among other topics. Of particular interest, though, is his emphasis on regional social networks—on understanding social organization through viewing the Coast Salish world as unified in several senses. "Affinal Ties, Subsistence, and Prestige among the Coast Salish," first delivered as a paper in 1959 and published in 1960, for example, shows the connections between subsistence and prestige economic activities (including potlatching) and the kinship system as well as how Coast Salish people in one region are connected to those elsewhere (Suttles 1960). William Elmendorf, another major scholar in Suttles' cohort, also embraced and developed this theme, particularly in his influential essay "Coast Salish Status Ranking and Intergroup Ties" (Elmendorf 1971). In Chapter 4 (Miller 2007), Chief Rocky Wilson employs this language of social networks, thus situating his own community within the larger Coast Salish world. Crisca Bierwert does the same thing in Chapter 6 (Miller 2007), where she discusses webs of kinship.

One could argue that Suttles' work clearly established both the significance of the study of Coast Salish peoples and the relevance of viewing a set of communities under the rubric of "Coast Salish" (although this term did not originate with him)—a topic historian Alexandra Harmon considers in Chapter 1 (Miller 2007). Previously, the Coast Salish region had suffered as an area of academic interest, not receiving the same attention as did other areas of the Northwest Coast. The Aboriginal occupants of the region were thought to be of less importance than were the Aboriginal occupants of other areas because they had been subject to early and intense assimilationist pressures by the settler populations, which eventually created Seattle, Vancouver, Victoria, Tacoma, and other large communities. For many who worked within a salvage paradigm (which was based on the conviction that Aboriginal life and peoples would soon disappear and that, therefore, any distinctive socio-cultural features should quickly be recorded), the region seemed less than fruitful, although descriptive ethnographic studies were conducted for the Klallam, Snoqualmie, Lummi, Skagit, and others. Typically, these "recipe" books were organized around reporting on a range of topics—curing, kinship, material culture, technology, oral traditions, and so on—rather than around advancing theoretical notions regarding the region. Real, individual people were largely absent, and, in their place, we were presented with a normative culture.

In addition, the Coast Salish world suffered from being regarded as a "receiver area"—an area that received cultural developments that had been created by supposedly "core" Northwest Coast groups such as the Wakashan speakers of the west coast and north end of Vancouver Island and the adjacent B.C. mainland. Suttles disputed this and theorized ways in which one might understand Coast Salish culture and the presence of dispersed, bilateral kin groups as a development related to local ecology rather than as the absence of a matrilineal clan system (which characterized groups further up the coast). The Coast Salish have commonly been depicted as the victims of raids by the more aggressive, better organized, and (implicitly) more important tribes to the north. In Chapter 9 (Miller 2007), Bill Angelbeck engages archaeological, ethnohistorical, and other materials to counter such claims and, in so doing, advances a more nuanced view of the Coast Salish. A final point, raised by Harmon (Chapter 1 [Miller 2007]), is that the concept "Coast Salish" may be too narrow. In Chapter 3 (Miller 2007), for example, Sonny McHalsie reveals the extent to which he and his ancestors maintained important relations beyond the Coast Salish world. Nevertheless, Harmon concludes, and both McHalsie and Rocky Wilson confirm, that affiliations within what we now know as the Coast Salish world were significant.

One could argue that Suttles created an orthodox view of the communities that had long been viewed as comprising a subregion of the larger Northwest Coast culture area. My intention here is not to identify Suttles as acting alone—a number of others of his generation and the one before (e.g., Erna Gunther, Marius Barbeau, Homer Barnett, June Collins, Diamond Jenness, Sally Snyder, Helen Codere, Wilson Duff, Marian Smith, and William Elmendorf) focused specifically on the Coast Salish in at least some of their publications and had much to say on a variety of issues. By his own account, in his student days Suttles was but one among many who were part of a Boasian legacy in the anthropology department at the University of Washington and who made their mark in Coast Salish studies (Suttles 1990:78). However, by virtue of his longevity and his influence on students, Suttles has arguably had a greater impact on the study of the Coast Salish than has any other scholar of his generation. He also provided much of the flavour of Coast Salish studies through having pioneered small but pivotal concepts. An example is the idea of "advice," a metonymic reference to the set of information regarding kinship, family history, mythology, and so on that is necessary for claimants to upper-class status and that young people would obtain through engaging in spiritual training, listening to stories, and accompanying adults in their daily activities. Advice would, in theory, not be available to lower-class people. The power of this simple idea is that it drew connections between diverse areas of sociocultural activity. In addition, Suttles' continuing influence reflects the great importance of his detailed ethnographies of economic life in contemporary tribal litigation—especially the landmark 1974 case, *United States v. Washington,* better known as the *Boldt* decision, in which Puget Sound tribes regained their treaty rights to half of the salmon catch.[2]

However, just as Suttles' legacy was firmly established, scholarship moved in another direction, as has Northwest Coast scholarship in general, in the period between the 1970s and the present (Mauzé, Harkin, and Kan 2004:xi). The turn of the millennium was yet another watershed in Coast Salish scholarship, with, in quick succession, the sudden appearance of several quite different monographs and edited volumes, including Jay Miller's (1999) *Lushootseed Culture and the Shamanic Odyssey: An Anchored Radiance*; Crisca Bierwert's (1999) *Brushed by Cedar, Living by the River* and her edited volume *Lushootseed Texts* (Bierwert 1996); Brad Asher's (1999) *Beyond the Reservation: Indians, Settlers, and Law in the Washington Territory, 1853–1889*; Alexandra Harmon's (1998) *Indians in the Making: Ethnic Relations and Indian Identities around Puget Sound*; and my own *The Problem of Justice: Tradition and Law in the Coast Salish World* (Miller 2001). These followed shortly after George Guilmet and David Whited's (1989) medical anthropology study of the Puyallup *(Those Who Give More)*; Daniel Boxberger's (1989) now classic political economy study of tribal fishing, *To Fish in Common*; and even William Elmendorf's (1993) *Twana Narratives: Native Historical Accounts of a Coast Salish Culture*, a presentation of first-person narrative materials that had been mined for his *The Structure of Twana Culture* (Elmendorf 1960). The Swinomish, together with their research partners, published a powerful and fascinating account of their culture and history—aimed at service providers—entitled *A Gathering of Wisdoms* (Swinomish Tribal Mental Health Project 1991).

These and other works signaled a new era and brought in en masse, and for the first time, real, named Aboriginal people and more detailed and theorized considerations of historical change. The photographs accompanying this chapter make these points visually and themselves comprise a record of Coast Salish lives and the dramatic changes to their communities. Figure 4 shows residents of Snauq, a community now encompassed by the Kitsilano neighbourhood of Vancouver, in various sorts of clothing and with distinct responses to the camera. A second photograph, Figure 5, depicts Upper Skagit people at work running cedar bolts downriver to sawmills sometime around 1900. Figure 6, taken about 1920, shows current Upper Skagit elder Vi Fernando as a toddler and Jessie Moses, a woman known for her powers of precognition and a powerful influence on current elders. Behind these figures looms sacred Sauk Mountain. The final photograph (Figure 7) shows Tom Williams in hop fields. He is remembered for bringing the Shaker Church to the Upper Skagit in the early twentieth century.

The Coast Salish peoples in most of the above-named works were shown in relation to other populations, particularly the settlers, rather than in isolation. Largely a stagnant field of study since the 1970s, Coast Salish research had come alive. No longer focused on salvage anthropology, strictly local issues, or assimilation (a genre perhaps best exemplified locally by Lewis' [1970] *Indian Families on the Northwest Coast: The Impact of Change*; and Hawthorn, Belshaw, and Jamieson's [1958] *The Indians of British Columbia: A Study of Contemporary Social Adjustment*), these books reveal the new connections between the larger scholarly fields and work conducted within the Coast Salish realm. The Coast Salish literature can again speak to larger scholarly and real-world issues. There are exceptions to this generalization, of course: significant research in the prior period included Pamela Amoss' (1978) *Coast Salish Spirit Dancing* and Michael Kew's (1970) dissertation concerning contemporary Musqueam. There was also the ethnobiological work of Turner (1975); a festschrift for UBC professor Wilson Duff, edited by Abbott (1981); Aboriginal leader Martin Sampson's (1972) brief study of Skagit history and ethnography; and the early, short writings of Kathleen Mooney (1976). Several others published valuable studies that included, but did not focus on, the Coast Salish, notably Rolf Knight's (1978) seminal work on Aboriginal peoples in the workforce and Paul Tennant's (1990) study of Aboriginal politics in British Columbia.

There has been, to date, no single volume that reflects the array of new topics, new interpretations, and new approaches to the Coast Salish, just as there had been no similar collaborative volume for the Northwest Coast since that edited by Tom McFeat (1966) and prior to the publication of Mauzé, Harkin, and Kan's (2004) *Coming to Shore*. Nor has there been an adequate reflection on how the legacy of early ethnographic studies influences our current scholarly understandings of the Coast Salish. These studies date back to the mid-nineteenth-century work of Horatio Hale (1846), the youthful ethnographer with the U.S. Exploring Expedition of 1838–1842; George Gibbs (1877), ethnographer with the U.S. boundary expedition and other government projects; the work of the eccentric and eclectic George Swan (1857); and the work of the "father of American anthropology," Franz Boas (1889); and others. It is equally important to consider the viewpoints of Aboriginal peoples themselves and how Aboriginal peoples have influenced scholarly perspectives. With this in mind, I have pulled together work by contemporary scholars who can comment on a variety of substantive issues, particularly the state of research, and whose work reflects both the influences of the Suttles generation of scholars and new ideas. Some of the contributors are now long-established scholars and others are of a newer generation.

History and Anthropology

Be of Good Mind has other aims as well as those mentioned above. Both the academic and popular literatures have commonly split the Coast Salish world in two, treating those living in Puget Sound and adjacent lands as constituting one world and those in British Columbia as constituting another. This practice fails to conform to the prior Aboriginal reality, before contact with whites and before treaties and borders. While it would be a mistake to argue that earlier scholarship failed to recognize the connections between peoples in what are now two separate nations, political factors have clearly influenced where people have engaged in fieldwork and what they have written about. For the most part, Americans have worked in the United States and Canadians in Canada. I want to make clear that there have been important exceptions to this observation: American Marian Smith, for example, conducted an ethnographic field school at the Seabird Island Reserve in British Columbia in 1945, as Crisca Bierwert points out in Chapter 6 (Miller 2007). Certainly, Suttles himself taught and researched in both countries and provided anthropological testimony on behalf of tribes on both sides of the international border. However, because much of the work during the period when Suttles got his start was descriptive salvage anthropology, it focused on discrete communities located in one country or the other. Meanwhile, political forces had pushed Aboriginal people to occupy reserves (the Canadian term) and reservations (the American term) whose borders had to remain within those of either Canada or the United States: there was to be no overlapping of federal borders. The Semiahmoo, for example, came to occupy only the Canadian portions of their territories, although they have maintained connections with their Lummi relatives in the United States. U.S. and British/Canadian policy did not allow for recognized groups to have land in both counties (thereby creating a legal question now tentatively being approached in courts in both countries). The creation of reservations and reserves led scholars to study these communities as free-standing political entities. Since the establishment of the international boundary in 1846, differences in Canadian and American contact histories and public policies have created significant differences between historically connected Aboriginal communities. Not surprisingly, regional historians have tended to focus on Aboriginal peoples residing in their region alone. In brief, the connections between communities and individuals across the entire Coast Salish world have not been adequately explored. Several contemporary scholars have explicitly concerned themselves with this problem and have sought to draw out the divergences and parallels. The chapters in this volume continue to address this shortcoming, including that of linguist Brent Galloway (Chapter 7 [Miller 2007]).

I am also interested in pulling together the work of historians, anthropologists, other social scientists, and community intellectuals to create an emergent picture of the Coast Salish realm. As in the case of cross-border studies, it is nothing new for scholars from various disciplines to work together or to mutually influence one another's work. There is a long history of this, but there are now new twists to it. First, professional historians appear to be paying more attention to the developing histories of particular First Nations and American Indian Coast Salish communities and people, although, as Alexandra Harmon points out in Chapter 1 (Miller 2007), no one has yet produced a synthetic history of the region. Examples of these new histories include the biography of Esther Ross, a profoundly important woman in the twentieth-century history of the Stillaguamish (Ruby and Brown 2001), and Daniel Marshall's (1999) *Those Who Fell from the Sky: A History of the Cowichan Peoples,* a community history. It is probably fair to say that the scholarly production of histories concerning the Coast Salish of Washington State is considerably ahead of those for British Columbia. Most notably, Alexandra Harmon (1998) has written a now widely influential history of the Coast Salish of Puget Sound, *Indians in the Making*. The gap is closing rapidly, however, and exciting new regional histories by Keith Thor Carlson (2003) and others, including John Lutz at the University of Victoria, will continue to dramatically transform our understandings of the area.

There are other reasons why the rapprochement of historians, anthropologists, and community intellectuals is occurring and why it is significant, including the fact that, over the past twenty years, both history and anthropology have changed as disciplines. Americanist anthropology, once driven by functionalist and then assimilationist academic agendas, has moved toward a more thoughtful consideration of the ways in which historical forces act on culture and on local peoples. One might even make this claim regarding anthropologists of the Northwest Coast, most of whom have been heavily influenced by Franz Boas' version of historical particularism. History, for its part, has increasingly embraced minority and social histories. This is evident in new hiring strategies at universities. For example, in 2004–2005 my own academic institution, the University of British Columbia (UBC), hired two young scholars whose primary interest is Aboriginal history. While an older generation of historians at UBC has played an important role in the production of Aboriginal history, this was not why they were brought to the university. Together, the two disciplines of history and anthropology, and their Aboriginal collaborators, have created the field of ethnohistory, a discourse that sprang out of the problems associated with providing evidence for the U.S. Court of Claims in the 1940s—a legal enterprise intended to speed up the resolution of land claims and treaty issues facing American tribes.

As Daniel Boxberger points out in Chapter 2 (Miller 2007), research among the Coast Salish has always been driven by concerns of public policy and litigation. This became evident following the *Boldt* decision, a large-scale legal proceeding in which Barbara Lane and many other formally trained researchers turned their attention to amassing various sorts of materials relating to the issue of treaty-period (i.e., mid-nineteenth-century) life. But academics have long worked for Aboriginal communities on legal matters. Sally Snyder, for example, carried out long-term fieldwork with Samish, Swinomish, Upper Skagit, Sauk-Suiattle, and other communities in the 1940s and 1950s, largely with litigation in mind. Later, she acted on behalf of these communities. As Boxberger describes in Chapter 2 (Miller 2007), Herbert Taylor of Western Washington University spent much of his career considering issues related to litigation. The intellectual problems presented in treaty, land, and other litigation have pushed scholars to more carefully consider questions of population size, the impact of contact on economic activities, the nature of social relations, the nature of private property, and many other issues. Litigation has also pushed scholars of different disciplines to create detailed and unified interpretations that are intellectually honest, that are in line with all available information (including Aboriginal viewpoints and oral documents), and that might be successful in court.

Most contemporary scholars of the Coast Salish have probably found themselves either producing materials for tribal litigation or testifying in court. Some have found this to be an onerous task and either refuse to participate or do so only once. Many contend that the demands of litigation—report production along with examination and cross-examination—provide greater scrutiny of academic ideas and arguments than does any other venue. The demands of litigation, in brief, have forced a newer, more carefully argued approach to a variety of issues about the Coast Salish area. As Boxberger indicates in Chapter 2 (Miller 2007), litigation may have profoundly altered the nature of scholarship as it relates to the Coast Salish. I might add that this appears to be largely for the good, in that it has precipitated new discussions and sharpened ideas, and it has also created a real-world forum within which to debate anthropological and historical ideas of very considerable importance. Problems have emerged too, including the ugly spectre of unprepared scholars testifying beyond their competence and/or being unaware of the differences between legal and academic understandings of particular words and concepts (Miller 2004). In addition, scholars have testified against each other in ways that are not always attractive or helpful, and many, including Colin Grier (Chapter 10 [Miller 2007]), remain wary of the relationship between law and scholarship. Academics have been accused of merely being mouthpieces for tribes/bands or for one or another government. Nonetheless, working together on litigation constitutes a third reason why history, anthropology, and Aboriginal forms of knowledge have usefully interpenetrated and why all are represented in *Be of Good Mind*. Boxberger (Chapter 2 [Miller 2007]) cautions, however, that some forms of traditional knowledge are not common property and that they should remain community-controlled resources of the sort articulated by McHalsie (Chapter 3 [Miller 2007]).

In Chapter 4 (Miller 2007), Rocky Wilson reveals more about the significance of legal engagement. His people, the Hwlitsum, are not yet recognized by the Canadian government, a circumstance that has caused his band to undertake litigation and that focuses his understandings of Coast Salish identity. He points out the participation of his band in Coast Salish social networks, the role of elders in creating internal recognition, and the importance of establishing one's place through honouring one's ancestors. His chapter also reveals the important and still unresolved issue of the existence of Coast Salish communities on both sides of the international border that lack official state recognition. Although this circumstance skews these communities' relationships with recognized tribes and bands, they rightly deserve to be recognized in this volume (see Miller 2003).

While historians are now making a big splash in Coast Salish studies, they are reading ethnographies, and anthropologists are reading histories. Beyond this, however, is the exciting development, at least from my perspective as an anthropologist, of a new generation of historians who have learned directly from community members themselves. This is not news for anthropologists; indeed, Valentine and Darnell (1999) suggest that Americanist anthropology is characterized by Aboriginal people's participating directly in theory making. Now, however, we have the prospect of historians trained in archival methods and informed by world-scale historical questions, who have added to their repertoire the insights of the community and a deep appreciation for Aboriginal epistemologies. This is a powerful combination. For historians, culture is never static, and they have challenged anthropological renderings in which culture appears to be so. Coast Salish culture (or, more aptly, cultures, there is no uniformity in the Coast Salish region) has seemed flat in the hands of anthropologists; the *Handbook* perhaps most thoroughly reflects this approach. While anthropologists have understood that Coast Salish culture changed prehistorically, and while none would argue that life four thousand years ago, during a period of mixed economic activity and before that of the intensification of salmon fisheries, would have been similar to life in 1750, not enough attention has been given to transformations in more recent cultural practice. For example, in Chapter 10 (Miller 2007) Grier indicates the extent to which archaeologists have uncritically applied ethnographic understandings to archaeological questions. He argues for "side-by-side" research. Critics may quickly dispute my contention and might, for example, point to studies of the rise of the Indian Shaker Church, the transformation of religious practices and concepts in the late nineteenth century, or to Guilmet, Boyd, Whited, and Thompson's (1991) study of the effects of disease on cultural transmission. But even these studies have not adequately dislodged the notion of an ethnographic present. The current dialogue with historians, however, appears to have begun to do this.

Simultaneously, histories appear more relevant and more respectful of community epistemologies and approaches to history. Keith Thor Carlson's work is perhaps most developed in this sense. Now a tenured faculty member at the University of Saskatchewan, Carlson worked for more than a decade as a historian for the Stó:lō Nation. During this period, he attended community spiritual events, listened to community members and leaders of all sorts, puzzled through community politics, and began to form a new idea of how identities had come to be what they are and what an indigenous historiography might be like. This is reflected in Chapter 5 (Miller 2007) and in previous publications, including the impressive and award-winning *A Stó:lō Coast Salish Historical Atlas* (Carlson 2001). Carlson has taken community oral histories of several sorts seriously and has wedded them to archival and ethnographic accounts. The product, exciting and provocative, is arguably an altogether new hybrid scholarship. Chapter 3 (Miller 2007), by Stó:lō cultural advisor Sonny McHalsie, shows in detail how he has learned to work with academics such as Carlson and to incorporate and re-analyze materials from previous generations of non-Aboriginal researchers. McHalsie points to the mutual sharing of published and unpublished materials (and suggests that unpublished notes are often more valuable than are the worked-over published materials, a topic taken up by Crisca Bierwert in Chapter 6 [Miller 2007]) and to the importance of mutual participation in spiritual life. For McHalsie, participant observation moves in both directions.

Carlson (Chapter 5 [Miller 2007]) and David Schaepe (Chapter 8 [Miller 2007]) point to another important feature of the post-1990 world and yet another reason to celebrate and encourage the new interdisciplinary scholarship—that is, the ability of communities to employ scholars directly. When I first began to work among Coast Salish communities in the 1970s, they were only tentatively engaging in research and had not fully begun to figure out ways in which they might work with scholars for mutually productive purposes.

The Puyallup, for example, had just seized a former BIA hospital and tribal tuberculosis treatment centre and were beginning to create a tribal archive. The Stó:lō, too, on the Canadian side, had recently forcibly seized a hospital located in their traditional territories, also formerly devoted to Aboriginal tuberculosis patients, and had begun to develop a research program and archive. Much of the visible and dramatic infrastructure of the communities, including large and attractive tribal centres, gaming and public auditoriums, gymnasiums, shopping malls, and new winter ceremonial longhouses, was not yet present. The implications of the legal victory of the *Boldt* decision were just beginning to become apparent in Puget Sound, and the B.C. bands were coming alive politically in opposition to the federal government's policy of radical assimilation and termination, which was announced by the Trudeau government's 1969 White Paper.

In the 1970s Vi Hilbert, now an Upper Skagit elder and then a language instructor at the University of Washington, had just begun her own engagement with a group of scholars interested in helping her develop materials about the oral traditions and cultures of the Coast Salish. By the mid-1990s, Hilbert's research group, including both community members and academics Pamela Amoss, Jay Miller, Andie Palmer, Crisca Bierwert, and many others, had produced several volumes and audiotapes. These materials directly reflected Hilbert's own teaching, which she received from her elders, including her aunt Susie Sampson Peter and her father, Charlie Anderson. The publications have had a considerable impact on the work of both those in her group, particularly on Jay Miller's (1999) *Lushootseed Culture and the Shamanic Odyssey,* and those outside, including Carlson. In fact, one might argue that Vi Hilbert has created her own orthodox and spiritually informed view of the Coast Salish peoples and cultures—one that complements Suttles' more academic and ecologically based perspective.

B.C. bands have entered into their own direct encounter with academics as their governmental infrastructure has developed and their capacity for employing academics has grown. In 1991, for example, the Stó:lō Nation invited anthropologists from UBC to help them with their research. At this point, the nation employed a single academically trained social scientist, the archaeologist Gordon Mohs, and early meetings between Stó:lō staff and UBC professors were held in a small trailer. There were fewer than ten Stó:lō staff at the time of the birth of the UBC graduate ethnographic field school, initially organized by Professor Julie Cruikshank and myself, in 1991. Less than a dozen years later, the Stó:lō staff had grown to well over two hundred, and the nation now employs academics of various sorts, including anthropologists and archaeologists, historians, archivists, GIS specialists, as well as community culture experts. This powerful group came to be known, in jest, as Stó:lō University, reflecting how its members dramatically changed the landscape of scholarship concerning the Coast Salish in Canada, publishing a series of significant books, including the *Atlas* (Carlson 2001) and *You Are Asked to Witness* (Carlson 1996), just as had Vi Hilbert and her research group in the United States. It is because of the groundbreaking work of Gordon Mohs, Keith Thor Carlson, Albert McHalsie, and many others that a disproportionate amount of research about the Coast Salish concerns the Stó:lō communities. *Be of Good Mind* reflects that reality.

Academics on both sides of the border have been called on to produce studies of Aboriginal economic practice to support litigation and to establish Aboriginal rights. In the 1980s, for example, Puget Sound sacred sites were mapped and documented for the purpose of protecting them from intrusive non-tribal economic activities, particularly logging. Later, the relicensing of Puget Power and Seattle City Light under the terms of the U.S. Federal Environmental Regulatory Commission (FERC) called for the production of traditional cultural property (TCP) studies. In Canada, the requirements of documenting tribal practice under the emerging case law of the 1990s have led to the production of traditional use studies (TUS). This sort of work has had the effect of informing academics of the depth of Aboriginal thinking and has created a heightened sensitivity to the cultural landscape. As several of the chapters in this volume reveal, particularly that of Stó:lō leader Sonny McHalsie, understanding the cultural landscape is a critical feature of the new interpretations of the Salish world. And in Chapter 8 (Miller 2007), Dave Schaepe suggests that contemporary Coast Salish community heritage resource policies constitute significant articulations of identity.

In brief, the scholarship of the contemporary period reflects a new engagement with the Coast Salish people themselves. In many cases, scholars are directly employed by tribes and bands; in other cases, they are under contract to prepare materials for litigation for tribal interests. Scholars are also occasionally employed to provide answers to legal questions posed by non-Aboriginal litigants. The demands of litigation have led to a new look at the landscape and a new vigilance. Within this framework, new questions are being asked and new concepts developed. An interesting example is the effort by Schaepe, Berkey, Stamp, and Halstad (2004) on behalf of the Stó:lō Nation to document Stó:lō practices and beliefs regarding air and water. This is part of the Stó:lō Nation's attempt to protect threatened sacred areas as well as the environment more generally, and it points directly to relevant, but poorly understood, features of Coast Salish identity.

For Coast Salish communities, all of this is occurring during a period of considerable political reawakening and tremendous cultural revival. For example, as recently as twenty years ago winter spirit dancing drew few new participants; today, there are many initiates from a number of Coast Salish communities, and hundreds crowd into longhouses for extended nights of watching and supporting the dancers. These forces, in addition to those internal to academic disciplines worldwide, have drawn together historians, anthropologists, archaeologists, linguists, tribal historians, and culture advisors. There remain issues that are particular to archaeology, and everyone is going to have to continue to rework his or her understandings of Coast Salish studies in light of new archaeological developments.

Archaeology, Anthropology, and History

The archaeology of the Coast Salish cannot be regarded as well-developed in comparison to the archaeology of some other regions of Aboriginal North America. Perhaps because of the rapid urban development in the region following white contact as well as compelling archaeological projects elsewhere, relatively few academic resources have been devoted to this subject. Even departments in large universities in the region, notably the University of Washington, the University of British Columbia, and Simon Fraser University (SFU), have done relatively little to follow the pioneering work of Charles Borden, Roy Carlson, and several others. Over the last decade and a half this has slowly begun to change. UBC established an archaeological field school in the late 1980s, working at several sites along the Fraser River and on the Gulf Islands, and has joined forces with SFU archaeologists to work on several projects. Some of these have the unusual feature of considering the archaeology of the Coast Salish across the international boundary (e.g., the study of the Chittenden Meadows in the Skagit region of both Canada and the United States). Tribes and bands have also come to rely on professional contract firms to obtain archaeological documentation. The resultant "grey" literature has frequently been entered as evidence in the legal record and has enhanced the overall understanding of the archaeology of the region.

Archaeology in the contemporary period is considerably transformed from what it was in earlier times. Now, neither academic nor contract archaeologists can proceed on their own accord in Aboriginal territory; community consent and participation is required, as it is with all forms of ethnographic research. In many cases, Aboriginal communities have created protocols for seeking permission and recording information for community use. In some cases, these protocols have been prepared with the co-operation of archaeologists themselves. In Chapter 8 (Miller 2007), David Schaepe looks at the participation of professional archaeologists in the conception and creation of the Stó:lō Nation cultural resource management program—including archaeological sites. Arguably, archaeologists of the Coast Salish are among the most responsive to the new environment of scholar-Aboriginal relations and among the most progressive in developing useful and mutually satisfying relationships with Aboriginal peoples in North America.

In many other regions, archaeologists and anthropologists remain much more resistant to incorporating Aboriginal peoples into their thinking and practice. This may reflect the fact that most of these scholars live in the Coast Salish region and that Coast Salish Aboriginal peoples are members of the larger community as well as of the tribe/band. They attend the colleges and universities and participate in academic affairs. Academics teaching courses about Aboriginal peoples see them in great numbers in their classes in the Coast Salish area, and community members themselves teach or give lectures in many of the courses. They push to have their voices and perspectives heard, and they have generously given their time so that scholars may learn from them. This is less true in many other areas, where academics live "away" and the scholarly discourse remains largely distinct from community concerns and voices.

Aboriginal participation, then, includes more than simply issuing or refusing permission to excavate archaeological sites. Community leaders now carefully consider what types of sites, and which sites in particular, need to be studied. There is a new utility to archaeology for Aboriginal communities; archaeological findings can be used to demonstrate continuity of occupation, the range of subsistence activities, and other topics significant in making land claims or, in the case of British Columbia, in supporting bands during the treaty process. Communities, then, have a direct interest in selecting projects that are of utility to them.

Further, communities directly contribute to the interpretation of sites. This is not new, but contemporary archaeologists have built community contributions directly into the initial planning and conceptualizing stage, so that there is constant feedback going on. The long collaboration of tribal expert Sonny McHalsie, historian Keith Thor Carlson, archaeologists Dave Schaepe, Michael Blake, and Dana Lepofsky in Stó:lō territory, and Robert Mierendorf in the adjacent U.S. National Park Service is one such example. Recently, a large-scale, long-term, federally funded "identity" project has been undertaken to examine the movements of Coast Salish people along the Fraser River, the point being to create a historical picture of the migrations, amalgamations, and fissioning that resulted in the contemporary Stó:lō people. Pat Moore has joined several other academics in the project to add linguistic reconstructions to archaeological and historical materials. McHalsie and the elders with whom he has worked have been able to connect features of the landscape to oral records that reveal the significance of the sites. The results of this project are not yet fully in, although McHalsie's chapter (Miller 2007) reveals the nature and significance of his contribution.

In Chapter 10 (Miller 2007), Colin Grier discusses his work in the Gulf Islands and his interest in household archaeology. His previous work (Grier 2003) has helped refine our understanding of how the Coast Salish world (or Salish Sea, in Russel Barsh's terminology) functions as a region by pointing out how island resources relate to riverine occupation. Grier's work also sheds light on ethnographic and ethnohistorical studies of the political organization of the Coast Salish peoples, since the early 1990s an area of lively debate (Tollefson 1987, 1989; Miller and Boxberger 1994; Miller 2001). Notably, his research also requires significant band co-operation with regard to granting permission, identifying sites, thinking through the uses of a site, and establishing a logistical system for his research team. Finally, Grier's work illuminates the operation of temporal corporate groups, an idea that I believe is underplayed in the literature. Here he focuses on difficult issues in the relationship between archaeology and ethnography. He points out that an uncritical imposition of ethnographic conclusions regarding Coast Salish social organization can obstruct the development of an adequate archaeology of the region. He calls for a

Coast Salish archaeology that is produced in conjunction with ethnography and, more broadly, with anthropology and that is independent of the ethnographic record. This would produce an archaeology that could contribute to ethnographic understandings and eliminate the teleological quality of Coast Salish studies, which have so strongly emphasized historically known peoples.

These examples of the integration of archaeology, linguistics, history, ethnography, and other disciplines reveal the significance of integrated, multidisciplinary research. Much more remains to be done, and the archaeology of the Coast Salish appears to be about to undergo significant revision. Robert Mierendorf's (1993) work in the U.S. North Cascades shows eighty-five hundred radio carbon years (calibrated 14C years before present) of Aboriginal occupation in the Ross Lake area, and use of high altitude Alpine regions and recent research in Yale Canyon at the Xelhálh site suggest the development of rock-wall fortifications along the Fraser River and the construction of a "castle-like" stone defensive site protecting a rich storage area (Schaepe 2006). Working out these ideas will require interdisciplinary efforts and will certainly affect our understanding of the Coast Salish peoples.

Who Are the Coast Salish?

Much of the new literature focuses on the critical question, "who are the Coast Salish?" and the related issue, "what are the connections between the contemporary peoples and the historic and prehistoric communities and cultures?" Either directly or indirectly, these questions are reflected in the chapters in *Be of Good Mind,* and they are important for a number of practical and intellectual reasons. First, Coast Salish communities, as I have suggested, are continuing their struggle to clarify and extend their legal footing in both Canada and the United States. The details of this are the topic of another book, but they influence current thinking. For example, in the second phase of the landmark *Boldt* decision, the shellfishing phase, in my own testimony and report I asked: "Who are the successors in interest to the treaty-period people of the Skagit?" This is not an easy question, applied as it is to a people who have long practised exogamous marriage (at least among those of high standing). Coast Salish society has been characterized by kinship ties that stretch over a large area and, in some circumstances, by use-rights to resources in various locales. Today, tribes and bands struggle internally over what constitutes a community and who ought to have membership. For example, over the last decade, various bands have drifted in and out of membership in the Stó:lō Nation, and the Stó:lō Nation and Musqueam band continue to differ over whether or not the latter ought to be regarded as part of the former (the Musqueam argue against this). In the United States and Canada, non-recognized tribes struggle to demonstrate their separateness from established tribes that claim to have incorporated their interests and their people in the nineteenth century.

Anthropologists, for their part, and, more recently, historians, have advanced several competing theories in an attempt to understand the social organization and identifying features of the various Coast Salish peoples. Suttles (1987) emphasizes the importance of the local kin group, which operated within a regional social network and which was based on lineage and the management of resources. Smith (1940) emphasizes mutual identity along watersheds, without formal regional leadership. Jay Miller (1999) points to the importance of spiritual practice and the role of shamanic practitioners in forming regional systems. And Tollefson (1987, 1989) suggests that at least some Puget Salish were organized into chiefdoms. Responses to this work (Miller and Boxberger 1994) argue that colonial processes may have pushed communities into creating more formalized alliances, as commonly occurred with several other Aboriginal regions of Native North

America. Yet others (Harmon 1998) emphasize how contact has altered, perhaps distorted, the ways in which Coast Salish peoples organize their identities. For his part, Carlson (2003) analyzes migrations and social class differences and their basis in cultural patterning in the early historic period.

Figure 4. Group near Jericho Charlie's home on Kitsilano Indian Reserve (Snauq): Mary (Yam-schlmoot), Jericho Charlie (Chin-nal-set), William Green, Peelass George, Jimmy Jimmy, and Jack (Tow-hu-quam-kee). *Major Matthews Collection, City of Vancouver Archives, P28N11*

It seems clear, however, that Coast Salish peoples have long constructed and maintained complex personal social identities that connect them to a variety of other groups. These include immortal beings regarded as ancestral kinfolk, immediate affinal and agnatic relatives, a larger set of more distant relatives, households, and fellow members of "villages" that are sometimes many kilometres in length but that have few structures. There are also patterns of affiliation based on common occupation of water systems; respect for particular regional leaders, use-rights, and resource procurement areas; and the common use of particular languages and dialects. In the contemporary period, the Coast Salish have some sense of common identity with fellow members of this Aboriginal language family, as is indicated by recent efforts to create a Coast Salish political network crossing the international border. To a great extent, though, patterns of identity and affiliations gain importance according to how they are deployed in daily life and, additionally, in times of great upheaval and change. Who the Coast Salish are depends upon the question being asked—a circumstance that has not been sufficiently recognized in the academic literature. It is this flexibility with regard to personal and group patterns of identity that has enabled the Coast Salish to adapt to the devastating problems resulting from contact (Kew and Miller 1999).

Harmon (1998) has rightly observed that, though tribes and bands exist in a form that was determined by the administrative practice of the colonizers, they have nevertheless become the focus of personal and group identity. Washington State tribes are "treaty tribes" in the sense that political and economic rights flow from the language in which treaties encapsulated them in the 1850s. These treaties structure the lives of individual Coast Salish peoples and families. Similarly, as Schaepe points out, the responses of B.C. bands and tribal councils to the current treaty process and land claims have had a similar impact. However, individuals on both sides of the border also closely identify with kin relations, and these cross tribal/band political boundaries. My own work with contemporary communities suggests to me that the significance of the local kin group, the "corporate group" which is based in the idiom of kinship but that implicitly excludes many potential kinfolk, has not been sufficiently considered. Because my research has largely been concerned with contemporary tribal internal politics, service delivery, and justice systems, my approach to these communities is quite different from that of those engaging in salvage anthropology and attempting to reconstruct largely dismembered ways of life. My work has shown that contemporary patterns of identity and organization, although not identical with earlier patterns, are powerfully influenced by them. An interesting example of this may be found in the Upper Skagit community in the rapid re-creation of family fishing co-operatives along the Skagit River following the regaining of tribal recognition soon after the *Boldt* decision (Miller 1989a). In Chapter 6 (Miller 2007), Bierwert points to the significance of extended kin groups as well as to the problems in retaining this sort of social pattern under mid-twentieth-century pressure to assimilate.

My claim is that the Coast Salish continue to form themselves into named corporate groups, known locally simply as "families." Further, many significant issues of contemporary social life might be best approached from an analysis of the ways in which these families interact. What follows is a short sketch of how this approach works and the sorts of questions it might address concerning the core question: who are the Coast Salish? These groups organize many fundamental features of the lives of their members, which is to say that they have corporate functions, including, in many cases, those affecting fishing, ritual life, regular small-scale reciprocity (such as babysitting, care of elders, borrowing cash, the lending of cars). These corporate groups are the entities within which "advice" is shared and taught. Elders gather goods for distribution at ancestral namings held for group members and other important ritual events, and members are initiated during winter dances in the group longhouse (if they have one). Senior members teach or demonstrate important skills, such as basket weaving and storytelling, to junior members. "Magic" is kept private within the group, and group members attempt to restrict access to personal information about health status and other vital issues. In one study (Miller and Pylypa 1995), paraprofessional mental health service providers reported that they were largely unable to provide services to members of outside groups because of the prohibitions against sharing information across family lines. In another case, a tribal basket-making project floundered because elders were unwilling to teach members of other families.

From this viewpoint, tribes and bands can be thought of as being composed of competing families, whose members' loyalties lie more with the families than with the political units that contain them. One political leader reported her efforts to ensure that the families co-operate for the purpose of mutual success (Miller 1989b). Families compete over a variety of internal resources, which are available solely through common membership within the larger tribal/band structure. These resources include seats on tribal/band councils; in both the Canadian and American communities, voting patterns show strong evidence of family loyalties (Miller 1992).

Figure 5. Running cedar bolts downriver to sawmills. *Ed Edwards Collection, Upper Skagit Tribe*

Further, families compete for available housing, access to health, social, and educational services, influence over community decisions, and tribal/band jobs. In one case in Canada, in recognition of the long-term practice of family leadership within the larger collective, the method of selecting band council members was adjusted to allow for the appointment of family leaders (Kew and Miller 1999). As is the case with many small-scale political systems elsewhere, families unite when necessary to compete with other tribes/bands, particularly regarding fishing allocations.

Unlike the northern matrilineal tribes in the northern Northwest Coast culture region, the Coast Salish have no clan system, with the result that distribution of members to family groups is not clearly channelled.[3] This fact points to the importance of examining individual, household, nuclear family, "family," and even band-level processes of affiliation. Interview data show that many, perhaps most, individuals carefully scrutinize their life chances within the family and the political unit (Miller 1989b, 1992). In many cases, individuals choose to move to a new location, sometimes to a new band or tribe, where, through bilateral kinship, they can claim membership in a different corporate family and where they might have either more resources available to them or a stronger position within the family. An individual's decisions are influenced by her stage of life, the stage in the life cycle of her nuclear family, her household, and the circumstances of the family she wishes to join.

Figure 6. Sauk Mountain, with Jessie Moses (looking down) and Vi Fernando (child). *Ed Edwards Collection, Upper Skagit Tribe.*

For the most part, families gain members in two ways: birth and recruitment. While members are not necessarily co-resident and may not even live in the same community, they practise regular generalized reciprocity (Mooney 1976), and they depend on one or more leaders who can offer them significant resources. These resources may include spiritual knowledge, "advice," financial assets, control of ancestral names (which may be given to appropriate family members), mastery of local norms of speech making, and various publicly identifiable phenomena associated with highclass status. Other resources may include control of locations for fishing camps, ritual roles, knowledge of the non-Aboriginal bureaucratic world, seats on tribal council, chances at tribal employment, influence in housing policy, and so on. Followers might gain access to these resources through their ties to leaders, but the connections to family leaders vary, and some tribal members are more socially and genealogically distant than are others. Leaders, in turn, offer their resources to family members but may shape their following through strategic allocations. A family, however, always remains a "moral" group rather than an instrumental one (Bailey 1980:73).

An important feature of the family is its size, and larger families are generally the most successful when it comes to competing with other families within a given polity. In tribal/band elections, for example, adult members can often be counted on to vote for family candidates. And, if a family is large, it is more likely than is a smaller family to have its members holding tribal/band jobs. But because families are not clans, they are not immortal: they follow cycles of birth, growth, and collapse. Families coalesce around able charismatic leaders, but they may splinter following the death of these leaders if there are no suitable candidates to take their place. Family leadership, then, is earned rather than ascribed. Over time, the named families in a community will change, and the presence of a particular surname is no more indicative of the existence of a corporate family group than is the presence of particular Anglo names in a Canadian telephone book.

Figure 7. Tom Williams (at left), founder of Upper Skagit Shaker Church, hop picking. *Ed Edwards Collection, Upper Skagit Tribe.*

The approach I suggest here is appropriate for examining contemporary internal political processes, for considering the lives of individuals, and for making sense of much of the confusion in the literature regarding how individuals identify themselves. It also provides insights into how and when individual members of polities gain access to services, a point medical anthropologist Jen Pylypa and I made regarding medical service delivery (Miller and Pylypa 1995). However, this is not a historical approach per se, although it relies on time depth; rather, it emphasizes the life cycles of individuals and other social units, and it relies on regarding Aboriginal communities from the vantage point of local-level politics. Further, it emphasizes the differences in how tribal/band members are positioned within their own communities, and it points to the importance of the analysis of power in understanding contemporary lives—all of which are issues that have been insufficiently developed in the literature. But this approach must be paired with those developed by historians (and others) to account for the processes of (neo)colonialism as well as with the political economic approaches developed by anthropologists and other social scientists. The latter are represented by Daniel Boxberger in Chapter 6 (Miller 2007).

The question "Who are the Coast Salish?" must, of course, be answered by community members themselves; the chapters by Sonny McHalsie and Rocky Wilson are part of an attempt to do just this. In Chapter 3 (Miller 2007), McHalsie discusses the complex and evolving process involved as he learns about his community and how he is connected to the landscape and his ancestors. He rejects shallow understandings of oral history, which claim that the use of outside sources constitutes a sort of contagion, and he reveals the complex relationship between oral and written materials. Showing how he has engaged scholars and scholarly writing, McHalsie points, as does Bierwert (Chapter 6 [Miller 2007]), to the value of fieldnotes as sources. In particular, he elucidates how the interests of linguists, who are intent on recording, analyzing, and preserving language, may diverge from his own interest in examining the social context within which language is used and of places and names. In Chapter 4 (Miller 2007) it is clear that Rocky Wilson is also informed by both the narratives of his elders and academic understandings.

Meanwhile, there is a growing debate concerning the role of various academic approaches and how they might help communities represent themselves to the outside world. In Chapter 2 (Miller 2007), Boxberger observes that, in legal settings, postmodern and poststructural approaches are of little practical value: they don't clearly address legal questions, they appear to lack the authority that courts demand of experts, and they employ a different notion of fact than do the legal systems in both Canada and the United States. They undermine the legitimacy of community self-representations within legal settings because opponents can point to internal disagreement and differing perspectives. For all of these reasons, such approaches simply don't work well in court. He argues that the reality is that legal settings constitute the primary forum for public debate, whether inside or outside the courtroom.

The counter-argument appears to be that communities must make representations to both the outside world and their own members during a period in which community diversity is considerably greater than was the case in previous generations. Coast Salish communities are no longer culturally homogeneous, if they ever were. Now, some members belong to the Shaker Church, others are Seowyn winter dancers, and still others are Pentecostals or Roman Catholics. Many participate in several spiritual and religious traditions, but many do not. Access to wealth and formal education divides communities in new ways. In this argument, pressures to exhibit internal cultural uniformity to the outside world have the potential to silence internal disputes (e.g., with regard to nascent justice systems) (Miller 2001). For this reason, foregrounding the social complexity of communities, as does Bierwert's poststructuralist writing, may be constructive and may potentially allow communities room to manoeuvre in future self-representations. Both positions—the legalistic and the poststructuralist—make important statements, however, and the question of how academics ought to position their research and their contributions remains open.

Conclusion

Wayne Suttles' *Coast Salish Essays* reflects the words and concepts of a lifetime of careful, thoughtful, and sometimes inspired work. The result of a long, fruitful collaboration with Aboriginal people and communities, it reflects Suttles' abiding interest in contributing directly to communities while developing his own intellectual program. Sadly, Suttles died in 2005 as *Be of Good Mind* was being prepared. Now it is time for a new collection of essays—one that teases apart the received wisdom, incorporating several voices and addressing a wide range of topics. In this sense, *Be of Good Mind* might be regarded as a sequel to Suttles' *Essays*—a sequel in which orthodoxy is replaced by heterodoxy and in which anthropology is paired with other disciplines. It is also time for Coast Salish literature to better connect with the broader scholarship regarding Aboriginal peoples, colonization, and globalization as well as to incorporate new forms of scholarly analysis. Once the influence of Boasian-style anthropology diminished in North America, the Northwest Coast culture area was widely thought to have become a scholarly backwater. Until recently this was particularly true with regard to the Coast Salish. The Northwest Coast has entered the broader scholarly imagination primarily with regard to the potlatch and exchange theory. This is most notable in French anthropology, such as Marcel Mauss' (1967) *The Gift* and Lévi-Strauss' (1982) structuralist renderings, some of which relied on examples from Stó:lō communities along the Fraser River. The influence of Northwest Coast art and material culture on European aesthetics has been noted (Clifford 1988). More recently, the work of Sergei Kan (1989), particularly his classic *Symbolic Immortality,* has signalled that the Northwest Coast is again pushing beyond its own borders. The foci of Northwest Coast scholarship—once on myth, art, the potlatch, descent systems, social inequalities, and winter ceremonies (Suttles and Jonaitis 1990)—are now elsewhere.

In the 1970s and early 1980s, at least one major university in the region chose simply to dump anthropology faculty members whose area of research was primarily the Coast Salish in favour of those who worked in more exotic and supposedly more intellectually exciting regions of the world, such as Papua New Guinea. But this appears to have been short-sighted and to reflect a lack of concern for the relationship between the local universities and local peoples, along with the old, lingering notion that the Coast Salish lack authenticity and are too assimilated to be of interest. During the 1970s and 1980s, little attention was paid to promoting the education of local Aboriginal people and to attracting them to a university that took their lives and view of the world seriously, never mind to respecting the fact that the universities themselves are built on Aboriginal traditional lands. In the 1970s, insufficient attention was paid to understanding how global trends are experienced or generated locally, and international indigenous concerns were yet to be articulated as a political force and the site of academic interest. These attitudes still persist in the academy and among contract researchers. To some, the Coast Salish world remains of little interest because, as I have been told (as were those many years before me), "There is nothing left to learn. They [members of some particular community] don't know anything now." The assumption is that the culture is preserved in recorded materials and best understood from written sources rather than from members of the communities themselves.

But anthropology has come to understand culture differently since the 1970s, and practitioners of the discipline now view culture as contested, as differently understood even in a single, apparently homogeneous community, and as best represented from several angles of vision. We can now appreciate more fully that culture is as it is lived and practised and that contemporary Coast Salish people *are* the bearers of culture as they know it and act on it. They are not simply lesser versions of their ancestors, even though community members themselves often articulate this viewpoint. Current scholarship recognizes the importance of describing and analyzing the ways in which the state and Aboriginal communities relate today, and the ways in which culture, however it might be thought of and represented, is brought to bear politically. More generally, we can now focus not on how Aboriginal people have been assimilated or exterminated but, rather, on how they have persisted, on how they have created hybrid forms of culture, and on how some forms of cultural practice have been sequestered from outside view. We can understand that some

34

cultural practices have been discarded and others enhanced. We can now work with a broad and interesting range of Aboriginal responses to contact and colonization rather than with the limited vocabulary of assimilation and resistance.

A period is now beginning in which a heightened rapprochement between disciplines can generate exciting new possibilities and in which Aboriginal concepts can play a direct part. There are now much richer answers to the question, "Who are the Coast Salish?" than there were a generation ago, and there is a new literature that enhances our understanding of the humanity of the community through accounts of individual leaders, innovators, and oral traditions. Attention is now being paid to the diversity of communities that were previously seen largely in terms of social classes, or adaptive responses to change, or as simply disappearing into the white world. It is hard to imagine what the issues will be in another twenty-five or fifty years. But the contemporary recognition of diversity allows for the development of insights into the growth of governance and community economic initiatives, as well as into the inequitable distribution of treaty rights to fishing and other resources. In addition, it sets the stage for contemplating what comes next in the Coast Salish world along the Salish Sea. I ask readers to "be of good mind" as they encounter the chapters herein. This is a phrase often heard in longhouse ritual, and, as Sonny McHalsie has said, it refers to the practice of avoiding bad thoughts (which can harm others) and of having faith that the work being undertaken together, in this case by scholars and community members, can continue.

Endnotes

[1] Salishan is a language family comprised of languages and dialects spoken by Aboriginal peoples of British Columbia, Washington State, Montana, Oregon, and Idaho. The language family is divided into Coast Salishan and Interior Salishan (or, commonly, Salish), and there are social and cultural differences between the constituent groups, which often overlap within this division. Today, most but not all of the languages are threatened with extinction. This volume is not intended as a reader on the particular communities either in the United States or in Canada; rather it addresses them as a whole. Within the Coast Salish language grouping in Canada there are fifty current bands, some of which have changed their names in recent years. Most of the Canadian bands have small populations and are organized into tribal councils, umbrella organizations that provide an economy of scale in the provision of services. The membership of these councils varies as bands occasionally withdraw or join. Currently, the Hwlitsum are actively engaged in attempting to gain federal recognition. There are twenty-four federally recognized Coast Salish tribes in Washington State, and several more are attempting to gain recognition. Among the prominent groups seeking recognition are the Steilacoom, the Duwamish, and the Snohomish. Some of the tribes are organized under the Small Tribes of Western Washington (STOWW), and most operate independently but participate in various intertribal consortia, such as the Northwest Intertribal Court system. Concerning the question of terminology—communities in Canada are commonly known as "First Nations" and those in the United States are commonly known as "American Indians" or "Native Americans." But terminology is complex and changeable. Many people continue to refer to themselves and others as "Indians"; some community members regard this term as disrespectful and colonialist. The term "Aboriginal people" is sometimes employed as a cover term and "indigenous people" is used to refer to groups worldwide. In practice, all of these terms are used in Coast Salish communities, although "Aboriginal" and "Native" are more commonly used in Canada than they are in the United States.

[2] It was anthropologist Barbara Lane, however, who authored the major reports presented for the tribes in this litigation.

[3] I do not wish to suggest that the presence of a system of clans fully determines the affiliation of individuals; indeed, research shows that there are many ways in which demographic anomalies can be addressed, people can be reassigned to a new clan, or clan membership can be manipulated.

References Cited

Abbott, Donald N., editor. 1981. *The World is as Sharp as a Knife: An Anthology in Honour of Wilson Duff.* Victoria: British Columbia Provincial Museum.

Amoss, Pamela. 1978. *Coast Salish Spirit Dancing: The Survival of an Ancestral Religion.* Seattle: University of Washington Press.

Asher, Brad. 1999. *Beyond the Reservation: Indians, Settlers, and the Law in Washington Territory, 1853–1889.* Norman, OK: University of Oklahoma Press.

Bailey, F.G. 1980. *Strategems and Spoils: A Social Anthropology of Politics.* Oxford: Basil Blackwell.

Bierwert, Crisca, editor. 1996. *Lushootseed Texts: An Introduction to Puget Salish Narrative Aesthetics.* Lincoln: University of Nebraska Press.

——— 1999. *Brushed by Cedar, Living by the River: Coast Salish Figures of Power.* Tucson: University of Arizona Press.

Boas, Franz. 1889. The Indians of British Columbia. *Transactions of the Royal Society of Canada for 1888,* 6(2):45–57.

Boxberger, Daniel L. 1989. *To Fish In Common: The Ethnohistory of Lummi Indian Salmon Fishing.* Lincoln: University of Nebraska Press.

Carlson, Keith Thor, editor. 1996. *You Are Asked to Witness: The Stó:lō in Canada's Pacific Coast History.* Chilliwack: Stó:lō Heritage Trust.

——— editor. 2001. *A Stó:lō Coast Salish Historical Atlas.* Vancouver/Chilliwack: Douglas and McIntyre/ Stó:lō Heritage Trust.

——— 2003. The Power of Place, the Problem of Time: A Study of History and Aboriginal Collective Identity. Ph.D. dissertation, University of British Columbia.

Clifford, James. 1988. *The Predicament of Culture: Twentieth Century Ethnography, Literature and Art.* Cambridge, MA: Harvard University Press.

Elmendorf, William W. 1960. The Structure of Twana Culture. *Washington State University Research Studies,* 28(3), Monographic Supplement 2. Pullman, WA: Washington State University.

——— 1971. Coast Salish Status Ranking and Intergroup Ties. *Southwestern Journal of Anthropology,* 27(4):353–380.

——— 1993. *Twana Narratives: Native Historical Accounts of a Coast Salish Culture.* Seattle: U of Washington Press.

Gibbs, George. 1877. Tribes of Western Washington and Northwestern Oregon. In *Contributions to North American Ethnology,* 1(2):157–361, edited by John Wesley Powell. Washington, D.C.: U.S. Geographical and Geological Survey of the Rocky Mountain Region.

Grier, Colin. 2003. Dimensions of Regional Interaction in the Prehistoric Gulf of Georgia. In *Emerging from the Mist: Studies in Northwest Coast Culture History,* edited by R. G. Matson, Gary Coupland, and Quentin Mackie, 170–187. Vancouver: UBC Press.

Guilmet, George M., and David L. Whited. 1989. *The People Who Give More: Health and Mental Health among the Contemporary Puyallup Indian Tribal Community.* Denver, CO: National Center, University of Colorado Health Sciences Center, Department of Psychiatry.

Guilmet, George, Robert T. Boyd, David L. Whited, and Nile Thompson. 1991. The Legacy of Introduced Disease: The Southern Coast Salish. *American Indian Culture and Research Journal* 15:1–32.

Hale, Horatio. 1846. *Ethnography and Philology: United States Exploring Expedition during the Years 1838, 1839, 1840, 1841, 1842.* Vol. 6. Philadelphia, PA: Lea and Blanchard.

Harmon, Alexandra. 1998. *Indians in the Making: Ethnic Relations and Indian Identities around Puget Sound.* Berkeley: University of California Press.

Hawthorn, Harry, C. S. Belshaw, and S. M. Jamieson. 1958. *The Indians of British Columbia: A Study of Contemporary Social Adjustment.* Toronto/Vancouver: University of Toronto Press/University of British Columbia.

Kan, Sergei. 1989. *Symbolic Immortality: The Tlingit Potlatch of the Nineteenth Century.* Washington, D.C.: Smithsonian Institution.

Kew, J. E. Michael. 1970. Coast Salish Ceremonial Life: Status and Identity in a Modern Village. Ph.D. dissertation, University of Washington.

Kew, J. E. Michael and Bruce G. Miller. 1999. Locating Aboriginal Governments in the Political Landscape. In *Seeking Sustainability in the Lower Fraser Basin,* edited by Michael Healey, 47–63. Vancouver: Institute for Resources and the Environment, Westwater Research.

Knight, Rolf. 1978. *Indians at Work: An Informal History of Native Indian Labour in British Columbia, 1858–1930.* Vancouver: New Star Books.

Lévi-Strauss, Claude. 1982. *The Way of the Masks.* Translated by Sylvia Modelski. Vancouver, B.C.: Douglas and McIntyre.

Lewis, Claudia. 1970. *Indian Families of the Northwest Coast: The Impact of Change.* Chicago: University of Chicago Press.

Marshall, Daniel. 1999. *Those Who Fell from the Sky: A History of the Cowichan Peoples.* Duncan, B.C.: Cowichan Tribes.

Mauss, Marcel. 1967. *The Gift: Forms and Functions of Exchange in Archaic Societies.* Introduction by E.E. Evans Pritchard. New York: W.W. Norton.

Mauzé, Marie, Michael E. Harkin, and Sergei Kan, editors. 2004. Editors' Introduction. In *Coming to Shore: Northwest Coast Ethnology, Traditions, and Visions,* xi–xxxviii. Lincoln: U of Nebraska Press.

McFeat, Tom, editor. 1966. *Indians of the North Pacific Coast.* Seattle: U of Washington Press.

Mierendorf, Robert R. 1993. *Chert Procurement in the Upper Skagit River Valley of the Northern Cascade Range, Ross Lake National Recreation Area, Washington.* Technical Report NPS/ PNRNOCA/CRTR-93-001. Sedro Woolley, WA: North Cascades National Park Service Complex.

Miller, Bruce G. 1989a. After the F.A.P.: Tribal Reorganization after Federal Acknowledgment. *Journal of Ethnic Studies,* 17(2):89–100.

———— 1989b. The Election of Women to Tribal Office: The Upper Skagit Case. Ph.D. dissertation, Arizona State University.

———— 1992. Women and Politics: Comparative Evidence from the Northwest Coast. *Ethnology*, 31(4):367–83.

———— 2001. *The Problem of Justice: Tradition and Law in the Coast Salish World.* Lincoln: University of Nebraska Press.

———— 2003. *Invisible Indigenes: The Politics of Nonrecognition.* Lincoln: University of Nebraska Press.

———— 2004. Rereading the Ethnographic Record: The Problem of Justice in the Coast Salish World. In *Coming to Shore: Northwest Coast Ethnology, Traditions, and Visions,* edited by Marie Mauzé, Michael E. Harkin, and Sergei Kan, pp. 279–304. Lincoln: University of Nebraska Press.

———— 2007. *"Be of Good Mind": Essays on the Coast Salish.* Vancouver, B.C.: UBC Press.

Miller, Bruce G., and Daniel L. Boxberger. 1994. Creating Chiefdoms: The Puget Sound Case. *Ethnohistory,* 41(2):267–293.

Miller, Bruce G., and Jen Pylypa. 1995. The Dilemma of Mental Health Paraprofessionals at Home. *American Indian and Alaska Native Mental Health: The Journal of the National Center,* 6(2):13–33.

Miller, Jay. 1999. *Lushootseed Culture and the Shamanic Odyssey: An Anchored Radiance.* Lincoln: University of Nebraska Press.

Mooney, Kathleen. 1976. Social Distance and Exchange: The Coast Salish Case. *Ethnology,* 15(4):323–346.

Ruby, Robert H., and John A. Brown. 2001. *Esther Ross: Stillaguamish Champion.* Norman: University of Oklahoma Press.

Sampson, Martin J. 1972. *Indians of Skagit County.* Mt. Vernon, WA: Skagit County Historical Society.

Schaepe, David. 2006. Rock Fortifications: Archaeological Insights into Precontact Warfare and Sociopolitical Organization among the Sto:lo of the Lower Fraser River Canyon, B.C. *American Antiquity,* 71(4):671–705.

Schaepe, David, Marianne Berkey, John Stamp, and Tia Halstad. 2004. Sumas Energy, Inc: Traditional Use Study – Phase Two: Stó:lō Cultural Relations to Air and Water. Stó:lō Nation with Arcas Consulting Archaeologists, Ltd.

Smith, Marian W. 1940. *The Puyallup-Nisqually.* New York: Columbia University Press.

Suttles, Wayne. 1951. Economic Life of the Coast Salish of Haro and Rosario Straits. Ph.D. dissertation, Department of Anthropology, University of Washington.

———— 1960. Affinal Ties, Subsistence, and Prestige among the Coast Salish. *American Anthropologist*, 62(2):296–305.

———— 1987. *Coast Salish Essays*. Seattle: University of Washington Press.

———— editor. 1990. *Handbook of North American Indians*. Vol. 7, *Northwest Coast.* Washington, D.C.: Smithsonian Institution.

———— 2004. *Musqueam Reference Grammar.* Vancouver, B.C.: UBC Press.

Suttles, Wayne and Aldona C. Jonaitis. 1990. History of Research in Ethnology. In *Handbook of North American Indians.* Vol. 7, *Northwest Coast,* edited by Wayne Suttles, pp. 73–87. Washington, D.C.: Smithsonian Institution.

Swan, George. 1857. *The Northwest Coast: Or, Three Years' Residence in Washington Territory.* New York: Harper. Reprint, 1972. Seattle: University of Washington Press.

Swinomish Tribal Mental Health Project. 1991. *A Gathering of Wisdoms.* LaConner, WA: Swinomish Tribal Community.

Tennant, Paul. 1990. *Aboriginal Peoples and Politics: The Indian Land Question.* Vancouver, B.C.: UBC Press.

Tollefson, Kenneth. 1987. The Snoqualmie: A Puget Sound Chiefdom. *Ethnology,* 26(2):121–36.

———— 1989. Political Organization of the Duwamish. *Ethnology,* 28:135–50.

Turner, Nancy. 1975. Food Plants of British Columbia Indians. Part 1, Coastal Peoples. *British Columbia Provincial Museum, Handbook* 34. Victoria: British Columbia Provincial Museum.

Valentine, Lisa Philips, and Regna Darnell, editors. 1999. *Theorizing the Americanist Tradition.* Toronto: University of Toronto Press.

Journal of Northwest Anthropology, Memoir 12:39–52 (2016)

3

Locating Aboriginal Governments in the Political Landscape*

Introduction

In the summer of 1992 chiefs of the Stó:lō bands located along the lower Fraser River wished to hold direct talks with federal Fisheries Minister John Crosbie.[sic] The chiefs were concerned that their allocations of fish were inadequate and that First Nations were obliged to uphold fisheries regulations which did not represent Native viewpoints and practices. Crosby was responsible for the Aboriginal Fisheries Strategy, a federal initiative designed as an interim measure allowing aboriginal fisheries on the Fraser while treaty negotiations and land claims were conducted. When Crosby declined to meet them, the chiefs took actions. They built a barricade blocking the CN railroad through Stó:lō territory near Sardis. The trains were halted, and railroad officials quickly complained about lost revenues, inconveniences, and dislocations for industry. Within two days, arrangements were made for the meeting the chiefs had requested. This event was but one of a number of direct and forceful actions taken by First Nations of British Columbia over the past several years to regain a voice in the management of their resource. The federal government's rapid response to the railroad blockade is an indication of the seriousness with which First Nations positions are now taken.

The First Nations of the lower Fraser River are a community whose influence on the river's future is likely to be distinctly out of proportion to their relatively small population. In this essay we describe why this is so by drawing attention to the unique circumstances of First Nations among the various residents of the Fraser Valley and how their culture affects the kinds of decisions they make. The political importance of First Nations has important implications for resource planning and use. In this regard ours is a cautionary tale. Treaty negotiations and the several comprehensive and specific land claims which First Nations have filed will alter the political and economic landscape of the Fraser Valley in ways that are not predictable. This uncertainty is particularly significant for resource planning and management as these assume a regime of property rights, which, in this case, cannot yet be known. Finally, we highlight the complexity of the political circumstances facing the residents of the Fraser Valley, and particularly the First Nations. We argue that population size is not the relevant variable in considering the future of First Nations participation in the Fraser Valley. The tiny residential clusters of Stó:lō people sit almost unobserved and seemingly insignificant within this populous region of cities, sprawling suburbs, and high-technology factory-farms. But the Stó:lō presence and their role in shaping the regional economy, arguably, outweigh all other residents. Their importance rests upon who they are, how they are organized, and what they own.

As the example of the railroad barricade shows, the First Nations remain important largely because of their ability to defend their aboriginal rights by making their views heard and exercising influence throughout the province and beyond. First Nations people and institutions have established direct working relationships with members of the print, television, and radio media, with scholars at universities and colleges, with governmental agencies, and with other First Nations within Canada and around the world. We argue that non-Natives who want to conduct successful planning and decision-making processes need to adapt and take First Nations positions and interests in account. To be able to adapt successfully, non-Natives need to appreciate how

* Authored by J. E. Michael Kew and Bruce G. Miller and previously published in *Seeking Sustainability in the Lower Fraser Basin: Issues and Choices* (Healey 1999:47–63).

First Nations make decisions within the context of their unique social and cultural organizations. This issue is considered here in relation to aspects of Aboriginal title and the cultural traditions of First Nations of the lower Fraser basin.

First Nations Rights in Property

The response of Department of Fisheries and Oceans officials to the Stó:lō blockade of CN tracks was not a mere bending of political will. Nor was the blockade itself just an example of posturing by disgruntled Indian fishers. Stó:lō people and government officials are well aware of the significance of court decisions over the last two decades, decisions that have given new meaning to the phrases "aboriginal rights" and "aboriginal title." All citizens, but especially those concerned with resource development and planning, should understand that Aboriginal rights include property rights protected by the common law of the land and the Canadian Constitution. They have been given practical support in legislation and the current executive policies of both provincial and federal governments.

From entry of the province into Canada, in 1871, until late 1990, successive British Columbia governments dismissed the idea of Aboriginal title. However, beginning with the Supreme Court decision in *Calder* (1973) and sharpened with the decision in *Guerin* (1984), a series of court cases has confirmed existence of Aboriginal title and begun to clarify its significance. Most important among these cases in their immediate consequences for resource users have been court injunctions granted to First Nations to stop logging, road building, expansion of rights of way, and so on, pending outcome of negotiation of outstanding claims to the territory or resources arising from Aboriginal title (see Tennant 1990:222–225).

The federal Office of Native Claims invited submissions of comprehensive land claims and began negotiations with the Nisga'a in 1976. But it was not until 1990, after it became clear that the courts would stop development threatening Aboriginal interests, that the province decided to participate in treaty negotiations. In 1993 the B.C. Treaty Commission, consisting of representatives of federal, provincial, and First Nations governments and acting as a body to facilitate negotiations of treaties, invited submission of *statements of intent* to negotiate a treaty. By the summer of 1994 more than 40 statements had been filed. These included statements from the Katzie, Musqueum, Tsawwassen and Yale within the study area (B.C. Treaty Commission 1993–1994). In the fall of 1994 the Stó:lō Nation, with 21 constituent bands extending from Langley to Hope, also submitted a statement of intent to the Treaty Commission (*Sqwelqwel te Stó:lō* 1995). These steps have set in motion the process of negotiating settlement of those property rights which Stó:lō peoples have in their Aboriginal territories, that is, the lands, waterways, and resources existing in or flowing through the area they and their ancestors have used for thousands of years.

In practical terms, the extent and nature of these rights will be the outcome of negotiations. The strength of First Nations bargaining positions and their claims at the negotiation table are presently supported most clearly in court decisions on the character of Aboriginal rights as they come before the courts to be tested. *Sparrow* concerned Musqueum salmon-fishing rights in part of the Fraser estuary, and *Van der Peet* addressed Stó:lō rights to sell salmon caught above the commercial fishing boundary. Of widest current interest are the B.C. Court of Appeal decision and arguments in *Delgamuukw* (a case brought by Gitksan and Wet'suwet'en peoples of the Skeena and Bulkley Rivers). Striving to achieve clearer understanding of the nature and scope of aboriginal rights, in law, Justice Lambert listed eleven relevant conclusions. One of their important features is the way in which Aboriginal rights are based in the specific socio-cultural system of each Aboriginal people. Justice Lambert writes, for example, that

> (c) Aboriginal rights arise from customs, practices and traditions of an aboriginal people so long as those customs, practices and traditions *form an integral part of the distinctive culture of the aboriginal people*, and have been nurtured and protected by their culture and society. (*Sparrow*)

> (e) Aboriginal rights as *part of the social fabric of the aboriginal society* continued after the assertion of sovereignty by the Imperial Crown, but they were no longer limited in the institutions which protected those rights to the institutions of the aboriginal society. When those aboriginal rights, in accordance with the Doctrine of Continuity, continued *as part of the social fabric of the aboriginal society* after Sovereignty, then, in addition to being protected by the institutions of the aboriginal society, they were also recognized and protected by the common law. (*Guerin; Sparrow*) (Lambert 1994, paragraphs 720, 722) [emphases added]

The aboriginal rights of the Stó:lō people are rooted in the continuing reality of Stó:lō culture; they are specific to their culture, not derived from others.

In summary terms we may say that Stó:lō people have claimed Aboriginal title to all of the lands and resources of the study area. What will they claim at the negotiating table? It is not our right to say, but a glance at other recently negotiated treaties in Canada would lead us to expect they will claim new and more direct ownership of what are now Indian reserves, ownership of additional lands, reparations for lands and resources taken over or used by others, guarantees of use of some resources, and participation as owners in decisions about future developments which impinge upon lands and resource use. In short, Stó:lō want a just share of the wealth of their lands. In treaty negotiations they will likely claim rights to participate as owners in all facets or levels of planning and governance of the area. They are presently only participating in a small way in discussions about disposition of allowable catch of Fraser River salmon.

Two additional points need to be made about Aboriginal rights because they are sources of misunderstanding by the public. The first should be obvious from what has already been written, but it continues to confuse people. Aboriginal rights are unique and exclusive to Aboriginal peoples, and they are legal rights defined within and guaranteed by the state, specifically by the common law and, since 1982, by the Canadian Constitution. Those voices which raise the cry of "equal rights for all" in opposition to recognition of Aboriginal rights speak from ignorance of their own history and society.

Finally, Aboriginal rights are communal rights. They are not personal but rest with a socially or culturally defined group. They are not marketable or transferable in an ordinary sense, like rights in land with a fee simple title, or shares in a joint stock company. The members of the Aboriginal group—band, tribe, nation—share the rights in common as a group. They come to have the rights by recognized membership in the group, commonly by birthright. This is the legal basis of the existence of First Nations as governments. It is what sets them apart from all other citizens and users of the study area.

First Nations' Distinctive Cultural Identity

Lower Fraser people identify themselves according to their village of residence (in most cases the bands have been assigned ancient village names), family affiliation, and as *whelmuxw* "Indians." Most of the band members in the study region also identify themselves as *Stó:lō*, meaning "river," hence "people of the river," a term which is ancient in usage (see Duff 1952:11). However, some First Nations near the delta portions of the river, Musqueam, Tsawwassen, Coquitlam, Katzie, do not identify themselves as Stó:lō, although they are closely associated in other ways with upriver kinfolk. For convenience in this essay, and with apologies to those concerned, we use the term Stó:lō to include all the Halkomelem-speaking people on the mainland, that is, in the study area.

First Nations of British Columbia, including those of the lower Fraser Valley, constitute an order of government in addition to federal, provincial, and municipal governments. The First Nations are not clearly controlled by either federal or provincial legislation. At the same time, the property rights of First Nations remain intact, un-extinguished by contact, conflict, or legislation. These property rights are themselves poorly defined and the subject of political negotiation and legal action.

The First Nations differ from the mainstream community in other ways as well. The First Nations are the most committed to place and are the most sedentary of the people living along the Fraser. Their long-term occupation of the valley, of some 10,000 years, and their belief that they will continue there into the future establish property rights but also influence their sense of how the resources may be appropriately managed.

British Columbians are slowly coming to grips with the errors and omissions of their own history books, to realize that Aboriginal title to the land has not been extinguished. Although Aboriginal title is now generally recognized, the same is not true for Aboriginal society and culture. Canada's century-long policy of forced assimilation of First Peoples, while it changed cultural systems and wrought immeasurable personal and social devastation, did not eradicate the people or their distinctive traditionally rooted cultural systems. But it did direct First Nations to conceal their own distinctiveness when necessary, to develop acceptable facades convenient for parades, to publicize examples of "successful" integrators. Such accommodations have helped Canadians believe what they wanted to believe, that assimilation is working—perhaps it hasn't quite finished—but "real" Aboriginal cultures are a thing of the past. This view is just as much in error as the view that Aboriginal title does not exist. Distinctive cultural forms continue among the Stó:lō as elsewhere among B.C. First Nations. Along with Aboriginal rights, these continuing distinctive cultures and the continuing reality of Stó:lō identity establish and ensure their place in the overall governance of the local region.

We will focus this brief discussion of Stó:lō culture on three distinctive facets of contemporary life: (a) kinship system, (b) world view and religion, and (c) political organization. We have found that within each of these fields, Stó:lō differ from their neighbours, and the three taken together constitute a core of Stó:lō culture today.

Kinship System

Stó:lō villages in earlier times consisted of clusters of large wooden houses, each the property of an extended family—a core of bilineally related kin (i.e., related by blood to two common family lines) and their spouses, extending through several generations. Nuclear family units each had their own area or open-sided compartment within the house for their own personal and communal arrangements for ordinary daily life. These small family units worked cooperatively and collaboratively with others in the household. Under the leadership of senior, respected members of the house, *siy:am*, the whole large group engaged in joint ventures where larger numbers of workers or supporters were needed.

The old style of "big-house" or "smoke-house" is still in use today, mainly for ceremonial purposes when large assemblies of people are necessary, and especially during the winter spirit dance season. At this time extended families once again may live within the house with the old form of domestic arrangements. Thus, in the absence of the old form of arrangements, within what appear to be conventional non-Native residential arrangements of separate suburban homes, the extended family structure and identity continue.

A distinctive feature of Stó:lō kinship is the conceptual framework underlying its system of terminology. This consists of a relatively small number of categories of blood kin (all those sharing a line of descent) extended widely. For example, all blood relatives of one's own generation are like siblings, and all of the parents' generation, except mother and father, are like aunt/uncle (one term). This part of the system is highly classificatory by generation.

Terms for affinal kin (those related by marriage) follow an entirely different structural pattern. Unlike English terms they are not simply modifications of blood-kin terms but refer to sets of spouse's kin and sets of affinals of one's own kin. Suttles (1987) has pointed out that these opposed sets of kin have conventional obligations and responsibilities of families linked by marriage. Here it is necessary to refer to the Stó:lō rules of marriage, which prohibit connections between blood kin. An important and well-known consequence of this rule is that local villages tended to be exogamous—appropriate marriage partners usually had to be sought outside the village and often outside the local area.

A secondary consequence of these patterns and the marriage rule is that both blood-kin and affinal-kin connections are widely distributed through many villages and over wide areas within and even beyond Stó:lō territory. Among the Stó:lō, the indigenous kin term system lays a great chart of kinfolk before each individual as a guide with which to identify and establish close and supportive associations.

The complex details of the terminology in Halkomelem are unfamiliar to many young Stó:lō, and, as with all kinship systems, the terminology is learned and known in a referential and non-analytic sense. Like all systems it is also subject to change. English glosses such as "cousin," "sister" or "brother" are now commonplace substitutes for two original terms which distinguish only relative order of birth among blood kin in one's own generation. But these English terms are used for a much wider circle of kin than when used by non-Stó:lō. The Stó:lō principles of kin structure are retained even with the English terms.

In this kinship system a key element is the common ancestor linking sets of blood kin. They are kinfolk and remain members of the family. Some kin terms change upon death, marking the condition of the individual and loss of the connecting link between living kin. Upon death the soul continues, and living family members, in taking care of their dead, keep in memory those members gone from the world of the living. Stó:lō kin groups may truthfully be said to extend over wide areas and to extend back through great spans of time.

Death marks a transition in status of a family member. Among the Stó:lō, funerals are occasions for congregations of hundreds of kinfolk and friends of the deceased's family. Family members are rendered support and assistance, including gifts or repayments of previously extended support, usually of money or foodstuffs, from affinal kin, friends, and distant family members. These are times when the "charts" of family kinship become visible social groups, occasions that are extremely important for older members to renew contact with kin, and for youths and children to meet and become newly acquainted with theirs (see Kew 1970 for additional accounts of rituals relating to death).

In addition to care given at funerals, decreased kin of importance to the family may be memorialized on a later occasion at which the family ceremoniously remembers and puts away mementos of the lost one. At funerals and memorials, and by many families as an annual act, favourite foods are fed to the deceased kin by a ritualist employed for the purpose. Such activities are also marked by the family acting together to invite and host guests from near and far.

Our observations of and participation in Stó:lō community activities during the period of study confirm the continuing role of these traditionally based activities. They continue to be vital to community life, just as they were 25 years earlier when first observed by the senior author, and as they presumably were in earlier times as well. The activities we were called upon to witness in the course of our research differ from earlier decades only in the large numbers of people now participating, and in the fact that today *tradition* serves more explicitly as a rallying theme for thinking about and directing actions towards independence and distinctive identity. Stó:lō people have resisted both explicit government policy of assimilation and pervasive assimilationist pressures of media and market (Carlson 1997).

The system of administration and dependent local governments subsumed under the band system administered by Indian and Northern Affairs may at first glance appear to have replaced the older local social system. But all the bands designated were established to replace one or more older village units, and the bands often retain those village names. Today, the normal day-to-day residences and households are usually occupied by nuclear family units. But band villages continue in the old pattern as well, with each extended family having connections with families in other villages from one end of Stó:lō territory to the other. They provide the living, dynamic fabric of modern Stó:lō social life in an ancient framework, and this sets them apart from other residents of the study region.

World View and Religion

No sphere of Stó:lō knowledge has experienced more direct and sustained attack than that of religious belief. Yet it too has survived and even experienced a resurgence in recent decades (Kew 1990). We will attempt to provide here a brief, analytic summary of key elements of the system, which is complex and firmly embedded in social relations. It is entirely appropriate when striving to understand another cultural system to begin with some fundamental metaphysical concepts. We begin with a review of traditional conception of the self, which is necessary to understand Stó:lō concern for health and well-being of individuals and their communities. The following analytic construction draws upon the work Jenness (1955), Duff (1952), Suttles (1955, 1958, 1960), Lane (1953), and Kew (1970), and field work by Kew.

According to Stó:lō belief, humans are set in the world in position which is essentially one of the weakness and dependence upon non-human powers. These are located in the world but outside the usual human sphere of activity—outside the home and village and ordinary centres of daily life. Non-human powers may be identified with animals, plants, or inanimate things and places. Powers are mysterious and unknowable except as they may reveal themselves in limited ways to humans. It is from the non-human sphere that humans obtain food, materials for manufacture, fuel, strength, luck, health, all that is necessary for life. A sense of dependence upon such necessities gives meaning to the rites of propitiation and thanksgiving which were indigenous and continue to be expressed, such as first salmon ceremonies, prayers of thanks for food, ritual bathing, and fasting. Christian prayers of thanksgiving expressing gratitude and respect for the source of well-being were readily adopted when introduced by missionaries. These prayers survive in Halkomelem and are regularly used at village and tribal ceremonies. The sun is recognized as a source or component of vitality. Its morning rays are beneficial and health-giving. Accordingly, elders continue to enjoin upon youth the practice of bathing in flowing streams or lakes in the light of the rising sun. The cycle of the day is repeated in the cycle of the year, with spring being a renewal and re-awakening like the sunrise of a day (see explanation by Peter Pierre of Katzie, in Jenness 1955).

All individual humans have a physical body and a number of other essential components whose identities may be translated as mind/sense, vitality/life-force, shadow/reflection, soul/ghost. It is essential to life and good health that these components be present and whole within the body. Any one may be detached by misadventure or by powerful external forces, especially during times of weakness such as sleep, infancy or childhood, physical injury to the body, and so on. Stó:lō recognize several different types of "doctors" or medico-religious specialists. Acting within the range of their appropriate expertise, these curers are able to diagnose illnesses and effect cures of those forms of illness due to loss or disruption of one of these essential aspects of the self. Curative procedures entail locating, returning, and adjusting the place and relationship of these aspects to the person; permanent loss of one of them will cause death, upon which the soul continues to exist as a spirit or ghost, remaining around the place of the body's interment.

In addition to these attributes of the normal healthy self, individuals may acquire additional attributes. They are known as *se'lye*, or in ethnographic terminology as "guardian spirits." In the Stó:lō view they are gifts to the individual from a particular spirit force or power in the non-human world. They may come unbidden and unsought to an individual, or as a successful conclusion to rigorous searching and purification during which an individual may remove from association with other humans, bathe frequently in fresh water, and fast. Seeking a *se'lye*, attaining one, or simply being visited by one, is a serious, not to say dangerous, act. For humans, the powers of the non-human world always have a dual character—they may be beneficent, providing health, strength, and good fortune, or they may be harmful, causing illness and death. Those individuals who acquire such powers follow specific courses of action in order to maintain their health. Some of the requirements, in the case of the spirit power, are entirely private and known only to the individual concerned. The power conveyed to individuals may include a song and accompanying dance. During winter months these are performed in public confirmation of power and in order to maintain a health-giving association with the power. Through the winter season hundreds of people attend weekly gatherings for *syewen* dancing. These are hosted by family or village groups and are convened in the "big-houses" or "smoke-houses," replicas of the old extended family dwelling.

This complex of belief and activity, focused on *syewen* dancing, constitutes a central linchpin in Stó:lō culture today. It verifies and displays at once, to the attendant congregation of people, the power of non-humans, the subordinate position of humans, and the ability of those favoured humans to fulfill critical, difficult roles which individuals must undertake in order to sustain favourable relations with the non-human world. The public performance of spirit-power gifts draws individuals together as one, sharing and reaffirming as a whole their intregrity and strength as a people.

Most Stó:lō people are nominal members of a Christian church, predominantly Roman Catholic. Although missionaries achieved remarkable success in earlier years and converted many, they did not extinguish indigenous ideas or activities. In recent decades, with the growth of the Stó:lō population and removal of prohibitory legislation in the Indian Act, there has been a substantial resurgence of open participation in the spirit-power ceremonies (Kew 1990:479–480). The continuance of Christian affiliation and participation in spirit dancing are no longer seen by either Stó:lō or many church officials as contradictory.

Self-Governance and Decision Making

The organization of decision making in First Nations is poorly understood by members of the mainstream community, a circumstance that impedes collaborative planning. The converse is not true, however, and First Nations have a long history of working within the confines of the mainstream governmental system. We suggest that attention to the way Native political processes are conducted could alleviate some of the burden carried by First Nations in finding common ground for the resolution of disputes and for routine politics. At the moment, Stó:lō and other First Nations leaders carry this load and have responded by making frequent public appearances to explain their own system to the mainstream society. Chief Clarence Pennier, for example, described Stó:lō governance to the Royal Commission on Aboriginal Peoples in August of 1991; Gwen Point made a presentation to education leaders at the Stó:lō longhouse on the Coqualeetza grounds in May of 1993. These presentations emphasize that the formal political structure decreed in the Indian Act is not the sole relevant political and decision-making unit. Governance works somewhat differently among the First Nations than for others of the Lower Mainland. This difference provides a resource to Native communities and potentially to mainstream society as well. At present, governance is both highly experimental and deeply traditional. More precisely, the present political structures are neo-traditional in that concepts with considerable antiquity continue as the basis for community social and political organization but are manifested in new ways. Chief Steven Point noted that "Our structure must be flexible, meaning the ability to change with the ever-changing needs of the people" (*Sqwelqwel* 1994a). Changes to the formal system of governance reflect three primary motivations at present. One is an interest in altering those aspects of the Indian Act election system which are incompatible with traditional practices. The second motivation is to create a political solidarity which is isomorphic with cultural identity (as we describe above) for the purposes of negotiating with the federal and provincial governments. The third is the creation of effective governmental and community institutions as part of the process of developing self-government.

In the fall of 1994, the Stó:lō communities completed the revision of the formal political structure. Two free-standing tribal councils, the Stó:lō Tribal Council and the Stó:lō Nation Canada, were merged into one, known as the Stó:lō Nation. The Stó:lō Nation is governed by the House of *Siy:am*, which is composed of respected leaders of the constituent families which make up the various bands. In one community, Ohamil, in the interest of moving closer to Aboriginal political practices, the election of band council members has been replaced by a selection of a *Yewal Siy:am* chosen by the family leaders, who acts as chair of the band council. Meanwhile, governmental and community institutions are being regularly created and developed. The Stó:lō health and social services division, for example, recently created *Xolhmi:lh*, a child welfare program, and *Tsu'ts'lwatil*, a life skills training program. Many other community health, planning, cultural, housing, and education programs have been created in recent years.

The present formal structure of governance is supported by an informal, much less visible system. This informal system is built on the broad networks of kinship and social relations which define the nation, and it clarifies group identity. Furthermore, the informal system underlies Stó:lō concepts of ownership. For example, rights to fishing and gathering locations or ceremonial prerogatives are thought to derive from participation in this system. Those people (known as *siy:am* or, in the words of Chief Sonny McHailsie, "wealthy, respected people") who stand at the centre of this regional system and who manage these social relations act as leaders independent of the formal political structure. Collectively they form a sort of consultative government with significant, even critical, influence on the formal political leaders, who rely on the ability of the informal leaders to articulate community values and to coalesce public opinion. The *siy:am* articulate these values at formal political events and at cultural and religious events.

The Coast Salish of southern British Columbia and northwestern Washington state have already been characterized as having a social system which enables its members to maintain contacts over a broad area. Consequently, resources are shared within a large universe of relatives (Elmendorf 1971; Suttles 1987). The traditional culture and current values emphasize the importance of marriage to someone with no genealogical connection within five or six generational links. Because Coast Salish communities are small and frequently composed of people with ancestors in common, present-day people, as was true of their ancestors, have been forced to seek marriage partners elsewhere. Members of one community regularly marry members of another, and individuals have relatives spread over the entire Coast Salish world and beyond (Allen 1976). This practice of intermarriage defines the borders of the Salish world, and marriage itself creates the basis for other significant social relations (Miller 1989).

In the traditional culture, a wedding established significant social obligations between affinal relations, not just the bride and groom, and travelers brought gifts of food or other commodities to their relatives. In turn, affinal relatives engaged in a common ceremonial life, attending funerals, weddings, potlatches, and winter-time Spirit Dancing together. The movement of goods within the region through gifting between affinal relatives and distribution at potlatches helped cement the moral connections between the members of the wide social network. This made the entire region, to a degree, a single system, through a pattern of reciprocity which continues to exist today (Suttles 1987). One observer, noting the common participation in ceremonial life throughout the region, spoke of the social networks as composing a Coast Salish "ritual congregation." These social relations between communities create a powerful integration of the larger Coast Salish community and provide the basis for group action.

The pattern of intermarriage links people in ceremonial life and also links the political elite—the hereditary chiefs—through ties of kinship over a wide area. Many of the chiefs of the lower Fraser from Yale to below Sardis and Chilliwack, for example, are related through common descent from a single nineteenth-century chief. These chiefs are today described as cousins, a term which denotes social closeness and a relationship which forms the basis for common action and, potentially, real solidarity in a sense similar to the sibling relationship in the mainstream community.

In addition to the properties of coherence and permanence of affiliation, Coast Salish social networks allow for short-term bouts of disaffiliation by individual members, communities, bands, or other constituent groups without substantively affecting the long-term social system, disrupting cultural continuity, or dissolving the boundaries of the Coast Salish moral universe. Examples of this in recent years include actions by bands to disaffiliate themselves from tribal councils or the refusal to participate in meetings of common interest to First Nations, such as fisheries meetings. Individual people, including leaders, sometimes practice what one Stó:lō chief called a "pulling-out strategy" to express reservations about decisions taken by the collective, or to influence internal political processes. Perhaps the most important aspect of this strategy is that, eventually, such people or groups are re-affiliated into the larger Coast Salish political community without penalty. Such actions are best understood as routine political actions rather than as schisms and ought not to be taken as evidence of political collapse or ineptitude. Instead, this property of the social network is a resource that allows for changing configurations of public opinion and for the establishment of alternative directions. One might argue that Stó:lō people can choose between alternative political approaches before a consensus gradually emerges among the leaders of the constituent bands. This property of the social network rests on the idea of permanence and continuity; the First Nations understand that their ancestors affiliated, disaffiliated, and re-affiliated over very long periods and that their descendants and heirs will do the same.

Present Stó:lō Formal Political Organization

The Coast Salish peoples of the lower Fraser River are, at present, organized into several political bodies. Bands hold formal recognition from the federal and provincial governments and are the entities that have title to any assets held in common by First Nations. Tribes are umbrella organizations composed of several culturally related bands. They exist to create an economy of scale in providing services to band members, to create a more powerful political presence in the province, and as a recognition of a common nationality among the member bands. In this sense, bands and tribes are creations of contact with non-Natives. The largest of the tribes in the region is the Stó:lō Nation referred to above. The Alliance Tribal Council, comprising seven bands, is another. The Stó:lō Nation is composed of 21 bands, with an aggregate population of about 6,000. A representative from each band is appointed to the House of *Siy:am*, or council of chiefs and councilors, which forms the legislative arm of the tribe. Six of the members of the council compose an executive (Special Chief's Council), with one selected as chief's representative and another as vice-chief. These six coucillors divide the portfolios, thereby creating a division of labour for the creation of policy. Among the important functions conducted by the Stó:lō Nation are the treaty negotiations with the federal and provincial governments, economic development, and mental and biomedical health services. Members of the various bands staff these units along with some non-band members. The Stó:lō Nation organization maintains affiliations with federal, provincial, and municipal authorities, with private institutions, and with a wide range of public planning bodies.

The sheer complexity of the tasks facing the tribal council organization is an important issue, and tribal councils remain underfunded and understaffed to carry out all of the requisite tasks (Robbins 1986). These disadvantages are mitigated somewhat by the fact that many employees and councilors concern themselves with a wider range of issues (and hold considerably more responsibility) than do comparable people in mainstream government. Over their careers, these people gain a broad sense of tribal government operations. Overlapping of personnel confers another sort of benefit: information ordinarily flows more quickly and freely than in other governments. This is in part because some councilors are also administrators and because many employees have responsibilities in more than one area. It is perhaps less characteristic of tribal governments than of the mainstream to have separate government agencies operating without knowledge of each other or under policies in conflict. However, on any given day an astonishing array of people with diverse interests interacts with the Stó:lō Nation, and staff must be ready to respond to the outsiders, in addition to dealing with the concerns and needs of members of the constituent bands.

The bands themselves are composed of extended families and organized around councils, whose head is a member of the Stó:lō Nation House of *Siy:am*. The councils are subordinate to the will of the general membership as expressed in annual (or more frequent) general meetings. Band councilors hold portfolios (education, economic development, and so on), and other band members join councilors in serving on a variety of committees which develop policy to propose to the councils and to oversee band operations. Committees are formed as needed to consider such topics as housing, the environment, youth programs, and economic development. Bands employ a staff of professionals such as planners and others to conduct programs. Bands, as do the tribal councils, maintain contacts with a variety of governmental and private agencies.

Most band and tribal councilors, administrators, and other employees are band or community members. As such, they regularly attend community events in which statements of important cultural values are forcefully made. Funerals are among the most frequent and important of these events, which also include potlatches, memorials, and school graduations. At such occasions senior people (elders), who are generally not part of the formal political apparatus at either the band or the tribal level, address the public. It is especially on such occasions that the formal and informal political systems intersect, and leaders of the formal system receive very direct instructions regarding their obligations to the community and the values of the community. A recent example of this occurred at the ceremony held to induct the members of the House of *Siy:am* after the creation of the unified Stó:lō Nation. Before the councilors were sworn into their new offices, witnesses were called. These witnesses validate the work carried out and have the obligation to testify to the nature of the event if called to do so in the future, but they also spoke directly to the audience and the new councilors, reminding them of their obligations and of the community support for them. Especially in recent years, non-community members are called upon as witnesses, an incorporative act which draws members of the mainstream political community in the Coast Salish world. For example, in July of 1993, several governmental officials, including B.C. cabinet minister Andrew Petter, attended the Hatzic Rock Celebration, held to commemorate the preservation of a sacred site, and were called as witnesses. These non-Native witnesses, too, hear the addresses of elders who articulate critical values and contemporary political stances of the community. On some occasions these meetings are held within a longhouse, a traditional site within which debate is held and differences are resolved, but also a site of spiritual significance. Within the longhouse, the messages carry additional meaning and enable the Stó:lō to convey the depth of their commitment to their values and traditional practices. It is especially within this setting that the fullest articulation of the formal and informal political structures occurs.

Conclusions: Stó:lō Resource Use and Planning

Stó:lō people have survived two centuries of colonization in which their original population was decimated by new disease, their lands occupied, their resources destroyed, their communities reduced in number and pushed aside to live on tiny pockets of Indian reserve lands under a culturally destructive system of administration. Measured by mainstream standards they are today undereducated, subject to high rates of unemployment, and poor. Yet, as we have indicated, family and community life continues to be distinctive and strong, and their society is rich in expressive tradition and dynamic in its political resources.

Canadians who look to the culture of the Stó:lō or other indigenous people for an easy solution to problems of environmental degradation, or who hope for a formula for sustainable development, are looking for the impossible. To First Nations people, with a long experience of colonial exploitation, such expectations are all too familiar. Nevertheless, there is a lesson to be learned without taking anything from the Stó:lō. It lies in understanding their culture and history as a whole. We find that the Stó:lō idea of interdependence or reciprocity between humans and non-humans embodies a philosophical theory which has merit. But it is, we suggest, not radically different from western systems theory which underlies the idea of ecology. Where the Stó:lō differ, however, is that their ideas are given immediate and forceful ritual expression in personal and social life. The unpredictable, precarious, and delicately balanced relationship of humans and all other forces is made evident and real in Stó:lō experience. Holding a balance has personal meaning and more directly informs their collective social and political action.

In large part this derives from the integrity of their community and the stability of their population in this place. They have existed in the lower Fraser Valley since "time immemorial," and they have no intention, as a people, of moving. They are born and die in their homeland. They invest their surplus wealth there, desire their children to live there, and plan their future to be there. They are committed, in a way no other residents are, to ensuring future viability of life in their homeland.

Stó:lō will continue to be important participants in the economy of the Fraser Valley. Their rights to their small reserves and to the use of remaining resources will continue whether treaties are concluded or not. Most activities of the Stó:lō Nation and band government are devoted to meeting the pragmatic ongoing needs of their communities: coordinating and administering education programs, health services, social welfare and child care, housing, employment and economic development, and so on. Band and nation agents coordinate the provision of services available through provincial and federal agencies, aiming to ensure adequate service for their people.

The Stó:lō also continue to develop policies and operate special programs to meet their own specific perspectives and needs, a process which has accelerated since the achievement of political unity under the banner of the Stó:lō Nation. Two tribal departments have particular responsibility for issues that influence the disposition of land and resources. These are Aboriginal Rights and Title, which is concerned with land claims, fishing, and self-government, and Culture and Heritage, which addresses spiritual and cultural activities. Both departments seek to protect culturally significant lands, such as the 18-acre site around the Hatzic Rock preserved in 1993. Stó:lō Nation personnel continue to document the impact of current and historic urbanization on their region—for example, the drainage of Sumas Lake earlier in the century (*Sqwelqwel te Stó:lō* 1995:9). Tribal environmental policies and economic development plans consider the impact of regional population growth, logging, the loss of fish habitat, contamination of lands, and the use of lands for housing. Tribal environmental planners note that "Aboriginal people hold the great responsibility of protecting the environment" (*Sqwelqwel* 1994b). In the Stó:lō view the health of the Fraser River is tied to the survival of Stó:lō culture, identity, way of life, and ultimately to Stó:lō sovereignty and the resolution of land claims (*Sqwelqwel* 1994b). Tribal planners are at present creating new economic uses of Stó:lō territory, particularly through a cultural tourism program.

In short, Stó:lō currently represent a distinct cultural and political component of the Fraser Valley population, one that has unique rights in lands and resources of the area, and one that will endure. Any planning for use of lands, waters, and resources in the valley affects Stó:lō interest. They can exercise power beyond the measure of their numbers alone to impede forms of development which threaten to impinge upon their rights. Thus, if planning for future developments in the valley is to be reasonably secure, Stó:lō must be consulted and involved.

Uncertainty of treaty negotiations and the unique nature of Stó:lō organization are sources of disquiet among other interest groups; they also open possibilities for creating new initiatives for resource sustainability. Rational planning in the study area with sustainability as a goal is impossible without the conclusion of treaty negotiations. The highly competitive nature of such business enterprises as commercial fishing, real estate development, and so on, coupled with uncertainty about the outcome of treaty negotiations, causes concern for many citizens. It is proper to ask the question, what will treaty negotiations mean for sustainability of resources in the Fraser Valley? Without presuming to speak for others, we believe the evidence suggests treaty settlements are essential to effective planning for sustainability. Conversely, sustainability, being one of the main reiterated objectives of First Nations' treaty positions, is entirely consistent with treaty making. Treaty making is essential because it provides relative security of tenure for all segments of the community. Further, sustainability and treaties are compatible because they promote local management, continued commitment and investment locally, and the use of internal and local mechanisms of social control.

References Cited

Allen, E. J. 1976. Intergroup Ties and Exogamy among the Northwest Coast Salish. *Northwest Anthropological Research Notes*, 10(2):161–172.

British Columbia Treaty Commission. First Annual Report. 1993–1994. Victoria, British Columbia.

Calder v British Columbia (AG). 1973. S.C.R. 313, [1973] 4 W.W.R. 1

Carlson, Keith Thor, editor. 1997. *You Are Asked to Witness. The Stó:lō in Canada's Pacific Coast History*. Chilliwack, BC: Stó:lō Historic Trust.

Duff, Wilson. 1952. The Upper Stalo Indians of the Fraser Valley, B.C. *Anthropology in British Columbia, Memoirs*, 1.

Elmendorf, William W. 1971. Coast Salish Status Ranking and Intergroup Ties. *Southwestern Journal of Anthropology,* 27(4):353–380.

Healey, Michael, editor. 1999. *Seeking Sustainability in the Lower Fraser Basin.* Vancouver: Institute for Resources and the Environment, Westwater Research.

Jenness, Diamond. 1955. The Faith of a Coast Salish Indian. *Anthropology in British Columbia. Memoirs* 3. B.C. Provincial Museum: Victoria.

Kew, J. E. M. 1970 . Coast Salish Ceremonial Life: Status and Identity in a Modern Village. Ph.D. dissertation. University of Washington.

——— 1990. History of Coastal British Columbia since 1849. In *Handbook of North American Indians,* Volume 7*: Northwest Coast*, edited by Wayne Suttles, pp. 159–168. Washington, D.C.: Smithsonian Institution.

Lambert, J. A. 1994. Reasons for Judgement of Mr. Justice Lambert (Dissenting). Court of Appeal of B.C. *Delgamuukw v. British Columbia (B.C.C.A.)*

Lane, Barbara. 1953. A Comparative and Analytic Study of Some Aspects of Northwest Coast Religion. Ph.D. dissertation, Department of Anthropology, University of Washington.

Miller, Bruce. 1989. Centrality and Measures of Regional Structure in Aboriginal Western Washington. *Ethnology*, 28(3):265–276.

R v Guerin. 1984. 2 S.C.R. 335

R v Sparrow. 1990. 1 S.C.R. 1075

Robbins, Lynn. 1986. Upper Skagit [Washington] and Gambell [Alaska] Indian Reorganization Act Governments: Struggles with Constraints, Restraints, and Power. *American Indian Culture and Research Journal,* 10(2):61–73.

Sqwelqwel. 1994a. Vol. 3(2).

52

Sqwelqwel. 1994b. Vol. 3(1).

Sqwelqwel te Stó:lō. 1995. Vol. 1(1).

Suttles, Wayne. 1955. Katzie Ethnographic Notes. *Anthropology in British Columbia, Memoirs 2.* Victoria: B.C. Provincial Museum.

———— 1958. Private Knowledge, Morality, and Social Classes among the Coast Salish. *American Anthropologist,* 60(3):497–507.

———— 1960. Affinal Ties, Subsistence, and Prestige Among the Coast Salish. *American Anthropologist,* 62(2):296–305.

———— 1987. *Coast Salish Essays.* Seattle: University of Washington Press.

Tennant, Paul. 1990. *Aboriginal Peoples and Politics: The Indian Land Question.* Vancouver, B.C.: UBC Press.

4

Creating Chiefdoms: The Puget Sound Case*

This essay deals with a regional problem that has gained force nationwide; namely, the reinterpretation of past cultural institutions to serve contemporary needs. There has been considerable treatment of the "invention of tradition" (see Clifford 1988), some sympathetic, some caustic. While scholarly attention is now focused on the political uses made by non-Europeans of cultural traditions (e.g., Hobsbawm and Ranger 1983; Hanson 1989), the reinvention by anthropologists of the Native American still occurs, sometimes collaboratively with the people whom they are studying. Just as governments created administrative units referred to as tribes for their own political reasons in the encounter between European and non-European societies (Suttles 1988:1), anthropologists continue to do so for their own reasons. We address several related issues: the importance of the problems associated with the use of theoretical models to place poorly known societies into types from which other undocumented cultural features can be attributed (Sturtevant 1983); the sometimes misleading assumption that anthropologists can easily deal with historical documents; and the valuable contributions that ethnohistorians and historians can make in these debates.

In two recent articles Kenneth D. Tollefson has argued for the recognition of chiefdoms in protohistoric Puget Sound (1987, 1989:Figure 5).[1] His work has been influential: Kehoe (1992) has included this material in her well known textbook, in the revised chapter on the Northwest Coast, and Isaac (1988:ii) noted that "the best case to date for the existence of a chiefdom on the Northwest Coast has been made by Kenneth Tollefson (1987) for the Puget Sound Indians." Furthermore, Tollefson's reassessment of the region may have important implications for current political issues, particularly the claims of several tribes to federal recognition[2] and the competition among tribes over the allocation of fish under the terms of a federal court decision.[3] Since Tollefson's argument purportedly refutes standard explanations it merits attention. We argue that his theoretical treatments of the chiefdom concept and the ethnohistorical reconstruction of Puget Sound social organization are misleading. We do not feel that present political needs require a reinterpretation of traditional Coast Salish social organization.[4] In this article we explore several problems with Tollefson's hypothesis and provide an alternative view of Coast Salish political structure that builds on previous scholarship.

In the final publication in his distinguished career, Northwest Coast ethnologist Philip Drucker hypothesized that the only political unit in native Northwest Coast culture was the local group (Drucker 1983:87). In order to understand Puget Sound Indian social organization in the mid-nineteenth century, we wish to expand on Drucker's view by showing how such local groups interacted to form a regional structure. The following outline of the local group concept is integrated with the related principles of bilateral kinship reckoning, the class/rank structure, marriage relationships, residence and seasonal movements, and the control of productive resources. We then show the relationship of the local group to the regional system of interaction, which may itself be regarded as having political implications (Miller 1989c).

*"Creating Chiefdoms: the Puget Sound Case" in *Ethnohistory*, vol 41(2). Bruce G. Miller and Daniel L. Boxberger. Pp. 267–293. Copyright, 1994, Duke University Press. All rights reserved. Republished by permission of the publisher. www.dukepress.edu <https://www.dukeupress.edu/>

54

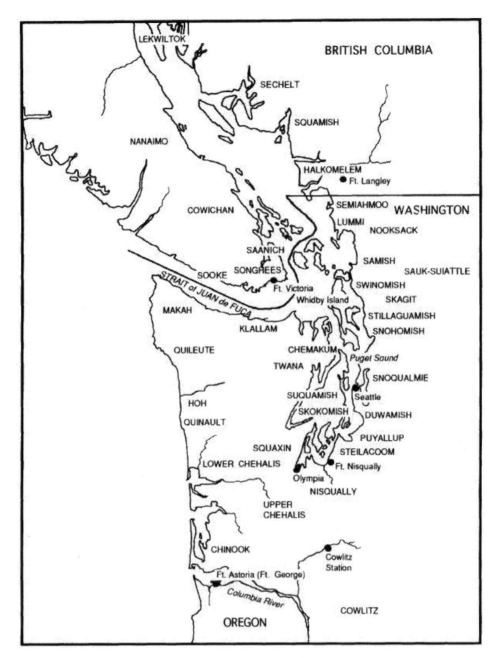

Figure 8. Map of western Washington and southwest British Columbia, ca. 1855.

Coast Salish Social Organization

Before the establishment of reservations, the native people of western Washington were predominantly semisedentary, traveling seasonally to various resource procurement areas, including fishing, shellfishing, and plant-gathering sites. While there was some variation, the general pattern was for several households to aggregate, usually during the winter months. In the early 1800s there also appears to have been some aggregation for protection from increased raiding activity by northern Northwest Coast tribes. While the establishment of permanent trading operations in the area in the early 1800s caused some social disruption, the general pattern of subsistence use continued much as before.

Although village aggregates existed, they were composed of households that were the core economic units, united by bonds of kinship to other, similar households. The household, in this context, refers to a set of individual families who shared the same structure while maintaining some forms of economic independence. However, the families within a household cooperated in certain types of subsistence or ceremonial activities, especially those requiring a great deal of labor or the accumulation of vast amounts of wealth. Generally an aggregate or village consisted of several households, more appropriately termed a "household cluster" (Barnett 1955:21). These aggregates comprised the "local group" and could be said to constitute the fundamental political unit of Puget Sound social organization. According to testimony presented in the 1920s, these household clusters ranged in size from one to fourteen households at treaty time (*Dwamish et al. v. United States*, 79 Ct. C. [1934]).

It is our contention that tribes did not emerge among Puget Sound Indians until necessitated by interaction with European settlers and with the United States government, especially during the early 1900s when political entities ("tribes") were a requirement in order to bring lawsuits against the federal government. Before that time it is likely that one most closely identified with the group with which one was residing. Allegiance and identification could, and often did, extend to other groups, the primary bond being a shared language and culture, not a unified political structure. Elmendorf (1960) suggested the concept of speech community as a means of understanding larger social groupings in western Washington.

> The chief bonds between the various villages within the speech community were a common language not spoken elsewhere, common customs, a common, single drainage-area territory, and a common ethnic and linguistic name…Other unifying factors were lacking. There was no political organization for the speech community, nor any traditional patterns of unified action among its constituent village communities. (Elmendorf 1960:255)

Consequently, some modern researchers suggest that the linguistic affiliation is a more useful concept than tribe (Kew 1981:62–63; see also Jorgensen 1980:1–2).

The speech community was the group within which individuals would tend to marry and also where the greatest sharing of resources and ceremonial interaction would take place. In Drucker's sense the local groups (which were politically interdependent units, but not under the authority of central leadership), were the groups that composed the village aggregates, and numerous village aggregates composed the speech community. The local group was either a single household or a number of households, varying in the strength and number of ties to other village aggregates. Local groups were fluid, and households sometimes broke off and joined other groups to improve their circumstances, ordinarily interacting with those speaking the same language.

Although an individual's immediate allegiance was to their household, this did not mean that members of a household necessarily cooperated in resource procurement activities. The nuclear family was the basic unit in the acquisition, preparation, and consumption of food. Many activities involved work crews or camp groups recruited from the extended kin group, often, but not necessarily, from the same household, or even from the same village.

The native people of western Washington shared similar kinship systems despite some cultural and linguistic differences. The kinship relationships were reckoned bilaterally, with generational emphasis predominating. Relationships could be extended laterally as far as an individual could reckon kin, although recognizable relationships beyond great-grandparent were rare. Since everyone has eight great-grandparents, this meant there could be literally hundreds of individuals descended from the great-grandparent generation. Inclusion in the kin networks of a spouse further increased the number of potential functional kin relationships. These extensive collateral-kin relationships meant that an individual would have relations in dozens of different villages, and it was not uncommon to have grandparents from four different local groups. Still, a person's primary allegiance was to their household of residence. Kin ties created a network of relationships that extended as far as an individual was capable of reckoning kin, and could be called upon for support.

The household tended to be composed of several families, probably with a patrilocal bias in residence patterns, and was generally headed by a senior man and woman who oversaw certain subsistence activities, especially the more labor-intensive fishing tasks such as the construction of a fish weir. The composition of households was not permanent. The data on the members are fragmentary, but it appears that several nuclear families joined by bonds of kinship (either through the houseowner or the owner's spouse) would come together to form a household. The households seemed most often to be composed of an owner and his sons, brothers, or male cousins, and their families (Collins 1949:155; Suttles 1951a:273; Barnett 1955:242), but any number of other collateral kin or affinal kin might also join the household. Households within a village aggregate were independent of one another, although they might cooperate for various purposes, such as defense, and might align with each other for other political purposes.

The role the local kin group played in determining access to resource procurement sites was affected by a complex interaction between free-access resources and restricted access to certain resource procurement locations that were held in trust by individuals for a larger kin group. An individual could access resources as far as their (or the spouse's) kinship networks extended. For practically everyone this included virtually the entire territory occupied by the speech community. Ownership of a fishing site (a fish weir or reef net location) placed certain obligations on the site owner to select crew members from among kin and housemates. Through this arrangement, however, the owner would gain enhanced status, and the ability to attract and support large numbers of kin (and some nonkin) would raise one's relative status among the local group. Often marriages were arranged with the intent of gaining access to particularly productive areas, thereby increasing the family group's options.

According to the ethnographic descriptions, western Washington Indian society was divided into three general social groups: the upper class, the lower class, and slaves. This ranking system can be visualized as an inverted pear (Suttles 1958), for the greater number of people belonged to the upper class while a smaller number belonged to the lower class, and slaves, while they certainly existed, were probably not common. Members of the upper class were expected to have proper deportment and a knowledge of their heritable, as well as inherited, privileges. An individual gained status by being of good family and having no trace of slave ancestry, by having some kind of private or guarded knowledge that often included gossip about other upper- or lower-class families, and by accumulating wealth, which was necessary for validating inherited privileges and gaining prestige. Some confusion exists over the so-called lower class. Suttles (1958) describes this group as those who have become impoverished or groups that have "lost their history." Little information is available on this group and, as Drucker suggests (1983:89), they may be an artifact of social disruption during the contact period.

The fur trade provided new forms of wealth and enabled some individuals to gain more power than they might have previously been able to acquire. Certainly the trade with the British caused some social disruption in the class system of the Puget Sound Indians. Consequently, the Indian tribes of nineteenth-century western Washington cannot be treated as isolated entities. Instead, we must place the analysis within the context of the growth of the European and American economy and its impact on the native people. Leaders such as Pat Kanim of the Snoqualmie, Snatlum of the Skagit, Duke of York of the Klallam, Leschi of the Nisqually, and Chowitsut of the Lummi, were innovators who took advantage of the changing circumstances.[5]

With the changes brought by the fur trade and subsequent developments, such individuals found new ways to value resources and to allocate access to them. These leaders took advantage of the shifting scene of the nineteenth century in generally similar ways, and some used their enhanced status and power to gain control over large areas. For example, in the first few years after the establishment of Fort Langley, the Skagit were not only exercising control over fur-producing areas but also controlling access to the fur trade (McDonald 1830).

While this understanding of Puget Sound social organization has long been generally accepted, Tollefson (1987:123–188), in a case study of the Snoqualmie, argues for a different view, claiming that the literature on Puget Sound Indians lacks an integrated political analysis for five reasons: (1) a failure to consider nineteenth-century historical data; (2) a limited understanding of the dynamics of kinship networks; (3) a theoretical lag in the development of political models in anthropology; (4) a rapid period of defeat and decline of the Puget Sound Indians; and (5) an inordinate preoccupation with the local village. He calls for the recognition of three distinct levels of political organization—the village, the district, and the chiefdom.

In a later study Tollefson argues that the anthropological studies have misunderstood the political organization of Puget Sound because they have overlooked five important ecological considerations: area topography, food resources, level of technology, population density, and political organization (1989:135). These are treated as interdependent variables in order to analyze their effect on the political organization in the form of a high chief administering a large area with the local segments under the administration of subchiefs. As the latter argument depends upon the model set up in the former to make its case, we would like to look at these two arguments together and demonstrate how the data have been either misused or misinterpreted.

The Nineteenth-Century Historical Data

The nineteenth-century historical data used by Tollefson appear to be limited to the 1840s and 1850s, and draw entirely on data recorded by Euroamericans and the oral testimony of descendants of Puget Sound Indians recorded in the 1920s and later. This approach ignores the fact that sole United States possession of the western Washington area was not a reality until 1846, and for at least a generation prior to this time the Puget Sound Indians had been in contact with employees of the Hudson's Bay Company. After acquiring land-based operations at Fort George (Astoria) in 1821, the British Hudson's Bay Company expanded operations to Fort Vancouver on the Columbia River (1824), Fort Langley on the Fraser River (1827), Fort Nisqually (1833), Cowlitz Station (1838), and Fort Victoria (1843).

Certainly the trade with these British forts caused some political upheaval among the Coast Salish of Puget Sound and beyond. The journals of the traders at the various forts are invaluable sources of information on the native people and lend considerable insight into their political structure during the time of first contact. For example, the Journal of Occurrences at Nisqually House contains daily entries on the activities of native people, and Dr. William F. Tolmie, a resident at Nisqually from 1843 to 1859, was an especially astute observer of native life (Dickey 1983; Carpenter 1986).

In addition, the earlier records of Spanish maritime expeditions provide other important clues to the nature of the political organization of the Coast Salish people of the Straits of Juan de Fuca, culturally similar and nearly adjacent to the Puget Sound groups under consideration by Tollefson. Suttles (1989:251) says that "there were great post-contact changes in the roles of leaders and in the scope of warfare." He concludes that "on the matter of chiefly authority, the accounts of Quimper, Pantoja, and Cardero offer no support for any revision of our views. The position that Central Coast Salish leaders were at the most village chiefs is not contradicted" (Suttles 1989:261). Furthermore, Suttles found that the Spanish evidence indicated that the threat of war was "probably an important feature of Central Coast Salish life even before the Lekwiltok menace. This threat may well have promoted the system of alliances and exchanges that culminated in the potlatch" (Suttles 1989:261).

None of the accounts Suttles studied mentioned fortifications, evidence that in the 1790s Lekwiltok (southern Kwakwala speakers) raiding into Central Coast Salish territory had not yet begun. However, Tollefson's (1987) reconstruction of a Snoqualmie chiefly order is built in good measure around the Snoqualmie Pat Kanim's military capacity, which appears from Tollefson's accounts to be largely focused on combating raids by "northern Indians." Following Gibbs (1967 [1855]), Tollefson (1987:127) notes that the warfare between the different tribes of Puget Sound was "never very bloody," which suggests that the highly elaborate Snoqualmie system of warrior schools, and linked defense systems, as described by Tollefson, likely developed after the Lekwiltok slave raiding began. "The Sound Indians were subjected to the annual slave raids conducted by northern coastal tribes. Systems of ditches and fortifications were constructed on Whidbey Island for an early system of defense against these northern tribes" (1987:127). The Snoqualmie administrative center at Tolt is said to have been selected for its impregnability, and the military center at Fall City is said to have been strategically located and protected by other Snoqualmie forts upstream and downstream. All of this may have existed (although there is no other evidence to substantiate it), but not in the period Tollefson indicates, and thus does not demonstrate a protohistorical chiefdom. The nature of the evidence by which Suttles (1989) draws his conclusions is as important as the conclusions themselves. Unlike much of Tollefson's data, which rely on twentieth-century reconstructions by informants raised in a different system, Suttles relies on the contemporary observations of the Spanish—most notably on those of Manuel Quimper, commander of a 1790 expedition, who said, concerning the people of Sooke Harbor and Port Discovery, that they "recognize no superior chief" (Suttles 1989:255).

Finally, Tollefson's assertion that the United States treaty makers of the mid-1850s recognized chiefs already in power (1987:126, 1989:135) requires some discussion. The most reliable observer of native life, and member of the Stevens treaty commission, George Gibbs, understood the social structure of the Puget Sound groups when he stated that they were "groups without political entities" (1877:185–87). In addition, two previous treaty-making sessions were disregarded. In 1850 and 1852 the Chief Factor of Fort Victoria, Sir James Douglas, negotiated twelve treaties with the Coast Salish of Vancouver Island (Duff 1969; Boxberger 1977). Douglas negotiated with each of the village groups in the area covered by the treaties and had all adult males sign the documents. This method was beyond the means of the Americans in 1854–55, and explains the explicit instructions given to Washington Territorial Governor Stevens to "unite the numerous bands and fragments of tribes into tribes" for the purposes of treaty making (Boxberger 1979:24).

In 1851 Anson Dart, Governor of Oregon Territory (which included what is now the state of Washington) signed treaties with the Chinookan people of the lower Columbia River; these people are of a different linguistic stock than their Coast Salish neighbors, but their social organization is similar. Like Douglas, Dart negotiated a relatively large number of treaties (ten) with the local village groups, and had all adult males sign. None of these treaties was ever ratified by Congress because they were made with "insignificant tribes" (Boxberger and Taylor 1991). We can therefore state, with some degree of certainty, that the predecessors of Governor Stevens had a very different view of the political structure of the Indians of the area, choosing to deal with the local villagers.

Further, Tollefson states that Stevens was instructed to "recognize or appoint chiefs" and that anthropologists have tended to "accept the 'appoint' and ignore the 'recognize' part" (1989: 135). Clearly, chief making was practiced by the Americans under Stevens. Some tribes assert to this day that the signators on their behalf had no right to sign for villages other than their own. Sampson (1972:22) notes the following example for the Sauk-Suiattle:

> At the time of the Point Elliott (Mukilteo) Treaty of 22 January 1855, Sta-ba-but-kin was the head chief. He and head chief, Waw-wit-kin, of the Sah-ku-meh-hu (Sauk) Tribe refused the treaty because they were not assured a reservation of their own, though Dahtl-de-min, a subchief of the Sauk Tribe, did sign it. Ki-ya-hud, chief of the Mis-skai-whwa, also refused to sign. This later caused a great deal of confusion.

The famous Chief Leschi supposedly refused to sign the Treaty of Medicine Creek, and so an "x" was placed on the document for him (Meeker 1905:240). Similarly, when Slabebtkud, an Upper Skagit leader, refused to sign, other Upper Skagits rejected his view and simply signed instead (Tollefson n.d.).

Perhaps most telling of all, while negotiating the Treaty of Grays Harbor (the one treaty Stevens failed to have the Indians accept) Tleyuk, the appointed head chief of the Lower Chehalis, refused to sign because his village site was not set aside as a reservation (Treaty Commission 1855). His refusal caused dissension among the other Indians present, and Stevens responded by tearing up the paper designating Tleyuk chief. According to the Annual Report to the Commissioner of Indian Affairs of 1858, Tleyuk had lost influence among the Chehalis (ARCIA 1858:585). These examples cast doubt on Tollefson's contentions about the Duwamish and Snoqualmie traditionally having chiefs, as there is no evidence to indicate that they differed significantly from other tribes in Puget Sound.

In his effort to show the existence of chiefs whose position did not depend on appointment by whites for the purposes of the treaty negotiations, Tollefson cites Chief Martin Sampson. But Sampson's (1972) work only denotes chiefs well into the postcontact period. He calls each village a tribe, refers to heads of villages as chiefs, and describes no systematic relationship between the chiefs. Concerning the subchief system established after the treaty period, Sampson wrote, "However, the authority of these men [chiefs] did not control the actions of the other chiefs" (Sampson 1972:24).

Tollefson (1987:124) incorrectly claims that Skookum George provided evidence in a 1923 deposition of a Snoqualmie chiefly system with a subchief over each band, and with the subchiefs ranked relative to one another. Skookum George testified, "The Snoqualmie lined up in that Treaty were Pat Kanim, Squaskim, Toaklim-Subskidem, Duquilsodt, my father. They were the leaders in the order named in that little tribe" (1923:11). It is not clear that this means they were ranked this way among the Snoqualmie.

Meanwhile, in a deposition (given at the same hearings before Walter F. Dickens, Superintendent of the Tulalip Indian Agency) a Skykomish man, Charles Jules, stated that "the Indians do not call each other chief, but when the one is a little better off, a little higher, then they look up to them." Finally, Jack Wheeler, in a legal affidavit dated 7 June 1923, asserts that each tribe of the Point Elliott Treaty had two chiefs—a head chief and an assistant to the head chief, which hardly suggests the existence of significant leaders and councils. Wheeler's testimony refers to the actual meeting of Indians from various areas at the treaty-making gathering. His translated affidavit reads as follows:

Q. Did the Indians have more than one Chief at that time?

A. There was more than one. Two of one tribe.

Q. Did each of these tribes that you have named have a Chief or two Chiefs?

A. Yes.

Q. Did the Governor treat with these Chiefs or did the Governor take up the matters with others of the Indians in a general council?

A. The Governor dealt with all of the Indians because they found out what it was.
(Wheeler 1923:4)

This ambiguous testimony lends no confidence to the view that an aboriginal system of chiefs and subchiefs existed in Puget Sound, or that any such putative leaders could be usefully described as chief. Jack Wheeler's testimony also refers to one "big Man-Chief," Slababubead (often called Slabebtkud), who withdrew without signing, and "his people did not agree with him" (Wheeler 1923:7). Others signed instead, suggesting that there were important limits on leaders' abilities to control the actions of their followers.

The Dynamics of Coast Salish Kinship Networks

Our primary problem with Tollefson's depiction of Coast Salish political organization is that he takes ethnographic evidence from the post-treaty period and extrapolates back to the early nineteenth century. By the 1920s the concept of chiefs and political organization with routinized positions of formal leadership was so ingrained into the minds of Puget Sound Salish that many believed it had always been so. Nevertheless, as the above cited evidence indicates, there were contradictory beliefs among the Indians as late as the 1920s. This is because reservations established by the 1870s were made up of people gathered together from numerous villages, and because even the landless Indians of the area (including those nonresident on reservations) had developed multitribal political groupings in response to the failure of the government to fulfill treaty obligations. Most notable among these organizations was the Northwest Federation of American Indians, created in 1914, including some forty "tribes" (Porter 1990:117). Other, smaller multivillage groupings were also formed prior to 1920, such as the Upper Skagit tribal council (Sampson 1972).

Nonetheless, the concept of tribes did not emerge among the Coast Salish until after these groups were restricted to reservations, and clearly the need for tribes to exist was reinforced among both reservation and nonreservation Indians during the land claims cases of the 1930s and 1950s (Boxberger 1989:12). Suttles's Lummi informants, for example, explicitly denied the existence of chiefs "before they were appointed by white missionaries and government men" (1951a:304).

Tollefson's case seems to rest on the idea that post-treaty tribal councils were patterned after the former chiefdoms, with elected members representing the various districts (1989:145). This form of elected representation is more adequately explained by the fact that extended family networks tend to elect members of their kin groups to tribal councils, and therefore it is not surprising that geographical representation is wide-spread (Boxberger and Miller 1989; Miller 1989b). In addition, post-treaty councils seem not to replicate precontact and protohistorical councils in their sexual composition. Following contact, and until the middle of this century, women were largely absent from positions of formal leadership (Miller 1989b), a circumstance that is contrary to an earlier period (Collins 1974a; Norton 1985). Such a change is an important divergence from aboriginal practice and shows the extent of change in the political culture by the time any so-called chiefdoms might have developed.

Models of the Chiefdom

Tollefson contends that there is a "theoretical lag in the development of political models in anthropology" (1987:123). Tollefson's use of the models of Service (1962) and Fried (1967) in setting out the criteria for chiefdoms and in attempting to show how the Snoqualmie and Duwamish fit the model appears to create just such a lag. Further, Tollefson's argument hinges on his criticisms of other anthropologists' "failure to apply the appropriate model to the appropriate time period" (1987:123). This is exactly the problem we have with Tollefson's argument for chiefdoms in Puget Sound.

Sturtevant (1983:3) pointed to some of the problems with Fried's now-dated evolutionary typologies of sociopolitical organization:

> Fried's methods can be described, with only slight caricature, as the use of a logic of social evolution to develop a scenario of stages, labeled with familiar terms, that are then illustrated with a few ethnographic and historical examples that come readily to hand. Misunderstanding this method of argumentation can lead to at least two dangers. One...involves the misinterpretation or misuse of social anthropological argumentation by lawyers, judges, juries, legislators, and bureaucrats. The other is that some historians and some archaeologists are misled into supposing that...if a poorly known society can be placed into one of the types because it seems to have one or a few of the attributes of that type, then significant other, undocumented, cultural features can be attributed to the poorly known society by drawing on social anthropological characterizations of societies of that type. (Sturtevant 1983:3)

The problems Sturtevant describes are exactly the sort we encounter in the reevaluation of Puget Sound political organization, and Tollefson's model is based on assuming or reading into the ethnographic record particular social practices because of the existence of others said to belong to the same level of sociopolitical organization. In recent years many authors have explicated criteria of chiefdoms (see especially Johnson and Earle 1987; Earle 1989), which has moved the theoretical discourse far beyond that of twenty-five years ago. A seminar on chiefdoms held in 1988 was especially influential in clarifying the "political process responsible for the creation and maintenance of regional polities" (Earle 1989:85). In respect to Native American societies these models must be applied carefully.

There is a growing awareness in the anthropology and history disciplines that Indian tribes can no longer be treated as isolated entities interacting with the environment. Processual analysis requires that we come to understand Indian tribes as the result of contact, not as ongoing processes interrupted by contact. This means that we must place this analysis in the context of the growth of the capitalist world economy and the impact it has had on people in local areas (Boxberger 1989: 9–10). The Indian tribes of Puget Sound were brought into being by interaction with the political and economic structure of the dominant society. Although local natural resources are an important variable, it is the manner in which whites and Indians competed over these resources that is the crux of analysis. In this way we can demonstrate that Indian tribes were created through political necessity, and the resulting interaction determined by the needs of the dominant society shaped and directed their growth and development, not the synergistic effects of native people and the natural environment. Therefore, an explanation is needed for the various aspects of contact-era Puget Sound culture that resembles chiefdom-like societies.

While examining the five ecological considerations presented by Tollefson, we will refer to the ten political strategies offered by Earle. The first two strategies deal with the attempt to control the means of production and distribution. In the case of Puget Sound, this involved access to and control of resource-use areas and efforts to improve subsistence production. Since chiefdoms are generally associated with agricultural production, Tollefson offers the practice of burning open areas, which resulted in the increased production of food plants, and the ready adoption of the potato into the diet after its introduction by whites. However, the practice of burning was found among many native groups that were clearly not chiefdoms, and the introduction of the potato was most certainly from the Hudson's Bay Company (Suttles 1951b). Smith (1950) notes that the Nooksack were more dependent upon root crops than the Puget Sound groups, and are believed to have introduced the potato to them after acquiring it from Fort Langley in the late 1820s. Evidence suggests that root crops were considered private property among the Nooksack (Smith 1950:337) and other Coast Salish, and most likely passed from mother to daughter (Collins 1974a).

As with the ownership of most productive resources, however, the root-gathering areas were held in trust for a larger kin group. With chiefdoms, the control of resource use in the form of agricultural production generally depends upon the creation of a surplus to support the chiefs' political control. Additionally, the surplus is often used to support a non-producing sector of the population (Earle 1989:85). This is clearly not the case in Puget Sound, where historical and ethnographic evidence indicate that productive resources were held in trust for a larger kin group, and kin could claim rights of access. Further, the right of access extended beyond the kindred and included any member of the village (Suttles 1951a:149; Boxberger 1989:17). Collins notes the following for the Upper Skagit:

> Land was divided into individual plots in these prairies, marked by sticks at the four corners. A daughter inherited the right to obtain roots from one plot from her mother. It was not necessary for women to live in the village...in order to harvest a crop. Use rights were based on descent; during the late summer, women with such rights came from widely distant villages. (Collins 1974a:55)

Snyder (n.d.), writing about Skagit people (including both Upper and Lower Skagit), described the gathering-area use rights that extended to areas into which a fellow-villager had married. Finally, the practice of the redistribution of wealth items through the potlatch must also be understood as changed by contact, and the potlatch no doubt accelerated as a means of dealing with surplus wealth acquired through the fur trade and wage labor introduced by whites (see Codere 1950; Drucker and Heizer 1967; Fisher 1977).

Earle (1989) contends that chiefs expand their control through conquest and alliances. Tollefson (1989) suggests that the position of chief was inherited, and gives one example that extends from the early American period to the present. However, many more examples could be given where the descent of Salish leaders shifted from kin group to kin group and has resulted in the transference of power within the reservation context. We might better think of the postcontact Coast Salish as forming ego-centered kindreds (Fox 1967:164–166) where ego (or a collective ego) forms a kin structure that controls either access to resources, access to the political structure, or both. Once ego is gone the kindred ceases to function, but new kindreds are regularly created and struggle for power and control (Miller 1989b).

Earle identifies chiefdoms as requiring principles of legitimacy both natural and supernatural, needing "an ideology that legitimizes the position of leaders as necessary for maintaining the 'natural' order of the world" (1989:85). Regarding how leaders in the Puget Sound were legitimized, Tollefson argues for the recognition of specific positions of power inherited through primogeniture, and states that at the Duwamish village of Stuck, the ethnographer Harrington referred to the residents as being "all chiefs," and adds that a "better designation would be aristocrats" (Tollefson 1989:142). The proper designation should be chief, as Harrington stated, but a qualified "chief," because that was the term applied by Euroamericans to any Puget Sound Indians of means in the late 1800s and early 1900s. For example, an army observer, William Trowbridge, noted that the Lummi, a group of some 450 (Gibbs 1967 [1855]:42) had 40 chiefs in 1853 (Trowbridge 1942:339). That chiefs constituted nearly ten percent of the population seems far more than was necessary to operate a chiefdom and incompatible with such a political system.

Concerning Snoqualmie leadership, Haeberlin and Gunther (1930:59) state that there was an intervillage council whose members "were scattered throughout the tribe" and who "met with the chief at some central meeting place." Whether these data, which Tollefson relies on, are accurate is a matter of concern. Haeberlin, an American ethnographer trained in Germany, gathered data from Puget Sound Indians in 1916 and 1917. Gunther translated his published work, supplemented it with her own field data, and republished it as co-authored in 1930. Gunther apparently disagreed with Haeberlin's assessment of the political structure of the Indians of Puget Sound; her footnote to Haeberlin's depiction states that the account seemed "oversystematized" (Haeberlin and Gunther 1930:59 n).

Chiefdoms also characteristically involve the control of internal and external wealth production and procurement (Earle 1989). The concept of private property was fairly well developed among the Coast Salish, particularly in regard to resource procurement sites. Many of the major fishing sites were considered the property of one or more individuals. Nonetheless, ethnographers agree that despite this property being owned, everyone in the village had rights of access. "Stewardship" is a better term than "ownership": an individual held the site on behalf of an extended kin group and all those with either consanguineal or affinal ties had the right to use the site. Clearly, the organizing principle is the extended bilateral kin group, or kindred. Certainly fishing sites were within the control of wealthy men, but "control" must be understood in this limited sense. Regarding other resource sites, particularly shellfish-gathering locations and plant-gathering sites, the control and ownership appears to have been with women. In this respect "control" is perhaps better considered as usufructuary rights. The evidence suggests that this control stayed within certain family groups (Snyder n.d., 1964; Collins 1974a).

Discussion

Aside from the problems in the application of his formal models of political evolution, residual problems remain in considering Tollefson's arguments. First, Tollefson employs a straw man in arguing that the orthodox position concerning political organization of the Puget Sound is the autonomous village, a claim he makes repeatedly (e.g., "the twentieth century ethnologists generally limit their political analysis to local autonomous villages" (1987:121)). Tollefson seems to be arguing that politics is viewed narrowly by other researchers when quite the opposite continues to be the case. For example, Miller (1989c) recently provided a model of the region based on a network analysis of social-relations sets, with the clear political implication that the ability to control the flow of communication is a form of political power. Miller's analysis flowed directly from the work of Elmendorf (1960) and Suttles (1960) who have long argued for viewing the Puget Sound and neighboring waterways as a region built around a network of social ties, including marriage, co-use of resources, ceremonial life, defense, in-law relations, and trade. Tollefson implies that scholarship has relied strictly on the outmoded analysis in which political processes are ignored in the concern for formal structures. Yet he overlooks the ways in which politics can be imbedded in other social relations and still be explicitly political.

Second, Tollefson misses the opportunity to point out that Pat Kanim of the Snoqualmie, and others like him, were innovators (see Suttles 1957 for a discussion of leadership and innovation). The efforts of individuals and groups to find new ways of valuing resources and allocating access to them is noteworthy, considering the monumental changes that Indian people have faced. By focusing on social action and the ability of actors to maneuver within the structural constraints of society, culture (Bailey 1988), and the new economic reality of the nineteenth century, instead of on formal political structures, as Tollefson does, one gets a very different view of Puget Sound political life.

Three nineteenth-century Skagit Valley leaders would have known Pat Kanim, because Snoqualmie, Snohomish, and Skagit summer procurement sites on Whidbey Island were in the same vicinity (Collins 1974a; Roberts 1975; White 1980). Collins (1974a, 1974b) described Snatlem as a noted missionary, warrior, and trader who succeeded in extending his power beyond his immediate kin group, largely through wealth gained as a middle-man in the exchange of goods and services with the white newcomers. He served as a missionary to his people, and was an eminent warrior in a difficult period of slave raiding (Collins 1974b:49–51). Snatlem, then, combined both the styles of charismatic leadership and traditional familial leadership that had characterized the Coast Salish to this point (Miller 1989a:3).

Pateus, one of those who signed the Point Elliott Treaty, made his mark as a war chief and through the strategic marriage of his daughter to Slabebtkud, another of the innovators. Pateus is said to have murdered those who angered him, sold relatives as slaves, disrupted ceremonial events, and performed other acts unacceptable to an earlier generation of Skagit leaders (Miller 1989a:3). He was a "disruptive leader," (a concept employed in Bailey 1988) who kept his followers, including his immediate entourage, continually off balance.

Slabebtkud was a religious innovator who used his connections with Catholic priests in the interior of Washington State to allow him to develop a cult and subsequently concentrate authority in his own hands in a way previously unknown. He developed a form of direct political cohesion in the Skagit Valley, including a system of subchiefs as described by Tollefson (1987) for the Snoqualmie. However, it is well documented that these actions represented a break from the earlier traditions of leadership (Collins 1974a), and accounts of a reaction to Slabebtkud's style leading to his murder are still told in the Skagit community. Strangely, Tollefson presents Pat Kanim as an innovator and skillful political actor in another account (Tollefson n.d.), but ignores this in his theoretical consideration of chiefdoms.

Third, what is meant in using the term chiefdom? Does the term illuminate or obfuscate the situation in the Puget Sound? Unfortunately, no one confronts the literature about Puget Sound and other Coast Salish chiefs to see what this suggests for the chiefdom model. Barnett's (1955: 246) description of Coast Salish chiefs is instructive: "He was an unassuming man and 'quiet' by which is meant that he spoke little, and only after mature consideration. He maintained his dignity but without hauteur...He was paternalistic, forwarding the best interests of his relatives....He was careful to avoid trouble but led the way when trouble was imminent. He was...generous." Collins (1974a:113, 1950:334) described Upper Skagit village-wide leadership as generally activity-based and episodic, with people serving as leaders for the duration of the activity for which they had special skills. Other members of the village submitted themselves to this direction because they derived benefits, not because the headman had coercive authority. Collins describes the family councils that could be called by the headman of a village as the "oldest sibling-cousin" (1974a). These councils included family members who lived in villages other than the one occupied by the headman, and who in some cases spoke different languages (thereby necessitating the use of interpreters). Such council meetings required unanimity for a decision to be taken. Collins's description is important because it can explain some of the large gatherings that Tollefson (1987) has interpreted as evidence of the influence of chiefs who are able to gather widely scattered people. Interpreting these events within the family council model is appropriate because it fits much more closely with the ethnographic descriptions. However, some of these large gatherings were not family councils, but rather were held in response to treaty issues, and reflect the ability of Coast Salish people to gather for the collective good without the order of a superior chief.

In addition, Roberts (1975:122) argued that in the aboriginal period authority was limited, but individuals sometimes exerted extensive power. She wrote that village headmen shaped extra-village relations through marriage alliances and also attracted useful personnel to the community as residents. In general, they worked to improve the rank of their group within the region by creating obligations on the part of smaller villages and limiting the actions of independent villages. Inherent in this description is the important fact that individuals could leave their villages and villagers could remove their headman or depart from their location (Snyder 1964). Leaders, then, did not exert coercive control over their followers. Followers were tied to them through kinship, not territory. However, an element exists in the process of the legitimization of leaders that appears to provide permanent advantage to leaders and their heirs. Only headmen had spirit-powers for a generalized "wealth" in addition to the powers for special skills (Snyder 1964:72). Individuals were obliged to validate these powers, however, which was not an automatic process; it required the cooperation of kin.

How does this information about leaders conform to what is known about chiefdoms? Isaac (1988:11–12), writing from a political economy perspective, notes that

> in their redistributive behavior, the leaders of the Northwest Coast polities were quite like the "big-men" described for (other) tribal societies, and very different from the chiefs of political chiefdoms. ...In a nutshell, the reasonably thorough and wide redistribution of the wherewithal that comes his way is the hallmark of a big-man, not of a chief. A chief is to a great extent insulated from the general redistributive demands because he is sustained by political office, a permanent structural position with certain inherent powers. A Chief can compel a following; he does not have to entice one. A big-man, in contrast, does not occupy a political office; he is literally a self-made man who attracts a following through his political skill and, above all else, his generosity. A chief can be "an appropriator and a concentrator," whereas a big-man cannot, because the political unit that a chief heads is not primarily a kinship unit. True, political relations in a chiefdom are often softened by a metaphor of kinship... Nevertheless, the political unit ("chiefdom") over which a chief rules is not composed primarily of his close consanguineal kin.... In short, a chiefdom constitutes itself territorially.... In contrast, where political scope is defined and confined largely by consanguinity, steady coercion is not possible—and we do not find chiefs. (Isaac 1988:11–12)

Isaac says that the prevailing ethic of generosity and the ideology of potlatching left "those in control motivated to share their exceptional bounty" (Isaac 1988:12), an ethic not characteristic of appropriating chiefs.

In several important ways, then, the protohistoric Puget Sound leaders do not appear to be chief like; their influence was limited (and in some cases seasonal), was kin-based rather than territorial, and the Puget Sound followers were not compelled to follow their leaders, while the leaders in turn could not compel a following.

A fourth issue is population size, an ecological variable regarded as important to understanding the emergence of chiefdoms. Tollefson (1989:139–40) bases his population estimates on a set of tenuous assumptions such as the following: "A consensus among Duwamish elders places the number of aboriginal villages at 28 and the number of longhouses in those village at 93: 62 medium longhouses and 31 large longhouses" (*Duwamish et al. v. U.S.* 1927:932–33). Tollefson (1989) suggests that medium-sized longhouses had six to eight firepits, and large-sized ones had eight to ten, and that six to eight people used each firepit. He thereby derives an aboriginal population of 5,000 (based on estimates ranging from 3,708 to 6,432). He then attempts to check these figures with "nadir population projections" as proposed by Dobyns (1966).

But there are problems with determining an aboriginal population from the memories of elders alive in the 1920s. Similar testimony of Upper Skagit elders, also in the case of Dwamish et al., provides the number of Upper Skagit villages: three villages and eight houses; six villages and thirty-two houses; twenty-seven villages and fifty-four houses; six villages and twenty houses; six villages and thirteen houses. No meaningful consensus exists among such data even though an average could be derived. Furthermore, the list of village names provided with this testimony taken in the 1920s is almost totally disjoint with those gathered by Collins in the 1940s (1987). Given the sporadic movement of longhouses because of flood, alterations in riverbeds, changes in political affiliation, and so on, whether the village sites existed at the same time or whether they existed in the protohistoric period at all remains uncertain.

Boyd's (1990:135) application of the Dobyns method in reconstructing Northwest Coast aboriginal populations gives estimates, albeit ones he describes as conservative, as 11,835 Lushootseed Salish (including what are now called the Skagit, Sauk-Suiattle, Snohomish, Swinomish, Duwamish, Puyallup, Nisqually, Squaxin, Steilacoom, and Snoqualmie, among others). The Duwamish comprise far less than half of the Lushootseed population that Tollefson's estimates suggest. The Lummi and Samish are listed separately at 1,975 people (Boyd 1990:136). Boyd notes that in what he calls the Georgia-Puget epidemic area, which includes the Duwamish and Snoqualmie Tollefson writes about, "the population decline... is the smallest estimated for any epidemic area on the Northwest Coast" (Boyd 1990:146).

Tollefson's estimate is based on the population data gathered by T. G. Bishop, organizer of the Northwest Association of Indians, who gave a figure of 320 Duwamish in 1916. Nadir ratios of twenty to one to ten to one give aboriginal populations of 6,400 and 3,200, respectively. These estimates assume a nadir population occurring about 130 years after contact, about 1910, and a reasonable survival ratio. Thornton et al. (1991:29) point out some difficulties in estimating aboriginal population fluctuations.

A fundamental problem with "working backwards" is the assumption that the populations neither grew nor declined from after the depopulation to the date of the known population size. Consequently, rates of population growth or decline prior to the depopulation as well as the role of fertility, and the implications of age structure of the disease mortality for population changes after reduction by disease episodes are all ignored. Each of these factors may influence population size following reductions due to mortality.

Conclusions

Anthropologists who have worked in the Coast Salish area in recent years hear claims that a tribe at one time exercised political authority over wide geographic areas (some modern Samish, for example, claim that their power extended from South Puget Sound to Alaska), which the previous generation of fieldworkers, with the sole exception of Haeberlin, never heard. In fact, the earlier informants stated quite the opposite, which makes evaluating the statements concerning political organization a difficult proposition, especially since contemporary people may not be using the same terminology as anthropologists use. As Sturtevant (1983:3) indicated in discussing Fried's concepts of chiefdom, there are important issues associated with labeling Indian populations with a typology of social organizations, in that such labels can lead to misinterpretation and misuse by legislators, judges, and bureaucrats. Furthermore, arguing that two such protohistorical chiefdoms existed suggests that the other peoples of Puget Sound, and indeed other Coast Salish, were likely organized into chiefdoms. These problems require great caution, especially in disentangling present-day claims made by Indian peoples. Given contemporary patterns of interaction and the development of a pan-Indian consciousness, reasonable claims can be made of a vast, overriding identity or commonality binding the Indian people of the Northwest Coast through contrast with non-natives, a common postcontact history, and so on. Extending claims backwards in time appears to be an invention of tradition, and, in any case, it is unclear what the connections between chiefdoms and present-day assertions of pan-Indian identity might be. Put more simply, Tollefson appears to have confused analytic units by confusing contemporary issues of personal identity with earlier issues of political organization. Contemporary Indian peoples' descriptions of their patterns of affiliation are not evidence of the existence of Puget Sound chiefdoms in the protohistoric period.

Endnotes

[1] The term Puget Sound refers to both a geographical region and a linguistic and cultural area. Suttles and Lane (1990) include the Indians of the Puget Sound among a grouping they refer to as Southern Coast Salish. Those west and north of the Samish are included among the Central Coast Salish.

[2] Tollefson and Penoyer's (1986) views of Snoqualmie ethnohistory are included in the Snoqualmie tribe's petition for recognition to the federal Branch of Acknowledgement and Research. Since such petitions involve a comparative component, it is possible that their view of tribal political organization will establish a standard used in other cases. "Guidelines for Preparing a Petition for Federal Acknowledgement as an Indian Tribe," published by the Bureau of Indian Affairs, 1978, details the criteria established under Title 25, Part 83, by which tribes are recognized. One of the seven specific criteria requires a tribe to "furnish a statement . . . which establishes that the group has maintained tribal political influence or other authority over its members as an autonomous entity throughout history until the present." The standard by which "political influence" is determined is the crux of the issue, and has been a problem for several tribes.

[3] Federally recognized tribes are eligible for inclusion in the treaty fisheries under the Boldt Decision. At present, tribes are engaged in negotiation and litigation over who may fish where. Demonstration of political control of a fishing ground in the treaty period of the mid-nineteenth century may help a tribe win the right to fish in a location and possibly gain primary rights there.

[4] While the authors take exception to reinvention of tradition for the present political agenda, this is not to be construed that we are unsympathetic to Indian rights issues. Both authors have, in fact, contributed to federal acknowledgment petitions on behalf of western Washington State tribes. We also wish to make clear that we do not believe such reinventions arise from conscious, willful attempts to mislead.

[5] Chief Seattle, of the Suquamish and Duwamish, is another example of a leader with wide influence. Seattle, the best known of all of the leaders of the treaty period, is not considered in Tollefson's study.

References Cited

ARCIA. 1858. Annual Reports to the Commissioner of Indian Affairs. Washington, D.C.: U.S. Government Printing Office.

Bailey, Frederick George. 1988. *Humbuggery and Manipulation: The Art of Leadership.* Ithaca, NY: Cornell University Press.

Barnett, Homer. 1955. *The Coast Salish of British Columbia.* Eugene: University of Oregon Press.

Boxberger, Daniel L. 1977. A Comparison of British and American Treaties with the Klallam. M.A. thesis, Western Washington University.

———— 1979. Handbook of Western Washington Indian Treaties: With Special Attention to Treaty Fishing Rights. *Contributions to Aquaculture and Fisheries, Occasional Paper* 1. Lummi Island, WA: Lummi College of Fisheries.

———— 1989. *To Fish in Common: The Ethnohistory of Lummi Indian Salmon Fishing.* Lincoln: University of Nebraska Press.

Boxberger, Daniel L., and Bruce G. Miller. 1989. Snohomish Social Organization: 1934–1950s. Report prepared for Snohomish Tribal Council, Anacortes, WA.

Boxberger, Daniel L., and Herbert Taylor. 1991. Treaty or Non-Treaty Status? *Columbia,* 5(3):40–45.

Boyd, Robert. 1990. Demographic History, 1774–1874. In *Handbook of North American Indians*, Vol. 7, *Northwest Coast*, edited by Wayne Suttles,pp. 135–48. Washington, D.C.: Smithsonian Institution..

Carpenter, Cecelia. 1986. *Fort Nisqually: A Documented History of Indian and British Interaction.* Tacoma, WA: Tahoma Research Service.

Clifford, James. 1988. *The Predicament of Culture: Twentieth-Century Ethnography, Literature, and Art.* Cambridge, MA: Harvard University Press.

Codere, Helen. 1950. Fighting with Property: A Study of Kwakiutl Potlatching and Warfare, 1792–1930. *Publications of the American Ethnological Society*, 18. New York: J. J. Augustin.

Collins, June McCormick. 1949. Distribution of the Chemakum Language. In Indians of the Urban Northwest, edited by Marian W. Smith, pp. 147–60. *Columbia Contributions to Anthropology*, 36. New York: Columbia University Press.

———— 1950. The Growth of Class Distinctions and Political Authority among the Skagit Indians during the Contact Period. *American Anthropologist*, 52:331–42.

———— 1974a. *Valley of the Spirits: The Upper Skagit Indians of Western Washington.* Seattle: University of Washington Press.

———— 1974b. *A Study of Religious Change among the Skagit Indians of Western Washington. Coast Salish and Western Washington Indians.* New York: Garland.

———— 1987. Personal telephone communication with Bruce Miller, Sedro Woolley, WA.

Dickey, G., editor. 1983. Journal of Occurrences at Fort Nisqually. Tacoma, WA: Fort Nisqually Historic Site.

Dobyns, Henry F. 1966. Estimating Aboriginal American Population: An Appraisal of Techniques with a New Hemisphere Estimate. *Current Anthropology*, 7:395–416.

Drucker, Philip. 1983. Ecology and Political Organization on the Northwest Coast of America. In *The Development of Political Organization in Native North America*, edited by Elizabeth Tooker, pp. 86–96. Proceedings of the American Ethnological Society, 1979. New York: J.J. Augustin.

Drucker, Philip, and Robert F. Heizer. 1967. *To Make My Name Good: A Reexamination of the Southern Kwakiutl Potlatch*. Berkeley: University of California Press.

Duff, Wilson. 1969. The Fort Victoria Treaties. *B.C. Studies*, 3:3–57.

Duwamish et. al. v. U.S. 1927. Testimony *(79 C. Cls. 530),* filed in 1926.

Earle, Timothy. 1989. The Evolution of Chiefdoms. *Current Anthropology*, 29:84–88.

Elmendorf, William W. 1960 The Structure of Twana Culture. *Washington State University Research Studies*, 28(3):1–565. *Monographic Supplement* 2. Pullman.

Fisher, Robin. 1977. *Contact and Conflict: Indian-European Relations in British Columbia, 1774–1890*. Vancouver: University of British Columbia Press.

Fox, Robin. 1967. *Kinship and Marriage*. Baltimore, MD: Penguin.

Fried, Morton. 1967. *The Evolution of Political Society: An Essay in Political Anthropology*. New York: Random House.

George, Skookum. 1923. Deposition of 4 June, Walter F. Dickens Hearings. Tulalip, WA.

Gibbs, George. 1877. Tribes of Western Washington and Northwestern Oregon. *Contributions to North American Ethnology*, 1. Washington, D.C.: Bureau of American Ethnology.

———— 1967 [1855]. *Indian Tribes of Washington Territory*. Fairfield, WA: Ye Galleon.

Haeberlin, Hermann and Erna Gunther. 1930. *The Indians of Puget Sound*. Seattle: University of Washington Press.

Hanson, Allan. 1989. The Making of the Maori: Culture Invention and Its Logic. *American Anthropologist*, 91:890–902.

Hobsbawm, Eric and Terence Ranger, editors. 1983. *The Invention of Tradition*. Cambridge: Cambridge University Press.

Isaac, Barry. 1988. Introduction. In Prehistoric Economies of the Pacific Northwest Coast. *Research in Economic Anthropology, Supplement* 3, edited by Barry Isaac, pp. 9–16. Greenwich, CT: JAI.

Johnson, Allen W., and Timothy Earle. 1987. *The Evolution of Human Societies: From Foraging Group to Agrarian State*. Stanford, CA: Stanford University Press.

Jorgensen, Joseph. 1980. *Western Indians*. San Francisco: W. H. Freeman.

Kehoe, Alice B. 1992. *North American Indians: A Comprehensive Account*. Englewood Cliffs, NJ: Prentice Hall.

Kew, Michael. 1981. Review of Ralph Maud, ed. The Salish People: The Local Contributions of Charles Hill-Tout, Vols. 1–4. *B.C. Studies,* 50: 60–65.

McDonald, Archibald. 1830. *Fort Langley Journal, 1827–1830*. Ms. Victoria: Provincial Archives of British Columbia.

Meeker, Ezra. 1905. *Pioneer Reminiscences of Puget Sound.* Seattle, WA: Lowman and Hanford.

Miller, Bruce G. 1989a. An Ethnohistoric Examination of Coast Salish Women in Leadership. Paper presented at the Annual Meetings of the American Anthropological Association, Washington, D.C., 15 November.

————— 1989b. A Sociocultural Explanation of the Election of Women to Formal Office: The Upper Skagit Case. Ph.D. dissertation, Arizona State University.

————— 1989c. Centrality and Measurements of Regional Structure in Aboriginal Western Washington. *Ethnology*, 28: 265–76.

Norton, Helen. 1985 Women and Resources of the Northwest Coast: Documentation from the Eighteenth and Early Nineteenth Centuries. Ph.D. dissertation, University of Washington.

Porter, Frank W., III. 1990. In Search of Recognition: Federal Indian Policy and the Landless Tribes of Western Washington. *American Indian Quarterly*, 14:113–32.

Roberts, Natalie. 1975. A History of the Swinomish Tribal Community. Ph.D. dissertation, University of Washington.

Sampson, Martin. 1972. *Indians of Skagit County.* Mount Vernon, WA: Skagit County Historical Society.

Service, Elman. 1962. *Primitive Social Organization.* New York: Random House.

Smith, Marian. 1950 The Nooksack, Chilliwack, and Middle Fraser. *Pacific Northwest Quarterly*, 41:330–41.

Snyder, Sally. n.d. Fieldnotes. Melville Jacobs Collection, University of Washington.

————— 1964. Skagit Society and Its Existential Basis: An Ethnofolkloristic Reconstruction. Ph.D dissertation. University of Washington.

Sturtevant, William C. 1983. Tribe and State in the Sixteenth and Twentieth Centuries. In *The Development of Political Organization in Native North America*, edited by E. Tooker, pp. 3–16. 1979 Proceedings of the American Ethnological Society, Washington, D.C.

Suttles, Wayne 1951a. Economic Life of the Coast Salish of Haro and Rosario Straits. Ph.D. dissertation. University of Washington.

————— 1951b. The Early Diffusion of the Potato among the Coast Salish. *Southwest Journal of Anthropology*, 7:272–285.

————— 1957. The Plateau Prophet Dance among the Coast Salish. *Southwest Journal of Anthropology*, 13:352–396.

————— 1958. Private Knowledge, Morality, and Social Classes among the Coast Salish. *American Anthropologist*, 60: 497–507.

———— 1960. Affinal Ties, Subsistence, and Prestige among the Coast Salish. *American Anthropologist*, 62: 296–305.

———— 1988. Testimony before the Senate Select Committee on Indian Affairs. 26 May.

———— 1989. They Recognize No Superior Chief: The Strait of Juan de Fuca in the 1790s. In *Culturas de la Costa Noroeste de America*, edited by J. Peset, pp. 251–264. Madrid: Turner.

Suttles, Wayne, and Barbara Lane. 1990. Southern Coast Salish. In *Handbook of North American Indians*, Vol. 7, *Northwest Coast*, edited by Wayne Suttles, pp. 485–502. Washington, D.C.: Smithsonian Institution.

Thornton, Russell, Tim Miller, and Jonathan Warren. 1991. American Indian Population Recovery following Smallpox Epidemics. *American Anthropologist*, 93: 28–45.

Tollefson, Kenneth D. n.d. Chief Pat Kanim. Ms.

———— 1987. The Snoqualmie: A Puget Sound Chiefdom. *Ethnology,* 26(2):121–136.

———— 1989. Political Organization of the Duwamish. *Ethnology*, 28(2):135–50.

Tollefson, Kenneth D., and F. D. Pennoyer. 1986 Snoqualmie Cultural Continuity Study: Federal Acknowledgement Petition. Washington, D.C.: Bureau of Acknowledgement and Research, Bureau of Indian Affairs.

Treaty Commission. 1855. Records of the Proceedings of the Commission to Hold Treaties with the Indian Tribes in Washington Territory and the Blackfoot Country. National Archives and Records Service, Record Group 75. Washington, D.C.

Trowbridge, William Petit. 1942. Journal of a Voyage on Puget Sound in 1853. *Pacific Northwest Quarterly*, 32:391–407.

Wheeler, Jack. 1923. Deposition of 7 June, Walter F. Dickens hearings. Tulalip, WA.

White, Richard. 1980. *Land Use, Environment, and Social Change: The Shaping of Island County, Washington.* Seattle: University of Washington Press.

Part III
Coast Salish Law

Colonial powers attempted to erode and erase Coast Salish legal orders, although not immediately. The following essays concern historic Coast Salish concepts and practices of justice and law and how these have transformed under duress. Chapter 5, *Justice, Law, and the Lens of Culture*, looks at the issues involved in invoking culture in restoring a tribal justice system. In recent years tribal courts have been established on the U.S. side and communities have attempted to build on these historic notions to create culturally specific legal systems. But, the various communities have interpreted their own past in quite different ways. Chapter 7, *Folk Law and Contemporary Coast Salish Tribal Code*, takes up these topics. In addition, some historic practices have been maintained and have regained strength. There are several attempts to re-establish a version of historic Coast Salish law in British Columbia. I include a chapter from *The Problem of Justice* that describes a failed effort, the South Island Justice Project, here published as Chapter 6. This diversionary program failed because it did not account for fundamental features of social organization, and victims of sex crimes were expected to receive counseling from elders of the family of the perpetrator. Chapter 8 examines historic Coast Salish practices of apology and cleansing from within their own legal practices and describes the way external efforts in the forms of church and state apologies can backfire. Chapter 9 concerns the complex of legal jurisdictions on the international border, including Washington state and U.S. federal law, B.C., Crown law, and tribal law. These contending jurisdictions, often unaware of each other, collide in the cases described here.

Figure 9. Repatriation ceremony of Sasq'ets from the Museum of Vancouver back to Sts'ailes (formerly Chehalis) in 2014.

Journal of Northwest Anthropology, Memoir 12:73–83 (2016)

5

Justice, Law, and the Lens of Culture*

It's a peculiar fact that contemporary tribal courts and justice initiatives undertaken by indigenous communities of the United States and Canada are infrequently examined through an ethnographic and historical lens. Studies by criminologists and legal scholars, important as they are in documenting the overrepresentation of indigenous people in prisons and legal systems or in teasing out complex issues of treaty law and jurisdiction, inadvertently deflect attention either from considering the difficulties facing indigenous people attempting to conceptualize their own prior localized legal practices or, more significantly, from how they wish to regulate their reserves/reservations. Frequently the latter is regarded as a nonissue because indigenous people's legal cultures are treated merely as the opposite of whatever people of European descent are said to be doing or, equally unproblematically, as a question of culture, reproduced through generations.

More ethnographic work is being done now to study both prior justice practices and to determine what contemporary community members view as significant about justice, an important development for several reasons. Indigenous communities in the United States do have tribal courts, and indigenous communities in Canada do engage in a variety of diversionary programs. It is a moment of potentially creative engagement, and in the Canadian dialogue at least, mainstream court officials claim they are looking to indigenous people for ideas for legal reform of the mainstream system. It is also a dangerous moment, although some are far along this path, in that indigenous communities are placed in the awkward position of developing programs for the self-administration of justice following a long period of disruption imposed by the state and of heightened differences between members of the communities based on wealth, education, religion, and so on. There is further danger in the difficulties struggling communities face in addressing internal diversity and in overcoming an inclination to use emergent legal/justice systems to address their relationship with the outside world (and to insulate themselves) rather than to address internal disputes or malfeasance. By this I mean that communities may choose to emphasize regaining control over legal processes, making a political statement about cultural differences, or foregrounding large-scale social dilemmas that are the outcomes of contact and colonization. None of these are the same as actually dealing with the nitty-gritty of regulating the community. Communities today face the dilemma of creating systems that can be regarded as legitimate by both community members and the mainstream justice system that provides funding. Other problems arise from the need to present complex prior local practices, inasmuch as they can be understood even by community members themselves, to the outside, while avoiding the problem of a simplification that boils out the flexibility once present in indigenous justice practices. In addition, some communities, particularly in Canada, are under pressure to import canned legal systems from elsewhere—including a Maori family conferencing model—that serve the interests of the state in being transportable, cheap, and controllable from the outside.

Continent wide efforts at the (re)establishment of indigenous justice practices are premised, in various ways, on the idea of cultural distinction, the notion that indigenous peoples have their own distinct ways of managing social relations and of conceiving of and maintaining humankind's place in the world. One implication of this perspective is that only indigenous peoples can administer justice to indigenous peoples because members of one cultural group

*Authored by Bruce Granville Miller, reproduced with permission and previously published in *Wicazo Sa Review*, 18(2):135–149 (2003). University of Minnesota Press.

cannot understand or empathize with those of another; an associated argument is that indigenous practices of justice are the opposite of whatever mainstream practices might be because they derived from distinct cultures. There may be some truth to these claims, but both widely held views are misleading, and in two senses. They do not logically follow from the premise, and, in addition, they lead in a dangerous direction, away from a careful consideration of prior indigenous justice practices and how these might be reworked for use today. The real world, the current world, of relations between indigenous groups and the mainstream societies of North America is more complex than can be captured by the ideas of cultural distinctiveness or social separateness; there have now been many decades of interpenetration of peoples and of ideas. Richard White (1991) and his student Alexandra Harmon (1998) develop this in his idea of the "middle-ground," as did Charles Menzies (1994) in his analysis of a polarized fishing community in which many, including himself, are descended, intellectually and biologically, from both Indians and whites.

My argument here is that innovative, community-driven justice initiatives must find a way to struggle against the impulse to misuse the idea of culture and engage in "us-them," oppositional, compartmentalizing, and dichotomizing thinking in developing new justice projects. Instead, perhaps ironically, establishing a recognizable, distinctive, identifiable indigenous program of justice requires a shared field of "we—you" interethnic discourse and interaction through a kind of complementarization (Eriksen 1993: 28). This perspective follows from the insight that the forms of group distinction referred to as ethnicity arise from conflict, yet require various continued forms of interaction. Ethnicity in this sense is relational rather than a discrete entity (Sider 1993; Comaroff 1996; Sharp 1996). Culture, the content of ethnicity, has particular relational properties; it marks off difference, but cultural boundaries are also transcended and culture transformed by contact. I make these comments even though indigenous peoples of North America are careful to distinguish themselves from ethnic minorities, and here I do not wish to represent that indigenous communities are merely one among many minorities; indeed, they have distinctive legal rights to self-government and claims to resources.

There are many reasons for the need for complementarization, but among them are the simple, practical realities that any justice program exists within a universe of neighboring legal jurisdictions and that community members have already internalized many European derived ideas of justice. First, there must be some form of mutuality so that jurisdictions can communicate regarding issues that cross boundaries. Indeed, indigenous jurisdiction can be regarded as severely restricted when it operates only within its own boundaries, legally barred from extending elsewhere, to the outside. Second, the holding of legal jurisdiction implies a connection to the whole infrastructure of contemporary society—of governance and administration, both within the jurisdiction and without. Indigenous communities, to grow institutionally, must develop cooperative agreements with other governments, including non-indigenous ones—to manage and regulate housing, water, employment, and so on. These activities are carried out in common with other jurisdictions. Third, the communication of cultural differences between groups, even groups that interact regularly and intensively but sometimes antagonistically, may involve a form of stereotyping of the other that itself generates a self-stereotyping. Self-stereotyping can lead to a cultural practice characterized by formalism and rigidity, unsuitable to the kind of maneuver and ambiguity that the practice of justice requires to avoid deadlock and to allow for the accommodation of conflicting cultural values at home. One example is the contradiction in Coast Salish communities between the emphasis on family solidarity and the existence of differences in social class and influence between family members. Another example is the unresolved tension between married women's affiliations to their natal and affinal families (Snyder 1964). These sorts of cultural contradictions require subtle management in times of difficulty or disorder; legal systems cannot simply support one and ignore the other in contemplating legal rights of individuals and families.

Shallow perceptions of the other are mutually entangling and misleading, and, as I noted, lead away from understanding the subtle systems of the regulation of human affairs that characterized prior systems of indigenous justice. In fact, one might argue that prior justice practices were themselves built on a careful examination of how both outsiders and insiders behave in order that community leaders might accurately predict and avoid the outbreak of conflict and control the consequent damage once human relations broke down. This idea is sometimes given in indigenous rhetoric as "maintaining and restoring harmony," but it is useful to emphasize the behavioral entailments and to view harmony as the outcome of human actions rather than merely as a state of affairs. The critical question is "What means did indigenous people of a prior period employ to achieve justice?"—in a practical sense, and which might be of use today—rather than "What is a state of harmony?"

My argument is leading toward considering just how culture is understood and deployed in the creation of justice programs; it is cultural differences, after all, that are said to necessitate distinctive indigenous justice regimes. In the indigenous world, culture is often said to be immutable, as I will show, and from this vantage point, law and culture are interwoven in that culture itself is said to be the law. The right regulation of society, then, in a manner reminiscent of the Confucian ideal of ordering of society (yet without the necessity of rigid hierarchy), resides in each individual occupying the proper niche and in the fulfillment of obligations to other entities, human or otherwise. In other tellings, culture can be divided into two components, each with implications for justice. Warry draws a distinction between custom, which is changeable, and tradition, which is not. "Customary processes, rules or penalties" are temporal applications of "traditional law which is a system of values embedded in social relationships, rather than a domain separate and discrete unto itself" (1998:176). For many indigenous people, culture is something inherited from the past, and about which contemporaries have an inadequate grasp (Bierwert 1999). Many social scientists use the idea of culture to consider the struggle between components of society (such as between men and women or between members of age groups or social classes) existing within a framework of a dominant, but changing, narrative of what culture is or ought to be. This perspective has been picked up within indigenous communities as well, sometimes in unexpected places. Cruikshank (1998) gives the story of an indigenous elder at a Yukon storytelling festival subverting white ideas of indigenous elderhood and the practice of storytelling by reading newspaper clippings about indignities suffered by her community at the hands of the mainstream society. In the present period of culture wars, of publicly deploying culture for political advantage, there is great utility for indigenous communities to emphasize difference and to flatten their renderings of their own culture (Harmon 1998). But there is also a price to pay in that the construction of legal regimes best rest on thoughtful, rather than shallow or misleading, perceptions of how people conceive how life ought to be lived, yet another understanding of culture.

Here I look briefly at the use of the idea of culture and its specific contents and how these connect to the creation of new justice initiatives in a single culture group, the Coast Salish of British Columbia and Washington State. The various Coast Salish communities from both sides of the border share more than cultural affinities. Members regularly marry into the other Coast Salish communities, attend the same winter ceremonials, Shaker Church services, funerals and naming ceremonies, and participate in the same summer canoe-racing festivals and powwows. In brief, the Coast Salish communities are very closely linked both socially and culturally, although there is, of course, variation in the cultural expression of communities and between families within the communities. However, differences in contact history and public policy have manifested themselves in the present differences in circumstances among the U.S. tribes and Canadian bands. In simple terms, the primary differences are that U.S. tribes are further ahead in most cases in the development of their structures of governance, in the development of service delivery, and in their rights to resources than are the Canadian bands. The Coast Salish peoples of British Columbia do not yet have formal treaty arrangements with the Canadian government, with a single exception, as do their relatives in the United States, dating from the period 1854 to 1856. There is at present a process of treaty negotiations under way, but it is unclear if this will actually produce any new treaties for the Coast Salish bands. In addition, the Canadian bands do not have criminal or civil jurisdiction over band members, even on their own lands, as do the U.S. counterparts. There are, however, several small-scale diversionary criminal justice projects. In these cases jurisdiction for the criminal acts is retained by the mainstream court but provisionally delegated to indigenous programs if all parties to the case agree (see Royal Commission on Aboriginal Affairs 1996, *Bridging the Cultural Divide*). I consider two of these in more detail and compare them to a Washington State tribal court (I take up these and related issues in more detail elsewhere; see Miller 2001 and 1994, 1995, 1997).

Communities' internal justice discourses contain a broad, confusing array of ideas from a variety of sources; these include ideas of healing originating in mental health service discourse, of harmony, of elderhood and the sacred. All are presented within the idiom of culture, however, and content derived from outside sources, such as psychological concepts or healing themes, becomes naturalized, folded into a Coast Salish presentation. In practice, none of these contemporary discourses leads to a careful consideration of two issues that seem to me to be critical to the development of tribal justice and sovereignty, issues that, by virtue of being espoused by the mainstream world, are not easily presented as indigenous or "cultural." These are, first, the administration of justice in a manner that allows the diverse community members to have a sense that they and their story are adequately represented in tribal justice processes, and second, that tribal government opens itself to democratic internal critique through judicial review of council legislation or by individual members.

Individual members of Coast Salish communities express frustration in many cases about the intractability and nonresponsiveness of tribal or band government to their personal problems and complaints. Members frequently rely on liberal, democractic values and on statements of primordial indigenous practice in their critiques. Examples include claims that tribal/band governments have violated rights to due process or to arm's-length judicial independence, ideas associated with European-derived justice, and that the governments violate the spiritual law of the community. In effect, there are parallel, interwoven discourses that acknowledge the borrowing between mainstream and indigenous societies, yet strategically and situationally reject such borrowing. It is this intermingling of ideas that most characterizes the current indigenous communities, a factor that is sometimes simply overlooked. Indigenous communities in some cases have promoted a conscious rejection of mainstream values and practices and, framing the discussion of their own indigenous practices in reaction to the mainstream, thereby distort their own legacy by emphasizing harmony and deemphasizing real-world problems. Particular ideas of culture produce claims to the sacred nature of justice practices and to primordialist discourses that uncritically incorporate concepts of healing, restoration, and elderhood without due regard for the relations of power between the various segments of the community. At its very worst, this idea of culture constitutes a direct silencing of community members who do not participate in an emergent spiritual and political orthodoxy. This potentially undermines the capacity of tribal governance to recognize diversity and community members' sense of fair, just participation in their own governance. I do not wish to suggest that all indigenous communities have fallen into these traps;

indeed, the opposite is true, and it is these differences, even within a single culture group, that provide grounds for optimism and something to be exchanged between communities.

The emergent justice practices of the Coast Salish communities of Washington State and British Columbia vary widely. I consider three distinct Coast Salish justice initiatives: a Washington State tribal court, a now-defunct B.C. diversionary justice program, and efforts by a B.C. tribal council to establish a "House of Justice" and related diversionary programs. All three initiatives employ the rhetoric of culture (and tradition) but vary in the attention given to the local play of power (particularly the role of elders and interfamily competition) and concern for community diversity, as revealed in both the practices of justice and the narratives concerning justice. All three communities are concerned with buffering their members from the intrusion of the state, but I argue that their differential success in doing this reflects their inclination to seriously respond to internal political processes. Material for this paper comes from my participation in the conceptualization of one Canadian Coast Salish initiative, the study of Coast Salish tribal courts in the United States, codes and constitutions, and analysis of framing and evaluation documents (Miller 2001).

The oldest of these three justice programs, the Upper Skagit Court, was established following a landmark legal decision, *U.S. v. Washington* in 1974 in which the tribe, and other tribes in western Washington, regained access to the salmon harvest as specified under the terms of western Washington treaties signed from 1854 to 1856. The ruling created the need for a venue in which to try fishing violations in order for the tribe to manage its own fishing interests along with the state and the federal governments. The tribe has acted on their legal jurisdiction under U.S. law by gradually expanding the repertoire beyond resource regulation, and now includes zoning, felony, and other legal issues within the system. The activities of the tribal justice system, including the court session, are today carried out almost exclusively on the reservation. The tribe employs its own judge and court officials, a circumstance that has arisen after several years of sharing resources with other local tribes within a legal services consortium. Tribal members and tribal employees have developed and fine-tuned tribal codes in order to both manage their relations with the outside and regulate activities within their own territories. For example, tribal code exists in areas in which they do not purportedly have jurisdiction under U.S. law, but to which local authorities acquiesce. This includes the release of tribal members incarcerated in county jail in order to attend funerals or the prosecution of major crimes in the events the federal court fails to act. The tribe has given particular attention to defining the legal relationships between components of the community—relations between families, between families and the tribe itself, and the legal individual within a universe of families. The Upper Skagit justice program emerged at the level of tribal government within the overview of the tribal membership as a whole.

A critical feature of the administration of justice is the process of "sorting-out" in which court officials examine community problems brought to them and provide a range of options for resolution. These options are as diverse as feasting between families and adversarial criminal prosecution. This "sorting-out" appears to diminish the problem of the translation into legally definable cases that plague local-level courts in the mainstream society and that appear to deny justice. This process has the effect, optimally, of providing a timely resolution to resolvable problems and of allowing disputants to employ processes and seek remedies from within the repertoire of culturally sanctioned traditions, or of seeking to redefine themselves and their adversaries as litigants within a formal, adversarial system. It also allows disputants to simmer down and potentially find their satisfaction in merely lodging a complaint or having a grievance heard. The critiques coming from opposite corners that tribal courts are either not indigenous (cultural) enough or not efficient (similar to mainstream courts) enough are both potentially addressed in this model. In effect, culture is not made problematic; there is no particular struggle over culture and its relationship to justice because culture can be understood and practiced in a variety of ways.

A very different program is the South (Vancouver) Island Justice Project, which emerged out of an effort in the 1980s to educate mainstream B.C. legal personnel about Coast Salish practices and concepts and became, in addition, a diversionary justice project in which cases could be treated by Coast Salish peoples themselves. There were several limitations to the program: cases had to come through the mainstream court, which maintained jurisdiction; all parties had to agree to the diversion; penalties and sanctions were limited. The defining characteristics were the separation between band elective government and the band elders who drove the program and the highly ideological effort to generate normative "tribal law" as a collaborative effort between a set of elders. This attempt dehistoricized Coast Salish oral traditions, which themselves have been reshaped to respond to new religious practices, such as the establishment of the Indian Shaker Church in the late nineteenth century, and to political and economic change. Further, the texts presented a collection of cultural teachings that did not easily allow shaping into practical application in the current world. The codification effort of these elders fell awkwardly somewhere in between customary process and traditional law, as Warry (1998) defined them. In addition, the codification was Edenic in nature, and was said to reflect unimpeachable, unchangeable verities. In particular, the system derived its sanction from the Syowen (winter ceremonial) world, leaving those outside this tradition beyond redemption. This is a summary of the elders' presentation of the grounds on which tribal law could be established:

> These laws that have been passed on to us by our parents and elders are law from *Hals* (Creator) and not made by man. They are held sacred by our people. These laws are for our survival and for protection of all our resources.

> These laws are received from *Hals* (Creator) after a purification period or a retreat of months or years of daily bathing in cold water, in streams or lakes, and living with nature during this period. Laws would come after *Hals* (Creator) feels that you are pure enough, then he would give you the law through one of the resources or through a vision. It is through total commitment, concentration and fasting of an individual that he is able to receive these laws from *Hals* (Creator).

> When one received a law from *Hals* (Creator) he would further bathe and fast to give thanks for the law or vision he has received. He must show his thanks for what he received for it should be for the survival of his family, the community, and the resources. Once this law is in place it is the responsibility of parents and Elders to uphold this law and pass it onto their children and their children's children.

> When these laws are upheld by individuals, families, and community, *Hals* (Creator) gives us bountiful resources. We do not show greed towards our resources but share with those in need. It is a way of saying thanks to *Hals* (Creator) for the laws he has given us for our survival and for the bountiful resources. (First Nations of South Island Tribal Council 1990)

Meanwhile, elders, selected in part for their abilities to speak Halkomelem, the local language, and their proximity to core program leaders, were used as supervisors of wrongdoers independent of their own placement in the community power structure. In an assessment of the project, community members spoke of generational rifts and abuse of power by families. Elders, on the other hand, reported a preference not to have political affiliations and their wish to be able to help everyone. This viewpoint seems sadly out of step with the reality of interfamily politics and the problems reported within the program. The unworkable system collapsed, in part, under the weight of critique from those living in urban settings who found the interpretation of tradition to be self-serving and self-protective and, consequently, found women and children without protection from wrongdoers who did not necessarily appear to be restrained. Project reviewers observed that "[p]ressure exerted by family or other community members regarding justice issues is consistently reported to have disturbed community members and service providers. Victims and offenders were likewise caught in the web of persuasion to deal with matters within the community." They noted that some victims did not come forward because they presumed that the offenders would simply be "counseled" by elders and remain in the community, perhaps as neighbors. "In some instances, women were reluctant to approach certain Elders who were convicted sex offenders, as the women felt their concerns would not be addressed." Further, the project review included a passage from an official report made during a preliminary review that makes clear the problem of the play of power and the misapplication of the system of elders:

> In conversation with community members, problems in the project arose during the phase in which victims were contacted to give their consent. Despite the highly confidential nature of the information shared at the diversion take-in meetings, allegations have been made that women who made disclosures of abuse to the police were subsequently approached by Elders who would try to persuade them not to use the criminal justice system. Apparently, this was often done by emotional blackmail, or "guilt trips."…In one instance, the victim was approached by a male Elder and was advised to "just put this behind her" and get on with her life.

> It was alleged that victims who persisted were sometimes bribed or visited by spiritual representatives who again tried to "persuade" them to drop the matter, sometimes through the use of "bad medicine." If the victims continued to persist [sic], we were told that the victim's abuser might be sent to intimidate them. (*[sic]* in original; reported in a.m. Research Services 1995:98)

The third example concerns the Stó:lō Nation, composed of about five thousand people organized into some nineteen bands along the lower Fraser River of British Columbia. The number of formally affiliated bands within the tribal council continues to shift gradually. The nation's justice initiatives arose in the 1990s out of three primary motivations: to create a justice program that could be put into place following treaty negotiations with the province and federal governments and thereby assert Stó:lō rights and title, to implement Stó:lō cultural practices as they pertain to justice, and to begin a process of restoring communities to a state of health, viewed holistically. Initial efforts included a study of Stó:lō people in incarceration, the creation of a House of Elders and a House of Justice to serve as advisers in the process, and a search for appropriate, interim, diversionary practices that could benefit members and families. This involved a small-scale application of a widely popularized and diffused New Zealand Maori Family Counseling model. In addition, as the nation took over service delivery, including educational, child welfare, and health services, efforts were made to incorporate current Stó:lō concepts of justice. Efforts were underway to consider how to create codes for a tribal system that would integrate Stó:lō cultural concepts.

In 1999, a diversionary justice program was initiated, following an earlier aborted attempt, and was named *Qwi:qwelstom,* "the Halq'emeylem word used to describe 'justice' according to the Stó:lō worldview. It reflects a 'way of life' that incorporates balance and harmony... Qwi:qwelstom is supported as an Aboriginal Justice Program that provides a means by which the Stó:lō people are achieving self-determination and self-governance as protected by Section 35 of the Canadian Constitution" (*Qwi: qwesltom: Stó:lō Alternative Justice,* 2001). The program, officially under the direction of the House of Justice and more immediately under an Elders' Council with indirect expertise in traditional forms of justice (none had participated directly while growing up), was created to address problems within the Canadian criminal justice system. Thirty-five facilitators underwent training in order to carry out "circles" for any of three different stages of the prosecuting process: replacing the trial process, making sentencing recommendations, or assisting in the reintegration of offenders back into their communities. Cases were to be referred from a variety of sources, including the mainstream police (RCMP), the Crown Counsel, probation officers, community members, and self-referrals. Cases were taken into the diversionary program when the offender expressed remorse; when the community showed willingness to deal with the offender; when resources were available to the offender, victim, and family members; and depending on "where the offender is in his/her own journey of healing," among other criteria. The Maori Family Group Conferencing materials remained central to the project, although the Qwi:qwelstom guiding principles were that the program was to be driven by Stó:lō people, supported by Stó:lō communities, and based on Stó:lō culture, customs, and traditions. The director of the project emphasized that Qwi:qwelstom was a "forum for balance, harmony, healing of all affected parties" (Wenona Victor, "Stó:lō : People of the River Conference III," Chilliwack, B.C., April 6, 2001). The core metaphor for the project was "Justice as Healing" (Stó:lō Nation Justice Programs, pamphlet, n.d.).

A carefully constructed special issue of the tribal newspaper, *Sqwélqwels ye Stó:lō,* entitled *Xyolhemeylh* (fall 1998), addressed criticism of the nation's health and family services program while describing a reorganization and centralization of tribal service delivery. The special issue also advanced the idea of "listening to the Nation's elders," several of whom were quoted in support of restructuring as a form of "working together." A program of "runners" was announced to facilitate the delivery of information from the tribal headquarters to the bands in order to replicate the aboriginal practice of sending messengers to announce potlatches and other major events. The special issue contained feature articles that described traditional life, culture, law, the role of elders, and how this was accommodated within the current and revised government structure. Meanwhile, privately, an elder who had served on a House of Justice corrections feasibility study questioned whether justice initiatives should occur at the nation level or at the level of individual bands (McMullen 1998:25).

The special issue provided a two-page statement of "traditional law," which I summarize here. The headline read, "Traditional Stó:lō People Conduct Their Lives according to the Seven Laws of Life: Health, Humility, Happiness, Understanding, Generations, Forgiveness, Generosity" (p. 6). Cultural traits said to be shared with many other native cultures were detailed: (1) spirituality—"[r]eflected in direct communications with the Creator"; (2) respect; (3) sharing of knowledge; (4) old ways—"[r]eflected in practices such as custom adoptions"; (5) listening, with the notation that "What is meant for you, it will stay with you." The accompanying text described the Stó:lō concept of "doing things in a good way" (actions that are conscientious, polite, kind, respectful), and noted that the elder or helper assists couples to resolve family conflict by

> speaking the truth to both members of the family without offending the feelings of either of them. The Elder or helper in this case will carefully balance the harsh truth (crude reality) with a softer version of the same truth (perceived reality) while still maintaining the integrity of the truth.

In traditional ways, conflict resolution and problem solving is achieved by assisting two or more parties to talk to each other and to listen to each other until an understanding and consensus is built….the traditional helper will focus on containing the level of anxiety, animosity, and anger from all parties so that each person can gradually see each other's position. The traditional process may also include STORY TELLING [uppercase in original]….the story told by the helper resembles the conflict experienced by the listeners and the listeners clearly see their own conflicts being unfolded in front of them. Often, the traditional helper will use his/her own life experience as an example so as to assist the "clients" to feel more comfortable with the helping experience….the traditional helper [thereby] acknowledges his/her own humanity including faults in character….The words selected by the helper are usually spoken from the heart rather than from the mind. Compassionate words that carry the unequivocal message of care allow the listener to become relaxed and more open to the healing words of the speaker.

This presentation introduced the idea of a "traditional helper" as a central figure. The presentation of "traditional law" was couched within the consensus/healing discourse, and overlaps with the "wellness" language of social services. A *Xyolhemeylh* editorial (*Sqwélqwels ye Stó:lō* 1, no. 5 [July 1998]:16), for example, presents Maslow's hierarchy of human needs in explaining the process of healing. Significantly, the presentation emphasizes the role of storytelling and the use of elders' personal narratives as examples. This account of aboriginal justice infuses ideology, including twentieth-century Western healing rhetoric, with the realities of prior indigenous practice and has significant implications for the real world, particularly the community debates about justice.

By 2001, Stó:lō justice initiatives were driven by a variety of ideas coming from within the communities that compose the nation and from outside. Some community members were fearful of the consolidation of authority within the nation. The nation paradoxically advocated Stó:lō traditional practices while importing systems from New Zealand with federal government encouragement and contemplating ideas from the Canadian prairies. An institutional structure had been established, with Houses of Elders and Justice, but some elements of the program were not yet institutionalized. Justice narratives and practices moved toward an explicit link to tribal social services through the Family and Child Services branch of tribal government. Some community members spoke from within the language of consensus, healing, and wellness. Others articulated a more conflictual stance based on the recognition of complex real-world problems of relations between families, observing that prior practice revolved around the use of senior people as mediators between opposed factions and noting the existence of class differences in behavior and in acting on social sanctions. Prior practice in this reading included violent sanctions, ostracism, avoidance, and thinly disguised aggressive play (Miller 2001). In contradistinction to the published tribal material, Stó:lō cultural advisor and historian Sonny McHalsie argued that both a class system and social conflict are deeply rooted within Stó:lō history and that oral histories provide a glimpse of powerful leaders capable of controlling and regulating others (McHalsie 1999).

Conclusion

My view is that features of the Upper Skagit tribal court provide a model worth considering further despite the widespread (although not universal) view in Canada that American

Indian political development had come at the cost of sacrificing indigenous practice. These communities nearly border one another; members marry one another and attend the same winter ceremonials. But despite these similarities their historical circumstances are so widely divergent that they have little clear sense of how indigenous governance operates across the international line; to that end, a dialogue across the international border is of real value. The ways in which the issue of culture is addressed remains one of the points of distinction. Upper Skagit has largely managed to avoid the trap of promoting elderhood independent of the consideration that elders, too, are socially positioned within their communities and that they participate in relations of power. Nevertheless, they employ elder council in tribal court in several ways. And, while Upper Skagit, in common with other indigenous communities, places emphasis on the resolution of social problems, they have not relied on an Edenic discourse as a way of distancing themselves from the mainstream. Indeed, they barely need to, unlike their relatives in Canadian Coast Salish tribes, which lack direct criminal and civil jurisdiction. I should add that the South Island Justice Project, which relied on such Edenic discourses, is still described as a model of diversionary justice by legal scholars and court officials. This is so even though the program collapsed under its own weight and the inability or disinclination of program developers to understand that indigenous communities are places of conflict and that justice concerns, in part, the resolution of conflict. Indeed, some members of the legal and academic communities presumed that prior justice practices remained wholly intact within communities and confused the resolution of a problem with "culture," as if an existing template provided an unambiguous answer to carrying out the practice of justice. Strangely, this example reveals the way in which indigenous communities become complicit with outside authority in promoting an image of indigenous society as cultural automaton, that is, the idea that people simply live in conformity with cultural norms, thereby avoiding conflict. In the long run, though, this complicity emerges as a means of domination in that communities that fail to directly address the mundane issues of carrying out justice, and in their rush to repudiate the outside and promote a sense of an Edenic past, delay the necessary work of furthering community sovereignty. This need not be the case, however. To my mind, community redemption, restoration, and sovereignty lie in addressing the commonplace details of life, and in discovering and acknowledging what has worked in the past and can work in the present.

References Cited

a.m. Research Services, Sheila Clark and Associates, Valerie Lannon and Associates, Inc. 1995. *Building the Bridge: A Review of the South Vancouver Island Justice Education Project, Final Report.* B.C. Ministry of Attorney General, the Department of Justice Canada and the Solicitor General of Canada.

Bierwert, Crisca. 1999. *Brushed by Cedar, Living by the River: Coast Salish Figures of Power.* Tucson: University of Arizona Press.

Comaroff, John L. 1996. Ethnicity, Nationalism, and the Politics of Difference in an Age of Revolution. In *The Politics of Difference: Ethnic Premises in a World of Power,* edited by Edwin N. Wilmsen and Patrick McAllister, pp. 162–184. Chicago: University of Chicago Press.

Cruikshank, Julie. 1998. *The Social Life of Stories: Narrative and Knowledge in the Yukon Territory.* Lincoln: University of Nebraska Press.

Eriksen, Thomas Hylland. 1993. *Ethnicity and Nationalism: Anthropological Perspectives.* Chicago: Pluto Press.

First Nations of South Island Tribal Council. 1990. Briefing Notes: An Introduction to Aboriginal Justice and the Function of an Elders Council. Presented at Cross-Cultural Awareness Workshop, Parksville/Nanoose, March 9–11, 1990.

Harmon, Alexandra. 1998. *Indians in the Making: Ethnic Relations and Indian Identities around Puget Sound.* Berkeley: University of California Press.

McHalsie, Albert (Sonny). 1999. That the Business was Done: Stories of Conflict and Leadership in Stó:lō Oral History. Paper presented at Stó:lō: People of the River II Conference, Chilliwack, B.C., October 22, 1999.

McMullen, Cindy. 1998. Bringing the Good Feelings Back: Imagining Stó:lō Justice. M.A. thesis, University of British Columbia.

Menzies, Charles. 1994. Stories from Home: First Nations, Land Claims, and Euro- Canadians. *American Ethnologist,* 22(4):776–91.

Miller, Bruce G. 1994. Contemporary Tribal Codes and Gender Issues. *American Indian Culture and Research Journal,* 18(2):43–74.

———— 1995. Folk Law and Contemporary Coast Salish Tribal Code. *American Indian Culture and Research Journal,* 19(3):141–64.

———— 1997. The Individual, the Collective, and Tribal Code. *American Indian Culture and Research Journal,* 21(1):107–30.

———— 2001. *The Problem of Justice: Tradition and Law in the Coast Salish World.* Lincoln: University of Nebraska Press.

Royal Commission on Aboriginal Peoples. 1996. *Bridging the Cultural Divide: A Report on Aboriginal People and Criminal Justice in Canada.* Ottawa: Minister of Supplies and Services Canada.

Sharp, John. 1996. Ethnogenesis and Ethnic Mobilization: A Comparative Perspective on a South African Dilemma. In *The Politics of Difference: Ethnic Premises in World of Power,* edited by Edwin N. Wilmsen and Patrick McAllister, pp. 85–103. Chicago: University of Chicago Press.

Sider, Gerald M. 1993. *Lumbee Indian Histories: Race, Ethnicity, and Indian Identity in the Southern United States.* Cambridge: Cambridge University Press.

Snyder, Sally. 1964. Skagit Society and Its Existential Basis: An Ethnofolkloristic Reconstruction. Ph.D. dissertation. University of Washington.

Stó:lō Nation. 2001. *Qwi: qwesltom: Stó:lō Alternative Justice,* pamphlet issued by Stó:lō Nation, April.

Warry, Wayne. 1998. *Unfinished Dreams: Community Healing and the Reality of Aboriginal Self-Government.* Toronto: University of Toronto Press.

White, Richard. 1991. *The Middle Ground: Indians, Empire, and Republics in the Great Lakes Region, 1650–1815.* Cambridge: Cambridge University Press.

Journal of Northwest Anthropology, Memoir 12:84–107 (2016)

6

The South Island Justice Project*

In the 1980s and 1990s, a third group of Coast Salish communities engaged in an attempt at diversionary justice. Under the authority of the mainstream judicial system, a limited number of criminal cases were diverted to a local indigenous system of justice. The now-defunct South Island Justice Project (SIJP) differed from those at Upper Skagit and at Stó:lō on many grounds; SIJP was not a freestanding system with its own jurisdiction (rather, jurisdiction was delegated provisionally and temporarily); it was not directed by a tribal government; it was not connected with treaty negotiations, as at Stó:lō; and it was not connected directly to the creation of governance in a larger sense. The very organization of the project reveals the depth of the difficulties in arranging legal relations between the constituent groups of society, issues addressed directly the Upper Skagits and Stó:lō, and in providing justice to a community diverse in religious practices, wealth, and education and marked by distinctions between generations and genders. The problems the SIJP encountered also reveal the difficulties members of the mainstream society have in comprehending the difficulties faced by indigenous communities as a result of contact and colonialism and the ways in which this incomprehension itself creates new problems. In many ways, the underlying perception within the mainstream society of indigenous culture, and therefore the practice of justice, as wholly intact and traditional, bound by custom, and homogenous, became an obstacle. The contemporary politics of nation-state-indigenous relations pushed community leaders into reinforcing these misperceptions.

The southeastern tip of Vancouver Island, British Columbia, is the homeland of Central Coast Salish peoples who are historically of Island Halkomelem and Northern Straits languages, both within the Coast Salish language family. In the mid-nineteenth century the speakers of Island Halkomelem were divided into several "tribes": the Nanoose, Nanaimo, Chemainus, Penelekuts, Cowichan, and Malahat, most consisting of more than one named group (Suttles 1990:455). The Northern Straits people of the period were composed of the T'Soūke (previously Sooke), Songhees, Saanich, Semiahmoo, Lummi, and Samish. The successor group to the Lummi and Samish live today in the United States, and the Semiahmoo are located on the mainland. Successors to the others, however, today make up the First Nations of South Island Tribal Council (SITC). In common with other Coast Salish peoples, the South Island people were organized into households composed of cooperative families related through both males and females. In stronger households, the core group of blood relatives composed a functioning "house" with heritable rights to resource stations, names, and ritual prerogatives under the direction of an elite. Society was divided into worthy or upper-class people, known as *sí:yá:m*, "worthless" people, and slaves. Suttles (1990:465) observed that conflict was common within and between villages. Injury or death, whether accidental or intentional, created the grounds for demanding compensation or became the cause of conflict, if compensation was not forthcoming quickly enough. Within a village, ongoing conflict was resolved by payments from the stronger party to the weaker party or the relocation of the weaker party. Conflict between people from different villages could lead to raiding led by professional warriors with spirit helpers (Suttles 1990:465). In common with other Coast Salish peoples, the smallpox epidemic of the late eighteenth century reduced the indigenous population, and Lekwiltok (Kwakwaka'wakw) raiders and slavers further reduced the population in the latter half of the century.

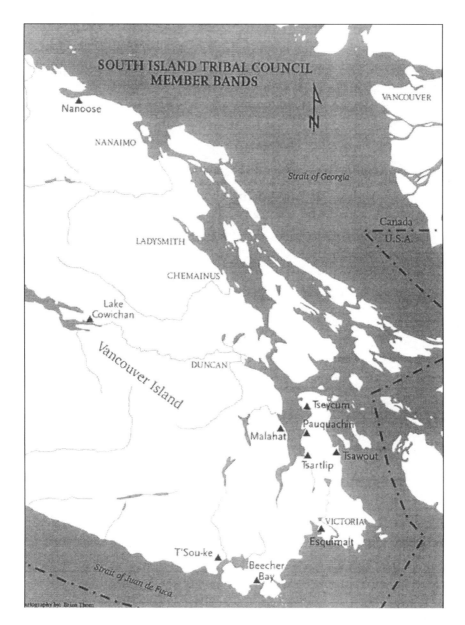

Figure 10. Map showing the locations of the South Island Tribal Council Member Bands.

The contact history of these communities is distinct from that of the other Coast Salish peoples. In 1846 the Treaty of Oregon split central Coast Salish territory into British and American sections, thereby placing the residents under separate administrative schemes. On the British (now Canadian) side, every large village was classified administratively as a band, unlike the policy of aggregation practiced in the United States. Following his appointment to the governorship of Vancouver Island in 1850, James Douglas began negotiations with nearby indigenous communities and concluded fourteen treaties with tribes near Victoria (Kew 1990a:159). One incentive to make agreements was the discovery of coals near the town of Nanaimo. The indigenous people were paid in goods in exchange for relinquishing rights to all of their lands except their villages and fields, and they retained rights to hunt and fish on unoccupied lands (Kew 1990a:159). Douglas purchased T'soūke, Songhees, Saanich, Vancouver Island

Clallam, and Nanaimo lands in 1850 and 1854, but no other titles were extinguished. Although the costs of negotiating the settlements were very small, the British government and the colonial assembly were unwilling to allocate more funds for treaties. However, Douglas continued to establish reserve lands in the hope of making treaties when funds became available (Kew 1990a:159). Meanwhile, settlement of the area continued, and the adjacent mainland was made a colony in 1858. After Douglas's retirement in 1864, Joseph Trutch was appointed the chief commissioner of land and works. Trutch held the view that "the Indians have really no rights to the lands they claim, nor are they of any actual value or utility to them; and I cannot see why they should either retain these lands to the prejudice of the general interests of the Colony, or be allowed to make a market of them either to Government of to individuals" (cited in Kew 1990a:160). Following the entry of British Columbia into Canada in 1871, Trutch continued his policies of limiting the size and location of future reserves as lieutenant governor. No further treaties or formal surrenders of land were completed. The process of creating reserves was not completed until the 1880s (Suttles 1990:471). The Songhees reserve in the city of Victoria was ceded for cash in 1910.

The Oblate order moved its headquarters from Puget Sound to Vancouver Island in 1858. Methodists were active among the Songhees and Nanaimos in the 1860s, and Anglicans among the Nanaimos. Fort Langley, a Hudson's Bay Company operation, was established on the Fraser River in 1827, attracting some interest from Vancouver Island people. By the 1860s, many south Vancouver Island indigenous people found employment as loggers, as mill hands, and in other enterprises, and others sold foodstuffs to whites. By the 1870s, men were employed in the fishing fleet and women in canneries, and there were successful farmers by the 1880s (Suttles 1954; Knight 1978). Many worked in hop and berry fields in the Fraser Valley and Puget Sound.

Despite these changes to the economy, important features of cultural life persisted. A Saanich potlatch held in 1876 attracted some three thousand indigenous people, and goods valued at $15,000 were distributed. Even after the prohibition of the potlatch, activity continued, and large potlatches were held on Vancouver Island until around 1912. However, the early twentieth century was a difficult time for people of south Vancouver Island. Economic opportunities dried up, and indigenous language use declined as a result of official repression, especially in schools. However, the Shaker Indian Church spread into the region, and Syowen (Spirit Dancing) experienced a revival with the incorporation of features of the potlatch (Suttles 1990:471–472).

With the creation of four major Indian agencies for British Columbia by 1886, the Coast Salish communities of Vancouver Island were assigned to the Cowichan Agency. Indigenous people of British Columbia, including the Coast Salish, came under the provisions of the federal Indian Act after confederation in 1871, an act amended in 1884 to prohibit the major indigenous ceremonies, including the potlatch and Winter Dancing. Provincial laws restricted indigenous people from homesteading and from the provincial franchise until 1949. The province treated indigenous people as noncitizens whose care was the responsibility of the federal government; provincial services were not extended to reserves, and children were excluded from public schools. When federal funds for the indigenous children in public schools became available, there was increasing school integration and, following World War II, integration of provincial services generally. Although the Indian Act had extended the federal franchise (citizenship) to war veterans and their wives who chose to waive their tax exemptions, this right was not extended generally to registered Indians, those with special legal status and of federal concern, until 1960.

Starting in the mid-1970s, bands began to organize themselves into regional organizations known as tribal councils in order to collectively focus on such issues as land claims, political lobbying, and the efficient provision of services to members. Among these regional groupings is the First Nations of South Island Tribal Council (SITC).

The Preamble

In 1988, immediately prior to the establishment of the South Island Justice Project (SIJP), the SITC was involved in a precedent-setting child custody case that was subsequently cited as "a good illustration of Aboriginal dispute resolution" (Michael Jackson, cited in Commission 1996:210). Jackson gives the following facts of the case (I summarize): The case concerned the custody of a child whose mother had died and who had previously requested that the child be brought up by her sister, a member of the Nuu-chah-nulth Nation (not a Coast Salish people), in order that the child learn family traditions and assume an appropriate position in the community. The boy's father, a member of a Coast Salish nation, wanted custody for similar reasons. The case went to before the court concerned whether the court should recognize the importance of early instruction to achieving high status, and, if so, whether the mother's family was more important than the father's. The SITC obtained intervener status in provincial court hearings and asked that a council of elders mediate the dispute. Terms of reference for mediation were agreed to by both parties, including establishing a council of elders agreeable to both families and chaired by the intervener, the chair of the tribal council; having the mediation occur in a neutral bighouse; and holding the meeting on Coast Salish territory. The families could call speakers and elders, and others could act as witnesses to the proceedings. The right to legal counsel as observers was retained, and the mediation would not be binding (Royal Commission 1996:210.)

A council of elders met with the parties; in Jackson's words, "The case history and the precedents in Coast Salish Aboriginal law were discussed," and the parties agreed to proposed resolution (Royal Commission 1996:211). A formal agreement was made up awarding custody to the father and acknowledging the role, advice, and influence of the grandparents on both sides and the special interest of the aunt. Further, the child was to be raised in respect to "customs and traditions of both families and cultures" (Royal Commission 1996:211). Access and visitations by relatives were provided for in the agreement.

The judge of the provincial family court was presented with a consent order giving the father custody, which was affirmed. Jackson concludes why this case was successful: "The parties were able to accept the recommendations of the Council of Elders because they have legitimacy as law-givers; the forum—The Big House—in which deliberations regarding the law and its application took place reflected the interconnectedness of Coast Salish families and its carving... encapsulates their shared history; the procedures in the Big House, the making of speeches which are listened to with respect and without interruption in the search for a consensus, draw upon time honored traditions of Coast Salish decision making" (Jackson, cited in Royal Commission 1996:213).

But, as I argue next, this case did not turn out to be a blueprint for indigenous justice Instead, the analysis of the case reflects an Edenic view of a society without a past in which serious conflict arose. Consensus, again, is treated unproblematically, and the idea of precedent in aboriginal law is without clarification (the concept arose later in representations of the SIJP). Nor is there any consideration of who the elders were, how they were selected, or what the relations of power or the existing state of relationship was between them and the litigants, issues that later came to haunt the SIJP. Elders, instead, are treated as an undifferentiated commodity. Finally, what is contested and politcal within a society (in this case the disposition of a child) is treated by outsiders as merely cultural (see LaRocque's discussion of the analogous process of the "culturalization of rape," [1997:89]).

This case is of interest here for two reasons: it helped pave the way for the South Island Justice Project, and this case and the SIJP are tied together through the central role of Chief Tom

Sampson, then chair of the SITC. Justice Edward O'Donnell, in his "Reasons for Judgement" (1988a), writes, "Through the leadership of Chief Sampson, the Tribal Council offered to the court and to the parties, to convene a Council of Elders to attempt to find a solution....It is my understanding that the institution of the Council of Elders had not been convened since possibly the 1920s in Southern Vancouver Island."

Justice O'Donnell (1988b) subsequently wrote Chief Justice I. B. Josephson of the Provincial Court of British Columbia to report on the success of the case, to describe the role of Chief Sampson and the Council of Elders, and to offer Chief Sampson as a liaison concerning "any questions as to Native Institutions and Concerns." Further, O'Donnell expressed his expectation that the report would be circulated to the provincial court judiciary. Seen retrospectively, the issues that were not attended to in this relatively simple case were precisely the ones that became most difficult for the SIJP. Secondly, the naive response of the judiciary and legal analysis in presuming an intact and consensual approach to justice on the part of the deeply divided and distraught present-day Coast Salish people facilitated the creation of a subsequent program that advanced a particular viewpoint without accounting for others.

The Project

The SITC was composed of the membership of nine (ten at one time) of the nineteen Vancouver Island Coast Salish bands. In 1992 membership came primarily from bands in the South Island area (Beecher Bay, Esquimault, Malahat, Pauquachin, T'Soūke, Tsartlip, Tseycum, and Tsawout) and included two nearby bands (Nanoose and Lake Cowichan). These small bands varied in size from 11 to 492 members and totaled just over 2,000 within an urban region of some 389,000 (a.m. Research 1996:2). The SITC represented "the majority of bands and the majority of the aboriginal population in the south Island" and was one of the oldest tribal councils in the province, founded in the early 1960s (Tennant 1992:5).

In the mid 1980s the SITC joined with the provincial justice ministry to explore ways to apply Coast Salish indigenous practices in the search for solutions to the problem of youth criminal behavior and to avoid their entanglement in the mainstream justice system (a.m. Research 1995). The circumstances were favorable for this. The report of the Justice Reform Committee, *Accessto* Justice, 1988, encouraged the provincial justice ministries (then known as the Ministries of Attorney General and Solicitor General) to make indigenous issues a priority. Local advisory councils, with indigenous representatives, were formed to examine the circumstances facing indigenous people as they encountered criminal justice in the province. The institute responsible for training provincial court judges for the four western provinces and two territories, the Western Judicial Education Centre (WJEC), and members of the University of British Columbia faculty, focused on indigenous issues (see UBC *Law Review* 1992). By the late 1980s, diversionary programs, funded by the province, were in place in British Columbia indigenous organizations, including elders groups, and oversaw the limited administration of justice in these programs. In one noteworthy case, considered above, a provincial court judge recognized the right of an elders council to rule on a child custody case. In 1989, following an annual workshop on indigenous issues sponsored by the WJEC, representatives of the WJEC and the SITC and other indigenous leaders on Vancouver Island made a commitment to bring together elders and justice system officials. University of British Columbia political scientist Paul Tennant, who participated in the program and wrote an evaluation, observed that the resulting Project "had its origins in 1989 in the thinking of three persons: Tom Sampson, the Chair of the First Nations of South Island Tribal

Council; B.C. Provincial Court Judge Douglas Campbell, the director of the Western Judicial Education Centre; and Sam Stevens, the Director of the University of British Columbia's Native Law Program" (Tennant 1992:1). Judge Campbell, program facilitator during the years 1988–94, observed that the project needed visionary leadership and "Tom Sampson had the vision" (telephone interview, 26 November 1998).

A proposal, submitted on behalf of the SITC, was funded by the federal Department of Secretary of State for a cross-cultural education pilot project. Other moneys came from the provincial Ministry of Attorney General. The cross-cultural education program forwarded the idea of a project to build on the partnership between the elders and the mainstream justice system. At the annual assembly of the SITC in July 1990, consent was given to seek formal approval for this plan. This followed on band resolutions in 1988 from nine bands interested in enhancing their communities' role in the practice of justice.

Additional funding proposals were drafted on behalf of the SITC, calling for further education sessions and a diversion program. The diversion program involved the creation of an Elders Council "to receive referrals from the community, police, Crown, corrections and the Court, and would recommend and supervise action to be taken within the traditional community in individual criminal and family law cases" (a.m. Research 1995:5). In March of 1991, the Education Committee combined both components, education and judicial, to be called the South Vancouver Island Justice Education Project (SVIJEP). Funding for eighteen months was received from the federal Department of Justice, the provincial Ministry of Aboriginal Affairs, the federal Department of Multiculturalism and Citizenship, and the British Columbia Law Foundation. Candidates for the diversion program came primarily from bands in the greater Victoria area, but other bands, particularly the Cowichan, were involved through participation of their elders on the Elders Council.

The SIJP proposed a series of project objectives, including using both Canadian and First Nations justice systems; improving the mainstream system's response to indigenous people; improved delivery of justice to indigenous people on south Vancouver Island; the integration of the Elders Council in each stage of justice delivery to indigenous people in criminal, youth, and family cases; the reduction of incarceration rates of indigenous people; the application of indigenous justice practices to alternative measures, diversion, dispute resolution, and family counseling; the promotion of cross-cultural education for justice systems professionals and indigenous peoples; and support of reform of justice delivery (a.m. Research 1995:6).

A small administrative and reporting structure was established. One part handled financial issues, and the Education Committee served as the administrative body. Two representatives on the board, the SITC chairperson and the regional Crown counsel, were key decision makers concerning the direction of the project (a.m. Research 1995:28). No formal reporting or accountability system was established to inform the SIJP sponsors, communities, or the justice community of the project developments. Instead, a process of "talking to one another" and the informal building of trust was relied on, and the authority of elders as "custodians of traditional First Nations' knowledge, custom, and law was recognized and accepted by the Committee" (a.m. Research 1995:28). Tennant notes that "the key initial players regarded maintaining the process as the way to achieve eventual agreement between the two cultures [indigenous and the mainstream culture of law] on specific goals and objectives…In this sense a plan was not part of the plan…the strategy was 'first relationships, then trust, then action'" (Tennant 1992:27).

Those selected to be project elders were a group of influential senior people who headed complex corporate multigenerational families (or family networks) and whose standing is recognized by the term *S'ul Hwen* (sometimes given as *sí:yá:m* in Stó:lō territory and *Si'ab* in Puget Sound). This group, including six prominent elders "who participated fully and continually in the Project," was invited by Tom Sampson in March of 1990 to the first meeting. Sampson, although himself a S'ul Hwen, did not serve in that capacity for the project but rather acted within his tribal council role (Tennant 1992:2). The home areas of the six project S'ul Hwen covered the whole of the Island Salish territory. The S'ul Hwen and their supporters sought to "continue and re-empower the traditional Salish teachings," although they were hesitant to allow discussion of teachings in English and in the bighouse with justice officials present (Tennant 1992:5).

A fundamental issue that confronted SIJP participants is the relationship between the elected band councils and the authority of family leaders and elders and, less directly, the role of the tribal council. The SITC and supporters, in Tennant's words, saw the SITC as "an advocate of tradition and as speaking for interests, values, and goals, not commonly or necessarily represented by Indian Act band councils" (Tennant 1992:6). The objective of the SITC leadership during the initiation and development of the project was to act as "agents of, and communication channels for, the *S'ul Hwen*," and then to withdraw from the project, to be replaced by the Council of the S'ul Hwen, which would become the "aboriginal voice and authority for the Project" (Tennant 1992:6). Significantly, neither reserve populations nor band councils were consulted in the process of creating the project because of negative perceptions by key indigenous project participants of Indian Act reserves, bands, and band councils. Nor were off-reserve band members or "front-line workers" (band staff engaged in projects aimed at aiding community members) included in the project design. The project was underscored by the view that "the only legitimate aboriginal communities are the traditional families, for whom the *S'ul Hwen* themselves, are, by definition, the only legitimate spokesperson" (Tennant 1992:6). Tennant concludes, "The *S'ul Hwen* and the leadership of the SITC are passionately concerned about the state of their peoples and view the Project as one important means of remedy. They see the traditional teachings not as ends in themselves, but as practical means of bringing guidance, meaning, and morality in place of anger, frustration, and suffering that is now so prevalent" (Tennant 1992:7).

There were two significant positions taken by SIJP members. Key indigenous project participants "explicitly disavowed" any idea of the creation of a separate indigenous justice system and even though the indigenous system was thought of as autonomous and freestanding, "the goal was to have it function in partnership with the justice system" (Tennant 1992:27). Second, an implicit strategy was to have the mainstream judges and courts serve as the agents of change and the WJEC act as the conduit for extending partnership principles to other communities (Tennant 1992:27).

Texts

The texts generated by the South Island Justice Project view justice as derived from the primordial teachings of Hals, or the Creator, which were given to humans during the myth time and which have persisted as underlying cultural values and as defining characteristics of Coast Salish peoples. "This hereditary system…acted as guidelines" (First Nations 1990:3). These teachings create a moral space, and abridgment of them is thought to diminish justice and offend the relations between members of the moral community. A committee of elders spent several years, beginning in 1987, codifying these orally transmitted teachings and created an intellectual framework for capturing central ideas and connecting to mainstream legal constructs. As is the case with other examples of codification of traditional law, this framework renders what were once fluid and localized processes of justice into a discourse suitable to advancing the viewpoint and, ostensibly, the political purposes or present-day elders. The framework privileged some elders and indigenous language speakers' position in their communities. The process also simplified the social and cultural reality of the community into a form that was accessible by mainstream community members and justice officials.

The elders expressed several concerns. Chief among these was that it was inappropriate for elected tribal council members to represent cultural values connected to justice to the mainstream legal system. Tom Sampson, one of the organizers and prime movers of the project, observed that "The elders weren't happy with our own leadership—they were more like the government, the DIA [Department of Indian Affairs]" (Sampson, interview). The extended family, rather than the tribe, was identified as the core of the community, and elected tribal or band leaders were seen as usurping the authority of family elders and leaders. Tennant writes: "In the view of those oriented towards tradition and towards the *S'ul Hwen,* the basic units among the Salish of the Island are not the 19 bands but the many extended families. In this view, it is the S'ul *Hwen,* not the band councils, who are the legitimate representatives of the Island Salish concerning all fundamental questions. Sampson and the Project S'ul Hwen consider there to be some 80 traditional families whose *S'ul Hwen* live in the south Island" (Tennant 1992:6). This viewpoint finds support in Coast Salish ethnography. Suttles (1987b:8) described fundamental ideas, values, practices, and knowledge of magic, genealogy, and proper behavior as "advice," which is passed along within families exclusively, and which varied in its details.

Elders involved in the project were further concerned that speakers of Halkomelem, the local Coast Salish language, conduct the project, a view based on the idea that justice concepts were directly embedded in language and not easily translatable, if at all. They expressed grave concerns about the alienation of land, the reduction of game and fish stocks, the imposition of outside law, Canadian law, the loss of control over youth in trouble, and the influence of families without proper instruction in Coast Salish practices. In general terms, elders were concerned for the decline of cultural practice, which was linked to the ability to use the productive capacity of the land. The elders' role as teachers of respect and proper behavior was itself connected to justice and regulation (Sampson, interview). Tennant summarizes the situation this way: "The *S'ul Hwen* and the leadership of the SITC are passionately concerned about the state of their peoples and view the Project as one important means of remedy. They see the traditional teachings not as ends in themselves, but as practical means of bringing guidance, meaning, and morality in place of the anger, frustration, and suffering that is now so prevalent (Tennant 1992:7). Other, more particularistic issues concerned elders, including "justice system [mainstream] involvement in traditional native activities," including Syowen (Tennant 1992:13).

In their briefing notes entitled "Introduction to Aboriginal Justice and the Function of an Elders Council," the authors note that "Aboriginal Justice is the standards and regulations pertaining to behavior and orally preserved and handed down through centuries since time immemorial" (First Nations 1990:2). At the heart of justice was law, which is said to "govern the people and family and community" (First Nations 1990:2). Judicial authority, by extension from the Creator, is given to the most powerful interpreters of the Creator's law and "centers around the 'Longhouse and our Elders'" (First Nations 1990:2). Sampson referred to the process of codifying law as "describing spirituality" (interview). Further, he stated, "We take the holistic approach. Our laws are not separate from spiritual healing and discipline. Everything fits together, all in one. We hold the Bighouse as paramount over all other things that we do." The South Island elders documents describe justice as "addressing standards of behavior. Our traditional laws are not based upon punishment. The Aboriginal Common Laws of our land focus upon reconciliation, rehabilitation, and education" (Sampson, quoted in Tennant 1992:4).

The family law itself is composed of three domains: spiritual issues (teachings), conservation (traditional), and economics (value) (First Nations 1987). For example, law concerning fisheries has spiritual, conservation, and economic components. Under the rubric of spiritual law, the documents report that "Thanks are given to salmon 'for the life it gives to our survival.'" Salmon is shared first with elders, then family, and then the community. "Later, salmon is shared with ancestors via the spiritual burning of food in respect of those gone before us so they would not harm us and in return they would help us in not having difficulty in harvesting our food for they are with *Hals* (Creator)'" (First Nations 1987:8).

Conservation law dictates that "We always allow a first run by for spawning"; "We harvest enough for family and community need or until Elders say we have enough"; "We move to different locations to avoid depleting stock as well as to acquire species not available in our area." In addition, conservation law regulates human-nonhuman interaction. "Widows, widowers and new Indian dancers stay away from fish habitat for one to four years depending on Tribal customs" in order to avoid the salmon being repulsed by humans and leaving an area (First Nations 1987:8). Conservation law also provides specifics concerning equipment used for harvesting, for instance, where weirs, dip nets, spears and gaffs or reef nets may be used."

Finally, there is an economic law concerning fisheries, a category that overlaps considerably with the conservation law but that incorporates the teaching "Do not waste any part of fish. We preserve, smoke, half smoke, sun dry and salt salmon" (First Nations 1987:8).

The summary of the elders' presentation of tribal law indicates the following:

These laws that have been past [sic] on to us by our parents and elders are law from Hals (Creator) and not made by man. They are held sacred by our people. These laws are for our survival and for protection of all our resources.

These laws are received from Hals (Creator) after a purification period or a retreat of months or years of daily bathing in cold water, in streams or lakes and living with nature during this period. Laws would come after Hals (Creator) feels that you are pure enough, then he would give you the law through one of the resources or through a vision. It is through total commitment, concentration and fasting of an individual that he is able to receive these laws from Hals (Creator).

When one received a law from Hals (Creator) he would further bath and fast to give thanks for the law or vision he has received. He must show his thanks for what he received for it should be for the survival of his family, the community, and the resources. Once this law is in place it is the responsibility of parents and Elders to uphold this law and pass them onto their children and their children's children.

When these laws are upheld by individuals, families, and community, Hals (Creator) gives us bountiful resources. We do not show greed towards our resources but share with those in need. It is a way of thanks to Hals (Creator) for the laws he has given us for our survival and for the bountiful resources.

In the view of the South Island elders, the sacred law creates a charter for the ongoing social organization of the community:

Indian Government Family Law, tradition and culture are dealt with, and developed in our traditional bighouse. At these gatherings all members are involved in decision making. If they have a proposal for action or questions, they would use their family spokesman and call upon several witnesses in support of their proposal or questions. Elders are always involved in decisions. (First Nations 1987:1)

A particular social role for elders is created because of their "knowledge of law given to us by Hals... [and] their knowledge of customs" (First Nations 1987:1). They held the opinion that "The elders are today and have been traditionally 'the Teacher, the lawyer and the Counsellor'" (First Nations 1990:4). The elders pointed to their own role in describing "Local and Private Matters (Disciplinary and Social) which involve elders in decisions made...because of their wisdom and knowledge of the laws and customs" (First Nations 1990:5). Further, law enforcement also falls into the domain of elders (together with parents), as does economics. The elders wrote, "In bartering for some of our resources our Elders and parents are the ones to decide what resources and how much to be bartered for" (First Nations 1990:5).

In addition, the elders described two other social roles that would support their own. One is spokespersons: "These persons are used, at the assembly, to voice the opinions or wishes of the general membership or family...These spokespersons must be knowledgeable of Tribal Affairs and Customs that have been given to them by the Elders" (First Nations 1990:5). A third social role, which derives from the teachings of Hals, is that of witnesses who are

> Persons...called upon when the membership want to voice their opinions at a gathering. They must be reliable because, when called upon at a later time, they must be able to recollect what was discussed and be able to relate that to a gathering. They must be able to thank those for their help or payback, and encourage others to carry and pass on this teaching to their children. Witnesses must have the respect of the Elders and general membership, and they must be knowledgeable of Tribal Affairs and Customs. (First Nations 1990:5)

Concerning the administration of justice, the elders recorded that "Justice is handled by the Elders of the community because of their wisdom and knowledge of the laws given to us by Hals (Creator). They are the ones to decide on discipline, depending on the seriousness of the violation." Further, "Parents and Elders are the ones to enforce laws given to us by Hals (Creator). Should it be decided that further action be taken in the enforcement of law, it can be done at a gathering, where a number are called upon to further advise the offender of the law he had broken" (First Nations 1990:4).

There is a pervasive sense that wrongdoing (my word) is primarily associated with children and youth, the pliable and the teachable, and that aboriginal law, then, is directed toward them. Tennant notes that the S'ul Hwen declined to accept cases concerning older people accused of major or violent crimes because they "won't listen to anyone" (1992:21). The exercise of justice lies with elders, who decide on discipline, sometimes in association with parents, and the system of authority is top-down, with communications flowing from elders to parents to children. "Aboriginal Common Law" is viewed primarily as a system of counseling with reconciliation, rehabilitation, and education as the major goals. There is no direct acknowledgment of the possibility of wrongdoing on the part of elders or other senior community members, despite the rich oral traditions that speak of dangerous warriors and even abuse by elders of grandchildren in their charge (see Snyder 1964). Indeed, there may be a connection between the intractability of problems of wife abuse and rape, clearly identified by women who objected to the project for its failure to protect them (a point I develop later), and the association made between justice and youth.

The South Island Justice Project, then, developed these features: the conception of law was "elder-driven," rather than linked to conceptions of rank and class that characterize Salish society. In this sense, age and seniority, rather than family status and personal achievement, were advanced. The laws themselves, although equated with common law, which is historical and changeable in its conception, were held to be primordial and unchanging in fundamental features.

There is a twist, however. These laws are thought to be revealed to elders following a process of personal purification and later taught to family members. In that sense, tribal law is not Mosaic, that is, revealed to the society as whole at one time and for all times. Rather, tribal law pertains to a particular family and, although this is not clarified in the documents, continue to be revealed to elders who could then proclaim tribal law that is both new and primordial (derived from X̱á:ls in the myth time.)

The system then, is directly connected through a specific spitual tradition, Syowen, which was thought to embed both the core spiritual concepts and the training and discipline that support moral behavior. The articulating model of justice that connected to the mainstream society discourses was that of restorative justice, with an emphasis on rehabilitation and reconciliation. In this case, reconciliation referred to a process whereby individuals acquiesced to the authority of current guardians of traditional law. Further, although the extended family was advanced as the basis of knowledge and authority, a composite group of elders stood in for family leaders in adjudication. The emphasis on rehabilitation placed the model squarely within the current "justice as healing" metaphor, which itself conjoins Western psychological and judicial concepts and indigenous social practice. Conley and O'Barr (1998) note, for example, that in the mainstream legal system, three discourses predominate, including healing, legal, and rehabilitative. In a similar vein, LaRocque (1997:85) queries whether the Hollow Water, Manitoba, mediation program had "fallen prey to contemporary, white, leftist/liberal, Christian and even New Age notions of 'healing,' 'forgiveness,' and offender 'rehabilitation.'"

Despite these unexplored connections to Western discourses, the aim of the project was to restore traditional life and the primacy of traditional values through the rejection of mainstream values and community elective leadership. However, explicit connections were also drawn to mainstream concepts. A fascinating development was the reference to indigenous law-and-order practices and personnel thought to parallel those of the mainstream society but not described in ethnographic literature as characteristic of Coast Salish life. Specifically, aboriginal Coast Salish law was described as "common law," "natural law," and "conservation law," and the death penalty was said to be extinguished and violators controlled by police. One sentence implicitly connects Coast Salish aboriginal practices and Western legal concepts by employing terms (*advocate, witness, clerk*) for Western court officials: "They [elders] deliberate over problem [sic] arising from causing offence to or violation of the community standards of behavior. The Elders are assisted by 'Spokesmen': who act as advocates. The affair is observed by 'Witnesses' whose function is to relate the events and proceedings to the families and communities. They act as clerk of the court and as our historians in this regard" (First Nations 1990:4).

Further, the justice process itself is described in a way that emphasizes overlap, making reference to an "appeal process" with stages, going first to an Assembly in Council of the Chiefs and Elders and then to an Assembly in Council of families and membership (First Nations 1990:4).

Project material advances the argument that Coast Salish traditional culture overlaps with contemporary progressive Western practice in several other significant ways as well. Here a paradox arises out of claims of difference and efforts to base authority on traditional practice and the connections drawn to Western legal categories. "An Introduction" states that:

> Many of the safeguards included in your legislation of recent decades have been significant in our traditional practices for centuries. 1. The Death Penalty: was extinguished as a form of punishment, centuries ago. 2. Inter-Tribal Warfare: As a means of political force was outlawed a century ago. *Violators could be addressed and dispatched by the police forces of our nations.* (First Nations 1990:5; emphasis mine)

However, First Nations ethnonationalist rhetoric frequently contrasts the absence of coercive authority and personnel associated with centralized power within First Nations and their presence in white society. Further, ethnographic notes from interviews with elders of the early and middle twentieth century make explicit mention of the execution of serious troublemakers within Coast Salish society in earlier periods, as described earlier.

Family law is, by inference, said to be "Indian Common Law" (First Nations 1990:5). Here, the term family law ought not to be confused with the idea of family law in the mainstream society, namely law that applies to family matters. Rather, the term refers to the primacy of the family in Coast Salish society and the idea that there is, in effect, no teaching that is not derived from family knowledge. Family law is further associated with *natural laws,* or "laws tied/based with nature" (First Nations 1990:3). The laws, however, were said to be "general" in that they apply to individuals and the community, not to families (Sampson, interview). "No one interferes with other families' teachings," and therefore the elders recorded what "all can agree on." In this sense, the laws were composite laws, or "laws lowest common denominator," in Sampson's terms.

Finally, the construction of "aboriginal common law" as revolving around "traditional conservation" as one of the three fundamental domains creates an explicit connection to current Western political thought and builds on perceptions of indigenous peoples, in contrast to Western peoples, in Fienup-Riordan's terms, as "original ecologists" (1990b:167).

Cases

Once a structure was created, the South Island Justice Project was in a position to begin to accept cases diverted from the mainstream justice system. The expectation was that counseling and dispute resolution functions were to arise from self-selection by clients and by a process of identification by the S'ul Hwen. The assistant Crown counsel and the regional Crown counsel were to identify candidates for consideration of the Council of S'ul Hwen, excluding non-Coast Salish and older people accused of major or violent crimes. The council would then decide whether to proceed with a case, and candidates and victims (both of whom had to consent to the diversion before it could occur) would be contacted prior to the production of a signed agreement between the candidate, SIJP coordinator, and Crown counsel. Clients would then be placed under the supervision of one or more S'ul Hwen, who would teach and counsel, supervise any community work, and arrange and witness apologies or restitution. The hope was that the relationship established or reestablished between client and victim would continue, thereby allowing the S'ul Hwen to monitor clients after the diversion process was complete (Tennant 1992:29).

Knowledge of an offender's or victim's family or family situation was the most important factor in the decision to accept or reject a candidate for diversion or sentencing intervention (a.m. Research 1995:43). Of a total of 184 cases brought forward, 26 offenders were selected for the project. The average age of the offenders diverted was twenty-six; there were 6 physical assault cases, 9 theft cases, 2 mischief cases, and 1 breach of probation. Diversion contracts called for community service in 13 cases, apologies in 11 cases, counseling in 11 cases, and abstinence from alcohol in 4 cases. All cases called for meeting with the program coordinator (a.m. Research 1995:49).

Among those selected, one candidate declined to participate, four candidates received warning letters, and, in a program review, three files could not be located (a.m. Research 1995:89). Three of the offenders (to use program terminology) agreed to be interviewed by program reviewers, who found quite varied responses. In one case, a 32-year old man, charged with spousal assault, reported that he was asked to do community work service in the Smokehouse *(Syowen* House), which he disliked because he already had respect for the elders and saw no need for Smokehouse intervention. However, he entered into a contract to complete his community work service, but there was no follow-up. This man told reviewers that traditional justice is "not the Smokehouse" and questioned how elders who do not know the offender could provide help (pp. 90–92). In another case, an aboriginal RCMP officer referred a second man, aged forty-one and charged with impaired driving, to the project. He met with a community elder who assigned him yard work. He enjoyed his regular discussions with the elder, who counseled him on a variety of topics. The program, this man believes, gave him a chance to straighten out and become sober (pp. 92–93). A third offender, a twenty-three-year-old man, was charged with auto theft and breaking and entering. He heard about the program while incarcerated and was released to meet with a group of elders. He was assigned and carried out tasks but did not find them relevant to his personal situation; nor did he find the experience with the project beneficial because, for him, "Nothing happened" (pp. 93–94). Legal scholar Mary Ellen Turpel, who visited indigenous justice programs across Canada in 1993, reported on a fourth offender in the SIJP, a twenty-eight-year-old man arrested for assault stemming from an episode of drinking. The man had left the reserve at age ten and had become an alcoholic at any early age. After being diverted to the SIJP he worked with elders for over a year, and according to Turpel's account of him (rather than self-accounts as reported in the project study), he had learned his place in the community and had developed responsibilities. Turpel concluded that "Through their compassion, teaching, and family reintegration, the elders have assisted this young man to gain control of his life…What happened was nothing short of a miracle" (Turpel, in Royal Commission 1996:105–106).

Reaction: The Issues

No victims could be identified and interviewed by the team of federally appointed reviewers of the South Island Justice Program, but interviews with a range of participants and community members were conducted. In all, seventy individuals were interviewed, two group interviews were held, and eighty-three case files were examined. Twenty-four respondents were "key participants" from various federal agencies; ten were service deliverers (such as social workers and health providers); eight were chiefs; eight were and twenty-eight were community members from ten communities (Royal Commission 1996:10–11). Respondents agreed unanimously that the goals of the project to improve relations between the mainstream justice system and the Coast Salish peoples, to make services more culturally sensitive, and to increase the capacity for the indigenous people to carry this out were valid and necessary. However, participants described the program as employing a "top-down" approach that did not adequately involve community members and front-line workers nor consider the variety of needs within the separate communities. Most (59 percent) felt that their expectations of the project's impact on Coast Salish communities and the criminal justice system were not met (a.m. Research 1995:S-3).

A number of issues emerged that related to the themes of the lack of agreement within the Coast Salish world and the orientation to family, as opposed to community, leadership. The respondents to the SIJP evaluation pointed out a number of community and criminal justice issues overlooked by the project. Among the most significant was that the project's "traditional" approach failed to adequately account for the current justice ideologies of the broad range of community members, some of whom are "without traditional values" (a.m. Research 1995:S-4). Respondents recommended a more extensive consultation with the community, including grassroots involvement. Community participation should have been sought out in the process of selection leadership and elders (a.m. Research 1995:S-6). Respondents emphasized that the justice services should be administered by a nonpolitical organization and operated according to the principles adhered to in the various communities in order that responses to the needs of the victims, offenders, and community members all be localized (a.m. Research 1995:S-7). One of the few respondents who believed that the project objectives were not obtainable gave as a reason "the lack of consensus among community members regarding the credibility of individuals providing service" and also mentioned "the lack of consensus within Coast Salish communities matters" (a.m. Research 1995:22).

The program review noted that the terms of reference for the project in two instances gave responsibility to the "First Nations Community," but the tasks of appointing the elders council and project liaison worker were instead carried out by the chair of the SITC. The evaluators wrote that "Two primary factors emerge from the responses which indicate that time and 'politics' significantly complicated and interfered with Project results" (a.m. Research 1995:32), noting that the specific objectives and administration of the project had not received band support in the form of council resolutions. The "credibility and objectivity" of the elders were controversial to respondents and, more broadly, within the communities. Respondents reported that "Elders were selected on a case-by-case basis for the objectivity and experience they could offer in a specific case; and Elders were hand-picked by SITC personnel on the basis of inter-personal relationships" (a.m. Research 1995:46).

The project review uncovered no instances of S'ul Hwen making sentencing recommendations to the court. However, "service providers and other community members mention inappropriate interventions by SITC representatives and Salish Elders in certain criminal matters involving Coast Salish citizens." The reviewers concluded that "real or perceived conflicts of interest and abuses of power by Project authorities at the critical stage of the Project's initiation devastated community members undermined the likelihood of Project success" (a.m. Research 1995:52). A case, not connected to the project, was given by respondents as an example of inappropriate intervention. The case concerned the attempts by some members of the SITC and some elders (some of whom were associated with the project) to intervene in the prosecution of a family member. The intervention took the form of a court's jurisdiction over the matter at a preliminary hearing. The challenge failed, and the matter proceeded through the mainstream system. The project evaluators note:

> It is said that at the time of this event, significant pressure was placed upon the victim(s), family and other community members to unite in the effort to have this matter treated in a traditional way. This suggestion and the proposed outcomes were perceived by many to be unacceptable. It failed to address the critical needs of the victim(s) while raising the alleged offender to "preferred justice" status. The serious nature of the alleged offense (i.e. sexual assault with multiple victims), the lack of resources to ensure public safety, and the lack of any defined principles or practices of the proposed "Tribal Justice" system, increased the concern among citizens.

> In addition, others point out that the event was a totally inappropriate forum for the exertion of political pressure respecting Aboriginal justice issues. This specific case and its surrounding events sparked a community concern that the driving force behind "the Project" was the [participant's] desire to intervene in justice on behalf of a member. (a.m. Research 1995:52–53)

A group of eight elders who responded in round-table discussion affirmed that the intent of the project was to "make an offender within the community a better person, not to find guilt." They reported that a number of people within Coast Salish communities spoke out against the project, and they attributed this to "misunderstanding" the project and to the inadequacies of those outside the Syowen tradition, who did not understand the teachings. Further, those who complained, in the elders' view, did so because of participation in the mainstream education system and their failure to receive "cultural education" (a.m. Research 1995:71). The consequence of this approach is that the program had a built-in limitation: only culturally well-groomed offenders need apply. In effect, there were implicit qualifying standards for participation, and one had to be good enough to be bad, to be an offender. In addition, a very limited conception of "tradition" was advanced: practitioners of religious traditions outside of the Syowen longhouse, such as members of the Indian Shaker Church, were thought to not qualify. In this view, no provisions were made for the vast majority of Coast Salish people who chose to attend school.

Other project respondents spoke of power relations, including generational rifts and abuse of power by families (a.m. Research 1995:58). Elders, on the other hand, reported their preference not to have affiliations and their wish to be able to help everyone (a.m. Research 1995:72). This viewpoint seems sadly out of step with the reality of interfamily politics and the problems reported within the program. A study of a tribal mental health program showed the significance of interfamily politics in community members' disinclination to share information with therapists across family lines (see Miller and Pylypa 1995). In addition, other studies show the inclination of community members to vote in tribal elections and to assess community resources along family lines (Miller 1992a).

A perhaps even greater difficulty for the project was what some critics felt were the implications for women. The project reviewers observed that "Pressure exerted by family or other community members regarding justice issues is consistently reported to have disturbed community members and service providers. Victims and offenders were likewise caught in the web of persuasion to deal with matters within the community" (a.m. Research 1995:97). They noted that some victims did not come forward because they presumed that the offenders would simply be "counseled" by elders and remain in the community, perhaps as neighbors. "In some instances, women were reluctant to approach certain Elders who were convicted sex offenders, as the women felt their concerns would not be addressed" (a.m. Research 1995:97). Further, the project review included a passage from an official report made during a preliminary review:

> In conversation with community members, problems in the project arose during the phase in which victims were contacted to give their consent. Despite the highly confidential nature of the information shared at the diversion take-in meetings, allegations have been made that women who made disclosures of abuse to the police were subsequently approached by Elders who would try to persuade them not to use the criminal justice system. Apparently, this was often done by emotional blackmail, or "guilt trips."... In one instance, the victim was approached by a male Elder and was advised to "just put this behind her" and get on with her life.

> It was alleged that victims who persisted were sometimes bribed or visited by spiritual representatives who again tried to "persuade" them to drop the matter, sometimes through the use of "bad medicine." If the victims continued to persist [sic], we were told that the victim's abuser might be sent to intimidate them. (a.m. Research 1995:98)

A *Vancouver Sun* (31 July 1992:84) headline read "Indians fear justice experiment will hush sex abuse charges," and the associated reportage provided more detail than the subsequent project review four years later, relying on reports from female community members. Women reported the cover-up of sex-abuse charges and the use of intimidation tactics. One woman told of "several cases where powerful families pressured women to use the alternative system, which involves the band's [sic] council of elders, rather than bring sexual assault charges to court. The newspaper account concluded, "But some native women wonder about how the council can handle cases of sexual assault given the history of denial by some elders."

Critiques by urban Coast Salish women, in addition to those coming from the reserve populations, eroded the viability of the program to the point that "detractors became bold and believed the Justice Ministry was on their side," in the words of Judge Douglas Campbell, and they "won the war [ended the program] by not fighting a battle" (Campbell, interview). Sharon McIvor, a lawyer and spokesperson for the Native Women's Association of Canada, for example, noted that "the nightmare for abused native women proves native men are not ready for self-government" *(Vancouver Sun*, 31 July 1992, B4, original in paraphrase). Project operations ended in February 1993, and the final report concerning the project was filed two years later.

In this I considered the "preamble," a much-publicized case of diversionary justice that was described in the academic literature and in justice circles as an example of indigenous justice at its best and that purported to show the facility with which elders councils could operate and deliver aboriginal justice. This case set the stage for the creation of an education project designed to teach mainstream justice officials about Coast Salish concepts, and this was followed by a diversionary justice project, the South Island Justice Project. The project, however, foundered through its failure to account for variability in beliefs and practices, for generational differences, for interfamilial suspicions and the consequent issues of confidentiality, and for the failure of intersubjective agreement about who belongs to the category of honored elder. In addition, the relations between band governments and tribal council were treated unproblematically. The outcome of the project renders unclear whether the "lowest common denominator" approach—taking only mutually agreeable concepts from the "law" of various families—is workable as a basis for a justice program.

Conclusion [from *The Problem of Justice*]*

This tour of aboriginal justice in Coast Salish communities of Washington State and British Columbia is constructed around the idea that colonial processes have transformed and distorted the politics of indigenous communities, including the ways in which community members understand their own prior practices of justice. Rather than providing a primordialist account of justice, I show the ways in which these understandings have changed historically and some of the consequences for the development of community-level justice. In particular, I point to the analytic value in treating the developments in indigenous justice as linked to the rise of the international ethnonationalist movements that effectively emphasize the moral claims to self-governance and appeals to retributive justice by minority ethnic groups. These claims are made in repudiation of European-derived centralized, rationalistic, bureaucratic, territorial, and universalistic nation-states. In addition, I employ the related concepts of resistance and accommodation within indigenous communities fractured by colonialism and domination and characterized by changing forms of internal differentiation and internal conflict.

Much of the debate within communities takes place at the level of claims to tradition and the sacred, cultural conceptions that remain invaluable as guides to community members and useful in managing relations with the outside world. Such debates, however, are less helpful in managing relations inside and in helping to create a justice forum in which community members as a whole may feel that their views are heard and that they have had what they feel to be an appropriate "day in court." The Coast Salish communities, with their own forms of internal differentiation in the period before contact, have been fractured in new ways, with new practices of internal domination. At the beginning of the twenty-first century, the problems of self-governance, particularly the management of justice systems that both promote and symbolize internal control, are exacerbated by these internal struggles and by the continuing pressures on indigenous communities imposed by the mainstream societies. A widely shared response among indigenous communities of both the United States and Canada has been to reorganize politically around the rhetoric of rejection of mainstream society's values and organizational practices with the hope of restoring the practices and values of earlier periods. But it is the act of rejection that has led away from the careful consideration of class, status, wealth, and power differences, features of life that are to wrongly said to characterize only mainstream society, in promoting justice practices instead organized around concepts of elderhood, healing, restoration, primordiality, and spiritual purity. Much of the discourse about elders (but not necessarily by elders) and about healing reflects reactions to the imposition by the outside world rather than the way life was lived at one time. The use of elders as a means to buffer communities from external influences has misrepresented their family roles and drawn attention away from working through the difficult problems of how families might relate to one another and how individuals relate to the community. I have not argued that discourses of health and restorative justice are destructive but, rather, that consensus cannot be assumed concerning what direction to head and that a fuller debate about these fundamental local issues is needed in creating valued systems of justice. Substantial agreement within communities will not arise from unchallengeable and didactic claims to authority through particular understandings of tradition. Instead, tradition remains a seductive trap.

Because justice and law arc not simply spiritual in nature, but rather are political as well, they concern defining crime and providing or denying access to legal processes. Disguising the workings of power and authority, I have argued, undermines the capacity of the new justice systems to achieve legitimization in the eyes of community members and to provide a real forum for the identification and resolution of problems. Much of the current discourse about justice is built on faulty notions, or at least public claims, of an earlier, Edenic society that cannot be emulated; such discourse is ultimately unnecessary and self-defeating. I have further argued that the present-day discourses obscure much of what might be of value from earlier Coast Salish concepts and practices of justice, particularly the ways in which landscape and ancestral names have been connected to thinking through problems and promoting resolution. These concepts are not forgotten by community members, however, and remain a significant resource for emergent formal terns. In fact, as I write this conclusion, a Stó:lō transformer rock near the Fraser River was inadvertently destroyed by the Canadian Pacific Railroad, and commentary by Sonny McHalsie and elders published in the *Vancouver* Sun in August 1999 emphasized the importance of the rock as a reminder to "do good."

In addition, the discourses I have described further contribute to a simplification and distortion of prior social and cultural practice that indigenous communities have been forced to undertake in order to establish legal authority, negotiate treaties, and claim lands. These self-representations potentially create problems for the future by becoming fixed in print and legally established but unable to meet the requirements of unforeseen legal battles. They create problems in the present by obscuring more subtle, less easily described, cultural practices that are central to Coast Salish thought and that give richness, flexibility, and strength, but that have little or no overlap with the conceptions of the mainstream society.

The importation of nonlocal alternative dispute resolution models of aboriginal justice, promoted by the state as an effective means of and cheaply diverting a portion of the problems of justice to aboriginal communities, remains a threat to communities developing their own programs. These models are not attuned to subtle local concepts of power and are premised on the concept that indigenous communities are fundamentally the same. Nader (1990; see also Nader and Ou 1998) has pointed to related problems: the models divert attention from systemic, endemic problems by identifying the struggles as localized and encapsulated and necessarily amenable to mediation or similar processes. Further, these models disguise differences of power, a significant problem for families struggling to maintain good relations and vigilant in watching that others do not gain an unfair advantage. The widely promoted Navajo Peacemaker program, perhaps unlike the Family Group Conferencing model, differs from the Western-style alternative dispute resolution system in the reliance on prayer, on lay rather than professional support people, in the use of a peacemaker who is not chosen on the criteria of neutrality, and in the seeking for consensus rather than the imposition of judgment by an arbiter (Nielsen 1998). But this program shares features with alternative dispute resolution in that it is aimed at a limited range of localized, personalized problems between individuals who can, ultimately, find common (referred to as consensus), rather than systemic issues or between groups and individuals who disagree in their fundamental understandings (Yazzie and Zion 1995, 1996; Nielsen 1998). This Navajo system provides limited guidance for the creation of a more comprehensive system.

In short, Canadian indigenous communities have been pushed into making inadequate, reified claims about their own prior practices to meet the demands of contemporary politics with the nation-state. Discourses have arisen that misrepresent ways in which indigenous practices overlap with Western legal and Western psychological thought and that boil the ambiguity and consequent flexibility out of the system. Further, by placing much of the discourse out of the way of open debate by employing the language of primordiality and sacredness, the ways in which the new justice initiatives advantage one group within society and place others at risk remain unexamined. A consequence of all of this is that tribal political movements concerned with removing indigenous communities from the coercive power of the state have come to rely on radically conservative (mis)representations. A comparative examination of the justice practices of neighboring Coast Salish communities of Washington State, which have considerably different political circumstances, reveals that misleading oppositions between Western and indigenous justice need not be the starting point for developments in British Columbia. Instead, features of both systems of justice can be incorporated into indigenous systems in a manner that can potentially accommodate the diverse interests and viewpoints of community members.

More specifically, I point to a series of justice issues that contemporary Coast Salish communities in two countries approach dramatically differently. Although much of this variation can be explained on historical grounds and by differences in national public policy, the variation is also an outcome of the personal conviction of community leaders such as those featured in chapter 5. These fundamental issues continue be debated everywhere in the Coast Salish world. The first of the issues concerns the authority by which tribal justice systems are created and operate and, by extension, the independence of their operation. Typically, the will of the community as a whole and tribal sovereignty are given as the source of judicial authority, backed by ancestral and spiritual sanctions. In this case, tribal government can incorporate the views of chiefs (elected or hereditary), elders, tribal bureaucrats and administrators, tribal members, and tribal officials. But the South Island debacle suggests the limitations of the extreme approach to justice that separates elders and elected tribal governments by placing sole authority in the hands of individual elders and elders councils as interpreters of traditional law and as judges and agents of restorative justice. Indeed, the former chief of the Cowichan band specified that the major failing of the SIJP was this division between elders and elected band councils (Alphonse, interview).

A second, profoundly difficult issue is the legal relationship between the competing constituent families that make up bands and tribes. Since families typically attempt to resolve internal difficulties without outside intervention, interfamily issues remain the greatest puzzle to be encountered in the administration of justice. In a broad sense, the relations between families cannot be resolved simply by dispute resolution practices (such as the Navajo Peacemaker program), which conceive of problems as personal, low level, and amenable to the creation of consensus between wronged parties and wrongdoers. The Navajo Peacemaker program specifies that crime be identified as between individuals, not between the individual and the state, as in Western justice, a frequently made claim concerning the nature of indigenous justice. But because tribal justice systems are an arm of governance by a sovereign or semi-sovereign entity (the only grounds on which tribes might actually have justice systems, as Doreen Maloney of Upper Skagit pointed out in her discussion with the Stó:lō), larger, more comprehensive issues must be incorporated within the scheme of justice. While indigenous justice may well once have been the sum of the total of the law as articulated by the separate families, as it was conceptualized in the South Island Project, this sort of family law does not address the big issues of the day. The present-day relations between families include fundamental concerns such as the problems of domination of the tribal council by large, powerful families; access to tribal jobs and services; access to tribal land and houses; and, more generally, how to define nepotism. In this sense, then, one can identify two entities: a corporate tribe (which is a creation of contact and was not a legal entity in earlier periods) and the various families. Families, in the current world, relate to one another not simply directly, but through the tribal structure of governance. It is this three-sided relationship that must be worked out and that cannot be addressed, as the south island case shows, by the creation of a third body, elders, which is thought to unproblematically stand outside of family politics. The Upper Skagit system, and potentially the Stó:lō approach, allow for the incorporation of elders as culture bearers and interpreters of history and law, without requiring or foregrounding this elder role.

A third issue is the conception of justice employed in tribal justice programs. A program strictly arranged around the metaphors of healing and restoration appears to be needlessly limiting and to have arisen from the rejection of Western justice. The more incorporative Upper Skagit approach, which allows for restitution and rehabilitation, as well as punishment, creates a wider range of ways to engage the justice system, as is appropriate to a diverse community.

A fourth issue is the association of tribal justice with a particular approach to culture and spirituality. If one regards the community as diverse, as I have done here, then the protection of diversity appears critical to the creation of a community where all have access to justice. At Upper Skagit, religious practitioners participate in code creation concerning areas of special interest to themselves and may be called in as culture experts at trial; likely something similar may emerge at Stó:lō. The case of the SIJP demonstrates that associating justice with a spiritual practice limits the numbers able to participate in a system, as wrongdoers and as participants of other sorts, and disenfranchises many. In this way, the justice system marginalizes itself and cuts out the possibility for a broad construction of justice.

The three cases show a variety of paths to the creation of law and the role of elders. Resolution by tribal council is one path to the creation of code. Another path, the use of "boilerplate" from other jurisdictions, has been criticized because it is said to erode traditional practices and to reduce tribal independence (Brandfon 1991). The material from the several Coast Salish tribes of Puget Sound, however, reveals how a process of tailoring code to fit local needs and viewpoints occurs. A study of tribal courts nationwide found that "Indian judges inevitably draw upon their own sense of justice and fairness in deciding cases and interpreting legislation, so their decisions reflect custom and tradition" (Cooter and Fikentscher 1992:562). As a consequence, "*Tribal law is distinctly more Indian as applied than written*" (Cooter and Fikentscher 1992:563, emphasis mine; see also Tso 1989; Vincenti 1995). The Puget Salish materials show other useful routes to code creation as well. Tribal justice committees can suggest particular needs that can be put on paper by legal advisers. At Upper Skagit, particular constituent groups have been consulted concerning legislation affecting them directly. This system allows the direct participation of elders on justice committees and as members of the tribal general council (all enrolled members) who can advance law at annual general meetings. Further, case law, although limited at present, provides a further location for elders to provide direction (as a group, as court-certified elders, or as called in on a case-by-case basis). The multiplicity of sources for code allows for community diversity and for continued debate.

At Stó:lō, the code-writing process is still rudimentary and conducted largely at the level of the "nation," that is, chiefs and senior officials working with tribal bureaucracy. Broad community consultation has not yet occurred, although efforts have been made. The *Sqwelqwels ye Stó:lō* (2, no. 6 [August 1999]: 14) called for suggestions for renaming Family Group Conferencing to reflect Stó:lō "ownership," and in March 2000 a "naming ceremony" was held in order that the alternative program receive an "official Halq emeylem name: *Qwi:qwelstom*," a term that "means to live in harmony, help one another to survive, to care and share amongst all people, if there are any disputes or conflicts it is resolved amongst family, elders, friends" (*Sqwelqwels ye Stó:lō* 3, no. 5 [May 2000]:1). Community workshops have been held to "develop policies and procedures that are specific to the Stó:lō people." The SIJP, on the other hand, avoided broad consultation and relied instead on the elders committee to articulate the law.

There are three final issues: the manner in which the systems articulate with the outside world, the related issue of the "reach" of the system, and, perhaps most significantly, the way in which internal problems and critiques are addressed. I present them here together because I have claimed that some efforts at justice are derailed by their attention to managing relations with the outside world (while, ironically, emphasizing their primordial nature), thereby eroding their capacity to come to grips with local issues of power and the critiques of constituents.

All three systems described here developed their own formal and informal strategies for dealing with the dominant mainstream society. This is perhaps easiest for the Upper Skagit and other tribes of Puget Sound that employ their own police, judges, and other justice personnel and that have entered into various agreements with other jurisdictions. These tribes have strengthened their jurisdiction by other means as well, including the creation of code in criminal areas in which they appear not to have jurisdiction under the Major Crimes Act. Perhaps most significantly, the codes and constitutions of the Upper Skagit and other tribes allow for the importation of federal, state, and other tribal law as they see fit, thereby helping to fend off the long arm of the federal justice system in those cases in which the tribal court would otherwise appear to have no remedy available. These two strategies have both extended the reach of the tribal courts and defended their systems from encroachment, but both strategies depend on deploying legal language that does not appear to be "traditional" in nature. Unlike the approach of the South Island Justice Program, these strategies of resistance do not rely on emphasizing differences with the mainstream law in content, in claims to moral priority, and in paradoxical and weak claims to parity through demonstrating comparability of Coast Salish and mainstream legal concepts. Instead, direct measures are made that rely on the realpolitik of understanding the loopholes in mainstream legal concepts and local and national politics. One might say that the outside world must be contended with, but not at the risk of ignoring the local.

Now, finally, what of the efforts to address internal critiques? The South Island Justice Project was tied to a construct, the primordial law as interpreted by elders, that placed itself above reproach. As a consequence, women's complaints about being coerced and complaints from both men and women of irrelevance were not effectively addressed. By seeking to remove itself from band politics, which was dismissed as merely hand in hand with the mainstream system, the SIJP instead ensured that local power politics would subvert the system.

In developing its own infrastructure, especially in the areas of child custody and the management of youth, the Stó:lō Nation is struggling to find ways to respond to the demands for local band authority and the demands by families for privacy and family autonomy over its own members. While the Stó:lō Nation promotes a particular view of justice, other voices are not dismissed and may well be accounted for in the imagined future of Stó:lō governance. Indeed, concrete actions have been taken by some of the constituent bands that have altered the method of selecting band councilors by moving from an elected system to a system of designated family leaders that is said to reflect earlier practices. These changes have been directed to the problems of power generally and specifically to the domination of elections by large families and the effective exclusion of small ones. Significant debate has arisen over the issue of the centralization versus regionalization of service delivery, a problem that gets at the issues of inclusion, equity, and the balance of power between large and small bands. Developments such as these reflect a willingness to address fundamental issues of justice, seen as the appropriate relations between constituent social units. It is not yet clear whether a means will develop for these debates to occur directly in the process of governance and the delivery of justice, and whether Stó:lō people will have direct means to critique Stó:lō central policy. The current ideology holds that all Stó:lō leaders serve to reflect the wishes of their band members, particularly elders. Those who fail to do so stand to be recalled from office. This view gives an inadequate accounting for community diversity, however, or of the play of power, central themes in this book.

As is the case with the Stó:lō, the Upper Skagit system allows for the removal of councilors who fail to meet the expectations of constituents at the time of elections. Groups within the tribe can participate in redrafting code directly affecting them. Those convicted in tribal court can appeal to a superior court within Indian country, but not at Upper Skagit. But there are limitations to the handling of internal critique. Although U.S. tribal courts have failed to create a "balance of powers" and to conduct judicial review of the legislation and executive orders of tribal government (Brandfon 1991), Upper Skagit allows its court to rule on tribal law produced by the council or through other routes. This avenue might develop further with time.

The implications of the debates about justice in Coast Salish territory are far-reaching and suggestive. They are far-reaching in that they concern fundamental questions of social reorganization in communities and nations around the world that have reassumed some measures of autonomy and whose citizens have shifted in jural status from colonial subject to national citizen. Worby and Rutherford (1997:65), writing about contemporary Africa, ask, "What kind of identities and what arenas of actions 'has the law'—in both its colonial and postcolonial manifestations—made it possible for subjects and citizens to imagine?" The Coast Salish are far from alone in their struggles with tradition and their efforts to imagine their own identities under state law and tribal law. The debates about justice are suggestive for other debates in indigenous communities in British Columbia, Washington State, and elsewhere, including those about efforts to transfer authority over education and health services from the state to tribes. Here, too, claims to authority by tradition mix with efforts to imagine a new, larger-scale, reconfigured society.

References Cited

a.m. Research Services, Sheila Clark and Associates, Valerie Lannon and Associates Inc. 1995. *Building the Bridge: A Review of the South Vancouver Island Justice Education Project, Final Report.* B.C. Ministry of Attorney General, the Department of Justice Canada and the Solicitor General of Canada.

Alphonse, Dennis, Cowichan elder and former Chief, 19 November, 1998.

Brandfon, Fredric. 1991. Tradition and Judicial Review in the American Indian Tribal Court System. *UCLA Law Review*, 38(4):991–1018

Campbell, Judge Douglas, November, 26, 1998 (phone).

Conley, John and William O'Barr. 1998. *Just Words: Law, Language and Power.* Chicago, IL: University of Chicago Press.

Cooter, Robert D. and Wolfgang Fikentscher. 1992. Is There Indian Common Law? The Role of Custom in American Indian Tribal Courts, Part II. *Center for the Study of Law and Society,* 46(3):509–580.

Fienup-Riordan, Anne. 1990. Original Ecologists?: The Relationship between Yup'ik Eskimos and Animals. In *Essays: Yup'ik Lives and How We See Them,* edited by Anne Fienup-Riordan, pp. 167–191. New Brunswick: Rutgers University Press.

First Nations of South Island Tribal Council. 1987. Aboriginal Self Determination, Indian Family Law, Tribal Indian Governments. [unpublished].

First Nations of South Island Tribal Council. 1990. Briefing Notes: An Introduction to Aboriginal Justice and the Function of an Elders Council. Presented at Cross-Cultural Awareness Workshop, Parksville/Nanoose, March 9–11, 1990.

Kew, J. E. Michael 1990. History of Coastal British Columbia Since 1849. In *The Handbook of North American Indians,* Volume 7, *Northwest Coast,* edited by Wayne Suttles, pp. 159–168. Washington, D.C.: Smithsonian Institution.

106

Knight, Rolf. 1978. *Indians at Work: An Informal History of Native Indian Labour in British Columbia, 1858–1930*. Vancouver: New Star Books.

LaRocque, Emma. 1997. Re-examining Culturally Appropriate Models in Criminal Justice Applications. In *Aboriginal and Treaty Rights in Canada: Essays on Law, Equality, and Respect for Difference*, edited by Michael Asch, pp. 75–96. Vancouver: University of British Columbia Press.

Miller, Bruce Granville. 1992. Women and Politics: Comparative Evidence from the Northwest Coast. *Ethnology*, 31(4):367–383.

Miller, Bruce G., and Jen Pylypa. 1995. The Dilemma of Mental Health Paraprofessionals at Home. *American Indian and Alaska Native Mental Health: The Journal of the National Center*, 6 (2):13–33.

Nader, Laura. 1990. *Harmony Ideology: Justice and Control in a Zapotec Mountain Village*. Stanford, CA: Stanford University Press.

Nader, Laura and Jay Ou. 1998. Idealization and Power: Legality and Tradition in Native American Law. In New Directions in Native American Law. *Oklahoma City University Law Review*, 23(1):1–29.

Nielsen, Marianne O. 1998. Navajo Courts, Peacemaking, and Restorative Justice Issues. *Commission on Folk Law and Legal Pluralism: Proceedings of Xll International Symposium*, Williamsburg, Virginia, pp. 167–184.

O'Donnell, Judge Edward. 1988a. Proceedings at Reasons for Judgment in the Matter of the Family Relations Act and Audrey Thomas and Allan John Jones. No. F-2808. Parkesville, B.C., 13 July.

——— 1988b. Letter to Chief Judge Josephson. 14 July 1988.

Royal Commission on Aboriginal Peoples. 1996. *Bridging the Cultural Divide: A Report on Aboriginal People and Criminal Justice in Canada.* Ottawa: Minister of Supplies and Services Canada.

Sampson, Tom. 18 November, 1998, elder and former chair of the South Island Justice Project.

Snyder, Sally. 1964. Skagit Society and Its Existential Basis: An Ethnofolkloristic Reconstruction. Ph.D. dissertation, University of Washington.

Sqwelqwels ye Stó:lō (2), no. 6 [August 1999]:14.

Sqwelqwels ye Stó:lō 3, no. 5 [May 2000]:1.

Suttles, Wayne. 1954. Post-Contact Culture Change Among the Lummi Indian. *British Columbia Historical Quarterly*, 18(1–2):29–102.

——— 1987. Private Knowledge, Morality, and Social Class Among the Coast Salish. In *Coast Salish Essays*, edited by Wayne Suttles, pp. 3–14. Seattle: University of Washington Press.

——— editor. 1990. *Handbook of North American Indians*. Vol. 7, *Northwest Coast*. Washington, D.C.: Smithsonian Institution.

Tennant, Paul. 1992. The South Island Justice Education Project: A Program Review Prepared for the Department of Justice. MS, June 30.

Tso, Tom. 1989. Process of Decision Making in Tribal Courts. *Arizona Law Review,* 31.

UBC Law Review. 1992. Special Edition on Aboriginal Justice. Vancouver, B.C.

Vincenti, C.N. 1995. The Reemergence of Tribal Society and Traditional Justice Systems. *Judicature*, 79(3):131–141.

Worby, Eric and Blair Rutherford. 1997. Law's Fictions, State-Society Relations and the Anthropological Imagination—Pathways Out of Africa: Introduction. *Anthropologica,* 39(1–2): 65–69.

Yazzie, Robert and James M. Zion. 1995. 'Slay the Monsters': Peacemaker Court and Violence Control Plans for the Navajo Nation. *In Popular Justice and Community Regeneration: Pathways of Indigenous Reform*, edited by Kayleen M. Hazelhurt, pp. 57–88. Westport, Connecticut: Praeger.

Yazzie, Robert and James M. Zion. 1996. Navajo Restorative Justice: The Law of Equality and Justice. In *Restorative Justice: International Perspectives*, edited by Burt Galaway and Joe Hudson, pp. 157–173. Monsey, N.Y.: Criminal Justice Press.

Journal of Northwest Anthropology, Memoir 12:108–124 (2016)

7

Folk Law and Contemporary Coast Salish Tribal Code*

An important issue facing leaders of elective Indian Reorganization Act tribal governments is how to establish efficacy and create legitimacy in the minds of community members by building the values and ethos of earlier periods into the operation of tribal government and courts. More specifically, DeLoria and Lytle have argued that the "[e]xtensive development of tribal customs as the basis for a tribal court's decision will enable these institutions to draw even closer to the people (Deloria and Lytle 1984:248)." This essay considers how governments have integrated folk law into the contemporary tribal codes developed over the last two decades by eight Coast Salish tribes of western Washington State. This study does not concern the manner in which colonial, national, or regional governments interpret folk law for use in mainstream courts or for tribal courts operated by the mainstream society. Rather, the focus is on how Indian people themselves approach the incorporation of folk law. The analysis presented here concerns code developed under the authority of tribal governments for use in tribal courts that hold significant, although not complete, jurisdiction.[1] The term *folk law* is used instead of *customary law* in order to refer to uncodified, lived law in use or previously in use at the local level. Customary law, on the other hand, is sometimes used to refer to elements of indigenous law codified by a colonial administration for its own benefit and purposes.[2]

In explaining the nature of the inclusion of folk law, current analyses of North American Indian tribal legal codes emphasize either the diffusion of legal concepts from the colonizing mainstream society or the ways communities attempt to manage their relations with the outside.[3] The commentary of tribal councilors and judges and a reading of the Puget Sound tribal codes, however, show that the variations between the codes of culturally similar peoples reflect the differences in approach taken by leaders and the circumstances facing each community. These eight closely related tribal communities consider their own prior "legal" practices in quite different ways in several important respects, a circumstance that suggests the utility of the latter approach of emphasizing how communities create codes in order to manage relations with the state. Roger F. McDonnell, for example, noted, concerning Canadian First Nations efforts to codify customary law, that

> as the relationships to the state are perceived to change, so too do the customs that…[a] culture group will stress…We must bear in mind that our focus on custom possesses a strongly relational, rather than substantive, dimension. (McDonnell 1992)

Constructions of folk law have changed as community circumstances change, and the strategic use of folk law will likely continue to be important in managing relations with the mainstream community.[4] It is possible to go further, however, and observe the nature of this relation and the subsequent content of folk law put into play in the tribal legal systems. The present Puget Sound codes manifest this outward-looking quality, and ideas of folk law are most broadly incorporated in code dealing with relationships with the outside world and with children. Folk law is most closely constrained or excluded regarding contentious problems that are internal to the community, engage incompatible or irresolvable concepts, and concern family survival

*Authored by Bruce Granville Miller. Reprinted from the *American Indian Culture and Research Journal*, Volume 19, Issue 3, by permission of the American Indians Studies Center, UCLA. © 1993 Regents of the University of California.

(especially the vexing problem of the allocation of resources). As is true elsewhere, community members hold ambiguous feelings about the interpretations, meaning, and application of folk law-feelings that are apparent in the codes themselves (LaPrairie 1992:290).

Among the crucial issues facing these tribes are how to organize the legal relationship between the constituent extended families in order to avoid the contemporary equivalent of blood feuds and to facilitate the equitable distributions of the material resources of the polity and maintain tribal cohesion in the face of an intrusive mainstream society. Because formerly seasonally mobile people are now encapsulated in communities without many of the advantages and resources common to the mainstream society, the extended families compete vigorously for the limited resources available to them as tribal members (Miller 1992). Further, the availability of resources new to tribes in the period since the 1960s (such as federally funded tribal employment or houses constructed under federal grants) has created new disputes, just as the long period of unavailability of resources following the appropriation of traditional resource areas in the late nineteenth century also generated new sorts of disputes (Miller 1992). When conflict arises within the communities, it is difficult for adversaries to avoid each other as was possible even a few decades ago. The ability to move away from the reservation is complicated by the issue of maintaining eligibility for social and health benefits and by the high financial and psychological costs of living elsewhere. These circumstances give rise to tension and exacerbate interfamily disputes in many Indian communities (LaPrairie 1992; Miller 1994a).

Meanwhile, social change, including the changing roles of women, shifting patterns of participation in the labor force, and the changing relationships between youth and elders, complicates the use of folk law and traditional forms of mediation.[5] In addition, a lack of community consensus on values, along with the creation of social class differences based on nontraditional criteria, are said to create grudges and violence. The role of elders is described as constrained; today elders are ordinarily restricted from disciplining members of other families. The cultural emphases placed on oratory and consensus are viewed as losing ground to adversarial debate (NICS 1991).

A commentary on traditional and informal dispute resolution processes produced by the Northwest Intertribal Court System (NICS) drew upon the ideas of a sample of elders from three of the constituent communities (NICS 1991). The 1991 NICS study shows the variability of viewpoints within the region and points out the context within which tribal code is designed to operate. The major problems of reservation life that are thought to require resolution today are identified as family feuds, alcohol and drug-linked problems, and neighborhood disputes. The NICS study links problems of substance abuse to poverty, powerlessness, and chronic depression.

While the aim of this study was to draw attention to informal processes of dispute resolution that might be of use, the study itself shows the difficulty in employing folk law to handle the contemporary circumstances. The three major categories of conflict reported by the NICS were either not faced in precontact times (in the case of alcohol and drug use and neighborhood disputes) or not easily resolvable under precontact period dispute resolution systems (in the case of blood feuds). Most of the cases that make it to the tribal court concern criminal actions that are likely beyond the ability of community members and informal community processes to handle.[6] Consequently, new processes for the resolution of community problems are contained in these codes.[7]

Code writers face the difficult task of reconciling folk law with the issues and legal demands of the present day. Despite all of the problems, however, tribal court systems appeal to folk law as a concept in order to gain legitimacy internally and as a source of inspiration and ideas.

Indeed, folk law is said to offer variegated and dynamic possibilities for tribal communities facing change (McDonnell 1992:301).

The Idea of Folk Law

The identification of folk law is inherently contentious because of the potential for variation in interpretation along gender, class, and other lines (see for example, Keesing 1992). There are particular problems in the treatment of Coast Salish folk law. Unlike some other groups of the Northwest Coast of North America and elsewhere, Coast Salish folk law is not easily identified by present-day community members, because it does not derive from the functioning of a chiefly system, clan system, the conduct of a redistributive system (sometimes referred to as the feast or potlatch), or taboos such as pollution rules. In addition, Coast Salish concepts of secrecy and the need to hold important knowledge privately within the extended family complicate the effort to identify folk law that receives broad approval within a community.[8] For the purposes of this paper, I rely on three primary sources of information concerning folk law: the ethnographic literature (including recent material produced by community members); my own interviews with tribal code writers, tribal court judges, and council members; and the Northwest Intertribal Court System study.[9]

Processes of Folk Law

Folk systems of law in the Coast Salish region included, and, to a degree, continue to include, a variety of sanctions, especially restitution in the form of negotiated payments, ostracism, and even violent recrimination. Public ceremonies of various sorts were also employed in the process of public debate and resolution of disputes and crimes. These ceremonies included potlatches, summer dances of spirit-powers (notably, in some areas, *sxwayxwey,* which cleanses an insult), and formalized fights. But underlying these institutions is a cultural emphasis on avoidance of conflict through proper training (glossed as "advice"), fear of shamanistic retaliation, the practice of avoidance, fissioning of villages to dampen conflict, and deference towards senior leaders (elders) noted for their ability to model conflict-avoidance behavior and to express cultural values in formalized oratory. Indirect social control and, ordinarily, an absence of physical coercion rather than regulations and sanctions were the hallmarks of these systems. These practices stemmed from a desire to restore the community rather than from abstract notions of punishment and deterrence.[10]

Changes in Folk Law

After contact with Europeans and Americans in the eighteenth century, new concepts of political organization, leadership, and law developed. Loosely affiliated villages were organized under coercive leadership, in some cases (see for example, Collins 1974). These changes produced some erosion of dispute resolution practices, including the negotiation of payments and games of resolution.[11] Nonetheless, significant elements of contact period practice remained through the 1940s, particularly for tribes without reservations, which were not under the direct and regular scrutiny of BIA Indian agents, police, and courts of Indian offenses. The Sauk-Suiattle, for example, maintained a council of elders until the 1940s, composed of upper-class men who talked to individuals who were engaged in conflict or were thought to be in violation of tribal law. Those who refused to accept the judgments produced in this process were "given the cold shoulder" or, if outsiders, were removed from the community. The elders relied on talking to the parties in dispute before the council meeting and generally offered advice rather than punishment in the hope of producing resolution (NICS 1991:88).

The Bureau of Indian Affairs (BIA) authorized the creation of externally controlled courts of Indian offenses (CFR courts) in 1883 for reservation communities, in part to fill a perceived leadership void following an apparent decline in traditional authority and to diminish the residual authority of traditional chiefs (Johnson and Paschal 1991:5). BIA authority over the court system was diminished with the passage of the Indian Reorganization Act of 1934. However, tribes were encouraged to establish governments and court systems modeled on those of the dominant society. These institutions were poorly funded (Johnson and Paschal 1991:3). The switch to a policy of self-determination in the 1970s was accompanied by efforts of tribes with independent courts and those within the BIA system to rewrite their codes for their own ends. Meanwhile, the Indian Civil Rights Act of 1968 imposed most of the federal Bill of Rights on tribes, thereby establishing new requirements for tribal courts and restricting the penalties that could be imposed. It became unlawful, for example, for a tribal government to enact a law that exacts punishment without a judicial trial (Johnson and Paschal 1991). Tribal courts, CFR courts, and traditional dispute settlement institutions and processes all exist in Indian Country at present. A more recent development is the consortium created by several tribes to streamline the delivery of legal services by providing centralized judicial, administrative, and support services.

The Incorporation of Folk Law

My reading of the eight Puget Sound codes and those of sixty other American Indian tribes shows that folk law is incorporated directly into the legal process through the recognition of official or semiofficial community experts (ordinarily elders or some subset of elders) who sometimes have expert standing in the tribal court. A separate survey of American Indian tribal codes found three major systems whereby folk law is incorporated in one legal domain, procedural rules (Johnson and Davies 1998). According to this analysis, in one type no expert system is established, but appeals can be made to concepts of custom if not already accounted for in the law. In a second type, an expert system is established. In a third system, a tribal custom advisor is appointed and serves as a court-appointed expert in the event of dispute or uncertainty.

Folk law is incorporated in the codes in varying degrees of formality and specificity, ranging from extremely vague and inoperable language to explicit procedural instructions. More specifically, the degree of inclusion of folk law can be sorted roughly into three levels. One is a minimal level characterized by tight regulation, which leaves little room for folk law or interpretation of tradition (several of the Coast Salish fish tax codes are of this sort). Another level is code that is ambiguous concerning inclusion or exclusion of custom, and a final level involves the actual incorporation of folk law as (currently) understood or analogous contemporary practice directly in the code (this occurs most frequently in youth codes). Finally, folk law plays a significant role in some domains of contemporary law and little or no role in others.

Background

The Eight Coast Salish Tribes

The eight tribes whose codes are reviewed here are located in the largely urban, north-south corridor of western Washington State, along the shores of Puget Sound and adjacent waterways. These tribes are composed of culturally similar peoples, linguistically Coast Salish, but with English-speaking memberships. The traditional economies of all eight tribes were built around fishing, hunting, and gathering, and a rank and class system was supported by elaborate religious and ceremonial life (especially potlatching and winter ceremonial activities). Emphasis continues to be placed on the harvest of salmon for subsistence and for ceremonial reasons and on cedar working.

The tribes range in size from about 200 to about 3,000, with a mean of 1,075 and a total of 8,600 people. All have elective councils (of five to eleven members) and relatively small reservations, although these vary in size from just a few acres to more than twenty thousand. Some important differences between the tribes are the result of federal policies. The eight tribes are all the successors in interest to communities that sent representatives to treaty negotiations in either 1854 or 1855, but several were restored to recognition by the federal government in 1973–74 after a lapse and consequently have small reservations created in the 1980s. Federal policy required the consolidation of diverse peoples onto reservations in Washington State, and all of the present-day tribes incorporated people from a variety of communities.

Federal policy has influenced these eight tribes in similar ways: All engage in regular relations with the Bureau of Indian Affairs and receive health services under the separate Indian Health Services, although some now have direct control of their medical system.

Tribal Court Systems

Seven of the eight tribes are members of a consortium of fifteen tribes, the Northwest Intertribal Court System (NICS), and the eighth, originally an NICS tribe, now has its own court system. The NICS was established in 1979 following the fishing litigation (*U.S.* v. *Washington*, 1974) that held that the treaties of the mid nineteenth century gave Indians of Washington State rights to half the salmon catch in state waters, thereby creating a need for fish and game codes and a legal setting for the prosecution of violators. The NICS courts operate under the provisions of the tribal codes and constitutions and federal law, and each tribe's court holds jurisdiction over civil, criminal, traffic, and fisheries issues involving both Indians and non-Indians. Federal law, especially the Major Crimes Act of 1885, muddies the issue of jurisdiction by restricting or creating concurrent jurisdiction with Indian courts in important criminal areas, including murder and other violent crime. Consequently, folk law concerning such crimes is not considered here.[12]

Each tribe has created its own processes to compose code, but there are a number of ways whereby code is ordinarily created. One route is through the tribal law committees, whose work is to consult with code writers in making recommendations to the tribal council. The council can then refine the language and vote to accept or reject the proposed legislation. It is particularly at the committee level that notions of folk law are entertained most significantly. However, code writers are frequently neither enrolled tribal members nor community members and find it a difficult task to fit the ideas emerging from the community and the law committee into the legal structure already in place. This process opens the possibility of miscommunication between committee and code writer. The tribal council, composed of elected representatives of the enrolled members, can pass legislation on its own initiative or vote on suggestions coming directly from the membership or from other sources. Finally, the general membership of the tribe can instruct the council to prepare legislation by vote at the annual general membership meetings.

Folk Law and Puget Sound Codes: An Overview

On the surface, the present-day legal codes appear to reflect a viewpoint quite different from that which motivated earlier community practices. There are few explicit provisions for mediation and negotiated restitution, which characterized earlier dispute resolution. Generally, the codes are built upon an adversarial model that balances the interests of citizens against each other in civil action or against the tribe in criminal prosecution. In most instances, the legal system places an emphasis on punishment and rehabilitation rather than on restitution. The codes provide limited opportunities for elders, and none for the upper class, to exercise the authority they held in previous periods as sanctioned arbiters of customary practice. The codes of the eight Puget Sound tribes provide for no formal standing appointment of experts or elders, with a few exceptions; rather, discretion about how to apply custom is ordinarily left with the judge. This suggests, first, that in the Puget Sound region, folk law is thought of as best embedded in dispute resolution practices that precede entry into the formal legal system and, second, that there is less reliance on folk law than in some other bodies of Indian law. Nonetheless, there is significant variation in how the eight tribes treat folk law.

Folk law is broadly contained within the codes through references to the extended family or family networks, and family is defined as many as seven ways in the legal codes of single tribes. How family is defined is critical, because tribal political life is conducted along family lines and in the idiom of kinship (Miller 1992). Furthermore, the extended family has always been the fundamental unit of dispute resolution, and the NICS study defines the family as "generally [including] parents, siblings, aunts, uncles, cousins to 3rd or 4th removed (also great and great-great) and in-laws" (NICS 1991:111). Family is consistently defined the most narrowly in the sections of the law dealing with economic issues (which regulate competition within the tribe), notably fishing, and most broadly in the sections dealing with provisions for youth and custody. These sections establish guidelines for the treatment of tribal youth in contact with the outside world of nontribal social service agencies and have the intention of limiting outside interference in tribal life.

Folk law is also constrained by provisions of the tribal bill of rights, usually contained in the constitution, that guarantee a wide range of individual rights. In some cases, the bill of rights includes economic rights of equal opportunity and access to resources. These bills contradict the emphasis on social class and extended families that characterized traditional society, especially the families' central role within Coast Salish social, political, and ceremonial organization, including control of access to resources.

Codes and Folk Law

The eight tribal codes contain twelve areas in which folk law, as identified in the NICS study, the ethnographic literature, or in interview, is treated as relevant in at least one of the eight contemporary codes, either through direct application or through analogous practice.[13] These twelve areas are (1) the allocation to extended families of use-rights to important resources that, under treaty law, are now tribally owned (but that, under folk law, are the property of individual families); (2) the rights of extended families to control the provision of care for children and the elderly; (3) the rights of extended families, through their leaders, to operate collectively in community political life; (4) the role of elders in adjudicating conflict (which is recognized today in the provisions for elders' councils or seats for elders as consultants to the tribal courts); (5) the prerogatives of elders in formal settings (which is recognized through the creation of legal distinctions that honor elders); (6)

114

regulation of tribal membership based at least in part on affiliation with constituent family networks and on participation in the life of the community rather than on imposed standards of blood quantum or descent from a base roll; (7) the use of restitution to resolve conflict and restore peace in the community; (8) the allowance for community input to the judge in legal proceedings (which approximates the earlier role of community meetings to discuss criminal behavior and to assign sanctions); (9) the allocation of community assets to fulfill ceremonial and spiritual obligations (which is approximated today by legal provisions for the allocation of funds for community ceremonial purposes); (10) the provision for the protection of particular features of the natural environment (through first salmon and other ceremonies that constituted a category of folk law in that the performance of such ceremonies regulated the harvest); (11) the allowance for the "spirit of tribal law" in judicial proceedings; and (12) the allowance for the "spirit of tribal law" in judicial rulings. Table 1 shows the absence or presence of these areas in the eight tribal codes, and Table 2 summarizes the raw scores for the inclusion or exclusion of folk law in order to indicate roughly the differences in approach in the eight tribal codes.

TABLE 1. FOLK LAW INCORPORATED IN TRIBAL CODE*

Issue	Tribe							
	A	B	C	D	E	F	G	H
Rights of Family net	+ −	−	+ −	+	+ −	+ −	+ −	−
Role of elders	+	−	−	+	+	+	+	+
Membership	+	+	+	+		−	+	+
Community input on case	−	−	−	+	−		−	−
Restitution	+	−		+	−	+	−	+
Protect Environment	+	+		+		+	−	+
Use-rights	+	−		−		−	−	+
Family net and child care	+	−		+ −		+	−	−
Honor elders	+	+		+	+		+	+
Ceremonial provisions	+	+		+	+		−	+
Spirit of tribal law-rulings	+	+		+	+	−	+	+
Spirit of tribal law-process	+	+		+	+	−	+	+

*Plus signs indicate that the code incorporates fold law; minus signs mean the code explicitly rejects. A blank cell indicates that the code is silent (neither implicit or explicit on the subject). A plus sign and a negative sign in the same cell indicates that the code embraces folk law at points and rejects it elsewhere.

Raw scores from this chart give a rough idea of the variation in the inclusion of folk law and traditional practice among the tribes' codes. The scores are tabulated in Table 2:

TABLE 2. RAW SCORES OF THE TREATMENT OF FOLD LAW IN CONTEMPORARY CODE

Tribe	Positive Score	Negative Score
A	11	2
B	6	6
C	3	2
D	11	2
E	6	2
F	5	5
G	6	7
H	9	3

These scores make clear the order of difference between tribal codes and suggest that the tribes might be roughly partitioned into three groups concerning the treatment of folk law in the contemporary code. Tribes A and D are the most inclusive, and B, F, and G the most exclusive. Tribes E and H fall somewhere in between, and the unelaborated code of tribe C is hard to categorize. The details of how folk law is treated by these eight tribes are more apparent through a consideration of each tribe's code.

The Eight Tribal Codes

The code of Tribe A incorporates folk law as thoroughly and poses as few constraints on traditional practice as any of the eight. The major areas in which folk law appears (in some form) are enrollment, fisheries law (in provisions for ceremonial fishing and the inheritance of fishing sites), and the youth code (for example, requiring the consideration of religious traditions in youth court hearings). In addition, the code is explicit in recognizing experts on custom, although formal bodies of cultural experts are not created. The Enrollment Ordinance specifies that the enrollment appeal board shall consist of "tribal council chairman, a tribal elder, the tribal judge, and the tribal enrollment clerk" (section 11). Presumably, the elder is an expert on folk law who is able to understand community membership in a broader sense than the strictly biological prescriptions of blood quantum. The Youth Code states that, in questions of uncertainty of interpretation, "tribal law or custom shall be controlling, and where appropriate, may be based on the written or oral testimony of a qualified elder, historian, or other tribal representative" (section 500, 13.3). Specific procedures for qualifying the elder or other community member are not included.

Nepotism rules (article IV, section 3 of the constitution) limit the regular expression of family corporate interests by requiring that no more than one immediate family member of any person on the tribal council shall become a candidate or serve on the council. Immediate family is defined as mother, father, brother, sister, spouse, son, or daughter. Significantly, cousins, traditionally regarded as classificatory siblings, are not excluded and would likely be included within one's family network. Volume 8, section 402 (Rules of the Tribal Court) uses language (which appears in the code of several tribes) that restricts the judge from seeking the advice or opinion of others regarding the merits of a case. This removes the judge from the local social context and creates an emphasis on deterrence, rather than on restoring the defendant to society and reestablishing social harmony, a principle aim of folk law, according to the 1991 Northwest Intertribal Court System study.

By contrast, the code of Tribe B, although lengthy, includes the least application of folk law. Article VI, section 1, of the constitution refers to the need to cultivate and preserve native arts, crafts, culture, and ceremonials, but there is no subsequent enabling legislation. Zoning ordinance 35 3.3.6.1 specifies that some areas of the reservation require protection because of the cultural heritage. A nonspecific passage, ordinance 49, title 1.2.2, states that "if the course of proceedings be not specifically pointed out by this code any suitable process or mode of proceedings may be adapted which may appear most comfortable to the spirit of Tribal Law." Finally, fishing ordinance 6.3 allows fishing permits for ceremonial permits for religious purposes. Other than this, the law is silent on the issue of folk law (or custom, as the law code refers to it). The heavy emphasis in the code is on ordinances regulating commercial development. Similarly, the code of Tribe C is quiet on the issue of folk law, a circumstance that appears to be the result of a general lack of elaboration. This very brief code, however, recognizes tradition in membership criteria (as do all of the other tribes), although there is a twist in that membership is granted to those on the official census of 1945 and to those born to any member who is a resident of the community. This creates an unusual burden for establishing membership, since membership is contingent on the direct, frequent participation in the life of the community of one's parent(s). This law corresponds to earlier concepts of community membership as deriving from participation in functioning corporate units, with membership established by both birth and marriage.

The code of Tribe D, as noted, has a relatively elaborate treatment of folk law (referred to variously in the code as custom, tradition, or tribal law). Judges are given broad latitude to apply folk law in two ways: If the course of legal proceedings is not specified in the ordinance, any suitable process may be adopted that appears in keeping with the spirit of tribal law; secondly, the judge has latitude in sentencing to conform to "traditional . . . remedies" (chapter IV of the Law and Order Code, section 4.5). In both cases, however, there is no further detail. Additionally, the Family Code (chapter 1.4.140) specifies that a "Qualified elder, Historian, or other tribal representative" who has been certified by the tribal council may testify concerning traditions and customs of the tribe. Also, the Family Code (part II, 2.1.010) contains an explicit recognition of traditional patterns of child care, which permit parents to place a child with another care-giver for a brief or a long period. This action by itself is not held to indicate that the child is in need of care action. Furthermore, part 111 (chapter 3.1.010) states, as an issue of intent, that termination of parental rights is never recognized, even in cases of extreme abuse or neglect because of tribal customs of child-rearing within "the supportive network of extended family and community."

There is a case of an explicit reworking of traditional themes to achieve similar outcomes as in the past. Chapter 1.8.010 of the Family Code establishes an Indian child welfare committee, in lieu of an elders' council, to recommend to the Indian child welfare worker measures to be taken to protect tribal families as the elders' council did in previous generations. Although elders may be on this council, the measure does not specify this.

Finally, sections of the law appear explicitly to overturn customary practices in the interests of contemporary needs. Section 3.02 of the fishing ordinance specifies that access to specific net sites and drift locations will be determined on a first-come, first served basis, instead of as allocated by the earlier patterns of family network control of locations.

The code of Tribe E treats folk law most significantly in two ways: by allowing for folk law where there is uncertainty in the code and through repeated reference to the "extended family." Other references are also included. Title 15–Youth Code 15.01.030 holds that, "[w]henever there is uncertainty or a question as to the interpretation of certain provisions of the code, tribal law or custom shall be controlling, and where appropriate may be based on the written or oral testimony of a qualified elder, historian, or other tribal elder."

The code recognizes the family network in several places. The Youth Code, title 15.02, defines extended family as follows:

> [T]his term shall be defined by the law or custom of the Indian youth's tribe, or in the absence of such law or custom, shall be a person who has reached the age of 18 years who is the Indian child's grandparent, grand aunt or grand uncle, aunt or uncle, brother or sister, brother-in-law or sister-in-law, niece or nephew, first, second, or third cousin or step parent.

The Youth Code (15.05.090) calls for consideration of the availability of resources for youth in the extended family and attempts to keep youth within the extended family in cases of termination of parental rights.

References to folk law show up in several other parts of the code. The fishing ordinance authorizes a special fishing permit for religious and ceremonial purposes; the liquor ordinance recognizes the importance of elders and programs for them through earmarking at least 15 percent of the tax received for elders' programs; and the gambling ordinance treats noncommercial, culturally sanctioned "traditional tribal games," which serve as a medium of conflict resolution (such as bone gambling), as separate from other forms of gambling. The code moves away from folk law in forbidding a judge from discussing a case or seeking advice within the community (title 10.04.010) and in the bill of rights (article IX of the constitution), which guarantees equal rights.

The code of Tribe F is unique among the eight in its specificity about where folk law stands in relationship to other systems of law:

> In cases otherwise before the trial and appellate court... decision on matters of both substance and procedure will be based on the following in the following order of precedent:
>
>   1. the constitution and bylaws...
>   2. Statutes...
>   3. Resolutions...
>   4. Customary law, custom, traditions, and culture of the... Tribe. (Title 9 Basis of Decision 9.4.01)

Furthermore, the law specifies that, in the absence of tribal ordinance or other law sufficient for a dispute or criminal procedure, then U.S. federal rules of procedure will apply, and the court will determine whether federal law is applicable. This is a much more concrete procedure than the vague references to the application of the "spirit of tribal law" that frequently occur in other codes, and folk law has a clearly limited role in the law. For example, unlike some other tribes, Tribe F includes no provisions in the membership code allowing the membership committees to grant membership on bases other than the formulistic requirements set forward (that is, reference to descent from someone on the 1934 roll, and of 1/8 blood quantum) in order that community recognition of membership may supplement the post contact emphasis on blood quantum.

Allowance for folk law does appear in title 12, the youth ordinance (typically the site of explicit references to custom), particularly in regard to the role of the extended family and protection of youth from interference by outsiders. Allowance for tribal law or custom is made through the written or oral testimony of a qualified elder, historian, or other tribal representative. However, as in the other cases where this language appears, the reference is to contact with outside service providers and agencies. The youth ordinance forbids service providers from holding tribal youth in detention, from criticizing the youth for expressions of their heritage, for hair styles or personal tastes; most importantly, the ordinance specifies that "[a] youth shall be permitted to attend the funeral and any related activities for his parent, guardian, custodian, or any member of his extended family..." This is a significant passage, because the various ritual observances surrounding death are among the most important of all Coast Salish practices. Title 12, chapter 12.06.010, in a section on placement preference for youth, gives the youth's extended family as second preference after parents. Title 11 defines "extended family member" as, "to the extent consistent with tribal law and custom, any adult who is competent to care for a youth, and who is the youth's grandparent, aunt or uncle, brother or sister, first or second cousin, step parent, or other family member including non-Indian people." Limits are placed on the relationships between extended family members in title 11, chapter 11.02.01, the amusement game and gambling ordinance (a person under 18 must be accompanied by a member of his/her immediate family or guardian). Title 12 defines parenthood as meaning biological parents or a person who has lawfully adopted a youth, including "adoptions under tribal law or custom."

> The code of Tribe G includes the familiar references to the use of folk law, such as this: [I]f the course of proceeding be not specifically pointed out by this code, any suitable process or mode of proceeding may be adapted which may appear most comfortable to the spirit of Tribal Law. (Title I General Rules 1.4.05)

Further, title 3.4.04 (civil procedure) allows the court to request the "advice of counselors familiar with these customs and usages" in the event any doubt arises about custom. The importance of elders and their standing in dispute resolution, noted in the Northwest Intertribal Court System study, is recognized through provisions exempting those over sixty-five from paying fish taxes on the first five thousand dollars of income per year and by allocating elders' programs 15 percent of income from the taxation of liquor.

But the code of Tribe G is ambiguous about the most significant of all traditional institutions, the extended family. Chapter 1.3.04, which deals with conflict of interest in the appointment and removal of judges, merely notes, "No Judge shall be qualified to act as such in any case wherein he has any direct interest," an idea imported from the mainstream society. Unlike other code, there is no specific reference to family membership nor definitions of membership given. However, section 1.8.08 is more specific and states that "no person shall be qualified to sit on a panel of the Court of Appeals in any case wherein he has any direct interest or wherein any relative by marriage or blood, in the first or second degree, is a party." Assuming that this refers to second cousins, even this definition of family is narrow in Coast Salish terms. Title 9.4.06 forbids a law enforcement officer from permitting any member of his immediate family from interfering with his duties or from discussing information obtained by virtue of his official position. Title 29.1.01 (elections) defines those "directly related" as son, daughter, husband, wife, mother, father, sister, or brother and restricts people directly related to a candidate from serving on the election committee. Other relatives are not so restricted.

The code makes a dramatic about-face in title 11.3.01 (domestic relations) in carefully separating the properties of husband and wife. Property and pecuniary rights of both, obtained before and after marriage, are not subject to the "debts or contracts" of the other. A husband or wife may "manage, lease, sell, convey, encumber as fully to the same effect as though he were unmarried...." This conforms to traditional patterns of inheritance, which privilege siblings and family network members who together form corporate groups for the management of resources, property, and incorporeal spiritual goods. Title 8, Juvenile Code, as is the case with other tribes, is more expansive in the application of family. The first priority in adoption procedures is given to "extended family members," a phrase that is not used elsewhere in the code and is not defined.

Notions of folk law are embedded directly in the code of Tribe H in several places. Section 4.500 of the sentencing guidelines provides that sentences "may be of a nature customary. . . [and] reflect traditional. . . remedies." The judge is given latitude in this regard, with the very important exception of fishing offenses. However, even the fishing ordinance recognizes traditional practice in giving preference for ceremonial fishing and in sanctioning the system of "traditional use sites," which by custom are held as usufructory rights. The code specifies that failure to use the site during one fishing season lays the site open to claim by others, a practice with some antiquity. All sites must be registered, and, in the event of dispute, the fish committee can order the area abandoned or shared. The hunting ordinance also gives priority to ceremonial hunting, especially for elders' lunches and for funerals. Further, "designated hunters" can provide for the elderly and infirm.

Notions of folk law also show up in the "utility sanction guidelines," which specify that sanctions be taken only if needed, with the minimum action necessary and after an effort is made to balance the interests of the tribe, the miscreant, and the neighbors. Finally, the ordinance establishing the juvenile court provides that a "principle of least restriction" be applied when dealing with juvenile offenders. In both cases, these provisions appear to coincide with traditional values of respecting personal autonomy, even for children, where possible. Further, children detained in facilities shall not be ridiculed for expressions of their cultural heritage and shall be permitted to attend the funerals of a named set of relations. This is the only place in the code where the family, as constructed culturally, is spelled out and includes sister, brother, mother, father, aunt, uncle, grandfather, grandmother, and cousin (it is notable that the code does not incorporate family otherwise and that this section of the juvenile code was later replaced).

The code retains a traditional flavor in the broad latitude it provides in defining membership. The adoption ordinance, section 2, allows the enrollment committee and the tribal council to "take into consideration other factors such as family blood lines, participation in the Tribe, tribal identification, and the applicant's personal identification with the...tribe in determining the quantum of...[tribal] blood..."

The code explicitly creates a nontraditional legal context in a variety of areas, including the following: in the guarantee of economic rights to individuals; in the imposition of impartiality and impersonality in court proceedings (prohibiting discussion between jurors and others involved in a case and in excusing witnesses with personal knowledge of a case); in allowing for termination of parental rights if a child is abandoned or willfully and repeatedly injured; in failing to mention extended families or networks in the provisions for appointing guardians for minors; in specifying that "any person who, lacking the legal right to do so, interferes with another's custody of a child, shall be guilty of an offence" (leaving out a role of extended family members); in requiring a high school diploma or GED (equivalency) for those under eighteen who wish to fish during school hours; in failing to include provisions making a married minor an adult (as occurs in several other codes).

Conclusion

One aim of this paper has been to show where, how, and to what ends folk law has been included in the codes of a group of tribes in Washington State with significant legal jurisdiction, including the right to create both civil and criminal code. Although many legal concepts and practices are clearly imported, the variability in emphasis in the eight codes demonstrates that they are best understood as responses generated by the communities to their own localized, historical conditions and not simply by a diffusionary model emphasizing the importation of Western legal concepts. Although the codes differ, they all provide legal mechanisms useful for the management of internal conflict and external intrusion. Tribal councils respond to the pressing demands placed on their communities by the outside world in part by developing tribal specializations that result from assessments of what is possible. Undersized, chronically underfunded tribal governments and staffs select among various possibilities in allocating personnel and resources; they do not hope to achieve everything at once.[14] Some governments (such as that of tribe D) devote much of their energy to cultural issues, others (tribe B) to economic development. Such decisions, in turn, influence the direction the legal system will take and the relative emphasis or de-emphasis of folk law.

The fact that folk law is least deployed in areas of ongoing dispute, especially the access of community members to tribal resources, and most developed in areas of least dispute, particularly concerning tribal youth and their relations with the mainstream community, reflects a lack of consensus within all of the tribes about the content of folk law and some reluctance to apply folk law in the present context. Tribes are, at present, experimenting in quite different ways with how best to regulate the relations between extended families, between generations, and between the tribe as a whole and the individuals who compose it. The experimental nature of the codes and the ambiguous feeling towards folk law are quantifiable: Six of the eight tribes have rejected community involvement in the judicial decision-making process; four tribes incorporated the concept of restitution, and three rejected it. There is also ambiguity about fundamentals of traditional social organization, or what might be considered folk law of inheritance and ownership: Use rights to resource sites are embedded in the law of only two tribes and were rejected by four others; extended families are rejected as institutions with rights of ownership (to some degree) by seven of the tribes, and rights and responsibilities for children of extended family members are acknowledged in three and restrained in four. However, six of the codes allow for the spirit of tribal law to be incorporated both in the legal process and at the stage of rulings. Six of the tribes have recognized the distinctive contributions of elders as experts in folk practice, although the provisions are quite unelaborated.

Some tribes, particularly tribes A and D, have chosen to recognize principles of traditional social organization in the law. Others (tribes B and H) have rejected this position and have emphasized universalism of access to resources as an issue of individual entitlement, without consideration of family organization. The use of various definitions of family within the codes of single tribes is a further indication of this ambiguity and of the complexity of creating code that emphasizes traditional values and addresses current issues. The use of a variety of definitions of family can be regarded as a significant strategy for sidestepping irreconcilable issues. All of the Coast Salish tribal law committees, whatever their approach, face difficulties in meaningfully merging folk law into tribal code.

Further research might be productively concerned with considering more closely the changing application of folk law in tribal legal systems as financial and political circumstances change and as tribal leadership changes. The current development of large-scale multimillion-dollar gaming operations by several of the tribes in question will produce new economic opportunities and new pressures on leaders that perhaps will result in an emphasis on economic development within tribal codes. Variations in tribal population and the degree of urbanization and institutional completeness ought to be considered. But equally important is what such analysis can reveal about community politics, especially the relationship between communal and individual rights, and vexing contemporary social and ethnographic problems of understanding intergenerational relations and changing conceptualizations of elder and resource management. Tribal codes, especially in their treatment of folk law, remain an underused resource for comprehending these issues.

ACKNOWLEDGMENTS

I wish particularly to thank Elbridge Coochise, chief justice of the Northwest Intertribal Court System, Ralph Johnson of the University of Washington Law School, and Ted Maloney, attorney for the Upper Skagit tribe, for their assistance. In addition, I thank the several tribal councilors and tribal law committee members who provided ideas. Any errors in fact and interpretation are my own.

ENDNOTES

[1] For a discussion of the constraints on the tribal courts and problems of jurisdiction, see Johnson and Paschal (1991: 166).

[2] The distinction between the concepts of folk law and customary law is important, because it draws attention to relations of power. Vincent notes, "It is useless . . . to look to 'customary law' for resistance to super ordinate institutions of power or privilege" (Vincent 1990, quoted in Just (1992:379). Tribal codes themselves make references to tribal law, custom, and tradition.

[3] Miller points out that there is little literature concerning the details of the new tribal code employed in the contemporary tribal court systems operated by tribes in the U.S. (Miller 1994b). Most of the current literature argues that Indian court systems rely on concepts imported from the mainstream legal system and consequently are largely devoid of folk law (see, for example, Brakel 1978; Barsh and Youngblood 1976; Christofferson 1991; O'Brien 1989; Lupton 1981; Svensson 1979. See Johnson and Lupton (1981) for a discussion of the early reliance of tribal codes on state and federal legal language.

[4] Although the historic relationship between mainstream legal systems and Coast Salish Indian communities remains largely unexamined, it is likely that Coast Salish people have long used legal systems for their own purposes. Asher noted the early use of white courts by Coast Salish Indians of Puget Sound interested in imposing sanctions on Indian assailants and also resisting white law when it was perceived as subverting tribal sovereignty (Asher 1993).

[5] Swinomish (1991) documents, for example, the changing relationship between grandparents and grandchildren and the erosion of grandparents' authority. In addition, those finding employment outside of the reservation communities have been largely unable to participate in folk law practices.

[6] See "Tribal Justice Survey, March 1995" (Unpublished manuscript, National American Indian Court Judges Association) for data concerning categories of cases entering the NICS courts.

[7] Several tribes within the Northwest Intertribal Court System have created peacemaker programs, also known as tribal community boards, as alternatives to the tribal courts and as a vehicle for the application of traditional dispute resolution processes (NICS 1991:1). Other tribes have rejected this idea.

[8] The Gitksan, a matrilineal people of northern British Columbia, for example, speak of a traditional set of laws that are upheld by house chiefs and that consider such topics as inheritance, land rights, adoption, resource access, and a range of criminal activities (Office of the Hereditary Chiefs of the Gitksan and Wet'suwet'en, "The Gitksan and

Wet'suwet'en," pamphlet, n.d.). The contemporary Nuu-chah-nulth describe traditional social practices of chiefly families as constituting Nuu-chah-nulth law in a variety of categories, including family laws (Haiyupis 1994),. A number of scholars have described the difficulty some communities have in identifying folk law, in translatingconcepts into English, or in gaining consensus on this topic. For example, McDonnell (1992:312) expresses concern about a process of the "creative elaboration of custom," the invention of tradition, and that codification will "do little more than promote the views and concerns of some natives over other". These are important concerns, but they are not the focus of this paper.

[9] Ethnographic sources that provide information concerning Coast Salish folk law in the contact period include Collins 1974); Elmendorf (1960); Gunther (1927); Smith (1940); Suttles, (1960). Recent, detailed, community-produced ethnographic accounts include Swinomish (1991) and NICS (1991).

[10] NICS (1991). Collins (1974:119) provides two categories in which corporal punishment was socially sanctioned. She gives an example in which a man who had killed by use of supernatural spirits was executed. Men and women guilty of incest were said to have been executed, but Collins provides no examples.

[11] See NICS (1991) for details of this erosion of dispute resolution processes.

[12] NICS Judge Elbridge Coochise has noted that Washington State has authority under PL 83-280 to prosecute major crimes but frequently fails to. Some tribes have responded by prosecuting these crimes themselves (personal communication, April 1995).

[13] Vi Hilbert, a well-known Upper Skagit elder, distinguished between ancestral rules and teachings in noting the relevance of legal innovation:

> We can't apply the rules of our ancestors to today's world, but the teachings of those rules can be adjusted to any time in history because they're done with honor and respect. Those are the two magic words: honor and respect (Hilbert, quoted in NICS 1991:12).

[14] Robbins described the struggles faced by tribal governments and administrations due to limited resources and the sorts of specializations that result (Robbins 1986).

References Cited

Asher, Brad. 1993. "They Are Satisfied if a Few Could Be Hung": Indian Legal Consciousness and White Law on Puget Sound, 1875–1889. Paper presented at the American Society for Ethnohistory Annual Meetings.

Barsh, Russel Lawrence and J. Henderson Youngblood. 1976. Tribal Courts, the Model Code, and the Police Idea in American Indian Policy. *Law and Contemporary Problems*, 40:25–60.

Brakel, Samuel J. 1978. *American Indian Tribal Courts: The Costs of Separate Justice*. Chicago: American Bar Association.

Christofferson, Carla. 1991. Tribal Court's Failure to Protect Native American Woman: A Reevaluation of the Indian Civil Rights Act. *The Yale Law Journal*, 101:169–85.

Collins, June McCormick. 1974. *Valley of the Spirits*. Seattle: University of Washington Press.

Deloria, Jr., Vine and Clifford Lytle. 1984. *The Nations Within*. New York: Pantheon Books.

Elmendorf, William W. 1960. *The Structure of Twana Culture. Washington State University Research Studies*, 28(3), Monographic Supplement 2. Pullman: Washington State University.

Gunther, Erna. 1927. Klallam Ethnography. *University of Washington Publications in Anthropology*, 1:171–314.

Haiyupis, Roy. 1994 Nuu-chah-nulth Family Law. *Ha-Shilth-Sa* (May 26), 6–7.

Johnson, Ralph and Richard Davies, editors. 1988. *Indian Tribal Codes: A Microfiche Collection of Indian Tribal Law Codes*, Seattle: University of Washington School of Law, Marian Gould Gallagher Law Library, Research Studies Series 5.

Johnson, Ralph W., and Susan Lupton. 1981. *Indian Tribal Codes*. Seattle: University of Washington School of Law, Marian Gould Gallagher Law Library, Research Studies Series 1.

Johnson , Ralph W., and Rachael Paschal, editors. 1991. *Tribal Court Handbook for the 26 Federally Recognized Tribes in Washington State*. Olympia, WA: Office of the Administrator for the Courts, State of Washington.

Just, Peter. 1992. *Law and Society Review*, 26:373–411.

Keesing, Roger M. 1992. *Custom and Confrontation: The Kwaio Struggle for Cultural Autonomy*. Chicago: University of Chicago Press.

Laprairie, Carol. 1992. Aboriginal Crime and Justice: Explaining the Present, Exploring the Future. *Canadian Journal of Criminology*, July–October:288–290.

Lupton, Susan. 1981. American Indian Tribal Codes. *Legal Reference Services Quarterly*, 1:25–41.

McDonnell, Roger F. 1992. Contextualizing the Investigation of Customary Law in Contemporary Native Communities. *Canadian Journal of Criminology*, July–October:299–316.

Miller, Bruce G. 1992. Women and Politics: Comparative Evidence from the Northwest Coast. *Ethnology*, 31:367–84.

——— 1994a. Women and Tribal Politics: Is There a Gender Gap in Indian Politics? *American Indian Quarterly*, 18:25–42.

——— 1994b. Contemporary Tribal Codes and Gender Issues. *American Indian Culture and Research Journal*, 18(2):43–74.

Northwest Intertribal Court System (NICS). 1991. Traditional and Informal Dispute Resolution Processes in Tribes of the Puget Sound and Olympic Peninsula Region. Unpublished manuscript.

O'Brien, Sharon. 1989. *American Indian Tribal Government*. Norman: University of Oklahoma Press.

Office of the Hereditary Chiefs of the Gitksan and Wet'suwet'en. n.d. The Gitksan and Wet'suwet'en. Pamphlet.

Robbins, Lynn. 1986. Upper Skagit [Washington] and Gambell [Alaska] Indian Reorganization Act Governments: Struggles with Constraints, Restraints, and Power. *American Indian Culture and Research Journal*, 10:61–73.

Smith, Marion W. Smith. 1940. The Puyallup-Nisqually. *Columbia University Contributions to Anthropology*, 32.

Swinomish Tribal Mental Health Project. 1991. *A Gathering of Wisdoms*. LaConner, WA: Swinomish Tribal Community.

Suttles, Wayne. 1960. Private Knowledge, Morality, and Social Classes among the Coast Salish. *American Anthropologist*, 60: 497–507.

Svensson, Frances. 1979. Liberal Democracy and Group Rights: The Impact of Individualism and Its Impact on American Indian Tribes. *Political Studies*, 27:421–439.

Tribal Justice Survey. 1995. March. Unpublished manuscript, National American Indian Court Judges Association.

Vincent, Joan. 1990. *Anthropology and Politics: Visions, Traditions, and Trend*s. Tucson: University of Arizona Press.

Journal of Northwest Anthropology, Memoir 12:125–138 (2016)

8

Bringing Culture In: Community
Responses to Apology, Reconciliation, and Reparations*

We live in an era of the proliferation of the use of apology and attempts at formal reconciliation by national governments and civil institutions, such as churches, to breach grievances with particular populations within the national borders. This is the case in Canada as well as the United States concerning indigenous peoples and other groups. Although these apologies are accompanied by various well-publicized ritualized events there is inadequate recognition by state officials of the preexisting and long-established cultural practices of apology in these indigenous communities. As a consequence, there can be a gulf between the practices of the state and local indigenous people's expectations regarding how apology and reconciliation should properly occur. These issues have received little direct scholarly attention.[1] My claim is that indigenous North Americans, and no doubt many others, already have ways of understanding how historical grievances should rightly be handled and that they have become less and less willing to put up with imposed, Western-derived models.

In this text, I describe historic Coast Salish ritual practices and the concepts regarding wrongdoing and redemption that underlie them. I draw out the implications, particularly the associated dangers, derived from these existing rituals for ritual work conducted by outsiders engaging Coast Salish peoples. Finally, I consider the responses of Coast Salish peoples to recent apologies and reparations in Washington State and British Columbia.[2] Despite the difficulties and potential traps, there can be positive benefits to considering existing cultural practices and incorporating them with top-down state-driven apologies.[3] Over the last few generations, Coast Salish leaders have developed their own ways of incorporating representatives of government and industry within local rituals of reconciliation. But, as I have noted, the state's use of rituals of apology to manage relations with constituent groups internationally creates the context for this development in North America, and so I briefly consider the insights and shortcomings of current scholarship on these issues.

Current Scholarly Approaches

To date, scholarly attention concerning apologies and reconciliation around the world has been largely directed to the politics of negotiation, international diplomacy, education and its role in reconciliation, the psychology of conflict, and national policies. These research initiatives are at the expense of the study of social justice from the ground up and from the vantage point of those who are not the newsmakers and largely without voice. Ehrenreich and Cole have noted that the Holocaust literature, for example, has given little visibility to the victim group, which has been treated as an amorphous mass (Ehrenreich and Cole 2005). They note further that there is a lack of direct documentation on the general, non-perpetrator/non-victim population in archives and oral histories. Torpey's seminal piece (2003) expressed concern for indigenous ideas of ownership of knowledge in the practice of reparations, but this falls short of considering directly indigenous ideas of the practice of ritual.

*Authored by Bruce Granville Miller. Reprinted from the *American Indian Culture and Research Journal*, Volume 30, Issue 4, by permission of the American Indians Studies Center, UCLA. © 2006 Regents of the University of California.

To the extent that rituals of reconciliation carried out by indigenous and other nonmainstream peoples have been recognized, they have been largely treated from an implicit neoevolutionary perspective disguised as historical analysis. For example, Olick and Coughlin (2003), although they concede that there are earlier precedents for reparation and apology, suggest that regret and apology are modern phenomena and not a characteristic of pre-modern societies that engaged in practices such as bribes, blood feuding, vengeance seeking, and compensation. However, other forms of political and ritual process have continued, although largely hidden from the view of a modernist dominant society convinced that its practices have supplanted earlier, less adaptive ones. Similarly, the rise of capitalism as the dominant contemporary economic system has not erased earlier forms of reciprocity and redistribution, forms that continue to coexist, although not as dominant forms of exchange.

However, there are others who share an interest in examining truth and reconciliation commissions, public state apologies, and state restitution efforts from the ground up and provide arguments outlining why this is important. Braithwaite observed that, when resolving what he called "micro forms of justice," top-down restorative justice works better when complemented by bottom-up restorative justice and that responses to global terrorism might be improved by pairing elite diplomacy with bottom-up justice in refugee camps (Braithwaite 2002). Likewise, Wilson (2001) argued that the South African Truth and Reconciliation Commission did not well serve the needs of the local community and had little effect on popular ideas of justice as retribution. He does not, however, consider culturally relevant approaches to justice, such as Coast Salish long-house rituals, that already exist and inform the viewpoint of local people and, in effect, provide the grounds on which a truth and reconciliation commission or any other state-sponsored initiative might be evaluated.

Avruch and Vejarano, in their review essay regarding truth and reconciliation commissions worldwide (2001), pointed to the issue of culture in such commissions, noting that "[c]ulture did not arise in our rough 'meta-analysis' of themes in the literature in anything like the way that justice, truth, reconciliation, and democratization did...[I]n fact the notion of culture hardly arises at all."[4] These scholars observed the attention given to the Christian-centeredness of the values driving the South African commission and concluded that "notions such as justice, truth, forgiveness, reconciliation...are always socially constructed and culturally constituted." Further, an avenue for further research lies in examining the challenges that arise working across significant cultural borders (Avruch and Vejarano 2001). The existing literature, in brief, stops short of carefully considering local culture.

Canadian Apologies

In the Canadian context, efforts at reconciliation have been made to various groups, including indigenous peoples and communities, by religious institutions and the state. These apologies are not limited to indigenous peoples, and in the spring of 2006 the Conservative government arranged apologies and reparations for the Chinese Canadians who were forced to pay a head tax in order to immigrate to Canada in the late nineteenth and early twentieth centuries. Indo-Canadians, Ukrainian Canadians, Japanese Canadians, and others have made demands for apologies.

In 1998 Jane Stewart, then minister of Indian Affairs and Northern Development, formally apologized on behalf of Canada for the damage done to indigenous people by the practice of sending children away from their homes and families to attend either church- or state-run residential schools. This practice ended only in the 1970s (Erasmus 2001:19). In these schools, ties to kin were damaged or broken, and the schools actively worked to eliminate language retention and erode indigenous cultural practice. In addition, in many instances physical, sexual, and other forms of abuse were practiced in the schools. The Canadian government funded a $350 million project to support what it termed community-based healing for individual victims of the residential schools. The intergenerational wounds from the residential school era are still fresh and are now widely discussed in indigenous communities.

The passive Canadian statement of reconciliation, however, is largely without "any real sense of responsibility or meaning" and leaves out questions of the control of land and resources in its stated emphasis on healing (Napoleon 2004:184–185). There is the suggestion that the statement is largely aimed at heading off lawsuits by residential school survivors.[5] Meanwhile, since the release of the statement of reconciliation the underlying relationship between the state and indigenous people remains unchanged (Erasmus 2001; Napoleon 2004:185). A promised $5 billion aid package for Aboriginal communities, known as the Kelowna Accord and negotiated by the Liberal federal government with indigenous leaders, was not included in the 2006 Conservative federal budget. Land rights negotiations remain stalled, with few settlements; treaty negotiations under the present treaty commission process in British Columbia have yielded no treaties; and bitter disputes between indigenous peoples and communities and the Canadian state flare episodically, such as the struggle over a parcel of land in Caledonia, Ontario in 2006.

In addition to concern about residential schools, a federal responsibility, there is also growing debate about the removal of thousands of children from their families by provincial authorities in the name of child protection. In the province of British Columbia, for instance, public ceremonies have been proposed as part of a reconciliation process by the Ministry of Children and Families' Strategic Plan for Aboriginal Services (Erasmus 2001:19). Val Napoleon argues that "Aboriginal communities will have to guard against substituting ceremony or ritual for substance," thereby overlooking underlying issues of power and reducing a ceremony to a "pretty band-aid on a gaping wound" (Erasmus 2001:19). But Napoleon further notes that one problem is that this is a one-way approach, and the ministry's efforts to learn about non–First Nations history and cultural values are not matched by an effort to expose ministry values, thereby perpetuating a myth of a cultureless ministry. Napoleon rightly concludes that it is through one's understanding of one's culture that other cultures are comprehended. She has, however, conflated the ministry's interest in connecting to elite indigenous political actors with genuine interest in community practice.

On the surface, many ordinary people respond positively to efforts at reconciliation and apology, although others emphatically reject this.[6] Some like the idea of monetary compensation for residential school abuses, for example, and many indigenous people have the strong sense that they should be financially compensated for wrongs committed against their person, family, nation, or against indigenous peoples generally (Carlson 1997:107). And well they should, given the scale of problems and the fact that the contemporary generation of First Nations and American Indian people have grown up with a very clear sense that compensation, within Western law, is achieved by equating harm with cash. They see in insurance claims, for example, that the loss of a limb or conjugal rights is tied to a specific dollar amount. In addition, Coast Salish family law has historically included the idea of compensation for damages. However, cash has been rejected as an unacceptable form of compensation for the alienation of land or the loss of resources in many cases. Many reject the idea of cash compensation for personal grievances.

The ways people respond to apologies and reparations reflect individual perceptions of the nature of power and state-indigenous relations. Often responses reflect local, personal feelings of hurt and dishonor following generations of abuse, disdain, and outright theft of resources. Many view the state proximally through their experiences with nearby representatives, school officials, or health professionals, for example, as opposed to viewing the state as distant from their lives or as a referee between competing interests, as in liberal theory.[7] They understand that the state relies on agents of normativity who regulate the body in a manner that reflects the values of communities other than their own. This understanding of the state as composed of local power holders is manifested in tensions in public institutions, such as hospitals or schools, and in barriers to access. These members of indigenous communities often personalize the insult felt by the actions of the unresponsive state and point to particular, grounded cultural practices (Miller 2003). This personalization is important in understanding the negative responses of some local people to formal and impersonal state apologies.

Existing Cultural Models of Reconciliation

Although these state-sponsored apologies are being carried out there remain significant existing models within indigenous communities concerning how conflict between constituent groups ought to be handled and that largely derive from prior practice—from current understandings of what was done in the "old days." The degree to which these perceptions are altered by contact with nonindigenes is not my central concern. Although indigenous peoples and leaders commonly speak in oppositional terms regarding Western and indigenous concepts of justice, this reflects more distaste for the current circumstances of indigenous peoples in North American society than an effort to discern carefully the history of the "middle ground" of mutual influence, as the historian Richard White has put it (White 1999).

It is these cultural models that are my concern. These ideas or models persist in people's minds; they suggest the right way to do things, even though people do not agree on the exact content of them. The practice of apologies, reconciliation, and the press for reparations have come at precisely the moment in which interest in indigenous ritual life is most heightened. This is not an accident, and these developments are related. They represent the increasing strength of the indigenous voice in Canada, liberation from restrictive rules and efforts at assimilation, and gradual realization that new practices within old frames of thought are possible. In recent years, a vigorous ethno-nationalist movement has arisen that has been built on the conscious rejection of Western governance even while Western-style administrative structures are widely adapted. These circumstances imply that attention to cultural models is all the more salient, more so today than ten or twenty years ago. One must also bear in mind that contemporary indigenous ritual life is increasingly associated with moral good, restoration of old ways, reestablishment of connections to an indigenous cosmology, the good path (as it is commonly termed in the Coast Salish community), community redemption, and repudiation of Western materialism.

Coast Salish Ritual

My examples of ritual come from the Northwest Coast, particularly the Coast Salish peoples of Washington State and the province of British Columbia; my work concerning tribal justice practices; and conversations on the topic of apologies with Coast Salish people in several communities.[8] In these communities people endlessly debate if political or cultural activities are being improperly conducted and, hence, if they are culturally correct. Bierwert (1999) observed the Coast Salish decentering of authority and the consequences of disputes about culture. To be wrong serves to invalidate the ritual "work" done and may convey the opposite message. In this case, the message received from the ritual practice of reconciliation could be the lack of a desire to reconcile. One of the analogues of reparations in indigenous life, the giving of gifts in repayment for wrongs, very specifically carries the cultural message that slight breaks of protocol can reverse the message.[9] It is hard to give gifts successfully, especially in those situations in which the problem between groups has been a wrongful, crude play of power. It is easy for the compensation to appear, yet again, as a manifestation of domination.

Shame Potlatching

A recent example of a ritual of reconciliation, and of the difficulty of gift giving, comes from a "shame potlatch" given by a tribal leader said to be powerful and domineering.[10] This man's effort to restore his name and his relations with his subordinates, people working under him in a department of the tribal government, by distributing gifts was undone by a subtle tone of superiority. Although he spent an estimated $10,000 to $20,000 on the affair, at least some guests left thinking the leader was all the more greedy, pompous, and destructive.[11] Giving gifts, after all, continues to demonstrate the wealth and power of the giver. It is hard to give humbly. It takes a mastery of the local idiom of oratory, timing, and shrewdness in picking "speakers" to present one's case, luck in that nothing else intervenes, and the goodwill of the guests—the witnesses to the affair who validate the outcome. If all goes well, there will be an implicit agreement to a new understanding of someone's place in the world. If it does not go well there is also a new understanding, not the one the host wished for but someone else's. These indigenous "reparation" feasts are political events; they are not pro forma. Someone may wish to disrupt the work on the spot and publicly present a more compelling or skillfully presented version of the truth than the host, a version to which the other guests might be willing to agree (Swinomish 1991:179). And the work is not concluded until long after the ritual event, when everyone has had a chance to criticize, find fault, and pick apart. Later, if the complainers are gradually silenced by an emerging agreement, then the tacit agreement achieved at the time of the potlatch is validated. It is difficult to change people's understandings and successfully assert a new social persona for oneself.

People from leading families who are leaders within the larger community normally carry out shame potlatching and other big-time ceremonial work. Lesser people from other families are willing to find fault, and there is a social-class element to this in the hierarchical and status-conscious Coast Salish society. Everyone can speak, but, ordinarily, elite people have the floor and the privilege of communication in important settings. In return, lower-class people have the privilege of looking carefully to see if the elite stumble—even minor slips can cause trouble, and these slips can require formal repair to one's reputation in the form of a potlatch. There is a history of using stories to lampoon the presumptuous elite who reveal themselves to be other than they claim when they are unable to conduct themselves properly in public.[12] The conduct of the elite is a potent theme all through Coast Salish society. Winter ceremonial initiates who slip while engaged in "dancing" their power and sing incorrectly are endangered spiritually. Similarly, leaders who lose their temper and warriors who kill too much and lose respect are the cause of revulsion rather than the objects of esteem or respect (Swinomish 1999:11; J. Miller 1999:94).

The relevance of this for the idea of state reparations is that reparations cannot be concluded outside of a formal, ritual setting. People are alert to and sensitive to the possibility of a slipup by the presumptuous elite. And, because reparations require a form of cross-cultural communication, there is a great probability that the representatives of the state will botch the job and appear presumptuous, arrogant, or foolish. It is hard for insiders to carry off ritual work before the scrutinizing gaze of the community, and it is all the harder for outsiders, even those who are well coached. Gooder and Jacobs point out that apologies are delicate, precarious transactions (Gooder and Jacobs 2000). One might object and argue that indigenous peoples, following a long, dark period of domination, would expect the idiom of the ritual to be Western. But this is not so, and a quick examination of ceremonial encounters even in the most Westernized settings incorporate indigenous symbolism. Indigenous people now expect the presence of their own symbols and protocols. To fail to include them would be to undermine the very point that reconciliation and, subsequently, reparation are meant to convey. Ritual action in the Western idiom would merely reinforce the differences in power that created the problems we face today.

Several years ago I carried out a ceremony to honor and thank a Coast Salish ritual man and elder who hosted a number of my graduate students who lived in his winter ceremonial house while conducting research with his nation (Miller 1998). He shared his knowledge, humor, and insights with my students, and I remain grateful. When I approached his family to discuss the ceremony, eventually held at the Museum of Anthropology at the University of British Columbia, they presumed that it would be done Coast Salish style, with speaking chiefs, witnesses, feasting, and gifts. There was no meaningful, other way to approach this. The event was fitted into the existing repertoire of "work," as ritual practice is called. There was some discussion about whether it was properly done in the format of a naming ceremony or an honor ceremony; eventually the latter choice won out. There was some oblique debate about whether regional up-river or down-river "saltwater" (located near the ocean) practices should be employed. The honored guest was from up-river, but the event was staged in a saltwater location, and there was one speaker from each. Rituals are negotiated all along, from conception to completion, which occurs some time after the event. Rituals are processes rather than single events.

Ritual work requires recognition of the permanence of the other party. There is no point in reconciliation or reparation with a fleeing adversary. These you merely dispatch, if you can, because adversaries do not occupy space in the moral universe. Reconciliation requires that one admit the possibility of the humanness of the other (in Coast Salish reckoning the other might actually be a nonhuman but be a powerful, sentient being nonetheless). Ritual work marks out the continuation of a relationship, one that has a past and a future. This, in turn, requires that the parties conduct further work to continue to cement the relationship; there is no unilateral ritual work (Miller 2001). One cannot impose reparations. Ordinarily, giving and receiving reparations assumes that one is willing to engage the other in a broad spectrum of activities that encompass the full humanity of the other. Simply, you exchange the most valuable commodities in one's possession and marry into the other's family. You participate in common defense from outsiders, contribute to mutual honor, and share the resources under one another's control. Although the other party will continue to control access to the riches of the environment, a party engaged in a moral relationship cannot be excluded (wealthy owners might, however, allocate a turn to use the fish weir in the middle of the night). There is an assumption of common contribution, even though parties will continue to engage in contests over one's place in the social hierarchy.

I believe this leads to an interesting contradiction. In traditional ritual life, the assumption is that parties to a dispute might reach a settlement, sometimes involving reparations in the form of gifts or labor, and restore the social breach and reestablish good relations. This isn't about reversing the social standing of the parties involved; traditional ritual life reflects a close reading of human motivations and possibilities. In the case of the Canadian state and First Nations, good relations cannot be restored, but they might be established. As of yet, there is only a little evidence that the apologies and pools of money for residential school victims reflect a notion that the state seriously wishes to change its relations with indigenes, and I think most indigenous people see it that way. There is considerable cynicism bred of lifelong experience. Although some people think of the state as a piggy bank waiting to be opened, perhaps others are aware that the state is limited. In effect, reconciliation rituals and reparations promise a future that the state neither understands nor is able to deliver. It is done in an idiom that neither reflects indigenous sensibilities nor conveys an appropriate message.

Family Feasting

Let's look more closely at the mechanics of a feast hosted by an extended family whose guests are members of an aggrieved family (Miller 2003:148). Someone may have been killed in a hunting accident, for example, causing a breach of relations between the families of the hunters. There is no misunderstanding of whose honor is at stake; it is the family whose member or members have committed the offense. The offense might be accidental or otherwise, but it doesn't matter. The issue at hand is the restoration of good, working relations between groups. There has been some behind-the-scenes work done to establish the terms of reference, if possible. You can't proceed beforehand, because to meet together otherwise would simply escalate the problem. The offending parties must willingly acknowledge their offense. There is an element of shaming here; it will not continue past the feast if done properly. Those who give offense are judged by the grace with which they respond to criticism. Speakers for both parties cautiously state their views of how things should be handled. They indicate what precedents there are and why precedents are slightly different than the situation the hypothetical speakers are dealing with. The feast is an exchange of food and thoughts. Exchange, as I have already noted, perpetuates a relationship rather than ends it. Details of the arrangement are given, and parties may arrange to compensate the other with labor and gifts. The entire offending family contributes to the effort, not merely those who committed the offense. The guests will agree that the issue is resolved properly, and, in theory, the issue will not be raised directly again.

The feast is not merely a public airing of grievances. Families attempt to reconcile differences in the tightest circles possible. The whole community is not invited to the feast unless outside help is needed. Once resolved, grievances are, in theory, not spoken of again publicly. There is no notion of justice performed by merely speaking or performing one's grievance and letting the culprits off the hook as in the South African Truth and Reconciliation Commission. In this case, the prosecution of lawbreakers for their confessions and meaningful compensation to those wronged were traded for the possibility of Christian redemption and public affirmation of the horror of crimes against oneself.

Longhouse Gatherings

There is another, related Coast Salish model of reconciliation besides shame potlatching and family feasting (Miller 2001:133). Here, an offender or "wrongdoer" agrees to meet in a longhouse to face a gathering of community elders and other community members. This is voluntary, but families exert pressure on members to protect their collective reputations and restore working relations with other families. The offender is "given strong words" by those whose opinions carry weight. This is often in the form of stories that contain implicit negative comparisons to those who exhibit good qualities and behavior. In this case, too, the offenders are judged by the grace with which they carry themselves. In theory, those who manage this well are judged favorably; they are redeemed and may even be celebrated for the achievement. If all goes well, terms of settlement are arranged, and the issue is regarded as completed.

Theories of Wrongdoing and Redemption

These three forms of reconciliation are built on local theories of the nature of wrongdoing and the role of redemption. Ritual life aims at treating particular kinds of dilemmas, and resolution depends on what causes people to do wrong. One Coast Salish theory is that low-class people do things wrong simply because they are not properly trained to conduct themselves in society (Miller 2001:140). It's worth noting, because of the implications for state apologies, that white people have historically looked like low-ranked people or even wrongdoers to the Coast Salish. They lose their temper in public, exercise authority openly and crassly, have few children (initially, early white traders and explorers didn't seem to have any wives at all—an obvious sign of inferior status), and point with their fingers (Harmon 1998). This latter practice is dangerous and rude because fingers can "shoot" harmful power. In short, people do wrong because they don't know otherwise and have not learned the public restraint that characterizes the elite; have been harmed by someone who wishes them ill (a form of intrusive magic); and are greedy and violate the cardinal rules of reciprocity. In prior periods, the material conditions of life were not so much different for upper- and lower-class people. For the most part, the difference lay in how people conducted themselves and the reputations they bore. Greedy people are thought to earn their own punishment by spiritual means; they will likely suffer infirmities or tragedies.

The relevant question now is: Why do white people (embodying the state) do wrong? The common answer is that whites are greedy—for land, salmon, anything. A Halkomelem (a Coast Salish language) term for whites is glossed as "hungry people," in reference to this greed (Carlson 1997:65, 82). They do wrong because they don't know any better. They don't reciprocate. They are overbearing and crude and are without the features of high-class people. What can you expect from them? The answer is more of the same. The hosting of a ritual for reparations or apology can't generate a result because it doesn't change the nature of the wrongdoer. In Coast Salish logic, it is not so much the gift that counts as what it represents, namely, a knowing repudiation of actions that have eroded the ability of groups to work together. The state appears shameless, however. Representatives have come to the ritual but seem to have a bad heart.

Coast Salish practices of reparation require that there be a reason for the wrongdoers to come forward. They may do so because they wish to redeem their family name or restore their place in the community or because their bad thoughts have caused harm to community members (Miller 2001:139–140). It is less clear what the motivations for the state are in participating in ritual life. At least one commentator, however, has connected the rise of state reparations with the growing inability of the state to carry out its core functions and the consequent need to get minority group support (Brookes 2003). Some indigenous people make this very connection and regard it as evidence that the state remains untrustworthy. Others note that the very conditions that promote apology rituals deny the possibility of transformation (Truiloot 2000).

Coast Salish culture emphasizes redemption and the capacity of individuals to transform in a way that contemporary mainstream culture does not. People can purify themselves and seek out spirit powers that can guide and empower. Individuals who have achieved this are new people and are conceptually not the same being. Individuals can take ancestral names that link them to others of the past and can make them new. People can be redeemed by the action of healers. Coast Salish stories speak of low-class people who surreptitiously overhear lessons given to upper-class young family members, act on these, and become great as a result. There are stories of people encountering immortal beings and attaining new capacities. People can work hard and gain the respect of community members through their ritual work. A common life course for contemporary middle-aged men is to transform themselves from lives of drinking and merrymaking into public figures acting for their family and community. Given the opportunities for redemption, and the emphasis on it, ritual practice without real change is all the more inappropriate.

Annalise Acorn, in her provocative book *Compulsory Compassion* (2004), observes that ritualized apologies in restorative justice settings can act to reinforce and maintain the existing inequality or state of disrepair. She notes that "it is therefore perplexing that conventional wisdom regards apology and forgiveness, in contrast to revenge and reprisal, as precisely what is need[ed] to heal the wounds of wrongdoing and to break out of a cycle of violence" (Acorn 2004:74). Further, she notes that apology and forgiveness saps the victim's energy for moving toward a more radical transformation in the relationship. Although Acorn primarily is concerned with restorative justice practices that concern one-on-one, private issues of wrongdoing and in which the victim may willingly comply and be fooled into believing in the sincerity of the wrongdoer's participation in the process, she also considers the implications for cross-cultural practice. She observes that it has become customary to begin with indigenous ceremonies such as prayers by elders in legal gatherings involving Aboriginal issues in Canada (for example, land claims proceedings). Nonindigenous participants, she says, look on with reverence. Although these shifts in ritual practice indicate some progress for indigenous peoples in Canada, nevertheless, "clearly, the currency here is not one of authentic respect. At stake is the ability to demand that others knuckle under and pretend to pay homage to your traditions—however much they may consider them at best quaint, possibly silly, or even downright offensive" (Acorn 2004:58). Such rituals, she concludes, are demonstrations of power relations but not just by indigenous peoples. These rituals remain tokens and "costless-to-whites" perks that are easier to grant than tangible and useful rights. Acorn has captured something of the truth in this, but has left out the average, nonelite community members who have their own interests in mind and do not sit on the stage during the proceedings, but watch the proceedings from below to note carefully the failures of the elite. In the case of state apologies, the careless elite are both the members of the indigenous community and the representatives of the state.

Gooder and Jacobs envision apologies as entangled with the postcolonial national agenda and primarily as vehicles for the white settler population to reconstitute the national imaginary by wiping out the actions of their shameful ancestors, thereby including themselves (Gooder and Jacobs 2000). Therefore, apologies are linked to social identity and the creation of a shared moral order and await the response of the other. For this reason, apologies require that the ways in which the other sees the world, in this case indigenous ideas of knowledge and of social relations, be taken into account.

The Present and the Future

The worldwide era of apologies is not yet ended and apologies remain politically significant. On 29 February 2006 the Washington State legislature, for example, issued a resolution passed by the Senate and House of Representatives to "acknowledge the injustices of the 1884 lynching of Louie Sam."[13] Louie Sam was a Stó:lō boy from British Columbia who was killed by a mob of Americans who were convinced that Sam had murdered a shopkeeper in nearby Nooksack, Washington. This story has remained with some elders for the last 122 years and research by historian Keith Carlson led to the making of a movie on this issue in 2004. The grand chief of the Stó:lō Tribal Council, the lieutenant governor of British Columbia, and the lieutenant governor of Washington all participated in a healing ceremony in Olympia, Washington, the state capital. A news release from the British Columbia Intergovernmental Secretariat of 1 March 2006 claims, John van Dongen, Minister of State for Intergovernmental Relations, is attending a ceremony in Olympia, Washington today...."In order to promote healing, it is important to come to terms and acknowledge historical wrong, as in the case of Louie Sam," said van Dongen. "Although these events may have taken place long ago, it's our moral duty to recognize these injustices so that Aboriginal people can fully participate in the great future we all have in British Columbia." The release cites a "new relationship with First Nations based on mutual respect."[14]

This event has a significant role in the education of the general public, but it is unclear what members of the community make of the ritual and the purported closing of the file by the high-and-mighty faraway, regardless of the ways in which community elite may use this event for political gain. If a mutually acceptable story regarding Louie Sam has been crafted and its acceptance signaled ritually, to whom is the story acceptable? Who has been given the chance to indicate acceptance or to contest the emergent story?

Some evidence regarding these questions comes from a discussion of state apology I conducted with a group of some twenty members of the Musqueam First Nation, located in Vancouver, British Columbia.[15] One person in attendance observed that the Canadian residential school apology described earlier didn't hold meaning for her because "they didn't consult the right people," meaning the school survivors. Another suggested that "too much damage has been done" for an apology to address the grievance. A third observed that the apology had to be understood within the larger historical context of loss of language and the destructive effects on parenting, and the apology, for this reason, was insufficient The relationship, in effect, is bigger than issues of residential schools, and schools can't be separated out. Another noted that the apology is "in the wrong language," meaning it should be in their own indigenous language because there is a history of the Crown "using tricky language," referencing legalistic English. Perhaps the most intriguing comment regarding apology and residential schools came from someone making comparative reference to both her own traditions and the South African Truth and Reconciliation Commission, noting that "the Nuns should come and speak the truth." The ritual, in her view, would have meaning if the parties actually involved (nuns and priests in the case of the Catholic residential school at Kuper Island where her family members were sent) participated and followed the longhouse practice of direct participation. Regarding the Louie Sam event, one indicated that the event "wasn't held in the right location" because it was away, from the place and the people where the lynching occurred. However, one man found the Louie Sam apology to be "ok" with him and suggested that "the family benefited."

There are reasons for cautious optimism about the possibility of the use of apology and ritual in reconciliation beyond that given by the lone man at Musqueam. In February 2006, I spoke to the Vancouver staff of the federal agency Indian Residential School Resolution Canada about the issues presented in this essay.[16] These federal employees, mandated to carry out alternative dispute resolution, promote reconciliation, and create agreements with churches whose school staff abused students, among other tasks, revealed through their questions, and in conversation after my talk, that some are largely uninformed about indigenous forms of knowledge and practice yet are willing to think about such topics. Others have already sought and found ways to make space for indigenous practice on its own terms in the conduct of government affairs. Still others, however, point out that government practices and protocols will continue to pose obstacles to conducting business in a way that connects to community practice. But at least they know this. A manager of this group hoped to go beyond academic talks such as mine and find ways to learn more directly, although he has not yet determined how this might be carried out. These responses give some hope that the government will become more open to the idea of thinking carefully about how it carries out its responsibilities to indigenous peoples. Further, the responses show an awareness that there are cultural differences between members of the mainstream and indigenous societies in their understandings of how social relations are best handled and even the insight that the current emphasis on apology as a political device derives from a particular historical moment.

In addition, there is a long history of Coast Salish Band and tribal leaders hosting events that they conduct in a traditional idiom in order to begin reordering political and economic relations with the mainstream society. It works this way: leaders invite important outsiders to their community to attend ritual events, sometimes held in winter longhouses. They cover the floor with blankets, thereby creating sacred space, place blankets over the shoulders of the visitors, and pin money on the blankets (Miller 1998). The visitors stand on the blankets. Speakers, hired for the occasion, call witnesses to the work and inform the visitors what they want for their community, employing techniques of ritualized oratory. The process creates liminal space, a transformed field, in which the visitors are receptive to the message in a way that they may not be otherwise. These ceremonies, however, are localized and ordinarily involve outside political and economic leaders from the immediate area. They typically don't involve national issues or leadership. They are time consuming and entail a measure of familiarity. They do, however, point to a model of ritual relationship that stands somewhere between those used by families in conducting relations with other families and those carried out in the halls of power, such as the Washington State acknowledgment of wrongdoing. Most significantly, as my examples suggest, many members of Coast Salish communities today believe that outsiders ought to negotiate with them in ways that are acceptable within their own communities. And rank-and-file members of communities continue to find ways to hold their own leaders responsible for doing so.

Conclusion

There may well be value in employing bottom-up restorative justice practices together with top-down efforts. For example, bottom-up justice in refugee camps might help dampen global terrorism. Local, bottom-up efforts at reconciliation, through apology or reparations and that take culture seriously, may better serve local needs and convey a more satisfying message than those derived from top-down rituals alone. In the Coast Salish case, attention to the specifics of local ritual practices and concepts and culturally specific theories of wrongdoing and redemption could build on local notions of the importance and possibilities of redemption and convey a message of inclusion of indigenous peoples within the contemporary society. There will be obstacles in carrying this out, including the difficulties associated with conveying the wrong message in ritual practice, but Coast Salish communities have already demonstrated, through incorporating outsiders into their own longhouse rituals, that representatives of the state and the community can engage each other in ways that can be satisfying and useful to community members.

Endnotes

[1] Two quite different events focused my attention on the issue of how indigenous peoples respond to the current state-sponsored attempts at restorative justice, apology, and reparation. One event was an international conference held in November 2001 at the Peter Wall Institute, University of British Columbia, regarding reconciliation and reparations. In good measure, guests responded to a seminal piece, "'Making Whole What Has Been Smashed' Reflections on Reparations," *Journal of Modern History* 73, no. 2 (2001) 333–58. See John Torpey (2003). In this book Torpey reviewed the sources and types of reparation politics and argued, following Habermas, for the creation of a shared history, a mutually acceptable story as the result of reparations. My focus, however, was ethnographic and focused on local reactions to large-scale politics. I raised the question of precisely how the mutually acceptable story is generated and what would be the forum in which this story is told. My paper "Indigenous Culture, Historical Grievances and

Reparations and Apologies" was delivered at the Peter Wall Institute for Advanced Studies Exploratory Workshop. Reparations for Historical Injustices, 2–4 November 2001. A second event concerned local responses to long-term injustice and historical grievances held just outside the old city walls in Jerusalem, Israel. This conference was the Adam Institute International Conference Attitudes Towards the Past in Conflict Resolution, held the week of 29 November 2001 My paper for the conference was "Indigenous Responses to Historical Grievances," and scholars speaking of historic injustices in Northern Ireland, Bosnia, Palestine, and elsewhere joined me.

[2] How community and national indigenous leaders treat this topic is much better understood than how nonelite community members view such events For example, lawyer Susan Alter has written a paper commissioned by the Canadian government entitled "Apologizing for Serious Wrongdoing: Social, Psychological, and Legal Considerations" (Law Commission of Canada, http.epe lac-bacca/100/200/300/icc-cdc/apology, 1999; accessed 20 March 2006), which considers in detail the legal and social implications of apology in providing direction to public officials She also points out that there are different kinds of apologies (personal and official) and suggests the need for cultural sensitivity in making apologies but fails to consider existing approaches to apology in First Nations communities.

[3] My concern is not to argue for a relativistic way of understanding culture or to contemplate universalism in light of the particularism of local culture See Eriksen (2001). Nor am I arguing that the world is merely composed of small, discrete cultures and I am not arguing that cultures are monolithic. Instead, culture is best understood as historically situated, contested, and a process. I am arguing for the significance of culture as a variable in reconciliation processes, which are very often or perhaps usually, cross-cultural affairs. Finally, I do not claim that contemporary rituals of reconciliation are flawed because they are Western-influenced or stem from Eurocentric social thought.

[4] Also see Borneman (1998) for a consideration of the analysis of culture in political change.

[5] Valpy (2002). This is not to suggest that underlying issues of relative power can be resolved by any ritual practice. Ritual generally papers over such differences but can be paired with substantive action.

[6] Swinomish Tribal Mental Health Project (1991:33). But see Rhonda Claes and Deborah Clifton (1998), who quote a residential school survivor who stated emphatically that he wants money in compensation but had no interest in an apology.

[7] Swinomish Tribal Mental Health Project (1991:29 and 68–69). See Paul Nadasdy (2003) for a discussion of Aboriginal perceptions of the state.

[8] This information comes from my own field notes concerning law I consider specific community responses in more detail in the following text.

[9] Swinomish Tribal Mental Health Project (1991:77–79). See Jay Miller (1999:104) for examples of consequences of improper ritual.

[10] See Jay Miller (1999:101) for historic examples.

[11] Personal communications, I wish to keep the sources anonymous. I don't want to provide identifying details regarding this instance of a shame potlatch, nor generally reveal the locations or identities of those commenting on the political actions of their own leadership Ethnographic details come from my field notes covering 1976 to the present.

[12] See Bierwert (1996), e.g., regarding the story of Crow, a social climber open to ridicule

[13] *Vancouver Sun* (28 February 2000), 1.

[14] New release, Intergovernmental Relations Secretariat, "B.C. to Attend Washington State Ceremony" (1 March 2006).

[15] I gave a two-hour talk and discussion with members of the Musqueam Nation, located in Vancouver, B.C., 15 March 2006, on "Apologies." The meeting was a session of "Musqueam 101," a weekly seminar held in the band center.

[16] Talk given to Indian Residential School Resolution Canada entitled "Ceremony and Protocol," 15 February 2006; the Vancouver office serves British Columbia, Alberta, and the Canadian North. This federal agency was established 7 June 2001. It is mandated to work with former students, families, and communities in support of projects that promote healing and reconciliation; use dispute resolution methods that are faster and less painful for the individuals; resolve claims and liaise with governments and churches in implementing the federal government's wider objectives of

healing and reconciliation; educate the general public; and work with church organizations to reach an agreement concerning their shared liability to compensate victims of sexual and physical abuse.

References Cited

Acorn, Annalise. 2004. *Compulsory Compassion: A Critique of Restorative Justice*. Vancouver, B.C.: University of British Columbia Press.

Avruch, Kevin and Beatriz Vejarano. 2001. Truth and Reconciliation Commissions. A Review Essay and Annotated Bibliography. *Social Justice Anthropology, Peace and Human Rights*, 2 (1–2):47–108.

Bierwert, Crisca. 1991. *Brushed by Cedar, Living by the River. Coast Salish Figures of Power*. Tucson: University of Arizona Press.

———— 1996. *Lushootseed Texts. An Introduction to Puget Salish Narrative Aesthetics*. Lincoln: University of Nebraska Press.

Borneman, John. 1998. *Subversions of International Order: Studies in the Political Anthropology of Culture*. Albany: State University of New York Press.

Braithewaite, John C. 2002. Thinking Critically about the War Model and the Criminal Justice Model for Combating Terrorism. Paper presented at the Law and Society Association Meetings, Vancouver, B.C., June.

Brooks, Roy L. 2003. Reflections on Reparation. In, *Politics and the Past On Repairing Historical Injustices*, edited by John Torpey, pp. 103–16. Lanham, MD: Rowman and Littlefield Publishers.

Carlson, Keith Thor, editor. 1997. *You Are Asked to Witness. The Stó:lō in Canada's Pacific Coast History*. Chilliwack, B.C.: Stó:lō Historic Trust.

Claes, Rhonda and Deborah Clifton. 1998. *International Child Abuse: Needs and Expectations for Redress of Victims of Abuse at Native Residential Schools*. Law Commission of Canada, www.lcc.gc.ca/research project/98/child abuse-en.aip. accessed 20 March 2006

Ehrenreich, Robert M. and Tim Cole. 2005. The Perpetuator-Bystander-Victim Constellation Rethinking Genocidal Relationships. *Human Organization*, 64(3): 213–24.

Erasmus, George. 2001. The Talking Stick. *Kahtou*, 10(2).

Eriksen, Thomas H. 2001. Between Universalism and Relativism' A Critique of the UNESCO Concept of Culture. In *Culture and Rights: Anthropological Perspectives*, edited by Jane K. Cowan, Mane-Benedicte Dembour, Richard A. Wilson, pp.127–148. Cambridge: Cambridge University Press.

Gooder, Haydie and Jane M Jacobs. 2000. On the Border of the Unsayable: The Apology in Postcolonizing Australia. *Interventions: International Journal of Postcolonial Studies*, 2(2): 229–47.

Harmon, Alexandra. 1998. *Indians in the Making Ethnic Relations and Indian Identities around Puget Sound*. Berkeley: University of California Press.

Miller, Bruce G. 1998a. Ties That Bind. Paper presented to the American Anthropological Association Annual Meetings, Philadelphia, 2 December.

——— 1998b. The Great Race. A Coast Salish Media Coup. *Pacific Northwest Quarterly*, 89(3):127–135.

——— 2001. *The Problem of Justice: Tradition and Law in the Coast Salish World*. Lincoln: University of Nebraska Press.

——— 2003. *Invisible Indigenes. The Politics of Nonrecognition*. Lincoln: University of Nebraska Press.

Miller, Jay. 1999. *Lushootseed Culture and the Shamanic Odyssey ~ An Anchored Radiance*. Lincoln: University of Nebraska Press.

Nadasdy, Paul. 2003. *Hunters and Bureaucrats, Power, Knowledge, and Aboriginal-State Relations in the Southwest Yukon*. Vancouver: University of British Columbia Press.

Napoleon, Val. 2004. Who Gets to Say What Happened? In *Reconciliation Issues for the Gitksan. Intercultural Dispute Resolution in Aboriginal Contexts*, edited by Catherine Bell and David Kahane, pp. 176–195. Vancouver: University of British Columbia Press.

Olick, Jeffrey K. and Brenda Coughlin. 2003. The Politics of Regret: Analytical Frames. In *Politics and the Past: On Repairing Historical Injustices*, edited by John Torpey, pp. 37–62. Lanham, MD: Rowman and Littlefield Publishers, Inc.

Peter Wall Institute. 2001. Making Whole What Has Been Smashed: Reflections on Reparations. *Journal of Modern History*, 73(2):333–358.

Swinomish Tribal Mental Health Project. 1991. *A Gathering of Wisdoms*. La Conner, WA: Swinomish Tribal Community.

Torpey, John, editor. 2003. *Politics and the Past On Repairing Historical Injustices*. Lanham, MD: Rowman and Littlefield Publishers, Inc.

Trouillot, Michel-Rolph. 2000. Abortive Rituals. Historical Apologies in the Global Era. Interventions. *International Journal of Postcolonial Studies,* 2(2):171–186.

Valpy, Michael. 2002. Native Lawsuits Fuel Costly Bureaucracy. *The Globe and Mail* (5 March 2002), sec. A:1–2.

White, Richard. 1999. *The Middle Ground. Indians, Empires, and Republics in the Great Lakes Region, 1650–1815*. Cambridge: Cambridge University Press.

Wilson, Richard A. 2001. *The Politics of Truth and Reconciliation in South Africa Legitimating the Post-Apartheid State*. Cambridge: Cambridge University Press.

Journal of Northwest Anthropology, Memoir 12:139–159 (2016)

9

AN ETHNOGRAPHIC VIEW OF LEGAL
ENTANGLEMENTS ON THE SALISH SEA BORDERLANDS*

The Salish Sea borderlands, straddling British Columbia and the State of Washington, are entangled in several legal orders, all asserting jurisdiction over geographic area and substantive issues. But these legal orders are often unaware of the other, or the impact of this entanglement on the Indigenous citizens of the various polities located directly on the border itself. Here I focus attention on the First Nations of Canada and the American Indians located in the Salish Sea and its drainage, from the mountains to the salt water. The naming of the water system comprising Puget Sound, the Strait of George, the Strait of Juan de Fuca, and smaller adjacent waters, as the Salish Sea in 2010 is recognition that the resident Coast Salish communities have constituted, historically, a zone of interaction between the constituent groups within a language family.

This work falls within the rubric of "law and society" research that, instead of featuring case law or treaty and constitutional arguments, or viewing a legal system as contained within the courtroom, examines the interactions of individuals or communities with representatives of the state and its legal systems, often low-level, and as seen from the ground up. This approach emphasizes the ways in which meanings become attached to law, how the legal regimes are contested and transformed, and the legal "consciousness" of everyday people (Buick and Sylby 1998; Merry 1999). I make this argument within the tradition of legal pluralism, although I do not regard the legal orders I describe here as on an equal footing[1] and I focus on the extension of Indigenous law into unexamined and unlikely corners. My approach is anthropological and ethnographic and follows on from my own studies regarding Coast Salish political life and legal orders since the 1970s. This research has been directly linked to tribal and band research interests, at the invitation of leadership, and sometimes directed towards legal venues.[2] This work follows the now well-established anthropological practice of working collaboratively with communities on issues selected by communities themselves.

The examples I present show the strength of the retention of Coast Salish ideas of law by members of the communities, the vehemence with which Coast Salish people believe these laws are still applicable, and the imaginative ways they attempt to integrate their historical legal concepts into the law of the dominant society.

The international border between the United States and Canada has been "hardened" with vastly increased surveillance practices since the catastrophic events of 9/11, but remains contested and permeable in unexpected ways. Now, creative Coast Salish leaders and rank-and-file communities members are drawing connections between their rights and obligations within their own law and those of the nations, Canada and the United States, within which they reside. Some of these efforts are merely symbolic but are still reflective of historic Aboriginal law. It is significant that they are not merely attempting to find their way through Canadian national or provincial law, or U.S. federal or state law. Rather, they are creating a new legal path, which takes seriously their own understandings and practices.

There is good reason for these developments. As Christie notes: "While some experimentation in living is both inevitable and worthwhile, within Aboriginal societies the broad strokes of how to live the good life have been worked out (Christie 2003)." Beyond this, I show

* Bruce Miller, "An Ethnographic View of Legal Entanglements on the Salish Sea Borderlands" (2014) 47:3 *UBC Law Review* 991–1024. Reproduced with permission.

the still limited ability of mainstream legal orders to "hear" the ideas of the Indigenous world (Borrows 2001) and the occasional ways in which it does.

The legal orders that sometimes contend for jurisdiction include the systems of law of the Coast Salish peoples themselves, the original peoples of the Puget Sound, Gulf of Georgia, the lower Fraser River, and portions of Vancouver Island, all regions that are contained within what I am calling borderlands. Coast Salish laws are both historic and codified in recent times. What is commonly called customary law, I wish to consider as *historic* law because "customary" supposes a timeless, unchanging order, and, further, to place law, portions of which have survived the colonizing processes, within history presumes movement and change during the difficult time since the arrival of settlers. On the U.S. side of the border, tribal code has been enacted by present-day federally recognized tribes and acted upon in tribal courts and inter-tribal appeals courts. On the Canadian side, tribal councils have created some legal apparatus, such as sentencing circles, in conjunction with Canada, and the First Nations Court in New Westminster. This is not tribally run nor tribally or Coast Salish specific (Whonnock 2011).

These three bodies of Coast Salish law overlap to some extent, particularly because the formal bodies, tribal code committees, composed of community members and legal advisors (created in the early days after the establishment of the tribal courts) have attempted to incorporate historic legal understandings within the new code.[3] They have partially succeeded, both in the language of the code and in the creation of legal procedures that allow for historical practices such as inter-family feasting (Miller 2001). Another example is the effort to incorporate historic ideas of the constituent elements of social organization with group rights into tribal code: the Upper Skagit code, for example, regulates fishing by recognizing extended family rights to riverside camp areas (Miller 1997a, 1997b). But the U.S. tribal codes created by Salish Sea Tribes have not entirely succeeded in reproducing either the concepts or the practices.

Coast Salish Law

Historic Coast Salish law is largely unwritten, although Puget Sound tribes have encoded portions for use in their own tribal courts, as I have noted. Unwritten legal orders, however, are far from unfamiliar to legal historians and Coast Salish law has distinctive features that are recognizable to legal practitioners.[4] First, although historically there were no buildings dedicated solely to the legal order—court houses, jails, and so on—and there were no permanent personnel associated with law—bailiffs, police, lawyers, judges—there were locations in which legal affairs could be placed out and particular high status people who could adjudicate between parties. Second, there were well-understood legal procedures—including inter-family conferencing, elders "panels", adjudication by neutral high status regional leaders, and even interpersonal song duels. Third, it was historically based on several principles, including non-interference with the rights of others, the role of elders and family leaders, respect for powerful (and potentially dangerous) spiritual beings, and privacy of spiritual identity. There was no state, and therefore no state involvement, and legal proceedings primarily involved families in relation to other families.

The historic legal order gave particular attention to issues of potential conflict—including control and management of resource areas, and the control and restriction of movement through one's territory and appropriate protocol for those travelling through. Law regulated rights to very important incorporeal prerogatives as well—including ancestral names, songs, and many other properties. And, the Coast Salish legal order employed sanctions for illegal behavior. This included compensation, exile, or in extreme cases, the right to take the life of someone poised to carry out further uncontrollable, destructive behavior. Coast Salish law, in fact, has much in common with the law of other small-scale societies, but with its own signature.

I do not intend a thorough discussion of historic Coast Salish law here. Nor do I wish to take up the debate about whether Aboriginal peoples of Canada had systems of law.[5] Rather, I point to the existence of a system that was historically understood throughout the Salish Sea and that was enacted in daily life. The Snuneymuxw tribal website puts it this way:

> Our relationships throughout the Coast Salish world are governed by our own laws and protocols, which reflect values of recognition, respect, and honour. Through those laws and protocols, Snuneymuxw self-determination and Territorial sovereignty is respected throughout the Coast Salish world.[6]

My writing here follows from a series of studies over the last 25 years on the issue of borders and Indigenous peoples (Miller 1997, 2006, 2011). I employ participant observations with Coast Salish communities on both sides of the border since the 1970s, address issues brought to my attention by community members and leaders, and discuss the results of my research, which included interviews with border officials. My own border crossings provide another lens to observe borderlands legal apparatus in action. Participation as an expert witness, or observer in some interesting, but largely under-the-radar law cases that turn directly on how the borderlands are understood and acted on legally, provides yet another perspective.

Calling on their own law is not new to colonized Coast Salish peoples dealing with the mainstream legal system (Asher 1995; J. Miller 1999), and in the current day the relationship to environmental issues in particular is well-established. For example, a writer on the West Coast Environment Law website notes:

> On Saturday, July 7 2012 the Tsleil-Waututh Nation and Squamish nation signed onto the Save the Fraser Declaration. In doing so, Tsleil-Waututh and Squamish joined more than 100 First Nations in asserting their own Indigenous Laws which effectively ban Tar Sands projects throughout their territories. (Statnyk 2012)

The Hozomeen Gathering

What follows are examples of less well-known engagements with historic law in the contemporary period. I start with a small, quiet example. One manifestation of Coast Salish law arose at a gathering of members of various communities whose ancestors had crossed the Cascade Mountains (as they are called in the United States) and the Coastal Mountains (the Canadian name) at International Point in the Skagit valley in September 2009. Event organizers, the Skagit Environmental Endowment commission, invited Washington and B.C. Aboriginal people, archaeologists, anthropologists, and other interested people. The two-day "Gathering at Hozomeen" focused on the long history of Indigenous involvement in the Upper Skagit River Watershed, a region that straddles the international border.

The region has always been a borderland between rival groups whose members travelled through to access resources, and in particular, the unique and valuable flint rock at Hozomeen Mountain. The Hozomeen chert (a flint-like rock deposit) was surface quarried and used for projectile points and other tools, and appears in the archaeological record of places throughout the region, including both sides of the international border (Mierendorf 1993). The area was a conflict zone well into the nineteenth century, and Upper Skagit tribal oral histories tell of violent conflict with Nlaka'pamux (previously called Thompson) people, who were thought to violate the protocols necessary to visit the region of the upper Skagit river and take game (Synder n.d.; Collins 1994; Mallone 2013).

These oral histories give a good sense of how features of Aboriginal law of the period can be characterized: passage of friends and relatives through the region was acceptable with notice and permission, but hunting without proper notice was certainly not. The punishment was reprisal in the form of attacks on hunting parties, with the heads of those killed put on stakes as a warning. The Upper Skagit oral histories indicate that the state of conflict with the Nlaka'pamux arose in response to protocol and hunting violations (from the Upper Skagit vantage point), not a general antipathy between peoples. Indeed, marriage between members of the group was not uncommon in the late twentieth century, long after warfare between Aboriginal groups had ended, although accompanied by jokes about heads on stakes (Miller 1985–1988).

The Gathering at Hozomeen was a curious event; many were aware that we were camping near the ancient quarry site (now underwater following the damming of the area to generate power for Seattle City Light and the creation of Ross Lake Dam) and that violent hostility characterized the region historically. The participants camped immediately next to the international border, indicated by the clear-cut of broad swaths of trees and markers on the trail leading from camp grounds on the U.S. side and the Canadian side. With permission apparently granted by U.S. authorities, represented by Park Rangers, participants enjoyed crossing back and forth, aware of the imposing hardened border at the official car crossings such as the Peach Arch at Blaine, Washington.

Elders from the various tribes and bands, including Swinomish, Upper Skagit, Nlaka'pamux, and others, made presentations. These elders, from communities all along the Skagit River valley from salt water to the mountains, uniformly spoke about named ancestors who crossed the pass, often to visit relatives. These talks foregrounded the rights and protocols by which this passage was made with the expectation that these would be acknowledged and understood by other Aboriginal participants. But, this was tempered by the recognition that under Canadian and U.S. law, rights and title to land and resources are not yet fully determined, and statements about passage, control, and related themes could be entered into the legal process.

In British Columbia, most bands do not have treaties and many are in the process of trying to clarify legally those territories they believe to have been theirs historically, and in the absence of any act of ceding them, still are. Claims of various bands often overlap, and the historic act of excluding and defending one's territory is evidence of exclusivity and title, rather than merely a right to pass through or use resources from a territory or waterway. In the State of Washington, treaties are long-established but treaty rights are still not fully determined. The Boldt Decision of 1974,[7] which allocated half of the salmon catch to tribes as an interpretation of nineteenth century treaties, was followed by a related decision concerning treaty rights to shellfish[8] and is now likely to proceed to a third area, hunting rights. This makes tribal members from both Canada and the United States wary about making statements, even about their own system of law, which might be misconstrued in a legal setting.

Nonetheless, in an event organized by the Skagit Environmental Endowment Commission, elders articulated their understandings of their own family and band or tribal histories and of Coast Salish laws regarding travel. Unspoken was contemporary national law, yet symbolically, in an area of contest over lands and resources between Coast Salish nations and the colonizers, Coast Salish law was articulated directly on the international borderlands.

The unequivocal and public statements of their right to travel across the U.S.–Canadian border by Coast Salish people at Hozomeen is reminiscent of medieval European law speakers who articulated the law at annual meetings of serfs and nobles, or at summer-time Icelandic gatherings at the Althingi. But it is also an example of historic and contemporary Coast Salish longhouse practice in which speakers state their understandings of rights to incorporeal properties such as ancestral names and songs, and corporeal properties such as land or the right to use particular resource stations. These statements are themselves articulations of law.[9]

Watt

The right of travel through Coast Salish territory, and hence the border crossing under Aboriginal law *and* U.S. and Canadian law, has come up in other guises. The case of *Watt v The Queen*[10] came before the Canadian judiciary in regard to Robert Watt, a member of the Sinixt (sometimes known as Arrow Lakes), whose members lived in what is now both Canada and the United States, but were declared legally extinct in Canada in the middle of the twentieth century, and are subsumed within the Colville Nation on the U.S. side (Pryce 1999). The Sinixt efforts to send Watt, a community member, to tend to their ancestral graves in Canada were rebuffed by his deportation, although band members claim the right to travel and reside within their historic territory and the obligation to look after their ancestors.[11] The Sinixt themselves put it this way: "After harassment and border crossing problems Sinixt Robert Watt leads a legal battle for the right to travel freely across International Boundary which divides the territory. He does this on behalf of all Sinixt people."[12] The Sinixt are not looking for the simple right of border crossing, which is guaranteed to Aboriginal peoples of Canada and the United States, but to have their territorial rights and their band in Canada recognized.

Fish and Water

One of the entanglements relating to law and borderlands in the Salish Sea concerns the movement not just of people, but of water and of salmon, some of which cross through U.S. waters prior to entering into Canadian waters and encountering both Aboriginal and non-Aboriginal fishers. This has led to competition over the resource and to litigation. Wadewitz has taken note of the problems at the border in an earlier period:

> In August 1895, George Webber, The U.S. customs inspector at Point Roberts, gazed out at the boundary waters between Washington State and British Columbia and lamented their porous nature. The Canadian salmon fishing boats that illegally traversed the water border particularly exasperated him. "If you try to get to them," he wrote, "they will steam away for a hundred yards across the line and then lay and laugh at you."
>
> The only way to catch them, Webber advised his superiors, was "to wait your chance, and the first time you can get aboard them in American waters to make the seizure." (Wadewitz 2012)

The Pacific Salmon Treaty between the United States and Canada was signed in 1985 in an effort to deal with such problems. The Pacific Salmon Commission is a 16-person body with 4 commissioners and 4 alternates each from the United States and Canada, representing the interests of commercial and recreational fisheries as well as federal, state, and tribal governments. On the U.S. and Canadian sides, members of Aboriginal communities have seats at the table of the body.

But problems have arisen in part because Indigenous law that managed the fish–human relationship prior to the imposition of foreign law was overlooked by the border-creation process in 1846. The diplomats who drew the border along the 49th parallel and out on a jagged course through the Gulf Islands failed to take into account the movements of tides and movement patterns and life cycle of salmon. With the rise of industrial fishing and new methods that allowed canning of salmon, overfishing became the norm and Aboriginal fishers found themselves largely pushed out of the harvest.

The dispossession of Aboriginal peoples from the fishery is well-known (Cohen 1986; Boxberger 1989; Harris 2001; Wadewitz 2012) but far less visible is the effort by a small, non-federally recognized band, the Hwlitsum, to protect their fishery in their homelands on the Lower Mainland of British Columbia and portions of the Gulf Islands. The Hwlitsum have an anomalous status within Canadian law. The members are largely individually status Indians but their existence as a band is not fully recognized, and, for the moment at least, is without a land base. They are, however, in phase two of the treaty process and a member of an intertribal council composed of Vancouver Island-based communities historically linked to them (Wilson 2007; Miller 2013). The Hwlitsum have acted within the mainstream legal system, documenting their resource locations in a "traditional use study" (Miller 2013), and have established a strength of claim to the territories used by their ancestors and by many present-day band members who fish, hunt, and gather. Consequently, they have asserted their right to be consulted in any development that might affect their ability to harvest or conduct traditional cultural practices under section 35 of the *Constitution Act*, 1982.[13]

Section 35 reads:

1. The existing aboriginal and treaty rights of the aboriginal peoples of Canada are hereby recognized and affirmed.
2. In this Act, "Aboriginal peoples of Canada" includes the Indian, Inuit and Métis peoples of Canada.
3. For greater certainty, in subsection (1) "treaty rights" includes rights that now exist by way of land claims agreements or may be so acquired.
4. Notwithstanding any other provision of this Act, the aboriginal and treaty rights referred to in subsection (1) are guaranteed equally to male and female persons.[14]

While subsequent case law has considered the specific meaning of "aboriginal rights",[15] the Hwlitsum argue that section 35 provides them the unfettered right to be consulted and to give testimony, for example, in the upcoming Canadian National Energy Board hearings regarding proposed pipeline expansion into the Salish Sea region and expansion of the Port of Vancouver, which lies squarely in their historic fishing waters.[16] In that testimony, they expect to make clear that their waters, and the species in those waters—including birds, fish, and shellfish of many sorts—will be irreparably harmed by an oil spill of even moderate size. And, they argue, the issue is vital because British Columbia lacks the capacity to respond promptly or in force to such a spill. Graham Knox, Emergency Response Coordinator of the B.C. Ministry of the Environment, confirmed in a meeting with Hwlitsum leaders, which I attended on the 12 September 2013 at the Cowichan First Nation Centre, that damage from spills will be unavoidable as the British Columbia has only 16 staff in the program for the whole of the province.

With the loss of shellfish and fish, they say, they will be unable to properly carry out ritual and spiritual life, which requires these foods to feed both ancestors (through burning in a ritual fire that sends the spiritual essence of the species) and the living (Miller 2013). Nor will they be able to carry out their stewardship function for territories they occupied and used, or their relationships with animal species and the immortal beings that also occupy the land and waterways. These responsibilities, they argue, are mandate by their law. Barsh refers to Salish Sea people's environmental laws and references "cleanliness" as the closest approximation to stewardship, because stewardship has spiritual connotations relevant to maintaining relations with the landscape (Barsh 2005:16). Although it may appear abstract, obligations to the land and water are fundamental to Coast Salish law, and is characteristic of Aboriginal thought generally, as Christie points out:

> The identity of these individuals (and the various communities they collectively comprise) is provided by the responsibilities they have, which work to weave the web of which they are parts. **There are, quite simply, things the individual *must* do, responsibilities to family, clan and community that *must* be respected and that *must* lead to action**. Responsibilities act to define a core of the identity of the individual, just as the existence of a society centred around responsibilities defines the identity of Aboriginal communities.[17]

The Hwlitsum draw on both Canadian constitutional law and Coast Salish law. They argue that they are following their ancestors, who responded to a shelling of their community in 1863 by the British Navy (Arnett 1999) by an attempt to protect their territory under their own law, which obligates them to do so (Wilson 2007). Chief Rocky Wilson is both a pragmatist in evoking Canadian law and a traditionalist in evoking the law of Coast Salish peoples, in particular regarding requirements of using harvested foods in ritual.

But, further, in their effort to fulfill their obligations to their land and waterscapes, and ultimately to their ancestors, the Hwlitsum met in 2013 with a U.S. tribe, the Makah Nation, located on the far northwest corner of the Olympic Peninsula of Washington state, for mutual assistance in creating an emergency response group for the waters (and fish) that flow between the United States and Canada. The Makah have a considerable presence in the emergency response field. In 2008 the Makah created their Office of Marine Affairs with funding from the federal Environmental Protection Agency and were given a voting seat on the Region 10 Response Team/Northwest Area committee. They prepared for training as "all hazard responders," in conjunction with the U.S. Coast Guard. The Marine Emergency Response Corporation employs three tribal members for duty on the 73-foot oil skimmer, *Arctic Tern*, and on the spill response vessel, *Loon*. The National Response Corporation employs two tribal members to maintain the 110-foot oil skimmer, *Cape Flattery* (Bowechop 2010; Miller 2013). The Hwlitsum and other Coast Salish groups of Canada commonly speak of the waters and resources as their own territories where their own resource laws must be maintained. Hence, they have invited cooperation to further their ability to meet their obligations.

All of this is a current example of the historical practice of family leaders acting as stewards of particular resource areas connected to their ancestral name, which sometimes required closing or limiting access to resource areas. Under Coast Salish law, these name holders had the unfettered right to control the resource for purposes of maintaining proper relations with the spirit beings who, constituted as fish and other species, offer themselves to people.[18]

"Like A Passport"

Coast Salish people continue to press for recognition of their own legal practices and concepts by federal officials, who sometimes respond positively, albeit without public notice. An unusual case occurred in August of 2009 when the Chief Justice of the Suquamish Tribal Court, Randall Steckel, organized a legal document to help a Canadian First Nations person from northern Vancouver Island cross back into Canada after departing from Suquamish territory in Washington. This person was in attendance at an inter-tribal (and international) canoe event known as Paddle to Suquamish, camping on Suquamish lands, when his or her tent was vandalized and travel documents stolen. The tribal police and tribal probation officer brought the situation to the attention of the Court. The Court ascertained the identity of the person in question by taking testimony on record of tribal people and the family. They determined that the person was a Canadian citizen and prepared a letter requesting Canadian border guards to recognize the identity as determined by the Suquamish Court. Judge Steckel reports that this person crossed through to Canada without difficulty and the letter was stamped by border service guards "like a passport."[19]

The Suquamish Tribal Court is an entity recognized by the Suquamish Tribe, other Coast Salish courts and inter-tribal appeals courts, the State of Washington, and the United States. It is not, however, known to Canadian authorities. However, representatives of Canada apparently chose here to recognize a U.S. federally-recognized tribe as a legal entity in this instance. The backstory is perhaps the interesting part: Judge Steckel recalls that the letter was created to facilitate the travel of a visitor to Suquamish territory and that Suquamish historic law and practice required safe travel out of Suquamish territory and back to the home of these guests. This form of historic law emerges out of the requirements of predictable, safe, and respectful interactions. (Historically, and in the present day, guests at major events such as potlatches are provided with enough food to return home.) Coast Salish law of travel imposed a burden of care on the Suquamish who acted here through their designated authority, the Tribal Court. Note the similarities to the discourse at the Hozomeen event, regarding rights of travel where proper protocol was recognized, except that in this case, the requirements of hosting are emphasized. Unlike the Mohawk of New York state and Quebec, this is not a case of an Indigenous-issued passport, and the Suquamish have no such document. It is a case of cooperation between tribal and national legal jurisdictions, and, consequently, Coast Salish law and state law, and of the innovation of new forms of relationship.

Fishing Rights Across the Border

A more direct challenge to U.S. and State of Washington law in the interest of Coast Salish concepts of property, ownership, and use rights came in the case of Steven Stark, a member of the Tsawwassen First Nation, a community of some 350 people located about 20 kilometers south of Vancouver and on the international border. The community is one of the few Aboriginal nations in British Columbia to have successfully gone through the B.C. Treaty process.[20] The Final Agreement contains a map of "Tsawwassen Fishing Area and Tsawwassen Intertidal Bivalve Fishing Area," which shows the Nation's fishing area and intertidal bivalve fishing area, bisected by the U.S. border, thereby cutting off large regions of its historic fisheries in Boundary Bay and the Straits of Georgia (all part of the Salish Sea).[21]

Mr. Stark was arrested in October of 2011 for fishing in U.S. waters and his load of Dungeness crab was seized. This arrest occurred in Boundary Bay, a body of water divided between Canada and the United States and within the historic waterscape of his band. Steven Stark's claim is that he may rightfully fish in this area just a few miles from his home. He hired a Bellingham, Washington criminal lawyer who prepared a defence, which included hiring me as an expert witness on Tsawwassen historic fishing territories and kin relations with U.S. tribes.

Counsel's argument in *Washington v Stark*[22] depended, in part, on whether Mr. Stark was fishing in historic Tsawwassen waters. In a report to the Superior Court of Whatcom County, Washington, I wrote (and later gave direct testimony to this):

> I have been asked to provide an expert opinion regarding whether the waters in which Mr. Steven Stark, huk-ka-luk-alle, when observed by the U.S. Customs and Border Protections agents, are within the usual and accustomed fishing grounds of the Tsawwassen First Nation. This area is in the vicinity of the waters off Point Roberts, 48 59 85 N 122 56 74 W. (See attached map). The Tsawwassen First nation is a treatied, federally recognized Indian band of Canada. The term "band" in Canada is equivalent to the term "tribe" in the United States and the Tsawwassen First Nation is the Canadian equivalent of the Lummi Nation or other recognized U.S. tribe.[23]

I concluded:

> It is my opinion that ancestors of the present-day Tsawwassen occupied and used territories adjacent to the international border at treaty-time; that they took marine resources from the waters of their territory; and that, specifically, this included waters off of Point Roberts, including what is now United States territory; and that Tsawwassen people of the time of the Treaty of Point Elliott customarily harvested in the area in question, namely off of Point Roberts and Blaine. Their overall harvest strategy included crab.[24]

The defence argument included the novel notion that Coast Salish tribes were densely connected through kinship and exchange such that treaty rights of the Coast Salish in the United States are extended to those Coast Salish groups within the Salish Sea that could demonstrate these connections. In a 20 December 2012 report to the Court, later accepted as evidence, I wrote:

> I have been asked to give an expert opinion concerning patterns of marriage between ancestors of the members of the Tsawwassen First Nation of the British Columbia, Canada, and the Lummi Nation of Washington State, United States, or other signatories of the Treaty of Point Elliott of 1855. There are three lines of evidence I draw on in making my conclusions. These are 1. Evidence from anthropological materials concerning the culture of the Central Coast Salish peoples, including patterns of travel, visitations to relatives, co-participation in winter ritual life, marriage. 2. Specific anthropological studies of marriage patterns of Coast Salish peoples. 3. Observations of a Tsawwassen family genealogist regarding her own family history and oral histories regarding relations with Lummi.[25]

And concluded:

> It is my opinion that mid-19th century ancestors of the Tsawwassen First Nation regularly intermarried members of the Lummi Nation, a signatory tribe of the Treaty of Point Elliott, that is a "treaty tribes," in local parlance. People from Lummi lived in Tsawwassen territory and visa versa. I have focused on Lummi here in drawing this conclusion but it is also my opinion that the Tsawwassen ancestors intermarried into other treaty tribes, including Swinomish and Nooksack (signatories to the treaty and federally recognized in 1974). These patterns have continued from treaty times into the present.[26]

Both of these arguments were made by reference to anthropological materials but directly reflect concepts contained within historic Coast Salish law. Marriage of Coast Salish people was historically to those outside of known kinship (sometimes given in terms of four or seven generations); closer marriage was incestuous and forbidden with severe sanctions imposed by Coast Salish law. This system of marriage underlies the network of ties within the Coast Salish world (Kennedy 2007) and the connections between the Tsawwassen and Lummi, for example. In addition, in-marriage provided recognized rights under Coast Salish law to portions of the territory of the in-laws, under a systems of protocol and management (Synder 1964). Notably, the criminal defence reproduced and depended on features of Coast Salish law.

Tsawwassen authorities initially did not back Mr. Stark, but recognized common cause in their difficulties with fishing near and crossing the border. Reporters noted:

> But Tony Jacobs, a member of the TFN legislative assembly, says that the new council—which reinstated his licence—is fully supportive of Stark. The border, he says, has only become an issue for TFN fishermen since 9/11. Like Stark, Jacobs' grandfather and father both fished around Point Roberts and throughout Boundary Bay. Jacobs is appalled at the severity of the charges Stark faces. "It doesn't matter if it's small or big," Jacobs says. "When you're dealing with the American authorities, anything to do with the border is just ridiculous." He hopes Stark wins the trial and TFN fishermen are granted more flexibility in terms of crossing the border.[27]

In my conversation with Stark in February of 2013, he expressed the desire to avoid a criminal conviction and to be able to fish in his traditional area. He spoke about the fisheries in light of the activities of his ancestors, noting that his father fished the grounds where he was arrested, as did other ascendants, including his great-grandfathers. He noted his kin connections and those of his ancestors to tribes now on the other side of the international border, including the Lummi and Nooksack, and his view that these connections remain constant, an essential part of the social fabric of Indigenous life. Stark spoke of the use of private family knowledge to fish in specific locations with specific, localized technology. He noted the connection between ancestral names (sometimes called "Indian names" and given within families) that are linked with the control of specific places and the place names also associated with these locations. The place names in the Coast Salish world commonly feature information about the physical nature of the place and historical or mythological details and show the relationship of the people to the land and waterscape. Under Coast Salish law, holders of these names (which are incorporeal family properties) were obligated to protect the animal and plant life and could preclude others from hunting, fishing, or gathering. Coast Salish law in this sense might be thought of as "decentralized law," in that there was, historically, no central government to enact law, and instead it arises out of interactions between these constituent families (Bierwert 1999; Napoleon 2005).

Stark, then, built from his own sense of family rights and obligations to the conclusion that despite the official Tsawwassen position regarding their historic fisheries as only in Canadian waters, there was every reason for him to be able to fish in the American portions of Boundary Bay. To him, fishing is both a family and tribal right. For Stark, these rights are tied to a particular protocol needed to access Aboriginal fishing territories, a protocol required of other tribes and bands as well as non-natives peoples. If these protocols are not followed, he noted, it is a "form of disrespect to the ancestors," and a form of "divide and conquer."[28] (Debates over fishing protocol arise in Coast Salish peoples' discussions of their role in fishing and open conflict occasionally breaks out between native people and with government officials.) Finally, Stark's feelings reflect the larger sense that the colonizers have damaged Aboriginal fishing to the extent that they have to go farther afield to find their catch, and should, by rights, be permitted to do this.

Stark's position gets at the larger question of how American and Canadian treaty and national law has converted what were once family rights to resource stations to strictly tribally-controlled rights, an issue noted by Barsh (2005, 2008) who argues against this development in Puget Sound:

> The importance of the incentive system embedded in traditional law is highlighted by the fate of Puget Sound salmon fisheries after judicial implementation of Coast Salish treaty fishing rights in 1974. The federal court rejected arguments that fishing sites are individually or family-owned, and chose instead to allocate fishing areas by "tribe." By court order, then, traditional custodians were divested of their control of access to fishing sites, and replaced by elected tribal leaders, tribal government bureaucrats and biologists. (Barsh 2005:12)

In effect, treaty law in the United States has erased features of historic Coast Salish resource law.

Stark further developed his position into a claim for the rights of the Aboriginal peoples of Canada to fish in U.S.-controlled waters because of his understanding of rights under the Jay Treaty.[29] One newspaper headline proclaimed, "One B.C. fisherman's fight for cross-border native rights".[30] Although Stark attempted, without success in court, to draw on treaty law, he paired it with Coast Salish law relating to property rights.

My conversations with Stark did not lead me to believe that this abstract Native right was his primary motivation. His motivations rest with the desire to make money fishing, his livelihood and that of many of his fellow Tsawwassen nation members, but also with his sense of his family hereditary rights. These rights, he says, were not negotiated away by his family, despite the new Tsawwassen treaty with Canada. "BC didn't own the land," he said, " there is no agreement to stay in our boundaries."[31]

In addition to the criminal charges within the State of Washington criminal justice system, Stark faced charges by Homeland Security, including a fine for illegally crossing the border in a boat. Stark notes that he was given 60 days to pay and informed that failure to pay is an admission of guilt. He says that he sent copies of his Status Card,[32] the Jay Treaty, and the 1974 Boldt decision. Stark believed that the terms of the Boldt decision would apply to those nations that are part of the social fabric of the Puget Salish tribes[33] and that under the terms of the Jay Treaty he could pass freely with his Status Card, which shows his membership in the Tsawwassen First Nation.

There are several interesting features to Stark's litigation and concerning what legal entity would properly have jurisdiction. Stark's belief was that historic Coast Salish law ought to be applied to his circumstances. This is not without precedent. Historic law, rooted in the relations between extended families that comprise the larger collective (Miller 2001) had previously been applied at the Peace Arch border through the actions of U.S. border officials to recognize the spiritual needs of "Babies," initiates into Winter Dancing. These initiates, whose gaze presents spiritual danger to others, were permitted for a period to pass through the border without being looked at if they had identification cards (this was before the requirement of a passport or a "hardened" drivers licence) and were under the supervision of the Longhouse elder accompanying them (Miller 1997). This was a significant recognition of the legal practices of the Coast Salish, which forbids interference with Babies. This feature of the border, and the local cooperation, has disappeared with the border hardening.

But Stark thought his family rights to particular locations on the land and water, as recognized by the ancestral law of his own nation (although not by the contemporary law of

Tsawwassen First Nation) ought to be upheld and believes that his family has not set them aside. Further, the Coast Salish legal regime, as it existed to regulate affairs between groups of Coast Salish, has itself not been extinguished on the Canadian side because most federally recognized groups have not entered into treaties modifying their rights and practices, although the Tsawwassen have done so. Many of the other Coast Salish bands have not ceded their land, nor with it, in Aboriginal reckoning, the law regulating that land. The historic system of law, Stark implies, continues.[34]

The legal entanglements included mainstream law as well. As counsel pointed out in his argument in *Washington v Stark*, state lower courts ordinarily do not consider international treaty law, which might apply in this case since Stark had crossed the boundary, and, he claimed, is outside their jurisdiction. In addition, because counsel argued (although not successfully) that Stark was fishing in a "right of way" in Indian country (itself a legal category), the federal government, not the State of Washington, alone retained the right to prosecute.

On the occasion of a preliminary hearing 23 May 2013, with imprisonment at issue, Stark was late in arriving. Homeland Security officials, apparently unaware or unconcerned, detained him at the border while he attempted to enter the United States to attend his own criminal trial. He was released in time to attend the later stages of the hearing.

Repatriation

A final example of the expression of Coast Salish law and its relationship with mainstream law and procedure comes from the case of a repatriation of a Sasquatch (properly spelled as Sasq'ets) mask from the Museum of Vancouver to the Sts'ailes (formerly Chehalis band) community located in the upper Fraser Valley. The Sts'ailes are closely identified with Sasq'ets; its image appears as the community logo and members have long reported sightings and interactions. The Museum was given the mask in 1939 by a White schoolteacher in the community, JW Burns, although it is not clear how Burns acquired the mask. A representative of the Sts'ailes wrote the Museum requesting repatriation and the mask was shown to Sts'ailes representatives at a repatriation of ancestral remains. On 11 December 2013, the four members of the Museum Repatriation Committee traveled to Sts'ailes to meet with Chief, members of the Council, and employees, and to attend events organized by the community.[35]

A search of Sts'ailes and Museum of Vancouver records uncovered some information regarding the provenance of the mask. It was carved in 1938 by a Sts'ailes community member and was paired with a head-to-toe costume. The carver had worn the Sasq'ets mask in public performance that year and there are several photographs of this performance. The Repatriation Committee learned far more during the December day at Sts'ailes. (I write as a member of the Board of Directors and chair of the Collections Committee, to which the Repatriation Committee is attached, and as one in attendance at these events.) The Chief noted that he is the grandson of the carver and a Council member described his own relationship to Sasq'ets.

In brief, in the 1930s the carver had had a spiritual encounter with Sasq'ets that led to his entry into the winter ceremonial dance (or Syowen ceremony). There, he learned a song and a dance that manifested the spiritual being and that became a part of his person (Amoss 1978). After the carver's death, the song, which is always personal to the spirit dancer, was "put away." Later, the song was transferred so that the song/dance could be performed in public. The council member reported that his own engagements with Sasq'ets were part of this transference (and transformation) and evidence that this was acceptable to Sasq'ets.

All of this information is important because it sets the stage for the creation of legal rights under Coast Salish law. At the December meeting, the Chief and council had organized a performance of the Sasq'ets song/dance to be held at an elder's Christmas lunch. This public performance by drummers and dancers constitutes a legal claim to the Sasq'ets mask because the performance can only be done by those with the rights to this spiritual, incorporeal property and its physical manifestations. The mask, song, and dance constitute a unity; they are inseparable components of this physical manifestation of the spirit being in its relationship to the human world. The council member had explained how rights to the performance were, in effect, ratified spiritually and the performance in December made this public. In theory, this claim to the right to dance the Sasq'ets mask could have been contested (it was not), although such contests do arise over incorporeal property, including ancestral names, in the contemporary Coast Salish world.

Drummers also performed an honour song, acknowledging the Museum committee members and their repatriation work. All of this constituted a formal request for repatriation. Here, in a legal order that has maintained performative features, a dance/song constituted the equivalent of a legal document. The Sts'ailes had shown their rights, had confirmed this publically, and had requested that the third element of the unity, the mask, be rejoined with the dance and song. This was done within the practices of the Coast Salish peoples.

The second piece of this story concerns mainstream law and administrative practice. Until recently, the Museum of Vancouver had no formal repatriation policy and had carried out no formal repatriations. The Board, in a phase of renewal of the Museum's mission in 2008–09, and at my urging and with the backing of the Director and professional staff, drafted a policy that was sent to the City of Vancouver legal department. The Board and the Director and professional employees act on behalf of the City, which owns the collection. The City eventually approved the new policy, which contains the terms under which repatriation can occur; in brief, when title is not clear or may have been unethically established, or if spiritual concerns of Aboriginal people are in question. The Collections Committee must approve the repatriation request (in some cases, a repatriation has been initiated by the Museum and a formal request from the First Nation has followed), which then recommends to the Board of Directors, which must also approve. While Canadian repatriations are not governed by federal law, as they are in the United States, there are still legal procedures and protections for the City-owned collection.

In this case, the Collection Committee approved the repatriation on 20 January 2013, as did the Board a short time later. The repatriation occurred on 14 May 2014 at Sts'ailes and the mask was again danced, to the evident delight of several hundred band members. On 7 June 2013, the Sts'ailes, further recognized the repatriation at the annual Sasquatch Days event held in conjunction with the town of Harrison Hot Springs, the Harrison Festival Society, and Tourism Harrison.

The Sts'ailes repatriation connects two bodies of law: mainstream property law as clarified in the repatriation policy (and, in another sense, the Museum's contract with the City to manage the collection), and Coast Salish law regarding incorporeal property and its physical manifestations. The process, however, was initiated out of Coast Salish law and practice and the family with the mask prerogative, and the council on behalf of the family explicitly made their claim to the mask within that law. Museum practice had only recently been adjusted to accommodate these Aboriginal legal orders.

Conclusion and Discussion

Sa'ke'j Henderson (2002:12) observed, "In its constitutional analysis, the [Canadian Supreme Court] has rejected…false assumptions of colonization, affirming that *sui generis*

Aboriginal law exists and is constitutionally protected by s. 35(1) of the *Constitution Act, 1982*." He noted that this has been the case since the Supreme Court "affirmed Aboriginal nationhood and its legal order" in *R v Sioui*,[36] but how does this work? Where and when are Aboriginal legal orders apparent in a borderland of considerable legal complexity and confusion, particularly since 9/11? Legal scholar Gordon Christie writes regarding the problems posed for Aboriginal law by liberal legal theory and critical legal theory, and the problems facing Aboriginal peoples within Canada more generally:

> It is not a problem of working out how Aboriginal interests can be translated into group rights and fit into the matrix of rights in Canada, just as it is not a problem of understanding these rights as reflective of group autonomy, and not a matter of recognizing that the "fluid and dynamic" interests of Aboriginal peoples can be better served through progressive democratic measures. **Rather, it is essentially a question about the ability of Aboriginal peoples to continue to define who they are, a potential for self-definition which includes their capacity to project their own theories and particular forms of knowledge.** (Christie 2009)

The cases I have given from the Salish Sea borderlands reveal the many ways Aboriginal peoples have recently sought to define themselves and project their own forms of law and knowledge. Many of these ways are hard to see, out of sight of mainstream lives, and difficult for mainstream people to understand, but they are constant, insistent, and subtly transformative. Even when the substantive issues are brought to public attention, Coast Salish law might not be understood to be at the heart of the matter.

There are counter-examples. The Museum of Vancouver repatriation is one example of the transformative process at work in the development of a repatriation policy and in the routine recognition of Aboriginal law and rights to incorporeal property. Museum staff members now treat ancestors (osteological material) held in the collection specifically according to Aboriginal protocol implemented through consultation.

But the legal scholar John Borrows has poignantly observed the legal restrictions imposed on the physical and intellectual mobility that is characteristic of the lives of Indigenous peoples. He writes that "most legal systems manipulate conceptions of mobility to deny or diminish Indigenous rights," and that these laws contribute to "removal from wider territories and relationship" (Borrows 2009). State law, he argues, blocks both physical movement of peoples and erases the underlying concepts. The examples here give a sense of the importance of movement for Coast Salish peoples historically and contemporaneously and the significance of the underlying Coast Salish legal order that has regulated this.

Several cases involve complex ways in which mainstream law is mobilized in support of Aboriginal practices and understandings, creating outcomes that are unexpected by the mainstream population. The Sts'ailes, whose efforts at repatriation of a mask have been detailed here, describe the connection between their legal order and their cultural and spiritual practices in their December 2013 newsletter:

> Lets'emo:t Sts'ailes Ikwe'lo. Xwem zwem sqalewel snowoyelh lam te mekw wates xaxa temexw te'i.

> We are all one mind, one spirit as Sts'ailes. We value being strong and balanced; our laws and teachings are for everything and everyone; everything is sacred to us.[37]

But note that the Sts'ailes have the expectation, as the mask case shows, that their law will apply in issues concerning their own society, and that, indeed, there are not reasonable alternatives. They acknowledge and work within Museum procedures dealing with collections (and the underlying notion of City of Vancouver ownership) but place emphasis on their own ways of understanding.

The location of the Coast Salish (most of the communities, in any case) on the Salish Sea borderlands increases the complexity of legal engagement. These cases, particular that of Steven Star, show Coast Salish people as occasionally subject to multiple legal jurisdictions, including tribal courts of Puget Sound, tribal constitutional law in British Columbia, state and federal law in the United States, and provincial and federal law in Canada as they attempt to live their lives under their own laws and practices, variously interpreted and enacted. Individual Coast Salish people, such as Stark and the canoeist at Suquamish, attempt to find their own way through the external legal systems. They act to transmit the moral legitimacy of their historic knowledge and ways of knowing while "strongly questioning and resisting the dubious neo-liberal and legal integrity of state policies" (Bardhoshi 2013). James Anaya, the UN Special Rapporteur on the Rights of Indigenous People, optimistically notes successes of Aboriginal people in asserting their laws:

Indigenous groups are asserting claims as distinct peoples with their own legal systems and associated cultural patterns and political institutions. In doing so, Indigenous peoples have made significant strides towards contributing to a greater pluralism in the global legal and political landscape—a pluralism in which Indigenous peoples and their legal systems are starting to find a place. (Anaya 2007)

Although Anaya is speaking primarily of the use of international law and protocol rather than in regard to national or regional law, his comments show that aboriginal people are engaging their own legal orders at every level. I will only note that Coast Salish peoples, at least, will no doubt continue to foreground their law. The sheer number of their current efforts to make their law visible testifies to this and one can only conjecture that even more Coast Salish individuals and communities will find new means to assert their law in an era in which communities (and inter-tribal groups such as the Union of British Columbia Indian Chiefs) have new legal and financial resources at their command.

Finally, I note that while there is a vigorous debate about whether it is possible or even desirable for Indigenous law, of the various sorts I describe here, to create space within mainstream law (see e.g., Johnston 1989; Borrows 2002, 2010; Napoleon 2005; Odis 2007:136; Miller 2011; Milward 2012; Duthu 2013), the fact is that Coast Salish people continue to project their law into public space. They seem compelled to do so because, as Christie writes, "the broad strokes of how to live the good life have been worked out."[38]

Endnotes

[1] Sally Engle Merry (1988) provides a succinct overview of legal pluralism and Paul Schiff Berman (2009) describes the "new legal pluralism", which considers normative, overlapping communities, some non-state, and their legal entities, and the transnational, emerging global legal system. Richard Wilson (2013) provides a concise critique. For a consideration of the interdisciplinary field of law and society studies, see Austin Sarat et al. (1998).

[2] For example, I worked with the Stó:lō Nation of British Columbia documenting their justice practices in the 1990s, with the Upper Skagit tribe of the State of Washington documenting their historic territories and practices of controlling access, and with the Hwlitsum band of British Columbia in documenting their historic social organization and resource practices. I organized a graduate ethnographic field school with the Stó:lō Nation at their request for eight summers in the 1990s to undertake research they identified. Discussions about the nature of collaboration with Aboriginal communities are frequently reported in the American Anthropology Association Newsletter and the Journals *Human Organization* and *Current Anthropology*. Good examples of the literature in anthropology include: Wayne Warry (1990); Luke Eric Lassiter (2008). My UBC colleague Charles Menzies (2004) has published his own views. For Gordon Christie's thoughts on the development of Indigenous legal theory and the participation of non-Indigenous scholars, see Christie (2009).

[3] See Bruce G Miller (1995, 1997, 2001). However, others contest the possibility that this can be achieved. See Larry Nesper (2007); Barsh (1999); Richland (2007).

[4] For other writing on this topic, see Brian Thom & Don Bain (2004); Brian Thom (2005); Barsh (2005, 2008); Northwest Intertribal Court System (1991); B. Miller (2001); J. Miller (1999); Elmendorf (1993); First Nations of South Island Tribal Council (1987). Internal documents such as the *Stó:lō Heritage Policy Manual* strongly reflect Coast Salish Law (Stó:lō Nation, 2003; approved by the Stó:lō Government House Chiefs & Councilors in 2003). "Indigenous Law in Coast Salish Traditions" was the subject of a conference hosted by Cowichan Tribes in 2010. In any case, much of Coast Salish Law is recognizable to the mainstream.

[5] See John Borrows (2005), who noted the "long history of recognition of indigenous legal traditions by those who encountered these societies". Further, Borrows (2010) observed that "[l]aws arise wherever interpersonal interactions create expectations and obligations about proper conduct".

[6] Snuneymuxw First Nation, "Coast Salish Culture", online: <http://www.snuneymuxw.ca>.

[7] *United States v Washington*, 384 F Supp 312, 1974 US Dist LEXIS 12291 (WD Wash 1974).

[8] *United States v Washington*, 873 F Supp 1422, 1994 US Dist LEXIS 20062 (WD Wash 1994).

[9] See Miller (2001); Thom (2005). Val Napoleon (2007) uses the term "legal order" to, as she puts it, "describe law that is embedded in social, political, economic, and spiritual institutions". The Coast Salish people's comments about the mountain pass and their law regulating access, including protocols, are embedded in all of these institutions.

[10] *Watt v Canada (Minister of Citizenship and Immigration)* (1998), 169 DLR (4th) 336, [1998] 2 FC 455 (TD).

[11] *Pryce (1999)*. The obligation to look after the graves of ancestors has its source in what Napoleon references in relation to First Nations as "divine" or natural law. See Napoleon (2007:5).

[12] Sinixt nation, "Timeline: 1990's", online: <http://sinixtnation.org/content/timeline>.

[13] *Constitution Act*, 1982, being Schedule B to the *Canada Act* 1982 (UK), 1982, c 11.

[14] *Constitution Act*, 1982, being Schedule B to the *Canada Act* 1982 (UK), 1982, c 11.

[15] Key early cases include, among others, *R v Sparrow*, [1990] 1 SCR 1075, 70 DLR (4th) 385; *R v Van der Peet*, [1996] 2 SCR 507, 137 DLR (4th) 289; *R v Gladstone*, [1996] 2 SCR 723, 137 DLR (4th 648; *Gitxsan Houses v British Columbia (Minister of Forests)*, 2002 BCSC 1701, 10 BCLR (4th) 126; *Homalco Indian Band v British Columba (Minister of Agriculture, Food & Fisheries)*, 2005 BCSC 283, 39 BCLR (4th) 263; *Huu-Ay-Aht First Nation v British Columbia (Minister of Forests)*, 2005 BCSC 697, [2005] 3 CNLR 74; *Timberwest Forest Corp v British Columbia (Deputy Administrator, Pesticide Control Act)*, [2–3] BCEA no 31 (QL), 2003 CarswellBC 3619 (WL Can); *Penelakut First nations Elders v British Columbia* (Regional Waste Manager), 2004 CarswellBC 2658 (WL Can), [2004] BCEA no 3 (QL); *Tsilhqot'in Nation v British Columbia*, 2007 BCSC 1700, [2008] 1 CNLR 112; *Musqueam Indian Band v British Columia (Minister of Sustainable Resource Management)*, 2005 BCCA 128, 251 DLR (4th) 717 [*Musqueam*]. Key later cases include *Delgamuukw v British Columbia*, [1997] 3 SCR 1010, 153 DLR (4th) 193 [*Delgamuukw*]; *Haida Nation v British Columbia (Mister of Forests)*, 2004 SCC 73, [2004] 3 SCR 511; *Taku River Tlingit First Nation v British Columbia (Project Assessment Director)*, 2004 SCC 74, [2004] 3 SCR 550 [*Taku River*].

[16] Hwlitsum Fieldnotes, (Miller 2013). The Hwlitsum have been accepted as an intervenor, and have scheduled appearances by elders, leaders, and experts, including myself.

[17] Christie (2009:111). The obligation to feed ancestors is another example of a form of prescriptive law, which Napoleon characterizes as divine or natural law. See Napoleon (2007:7).

[18] For discussions of historical and contemporary social organization and resource control and human relations to animals, see Wayne Suttles (1987); Bierwert (1999). Brian Thom (2009:185) provides details about hereditary names and resources. See also Homer Barnett (1955:134).

[19] Interview of Judge Randall, Suquamish Tribal Court (December 2013) [unpublished; on file with author].

[20] See *Tsawwassen First Nation Final Agreement Act,* SC 2008, c 32; *Tsawwassen First Nation Final Agreement Act,* SBC 2007, c 39.

[21] *Tsawwassen First Nation Final Agreement Act,* SBC 2007, c 39., Appendix J-3.

[22] *Stark*, 23 May 2013, Bellingham, Wash 11-01-012258-8 (Whatcom Co Super Ct).

[23] *Stark*, (23 May 2013), Bellingham, Wash 11-01-012258-8 (Whatcom Co Super Ct). (Report by Bruce Miller, 1 October 2012).

[24] See note 23.

[25] *Stark,* (23 May 2013), Bellingham, Wash 11-01-012258-8 (Whatcom Co Super Ct) [*Stark*]. (Supplemental report by Bruce Miller dated 20 December 2012).

[26] See note 25.

[27] Joel Barde & Carlos Tello, "One B.C. fisherman's fight for cross-border native rights" *Vancouver Sun* (13 May 2013),online: <http://www.vancouversun.com/news/fisherman+fight+cross+border+native+rights/8379487/story.html>.

[28] Interviews with Steven Stark, May 2013 [Interviews with Stark].

[29] More formally, *The Treaty of Amity, Commerce and Navigation, United States and Great Britian*, 19 November 1794, 8 US Stat 116.

[30] Barde and Tello (2013).

[31] *Stark,* (23 May 2013), Bellingham, Wash 11-01-012258-8 (Whatcom Co Super Ct) [*Stark*]. (Supplemental report by Bruce Miller dated 20 December 2012).

[32] Aboriginal Affairs and Northern Development Canada (AANDC) notes, "[T]he Certificate of Indian Status, more commonly referred to as the Status Card, is an identity document issued by AANDC to confirm that the cardholder is registered as a Status Indian under the *Indian Act*": AANDC, "Indian Registration, status and Status Cards", online: <https://www.aadnc-aandc.gc.ca>.

[33] For an argument for Boldt rights in Canadian courts, see Douglas C Harris (2008).

[34] *Stark,* (23 May 2013), Bellingham, Wash 11-01-012258-8 (Whatcom Co Super Ct) [*Stark*]. (Supplemental report by Bruce Miller dated 20 December 2012).

[35] The following account comes from my fieldnotes of a trip to Sts'ailes in 2013.

[36] Henderson (2000), citing *R v Sioui* [1990] 1 SCRp 1025, 70 DLR (4th) 427 at 1053.

[37] "Sts'ailes Mission Statement", *The Beating Heart: Sts'ailes Community Newsletter* (December 2013) online: <http://www.stsailes.com>. Similarly, Borrows (2010:6) writes, "Many Indigenous peoples believe their laws provide significant context and detail for judging our relationships with the land, and with one another".

[38] Christie (2003:91). This is the case elsewhere, although not my focus here. See e.g., Leslie A Robertson and Kwagu'l Gixsam Clan (2012:403; noting the insistence of Kwakwaka'wakw people to honour the laws of their potlatch).

156

References Cited

Amoss, Pamela. 1978. *Coast Salish Spirit Dancing: The Survival of an Ancestral Religion.* Seattle: University of Washington Press.

Anaya, James. 2007. Indigenous Law and Its Contribution to Global Pluralism. *Indigenous Law Journal*, 6(1):3–12.

Arnett, Chris. 1999. *The Terror of the Coast: Land Alienation and Colonial War on Vancouver Island and the Gulf Islands, 1849–1863.* Vancouver: Talon Books.

Asher, Brad. 1995. A Shaman Killing Case on Puget Sound, 1873–1874. American Law and Salish Culture. *The Pacific Northwest Quarterly*, 86(1):17–24.

Barde, Joel and Carlos Tello. 2013. One B.C. fisherman's fight for cross-border native rights". *Vancouver Sun* (13 May 2013), online: <http://www.vancouversun.com/news/fisherman+fight+cross+border+native+rights/8379487/story.html>.

Bardhoshi, Nebi. 2013. Legal Dynamics in a Border Area: Between Customary Law and State Law. *Journal of Legal Anthropology*, 1(3):314–332

Barnett, Homer. 1955. *The Coast Salish of British Columbia.* Eugene: University of Oregon Press.

Barsh, Russel Lawrence. 1999. Putting the Tribe in Tribal Courts: Possible? Desirable? *Kansas Journal of Law & Public Policy*, 8(2): 74–89.

————— 2005. Coast Salish Property Law: An Alternative Paradigm for Environmental Relationships. *Hastings West-Northwest Journal of Environmental Law and Policy*, 12(1):1–29.

————— 2008. Ethnogenesis and Ethnonationalism from Competing Treaty Claims. In *The Power of Promises: Rethinking Indian Treaties in the Pacific Northwest*, edited by Alexandra Harmon, pp. 215–243. Seattle: University of Washington Press.

Berman, Paul Schiff. 2009. The New Legal Pluralism. *Annual Review of Law and Social Science*, 5:225.

Bierwert, Crisca. 1999. *Brushed by Cedar, Living by the River: Coast Salish Figures of Power.* Seattle: University of Washington Press.

Borrows, John. 2001. Listening for a Change: The Courts and Oral Tradition. *Osgoode Hall Law Journal*, 39(1):1–38.

————— 2002. *Recovering Canada: the Resurgence of Indigenous Law.* Toronto: University of Toronto Press.

————— 2005. Indigenous Legal Traditions in Canada. *Washington University Journal of Law and Policy*, 19(167):167–223.

————— 2009. Physical Philosophy: Mobility and the Future of Indigenous Rights. In *Indigenous Peoples and the Law: Comparative and Critical Perspectives*, edited by Benjamin Richardson, Shin Imai , and Ken McNeil, pp. 403–419. Oxford: Hart Publishing.

————— 2010. *Canada's Indigenous Constitution.* Toronto: University of Toronto Press.

Bowechop, Chad. 2010. Makah Tribal Council's Office of Marine Affairs. *Proceedings of the Marine Safety and Security Council*, 67(1):51–52.

Boxberger, Daniel L. 1989. *To Fish in Common: The Ethnohistory of Lummi Indian Salmon Fishing*. Lincoln: University of Nebraska Press.

Christie, Gordon. 2003. Law, Theory and Aboriginal Peoples. *Indigenous Law Journal*, 2 (Fall):67–115.

———— 2009. Indigenous Legal Theory: Some Initial Considerations. In *Indigenous Peoples and the Law: Comparative and Critical Perspectives*, edited by Benjamin J Richardson, Shin Imai, and Kent McNeil, pp. 195–231. Oxford: Hart Publishing.

Cohen, Fay G. 1986. *Treaties on Trial: The Continuing Controversy over Northwest Indian Fishing Rights*. Seattle: University of Washington Press.

Collins, June McCormick. 1974. *Valley of the Spirits: The Upper Skagit Indians of Western Washington*. Seattle: University of Washington Press.

Duthu, Bruce. 2013. *Shadow Nations: Tribal Sovereignty and the Limits of Legal Pluralism*. Oxford: Oxford University Press.

Elmendorf, William W. 1993. *Twana Narratives: Native Historical Accounts of a Coast Salish Culture*. Seattle: University of Washington Press.

Ewick, Patricia and Susan S. Silbey. 1988. *The Common Place of Law: Stories from Everyday Life*. Chicago: University of Chicago Press.

First Nations of South Island Tribal Council. 1987. *Aboriginal Self Determination, Indian Family Law, Tribal Indian Governments* [unpublished].

Stó:lō Nation. 2003. *Stó:lō Heritage Policy Manual*. Chilliwack, B.C. Online: Stó:lō Research and Resource Management Centre <http://www.srrmcentre.com>.

Harris, Douglas C. 2001. *Fish, Law, and Colonialism: The Legal Capture of Salmon in British Columbia*. Toronto: University of Toronto Press.

———— 2008. The Boldt Decision in Canada: Aboriginal Treaty Rights to Fish on the Pacific. In *The Power of Promises: Rethinking Indian Treaties in the Pacific Northwest*, edited by Alexandra Harmon, pp. 128–153. Seattle: University of Washington Press.

Henderson, Sa'ke'. 2000. Aboriginal Law Now a Source of Constitutional Law. *The Lawyer's Weekly* (20 October 2000).

Johnston, Darlene. 1989. *The Taking of Indian Lands in Canada: Consent or Coercion?* Saskatoon: University of Saskatchewan Native Law Centre.

Kennedy, Dorothy. 2007. Quantifying 'Two Sides of a Coin': A Statistical Examination of the Central Coast Salish Social Network. *BC Studies*, 153(1):3–34.

Lassiter, Luke Eric. 2008. Moving Past Public Anthropology and Doing Collaborative Research. *NAPA Bulletin*, 29:1–70.

Malone, Molly Sue. 2013. *Where the Water Meets the Land: Between Culture and History in Upper Skagit Aboriginal Territory*. Ph.D dissertation, University of British Columbia.

Menzies, Charles R. 2004. Putting Words into Action: Negotiating Collaborative Research in Gitxaala. *Canadian Journal of Native Education*, 28(1–2):15–32.

Merry, Sally Engle. 1988. *Law and Society Review*, 22(5):89–96.

——— 1999. Pluralizing Paradigms: From Gluckman to Foucault. *Political and Legal Anthropology Review*, 22(1):115–122.

Mierendorf, Robert R. 1993. *Chert Procurement in the Upper Skagit River Valley of the Northern Cascade Range, Ross Lake National Recreation Area, Washington.* Seattle: National Park Service.

Miller, Bruce G. 1985–1988. Fieldnotes from visits to Upper Skagit, WA, Community.

——— 1995. Folk Law and Contemporary Coast Salish Tribal Code. *American Indian Culture and Research Journal,* 19(3):141–164.

——— 1996–97. The 'Really Real' Border and the Divided Salish Community. *BC Studies,* 112:63–79.

——— 1997. The Individual, the Collective, and Tribal Code. *American Indian Culture and Research Journal,* 21(1):107–129.

——— 2001. *The Problem of Justice: Tradition and Law in the Coast Salish World.* Lincoln: University of Nebraska Press.

——— 2006. Conceptual and Practical Boundaries: West Coast Indians/First Nations on the Border of Contagion in the post-9/11 Era. In *The Borderlands of the American and Canadian Wests: Essays on Regional History and the Forty-ninth Parallel,* edited by Sterling Evans, pp. 49–66. Lincoln: University of Nebraska Press.

——— 2011. *Oral History on Trail: Recognizing Aboriginal Narratives in the Courts.* Vancouver: University of British Columbia Press.

——— 2013. Fieldnotes from Hwlitsum.

Miller, Bruce Granville, et al . 2013. *The Hwlitsum First Nation's Traditional Use and Occupation of the Area Now Known as British Columbia* (Hwlitsum Marine Traditional Use Study), vol 2 [unpublished].

Miller, Jay. 1999. *Lushootseed Culture and the Shamanic Odyssey: An Anchored Radiance.* Lincoln: University of Nebraska Press.

Milward, David Leo. 2012. *Aboriginal Justice and the Charter: Realizing a Culturally Sensitive Interpretation of Legal Rights.* Vancouver: University of British Columbia Press.

Napoleon, Val. 2005. Delgamuukw: A Legal Straightjacket for Oral Histories? *Canadian Journal of Law and Society,* 20(2):123–155.

——— 2007. *Thinking About Indigenous Legal Orders.* West Vancouver: National Centre for First Nations Governance.

Nesper, Larry. 2007. Negotiating Jurisprudence in a Tribal Court and the Emergence of a Tribal State. *Current Anthropology,* 48(5):675–699.

Northwest Intertribal Court System. 1991. *Traditional and Informal Dispute Resolution Processes in Tribes of Puget Sound and Olympic Peninsula Region.* Edmonds, WA: Northwest Intertribal Court System.

Otis, Ghislain. 2007. Territoriality, Personality, and the Promotion of Aboriginal Legal Traditions in Canada. In *Indigenous Legal Traditions*, edited by Law Commission of Canada, pp. 136–160. Vancouver: University of British Columbia Press.

Pryce, Paula. 1999. *Keeping the Lake's Way: Reburial and the Re-creation of a Moral World among an Invisible People.* Toronto: University of Toronto Press.

Richland, Justin B. 2007. Pragmatic Paradoxes and Ironies of Indigeneity at the 'Edge' of Hopi Sovereignty. *American Ethnologist,* 34(3): 540–557.

Robertson, Leslie A., and Kwagu'l Gixsam Clan. 2012. *Standing Up with Ga'axsta'las: Jane Constance Cook and the Politics of Memory, Church, and Custom.* Vancouver: University of British Columbia Press.

Sarat, Austin, David M. Engel, and Marianne Constable, editors. 1998. *Crossing Boundaries: Traditions and Transformation in Law and Society Research.* Evanston, III: Northwestern University Press, American Bar Foundation.

Snuneymuxw First Nation. n.d. Coast Salish Culture. online: <http://www.snuneymuxw.ca>.

Snyder, Sally. 1964. *Skagit Society and Its Existential Basis: An Ethnofolkloristic Reconstruction.* Ph.D. dissertation, University of Washington.

———— n.d. Fieldnotes. Melville Jacobs Collection, Suzzallo Library at University of Washington.

Statnyk, Kris. 2012. Tsleil-Waututh Nation and Squamish Nation Sign Save the Fraser Declaration. *Environmental Law Alert Blog*, online: West Coast Environmental Law <http://wcel.org>.

Suttles, Wayne. 1987. *Coast Salish Essays.* Seattle: University of Washington Press.

Thom, Brian. 2005. *Coast Salish Senses of Place: Dwelling, Meaning, Power, Property and Territory in the Coast Salish World.* Ph.D. dissertation, McGill University.

———— 2009. The Paradox of Boundaries in Coast Salish Territories. *Cultural Geographies,* 16(2):179–205.

Thom, Brian and Don Bain. 2004. *Aboriginal Intangible Property in Canada: An Ethnographic Review.* Ottawa: Industry Canada.

Wadewitz, Lissa K. 2012. *The Nature of Borders*: *Salmon, Boundaries, and Bandits on the Salish Sea.* Seattle: University of Washington Press.

Warry, Wayne. 1990. Doing Unto Others: Applied Anthropology, Collaborative Research and Native Self-Determination. *Culture*, 10(1):61–73.

Whonnock, Karen L. 2011. A Tale of Two Courts: The New Westminster First Nations Court and the Colville Tribal Court. *UBC Law Review*, 44(1):99–110.

Wilson, Raymond (Rocky). 2007. To Honour Our Ancestors We Become Visible Again. In "*Be of Good Mind": Essays on the Coast Salish,* edited by Bruce Granville Miller, pp. 131–137. Lincoln: University of Nebraska Press.

Wilson, Richard A. 2013. Book Review of *Global Legal Pluralism: A Jurisprudence of Law Beyond Borders* by Paul Schiff Berman. *Journal of Law & Society*, 40(4):706–711.

Section IV

Gender and Political Life

The period since the 1970s has seen a rebuilding of Coast Salish community institutions, and this has been paired with the rise of women in formal tribal/band political office. Gender attributions and roles have themselves rapidly shifted in the changing economy. These papers are built on empirical data (elections results), interview data, and analysis of Coast Salish social organizational features—particularly the family groups. Chapter 10, *Women and Politics: Comparative Evidence from the Northwest Coast* uses data from Coast Salish communities from both sides of the international border to examine this rise and shows relationships between women's electoral success and the size of the community, large male income, and other variables; a discussion of this journal paper has been featured for some years in the Carole Ember and Melvin Ember text, *Anthropology* (Figure 12). Chapter 11 concerns the ways gendered issues have been treated in the new tribal codes and Chapter 12 considers Coast Salish women and politics in light of trends developing world wide.

Figure 11. Male and female greeting figures at the Stó:lō Nation (2014).

■ new perspectives on gender

Women's Electoral Success on the Northwest Coast

Political life has changed dramatically since first contact with Europeans for most Native American groups, including the Coast Salish of western Washington State and British Columbia. With impetus from the U.S. and Canadian governments, each of the recognized Coast Salish communities now has an elected council. But who is getting elected? Even though women did not have much of a role in traditional politics, now the Coast Salish groups are electing a lot of women. From the 1960s to the 1980s, women held over 40 percent of the council seats in the 12 Washington State groups, and in the 1990s, women held 28 percent of the seats in the 50 British Columbian groups. The proportion of women on the councils varies from 6 percent among the Tulalip to 62 percent among the Stillaguamish. What accounts for the women's electoral success? And why does that success vary from one group to another, even though the groups are closely related culturally?

According to Bruce Miller, who did a comparative study of women's electoral success in Coast Salish communities, women generally have more of a political role now perhaps because new economic opportunities in the service and technical sectors allow women to contribute more to the household economy. But why do women win proportionately more council seats in some communities than in others? Miller found that women win proportionately more seats in communities with less income, the least income derived from fishing, and the smallest populations. Why should lower household income predict more electoral success for women? Miller suggests that it is not so much the amount of income but rather the degree to which women (compared with men) contribute to household income. In groups with economic difficulties, the jobs women are able to get play a vital role in the household. Federally funded programs such as the War on Poverty helped women to acquire technical skills and jobs. Simultaneously many men in some communities lost their jobs in logging and agriculture.

But a high dependence on fishing income seems to favor men politically. Families that operate vessels with a large drawstring net to catch fish at sea can make hundreds of thousands of dollars a year. Men predominantly do such fishing, and where there is such lucrative fishing, the successful men dominate the councils. Even though women may have jobs too, their income is not as great as the successful fisherman's.

Why should women be more successful politically in smaller communities? Miller suggests that women have a better chance to be known personally when the community is small, even though working outside the home in technical or service jobs cuts down on the time women can devote to tribal ceremonials and other public events.

Does female income relative to male and community size help explain the relative political success of women elsewhere? We do not know yet, but subsequent research may help us find out.

Source: B. G. Miller 1992.

Women as well as men serve on political councils in many Coast Salish communities. Here, we see a swearing-in ceremony for the Special Chiefs' Council in Sardis, British Columbia.

Figure 12. Highlights of the 1992 article on women and Northwest Coast politics have been included in the textbook, *Anthropology* (Ember, Carol R., Melvin R. Ember, and Peter N. Peregrine. 2010. New York: Pearson North America).

Journal of Northwest Anthropology, Memoir 12:162–178 (2016)

10

Women and Politics: Comparative Evidence from the Northwest Coast*

In recent years women have attained an increasingly important role in the formal political structures of the Coast Salish communities of western Washington State and British Columbia, a development that has been reported among other North American Indian groups (Kidwell 1975; Green 1980;Verble 1981). In the period 1962 through 1987, women held over 40 percent of council seats in the twelve western Washington tribes administered under the Everett office of the Bureau of Indian Affairs. Women won 28 percent of council seats in the 1990s in the 50 British Columbia Coast Salish bands. In both cases, these figures represent huge, unexpected increases over earlier periods, and there is little local precedent for this contemporary development. Women did not play a routine public political role in this region in the post-contact period, with few exceptions, and perhaps not in the aboriginal period (Haeberlin and Gunther 1930; Smith 1940; Collins 1974). Indeed, white society and government policy actively discouraged women's participation in government (Roberts 1975; Donaldson 1985).

Further, Coast Salish societies are not organized into matrilines which are said to validate and elevate the status and autonomy of females in northern Northwest Coast societies (Mitchell and Franklin 1984:22). Nor is there a clear rank system that promotes women's careers. Although in earlier decades some talented women inherited leadership positions from family members and exercised their authority publically, the presence of so many women in high office is, in Alber's words, "a contradiction in the nature of female status in modern reservation settings" (1983:176).

The dramatic increase in the elective political role of women is an important element of contemporary Coast Salish life. Yet, just as remarkable as the overall incidence of women's success is the variability between culturally related tribes and bands in women's access to public authority. Consequently, the foci of this work are the electoral trends in both Washington and British Columbia and the variables that act on women's chances of election. Comparative data show both the importance and limitations of male income, tribal size, median household income, and local historical differences in the relationship of Indian groups to white governments, in assessing the political chances of Indian women. Three brief case studies are presented to clarify the comparative analysis. Elsewhere (Miller 1989, 1990, 1992), I analyze these same issues from other viewpoints (the political and managerial strategies employed by individual women, the influences of community social organization on elections, voting patterns, and the development of tribal legal codes) in order to show how women affect the structure of the state (Silverblatt 1991) and act to shape their own communities.

The Coast Salish data cast light on larger theoretical issues concerning Indian women and the state. Coast Salish women have a markedly different relationship to the state than do the men of their communities and are situated, as are many women, at the "boundary between kinship relations and state structures in a way in which men are not," (Moore 1988:184) and which ordinarily works against the political participation of women. Despite this, and even because of it, Indian women have emerged in recent decades in political roles as cultural brokers mediating between government institutions and their own communities in ways other women and men have not. How this works varies, and is the subject of analysis by Albers (1983, 1985) and Powers

*Authored by Bruce Granville Miller and previously published in *Ethnology*, 31(4):367–383 (1992).

(1986) writing about the Sioux, Lynch (1986) on the Northern Paiute, Knack (1989) on the Southern Paiute, and Fiske (1989) on the Stoney Creek Carrier. Closer to the Coast Salish, Ackerman (1988) has analyzed the political participation of Colville (Plateau) women, and Klein (1976, 1980) of Tlingit women. These studies are not designed to sufficient data to clarify electoral trends, a short-coming in the literature that I seek to remedy for the Coast Salish. Further, both Ackerman and Klein base their arguments for high rates of public office-holding on an absence of gender bias. Relatedly, Albers, in an overview on the literature on Indian women and contemporary political life writes:

> there is the fact that many forms of work and leadership are not sex-typed in a fixed and narrow way. Generally speaking, American Indian women have not been stigmatized for working outside the home or for getting educations that qualify them for professional jobs... Other conditions being equal, women have as much chance as men to seek elected and appointed offices. (Albers 1989:160)

The Coast Salish data show that although women are not stigmatized in the political arena for working outside the home, for training, or education, there are highly localized notions of politics and gender. Indeed, elements of public political life have come to be associated with women in some communities and with men in others. Consequently, explaining the temporal and localized variations in women's access to public office requires examining gender bias and sex-typing.

Many Coast Salish women have benefitted from favorable conditions which arose unexpectedly in the 1960s through new federally funded training programs and related employment opportunities. These women learned technical skills while in tribal service that are applicable to tribal political life and have gradually emerged as managers, or "technocrats," who receive community-wide, as opposed to partisan, political support because of their ability to contribute to the well-being of community members. Technocrats, for example, are acknowledged for community members in dealing with bureaucracies (such as schools and authorities) and for their ability to attract federal and state funding to the reservation. The technocrats have been, almost without exception, women who have gained their experience through federal opportunities provided by War on Poverty funding.[3] The technocrats' relatively high and stable incomes allow women to play an important role in their families and communities and to fulfill the community ethic of "collectivism" (Mooney 1979). In addition, the simultaneous pattern of loss of men's jobs in logging, agriculture, and nonskilled labor (Miller 1989) has enabled (or perhaps more accurately, obligated) women to fill the economic void. Other women exercise control over the distribution of resources within family networks and have thereby become family heads and gained family support in elections.[4]

Western Washington State

The twelve tribes affiliated with the Everett Office of the Bureau of Indian Affairs have been selected for study because of their similar histories of contact, important cultural similarities, and because of a regional pattern of intermarriage and ceremonial exchange. All but one, Nooksack, are regarded as Southern Coast Salish (Suttles and Lane 1990), but are treated collectively in analyses of ceremonial life since 1900 (Kew 1990). Tribes vary in their relationship to the state, in size, in wealth, and in women's electoral success, and dissimilarities allow for the examination of the effects of the differences on the political chances of women. Table 3 shows the results of elections to tribal councils for the twelve tribes from 1962 to 1987. The results range from 6.1 percent female councilors at Tulalip to 62.2 percent at Stillaguamish. The average for all twelve tribes is 41.4 percent.

The data can be rearranged to focus on the electoral success of women as a percentage of each council, rather than by raw totals (Table 4). This is important because councils vary in size. Seen from this perspective, progress in women's electoral success has stabilized, or is even declining very slightly.

TABLE 3. ELECTION RESULTS, 1962–1987*

Tribe	# Women	%	# of men	%	Total
Tulalip	6	6.1	92	93.8	98
Swinomish	48	32.0	102	68.0	150
Sauk-Suiattle	27	60.0	18	40.0	45
Puyallup	29	39.2	45	60.8	74
Nooksack	40	38.8	63	61.2	103
Nisqually	43	55.1	35	44.9	78
Muckleshoot	70	62.0	43	38.0	113
Lummi	13	8.0	149	92.0	162
Port Gamble	15	27.3	40	72.7	55
Stillaguamish	28	62.2	17	37.8	45
Suquamish	20	39.2	31	60.8	51
Upper Skagit	48	53.3	42	46.7	90
Totals	479	41.4	677	58.6	1,159

Results by Decade: Raw Totals Women on Council		
1960s... 97	of	393...29.1%
1970s...180	of	467...38.5%
1980s...117	of	260...45.0%

*These data were obtained from records of the Everett Office of the Bureau of Indian Affairs, Everett, Washington. First names were used to determine sex.

TABLE 4. PERCENTAGE OF WOMEN ON COUNCIL*

1960s	29.3%
1970s	45.2%
1980s	41.7%
Total, all decades	40.8%

*This table uses tribal council averages. Data were gathered from records of the Everett Office of the B.I.A. The age of council members is not indicated from these data and sex is determined by names.

Historical Considerations

Five of these tribes (Sauk-Suiattie, Pt. Gamble, Nooksack, Stillaguamish, Upper Skagit) are composed of the descendants of people who were unable or chose not to participate in the 1855 Treaty of Pt. Elliott and consequently were "landless"; that is, without reservations and with unclear relationships with the federal government until the 1970s (Ruby and Brown 1986; Marino 1990; Porter 1990). Taken as a whole, the tribes recognized by the federal government in the 1970s have more women on their tribal councils (an average of 48.3 percent) than those tribes that were recognized in the middle of the nineteenth century (average 34.5 percent). However, the differences in election rates by sex between the two groups are not statistically significant (at the .05 level, using the Wilcoxon U test).

Nonetheless, it is no accident that the two tribes with by far the fewest women on their councils were bound to reservations and received recognition in the nineteenth century. These are Lummi, with 8.0 percent women on the council, and Tulalip, 6.1 percent. Tribes which obtained reservations in the nineteenth century were often left near significant traditional fishing areas and have access to these areas today. In addition, such tribes often hold primary rights, which provide control over the timing of the sporadic bouts of fishing permitted under agreements between the tribes and the state. By contrast, recently acknowledged tribes are much less likely to have favorable fishing sites, or to have primary rights in these locations (Boxberger 1989). As explained below, the location of fishing determines the appropriate technology, and ultimately the size of the catch available to an individual. These factors in turn influence the distribution of resources within a community, and thereby influences women's electoral chances.

The period of acknowledgement is also important in that Lummi, Tulalip, and other tribes federally sanctioned since the nineteenth century, have considerable continuity in male leadership. Post-reservation councils were almost exclusively male, and U.S. policy and western values actively promoted this (Roberts 1975; Donaldson 1985). These councils, while weak in comparison to surrounding community governments, dealt with serious issues such as membership, policing of the reservation, relations with neighboring communities, and tribal economic development. Post-contact history thus created precedents favoring male access to political authority and limiting women's access to political power.

By contrast, women provided much of the political leadership in some of the tribes, including Sauk-Suiattle and Stillaguamish, which were not acknowledged until the 1970s. Women played important roles in the crucial fight for federal recognition (Ruby and Brown 1986). Prior to acknowledgement, membership was dispersed for lack of a tribal land base and because of local economic conditions, and the tribal governments exercised little power over members or resources. Women's history of political involvement has helped women today in the elections for seats on the new formal councils established after recognition, and both Sauk-Suiattle (60.0 percent) and Stillaguamish (62.2 percent) women have high rates of electoral success. There is variation in this, and one cannot argue simply that male involvement increases as the financial stakes increase, as, Hansen (1979) has demonstrated for Seattle urban Indian institutions. At Upper Skagit, another tribe acknowledged in the 1970s, women provided valuable leadership during the difficult period before acknowledgement, but were limited to roles as nonvoting secretaries and treasurers on the Tribal Council (Miller 1989).

In some instances, the new constitutions written in the 1970s legally enfranchised women and enabled their participation on the council. At Upper Skagit, for example, enfranchisement occurred after the return of families (who had departed for economic reasons) to regular participation in tribal life. Members of these families subsequently helped alter the tribal political culture to allow for women's direct access to public authority, an outcome not intended at the time the constitution was prepared (Miller 1990). Women from these families ran for office with family support and one woman successfully overcame resistance to her candidacy by the unprecedented act of sending out timed political mailings to tribal members.

Despite these historical differences between tribes, the regional data show several variables, especially size and economy, which are related to women's electoral chances.

Median Household Income

The most useful measure of community prosperity for which data are available is the median household income. The entire community is reflected and the data include all sources of income. Reliable data are available from the 1980 Census (General Social and Economic Characteristics, Washington) for six tribes and Skagit System Co-operative information (1980 Report) provides data for two more, including the Sauk-Suiattle and Upper Skagit. The median household incomes for these tribes varies from $4,542 to $15,956, in 1980 dollars, which reflect important differences in the ways families can operate.

The ability of women to win seats varies according to median household income (Spearman's rank order correlation +.742, stat. significant at .05). Women win more seats in poorer tribes, which suggests that women have succeeded politically in good measure because of the new economic and educational resources available to them (Miller 1989, 1990). These new resources show up as most important in poorer tribes where women's contribution to and control over the distribution of family resources is most important. Data show the most important of the financial resources are income from employment and fishing, and to a lesser degree, income from social assistance programs administered by the state and federal governments.[5]

Male Income

The size of fishing income is a second important feature of economic life, as Boxberger (1989:300) noted for the Lummi:

> in fairly closed fishing communities the more prolific fishers utilize their success to create a political following. By carefully selecting crew members and by assisting others to enter the fishery, a strong faction is create…. A parallel structure exists at

Lummi, where a small faction of the tribe, the purse-seine operators who take over 60% of the total Lummi fish harvest control the decision-making body of the tribe...

By "decision-making body of the tribe," Boxberger (1989:300) refers to the tribal council, noting that seven of eleven council members are from "influential families that operate purse-seine vessels." Purse-seining technology enables these men to achieve significantly higher income than gill-net fishers; some earning several hundred thousand dollars a year. Gill-net fishers, by contrast, cannot harvest enough fish to make large incomes, and gross about $25,000 (personal communication, Doreen Maloney, Upper Skagit fisheries manager). I suggest that the relatively large income of the purse-seiners mitigates the contributions of technocrat women, whose much smaller income is thereby less important to their family and community, as Table 5 shows.

TABLE 5. LARGE FISHING INCOME AND WOMEN'S ELECTORAL RESULTS.

Tribe	Presence of Large Fishing Income (purse-seining)	Relative Political Success of Women
Sauk-Suiattle	No	High (60.0% of council)
Upper Skagit	No	High (53.3% of council)
Swinomish	Yes	Mid (32.0% of council)
Lummi	Yes	Low (8.0% of council)
Tulalip	Yes	Low (6.1% of council)

Size of Tribe

The electoral success of women also varies with the size of the tribe (Spearman's rank order correlation +.797, stat. significant at .01). The tribal populations in the study range from about 260 to about 3100 (Ruby and Brown 1986) and, according to council women, three related factors are at work. First, the size of tribes influences the way in which people relate to one another and to women candidates, especially technocrats who are not well integrated into tribal day-to-day life and ceremonial life. Technocrats are simply not known personally by many of the voters in large tribes and succeed less frequently than in small ones. This supports the proposition (Newland 1975; Rix 1987) that women candidates do better in small political arenas than in larger polities. As Newland (1975:16) noted, in small political fields women are more likely to "...be judged for personal qualities rather than according to sexual or other stereotype." Women who have been public office holders and residents of more than one reservation have related the differences in running for office to differences in size (Miller 1989). Second, on smaller reservations, large family networks are able to provide enough votes to win elections for family heads, male or female; this is not so easily the case on larger reservations (Miller 1989). Third, small reservations have a smaller pool from which to draw capable people for tribal service and members may, at least in some circumstances, use whomever they can.

British Columbia

The electoral situation is somewhat different among the culturally related Central Coast Salish of British Columbia and women's successes there have come more recently than in Washington State. As in Washington State, women's access to political authority is responsive to fluctuations in the local economy and in the availability of training opportunities. Another similarity is the tremendous variability of women's electoral successes. Table 6 shows that the rate of increase has been about 5 percent per decade.

TABLE 6. WOMEN'S ELECTORAL RESULTS FROM FIFTY B.C. COAST SALISH BANDS, BY DECADE*

Decade	Women on Council
Pre-1960s	6.5%
1960s	11.0%
1970s	16.0%
1980s	21.7%
1990s	28.0%

*These data are taken from Department of Indian Affairs records. Sex has been determined by first name. 1990s data are limited to 1990 and 1991. Linguistic affiliation was used to select the 50 bands. Nuhalk (formerly Bella Coola), which is not adjacent to other Coast Salish-speaking bands, has not been included.

The 1986 census data help explain the overall trend in British Columbia towards the increased election of women (Table 7). The data show both a clear division of labor and a partitioning of categories of post-secondary training. Jobs are highly partitioned by sex and more than half of all jobs are held in gendered occupations (56.6 percent of all job holders are in categories dominated (2/3 or more) by either men or women).

Education is also highly partitioned; 84.4 percent of people are trained in an area in which one sex predominates (2/3 or more) (Table 8).

The political meaning of this division of training and labor varies locally along several dimensions, as it does in Washington. Training in certain occupations, especially clerical work, provides a suitable preparation for election to band councils because it physically places one in the band center and familiarizes people, especially young women, with bureaucratic functioning and providing services for band members. The employment areas in which men dominate are management, construction, primary industries, and transportation. Women predominate in clerical, health, and teaching jobs, which are frequently located in places where community management is centered. Although census data show men hold many more jobs than women (62.6 percent of jobs are held by men), white-collar work is more important for elective office.

TABLE 7: JOB HOLDING BY SEX*

Predominantly Male Jobs	Predominantly Female Jobs
Construction (100% male)	Clerical (85.1%)
Primary industries (94.3%)	Health care (66.7%)
Transport (78.6%)	Teaching (59.3%)
Management (64.5%)	————

*Data are from the 1986 Canadian census (N=2100) not reported by Band, but by census subdivision, which includes non-Natives, Native band members, and Native non-band members. Subdivisions with less than 75 percent Natives have been excluded from this table. For reasons of confidentiality, Statscan policy is to withhold data for subdivisions of less than 100, and consequently small bands, and small reserves of larger bands, are not accounted for.

TABLE 8: AGGREGATE EDUCATION DATA*

Predominantly Male Areas of Training

1. engineering and applied science (100% male)
2. engineering and applied science-technical and trade (62.4%)

Predominantly Female Areas of Training

1. health (80% female)
2. education, recreation, counseling (71.4%)
3. (tie) agriculture and biological sciences-technical (66.7%)
3. (tie) humanities (66.7)%

*Training refers to post-secondary qualifications (N=805).

For those 23 bands for which 1986 census data are available, 555 of 1965 jobs (28.2 percent) are government service jobs.[6] This figure gives some idea of the importance of these jobs to the local economies. In many poor communities, clerical work provides stable and locally significant salaries, as is the case in Washington State, In addition, clerical work shows up in interview data as an important avenue to tribal electoral success, and it is primarily women who perform this work (Miller 1989).

Within British Columbia there is interesting variation: three band councils have persistently remained all male (Malahat, Nanoose. Scowlitz); 24 band councils have remained heavily male; four councils have moved from all-male to predominantly or entirely female (Katzie, Lakahahmen, Musqueam, Ohamil); five councils changed from male to a rough parity (Beecher Bay, Cowichan, Skwah, Skway, Union Bar). One council has consistently remained mixed (Semiamhoo).

In those tribes with few or no women on the council, there is an important difference in income by sex: in each of the seven bands for which appropriate 1986 census data are available, there are a significant number of men earning the top reported incomes in the census figures ($35,000 a year or more) and no women earning over $25,000 or $30,000. In the case of Sechelt, for example, the census reports ten such high male income earners and no women; at Seabird Island, five such men and no women over $25,000. These kind of income differentials were found in the Washington State case to mitigate the importance of women's stable, but smaller, incomes from band employment.

Although a strong negative relationship exists between median household income and the electoral successes of women in Washington, the British Columbia data are insufficient to confirm or reject this finding. Of the 50 bands included in the study, the census provides sufficient and appropriate data for only eight.

As with Washington tribes, the level of success of women candidates is related to size, but not as convincingly. How this works is quite revealing: women as a group began to win seats earlier and more regularly in the very smallest tribes. Women held 35.1 percent of council seats in 1989 in the fourteen tribes of 100 or fewer members. Otherwise there is no systematic connection between size and election to the council.

On the other hand, band size is closely related to the issue of the election of band chiefs. Of the seven women serving as elected chiefs in 1991, all but one were from small bands, with a mean population of 255. Of the 48 bands reported to have had a chief in 1989, seven, or 14 percent, have women chiefs, which is exactly 50 percent of the ratio of women councilors. Women were somewhat more likely to win election as chief in bands where women generally did well in elections and these bands averaged 37.9 percent women on council. A plausible explanation for the lower rate of election of women to the position of chief, or chair, is that the position is gender-typed in many communities because of the association with public speaking (Miller 1989).

TABLE 9. 1990 BAND MEMBERSHIP SIZE AND ELECTION RESULTS BY SEX*

Band Size	Number	Women on Council
Small (9–378)	38	31.3% (77 men, 35 women)
Medium (429–840)	10	22.7% (51 men, 15 women)
Large (2131–2451)	2	27.6% (21 men, 8 women)

*1989 data from the Department of Indian Affairs publication, *Indian District and Tribal Councils, British Columbia Region* (1990).

To some degree, these data reinforce the conclusions drawn from the Washington data. Tribes with a very limited labor pool may draw on all available capable people to fulfill band responsibilities, independent of extraneous features such as gender. Further, women candidates in these communities benefit from their face-to-face acquaintance with all adults so that people may be less likely to vote categorically. Finally, members of family networks are able to vote their representatives onto the councils, as was the case in Washington. Despite all this, the three British Columbia bands without women councilors are all small (Nanoose, with a population of 151,

Scowlitz with 179, Malahat with 205) and, as the Katzie case (below) shows, other variables such as the development of tribal services, may be required before alteration in the post contact pattern of male domination of formal political life occurs.

Case Studies

Three communities are included in this study; the Upper Skagit Tribe of Indians and the Lummi Nation, both in Washington State, and the Katzie Band in British Columbia. These communities have a great deal in common; e.g., all are located on or near ancestral lands and are organized around the harvest of fish. They are now surrounded by bedroom communities for burgeoning metropolitan areas. Members of all three, but especially Lummi and Katzie, and Lummi and Upper Skagit, participate in the same network of intertribal life, and are in direct contact in religious, ceremonial, social, familial, and recreational activities.

Katzie

There are differing circumstances for the three communities. Katzie, like other Canadian bands, has been subject to a set of imposed membership criteria under the Indian Act, and until 1985 women lost their recognition as official Indians by marrying any nonstatus person. Non-native women marrying status men, on the other hand, were placed on the Band rolls (lists of officially recognized members). British Columbia policy called for the placement of Natives onto small, local reserves, and today there are five Katzie reserves located along the Fraser River. Although this is changing, Canadian policy has not permitted Native commercial fisheries, thereby restricting Natives to a ceremonial and subsistence catch. Further, the provincial government has not engaged in treaty making with the vast majority of British Columbia Native peoples; consequently, the Katzie government provides fewer governmental services than do the Washington tribes. Nonetheless, the Band is moving towards institutional completeness; a development associated with the political success of women in Washington State and at Katzie.

At present there are about 300 members, most living on the main reserve in the rapidly developing Pitt Meadows area 30 miles east of Vancouver. Department of Indian and Northern Affairs data, going back to 1956, show that the Band Council was entirely male until 1986, with the lone exception of a woman who served as Chief from 1971 to 1974. Nine different men held office during this period. In 1980 the Council expanded from three members to four. From 1986 to the present, the council has been entirely female, with the exception of the chief. Six different women have served on the council since 1986.

The dramatic alteration in the sexual composition of the band council coincides with a whole new set of tribal responsibilities and with the construction of a new band center in 1984. Prior to this, the activities of the Band were carried out in the house of the then Chief. The new "full-fledged band-office," a term employed by one councilor, included a program of community services and the personnel to conduct the services: a book-keeper, community health representative, social worker, and secretary. The new responsibilities drew women to fill them, and these women are now the Band councilors. As in other communities, the council women have noted the importance of membership in a large family to winning tribal elections, but it is the association with band activities that has facilitated their entry into the Council. One of the three women councilors in 1991 observed: "Well, band members have seen me work with kids the better half of my life, so I guess they have trust in me, and elected me in." This councilor worked for the Band on education programs for three years prior to election. Another received Department of Indian Affairs funding for training and performed clerical work for two years for the Band before election to the council. The third was the Band book-keeper for two years prior to her election in 1986. This career trajectory is quite similar to that of elected women in Washington State.

Although Katzie lacks a treaty-based band fishery, unlike the Washington tribes, the increased time commitment of governance is said by the councilors to have partitioned job holding between fishing (at least the on-water portions of fishing as opposed to net and boat tending, and other related tasks) and tribal management and, consequently, created an ad hoc gender-linked division of labor. The time requirements of fishing, to the contrary, are not said to influence office-holding in Washington State tribes, where fishermen routinely win elections (Miller 1989).

The council women at Katzie do not claim that political work is gender-specific, as council women and other tribal members at Upper Skagit do. Nonetheless, one council woman noted that "women are more sensitive to any kind of issue" and that women are most likely to defend family interests against the outside world. Further, women are more likely to "really go in and fight," which she explained was an attribute that attracted political support. Another noted that "women I admire is someone who can take charge..." and further, that people look for councilors who "will take charge and not be afraid to speak out." The third linked emotion and action: "They say a woman takes it to heart if something happens, we think on both sides. I guess they say its typical to get emotional over an issue and end up sitting there crying, you know, just take it to heart." Women are culturally cast as emotional actors who can rise to the occasion more readily than men in the context of defending the band's interests to the outside world.

By 1991 changes in the composition of the Band due to the establishment of a procedure for outmarrying women to regain Indian status and band membership, under provisions of federal Bill C-31, had not yet significantly altered the political scene, although male and female members of a large and potentially significant family network had returned to the main reserve. However, it is probable that the long-term removal of Native women from band rolls had hampered women's ability to compete politically before 1986.

Upper Skagit

The Upper Skagit reservation is located near Sedro Woolley, Washington, along the Skagit River. There are about 540 members, and almost 200 live on the small, 74-acre reservation. The bulk of the others live in the surrounding Skagit County. The position of hereditary Chief was established sometime before the 1855 Treaty of Point Elliott (Collins 1974) and the all-male council, established about 1915, relied on the chief to select new council members. New councilors were confirmed by acclamation at the annual general tribal meeting. This system was replaced in 1974 by an elected council and a new constitution which enfranchised women.

Upper Skagit is where the most explicit link is made between the culturally defined attributes of women and the requirements of political life. Interview data show that community men and women (but especially women and men other than elders) associate self-control (nonemotional behavior), concern for children, and knowledge of the external culture with women. These traits are closely associated with local notions of ideal political traits, and many men and women assert that women are most suited for political work (Miller 1989).

There *is* an interesting comparison between how Upper Skagit and Katzie people speak of women and politics. In both cases, women are said to be best suited to intervene with the outside world. At Upper Skagit this is linked with self-control and rationality; at Katzie, to an energetic and emotional response to external intrusion. The difference may simply reflect the somewhat longer history of governance at Upper Skagit and the greater elaboration of the tribal bureaucracy.

At Upper Skagit women are more involved than men in tribal politics in significant ways and several trends stand out since 1974: (1) Women run for office at much younger ages, with 46 percent of women who have served on council elected for the first time before age 30, compared to 13 percent for men; (2) Women vote at a higher rate than do men, especially among elders. Women over 58, for example, vote at a rate representing 92 percent of their expected proportional vote, compared to a rate of 56 percent for men over 58; (3) Women actively support women. In 1987 women cast 62 percent of all ballots in the tribal election and reported a preference for female candidates. For these, and other reasons, women have come to dominate council elections, with a stable female majority in the seven-person Council (Miller 1989). Since 1974, the most successful candidates have been family candidates, from family networks large enough to win an election and technocrats.

Upper Skagit has treaty rights to fishing under the terms of the 1855 Treaty of Point Elliott. Treaty fishing is limited to the Skagit River, however, and only gill-netting and dip netting techniques may be employed. The start-up costs are considerable and the fluctuation in the size of the runs and the price paid for fish makes survival as a river gill-netter a difficult proposition (Robbins 1980). Consequently, the relatively stable and large incomes of female technocrats are important in an otherwise poor community, and there is no large source of male income to offset this, as at Lummi. A summary of tribal job holding makes this clear: in 1987, 45 jobs were full-time and twenty more were part-time, with men clustered in the seasonal tribal jobs. Men held outdoor jobs on the fire-crew, wood-crew, box-making crew, tending the salmon pens, and in maintenance. Thirteen women and six non-Native men held the higher-paying, permanent, white-collar technical jobs. These jobs are tribal manager, health services director, tribal planners, fisheries and tribal enterprise managers, community health representatives, and clerical positions (Miller 1989). By 1991, there were 50 full-time employees, of whom 33 were Indian. Twenty-seven of these positions were service staff, indoor jobs, and the vast majority were women (Upper Skagit Indian Tribe General Council Report. January 25, 1992).

As in the British Columbia case, holding "inside" tribal jobs increases one's suitability for the council in several ways. Jobs provide income which can be dispersed within the family network, thereby supporting relatives in ceremonial life and enhancing one's own and the status of one's family. Job holders gain access to information about tribal politics, such as knowledge of jobs, tribal code, fishing and hunting openings, and new programs. Further, workers receive training and experience in skills needed by family members, such as how to obtain and use tribal, state, and federal social and legal services.

Lummi

The Lummi Nation is a larger tribe of about 3100 located near Bellingham, Washington. In recent years the tribal council has been dominated by men who operate the purse seining fleet and thus are able to employ people and provide leadership for relatives (Boxberger 1989). These men are at the center of large, important family networks. Few Lummi women have won elections, but a cohort of women has advanced to leadership in the nonelectoral sphere of government operations with the training provided through federal funding (Miller 1990). Women have fared poorly in elections despite repeated efforts and campaigns aimed at the promotion of the general community welfare (*Squol Quol*, January 25, 1990, the Lummi tribal newspaper). After several years of trying for office a recent successful female candidate described her path to public office, her aspirations, and perhaps worries about the difficulties of getting elected:

Dear Lummi People, Have you heard a rumor lately! One rumor is real—I hope to be on the Lummi Council this year…I've enjoyed many years of serving on Lummi committees and boards, and serving the people through tribal programs. By volunteering and getting job experience, and getting education. I've been learning about Tribal Government. *(Squol Quol* January 25, 1990)

In 1990 the Lummi Nation entered into a phase of the Tribal Self-governance Demonstration Project in which they are directly allocated $2 million of federal money without the oversight of the Bureau of Indian Affairs *(Bellingham Herald,* May 20, 1990). This required that the tribe assume new administrative responsibilities over programs such as Head Start, a preschool program, and the tribal court. The increased control over services has not meant the addition of new ones, and Lummi provided a full array of services to tribal members prior to the Demonstration Project. The long-term effects of this project on community organization are unclear.

At Lummi, it appears that the significance for women's electoral chances of both the stable income associated with tribal management and of institutional completeness itself are overwhelmed by the incomes earned by purse-seiners. What is less clear is why women are not skippers of purse-seine boats. It is possible that it is more difficult for women to gain bank loans to purchase the vessels, and that many talented women who would make able skippers instead go into tribal administration. Historic records indicate that fishing was predominantly, but not solely, a male activity (Suttles 1951). These ideas may be embedded in the differences between sanctioned female dip netting, small scale gill-netting, and set netting on the one hand, and male off-shore purse-seining, on the other.

Discussion

The modern state is said to be predicated upon gender differences (Moore 1988). In the nineteenth and most of the twentieth century, Federal policy and administration has increasingly placed women under the control of men, both formally and informally, and dramatically increased the presence of the state in the lives of Native people on both sides of the Canadian international border. The treaty-making process in Washington State, which involved the selection or acknowledgment of male leaders only, the ideologies and actions of missionaries acting as government officials, the practices of the residential schools, the design of federally imposed post-Indian Reorganization Act tribal governments in the U.S. and Indian Act governments in Canada, and federal policies of allotting land to male-headed households, all have relatively advantaged men and intruded into Indian life (Mitchell and Franklin 1984; Donaldson 1985; Miller 1989; Marino 1990). The penetration of the modern state has had contradictory effects, however, in both increasing control over women and also "engendering" the political (Everett et al. 1989:183), largely unintentionally. Recent events have reversed the pattern of male control over women, even though policy has continued to be intended to be gender-neutral or guided by the assumption that male contributions to the household are primary. While Indians were explicitly intended to be part of the U.S. War on Poverty under the Johnson administration, programs (Prucha 1984:65) such as CETA and Indian Community Action Program (ICAP), which disproportionately benefitted the careers of Coast Salish women, were not directed to women (Miller 1990). Program analysts, in fact, described the high representation of women as a flaw in the programs (Sorkin 1971:131). Local concepts of gender, however, have transformed the state's actions.

Furthermore, state-provided access to education and technical training and tribal jobs are central to the changed circumstances in the lives of some of the women in these Coast Salish communities. Unlike the Navajo (Shepardson 1982; Lamphere 1989), where women's lives have also been altered by the creation of clerical, service, and professional jobs with the tribe, the Bureau of Indian Affairs, and the Indian Health Service, Coast Salish women have translated these new circumstances into formal political success.

Conclusion

In Coast Salish territory the recent political successes of women are tied to the economic opportunity structure available to women in recent years, and the resultant ability of women to either play central roles in family networks or attract a political following by virtue of expertise. This is not to argue for a simple economic determinism, however; there is considerable variation in women's electoral results and local circumstances influence the political meaning of such opportunities. In both Canada and the U.S, women are found to do generally better in smaller tribes, in tribes where there is no disproportionate male income available, and in tribes with a relatively high degree of institutional completeness Women's success is negatively associated with median family income in the U.S. tribes, but this finding could not be tested in Canada. Nonetheless, these variables tell only part of the story and appeals to particulars of tribal history are necessary especially the issue of tribal recognition and the consequent change in tribal government.

There is variation in how political life is linked to attributions of gender. Members of one U.S. tribe associate political life with women, yet, members of another, nearby tribe make no such connection and vote in few women. By contrast, members of a Canadian band have begun to vote in primarily women, but appear to draw no implications for the gender system from this, other than as matter of division of labor. This variability suggests that the access of Coast Salish women to political authority will continue to fluctuate with changes in federal policy and the economy, but also that women act to take advantage of opportunities and to create associations between femininity and political life.

Moore (1988:134) wrote that "One of the more salient features of women's position in society is that they often have political authority, but they frequently lack force, legitimacy and authority." However, Coast Salish women now exercise authority broadly, including the administration of the most economically vital and symbolically important resource of all—to people tied spiritually and symbolically to salmon—the fisheries.

Endnotes

[1] Financial support for this research was provided by a Jacob Javits Fellowship, 1987–89, and by a University of British Columbia H58 grant, 1991. This support is gratefully acknowledged. I thank Brian Foster, Jo-Anne Fiske, and GiGi Weix for their comments on an earlier draft.

[2] Mitchell and Franklin (1984) argue that women did not carry out political roles, but Norton (1985) reports that Northwest Coast women's participation is overlooked.

[3] Miller (1990) shows the importance of training and employment opportunities provided by the War on Poverty for reservation residents and Hansen (1979) for urban Indian women. This is a widely reported development, as noted by Albers (1989). Among the most important of these federal programs for women were the Comprehensive Training and Employment Act (CBTA) and the Indian Community Action Project (ICAP). An example of one such technocrat

council member is Mrs. Jones (a pseudonym), who grew up with the intention of simply working in the home. However, as new opportunities became available under CETA funding she developed clerk-typist skills and gained employment in a new tribal program. Her supervisor, a tribal member, noticed her ability and encouraged her to receive additional training and schooling. Several years later she was selected to fill a vacancy on the council, and then won election in her own right. Eventually she became the head of a multi-million dollar, inter-tribal program.

[4] For details of the role women play in family networks and how they attract a political following, see Miller (1989, 1990). In brief, the core political units of Coast Salish communities are extended family networks whose members are recruited bilaterally and who actively depend on leaders with relatively large and stable incomes. Leaders provide aid and assistance to family members and represent family interests in tribal politics, as part of a larger pattern of reciprocity. The movement of capital through family networks is often enough to enable members to meet ceremonial obligations, keep fishing boats operating, or fuel cars so that people can travel for ceremonial, recreational, or vocational purposes. Men or women standing at the center of these networks are acknowledged as leaders and draw the support of family members when running for the council. Another path to council election is taken by technocrats who are not members of family networks with enough adult voters to support their candidacy, but who draw votes from community members who recognize their contributions and who may wish to defeat candidates from large families. These processes are detailed elsewhere in an analysis of voting patterns (Miller 1992).

[5] The most important of the new economic opportunities for women is tribal employment. Upper Skagit data show that assistance income is not a primary source for individuals or households, in part because of the difficulty of obtaining it. Robbins's (1986) Upper Skagit community survey found that only 7.3 percent of individuals received social security-SSA income, 1.5 percent received public assistance or welfare, and 3.5 percent got unemployment compensation. Additional resources that women control and distribute within their family networks are WIC (Women, Infant, Child) funds provided to meet nutritional needs, and the monthly food packages known as commodities. These packages are Federally funded and administered by the Small Tribes of Western Washington.

[6] Bands are partly enumerated in those cases where some of the band's reserves are too small to report data. Other reserves are excluded because of the high percentage of non-Natives.

References Cited

Ackerman, L. A. 1988. Sexuality Equality on the Colville Indian Reservation. In *Traditional and Contemporary Contexts. Women in Pacific Northwest History: An Anthology*, edited by K. A. Blair, pp. 152–169. Seattle: University of Washington Press.

Albers, P. 1983. Introduction: New Perspectives of Plains Indian Women. In *The Hidden Half: Studies of Plains Indian Women*, edited by P. Albers and B. Medicine, pp. 1–28. Washington, D.C.: University Press of America.

———— 1985. Autonomy and Dependency in the Lives of Dakota Women: A Study in Historical Change. *Review of Radical Political Economics*, 17:109–134.

———— 1989. From Illusion to Illumination: Anthropological Studies of American Indian Women. In *Gender and Anthropology*, edited by S. Morgan, pp. 132–170. Washington, D.C.: American Anthropological Association.

Boxberger, Daniel L. 1989. *To Fish in Common: The Ethnohistory of Lummi Indian Salmon Fishing*. Lincoln: University of Nebraska Press.

Collins, June McCormick. 1974. *Valley of the Spirits: The Upper Skagit Indians of Western Washington*. Seattle: University of Washington Press.

Donaldson, L. C. 1985. Change in Economic Roles of Suquamish Men and Women: An Ethnohistoric Analysis. M.A. thesis, Western Washington University.

Everett, J., K. Staudt, and S. M. Charlton. 1989. Conclusion. In *Women, the State, and Development*, edited by S. M. Charlton, pp. 177–190. Albany: State University of New York Press.

Fiske. J. 1989. Gender and Politics in an Indian Community. Ph.D. dissertation, University of British Columbia.

Green, R. 1980. Native American Women. *Signs*, 6:248–67.

Haeberlin, H., and E. Gunther. 1930. The Indians of Puget Sound. *University of Washington Publications in Anthropology*, 4(1):1–83. Seattle.

Hansen, K. 1979. American Indians and Work in Seattle: Associations, Ethnicity, and Class. Ph.D. dissertation. University of Washington.

Kew, J. E. Michael. 1990. Central and Southern Coast Salish Ceremonies Since 1900. In *Handbook of North American Indians*, Volume 7: *Northwest Coast*, edited by W. Suttles, pp. 476–480. Washington, D.C.: Smithsonian Institution.

Kidwell, C. 1979. The Power of Women in Three American Indian Societies. *Journal of Ethnic Studies*, 6:113–121.

Klein, L. 1976. "She's One of Us, You Know": The Public Life of Tlingit Women: Traditional, Historical, and Contemporary Perspectives. *The Western Canadian Journal of Anthropology*, 6:164–183.

——— 1980. Contending with Colonization: Tlingit Men and Women in Change. In *Women and Colonization: Anthropological Perspectives*, edited by M. Etienne and E. Leacock, pp. 88–108. New York: Praeger.

Knack, M. C. 1989. Contemporary Measures of Southern Paiute Women and the Measurement of Women's Economic and Political Status. *Ethnology*, 28:233–248.

Lamphere, L. 1989. Historical and Regional Variability in Navajo Women's Roles. *Journal of Anthropological Research*, 4:431–456.

Lynch, R. N. 1986. Women in Northern Paiute Politics. *Signs*, 11:352–366.

Marino, C. 1990. History of Western Washington Since 1846. In *Handbook of North American Indians*, Volume 7: *Northwest Coast*, edited by W. Suttles, pp. 169–179. Washington, D.C.: Smithsonian Institution.

Miller, B. G. 1989. A Sociocultural Explanation of the Election of Women to Tribal Office: The Upper Skagit Case. Ph.D. dissertation, Arizona State University.

——— 1990. An Ethnographic View: Positive Consequences of the War on Poverty. *The National Center for American Indian and Alaska Mental Health Research*, 4:55–71.

——— 1992. Tribal Law and Coast Salish Gender Systems. Paper presented at the 45th Annual Northwest Anthropological Conference, April 16, Burnaby, British Columbia. Is There a Gender Gap in American Indian Elections?

Mitchell, M., and A. Franklin. 1984. When You Don't Know the Language, Listen to the Silence: An Historical Overview of Native Indian Women in B.C. In *Not Just Pin Money: Selected Essays on the History of Women's Work in B.C.*, edited by B. K. Latham and R. J. Pazdro, pp. 17–35. Victoria: Camosum College.

178

Mooney, K. 1979. Ethnicity, Economics, the Family Cycle, and Household Composition. *Canadian Review of Sociology and Anthropology*, 16:387–403.

Moore, H. L. 1988. *Feminism and Anthropology*. Minneapolis: University of Minnesota Press.

Newland, K. 1975. Women in Politics: A Global Perspective. *Worldwatch Paper*, 3.

Norton. H. H. 1985. Women and Resources of the Northwest Coast: Documentation from the 18th and Early 19th Centuries. Ph.D. dissertation. University of Washington.

Porter, P. W. 1990. In Search of Recognition: Federal Policy and the Landless Tribes of Western Washington. *American Indian Quarterly*, 14:113–132.

Powers, M. 1986. *Oglala Women: Myth, Ritual, and Reality*. Chicago: University of Chicago Press.

Prucha, F. P. 1984. *The Great Father*: *The United States Government and the American Indians*. Lincoln: University of Nebraska Press.

Rix, S. E. 1987. *The American Woman 1987–1988: A Report in Depth*. New York: Norton.

Roberts, N. A. 1975. A History of the Swinomish Tribal Community. Ph.D. dissertation, University of Washington.

Robbins, L. 1980. Upper Skagit Fishing Households: Location, Composition and Multiple-Family Cooperation. Ms. prepared for the Upper Skagit Tribal Council.

——— 1986. Community Survey. Ms. prepared for the Upper Skagit Tribal Council.

Ruby, R. H., and J. A. Brown 1986. *A Guide to the Indian Tribes on the Pacific Northwest*. Norman. University of Oklahoma Press.

Shepardson, M. 1982. The Status of Navajo Women. *American Indian Quarterly*, 6:149–169.

Silverblatt, L. 1991. Interpreting Women in the State: New Feminist Ethnohistories. In *Gender at the Crossroads of Knowledge*, edited by M. di Leonardo, pp. 140–174. Berkeley: University of California Press.

Skagit System Cooperative Report. 1980. Ms. in Upper Skagit Tribal Archives.

Smith, M. 1940. The Puyallup-Nisqually. *Columbia University Contributions to Anthropology*, 32. New York.

Sorkin, A. 1971. *American Indians and Federal Aid*. Washington D.C.: Brookings Institute.

Suttles, W. 1951. Economic Life of the Coast Salish of Haro and Rosario Straits. Ph.D. dissertation, University of Washington.

Suttles, W., and B. Lane. 1990. Southern Coast Salish. In *Handbook of North American Indians*, Volume 7, *Northwest Coast*, edited by W. Suttles, pp. 48–502. Washington, D.C.: Smithsonian Institution.

Verble, S., editor. 1981. *Words of Today's American Indian Women: Ohoyo Makachi*. Washington, D.C.: U.S. Department of Education.

Journal of Northwest Anthropology, Memoir 12:179–199 (2016)

11

Contemporary Tribal Codes and Gender Issues*

This paper makes three related points: first, that many of the present-day legal codes of U.S. Indian tribes are unexpectedly innovative and representative of contemporary indigenous view points, especially in the ways in which individual rights are conceived; second, that the variability in the way the codes treat issues of special concern to women demonstrates the extent of the imprint of local tribal people on their own codes; and third, that analysis of the implications of tribal codes for Indian women is a valuable and hitherto undeveloped avenue in clarifying women's circumstances. I address these points by comparing the categories of code that eight western Washington tribes have created and by looking at a set of legal issues that particularly influence women's lives. This essay is intended as a preliminary effort to make use of legal materials in the analysis of contemporary Coast Salish life.[1] The codes of these eight tribes vary in their overall emphases, in their legal treatment of family networks, in the rights of parents, and in attention given to women's issues generally.

In 1985, William Rodman commented that legal innovation in small-scale societies "is a topic so few anthropologists have studied that a summary of relevant sources takes only a few paragraphs"; he noted further that "[l]egal scholars use 'innovation' exclusively to denote changes that the state introduces, never changes that local people make of their own accord..." (Rodman 1985). Rodman correctly argued that the trend towards "legal centralism" (a state-centered view of the law and an emphasis on the coercive nature of the state have made it difficult to perceive indigenous legal innovation. Further, Vincent (1990) wrote that the anthropology of law has turned to the study of historical legal change "in the guise of legal pluralism," thereby resurrecting diffusionist theory and diverting attention from local developments.

The study of tribal law and legal innovation among native North Americans appears to be similarly burdened. What little is written about Indian legal systems suggests co-option by the mainstream political system of tribal governments (under whose authority tribal legal systems are developed) and a disproportionate influence of the non-native legal system through the importation of legal language (or "boilerplate") (Weber 1982; Matsuda 1988; O'Brien 1989; Fleras and Elliot 1992). Barsh and Henderson (1976), for example, argued that the procedural codes of tribal courts are forced for financial reasons into conformity with model codes derived from those followed in federally administered Bureau of Indian Affairs (BIA) courts. These model codes, they reason, are built on a "police idea" of law and order, with little civil code. Through this process, Barsh and Henderson conclude, the state works to limit the scope of Indian law and sets Indians against their own government. O'Brien's view of contemporary Indian law exemplifies this approach:

> When tribes started replacing the Code of Federal Regulations with their own codes, few had the expertise or the resources to do a professional job of establishing new tribal laws. As a result the codes in operation on many reservations today look much like the federal code they replaced: they are outdated, Anglo-oriented, and poorly reflective of tribal philosophy and culture. (O'Brien 1989)

*Authored by Bruce Granville Miller. Reprinted from the *American Indian Culture and Research Journal*, Volume 18, Number 2, by permission of the American Indians Studies Center, UCLA. © 1994 Regents of the University of California.

One analyst recently addressed the issue of how women are faring in tribal courts but started from the unstated assumption that women are unable to exercise political power in tribal communities and that, consequently, women's only remedy for a male bias in tribal codes and courts was through the intervention of a reworked Indian Civil Rights Act. This work includes virtually no analysis of tribal codes themselves (Christofferson 1991).

Although there are sizable literatures on the topics of federal, state, and provincial laws concerning Indian people, and on customary law, little literature exists concerning the law that applies in Indian courts. The analysis of a 1978 publication of the American Bar Foundation still holds true:

> There is a wealth of literature, including "legal" literature, on Indian matters, but it rarely deals with contemporary issues. Apart from a few short pieces dealing mainly with the theory rather than practices, there is no legal literature on the present-day tribal court system. Instead the bulk of it concerns jurisdictional issues and treaty rights or land or water use....In addition, there are studies with an anthropological focus—typically, historical quests to uncover the traditional "law-ways" of selected tribes....Practically the only works that deal specifically with the contemporary tribal court system are the reports of the Senate Hearings on the Constitutional Rights of the American Indian (Hearings before the Subcomm. on Constitutional Rights of the Senate Comm. on the Judiciary, 87th Cong., 1st sess., 89th Cong., 1st sess. [1961–65])[2]

The emphasis on understanding Indian codes from the perspective of Indian-white power relations, while necessary, places the analytic frame outside the Indian communities and has the unfortunate result of causing the contents of the codes to be overlooked. Although analysis of tribal law is now overdue, there is still the chance to examine the contemporary tribal code while it is in its infancy, to understand the forces internally acting on its creation and development, and to gain an understanding of the direction the law is headed (Miller 1993).

Tribal codes are best understood as innovative and responsive to highly localized circumstances, variable from tribe to tribe. If nothing else, tribal codes are not simply boilerplate, although on cursory examination they may appear to be so. Even in those cases where code is imported from the mainstream system, it is often quickly adapted to local circumstances. In part because these codes are so recent (as described below), they are still relatively uncluttered and the discernible products of individuals and can be thought of, with due caution, as road maps for the visions of political and other leaders for the future of their communities.[3] Perhaps most significantly, many contemporary tribal leaders and tribal councils have found their own balance points between collective and individual rights, a balance that varies considerably between tribes.[4]

More specifically, for several reasons, analysis of the legal codes provides new leverage that is helpful in understanding multiple dimensions of the gender systems operant in reservation communities. First, the new codes crystallize, for the moment, issues that communities have heretofore struggled over and have often left unresolved. Second, the laws themselves have a direct, immediate impact on the behavior and lives of women and men. Third, as is true of legal systems elsewhere, embedded in these new systems are notions of what it means to be male and female. The laws create male and female "legal statuses"—statuses that themselves come to influence how community members construct gender and organize gender relations (Menkel-Meadow and Diamond 1991). Finally, the codes regulate issues thought to be generally of concern to women, including violence towards women and children, divorce, spousal support, inheritance and ownership of real property, responsibility for children and elders, custody, access to positions of public authority, access to tribal membership, the availability of social and other services, and so on.

The Study

This study is built around interviews with tribal code writers and tribal councilors and a reading of the published codes of eight small Coast Salish tribes in northern Washington State, which range in size from about three hundred to three thousand enrolled members (Johnson 1981) In 1979, the tribes participated in creating the Northwest Intertribal Court System (NICS), which provides judicial services for the member tribes, including supplying the judge, but each tribe maintains its own laws. One of the eight tribes, Lummi, is no longer a member of the NICS. The NICS is described in more detail below.

The eight Coast Salish tribes (Nisqually, Lummi, Skokomish, Sauk-Suiattle, Upper Skagit, Tulalip, Muckleshoot, Nooksack) are situated in close proximity to metropolitan centers, and members live both on the small reservations and in the nearby cities and towns. Many members of the eight tribes live traditional religious and ceremonial lives, engage in subsistence harvests of shellfish, plants, and other materials, and participate in the regional system of social relations. Although tribal members participate in the local economy, all eight tribes place a heavy emphasis on the commercial salmon harvest. Perhaps most germane to this study is that communities are themselves organized into competing, temporal family networks. Family leaders, both men and women, help coordinate family economic activities, including fishing, provide for the sharing of resources and labor, and help in the arrangement of the ceremonial and spiritual life of the members of the family network. Family networks typically create voting blocs in tribal elections, and the legal regulation of these units is a critical issue (Miller 1992).

Historical Background

Customary Law and the Tribal Court System

Customary law in the Coast Salish region employed a range of sanctions to control behavior and restore communities in the event of a breach. These sanctions included restitution, ostracism, social pressures, and even violent recrimination (NICS n.d.; Miller 1993). Public ceremonies were (and continue to be) carried out in the process of the public debate and resolution of conflicts. The region has been characterized by a cultural emphasis on the avoidance of conflict through proper training in the absence of coercive authority (see the NICS report [n.d.] for a fuller treatment of the topic). After several decades of contact with Europeans and Americans in the nineteenth century; new concepts of political organization, leadership, and law developed. For example, a mid-nineteenth-century Skagit innovator, Slabebtkud, organized loosely affiliated villages and imposed rule based on coercion. He established a system of subchiefs who enforced new, Christian influenced concepts through the threat of incarceration in stocks (Sampson 1972; Collins 1974).

In 1883, the U.S. Bureau of Indian Affairs (BIA) authorized the creation of Courts of Indian Offenses (CFR courts) for reservation people in order to fill a perceived leadership void following an apparent decline in traditional authority and to diminish the residual authority of traditional chiefs (Burnett 1972; Johnson and Paschal 1991). The BIA exercised great authority over this court system, selecting the police and judges and promulgating the rules and procedures. BIA authority over this court system was diminished with the Indian Reorganization Act of 1934. Tribes were encouraged to establish governments and court systems modeled on those of the dominant society, although the BIA is said to have simply imposed its own bylaws on "tribes... ill-prepared for self-government" (Burnett 1972:565). Later, particularly during the termination period of the 1950s when federal policy aimed at ending trust relationship between tribes and the federal government, little money was available for tribal legal systems (Burnett 1972:590; Johnson and Paschal 1991:3).

In the 1970s, federal policy again produced contradictory effects on Indian courts. The new federal policy of encouraging tribal self-determination was accompanied by the efforts of tribes with independent courts and those with CFR courts to rewrite their codes for their own ends. However, the Indian Civil Rights Act of 1968 imposed most of the federal Bill of Rights on tribes, thereby reducing self-governance and imposing new requirements on tribal courts. For example, it became unlawful for a tribal government, without a jury trial, to enact a law that imposes punishment (Johnson and Paschal 1991:3). The passage of the Self-Determination Act of 1976 required that further regulations be adopted. In some cases, specific provisions must be contained in tribal law so that jurisdiction can be obtained (i.e., provisions for the detention of criminals, specific provisions for recourse under the law) or so that funding requirements can be fulfilled. Today tribal courts, CFR courts, and traditional dispute settlement institutions all still exist in Indian Country.

The Northwest Intertribal Court System

The Northwest Intertribal Court System, a judicial services consortium, was established in 1979 following the fishing litigation *(US* v. *Washington,* 384 F Supp. 312, 1974) that held that the treaties of the mid-nineteenth century gave Indians of Washington State half the salmon catch in state waters. The ruling created a need for fish and game codes and a venue to adjudicate violations. The NICS courts exercise general jurisdiction over tribal members, as limited by the tribal code and constitution and by federal law. In the case of Upper Skagit, for example, NICS courts hold jurisdiction over civil, traffic, fisheries, and some elements of criminal domains for both Indians and non-Indians. The tribal council is responsible for passing tribal code and is assisted in its work by hired code writers and by suggestions from the community itself. In some cases, tribal councils have created formal advisory boards to advise the code writers. There is, as yet, limited development of case law.

Court is convened on the Upper Skagit reservation once a month, or more often if needed, at the community center on the reservation near Sedro Woolley, Washington. The court staff includes one part-time clerk and one part-time deputy prosecutor. NICS provides the other personnel, most notably the judge. In this case, the source of the law is the tribal constitution, approved in 1974 and amended in 1977, and customary law. The tribal code may "codify or refer to customary practices. The sitting judge may also have discretion to consider and apply custom in individual cases" (Johnson and Paschal 1991:37). In fiscal year 1990, the Upper Skagit court, which serves 540 tribal members, heard 43 criminal cases and 15 civil cases, NICS data (which does not include Lummi, the largest of the tribes) give some measure of court activity, The data show that, in 1990, the court heard 147 criminal cases (ranging from 8 to 43 per tribe, with a mean of 21) and 21 civil cases (with a range from 0 to 15; six of the seven tribes had no civil litigation).[5]

The formal court system is thought to be used as a last resort after a variety of informal mechanisms have been exhausted, especially in the case of intrafamily disputes.[6] In one case, for example, the NICS judge ordered a young married couple to "work out their problems" after a restraining order was brought against the husband at the suggestion of tribal social service staff. Interfamily disputes, public disorder, fishing violations, and vandalism are more likely to end up in court than intrafamily problems. For these reasons, court hears more criminal cases than civil. There is, so far, a limited infrastructure of lawyers versed in tribal law to help bring civil action in the NICS court, and the formal court system is not easily accessible to ordinary people. In addition, the NICS prosecutors are frequently non-Indian and nonresident and must work with police reports, thereby making the application of nonjudicial remedies more difficult. Also, the presence of non-Indian tribal police, who are largely unaware of community processes, produces a formal treatment of cases and increases use of the courts.[7] These features of the legal system, by their very nature, exacerbate the alienation that some people feel from their own community institutions and make protection of the rights of the relatively powerless, including some women, difficult, especially in establishing civil litigation.

Underlying the tribal system of laws is the system of law enforcement. According to Upper Skagit records, in 1991 officers were on active duty patrol 16.9 percent of hours, a total of 1,478 hours, compared to the 2,551 in 1990.[8] However, 55 cases involving violations of tribal laws and ordinances were logged in 1991 compared to 87 in 1990. Of the 155 offenses, 86 involved adults, and 52 of these were alcohol related. Forty-six incidents involved juveniles; 22 of these were alcohol related. Subsequently, 13 adult males, 5 adult females, and 4 each of juvenile boys and girls were referred to the NICS prosecutor. The offenses are categorized in Table 10.

TABLE 10. OFFENSES, UPPER SKAGIT 1990–1991*

Category	1990	1991
	[n=87]	[n=155]
Mixed	5.7%	5.8%
Property	12.6%	8.4%
Public Order	35.6%	37.4%
Offenses Against Persons	19.5%	13.5%
Other Offenses	26.4%	34.8%

*Source: 1991 Upper Skagit Tribal Police FY91 Activities Report, 25 January 1992.

The NICS and Upper Skagit data conform to the generalization that a high volume of cases of alcohol-related crimes against persons are brought in tribal court (Brakel 1979). Crimes against persons are often offenses against family and children, and these data point to the importance of tribal code for women.

Legal Statuses

The eight sets of tribal codes and constitutions create complex, overlapping systems of legal statuses, about which some generalizations can be made. Men and women are treated by the codes as undifferentiated individuals with entitlements (interests in community-held resources of various sorts). These legally distinct individuals are restrained in their interests by two other sets of interests, those of the tribe and also, in limited ways, the rights of family networks. Secondly, men and women are legally members (citizens) of the tribe (and, separately, of the community and, as such, are entitled to residence in Indian Country and to shares in community assets (such as fisheries resources, education programs, Indian Health Service care, and reservation housing). Community membership alone does not confer these entitlements. Thirdly, in most codes, men and women have legal standing as extended family (or family network) members. As such, in some tribes people are entitled to make claims to fishing locations (under customary provisions of use-rights) and hold rights to oversight of the children of the family network. In addition, the law places restrictions on citizens on the basis of kinship affiliations, which overlap in various ways with membership in corporate, temporal family networks. For example, several of the codes restrict individuals from running for office in the event a relative is a council incumbent. Finally, people are legally parents, with an array of parental rights and obligations.

The various legal statuses an individual may occupy are not fully compatible (in part because of the long history of federal policy and court rulings that have imposed and reconstructed concepts of membership), a circumstance that leads to significant disagreement in the communities. Some people residing on the reservations are legally members of the community but not members of the tribe. (Some are legally members of other tribes; others are non-Indians.) A further complication is that some nontribal members who are resident on the reservation are family network members and hold legal rights as such. They may, for example, have priority in adoption or in provisions for the care of family network children, or may have legal rights to attend family-sponsored ceremonial events while incarcerated. (The jurisdictional complexities of Indians who are not members of the tribe in whose territory they reside are not yet resolved and have been complicated by *Duro* v. *Reina,* 495 U.S. 676, 1990, and subsequent legislation; Quinn 1993).

These incompatible statuses give rise to role conflict. A debate arose recently on one reservation, for example, over whether community members who were not tribal members were entitled to treaty fishing rights, a vital resource. Tribal council members split over this issue by sex, with three women arguing to allow these community men to keep fishing (and thereby provisioning Indian family members and three council men arguing against granting permission. In this case, women's status as tribal members was in conflict with their role in provisioning family members. Table 11 summarizes the primary generalizable legal statuses that individuals occupy, and the associated legal entitlements.

The legal codes differentiate on the basis of age and other criteria. Legal minors are distinguished from adults in a variety of ways. Voting for public office is a privilege available to tribal members over 18; children are restricted from fishing and hunting (with some exceptions when supervised); and, in some cases, children's movements are restricted by curfews. But some of the codes (Skokomish, Tulalip, Upper Skagit, Nooksack, Muckleshoot) allow for the formal age requirements of adulthood to be set aside under certain circumstances. In two of the codes (Skokomish, Tulalip), children can be emancipated when acting as a household head—a circumstance of special importance to females, who frequently begin families in their early teens and who assume responsibility for the provisioning of their offspring (Miller 1989). Emancipation releases minors from restrictions on fishing or hunting by virtue of age.

Adult men and women also assume secondary legal statuses as owners of real property, as heirs to the property of others within the community, as members of a regulated community that provides rights to safety and comfort, as voters and potential tribal councilors, as official tribal committee members, and as jury members or witnesses. The implications of each of these legal status are somewhat different for men than for women, as indicated below.

TABLE 11. LEGAL STATUSES

Legal Status	Key Legal Entitlements
1. Minor	Some rights to participate in customary practice
2. Adult (as defined by activity)/emancipate minor	Fishing, hunting, voting rights
3. Kinfolk	Limitations imposed (nepotism rules)
4. Parent	Limited rights to control of offspring
5. Household head	Emancipation, rights to resources (if tribal member)
6. Community member	Residence, some services
7. Family network member	Some rights regarding children some customary resource use-rights
8. Tribal member	Vote, office-holding, rights to collective resources, jobs

Regional Generalization

Analysis of the Subject Index of Tribal Codes

The codes of the eight tribes vary in their inclusiveness, due in part to the variation in institutional completeness of tribal governments and in the range of services provided. But the raw fact that tribal governments have enacted codes in some areas and not others reflects the interests and specializations of these governments. Table 12 displays the content of the tribal codes by heading.

These data can be comprehended by grouping the codes, thereby allowing for a very rough measure of the interests and intentions of particular tribes. The codes are grouped in Table 13.

Once categorized, raw counts in each of the four categories for each tribe can be computed, giving a picture of the emphases of the tribal councils, under whose authority codes are created. Table 14 presents these results.

Briefly, these data show the divergence among the codes. Lummi has the most comprehensive code (sixteen areas), with code in all four areas categorized as "Peace and Safety." The Upper Skagit and Muckleshoot codes are second and third most complete, respectively (ten and nine areas), and well-developed in the areas peace and safety. On the other extreme, the Tulalip and Nooksack codes focus on economic development and regulation. The Tulalip code is silent on issues of peace and safety, and Nooksack nearly so (one area). The Nisqually code is by far the least developed of the eight (code in two areas) and contains little concerning peace and safety. The Sauk-Suiattle code is also relatively unelaborated (six areas) but has code in two of the peace and safety areas. The analysis thus far shows somewhat roughly the differing emphases between the tribes' codes. The next step is to look more closely at how the codes treat issues particularly relevant to women's lives.

TABLE 12. SUBJECT INDEX OF TRIBAL CODES

Subject	Tribe							
	Lummi	Muckleshoot	Nisqually	Nooksack	Sauk-Suiattle	Skokomish	Tulalip	Upper Skagit
Administration	X							
Building	X						X	
Business		X		X		X	X	
Domestic Relations	X				X			
Elections					X			X
Enroll/member					X	X		X
Exclusion	X	X	X		X			X
Fish/Hunt	X			X		X		X
Gaming	X			X				
Housing	X	X		X		X		X
Juvenile/children	X	X		X		X		X
Labor/employ	X							
Tenant	X			X				
Liquor/tobacco	X	X		X				
Natural resources					X	X		
Probate	X							
Sentence			X					
Tax		X		X		X		X
Traffic		X				X		X
Tribal Enterprise								X
Utilities					X			X
Water								
Zoning		X					X	

TABLE 13. CATEGORIES OF LEGAL CODES*

Category	Type of Code
A. Economic Development	Business, fish, gaming, natural resources, enterprise, tax
B. Regulation	Building, housing, landlord/tenant, probate, sentencing, utilities, water, zoning, liquor
C. Peace and Safety	Domestic relations, juvenile, exclusion, traffic
D. Governance/Politics	Administration, elections, enrollment, labor

*Laws concerning exclusion from the reservation are included in category C because they have most to do with public safety, ordinarily the only grounds on which nonmembers may be excluded.

TABLE 14. EMPHASES OF TRIBAL CODES—RAW SCORES

Tribe	Type				
	A. Econ. Dev.	B. Regulation	C. Safety	D. Govern.	Totals
Lummi	3	7	4	2	16
Muckleshoot	3	3	3	0	9
Nisqually	0	1	1	0	2
Nooksack	4	3	1	0	8
Sauk-Suiattle	1	1	2	2	6
Skokomish	4	1	2	0	7
Tulalip	2	2	0	1	5
Upper Skagit	3	2	3	2	10
Totals	20	20	16	7	63

Legal Codes and Gender Issues

Inheritance

Here the focus is on a subset of particular legal issues important to understanding women's circumstances. The first such issue is inheritance. Generally, tribal codes follow state law in matters of property inheritance, but there are some important exceptions, especially in areas that state law does not cover. One such exception is the issue of the inheritance of traditional resource procurement stations, particularly along waterways. The eight tribes vary significantly in how this issue is treated. At Skokomish and Upper Skagit, these rights are directly embedded in the code, along with provisions for the reallocation of fishing stations in the event of abandonment of the site. Since traditional fisheries resource use-rights are primarily inherited patrilineally (with the exception of female-set net sites), the pattern of inheritance favors men who can control the disposition of the grounds. With the loss of tribal land to white settlers in the nineteenth century, women have lost control of gathering grounds, the primary female-controlled resource. The Lummi, Sauk-Suiattle, Muckleshoot, and Tullalip codes are silent on this issue, and traditional use-rights are not protected legally.

A second exception to the institution of the mainstream society's patterns of inheritance is the section of the Lummi code that concerns spousal relations. Title II of the Domestic Relations Act, 11.3.01, specifies,

> Property and pecuniary rights of the husband before marriage and that acquired by him afterwards by gift, bequest, devise or descent, with the rents, issues, and profits thereof, shall not be subject to the debts or contracts of his wife, and he may manage, lease, sell, convey, encumber as fully to the same effect as though he were unmarried…

Section 11.3.02 provides the same terms for the wife.[9] In the case of the other tribes, state law obtains concerning spousal legal obligations. The Lummi code, however conforms to the aboriginal practice of the separation of the property of spouses at the time of divorce or death and to have divorce easy and protecting the critical connections between sibling sets and family networks. The code may have the additional effects of protecting the interests of Indians from non-Indian spouses and of preventing the alienation of extremely valuable property—purse seine boats—from male owners at the time of divorce.[10]

Although inheritance of material objects at the time of death had not been an important practice among Puget Sound Salish, with many items distributed to people beyond the immediate family and household, valuable incorporeal objects were traditionally inherited (Collins 1974). Indian names and control of resource procurement sites are among the most important (Smith 1941). The effect of the new pattern of inheritance, with the exception of Lummi, is to narrow the claims women may make as sisters and senior members within family networks (with important influence over the disposition of family possessions and the labor of kin) and to reinforce their position as wives and mothers, with primary inheritance coming from a spouse rather than a brother, sister, or parent. In practice, this may be an advantage or a disadvantage for individual women (some women have benefited through amassing large land holdings through consecutive marriages to short-lived men). But, on balance, these inheritance patterns, although gender neutral in appearance, have differential impact. Modern inheritance practices reinforce the subordination of women to male cohouseholders (affinal relatives) and deemphasizes women's potential for superordination as senior members of a corporate family group.

Regulation of Work

A second important domain of the law concerns the regulation of work. Four of the tribal codes (Upper Skagit, Tulalip, Nisqually, Muckleshoot) contain specific provisions under the tribal bill of rights for equal access by individuals to economic resources and programs of the tribe. Of the eight, the Upper Skagit code is the most focused on the issue of safeguarding the rights of workers to gain access to tribal jobs and protecting them from harassment while working. Both provisions are crucial for women because, at Upper Skagit, as at the majority of Coast Salish tribal and band offices, the bulk of tribal employees are female (Miller 1989, 1992). The Upper Skagit bill of rights provides economic rights to individuals that are not accorded to family networks. The code protects individuals from criticism by community members in the conduct of their work. Chapter 6 of the Law and Order Code (6.530—Verbal Threat to Public Officials) specifies, "Any person, who shall, when speaking to a public official, including a council member, employee, judge, prosecutor or other public official threaten such person with an act of violence or otherwise try to influence an official act by means of a verbal threat shall be guilty of an offense..." Similar language is used in two other places to prohibit threats to officials and employees. These provisions were created with the expressed purpose of providing a work place free of disruption by factionalized conflict and to ensure a productive community.[11] The effect is to provide for safety in a work place occupied largely by women. Several tribal codes contain references to threats against officials (judges, police, or elected officials) but, significantly; not rank-and-file tribal employees. These include Lummi, Muckleshoot, and Nooksack. There is no such language in the Skokomish, Tulalip, and Nisqually codes, leaving employees without special legal protection from harassment.

Finally, the Tulalip code contains provisions aimed at increasing employment on the reservation. Ordinance 61 charters a "Tulalip Construction Company" and provides for educational activities designed to furnish training in jobs related to the construction industry. These provisions appear to favor male employment as an issue of tribal policy, since the Coast Salish construction work force is overwhelmingly male (Miller 1992).

Political Enfranchisement

Political enfranchisement of women and replacement of postcontact male quasijudicial bodies by the system of tribal courts and codes are areas of the law with significant impact on women's lives. For example, the all-male Elder's Council that adjudicated community issues and established sanctions for transgressors among the Sauk-Suiattle of the postcontact period is now replaced by the court system (NICS n.d.). Sauk-Suiattle women may now influence the direction of the legal community through election to the council or participation on advisory committees.

Similarly prior to the creation of a constitution in 1974, Upper Skagit women were disenfranchised from the formal political system, although individual women maintained significant influence in the community (Collins 1974; Miller 1992). The system of selection of tribal councilors left women out: Sitting councilors, under the direction of the chair, nominated candidates who were then ratified by the general membership of the tribe through a process of acclamation. Women served as nonvoting secretaries and treasurers on the council (Miller 1989). Immediately after enfranchisement, women ran for public office and, by the 1980s, regularly won the majority of seats. No legal barriers have been posed for women in voting, and, in fact, women control the process of establishing eligibility to vote through tribal membership. Strong evidence suggests that many community members now associate femininity with political life, a rapid transformation of gender ideology (Miller 1989). The changes in the constitution altered the nature of women's citizenship and their access to politically important institutions. Women are now full participants as voters and councilors, as well as jury members and members of tribal committees.

Child Care Responsibilities

Another significant area of legal activity has been the creation of laws regulating the behavior of children on the reservation and the associated definition of parental obligations. Ordinarily, children are most closely associated with women, who perform the bulk of child care. For many women, child-care responsibilities begin as a preteen looking after younger siblings. Many, although not all, women continue to carry out child care through young adulthood and into grandmotherhood. Laws affecting the behavior of children, then, differentially affect women and the organization of their daily lives. The creation of penalties for parental negligence, including fines and possible loss of custody, has been a hotly contested issue, with different resolutions on different reservations. Some men on the Upper Skagit reservation have employed a discourse of traditionality, arguing that strict guidelines for the behavior of children violate traditional cultural values by failing to recognize the autonomy of children and by rejecting cultural patterns of reliance on a network of relatives to ensure that children come to no harm. This argument holds that requiring parents alone to oversee the behavior of children releases other men and women from their duties toward related children. Despite these claims, Upper Skagit code has moved toward defining parental obligations to include both parents and to exclude extended family members, and towards requiring that children be protected from their own actions and the actions of other people. Code therefore may redefine the concept of childhood by moving away from emphasis on children's personal autonomy and on oversight by the extended family.[12]

Chapter 3 of the Upper Skagit Children's Code provides for termination of parental rights in the event of abandonment; willful, repeated physical abuse that creates a substantial risk of death; sexual abuse; or consent of both parents. Chapter 5 of the same code provides for guardians to be appointed for minors, with no rights for family network members. Upper Skagit has also enacted a series of codes designed to protect children's rights, each of which imposes burdens on parents. Chapter 5.110 of the law and order code forbids leaving children under ten years of age unattended in a car; 6.160 forbids desertion and nonsupport of a child; and, significantly, 6.130 specifies that "[a]ny person who, lacking the legal right to do so, interferes with another's custody of a child shall be guilty of an offense..." This last is the clause that most effectively removes children from the oversight of extended family members (that is, extended family involvement without the consent of the parent). Finally, the fishing ordinance forbids those under eighteen from fishing during school hours unless holding a GED (high school equivalency) certificate.

Other tribes' codes regulate the behavior of children but do not specify the legal obligations of both parents even in those cases where the obligations are spelled out. Since women are more likely to have custody of children, this appears to create a burden for women but not men. Sauk-Suiattle and Skokomish, in particular, have created legal structures concerning children and care responsibilities that are quite different from those of Upper Skagit. Section 1.4.060 of the Sauk-Suiattle Family Code contains the broadest possible definition of extended family membership in the context of provisions for responsibility for youth. This definition reads as follows:

Extended Family Member: a person who has reached the age of eighteen years, or who is of sufficient maturity to care for a child, and who is the Indian youth's grandparent, aunt or uncle, brother or sister, brother-in-law or sister-in-law, niece or nephew, first or second cousin, or step-parent, and any other person who is considered a family member under tribal law or custom; a non-Indian relative who is an accepted member of the Sauk-Suiattle Indian community and would be considered a member by tribal custom shall also be considered part of the youth's extended family...

Elsewhere (Family Code 3.1.010), the Sauk-Suiattle code specifies that termination of parental rights is not permissible under any circumstances and that the "supportive network of extended family..." as defined above, is to provide care. Family Code 2.1.010 mentions "raising another person's child" as a customary alternative that does not terminate parental rights and as not necessarily indicating a need for legal "care action." Family Code 3.2.110 specifies that extended family members are preferred in the appointment of guardians for youth. The Law and Order Code, section 5.035, establishes a curfew forbidding children under fourteen from appearing "on the streets, highways, roads, or other public places without responsible adult supervision between the hours of 10 PM and 6 AM," placing the burden on the parent or guardian. In addition, Sauk-Suiattle has ordinances (Law and Order Code 5.110), identical to those of Upper Skagit, forbidding leaving children under the age of ten unattended in a car and concerning desertion and nonsupport (6.160).

For both Upper Skagit and Sauk-Suiattle, the new codes place heavy responsibilities on adults for the protection and support of children. In the former case, the responsibility rests strictly with the parents, and ordinarily this means the mother. Other family members are not only not legally responsible but are explicitly excluded from entitlement. In the latter case, a wider range of kinfolk are entitled to intervene in the lives of children.

Parental Rights and the Establishment of Paternity

A closely related and critical domain for understanding women's and men's legal status is that of parental rights. Once again there is tremendous variation in how these issues are handled. The codes range from not incorporating this category of law at all (Tulalip), or including few specifics (Nooksack recognizes termination of parental rights and calls for the placement of children with extended family members, where possible), to complex efforts to define paternity and to create legal obligations to testify in court about paternity (Muckleshoot).

A few generalizations may be made. Most of the codes either state explicitly or imply that parental rights are considered individually; that is, either a father or a mother may have such rights terminated (Lummi, Upper Skagit, Muckleshoot, and Nooksack specifically allow for termination), although in Sauk-Suiattle termination is explicitly rejected. Mothers are thereby able to assume sole custody in the event of the unsuitability of the father. Most of the codes specify that children must be supported, leaving open the prosecution of delinquent parents, ordinarily fathers. These circumstances, although gender-neutral on the surface, provide some legal protection for women's relationships with their minor offspring.

A related issue is where provisions for child support are placed within the code. Particular problems arise where child support is handled under criminal law. In these cases, the police must decide whether to pursue the issue (a serious problem in light of police understaffing); criminal convictions depend on a higher burden of proof than civil cases, thereby increasing the difficulty of obtaining legal relief and getting child support; and a criminal conviction carries a stigma and may actually make it difficult for a man to obtain a job and carry out his legal and financial obligations. Beyond these points, the codes diverge.

The Muckleshoot code is unique in its remarkable emphasis on the question of establishing paternity. Parenthood is defined through biology or adoption, except that the legal status of parenthood is not extended to a father whose paternity is not established by the court, through public records, or acknowledged by him. This places an obligation on the mother to take the father to court to prove his fatherhood and establish his legal responsibilities to his child. However, a legal mechanism exists to establish paternity, regardless of the marital status of the mother and alleged father. A second clause creates additional problems for women: Any person who has sexual intercourse on the reservation thereby places himself or herself under the jurisdiction of the tribal court with respect to any resulting children. This potentially places a very difficult, almost unmanageable, burden on women to establish jurisdiction and resolve issues of child support. Evidence regarding paternity can be taken from statistical probabilities, medical or anthropological evidence, or, simply, reputation in the community concerning paternity. Furthermore, a presumption of paternity is made if the mother and the purported father are married and the child is born within three hundred days of termination of the relationship; if they cohabited or attempted to marry by state or tribal custom and the child is born within three hundred days; or, finally, if the child is under eighteen and the purported father receives the child in his home and "openly holds the child as his to the community." The last provision appears to allow for establishment of paternity under conditions adverse to the interests of the mother, while simultaneously making it difficult to establish paternity when the man wishes to avoid it. In addition, no provisions are included to compel a father (or mother) to make child support payments. Despite the problems, the focus of the Muckleshoot code is not to enfranchise extended family members—provisions useful for men who wish to place the burden for child care elsewhere—but rather to create a mechanism, albeit a difficult one, to place legal obligations on fathers. Furthermore, the Muckleshoot law deals with nonsupport in the civil, not criminal, sections of the code.

The Sauk-Suiattle code provides no rights for the unmarried father whose paternity is not established or acknowledged. This code does not clarify who must make the acknowledgment, and the implications vary considerably if the testimony of the mother, father, either, or some third party is sufficient to establish paternity. Nonsupport, neglect, or desertion of children is handled within the criminal code.

The Nisqually code adds another, quite significant, twist (and burden to women) by limiting tribal membership to the children of women who are resident in the community at the time of birth. Women who are mobile for employment or other reasons thus jeopardize their offsprings' tribal membership, a hardship that does not apply to men, who may live elsewhere for employment and have offspring born to mothers resident on the reservation.

The Upper Skagit code provides for the termination of parental rights under specific circumstances (including sexual and repeated physical abuse) and makes desertion of children a criminal offense.

The Lummi code's domestic relations approach to the issues of parental rights and marriage explicitly creates what appears to be the most advantageous circumstances for women of all of the eight codes, although there is no paternity section as such. Civil procedures are established to order payments from delinquent parties—a clause that is not directed to domestic relations issues but that potentially creates a way for women to seek child support payments from fathers. The code provides for arrangements to be made for custody, visitation, maintenance of a spouse (gender is not specified), and child support. Further, the code creates a legal obligation to support one's child, even those born out of wedlock (under common law, tribal custom, or as established by intent to live together). Additionally, parental rights may be terminated for either the mother or father. The Lummi code also restricts categories of marriage partners: People of the same sex are excluded, as are a range of other people who, in earlier times, would have been included in the pool of potential spouses through the Coast Salish institutions of the sororate and levirate (Collins 1974). This code eliminates obligations of women to affinal relatives through these earlier marriage proscriptions. Finally, the code separates the property and legal obligations of wives and husbands to each other during marriage and at divorce.

There are several difficulties in the Lummi code for women with children. One problem with Title 5, Code of Offenses (5.6.01 Offenses Involving Children), is determining whether the father is financially responsible for his offspring if the parental couple has split up and the father is not residing with the child. Secondly, criminal rather than civil proceedings are required if a man, "because of habitual intemperance or gambling, or for any other reason, refuse or neglect to furnish food, shelter, or care, to those dependent upon him..." These features of the code potentially make obtaining child support difficult.

The Tulalip code creates no youth court, has no provisions against nonsupport or for establishing paternity; nor regulations against child abuse. Issues concerning women and children are not the focus of this code. However, as is the case with the Nisqually code, a clause in Article II, section 2 of the membership code specifies that membership is contingent on being born to a member of the Tulalip tribes who is a resident of the reservation at the time of birth. This creates difficulties for women, but not men, who wish to move for employment.

The issue of emancipation is related to the topic of parental rights. Minors may sever the parent-child bond through actions of their own, just as parents may seek to avoid parental responsibilities or the tribal court may end parental rights. In most of the tribes, marriage creates the status of adulthood, independent of age (this is explicitly rejected in the Upper Skagit code). In addition, children who are self-supporting or who live apart (these are regarded as simultaneous conditions) or are heads of households may be emancipated (Muckleshoot, Nooksack, Skokomish, Tulalip). This raises three points: First, emancipation is an advantage for minor females seeking to care for themselves and their children, in that it removes them from a whole series of restrictions that could obstruct their working careers (such as attendance at job training programs and age-linked restrictions from treaty fishing and hunting). Emancipation also removes restrictions as to the types of contracts that minor women can be bound or can enter into. Thus an emancipated woman could execute legal obligations necessary for self-sufficiency, such as buying a car or renting an apartment. Second, the code also creates the grounds under which parental obligations be can overturned. Negligent parents, who are most likely to be the ones whose children establish separate residence, are, in effect, rewarded for their negligence by the diminution of their obligations. Third, emancipation creates a mechanism for older children to get out of abusive situations without being placed in foster care.

Peace and Safety

As with the other issues, there is significant variability in how conditions of peace and safety are achieved on the reservation and in the meaning of these provisions for men and women. A wide range of regulations have been created to ensure peaceful communities. One significant passage for women is contained in the Lummi code (Upper Skagit has a similar code; the others do not), Title 5.1.08, which specifies,

> In the practice of the culture, traditions, or religions of the Lummi people, no person shall be subjected to any of the following: (1) brutal treatment, including... hitting, clubbing...biting...(3) deprivation of medical treatment...(4) forcing any person to take part in any activity relative to traditional culture or religious practices against their will.

These provisions refer to the involuntary seizure and initiation of tribal members into Winter Spirit Dancing societies, occurrences that have produced death and injury in the recent past (precipitating legal action) and that are believed by some women to be differentially abusive to women.[14] Physical contact is used in order to bring a spirit power to the initiate. In addition, the Lummi code (Juvenile Code 8.6.07) establishes legal requirements to report abuse or neglect of children and permits termination of parental rights for cause (8.7.01). Other Lummi code serves to regulate the community, including the following: Chapter 20.6, Illegal Activities, expressively forbids furnishing liquor to minors; the Code of Offenses 5.4.03 requires advance notice and approval for holding public dances, games, or gatherings; and the Housing Authority Declaration of Need 32.2.01 declares the need for "decent, safe and sanitary dwellings, which cannot be relieved through the operation of private enterprise."

Nooksack code (Title 53, Gambling Ordinance, 53.01.010) includes the statement that "in order to safeguard the public health and morals on tribal lands it is necessary to prohibit certain undesirable forms of gambling and to regulate the incidence of those acceptable forms of gambling... " (Nooksack has since opened a public gambling casino.) The code also regulates liquor sales and bans the sale of alcohol, marijuana, and drugs to children (Title 20, Crimes 20.02.040). These passages are commonly incorporated into the legal codes of the eight tribes, except Nisqually and Tulalip.

Finally, the codes deal with rape in several ways. These provisions must be understood in light of the federal Major Crimes Act, which gives federal courts jurisdiction over seven areas of violent crime committed on reservations. However, in an effort to assert autonomy and in the event the federal court fails to prosecute, tribes have created their own code, and criminal provisions are created for rape in most of the codes. The Lummi code forbids attempted rape or rape or assisting another. Muckleshoot (Title 5 of the criminal code [5.1.50]) forbids "any person who willfully and knowingly by force or violence rapes, attempts to rape another, or assists..." Sauk-Suiattle and Upper Skagit forbid forcible sexual intercourse. Tulalip, Nooksack, Nisqually, and Skokomish have no relevant code. The Muckleshoot code adds the burden of demonstrating a mental element and allows for the defense of a "reasonable and honest mistake." It is remarkable that such code has developed at all in the absence of clear jurisdiction.

Conclusion

To date, no developed literature exists concerning the legal codes of U.S. tribes, and attention concerning legal issues affecting Indians has been focused elsewhere. The variability of the present-day Puget Sound tribal codes considered here puts to rest the notion that the codes merely reflect imposed legal concepts of the mainstream society, a view that implies uniformity The fact that the communities considered in this study—with similar traditional cultures and engaged in regular social interaction—have chosen differing routes in establishing their own legal codes argues against such a position. It is true that the use of formalized court systems and the employment of non-Indian code writers does not reflect aboriginal practice, but these facts are not sufficient to allow generalizations about the nature of the codes. This paper suggests three methods to begin the process of understanding the nature of the codes and the implications for women: analysis of legal statuses, comparative examination of the domains of code, and consideration of code.

The eight codes vary significantly in how they balance the rights of individuals and the rights of extended family networks. One aspect that the codes have in common is that they do not rely solely on traditional family networks to provide safety and peace in the community. However, while some codes, such as that of Sauk-Suiattle, broadly incorporate the rights of family networks, the emphasis of other codes, particularly the Upper Skagit, is to regard entrenched family networks as potentially the locus of women's difficulties and to restrain the exercise of influence and authority of kin groups in order to enhance women's lives.[14] Under the Upper Skagit code, women are affirmed as heads of households through their eligibility for tribal housing, jobs, and services, independent of male relatives. Women are given explicit protection as wage earners on the reservation, thereby facilitating their contributions to the reservation's families and to the economy. Such restraints on family networks contradictory implications for women, however: Although restraints provide protections for women, they also limit the powerful roles women have played as influential sisters of significant men and as senior members of family networks.[15]

Among the eight codes included in this study, significant differences exist in overall emphasis and elaboration.[16] Some tribal codes focus on economic development and community regulation, with little attention given to women's issues. Other codes are more directed to peace and safety issues. The differentiation in approach has implications for women, particularly regarding such issues as the rights of parents, legal protections accorded women in the workplace, and procedures for establishing paternity and obtaining child support. Among the codes, the Lummi code is notable for its attention to women's issues, even though women have achieved limited success in tribal elections (Miller 1992). The code provides for women's control of their own productivity, for the protection of children, and for child and spousal support. The Upper Skagit code is similarly notable for the protection provided for women in the workplace.

Generally, tribal codes reinforce women's double burden of responsibility to home and work, particularly through the provisions regarding child care. But the codes simultaneously allow a full expression of women's activities: Under the current codes, women are legally full citizens, with the rights to vote and run for office. Older, postcontact feminine ideals of passivity and lesser involvement in spiritual life are not the basis of present legal constructions. In fact, legal avenues have developed that recognize the differing life courses of young men and women (Snyder 1964; Collins 1974). In earlier generations, young women were secluded from public life at adolescence; today provisions allow for women's early careers as mothers and wage earners through procedures for emancipation.

This examination of eight tribal codes shows the relevance of further study of codes in understanding contemporary women's lives. Subsequent research should give attention to the relationship between the rights of individuals and of the collective, noting carefully how the extended family (or other collective body) is defined in various passages of the code. In the Puget Sound case, the extended family is defined as many as seven ways in single codes, thereby allowing restraints on the networks in some areas and facilitating the networks in others. Future work might employ a comparative perspective in order to provide useful material for band councils developing legal structures in Canada and elsewhere. In addition, the development of legal histories can clarify the issue of the interaction between political actors and legal systems in order to provide insights into the factors influencing code construction. Examination of the relationship between the gender composition of tribal councils and tribal code, and of the community economic structures and the code would be particularly valuable.

ACKNOWLEDGMENTS

I would like to thank Ted Maloney, Upper Skagit tribal attorney and code writer, and Doreen Maloney, Upper Skagit councilor, for their observations concerning the Upper Skagit legal system; also, Talus Woodward, a tribal code writer; Emily Mansfield, NICS attorney and tribal code writer; and Catriona Elliott, my research assistant for this project. Any errors of fact and interpretation are my own. I also wish to thank the tribal council women from several tribes, anonymous here, who have discussed tribal political life.

Endnotes

[1] This study does not include analysis of the workings of the court and is not directed to explain why tribal codes differ. Although both are useful topics, the focus here is on the codes themselves. See Chief Justice Tom Tso (1989:225–235), for details of the working of the Navajo court; and Miller (1993). Analysis of actual trials would supplement the work presented here, a point made by Peter Just (1992).

[2] Samuel J. Brakel (1979). See also Susan Lupton (1981).

[3] In *Law as Process: An Anthropological Approach,* Sally Falk Moore (1978) observed that it is misleading to seek out core ideas in the law that express important social values because of the slow construction of the law through aggregation. Nonetheless, I argue that despite the fact that much of the law does not result from a rational, considered process, the newly emerging codes clearly reflect the values and aims of influential community leaders. For example, one Upper Skagit tribal councilor held specific concerns that protections be provided tribal employees in order that the community be productive. Her concerns were addressed in specific code. Sometimes the interests of the councilors are more personal. I was told of a case in one of the tribes in which a councilor pushed for code that would accommodate the interests of her underaged son. This is not ordinarily the case, however. These leaders and their values are more fully addressed elsewhere (Miller 1989, 1992).

[4] Harry Chesnin, a Seattle lawyer involved in the process of code writing in Puget Sound since the 1970s, has pointed out that variation in tribal codes may reflect the period in which code was written and the personal outlook and interests of particular code writers hired by the tribes. Code writers, however, clearly assign priority to the interests of the councils and advisory committees. The writers are given guidelines and frequently asked by the tribal councils to revise code, particularly in the last decade.

[5] Data compiled from Johnson and Paschal (1991).

[6] Ted Maloney, Upper tribal attorney and sometime code writer, personal communication.

[7] Public Law 83-280 (1953) empowered states to jurisdiction over Indian reservations in several legal domains. Subsequently, Washington State enacted RCW 7.12.010, requiring tribal consent to do so. The Muckleshoot, Nisqually, and Tulalip tribes among those under consideration here, came under these terms. The Upper Skagit, Nooksack, and Sauk-Suiattle reservation were created later, and it is unclear if PL. 280 applies. Tribal and state Jurisdiction are concurrent under PL. 280, creating the possibilities for a "race to the courthouse, and a race to final judgment" (Johnson and Paschal 1991:9).

[8] Upper Skagit Tribal Police Report, 1992 (unpublished ms.).

[9] The Lummi code differs from Washington State code concerning common property in that the Lummi code provides for separability of property acquired during marriage. The more important issue is that the present Lummi code is in accordance with traditional practice.

[10] These male boat owners have composed the majority in the tribal councils, a fact noted by Boxberger (1989).

[11] Personal communication, Ted Maloney.

[12] See Sally Snyder (1964), Collins (1974), Miller (1989), Amoss (1978) for details of male and female life course.

[13] Coast Salish men who were involuntarily "grabbed" have also recently complained of assault in winter ceremonials. A recent case involved Thomas of the Lyackson band in British Columbia. He was awarded $12,000 in damages by the British Columbia Supreme Court (*Vancouver Sun*, August 1992). It is important to note that not all community members have a negative view of winter ceremonials. There are many participants and supporters.

[14] This strategy does not appear to be accounted for in the literature. One analyst argued, for example, that principles of legal and political individualism have been "extended" into tribal governance as a result of the Indian Bill of Rights of 1968 and at the expense of group-based rights (Svensson 1979:421–439). This approach fails to entertain the possibility that innovators within communities may see advantage in reconstructing the relationship between group and individual entitlements.

An interesting comparison may be made with Coast Salish communities of southern Vancouver Island, immediately adjacent to those in Washington State, who lack the jurisdiction to establish their own court systems. Experiments in alternative justice systems that divert charges from the mainstream societies' court system to a band's male-dominated council of elders have foundered on charges of abuse of the system by powerful family networks. Women have criticized the system for covering up sexual abuse of women and perpetuating the influence of the family system. A reporter noted that one woman "says she knows of several cases where powerful families pressured women to use the alternative system, which involves the band's council of elders, rather than bringing sexual assault charges to court. Mavis Henry, a member of the Pauquachin band of southern Vancouver Island, stated, 'It can happen in subtle ways... A family will offer to buy a car or do repairs on your house in return'" *(Vancouver Sun,* 31 July 1992). The article points out that other women were forced to move from their reserve. The implication of the article is that large, politically powerful families attempt to coerce assault victims into using traditional systems of restitution or to completely bury their charges of abuse. In a related debate, Joanne Fiske, in "Child of the State, Mother of the Nation: Aboriginal Women and the Ideology of Motherhood" (a paper presented to the Joint Meetings of the Atlantic Canada Studies and B.C. Studies Association, 21-24 May 1992), has shown how Carrier and Micmac women have relied on metaphors of motherhood in making claims to a present-day political position for women based on "sexual equality [of] folk laws instead of ... state law" (p. 5). In this discourse, motherhood is represented as traditionally the dominant social identity in the community, the font of cultural knowledge, and the source of band identity. Further, these claims are said to be made "not as women seeking individual rights as against their male peers" (p. 24) but in the struggle against the intrusion of the state. "It is because of their [women's] *collective* responsibility for future generations that they seek sexual equality ..." (Fiske 1992). In this case, traditional kinship structures are viewed as the source of women's protection, and new systems of justice are seen as creating difficulties. See also Teressa Nahanee (1992:5–7); Faith et al., (1991); and Moss (1990).

[15] Such family networks persist as underlying political structures, but women as individuals are free to amass resources outside of this system of resource ownership and control. Many women have responded by directing their resources back within the family network through regular patterns of generalized reciprocity, and others have emphasized development of careers as cultural mediators and technical experts.

[16] There are other background similarities between codes. None of the eight legal systems is based on an explicit notion of differences between the sexes. None relies on special theories of femininity or masculinity. Women are not excluded from voting because of theories of differential intellect or moral development, although some codes recognize differing circumstances for men and women in limited ways. Women are not partitioned into legal categories with separate rights. (For example, married and unmarried women are not treated separately except as this applies to the emancipation of youth.)

References Cited

Amoss, Pamela. 1978. *Coast Salish Spirit Dancing: the Survival of an Ancestral Religion.* Seattle: University of Washington Press.

Barsh, Russell Lawrence and J. Youngblood Henderson. 1976. Tribal Courts, The Model Code, and the Police Idea in American Indian Policy. *Law and Contemporary Problems,* 40:25–60.

Boxberger, Daniel L. 1989. *To Fish in Common: The Ethnohistory of Lummi Indian Salmon Fishing.* Lincoln: University of Nebraska Press.

Brakel, Samuel J. 1979. *American Indian Tribal Courts: The Costs of Separate Justice.* Chicago, IL: American Bar Association.

Burnett, Jr., Donald L. 1972. An Historical Analysis of the 1968 'Indian Civil Rights' Act. *Harvard Journal on Legislation,* 9:556–626.

Christofferson, Carla. 1991. Tribal Court's Failure to Protect Native American Women: A Reevaluation of the Indian Civil Rights Act. *The Yale Law Journal,* 101:169–185.

Collins, June McCormick. 1974. *Valley of the Spirits: The Upper Skagit Indians of Western Washington.* Seattle: University of Washington Press.

Faith, Karlene, Mary Gottfriedson, Cherry Joe, Wendy Leonard, and Sharon McIvor. 1991. Native Women in Canada: A Quest for Justice. *Social Justice,* 17:167–188.

Fleras, Augie and Jean Leonard Elliott. 1992. *The Nations Within: Aboriginal-State Relations in Canada, the United States and New Zealand.* Toronto: Oxford University Press.

Johnson, Ralph W. 1981. Introduction. In *Indian Tribal Codes: A Microfiche Collection of Indian Tribal Codes,* edited by Ralph W Johnson. Seattle: Marian Gould Law Library, University of Washington School of Law, Research Studies Series.

Johnson, Ralph W., and Rachael Paschal, editors. 1991. *Tribal Court Handbook for the 26 Federally Recognized Tribes in Washington State.* Olympia: Office of the Administrator for the Courts, State of Washington.

Just, Peter. 1992. History, Power, Ideology, and Culture: Current Directions in the Anthropology of Law. *Law and Society Review,* 26:373–411.

Lupton, Susan. 1981. American Indian Tribal Codes. *Legal Reference Services Quarterly,* 1:25–41.

Mari, Matsuda. 1988. Native Custom and Official Law in Hawaii. *Law and Anthropology,* 3:135–146.

Menkel-Meadow, Carrie and Shari Seidman Diamond. 1991. The Content, Method, and Epistemology of Gender in Sociolegal Studies. *Law and Society Review,* 25:221–238.

Miller, Bruce G. 1989. A Sociocultural Explanation of the Election of Women to Tribal Council: The Upper Skagit Case, Ph.D. dissertation, Arizona State University.

——— 1992. Women and Politics: Comparative Evidence from the Northwest Coast. *Ethnology,* 31(4):367–383.

——— 1993. The Northwest Intertribal Court System and Indian Law. Paper presented at the 46th Annual Northwest Anthropological Conference, Bellingham, Washington.

Moore, Sally Falk. 1978. *Law as Process: An Anthropological Approach.* London: Routledge and Keegan.

Moss, Wendy. 1990. Indigenous Self-Government in Canada and Sexual Equality under the Indian Act: Resolving Conflicts Between Collective and Individual Rights. *Queens Law Journal,* 15:279–305.

Nahanee, Teressa. 1992. Do Native Women Need Charter Rights? Priorities: A *Feminist Voice in a Socialist Movement,* 20: 5–7.

Northwest Intertribal Court System (NICS). n.d. Traditional and Informal Resolution Processes in Tribes of the Puget Sound and Olympic Peninsula Region. Unpublished ms.

O'Brien, Sharon. 1989. *American Indian Tribal Government.* Norman: University of Oklahoma Press.

Quinn, William. 1993. Intertribal Integration: The Ethnological Argument in *Duro v. Reina. Ethnology,* 40:34–69.

Rodman, William L. 1985. A Law Unto Themselves: Legal Innovation in Ambae, Vanuatu. *American Ethnologist,* 12: 602–624.

Sampson, Chief Martin. 1972. *Indians of Skagit County.* Mount Vernon, WA: Skagit County Historical Society.

Smith, Marian W. 1941. The Coast Salish of Puget Sound. *American Anthropologist,* 43:197–211.

Snyder, Sally. 1964. Skagit Society and Its Existential Basis: An Ethnofolkloristic Reconstruction. Ph.D. dissertation, University of Washington.

Svensson, Frances. 1979. Liberal Democracy and Group Rights: The Legacy of Individualism and Its Impact on American Indian Tribes. *Political Studies,* 27:421–439.

Tso, Chief Justice Tom. 1989. Process of Decision Making in Tribal Courts. *Arizona Law Review,* 31:225–235.

Vincent, Joan. 1990. *Anthropology and Politics: Visions, Traditions, and Trends.* Tucson: University of Arizona Press.

Weber, Sandra Robinson. 1982. Native-Americans Before the Bench: The Nature of Contrast and Conflict in Native-American Law Ways and Western Legal Systems. *The Social Science Journal,* 19:47–57.

Journal of Northwest Anthropology, Memoir 12:200–214 (2016)

12

Women and Tribal Politics:
Is There a Gender Gap in Indian Elections?*

Since the 1980s scholars have labored over the problem of understanding differences in voting habits of men and women in mainstream American society. The stimulus for this new interest was the discovery of a "gender gap" in the 1980 United States presidential election: six million more women voted than men, and men and women expressed significant differences in candidate preferences. Men and women are said to have somewhat different opinions on political issues generally, and on the qualifications for public office, largely the result of disparities in economic positions (Renzetti and Curran 1992:252). Few comparable data on electoral processes in Indian communities have been published (Bateille and Sands [1984], and Green [1980] point out that there is little material on Indian women generally) and it is unclear from the literature if there is an Indian "gender gap" in routine political life.[1]

This article focuses on voting behavior and election strategies over the last two decades in a Coast Salish community, the Upper Skagit Tribe of Indians, in Washington State, in order to suggest one possible way to reorient the study of tribal political life and of the political participation of women. Indian political life is not the same everywhere, nor even among culturally similar tribes and bands. Indeed, the evidence shows otherwise (Miller 1989a, 1992, n.d.).

Nonetheless, this paper is a start towards supplementing the vast literature that treats contemporary Indian politics in a variety of ways: through an emphasis on symbol systems (Fowler 1982; Boelscher 1988), as underpinned by mythology (Powers 1986; Ridington 1990), as traditional (Voget 1980; Tollefson 1987); as altered by outside forces that assimilate communities (Spicer 1967; Clifton 1972), "decapitate" leadership (Garbarino 1980; Stearns 1981), or co-opt tribal governments (Biolsi 1991; Carstens 1991); or, finally, through an emphasis on adaptive responses and resistance to interference (Jorgensen 1972; Bee 1981; Tennant 1990). None of these approaches places special emphasis on a feature of contemporary politics that candidates for tribal office know well: elections are won by understanding the electorate.

Indian women's political participation in contemporary tribal government has been most usefully analyzed from a feminist perspective (Klein 1976; Albers 1983; Fiske 1989; Knack 1989), but this work includes little analysis of voting patterns and candidates' strategies. Further, the approach taken here avoids the speculation that frequently accompanies the usually very brief descriptions of Indian women's political life in the anthropological literature. The following passage, for example, mystifies Okanagan Indian women's political participation by attributing the women's successes to marginality and to belonging to a symbolic category that supposedly exempts political women from voters' ordinary considerations:

> The most important structural change…was the election of the first woman to council in 1983, and two in the 1985 elections…these women were successful, in part at least, because they had learned basic strategies of winning support from the electorate. They are all outsiders who had married into the band, which suggests that the band elected women to office who were marginal to the community, thus placing them in a symbolic category that made them different from local Okanagan women. (Carstens 1991:253)

*Authored by Bruce Granville Miller, reproduced with permission and previously published in *American Indian Quarterly*, 18(1):25–41 (1994). University of Nebraska Press.

Although many of the issues the community members face differ from those in the majority culture, there are important similarities in voting trends. In the Upper Skagit community, women vote more often than men and have somewhat different views of the qualifications of women for public office. An important difference with the United States elections, however, is that women win tribal council elections much more frequently (women held 53.6 percent of tribal council seats between 1975–1992) than do women in state or federal elections. In both cases, women were enfranchised relatively recently (in 1920 in the case of the majority culture and 1974 in Upper Skagit elections) and so the political involvement of women has required overcoming an earlier system which excluded them.

Indian communities, as elsewhere, have their own political dynamics and I will attempt to clarify just how women engage themselves in politics by first considering the social organization of the community, especially the family network system, and subsequently describing trends in voting, characteristics of women office holders, and how women position themselves to run for office. I argue that women have several electoral advantages over men due to features of social organization and demography in a small community.[2]

The Research

The data for this analysis were gathered primarily during two years of fieldwork on the Upper Skagit reservation, 1986–87. The data include the voting records contained within the tribal archives (lists of eligible voters, lists of those who voted in each election, and tallies of votes for each candidate), interviews from a randomly selected sample of thirty eligible rank-and-file male and female voters, and interviews with thirteen past and present tribal councilors. A years' service as a home-based early child education teacher and later as an ethnohistorian for the Tribal Council provided opportunities to talk informally with community members about how they viewed community politics, family organization, and local gender relations. Regular visits to the reservation since 1987 have helped in the analysis of the tribal political culture.

The Setting

The Upper Skagit Tribe of Indians is a federally recognized tribe in the Skagit River valley on the western flank of the Cascade Mountains of Washington State. Tribal members live primarily along one hundred or so miles of the river, their aboriginal homeland, and, since 1984, have a reservation near Sedro-Woolley, Washington. Upper Skagits, along with other local Indian people, signed the Treaty of Point Elliott with the United States in 1855, but the bulk of the tribe refused to move onto a reservation and instead moved upriver, away from White contact. In 1926 the Upper Skagits constructed an Indian Shaker Church near the town of Concrete, and this became the central meeting place. The most important sources of income were from fishing, logging, and agricultural work. Over time, some tribal members moved from the valley to find work, especially after the State of Washington began to actively obstruct Indian treaty-based fishing. In 1974, a landmark case, *US v. Washington,* known as the Boldt decision, overturned state fishing regulations and awarded 50 percent of the harvestable salmon and steelhead runs to Indian fishers, to be divided among the federally recognized tribes.

The Upper Skagits received recognition that year and with it, fishing rights. This sparked a revitalization in Upper Skagit society; members returned to the valley, and a constitution and bylaws were written. Elections were held in 1975 to create the first modern tribal council replacing an earlier council which included women only as non-voting secretaries and treasurers. The seven-member council holds staggered elections for three-year terms and the chair and vice-chair are elected annually from among council members by the general electorate. Today about 170 of the approximately 540 members live on the seventy-five acre reservation, and most of the rest live nearby in Skagit County. The tribe operates a range of services for members, including education, health, and other social services, and provides jobs for about fifty people in tribal industries and administration. The tribe is part of the Northwest Inter-tribal Court System, and the multi-tribe Skagit System Cooperative for fisheries management. (More detailed descriptions of the community are in Snyder 1964; Sampson 1972; Collins 1974; Robbins 1986; Miller 1989a, 1989b, and 1990).

Politics and the Family System

The family network system is at the heart of tribal social organization and politics, and family network members look after their mutual well-being.[3] Family networks are based on an ethic of "Indian collectivism" (Mooney 1976) and control material and ceremonial resources. These family networks, or families as they are called locally, support members in ceremonial responsibilities such as entry into the sacred winter Spirit Dancing and in honoring and "feeding" family ancestors. Families are also important economic units and form fishing cooperatives. While in previous eras the families fished, lived, and moved together (Snyder 1964; Collins 1974), today members are no longer co-resident. As in the past membership is negotiable, and in theory one could belong to one of several family networks. Networks form around leaders, often a sibling set, who use important inherited resources and their personal abilities to benefit their followers. Over time, the successful networks expand through in-marriage and the production of off-spring to become large and prosperous enough to compete as a group within the village and region.

While previously families competed for status through the potlatching system (which continues to the present), emphasis is placed today on the competition for resources with other family networks. This competition is significant: the presence of family members in political office is thought by many community members to make it easier to obtain tribal employment, for prompt access to vital information about tribal programs, and to advance one's viewpoint about important issues such as fisheries policy. Tribal members worry about the potential for nepotism and the possibilities for corruption if any one family gains multiple seats on the council.[4] Family networks are not permanent units, and undergo a process of fissioning, often as leaders age. The contemporary tribal community is, to some measure, an aggregation of corporate family networks, but with a minority of people unaffiliated with a corporate family network.

Male council members, like their forebears, play a role in tribal level politics by virtue of their leadership within their own family networks. Women, too, must take into account the family system when running for office, but have done so somewhat differently than men. Some have run for office as traditional family heads, but the majority are "technocrats" (those with specialized education, training, and expertise in dealing with external bureaucracies) who attract community-wide political support. With one exception, male councilors have not been technocrats.

Interview data show the significance of family networks to voters. Seventy-two percent of the sample of tribal members interviewed said they vote for members of their family network as the first priority. An additional 12 percent (all people who are not affiliated with a family network) said they vote for members of their immediate family if one is running. Only 17 percent did not claim to vote for family network members as a priority, and all are members of families that have fissioned and no longer act corporately. Everyone described Upper Skagit politics as family-based, and 93 percent said that they vote to defeat candidates of big corporate families.

To compete politically, family members must select and support family candidates or simply support family members who choose to run. An illustration of this comes from the 1992 election: a family that had unsuccessfully supported its own candidates attempted to make certain everyone was aware of their latest candidate's affiliation by writing the family network name in parentheses next to the candidate's surname on the bulletin board in the tribal center announcing the candidates. Perhaps this helped; he won by a single vote. Some families have been very successful in motivating and organizing members to show up to vote for family members, and other families have been generally unable to "get out the vote" on election day.

Analysis of Upper Skagit election data makes clear the influence a single family network can have in the elections. In 1987 there were 382 eligible Upper Skagit voters and of these, 156 had never voted, 226 voted at least once, and 145 were regular voters who have voted in half or more of the elections for which they have been eligible. In the thirteen years since recognition and the formation of a new council the mean number of actual voters was 87, with a high of 124 and a low of 56. For these same elections the mean number of votes given a winning candidate was 50, with a high of 68 and a low of 39 in a given year. The most votes ever received by a winning candidate is 70 and losing candidates have received a mean of 24 votes.

These data show that the number of votes required to win an election was well within the reach of a large family even if few others voted for their candidate. If there is no competition from one of the other large families, and in the absence of effective coalitions, there is no effective opposition to candidates of the large family networks, each of which has been able to produce as many as 60 votes. (See Miller 1989a for a discussion of the number of votes potentially available to families; one of the three large families collapsed as a corporate group in the 1980s after several decades as the most politically prominent.) As of 1987, the three large families have had thirteen members serve sixty-five and a half years and all other families combined have had fourteen members serve thirty-one and a half years.

Analysis of head-to-head electoral competition provides another indication of the ability of large families to elect their members to the council. For the purpose of this analysis, candidates were grouped into three categories:

- technocrat candidates
- heads of families (large and small)
- family candidates (who were not family heads).

The most successful candidates have been technocrats, who generally defeated candidates from the other categories. Large family candidates usually defeated small family candidates (80 percent of the time). In general, small families ordinarily do not present candidates of their own leaving large family candidates to battle the technocrats. Sometimes technocrats are also large family candidates, a virtually unbeatable combination. Three of the women who have served as councilors were heads of large families, and three more were technocrats who were members of large families. Four women who are not members of large families have won election as technocrats.

Women, Family Networks and Community Well-Being

Upper Skagits recognize the need for the preservation of the larger tribal entity as well as their own family network, and there is a near universal feeling that the interests of the tribe must be protected. Members are aware of the importance of the tribe in obtaining fishing rights, economic opportunities, housing, and energy assistance and that the majority of these opportunities did not exist before the new constitution was formed in 1974. Pressure on politicians to uphold tribal as opposed to family interests is indicated by the sort of language used in charges community members occasionally directed against politicians and administrators. Recall petitions in 1981 and 1989, asking for the removal of council members, were put into terms of violation of the common good.

In response to the problem of reconciling apparently conflicting interests between family network and tribe, many Upper Skagits adopted a personal strategy of primary investment in the family and secondary investment in the tribe, as the interview data show. Tribal members have supported tribal interests without hindering their own family interests by voting for "neutral" candidates. These neutral candidates are ones who are not members of the large, powerful families and are often technocrats. By voting for neutral technocrats, tribal members (1) diminish the control exercised by other families over the tribal council and resources, and (2) support someone with the technical skills needed in tribal administration who has the added benefit of not being a member of a large family.

The neutral vote is a very important element in tribal elections at Upper Skagit. Most informants (85 percent of the sample) reported using the strategy of voting for neutrals because they feared what could happen in the event of domination of the council by one family and because the neutral vote helps maintain balance on the council. The neutral vote is especially important to the election of the technocrats, the only category of candidates from small families who are able to win consistently.[5]

There is another category of neutrals as well, those candidates who are not likely to take strong political positions and hence not likely to alter the political balance of power. These neutral candidates received support in order to block another candidate from upsetting the council balance in favor of one family. Neutral council members themselves acknowledged the nature of their political support and their own political roles.

Candidate strategies in response to these characteristics of the electorate have included carefully choosing a vacant position to run for in order to avoid large-family opponents who appeared to be difficult to beat. Election results show that neutral technocrat candidates have positioned themselves carefully, winning their match-ups with other candidates 78 percent of the time.

Voting Patterns

Analysis of the family network system reveals one dimension of the political system at Upper Skagit, but there are other dimensions which clarify the manner in which women and men choose to participate in public life as candidates and as voters. Interview data (Miller 1989a) show that women start their work careers earlier than do men, even if they have children, and begin serious involvement in the public life of the community, as employees and politicians, earlier than men do. Women enter into service on the tribal council earlier and are more likely to vote. Furthermore, women running for tribal office at Upper Skagit have several advantages resulting from tribal voting patterns. While there is only a weak positive correlation between the percent of the vote cast by women in a given year and the number of women elected, women nevertheless have disproportionate influence on election day.[6]

Participation in Voting by Sex

In the first years under the new constitution male and female voting was quite even, with 1981 the high point for male voters. Men cast sixty-six votes, 53 percent of the vote that year, their largest percentage ever. The next year, 1982, was almost evenly matched in voting participation by sex, with a difference of one vote. Men cast forty votes in 1982 and have cast fewer votes each year since then. Women took over as the majority voters in 1983, with 57 percent of the vote, and cast a high of sixty-three votes in 1987 (62 percent). After 1981 the composition of the council, which had been predominantly male (twenty-four seats won by men, seventeen by women) became primarily female. Women held a majority on the council from 1981–1992, when men gained a 4–3 majority.

Women voters did not generally report a bias in favor of females for tribal office, but they were much less likely than men to report a bias against women. Forty-three percent of the men in the sample reported some bias against women in office (varying from believing women should not hold office to preferring men) compared with 10 percent of women. Twenty percent of women reported a bias in favor of women in office, as did 10 percent of men. Since women are less apt to be biased against women, a female majority in the electorate is an advantage for female candidates. Despite the bias against women by some men, and even a few women, most men have voted for female candidates at some point and hence women were able to win the majority of council seats in 1981 when more men voted than women. In 1984, when six of seven councilors were women, some members of the community (both men and women) perceived this council as having too many women. Since then the council's sex composition has been more balanced.

Participation in Voting by Age Group

Participation in the electoral process at Upper Skagit generally declined with age, especially for men. The political impact of the differential voting by age is significant for two reasons, even though it was created in part by anomalies in the sex and age structure of the tribe (there is a disproportionately large group of young women). First, because men voted less than women as they age and because women were less biased against female candidates, there has been an advantage for women candidates. Second, older men, who were the most likely to oppose women candidates, voted the least. The proportion of women who voted in early adult life is low, reaching its highest point in the middle years, and staying strong through old age. For men, participation was also greatest in the middle years and trailed off in old age. This contrasts with levels of absolute participation in which young women comprised by far the largest group of voters, followed by middle-aged women, young men and old women. A comparison between Table 15 (showing raw voting results) and Table 16 (which shows the tribal sex and age structure) allows the computation of the relative rates of voting by age and sex (Table 17) and controls for differences in cohort size.

TABLE 15. VOTING IN TRIBAL ELECTIONS BY AGE AND SEX*

Age Group	Women	Percent	Men	Percent	Total	Percent
18–27	134	15.2	107	12.1	241	27.4
28–37	90	10.2	101	11.5	191	21.7
38–47	101	11.5	73	8.3	174	19.8
48–57	51	5.8	66	7.5	158	13.3
57–over	93	53.2	65	7.4	158	17.9
Totals	469	53.2	412	46.8	881	100

*Column totals represent the number of voters within each age group, 1975–1987.

TABLE 16. TRIBAL SEX AND AGE STRUCTURE

Age	Female	Percent	Male	Percent	Total	Percent
18–27	51	17.1	30	10.1	81	27.2
28–37	36	12.1	39	13.1	75	25.2
38–47	27	9.1	20	6.7	47	15.8
48–57	16	5.4	24	8.1	40	13.4
58–over	27	9.1	28	9.4	55	18.5
Totals	157	47.3	141	52.3	298	100.1

TABLE 17. RATIO OF VOTING TO COHORT SIZE*

Age Group	Women	Men
18–27	.89	1.20
28–37	.84	.88
38–47	1.26	1.24
48–57	1.07	.93
58–over	1.16	.79

*Table 17 reports the ration of voters to the percentage of the population for each age group. Women ages 18 to 27, for example, make up 15.2 percent of the voters and 17.1 percent of the adult population, and, therefore, have a score of .89.

Age Characteristics of the Council Members

Women councilors have been, on average, younger than their male counterparts both at the time of first election (thirty-two versus thirty-nine) and as measured by the mean age of councils (thirty-nine versus forty-seven). In the years 1975–1980 council women averaged thirty-three years of age and in the period 1981–1987, forty-seven. The average age of women councilors now falls right in the middle of the female cohort (thirty-eight to forty-seven) that participates the most on a percentage basis. Women of all ages have held political office, and the bearing of children has not been an impediment to holding office. Until recently the average age of women councilors was well within the prime childbearing years. The data refute the notion that political leadership is the provenance of elders or any other age group. Women have ranged in age from 18 to 63 with the distribution as reported in Table 18.

TABLE 18. AGE OF COUNCILWOMEN

Age Group	Number of Councilwomen
18–27	4
28–37	18
38–47	15
48–57	8
57–over	5

With the exception of the anomalous year of 1983, councilmen have always been older than councilwomen. The gap has narrowed considerably, however, and this increase in the average age of women councilors resulted in part because of the repeated election of a professional elite (technocrats) whose members have aged since their first election. In addition, men are not usually elected to the council for the first time under the age of thirty (13 percent) while nearly half of the women (46 percent) are first elected under thirty. The earlier involvement of women in community affairs is, of course, a political advantage for women. They have a longer period in which to develop their careers, more opportunities to run, and the early involvement of women in political life helps to identify women with politics and to legitimize women's political participation.

Ideal Councilor Characteristics

As the requirements of political leadership have changed (since 1974 more formal education is required of those leaders who make decisions concerning all of the new social, educational and administrative systems) the community members' concepts of what sort of person is needed on the council has also changed. The most interesting development has been the emergence of an overlap between characteristics regarded as feminine and what is regarded as important in political leaders. Although, as noted above, a sizable number of men reported some bias against women in public office, men and women in all age groups nevertheless held strikingly similar notions of ideal female traits and the most significant of the ideal traits of political leaders (Table 19).

TABLE 19. QUALITIES ADMIRED IN MEN AND WOMEN*

Admired in Men	Admired in Women
1. Joking/outgoing 66%	1. Care for Family 100%
2. Job Holding 61%	2. Job Holding 100%
3. Traditional 55%	3. Traditional 71%
4. Care for Family 55%	4. Education 50%
5. Education 50%	5. Reserve 30%

*The rank ordering reflects the number with percentage of informants who listed the qualities among the most important.

The interview data show important associations between the qualities admired in women, women's role in family life, and qualities admired in political leaders. This linkage reinforces women's political chances (even though it represents a contradiction for those who express a generalized preference for male candidates). Specifically, women were more generally expected to take care of matters of importance (especially care of the family and earning money) and to have the traits of objectivity and calmness thought necessary to do so. Women were not admired for jocularity and an outgoing personality (0 percent of the sample reported this trait), traits which can complicate carrying out job and family responsibilities because of the time demands associated with them.[7] Men were most admired for personal qualities—affability and humor—and relatively less for their participation in instrumental areas such as care of families and holding jobs. Unlike women, men were not admired for traits associated with political life—impartiality, calm, and reserve (0 percent).

Most significantly, the data show (Table 20) that the qualities associated with political leadership are not only those that are admired in women but, even more specifically, are the traits of technocrats. Education, technical abilities (especially the ability to deal with bureaucracies), and impartiality may describe the technocrats, but they also are the traits highly valued in political leaders. The third most commonly admired trait of leaders, the ability to communicate with tribal members, is a trait associated with traditional leaders.

The broad similarity in views about political leadership held across generations and between the sexes is an indication of the importance of such views. There are some generational differences in viewpoint, however, with men fifty-five and over at variance with others. Men and women thirty-one to fifty-five years old all viewed technical abilities (and the ability to deal with bureaucracies) as a fundamental attribute for political leaders, a perspective widely but not universally held by younger adults (67 percent) and rejected by many in the oldest cohort (fifty-five and over). This variability in perspective may be explained by the perception of men over fifty-five that their traditional knowledge is being slighted by tribal administrators, councilors, and committees. The association between importance placed on the ability to communicate with tribal members and political leadership is somewhat more complicated by sex and generational differences. A major form of communication, public speaking, is associated with masculinity and perhaps as a consequence more men than women identified this as an ideal characteristic of leaders. Men fifty-five and over consistently identified public speaking as an important ability for political leaders. There is little intergenerational variation about the importance of formal education for political leadership.

TABLE 20. QUALITIES ADMIRED IN POLITICAL LEADERS*

1. Objectivity/Impartiality— 95%
2. Knowledge of dealing with bureaucracies (such as the Bureau of Indian Affairs, social services, Indian Health Services, and the state of government)—82%
3. Ability to communicate with tribal members—71%
4. Education—61%
5. Knowledge of tribal of traditions—33%
6. Knowledge of the reservation—26%
*Percentages are of those reporting the quality.

Who are the Female Leaders?

The women who have served on the council have been partially characterized thus far; they typically began their political careers at an early age, some were traditional family leaders, but most possessed technical skills of great importance to the tribal community. They held jobs and were skillful at positioning themselves against other candidates. The women had incomes which were similar to those of males on the council and were considerably higher and more stable than the average for the tribe (Table 21). Technocrat council women were also much less likely to have a leadership role in traditional religious life (such as the Shaker Church or winter ceremonial activities) (0 percent) than were family-head council women (66 percent) or multiple-term councilmen (75 percent). The time commitments of leadership in traditional life remain largely incompatible with council responsibilities in technical fields, such as fisheries management. In addition, traditional councilwomen had several close male relatives (within one genealogical link) who have served on the council (an average of 3.5 such relatives), while technocrats, who averaged the same as women in general (1.0), did not.

Women on the council showed no significant difference from other women in most of the features of marriage, such as the average age at first marriage or number of marriages. Technocrats (83 percent) were far more likely to marry people with technical or professional skills than were other women (8 percent), councilmen (6 percent) or non-councilmen (8 percent). Interview data show that these spouses were a reservoir of income and information for technocrat women and increased their ability to act as culture brokers, mediating between the outside world and the tribal community. Finally, the technocrats (100 percent) had far more professional and college training than traditional councilwomen (0 percent), non-councilmen (0 percent), councilmen (20 percent), and non-council women (20 percent).

Councilwomen, then, typically have resources unavailable to the vast majority of tribal members, especially access to important information and stable, relatively large incomes. These sorts of resources have their political utility, and contribute to women's electoral chances by reinforcing their ability to contribute to their families and community.

TABLE 21. EMPLOYMENT STABILITY*

	Mean		Median	
	Not on Council	On Council	Not on Council	On Council
Men (%)	48%	87%	53%	89%
Men (n)	13	8	13	8
Women (%)	45%	79%	37%	88%
Women (n)	10	10	10	10

*This measure of stability is a percentage of years of employment (age 18 and over) and is expressed as an average within a group. Difference between the council and non-council groups were statistically significant at .025 using a chi-square test, and setting the level for high stability at 80% and low stability at less than 80%

Discussion

Perhaps the most obvious and salient comparison of the majority culture political system to that of the Upper Skagit reservation is that while women continue to face obstacles in the mainstream a variety of factors have emerged at Upper Skagit favoring women's political chances. One explanation of the low rate of electoral success of mainstream women emphasizes that women have greater difficulty meeting the demands of public life and must shoulder a double work load. Perhaps as a consequence, women typically enter politics later, after children are grown, or while divorced, single, or widowed (Renzetti and Curran 1992:260). This is not the case for Upper Skagit women, who begin their political careers early in their lives, in spite of what could be called a "quadruple work load" of council duties, domestic chores, employment obligations, and treaty-fishing. Councilwomen receive help from family members or hire child-care providers in order to fulfill their tasks.

Another argument for the gender gap in office holding in the majority culture points to prejudice and discrimination against women by the electorate and within public office (Renzetti and Curran 1992). It is worth noting that other Coast Salish tribes, immediate neighbors to the Upper Skagit, seldom elect women (such as Tulalip, with 6.1 percent women on the council 1962–1987, and Lummi with 8 percent) and some female candidates there have pointed to hostility to women on the part of voters. Other neighboring tribes are much more similar to Upper Skagit (for example Sauk-Suiattle, 60 percent women and Nisqually, 55.1 percent).[9] At Upper Skagit, other variables have become more important in determining the outcome of elections than what some Upper Skagit women perceive as sexism in the community.[10]

The problems of running against incumbents in political office is said to be a primary reason few women win in the majority culture (Stockard and Johnson 1992:24). Incumbency works somewhat differently in Indian communities than in the mainstream. The primary advantage of incumbency in the mainstream is the greater ability to raise money for campaigning. This is not an issue in the small-scale Upper Skagit society or, indeed, other small communities. Upper Skagit women have not faced the problem of overcoming an entrenched set of incumbents; rather, several have themselves developed political advantages through their knowledge of the political and bureaucratic scene. The Upper Skagit community has not voted out incumbents as a regular practice, as has been widely reported in Indian communities (Dobyns 1981; Bee 1990).

Instead, at Upper Skagit patterns of voting and widely held attitudes are favorable to women as candidates. As in the mainstream culture, there are more women voters. In addition, women are more likely than men to vote, are less biased against women candidates, and are elected at an earlier age. Women form a substantial majority of the electorate and stay involved in the tribal elections longer. Since primarily women seek out the training and career development which suits them to be neutral technocrat candidates (Miller 1989a), the family network system serves to funnel votes to women. A further advantage for women is that ideals of femininity, shared by men and women, closely approximate the emergent ideals of political leadership.

As is the case of the majority culture, the Upper Skagit data point to the value of considering how candidates for political office use their knowledge of community voting preferences, ideals of leadership, and demographic variables in seeking public office. Upper Skagit technocrat candidates calculate the size of voting blocs and the ability of particular families to turn out the vote, determine which council slot to run for (whom to run against), estimate voter turnout by age and sex, calculate how episodic events such as fishing season will disrupt the voting turnout, construct and target timed political mailings to potential supporters, and assess their own ability to draw votes in light of their own family affiliations and contributions to the community.

Unlike the majority culture, Upper Skagit women and men tend to seek out the same traits in candidates. Members of both sexes experience the same problems of low-income and poverty, engage in the same mutual-aid networks, and identify similar issues as critical to the Upper Skagit community. Perhaps because rank-and-file men and women are relatively undifferentiated by income and life-chances there is agreement on the necessary qualities for leadership. Women are not undervalued or underused politically as is the case in the majority culture. Is there a political gender gap at Upper Skagit? While there are differences in the sorts of leadership men and women provide and in voting behaviors, neither are excluded. The gender gap is a different one than that of the mainstream society.

Endnotes

[1] Recent events in Canada vividly demonstrate that responses to public policy *issues* affecting the internal politics of Indian communities sometimes divide along sex lines. In the 1970s and 1980s, men and women had different views of a particularly thorny issue facing Indians: under the Indian Act female members of Indian bands were removed from federal Indian status upon marriage to non-status men. Indian men, on the other hand, faced no such obstacle and in-marrying, non-status women were given Indian status. In 1985 the federal government attempted to resolve this discrepancy between the treatment of men and women by amending the Indian Act (Bill G31). Some male-dominated band councils responded by refusing to reinstate women into band membership, even though the women had regained their federal recognition as status Indians (Frideres 1988:13). In 1992 spokespersons for aboriginal women's groups criticized the Canadian constitutional negotiations, and the position taken by the male leadership of the Assembly of First Nations, for excluding Native women from the bargaining table and called for the extension of the federal Charter of Rights and Freedoms to future Native self-governments. Sharon Mcivor, acting speaker for the Native Women's Association of Canada, feared the lack of protection for Native women by male-dominated aboriginal governments (*Vancouver Sun,* July 13, 1992). The responses to Bill C-31 and the constitutional debates in Canada make clear that political differences between Indian men and women may be significant in both community and national affairs.

[2] Elsewhere I examine several related issues including regional electoral results and economic issues (1992), federal funding and women's political chances (1990), and women, politics, and tribal legal systems (1994a, b), and specifics of the family network system (1989a).

[3] I use the term family networks to refer to the collectivity of people who are linked by the idiom of kinship and through regular patterns of reciprocity. Community members refer to these collectivities as families, a term that does not mean households or nuclear families. The terms family network and family are used interchangeably in the paper.

[4] Accusations of nepotism and corruption, of course, do not necessarily reflect reality. While it is true that the three large family networks have had many of their members engaged in tribal employment, this reflects in part the fact that the families constitute a significant percentage of the tribal population. A separate committee, designed to have broad community representation, has been established by the council to oversee hiring for tribal jobs to address the issue of nepotism.

[5] One woman councilor, a "neutral" from a small family, attributed her own election and re-election to the council to being quiet, both generally and at council meetings.

[6] A Kendall's Tau test gives a correlation of +.345, not significant at .05, between the percent of the vote cast by women and the number of women elected.

[7] To be known as outgoing, humorous, and light-hearted one must be willing to spend time with other community members in ways which are not directly task-oriented. Whitehead (1986) used the phrase "reputational work" to describe the effort and time spent developing social connections (often by just hanging around) in another society, and the phrase seems apt, especially for young men. As the phrase suggests, however, this activity may have a pay-off over the long run through the production of tribal solidarity (family lines are crossed in the socializing required in reputational work) and in helping to coalesce public opinion on issues of importance to the community. Reputational work, however, can be thought of as more in line with the requirements of leadership in a previous period before the present administrative structure developed.

[8] The sample size of the formal interviews is too small to make more than informed judgments about the viewpoints of men and women 55 and over. However, I rely on other information obtained during my work at Upper Skagit in making my arguments.

[9] Amoss (1985) has argued for the importance of "cultural texts" as one determinant of behavior among Indian people of Puget Sound, a view that my data support. Underlying gender attributions have undoubtedly helped shape the way men and women have responded to economic and educational opportunities, and ultimately, chances in tribal politics. However, I argue elsewhere (Miller 1992) that attributions of masculinity and femininity vary somewhat even between Coast Salish communities in close proximity. The division of labor at Upper Skagit has both a situational component (individual actors, especially technocrats, have taken advantage of opportunities and built on existing skills to advance their careers) and a gendered component in that community members have several very specific gender-linked expectations of men and women. There is some reason to believe that women have taken advantage of a differential role flexibility to move into the newly created categories of work and to legitimize their employment in terms of cultural expectations of women, an issue I take up in more detail elsewhere (Miller n.d.).

[10] Upper Skagit women frequently described their community as suffering from sexism. The issues they raised ranged from a desire for a more equitable division of housework to more serious problems of domestic violence.

References Cited

Albers, Patricia. 1983. Sioux Women in Transition: A Study of Their Changing Status in Domestic and Capitalist Sectors of Production. In *The Hidden Hall: Studies of Plains Indian Women*, edited by P. Albers and B. Medicine, pp. 175–234. Lanham Park, MD: University Press of America.

Amoss, Pamela. 1985. Coyote Looks at Grandmother: Puget Salish Grandmothers. Paper presented at the 85th Annual Meetings of the American Anthropological Association, Washington, D.C.

Bateille, Gretchin M., and Kathleen Mullen Sands. 1984. *American Indian Women: Telling Their Lives*. Lincoln: University of Nebraska Press.

Bee, Robert. 1981. *Crosscurrents Along the Colorado: The Impact of Government Policy on the Qpechan Indians*. Tucson: University of Arizona Press.

———— 1990. The Predicament of the Native American Leader: A Second Look. *Human Organization*, 49(1):56–63.

Biolsi, Thomas. 1991. "Indian Self-Government" As A Technique of Domination. *American Indian Quarterly*, 15(1):23–27.

Boelscher, Marianne. 1988. *The Curtain Within: Haida Social and Mythical Discourse.* Vancouver: University of British Columbia Press.

Carstens, Peter. 1991. *The Queen's People: A Study of Hegemony, Coercion, and Accommodation Among the Okanagan of Canada.* Toronto: University of Toronto Press.

Clifton, James. 1972. Factional Conflict and the Indian Community. In *The American Indian Today,* edited by S. Levine and N. Lurie, pp. 184–211. Baltimore, MD: Penguin.

Collins, June McCormick. 1974. *Valley of the Spirits: The Upper Skagit Indians of Western Washington.* Seattle: University of Washington Press.

Dobyns, Henry. 1981. Patterns of Indoamerican Chief Executive Tenure. *Human Organization,* 40:78–80.

Fiske, Joanne. 1989. Gender and Politics in an Indian Community. Ph.D. dissertation, University of British Columbia.

Fowler, Loretta. 1982. *Arapahoe Politics: 1851–1978.* Lincoln: University of Nebraska Press.

Frideres, James S. 1988. *Native Peoples in Canada: Contemporary Conflicts.* Scarborough, ON: Prentice-Hall Canada.

Garbarino, Merwyn S. 1980. Independence and Dependency Among the Seminole of Florida. In *Political Organization of Native North America,* edited by E. Schusky, pp. 141–162. Washington, D.C.: University Press of America.

Green, Rayna. 1980. Native American Women. *Signs,* 6:248–267.

Jorgensen, Joseph G. 1972. *The Sun Dance Religion: Power for the Powerless.* Chicago: University of Chicago Press.

Klein, Laura. 1976. She's One of Us You Know: The Public Life of Tlingit Women. *Western Canadian Journal of Anthropology,* 6:164–183.

Knack, Martha. 1989. Contemporary Measures of Southern Paiute Women and the Measurement of Women's Economic and Political Status. *Ethnology,* 28(3):233–248.

Miller, Bruce G. 1989a. A Sociocultural Explanation of the Election of Women to Formal Political Office: The Upper Skagit Case. Ph.D. dissertation, Arizona State University.

———— 1989b. After the F.A.P.: Tribal Reorganization After Federal Recognition. *Journal of Ethnic Studies,* 17 (1): 89–99.

———— 1990. An Ethnographic View: Positive Consequences of the War on Poverty. *American Indian and Alaska Native Mental Health Research,* 4(2):55–71.

———— 1992. Women and Politics: Comparative Evidence from the Northwest Coast. *Ethnology,* 31(4):367–384.

———— 1994a. Tribal Law and Coast Salish Gender Systems. *American Indian Culture and Research Journal,* 18(2):43–74.

——— 1994b. Contemporary Native Women: Role Flexibility and Politics. *Anthropologica,* 35(1):57–72.

Mooney, Kathleen A. 1976. Social Distance and Exchange: The Coast Salish Case. *Ethnology,* 15(4):323–346.

Powers, Marla N. 1986. *Oglala Women: Myth, Ritual, Reality.* New York: University of Chicago Press.

Renzetti, Claire M., and Daniel J. Curran. 1992. *Women, Men and Society.* Boston: Allyn and Bacon.

Ridington, Robin. 1990. *Little Bit Know Something.* Vancouver: Douglas and Mcintyre.

Robbins, Lynne A. 1986. Upper Skagit (Washington) and Gambell (Alaska) Indian Reorganization Act Governments: Struggles with Constraints, Restraints and Power. *American Indian Culture and Research Journal,* 10(2):61–73.

Sampson, Chief Martin. 1972. *Indians of Skagit County.* Mount Vernon, WA: Skagit County Historical Society.

Snyder, Sally. 1964. Skagit Society and its Existential Basis: An Ethnofolkloristic Reconstruction. Ph.D. dissertation, University of Washington.

Spicer, Edward H. 1967. *Cycles of Conquest.* Tucson: University of Arizona Press.

Stearns, Mary Lee. 1981. *Haida Culture In Custody.* Seattle: University of Washington Press.

Stockard, Jean and Miriam M. Johnson. 1992. *Sex and Gender in Society.* Englewood Cliffs, NJ: Prentice Hall.

Tennant, Paul. 1990. *Aboriginal Peoples and Politics.* Vancouver: University of British Columbia Press.

Tollefson, Kenneth. 1987. The Snoqualmie: A Puget Sound Chiefdom. *Ethnology,* 26(2):121–136.

Voget, Fred W. 1980. Adaptation and Cultural Persistence among The Crow Indians of Montana. In *Political Organization of Native North Americans,* edited by E. Schusky, pp. 283–297. Washington, D.C.: University Press of America.

Whitehead, Tony and Mary-Ellen Conaway. 1986. *Self, Sex, and Gender in Cross-Cultural Fieldwork.* Urbana: University of Illinois Press.

Part V
Coast Salish Relations
with the Mainstream

The renaissance of the Coast Salish world over the last three decades has been profound and the relationships with the Canadian and American state, and with the mainstream populations, have been fraught but also transformative. These selections examine strategies employed by Coast Salish peoples in their routine relations with the others and in the battles in court over resources and control of the landscape. Perhaps the most fascinating of these efforts was the canoe v. rowing shell race created by Swinomish Chief Tandy Wilbur in response to the effects of the depression and the cancellation of the rowing schedule of the University of Washington, the defending Olympic champions. A publicity stunt aimed at gaining war contracts for the Tribe, the race garnered national attention. Chief Wilbur's actions follow a distinctive format of creating space for Coast Salish peoples to project their ideas. This is the topic of Chapter 15, *The Great Race of 1941: A Coast Salish Public Relations Coup*

Another Coast Salish group attempted unsuccessfully to save a distinctive feature of their mythic landscape and I describe the legal issues that arose, including my own expert testimony, in Chapter 16, *Culture as Cultural Defense: A Sacred Site in Court.* Newspaper coverage of Coast Salish people shifted dramatically following the landmark *Boldt* decision regarding the division of the salmon harvest in Puget Sound. I use a content analysis of the entirety of the coverage in the Skagit Valley from the early twentieth century until the 1970s in Chapter 14, *The Press, the Boldt Decision, and Indian-White Relations* to show what these damaging changes have been. In addition, I describe the approach of a Canadian court to understanding the history of Indigenous peoples and the subsequent problems in the landmark *Delgamuukw* case in British Columbia. This essay, Chapter 13, *Anthropology and History in the Courts,* is my introduction to a special issue of *BC Studies,* which I put together following the decision. Finally, I use a figure from literature, Peter Pan, to show the damaging implications for Coast Salish people of the differences between the power of memory and oral traditions among Indigenous peoples and the institutional forgetfulness of the state; Chapter 17, *Story of Peter Pan, or Middle Ground Lost* was *a BC Studies* publication.

13

Introduction to Anthropology and History in the Courts*

Five of the papers in this collection deal with the use of the disciplines of anthropology and history *in Delgamuukw v. B.C.,* a case heard in the British Columbia Supreme Court. More commonly known as the McEachern Decision after presiding judge, Chief Justice Allan McEachern of the B.C. Court of Appeal, the outcome was made public on Friday, 8 March 1991, with the release of Mr. Justice McEachern's 394-page *Reasons for Judgment.* No effort is made to analyze the legal decision itself; that work is better left to legal scholars and to the First Nations communities. What follows concentrates instead on the court's use of the materials submitted to it by historians and anthropologists. It comes to the conclusion—let there be no doubt concerning the matter—that those materials were improperly utilized and badly understood.

The *Delgamuukw* case is an important one for several reasons. Brought to court by fifty-one hereditary chiefs of the Gitksan and Wet'suwet'en, representing 6,000 people organized into 133 Houses, this was the longest aboriginal title case in Canadian history: 374 days spent in court and 141 days spent taking evidence out of court. A massive territory, 54,000 square kilometres of crown land along the Skeena River in northern British Columbia, was at stake. The case began in Smithers in May 1987 and concluded in Vancouver in June 1990, with the decision rendered ten months later. The court proceedings, however, represent merely one step in a much longer process. For over 100 years the Province had refused to negotiate land title settlements with First Nations people of British Columbia. In November 1977 the Gitksan-Wet'suwet'en Declaration of ownership and jurisdiction was accepted by the federal government for negotiation. However, the Province of British Columbia failed to act on the Declaration, and the chiefs sought the only available remedy. In October, 1984, fifty-four hereditary chiefs representing seventy-six Houses took the province to court.[1]

The chiefs, through their legal counsel, argued that their traditional law remains in effect in their territories unless changed with their consent. Judge McEachern rejected both the claim and the theory underlying the claim, holding that Aboriginal people were never sovereign over these lands; that they held no Aboriginal title to the land, and instead had weaker use rights to the land; that use rights were limited in area; and that extinguishment of these use rights could occur by inference during the colonial period through land ordinances, proclamations or other means. *Delgamuukw* is the latest in a long line of legal decisions that deal with self-government and Aboriginal and treaty rights of First Nations in Canada, the United States, and other of the former British colonies. *Delgamuukw* represents a retreat from the findings of courts in all of these jurisdictions. Most notable among the Canadian Supreme Court decisions concerning British Columbia are the 1973 *Colder* case, in which the court split over the issue of whether the Aboriginal title of the Nishga had been extinguished in the colonial period, and the 1990 *Sparrow* case, in which the Aboriginal right to fish was held not to have been clearly and plainly extinguished by legislation.

Delgamuukw is important in that the litigants hoped to gain some measure of control over the natural resources of their region. The Skeena Fisheries Commission, made up of Gitksan and Wet'suwet'en chiefs, the Tsimshian Tribal Council, and the Lake Babine band, was established to manage the Skeena watershed area under their own fisheries management and harvest

*Authored by Bruce Granville Miller, reproduced with permission and previously published in *BC Studies*, 95:3–6 (1992).

philosophies. First Nations control over areas important for their forestry products, ceremonial uses, medicinal herbs, and game were linked to success in the suit.

But *Delgamuukw* is notable for reasons other than these quite predictable ones. The full-blown presentation of Gitksan and Wet'suwet'en oral tradition provides one of the richest sources of information about First Nations societies to date. Such a presentation required a concerted effort by the plaintiffs to provide the most thorough and authoritative testimony possible. By doing so, as Dara Culhane (1992) points out in this volume, "the Gitksan and Wet'suwet'en approached the court and the proceedings with dignity, sincerity and integrity." Michael Kew (1989:98) noted in a review of *Gisday Wa and Delgam Uukw, The Spirit in the Land,* the opening statement of the hereditary chiefs, that

> the case is also unique for the extent and breadth of the evidence from the people themselves…It contains a full record with unsurpassed detail of territory, history, and organization of all the houses (the primary political units), and it is given in the words and under direction of the people themselves. It is not a construction by outsiders.

Chief Justice McEachern's rejection of this testimony and the associated testimony of anthropologists and other academics is therefore a particularly heavy blow to both the First Nations and academic communities. It is most important that such valuable testimony be understood in a light different from that cast by the *Reasons for Judgment.*

In addition, the language employed in the *Reasons for Judgment* to describe Gitksan-Wet'suwet'en people and society and the logic underlying such descriptions shocked and outraged First Nations and academics, a fact noted in the pages of the nation's newspapers. Judge McEachern's reference to the "nasty, brutish and short" lives of Gitksan-Wet'suwet'en people in the nineteenth century and the notion that these people lived without the regular workings of an organized society received wide attention. *The Weekend Sun* reporters Mark Hume and Scott Simpson, for example, write of the fact that "with tears in their eyes, some of them shaking with anger, Indian leaders reacted with shock and dismay to the judgement of Chief Justice Allan McEachern" (9 March 1991). Reporter Ken MacQueen captured the sentiments of many scholars when he wrote that the ruling "has so angered and disgusted many of Canada's leading anthropologists that they are considering legal action" *(Vancouver Sun,* 13 July 1990).

The conduct of the trial and the manner of publication of the *Reasons for Judgment* are also noteworthy. In his chapter, Robin Ridington, a first-hand witness to much of the trial, describes the treatment of the chiefs during the case by a judge who did not understand the value of their contribution to the proceedings. Others, including Bruce Miller in this volume, have commented on the attractive packaging of the decision, the deceptively simple quality of its language, and the fact that it was priced to sell for $20. Apparently intended for wide distribution, it may provide a misleading account of First Nations history and culture to large numbers of people.

The first piece in this collection is the text of an address given 9 April 1991 at the Museum of Anthropology on the campus of the University of British Columbia. Dora Wilson-Kenni, Yagalahl, of the House of Spookw, served as a member of the Gitksan-Wet'suwet'en litigation team and monitored the trial in Vancouver. She describes the feast system, the importance of the oral testimony, and her strong reaction to the legal process. She comments that "we had to prove that we existed. We had to prove that we were a people and that we had a language…I'm sitting here. Can't you see me?"

The other contributors to this collection are four anthropologists and one historian. Robin Ridington, Julie Cruikshank, and Bruce Miller are all anthropologists at the University of British Columbia; Dara Culhane is a doctoral candidate in anthropology at Simon Fraser University. Robin Fisher is an historian at Simon Fraser University. Fisher examines the *Reasons for Judgment* in historiographie context and argues that although the Judgment appears to applaud the work of historians, there are serious problems with the judge's "scissors and paste" methodology and consequently with the conclusions reached. Fisher likens Judge McEachern's view of history to views current in the 1930s and notes that Judge McEachern overlooks the important work in understanding the history of British Columbia of the last two decades.

Ridington presents his account of the trial itself as a way to frame the use of anthropological testimony and the testimony of the hereditary chiefs. Cruikshank provides an overview of the approaches to the analysis of oral tradition in order to examine the judge's treatment of the Gitksan-Wet'suwet'en oral histories known as *adaawk* and *kungax.* She comments on his creation of his own brand of scholarship while dismissing the commonly accepted principles of research. Cruikshank calls this an "invention of anthropology." Miller employs Bourdieu's concept of common sense in order to make clear the logical underpinnings of the judge's opinion and the political implications of over-simplification and reliance on the "dominant discourse." Culhane focuses on the court's use of testimony and especially on the performance of Dr. Sheila Robinson, a cultural geographer employed by the Crown to provide anthropological testimony. Culhane points out that the testimony of Robinson, a non-anthropologist with no record of publication or fieldwork in the relevent areas, found favour with the court, while that of Hugh Brody, Richard Daly, and Antonia Mills, all well known and actively publishing in the field, was dismissed.

Important issues, these commentators make clear, are at stake in all of this. Let us now look at what those commentators themselves have to say in order to see, at length and in detail, what those issues are.

Endnote

[1] The Gitksan and Wet'suwet'en Information Packet. Prepared by the Office of The Hereditary Chiefs of the Gitksan and Wet'suwet'en People. Unpaginated. No date or place of publication given.

Reference Cited

Culhane, Dara. 1992. Adding Insult to Injury: Her Majesty's Loyal Anthropologist. In *BC Studies*, 95:66–92. Vancouver, B.C.: University of British Columbia.

Kew, J. E. Michael. 1989. Review of GISDAY WA and DELGAM UUKW, The Spirit in the Land: The Opening Statement of the Gitksan and Wet'suwet'en Hereditary Chiefs in the Supreme Court of British Columbia, 11 May 1987. *Culture,* 9(2):198–99.

Journal of Northwest Anthropology, Memoir 12: 219–235

14

The Press, the Boldt Decision, and Indian-White Relations*

This article examines newspaper coverage of Indians in the Skagit Valley of northwest Washington State. Many Indian people there have expressed unease towards the local newspapers and have suggested that the papers have damaged relations between Indian and non-Indian people over a long period, but especially during a treaty-related battle over salmon fishing which led to the so-called Boldt decision (*US* v. *Washington*, 384 F. Supp. 312,1974).[1] Such unease is understandable: this study of local newspapers shows that the nature of contemporary reporting and the historical context of reporting are important to understanding the region's intergroup relations. A content analysis of all articles concerning local Indians in the two most significant community newspapers, the *Concrete Herald* and the *Skagit Valley Herald*, going back to the early part of the century shows that reporting changed during and following the controversial court hearings.[2] Specifically, the nature and volume of reporting about Indians and Indian issues changed significantly during periods of intense interethnic group competition over salmon resources. Relatedly, the volume of reporting about tribes that are not federally recognized as political units (and therefore are ineffective competitors for resources) was less than that of acknowledged tribes.

Newspaper reporting in this location helped protect the interests of the dominant ethnic group and affect public attitudes by providing particular perspectives on the issues.[3] This is not to suggest, however, that the management or staff of either newspaper acted conspiratorially. Indeed, the reporting simply may have reflected unexamined biases of the white reporters and an internalization of prevalent images of Indians. The goal here is to determine what images of Indians were encountered by readers of the local newspapers and how these images varied over time, independent of any motives on the part of newspaper personnel.

Although this essay presents the results of a case study, the circumstances for Indians of the Skagit Valley were similar to those faced by Indians throughout the United States and Canada who are struggling for control of valuable resources, especially fishing, hunting, mining, water, and gambling (important examples include conflict over the Gitksan-Wet'suwet'en land claim in British Columbia and Chippeweyan fishing, hunting, and timber rights in Wisconsin). The value of the Skagit Valley case, then, is that although it does not provide a broad database for establishing general rules of newspaper behavior, the study does show that examining the role of the local media (and the use of content analysis methodology) may help in understanding the actions of participants in Indian-white disputes over resources. There are good reasons to believe the Skagit Valley reporting has much in common with the coverage of Indians by local newspapers elsewhere. A significant body of research, discussed below, has found media coverage of Indians (and other minorities) to be considerably different from coverage of the majority population and commonly to fail to provide an image of routine life. Instead, the focus is frequently on conflict and deviance. The approach taken here is informed by this literature, but understanding of how the media affects Indian-white relations can be refined by specifically comparing the coverage of Indians in resource-extraction areas during times when Indians are largely powerless and when they are serious claimants to vital resources.

*Authored by Bruce Granville Miller. Reprinted from the *American Indian Culture and Research Journal*, Volume 17, Issue 2, by permission of the American Indians Studies Center, UCLA. © 1993 Regents of the University of California.

Indian-White Relations and the Boldt Decision

The Boldt decision in 1974 ended almost a century of illegal obstruction by Washington State of treaty-based Indian access to salmon fishing: a resource central to Coast Salish Indian identity, spiritual life, and livelihood.[5] The federal court affirmed Indian treaty rights to fish in off-reservation locations and allocated half the Washington salmon catch to Indian fishers. The Indian share of the salmon harvest thereby increased about tenfold, a staggering windfall and a huge surprise to both Indians and whites.[6] The importance of the decision for the affected Indian and white communities can hardly be overstated.

The decision stands in contrast to a long history of alienation of Indian control over the resources of the Skagit Valley and a decline in Indian political fortunes, a process that began shortly after the United States gained clear title to the Oregon Country, including the Skagit Valley, in 1846. Governor Stevens negotiated treaties with Indians in order to open the area quickly, and pioneer settlement, mining, trading, and missionary activities started promptly. In 1855, Skagit Valley Indians signed the Treaty of Point Elliott, thereby ceding lands to the federal government. Congress ratified the treaty in 1859 and created the Swinomish Reservation in 1873. However, most Upper Skagit and Sauk-Suiattle avoided settling on the reservation, stayed out of regular contact with whites until after 1875, and eventually became known as "landless Indians." Subsequently, conditions deteriorated for both reservation and landless Indians. By the early twentieth century, with the loss of lands, fishing areas, and gathering sites, with populations diminished, and with control resting with Indian agents, Indians faced serious economic and political difficulties. Some gradually drifted out of the Skagit Valley in search of employment.[7]

The relative powerlessness of the Indian communities left non-Indians unprepared for the sudden turn of events brought about by the Boldt decision, and the shocked white community reacted immediately. Non-Indians, who had long since come to regard the salmon harvest as virtually their own, were suddenly faced with the possible prospect of being forced out of the fishing industry or facing large reductions in their catch (Knutson 1987). Hostility became so serious that Indians armed their fish camps after enduring attacks on themselves and their equipment.[8] Many whites displayed their reaction to the decision with bumper stickers proclaiming "Can Judge Boldt" on their cars. A widely held view was that the Boldt decision had given an unfair advantage to Indians in the fisheries.

The reactions in the Indian communities were equally profound, but the consequences were not felt immediately. The symbolic dimension of the decision was apparent right away: Fishers with a deeply felt tie to the Skagit River and the salmon were relieved to be able to openly carry on an activity so central to their identity. The economic transformations created by the decision were just as significant. The Boldt ruling was vitally important to Indian fishing communities,[9] in part because the local economies were so weak and employment opportunities limited.[10] The direct impact of the decision is exemplified in Boxberger's study of the Lummi Nation, a group located northwest of Bellingham, thirty miles from the Skagit Valley (Boxberger 1989). Since the late nineteenth century, the Lummi fishing fleet had fluctuated in size in response to the needs of the non-Indian community. After the Boldt decision, the Lummi fleet expanded independently and rapidly, as was the case in the nearby Indian communities of Skagit County. Today, some members of the Lummi, Swinomish, Tulalip, and other tribes operate highly profitable purse-seine operations. The Upper Skagit and Sauk-Suiattle, however, are limited to treaty-fishing on the Skagit River and therefore have developed less profitable gill-netting fleets. Still another important effect of the Boldt decision was the consequent return migration to the reservation. Many Indians of the Skagit Valley and elsewhere have been able to return to their ancestral lands, increasing populations on reservations and ending what one tribal leader called a "brain-drain" (Miller 1990).

The Boldt decision affected the several Indian communities in different ways. Although the decision is of great benefit to the recognized tribes, it led to the complete severing of relationships between the federal government and the landless tribes and to the elimination of landless tribes from the salmon harvest. Some tribes, including the Upper Skagit and Sauk-Suiattle, gained official recognition in 1974, and are included in the salmon harvest. The Samish and Snohomish were excluded, and other tribes took over their traditional fishing areas during a long and sometimes acrimonious process of dividing fishing areas and allocations between eligible tribes, a continuing process known as the "fish wars."

The Boldt decision has varying significance to non-Indian communities as well. Gaasholt and Cohen found that Indian-white relations in Seattle center around the controversy over Indian fishing rights but that public attitudes of Seattleites toward Native Americans did not appreciably deteriorate after the Boldt decision (Gaasholt and Cohen 1980). Small, white fishing communities, on the other hand, are more heavily dependent on fishing income, and therefore treaty rights issues are relatively more important to ethnic relations. The reporting in urban Seattle, with its more diversified economy, appears to be qualitatively different from that in the resource procurement areas, just as it varies between Vancouver and outlying areas in British Columbia.[11] This study, therefore, is concerned with reporting in the areas where the most heated battles over resources take place.

The Study

Research for this study included a thorough search of all the extant issues of two local newspapers for articles referring to local Indian people and tribes. The papers have been published continuously since the early part of the century and have circulated in areas with both federally recognized and nonrecognized tribes. Back copies of the weekly *Concrete Herald* are available since 1914. The circulation in 1988 was approximately 1,500, and the population of the town was 580 within city limits (Roberts 1987). This newspaper serves the upper reaches of the Skagit Valley, including the community of Concrete. The Skagit Valley *Herald* is based in Sedro-Woolley, Washington, and began publication as a daily in 1888, but back copies prior to 1911 are not available. In 1956, the previous name, *Mount Vernon Herald*, was dropped, and the present name came into use. Circulation was 16,500 in 1988. Sedro-Woolley had a population of only 6,290, but Skagit County, the target area of the newspaper, had a population of 68,200 in 1985. Whites comprised 94.6 percent of the population in 1984, and Indians were reported at 1,407, or 2.1 percent, although this undoubtedly is an undercount (Roberts 1987:9).

This study uses thematic analysis rather than other indicators of reporting such as headline, key word, placement in the paper by page, orientation, or attention (space) analysis. Fedler reported that minority groups, contrary to expectations, receive a proportional share of the space in the newspapers he surveyed (Fedler 1973). This is simply not the case for Indians of the Skagit Valley, especially before the 1960s. For example, Indians received only a handful of mentions in either paper between 1911 and 1961; consequently, there is no utility in studying the coverage from this angle. Both newspapers devoted only the front page to hard news for decades, reserving other pages for sports, gossip, advertising, comics, and other categories, so the great majority of articles about Indians are from the front page.[12]

Procedures

Articles are classified according to the dominant single theme and grouped by period. The formal analysis does not include editorials and letters to the editor. In the case of the *Skagit Valley Herald*, the six themes are as follows: (1) lore, which includes discussions of precontact Indian technology, stories, legends, and pioneer accounts, with an implicit assumption that Indian life as so depicted is now gone; (2) Indian antisocial actions that involve arrests, drinking, and violence (these articles may imply an anti-Indian sentiment); (3) politics, including treaty rights, especially fishing, hunting, and land claims, and Indian political organizations; (4) civic affairs, including white interventions on behalf of Indians, such as the construction of hospitals, schools, roads, or the bestowal of awards on Indians as Indians; (5) obituaries; and (6) other, a residual category. The analysis of the *Concrete Herald* employs the same categories, except that the civic theme did not arise.

Several examples illustrate the nature of the reporting. A 1923 *Mount Vernon Daily Herald* piece under the headline "Shaker Religion Queer Orientation" emphasized antisocial behavior. The accompanying text emphasized the violent shaking supposedly associated with the Shaker religion and claimed that this Salish Indian religion is "one of the strangest in the land." A 1915 frontpage lore article on the annual hops harvest, formerly a major local industry, noted that "the sound of the merry Indians and the sight of the long rows of boxes, Indian baskets, barrels, dinner pails, Indian babies…brought back memories." The accompanying photo was captioned,

> Remnants of a pioneer industry and a race of people, both of which once flourished in the Valley of the Skagit. Indians no longer dodge the picture man. This young brave and his family posed for *The Herald* camera.

A 1927 front-page lore piece in the *Mount Vernon Herald* entitled "Characteristics of Early Skagit Indians Are Told" recounted that "[s]uperstition was formerly among the Indian's most conspicuous infirmities." A 1936 front-page obituary entitled "Aged Indian's Death Recalls Early Day Skagit Slaying" combined qualities of both lore reporting and Indian violence:

> Paul Jesus, one of the Skagit's colorful Indian characters, died Saturday at the advanced age of 99…The passing of Paul Jesus recalls an Indian murder case in the early court records of Skagit county. In July 1897, four Indians were arrested for murder…

The article concluded with a discussion of how drinking and witchcraft contributed to the murder.

The *Mount Vernon Daily Herald* of 23 September 1937 contained two front-page stories concerning Indian antisocial behavior: One was entitled "Indian Shoots Self While 'Showing Off' with Rifle at Party," the other, "Indians Buy Wine; Two Men Are Arrested." A characteristic *Concrete Herald* piece of the same period, April 1933, recounted the death by drowning of two Indian ferrymen related to an episode of drinking.

A 1946 front-page article described an Indian gathering held to discuss state violations of treaty rights:

> In the light of the three huge bonfires which glaringly lit the center of the large room and threw weird shadows into the corners, bizarrely painted and costumed dancers performed the ceremonials to the rhythm of drums and the accompaniment of wailing chants.

A 22 February 1974 piece in the *Skagit Valley Herald* exemplified reporting on contentious treaty issues in the ten days immediately after the Boldt decision and suggested that the Indians might already have ruined the fish run. The front-page headline read "Loss of fishing, hunting controls told by official," and the text reads,

> A recent court ruling highly favorable to Indian fishing rights could affect "every citizen in the state," a Washington State Game official told Sedro-Woolley Rotary members at a meeting Tuesday...Wallace Kramer informed the local group that the...Indians have the potential to bankrupt local citizens...We don't know if they [Indians] have decimated the run yet.

Hypotheses

The study uses significant local events to partition the data and highlight trends in reporting (Table 22). The first period is 1911–1929. The second is 1930–60, beginning with the onset of the Great Depression, an event that shifted attention from Indian issues nationally. The third period is 1961–64, when Skagit Valley Indians publicly challenged state restrictions placed on treaty fishing rights. The final periods are 1965–71, a relatively quiet period in the Skagit Valley, and 1971–present, the start of the court proceedings leading up to the Boldt decision, and a period of active conflict over fishing, hunting, and the establishment of the Upper Skagit and Sauk-Suiattle reservations.

TABLE 22. PERIODIZATION OF REPORTING IN THE SKAGIT VALLEY NEWSPAPERS, 1911–PRESENT

1911–29	Predepression
1930–60	Depression, World War II, and period prior to publicized arrests for fishing
1961–64	Heightened struggle over fishing rights
1965–70	Quiet period before further struggle over treaty rights
1971–present	Ongoing struggle over fishing, hunting, and control of tribal land

The volume of reporting dramatically increased during times of overt conflict and competition between whites and Indians over land, fishing, hunting, and political and legal jurisdiction. In addition, the nature of reporting, by volume and by type, changed during these periods of active competition, as demonstrated in two ways. The hypothesis states that variation in types of reporting is unlikely to be due to chance. When the news is divided into those articles addressing or not addressing resource competition and when articles are partitioned into periods of contention and noncontention, a chi-square test gives statistically significant results (>.001) for the *Concrete Herald* and the *Skagit Valley Herald*, and for the two taken together. Second, a test of the variation of volume of reporting can be made by comparing the volume in these periods. Because both of these newspapers have gradually increased in size and coverage and because the contentious issues fall generally into recent times, this test would be biased. A more accurate test is to compare the volume of reporting immediately before and after the advent of heightened competition between ethnic groups. The clearest test is the comparison of the immediate pre-1961 (1959–60) reporting and the reporting of 1961–62, since serious conflict continues in the post-Boldt decision years (1974 onward). In the case of the *Skagit Valley Herald*, reporting on Indians is five times greater in the years 1961–62 compared to 1959–60, and for the *Concrete Herald* the increase is 2.7 times.

Analysis of Reporting

There is very little reporting of any sort about Indians prior to the 1930s in the *Skagit Valley Herald*, despite the fact that the Indian population was still considerable (Table 23). The 1,475 or so Indians at the time of the treaty in 1855 had been reduced (Lane and Lane 1977), but a Bureau of Indian Affairs census of 1921 showed 177 Upper Skagit and 200 in 1925.[13] There were a reported 208 Swinomish in 1909 and 285 in 1937 (Ruby and Brown 1986).

TABLE 23. INCIDENCE OF REPORTING ON INDIANS WITHIN SIX CATEGORIES IN THE *SKAGIT VALLEY HERALD*, 1911–1983*

Period	Obituaries	Lore	Antisocial	Political	Civic	Other
1911–29	2	10	1	12	0	8
%	6%	30%	3%	36%	0%	24%
1930–60	5	25	32	38	20	6
%	4%	20%	25%	30%	16%	5%
1961–64	0	7	18	31	1	1
%	0%	12%	31%	53%	2%	2%
1965–70	0	6	2	12	8	2
%	0%	20%	7%	40%	27%	7%
1971–83	4	7	29	181	4	50
%	1%	3%	11%	66%	1%	18%
Totals (522)	11	55	82	274	33	67
%	2%	11%	16%	52%	6%	13%

*Table 23 reports raw counts of articles within each category and, immediately below, the percent of the total for each period.

Skagit Valley Herald

Although local Indian activities scarcely showed up in reporting before 1930, some articles appeared about Indians living elsewhere. There was coverage of local *powwow* and *potlatch* events, terms used by the Indians to refer to their own important gatherings, but the newspaper reports did not refer to these. Instead, the articles dealt with large annual community festivals that had usurped the Indian terms in the 1910s. During the 1930s, reporting on Indians increased but then slowed down and almost disappeared during the years of World War II.

In 1961, the year Indian fish protests and fish-ins began, the pace of reporting about Indians quickened. This was, in part, a response to a court ruling that opened the way for off-reservation fishing by Indians without state regulation. In 1961–62, thirty-one articles on fisheries and the treaty and eighteen articles on antisocial Indian behavior appeared. There are no civic articles in either year, and they do not appear again until 1965, after the fishing controversy had died down. Civic articles, which had a heyday in the years 1930-60, occurred in small numbers during contentious periods. The paper published eight lore articles in those years, no obituaries, and one "other." Altogether, 84 percent of articles in the years 1961–62 depicted Indians engaged in activities that potentially threatened the welfare of the community. The predominant media images were of Indians who were antisocial or who challenged the status quo by bringing up treaty issues (which inherently are litigious, having to do with the legally binding division of resources within the region); these evidently were regarded as reportable, public issues only when Indian claims to a greater share appeared. Twelve percent more articles concern precontact life treated as quaint. Only one article addressed any other aspect of the lives of Indian people or of Indian tribal government.

With the start of court proceedings came a tremendous outpouring of articles on the fisheries issues. One hundred eighty-one articles appeared on this topic between 1971 and 1983, dwarfing all other categories reporting on Indians. Twenty-nine articles concerning antisocial Indian behavior appeared in the *Skagit Valley Herald* after 1971 and, again, only a few other articles (4 obituaries, 7 lore articles, and 50 "other" articles). Editorial policy condemned the Boldt decision in 1974 ("The Treaty Shouldn't Apply"). Other parts of the paper supported this view: A front-page query posed the question, "Should the State Control Fishing?"; a full-page spread claimed, "Observers Say Enforcement Is One Sided'' (the text asserted that Indian enforcement of Indian fishing quotas was lax), and accompanying photos showed happy Indian fishermen "making up to $600 a drift." This was contrasted with photos of whites who were forced out of fishing.

As with the earlier 1961–62 period, the great bulk of reporting (77 percent) in the years 1971–83 concerned either antisocial Indians or litigious Indians. There was another development as well. By 1978, after the Supreme Court had rejected an appeal of the Boldt decision and the matter was effectively closed legally, the paper regularly printed the opinions of the Indians about fisheries and treaty matters and published photos and interviews with Indians. The articles that fall into the "other" category are predominantly from the 1980s and are varied in content. One, for example, described the dedication of the new tribal center in 1982; a 1986 piece described a smoked fish business operated by the former Upper Skagit tribal chair; several in the early 1980s described zoning issues relevant to the Upper Skagit; and several in 1979 dealt with tribal efforts to intervene in the construction of a nuclear energy facility in the Skagit Valley. A 1978 article described the results of a nutritional study showing poor diets among Indians of the Skagit Valley, and a 1977 article described training given members of tribal police forces.

Nonacknowledged Tribes

The *Skagit Valley Herald* and its predecessor did not identify by name a formerly unrecognized tribe, the Upper Skagit, or the Upper Skagit tribal government, until 1924, when an article misidentified the chief who signed the Treaty of Point Elliott in 1855. The next report concerned a 1926 tribal meeting at the Shaker Church. Articles in the 1930s and early 1950s mentioned Upper Skagit racing canoes several times. Other than this, coverage of the Upper Skagit was almost nonexistent until the 1970s. The Sauk-Suiattle were treated as an Upper Skagit subgroup, receiving little separate attention.

The paper gave little coverage to the two tribes that achieved federal recognition in 1974. However, after 1977, the paper began reporting Upper Skagit Council viewpoints. Even in 1988, however, the newspaper did not routinely cover tribal events such as elections, although such coverage occurred sporadically, and a new city editor attempted to initiate a policy of covering tribal events. The paper gave considerable coverage to the effort to establish a reservation, an action hotly contested by the county and city governments. The choice to devote space to coverage of the proposed reservation can be understood within the ethnic resource competition framework, since reservation status took the land off the tax rolls and deprived the local white authorities of legal control over Indian populations. After tribal lands achieved reservation status, the council became free to write and apply their own code for tribal land and to police their own population. Coverage of the Upper Skagit and Sauk-Suiattle, then, did not seriously begin until after official governmental recognition. Newspaper coverage reflected the intentions of United States policy in giving attention primarily to Indians with a recognizable political status (and with the associated policymaking, corporate, political capacity), rather than to members of groups who are Indian as a matter of identity and descent.

Concrete Herald

The second paper, the *Concrete Herald*, went through several long periods of little reporting (Table 24). What reporting there was prior to 1961 emphasized obituaries, antisocial actions, and lore (78.6 percent of all articles). It is noteworthy that, through 1976, the only photos of Upper Skagit people or events were of canoe-racing or of people standing by canoes; as of 1986, five of the nine photos have included canoes, symbols of the past. From 1961 on, the focus was on treaty rights, especially fishing (66.7 percent). Obituaries, lore, and antisocial reporting diminished significantly.

As is the case with the *Skagit Valley Herald*, the early response to open conflict with Indians was a partisan white position. During the fish trouble of 1962, the front page announced "the gloomy conclusion that everything that could be done was done [to halt Indian fishing]. . . . Indians have the law in their favor. The only hope now is for Congressional action." Several articles in 1962 assigned full blame to the Indians for the decline of the fish run, even though the scientific community took a different view. For example, one headline read, "Net Fishing Kills Fish Runs." *Herald* articles assigned no part of the blame to the substantial white fishing fleet and white sportsfishers, nor did it point out that, for several decades, Indians, including Upper Skagit, had been all but removed from fishing.[14] In a similar vein, the settlement in 1968 of a century-old conflict over payments for lands ceded under terms of the Point Elliot Treaty of 1855 produced a headline of "Skagit Tribe Offered Grant." This headline implied that payment for lands was a gift of the government offered in the form of a grant, reinforcing the idea that Indians were unfairly taking advantage of their unique status. After 1977, the tone of the paper slowly shifted, and Upper Skagit views began to be aired. Reporting of antisocial behavior ceased, and an editorial of

1987 supported the right of the Upper Skagit to fish in cooperation with whites, albeit long after Washington State and the tribes had reached cooperative agreements on fishing and management programs.

TABLE 24. INCIDENCE OF REPORTING ON INDIANS WITHIN FIVE CATEGORIES, IN THE *CONCRETE HERALD*, 1914–1988

Period	Obituaries	Lore	Antisocial	Political	Other
1914–29	5	1	5	1	4
%	31%	6%	31%	6%	25%
1930–60	9	16	7	3	5
%	23%	40%	18%	8%	13%
1961–64	1	1	6	12	1
%	5%	5%	29%	57%	5%
1965–71	2	0	0	2	0
%	50%	0%	0%	50%	0%
1971–88	1	3	0	24	5
%	3%	9%	0%	73%	15%
Totals (114)	18	21	18	42	16
%	16%	18%	16%	37%	14%

Nonacknowledged Tribes

The *Concrete Herald* was very slow to recognize the Upper Skagit Indians whose aboriginal base was Concrete and who maintained the Shaker Church, their ceremonial center and tribal meeting place, in that town. The first specific mention of the tribe as a contemporary group was in 1918. The newspaper mentioned the tribe several times again in the thirties and fifties in stories on canoe-racing. Reporting increased dramatically after the emergence of the fishing issue in 1961–62, when nonacknowledged tribes were permitted to participate in the salmon fisheries, and again in the mid-1970s, after the Boldt decision heated up the fishing issue.

Discussion

Accounts of Indians in newspaper reporting have attracted some attention from social scientists and journalists, and generally the Skagit County findings are in line with earlier work. Most notably, other studies have shown an emphasis on conflict and Indian antisocial behavior in newspapers and have demonstrated the significance of the manipulation of Indian images by the press (Haycock 1971; Pride 1973; Green 1975; Wilson 1976; Scanlon 1977; Berkhofer 1978; Murphy 1979; Murphy and Avery 1983; Clifford 1988). Research indicates that newspaper representations of minority people play a role in the development of both public images and the self-image of minority groups (Osler 1974; Singer 1985; Lerner and Simmons 1996). Significant themes in the analysis of reporting are the limited repertory of storylines and the emphasis on Indian dependency on the government (Singer 1985). In addition, some work questions the accuracy of information presented about Indians. *Wassaja*, a newspaper with nationwide circulation, written by Indians about issues in Indian Country, reported that non-Indian reporters and columnists for newspapers of British Columbia "have attacked Indian fishing rights, misleading the public, and peddling misinformation."[15] 1975 analysis of reporting about Indian issues in non-Indian newspapers in New Mexico "found such coverage to be little short of a disgrace..."[16] This study examined seven newspapers, including the *Gallup Independent*, and found that only one newspaper employed an Indian reporter.

The type of coverage of minorities is different from that of the white population, as Fedler notes (Fedler 1973). The newspapers that he studied did not often run articles on routine aspects of the lives of minority people, such as meetings or community and individual honors, as they did about whites. Other newspapers have also neglected to report on routine life, and perhaps this is a persistent feature of reporting about Indians. Knack noted

> Just as biases become evidence, so too does the systematic failure of the newspapers to report certain events and information which was available to them. Omissions included the total absence of articles on the day-to-day home life of native families. There was no sense of the structure of the Indian community or of social or political relationships within it. (Knack 1986:91)

Knack showed not only that newspaper reporting mirrored the subordination of Indians within the dominant hierarchy of southern Nevada, but that newspapers were an instrument in establishing this relationship (Knack 1986:92). One might add that reporting reinforces the ethnic dominance hierarchy through its effects within the Indian communities as well. Some tribal members (especially members living off reservation) have internalized a negative impression of tribal life similar to that typically presented by newspapers. Newspaper reporting is the major source of information for many tribal members about Indian affairs; it influences their interest in participating in tribal events and in interacting with other tribal members.[17]

Additionally, other analyses focus on the generally conservative nature of the media. The content of editorial and "op-ed" pages are said to be "determined by the sense of purpose vis-a-vis the target audience: Enemies singled out for attack are always outside the social and political boundaries occupied by the significant gate-keepers..." (Altheide and Snow 1979:237). Further, most newspapers, in one view, are protective of entrenched interests and positions and are cautious because they depend on the routine assistance of politicians and organizations.[18] Not all newspapers operate to protect entrenched interests, however, nor are they all engaged in similar relationships with the political structure; an example is the *Observer*, a newspaper published in the Queen Charlotte Islands, British Columbia.[19] Nevertheless, as was the case in another study of reporting about Indians, both Skagit Valley papers show an overwhelming tendency to depict Indians as "individuals whose relationships to…society are essentially mediated by dependence on government and by presumably aggressive…claims. The second major image component presented is that of conflict-deviance" (Singer 1985:357).

Altogether, exactly 50 percent of the reporting over the last seventy-five years concerned fishing, hunting, and other treaty rights. Another 15.8 percent of reporting depicted antisocial Indian behavior. Nearly two-thirds (65.8 percent) of all reporting fell into these two categories. Little attention was given to routine reporting of Indian lives and governance, such as participation in ceremonies, episodes of intergovernmental cooperation, school events, or economic development planning.

The failure of these two newspapers to report about Indians' lives during noncontentious periods supports the premise of this work. Whole years passed without any reference to Indians who were unable to oppose state of Washington fisheries regulations effectively. It is worth noting that the Upper Skagit and Sauk-Suiattle themselves may not have been interested in being the subjects of reporting, especially since they were then nonreservation Indians otherwise out of the view of white authorities.[20]

The nature of reporting has special relevance for nonacknowledged tribes. The *Skagit Valley Herald*, which ran under the motto, "News Without Prejudice," sporadically supported the treaty rights of Indians, as in an editorial in 1922 and an article in 1924. The 1920s was a decade in which nonacknowledged, landless tribes attempted to receive cash compensation for lands and property surrendered under treaties of the previous century. These claims did not place local Indians and non-Indians in direct competition, however; no land would change hands, and any potential payment would have been made by the federal government and likely would have filtered into the white communities and businesses. The Upper Skagit and Sauk-Suiattle began to have a visible presence in the community newspapers only after federal acknowledgment in the 1970s.

At present, there are some two hundred nonacknowledged tribes in the United States (Miller 1991), and the Skagit County data suggest that these tribes may have difficulty obtaining local recognition of tribal activities and using the newspapers as a means of maintaining communication between members, as is the case with the Snohomish tribe of Washington State.[21] Although the Samish, also of Skagit County, have been notably successful in recruiting coverage from the *Anacortes American*, a local paper, their success is a result of sophisticated and unusual attempts to gain media attention, such as "declaring war on the United States" and declaring the Samish an endangered species.[22]

Conclusion

Newspapers must be regarded as participants in the sometimes heated competition between whites and Indians over the resources of the Skagit Valley. Just as the size of the Indian fishing fleet was altered by government regulation to serve white interests, the changing image of Indians systematically served white interests. The finding that the attitudes of non-Indian people in Seattle toward Indians did not deteriorate after the Boldt decision can be understood in view of localized differences in the importance of the contested resources (Gaasholt and Cohen 1980). More than fifteen years later, repercussions of the Boldt decision continue to influence attitudes in the Skagit Valley, and these attitudes still create regular difficulties for members of Indian communities.[23]

Just why were Skagit Indians distrustful of the local newspapers? The Skagit county newspapers, whether by conscious policy or not, managed the image of Indian people in a variety of ways, particularly by failing to report routine events, by helping in the usurpation of Indian symbols, and by emphasizing negative and contentious behavior. These two newspapers manipulated the image of Indians by responding directly and immediately to the demands of the non-Indian community in times of serious conflict and providing the majority culture a highly abstract view of Indian culture. These newspaper practices left the white community inadequately informed about details of federal Indian-white relations that would have broadened understanding of local events such as the sudden increase of Indian fishing or the establishment of the Upper Skagit and Sauk-Suiattle reservations. The failure over the years to report Indian events and accomplishments routinely perhaps contributed to the present-day conflict experienced by many Upper Skagit and white residents of the Skagit Valley. The "invisible" Indians, particularly those from nonacknowledged tribes who pressed for their treaty rights in the 1960s, surprised the white inhabitants who believed there was little real Indian presence in their area.[24]

This study suggests that tribal media-management strategies might take into account the long-term imagery of Indian people created by the local media. Since newspapers are predisposed to report in already-established categories, press releases and news creation efforts will be more likely to succeed if they work within this context (Altheide and Snow 1979). An effort to establish an image of routine Indian life may help mitigate contentious reporting during episodic, treaty related periods of heightened antagonism and may produce public relations benefits with regard to tribal members living away from the reservation.[24]

ACKNOWLEDGMENTS

The author wishes to thank Lynn Robbins, David Altheide, and Rebecca Bateman for their comments on this essay. An earlier version was presented at the 44th Annual Northwest Anthropological Research Conference, 28 March 1991, in Missoula, Montana.

Endnotes

[1] Members of several Indian communities expressed these opinions to me during a period of fieldwork, 1986–89, in which I studied political processes on reservations of northern Puget Sound, especially in Skagit County. Several of these people made sure I understood the importance they attached to the issue of newspaper coverage of Indian communities, and the Upper Skagit summer youth program provided several teenagers to help in the laborious examination of back issues. Andy Fernando, former Upper Skagit Council chair, remarked in 1986 that he left his job as a reporter for the *Bellingham Herald*, published about twenty-five miles north of the Skagit Valley, in part because of anti-Indian bias at the newspaper.

[2] The methodology of content analysis does not provide a direct sense of the effects of reporting or of the Boldt decision on individuals. Depicting the human side of the story is not the aim of this article. Accounts of the Indian experience in Skagit County can be found in the works of Chief Martin J. Sampson (1972), Roberts (1975), Fernando (1986), and Miller (1989).

[3] Martha C. Knack detailed the role of the press in protecting white interests in "Newspaper Accounts of Indian Women in Southern Nevada Mining Towns" (Knack 1986). Many other social institutions and processes influence public attitudes and the outcomes of struggles over land and resources, of course, but the focus here is on the press. The related issues are beyond the scope of this work. Nonetheless, Altheide and Snow emphasize that understanding the behavior of the media, including the response to pressures on the media from the outside, is crucial for several reasons (Altheide and Snow 1979); Altheide (1987 and 1991). Altheide and Snow describe what they call "media logic" in arguing that the media cannot be understood as just another variable in the process of social change. The format (style, focus, and grammar of communication) creates a perspective for presenting as well as interpreting phenomena and is integrated by individuals as a form of logic. This logic influences how people perceive, interpret,

and act. Consequently, media function to determine what subjects will be discussed and will be deemed relevant for the community. Media coverage becomes the source of official and unofficial information and historical accounts, and legitimizes current practices (Altheide and Snow 1979:237–38).

[4] See Daniel L. Boxberger (1989) for a history of state intervention.

[5] Northwest Coast Indians, including Coast Salish, have sometimes been called the "Salmon People," referring to a spiritual link to the fish and to the importance of salmon to the economy and diet.

[6] Knutson (1987) notes that Indian fishers took only 5 percent of the catch in the early 1970s.

[7] For histories of the postcontact period, see Sampson (1972), Collins (1974). Roberts (1975), Cohen (1986), and Miller (1989)

[8] Some Indian fish camps are still armed and fishers alert to intrusion by outsiders. This aspect of the events surrounding the Boldt decision did not appear in newspaper coverage. Many whites left the salmon fishing industry, some under a fishing boat buy-back program established by the state.

[9] The Boldt decision is important to Indian communities located elsewhere as well. Despite the hostility it generated, the decision is notable in creating the basis for successful cooperative management of the fisheries resource by the state, Indian tribes, and white fishing interests. The decision is a model for the resolution of other claims to resources based on treaty or aboriginal rights in the United States and Canada. See Cassidy and Dale 1988).

[10] Two of the major sources of employment in the Skagit Valley, logging and agricultural work, significantly diminished in the 1980s, and few Indian laborers have found employment in the skilled labor positions. See Judy Roberts (1987:10).

[11] A 1990 study by Nels Pedersen, a Danish graduate student, tentatively suggests variation in reporting between Vancouver and outlying areas (manuscript in author's possession). Reporters for the urban *Vancouver Sun* are far more likely than those in outlying areas to represent views sympathetic to Indians or to attempt to print Indian viewpoints. Sun reporters are assigned full-time to the "Indian beat." However, there may be limits to accurate treatment of the Indian community. One well-informed reporter, Terry Glavin, claimed disapprovingly in a public lecture at the University of British Columbia that he was removed from covering Indian issues in 1991 because his editors felt he was "burnt out," meaning he was too close to the Indian communities and his work lacked objectivity.

[12] It is beyond the scope of this study to consider in detail the history of editorial policy, ownership, and overall political tone of the two newspapers. Both papers have consistently focused primarily on local events and from a conservative perspective. For example, the *Skagit Valley Herald* ran a series of articles entitled "Silly Wives of History," starting immediately after women won the right to vote. During the years 1913–1919, front-page articles encouraged participation at Ku Klux Klan events held locally. Editorial policy opposed the formation of the United Nations, and the paper completely omitted reports on the Russian Revolution until after the fact.

[13] Tulalip Indian Agency records. Offices of the Bureau of Indian Affairs, Everett, Washington, no record number given.

[14] Boxberger (1989), Knutson (1987). There is an interesting parallel between events in British Columbia in the summer of 1992 and the accusations that Skagit Valley Indians had fished out the Skagit River within days of regaining treaty rights to fish in usual and accustomed locations. Shortly after bands received an allocation for commercial fishing on the Fraser River for the first time ever, the *Vancouver Sun* reported that the Fisheries Council of B. C. and the United Fishermen and Allied Worker's Union charged the Indians were responsible for the disappearance of one million salmon.

[15] *Wassaja*, 7(2):16 (1979).

[16] *Wassaja*, 3(6):10 (1975).

[17] Tribal members who have internalized a negative impression of their own tribe have not rejected their tribal identity but may be dissatisfied with tribal political leadership and reservation lifestyle. One off-reservation man, for example, rejected the "welfare mentality" of the reservation, a complaint voiced in the local newspapers. Many off-reservation tribal members, even those living nearby, reported that their major source of information about tribal activities, other than activities of their relatives, is the local newspapers (fieldnotes, 1986).

[18] It is likely that the media will grow in importance as a factor in the competition over resources between Indians and non-Indians. In British Columbia in 1990, for example, Indian, federal, and provincial authorities attempted to use the

media to provoke public opinion prior to negotiations over land claims and sovereignty. The federal Indian affairs minister talked of a "multibillion-dollar" cost for settling the land claims (*Vancouver Sun*, 5 December 1990). In response, one Indian leader, then chairman of the First Nations Congress, claimed in a widely reported public address that Indians should have killed the first white settlers and that delaying the land claims would increase the cost one hundred times (*Vancouver Sun*, 12 December 1990). Efforts to use the press are not new, but such scenarios may multiply as the economy remains weak and treaty issues remain unresolved. Pressure began to build in the 1970s, a decade characterized by a resurgent demand for Indian resources, including coal, uranium, fish, and water, by the non-Indian community in both the United States and Canada. (See Stephen Cornell 1988). This was also a period of a dramatic nationwide increase of Indian political activity and of a substantial reorganization of Indian-white relations more directly influenced by the actions of Indians themselves than in earlier periods (Cornell 1988:12). Meanwhile, governmental controls over Indian people and resources are less direct under the present United States policy of Indian self-determination and under new Canadian policy initiatives than it was in earlier periods (Cornell 1988). Consequently, influence over political and legal processes will depend more on the mobilization of public opinion than on the authoritarian, coercive measures of the past.

[19] The relationship between the people of the Queen Charlotte Islands and the only newspaper, the Observer, is quite different from that in Skagit County. The Queen Charlotte Islands stand variously 50 to 75 miles off the coast of British Columbia and are home to small populations of native and nonnative people. There are some 5,470 residents of the islands, including 867 Haida (Statistics Canada: 1986 Canadian census). The circumstances are similar to those in Skagit County in several ways (Stearns 1960:261–266). Both areas are rural and depend heavily on fishing and logging, industries in decline. What is different is the relatively greater percentage of Indian population on the islands and a shared Indian and white interest in preservation of some of the islands' lands, which culminated in the creation of a national park on Moresby Island in 1989.

The Observer is a weekly that sometimes has no reporting staff, instead relying on unsolicited letters, press releases, and articles; therefore, it reflects public opinion, including Indian opinion, more directly than do the Skagit County papers. Pinkerton, an anthropologist specializing in resource management, analyzed the newspaper coverage (Pinkerton 1983). During the years 1971–1973, there was little discussion in the paper of forestry issues or Haida land claims, the British Columbia equivalent of treaty issues in Washington State. But starting 1974–1976, a debate arose concerning the use of island land and the relationship of the issues to Haida land claims. There was a fivefold increase in the mentions of forest management issues in the *Observer* during this period, and an elevenfold increase in discussions of Haida land claims. The majority of letters were critical of forest management practices and policies, which largely were determined off the Islands. As the issue of Haida land claims developed, the nature and volume of reporting changed. In Pinkerton's words,

> *Observer* coverage of forest management, in letters, editorials, and articles, increased from a middle high period of 35 mentions a year, in 1975, to 126 mentions in 1979…[T]he percentage of mentions criticizing the companies or government…exceeded 50%…The percentage of mentions which were hostile reactions to the criticism remained at about 30%. By 1980, however, none of this hostile criticism was coming from local residents. All of it was coming from the companies and the government. The power level of respondents to the newspaper rose, and higher authorities began to write as the stakes increased. By the time the minister of forests was taken to court in 1979, the newspaper had helped create crucial changes in public opinion on the islands, which placed the role of the logging companies and the government.

The power level of respondents to the newspaper rose, and higher authorities began to write as the stakes increased. By the time the minister of forests was taken to court in 1979, the newspaper had helped create crucial changes in public opinion on the islands, which placed the role of the logging companies and the government under scrutiny.

Several observations may be made concerning this case. As with the two Skagit County papers, coverage of treaty or aboriginal rights-related issues dramatically increased as these issues became more salient. Elements of the nonnative power structure attempted to use the paper to sway public opinion, but, unlike in Skagit County, hostile opinion came only from off-island, and the small populations of Indians and non-Indians found common cause in opposition to off-islanders. As was the case in Skagit County, the newspaper reflected local interests. A land claim issue not centered around local resource competition did not inspire a racially polarized response in the press, even though the volume of reporting about treaty-related issues increased. In sum, the Queen Charlotte Islands case is a counter-example, and shows conditions under which a paper does not make life difficult for Indians, as the Skagit County papers have. It is notable that the *Observer* ran articles on routine elements of Indian life before the land claim issues arose.

[20] Because of their landless status, the Upper Skagit and Sauk-Suiattle were largely free of the restraints on ceremonial events, such as Spirit Dancing, that were imposed on reservation residents by Indian agents.

[21] This is a conclusion in a study by Daniel L. Boxberger and Bruce G. Miller, "Snohomish Social Organization: 1930s–1950s" (Unpublished ms.).

[22] Ken Hansen, former tribal chair, personal communication.

[23] For example, school children face regular harassment because of the fisheries situation.

[24] The major history of the region, JoAnn Roe (1980), makes scant reference to Indians of the area and fails to mention many tribes altogether. Longtime residents of the upper Skagit Valley, where the nonrecognized tribes are located, frequently report that they were unaware that any Indians still exist in these locations (fieldnotes, 1989).

[24] The Samish management of the press is an example of a successful effort by a tribe to enlist support from the local media. Routine events are reported, and the *Anacortes American* supports Samish efforts to obtain federal recognition. The town of Anacortes stands to benefit from Samish recognition through the flow of money to the Samish from federal programs. The Samish are not direct competitors with white fishers, though. Under the terms of the Boldt decision, the Samish, if recognized, would potentially be included in the (Indian) treaty share of the salmon harvest.

References Cited

Altheide, David L. 1987. Ethnographic Content Analysis. *Qualitative Sociology*, 10(1):65–77.

———— 1991. The Mass Media as a Total Institution. *Communications*, 16(1):67–71.

Altheide, David L., and Robert P. Snow. 1979. *Media Logic*. Beverly Hills, CA: Sage Library of Social Research.

Berkhofer, Robert F. 1978. *The White Man's Indian: Images of the American Indian from Columbus to the Present*. Lincoln: University of Nebraska Press.

Boxberger, Daniel L. 1989. *To Fish in Common: The Ethnohistory of Lummi Indian Salmon Fishing*. Lincoln: University of Nebraska Press.

Boxberger, Daniel L., and Bruce G. Miller. n.d. Snohomish Social Organization: 1930s–1950s. Unpublished ms.

Cassidy, Frank and James Clifford. 1988. *The Predicament of Culture: Twentieth Century Ethnography, Literature and Art*. Cambridge, MA: Harvard University Press.

Cassidy, Frank and Norman Dale. 1988. *After Native Claims: The Implications of Comprehensive Claims Settlements for Natural Resources in B. C.* Port Redrew, BC: Oolichan Publishing.

Cohen, Fay G. 1986. *Treaties on Trial: The Continuing Controversy over Northwest Indian Fishing Rights*. Seattle: University of Washington Press.

Collins, June McCormick. 1974. *Valley of the Spirits: The Upper Skagit Indians of Western Washington*. Seattle: University of Washington Press.

Cornell, Stephen. 1988. *The Return of the Native: American Indian Political Resurgence*. New York: Oxford University Press.

Dale, Norman. 1988. *After Native Claims: The Implications of Comprehensive Claims Settlements for Natural Resources in B. C.* Port Redrew, B.C.: Oolichan Publishing.

234

Fernando, Andres. 1986. Introduction. In *Treaties on Trial*, edited by Fay G. Cohen, pp. xv–xxvi. Seattle: University of Washington Press.

Gaasholt, Oystein and Fay Cohen. 1980. In the Wake of the Boldt Decision: A Sociological Study. *American Indian Journal,* 9:9–17.

Fedler, Fred. 1973. The Media and Minority Groups: A Study of Adequacy of Access. *Journalism Quarterly,* 50:109–117.

Green, Rayna. 1975. The Image of Indian Women in American Culture. *Massachusetts Review,* 16:698–714.

Haycock, Ronald Graham. 1971. *The Image of the Indian.* Waterloo, ON: Waterloo Lutheran Press.

Knack, Martha C. 1986. Newspaper Accounts of Indian Women in Southern Nevada Mining Towns. *Journal of California and Great Basin Anthropology,* 8:83–96.

Knutson, Peter. 1987. The Unintended Consequences of the Boldt Decision. *Cultural Survival Quarterly,* 11(2):43–47.

Lane, Robert B., and Barbara Lane. 1977. Indians and Indian Fisheries of the Skagit River System. Ms. in Upper Skagit Archives.

Lerner, M. J., and C. H. Simmons. 1966. Observer's Reaction to the Innocent Victim: Compassion or Rejection? *Journal of Personality and Social Psychology,* 4: 203–210.

Miller, Bruce G. 1989. After the F.A.P.: Tribal Reorganization after Federal Recognition. *Journal of Ethnic Studies,* 17(2):89–100.

——— 1990. An Ethnographic View: Positive Consequences of the War on Poverty. *American Indian and Alaska Native Mental Health Research,* 4:55–71.

——— 1991. The Forgotten Indians and Federal Recognition. *Friends Journal,* 37:22–24.

Murphy, Sharon. 1979. American Indians and the Media: Neglect and Stereotype. *Journalism History,* 6:39–43.

Murphy, James E., and Donald R. Avery. 1983. A Comparison of Alaskan Native and Non-Native Newspaper Content. *Journalism Quarterly,* 60:316–22.

Osler, Andrew. 1974. An Analysis of Some News-flow Patterns and Influences in Ontario. In *Reports of the Royal Commission on Violence in the Communications Industry,* vol. 7, *The Media Industries: From Here to Where?,* pp. 47–70. Queens Park, ON: Publication Centre, Ministries of Government Services.

Pinkerton, Evelyn. 1983. Taking the Minister to Court Changes in Public Opinion about Forestry Management and Their Expression in Haida Land Claims. *BC Studies,* 57:68–85.

Pride, Richard A. 1973. Race Relations in TV News: A Content Analysis of the Networks. *Journalism Quarterly,* 50:318–328.

Roberts, Judy. 1987. Low-Income Needs and Community Resources Assessment. Document prepared for the Skagit County Community Action Council.

Roberts, Natalie A. 1975. A History of the Swinomish Tribal Community. Ph.D. dissertation, University of Washington.

Roe, JoAnn. 1980. *The North Cascadians*. Seattle, WA: Madrona Publishers.

Ruby, Robert H., and John A. Brown. 1986. *A Guide to the Indian Tribes of the Pacific Northwest*. Norman: University of Oklahoma Press.

Sampson, Chief Martin J. 1972. *Indians of Skagit County*. Mount Vernon, WA: Skagit County Historical Society.

Scanlon, Joseph. 1977. The Sikhs in Vancouver: A Case Study in the Role of the Media in Ethnic Relations. *Ethnicity and the Media-An Analysis of Media Reporting in the U. S., Canada, and Ireland*. UNESCO.

Singer, Benjamin D. 1985. Minorities and the Media: A Content Analysis of Native Canadians in the Daily Press. *Canadian Review of Sociology and Anthropology*, 19(3):348–59;

Sterns, Mary Lee. 1990. Haida Since 1960. In *Handbook of North American Indians*, Vol. 7, *Northwest Coast,* edited by Wayne Suttles, pp. 261–266. Washington, D.C. Smithsonian Institution.

Wilson, Charles R. 1976. Racial Reservations: Indians and Blacks in American Magazines, 1865–1900. *Journal of Popular Culture*, 103:70–79.

Journal of Northwest Anthropology, Memoir 12:236–248 (2016)

15

The Great Race of 1941:
A Coast Salish Public Relations Coup*

On November 29, 1941, two 11-man Indian racing canoes—the famous *Lone Eagle* and the *Susie Q*—and two University of Washington (UW) eight-oared shells lined up to race through the Swinomish Slough in La Conner, Washington. A small crowd watched the race from the shore, and a much larger audience read about it in the next day's *Seattle Times*. More than 50 years later, it is not clear how this "Great Race" was conducted, how far the boats raced, who won, or even whether there was meant to be a winner. This small drama, however, reveals something of the nature of relations between the Indian and mainstream communities of western Washington during the Great Depression and its immediate aftermath. The race serves as an example of media management and the public relations strategy carried out by one Indian leader in his efforts to address pressing issues within the Indian community and improve relations with the mainstream society. His strategy, although ordinarily implemented less dramatically, remains characteristic of leaders from the Coast Salish communities of Washington and British Columbia.

Information about the 1941 Great Race comes primarily from interviews with five UW oarsmen; Al Ulrickson, Jr., the son of the head coach and a boy at the time; and Bud Rainey, the freshman coach. I have also consulted Smokey Lyle, one of the pullers (Indian paddlers) in the race, and I have talked with Emmett Oliver, who raced in the *Lone Eagle* canoe in an earlier period. The Indian leader who conceived of this race, Tandy Wilbur of the Swinomish reservation, is now deceased. However, Natalie Roberts's 1975 monograph largely based on her work with Wilbur is most helpful in understanding twentieth-century Swinomish history from his perspective.[1]

The Great Race is a twentieth century story, but it includes themes developed earlier in both Indian and settler societies. Since much of the coast was inhospitable to overland travel, Northwest Coast Indian cultures emphasized water travel. Puget Sound itself is a complex of waterways, and Indians traveled and transported goods in canoes of several sorts, using paddles, sails, and poles for propulsion. In addition to this tradition of canoeing for transportation, there remain important cultural beliefs and practices surrounding canoes and canoeing. For instance, the act of felling the tree for the canoe continues to be a spiritual event, as is the process of building the canoe. Canoe builders are people of high status, and canoes have long been important items in potlatches and trade (Lincoln 1991).

In the early twentieth century, with the construction of roads and railroads, the need for canoeing diminished. However, canoes remain a part of many Indian cultures. As Emmett Oliver, a Quinault, observed in 1991, "The canoe represents Native life at its fullest" (Oliver 1991:248). A new canoeing tradition sprang up in the early part of the century, when organized canoe regattas were staged, often at civic events that drew large crowds of nonnatives. The biggest event, held from 1929 to 1941, was at Coupeville, Washington.[2] Winners received cash prizes, and several towns such as Coupeville, sponsored races in order to draw tourists.[3] Races on the Swinomish Slough were sponsored partly by La Conner businesses (Roberts 1975:259).

*Authored by Bruce Granville Miller, reproduced with permission and previously published in *Pacific Northwest Quarterly*, 89(3):127–135 (1998).

In those days—as well as today—skippers, the captains of the canoes, brought in talented athletes, sometimes from outside their own tribal communities but ordinarily with some kinship connection, to race in a particular canoe. The *Lone Eagle*, one of the canoes in the 1941 race, had a long and colorful history and attracted outstanding pullers. Emmett Oliver, for example, a collegiate football player, was working in the La Conner vicinity for the summer and was invited to pull in the *Lone Eagle* for the 1934 season. The *Lone Eagle's* victories depended on coaching, tradition, and dedication on the part of supporters, in addition to good athletes. Two brothers, Vic and Willie Jones, and their father, Earl Jones, of Lummi, Washington, were driving forces behind the successes of the *Lone Eagle*. Vic Jones reportedly loaded war canoes on his fishing boat to transport them to Victoria, B.C., for races against Canadian Indians. Norb James built racks for his truck to transport the *Lone Eagle*. Stories about particular canoes are told within communities, and the tales contain elements of spiritual enhancement and efficacy, properties both of the athletes and, significantly, of the canoes. Names of canoes are often preserved for generations and given to replacement canoes.[4] In sum, there is a long and significant tradition of canoeing in Coast Salish culture.

There is also a long and significant tradition of boatmanship among the non-aboriginal population of western Washington. This tradition began with Vancouver, Wilkes, and other early white visitors, who employed small boats to explore and map the area. Nonnative settlers arriving in the middle and late nineteenth centuries learned about the local waterways from Indians and hired them to transport goods and people. Later, the settlers took on these tasks themselves, employing a mosquito fleet.

*   *   *

A new chapter in the history of boatmanship began in 1911. George Pocock, a young descendant of English boat builders and scullers, came to British Columbia to build boats and organize races for the Vancouver Boat Club. In 1912, Pocock and his brother moved to Seattle to work with Hiram Conibear, coach of the University of Washington rowing program, which had been established in 1904 (Newell 1987). The combination of Pocock and Conibear was just what was needed to propel the Washington Huskies to the center of the American rowing world, to make them competitive with the eastern powers in the sport.[5]

In 1936, at the height of an economic depression that devastated the nation, the University of Washington crew, representing the United States, narrowly defeated the Italians to win the Olympic championship in eight-oared shells. This event galvanized the population of Washington State in a manner that is difficult to imagine today. Several of the Washington oarsmen of the period believed that their coach, Al Ulbrickson, Sr., could easily have been elected governor. This was not mere hyperbole: newspaper coverage reveals the profound symbolic significance of the event. In 1936 there were no major-league professional teams on the West Coast, and the major contender for media coverage in the Washington papers was collegiate football, a sport that does not award Olympic medals.

The coxswain of the 1941 varsity crew, Vic Fomo, noted that 250,000 spectators attended one of his intercollegiate races on Lake Washington.[6] So large an audience is not unlikely; in the 1980s 100,000 people attended an Opening Day Regatta in which the Huskies rowed against the Soviet national team. In the 1930s and 1940s the Washington Huskies were the biggest show in town, and even their workouts were reported in detail by the newspapers. On the very day of the Great Race, November 29, the lead headline of the *Seattle Times* sports section read, "Raney

Selects Frosh Oarsmen." Al Ulbrickson, Jr., noted that the "whole community identified with" rowing, adding that it was "a focus of Northwest culture."[7] The popularity of the Husky rowing program of that period underscores the utter implausibility of having these media stars race against Indian canoeists unknown to the mainstream community.

Figure 13. This photo of the Great Race, published in the *Seattle Times*, November 30, 1941, shows the Huskies badly out of sync and two oarsmen looking to the side, indications that the photo was not taken during the actual race. (Author's collection)

In both Swinomish and mainstream societies, boats and racing were powerful, evocative symbols. For Indians, canoes—with their origins in sacred cedar trees—represented a connection to the land, to the water, and, more generally, to an aboriginal world view. For the mainstream society, the rowers represented the vigor of a community then based in good measure on the primary industries of fishing, farming, and logging and intimately connected with the sea. The successes of the crew demonstrated the ability of the Washingtonians to persevere under adversity and to compete on equal footing with other, more prosperous and powerful parts of the United States. There was, however, an overlap in Indian and mainstream societies' interest in small boat racing, and the Swinomish leader Tandy Wilbur acted on this in promoting the Great Race.

Wilbur's motivations for staging the event appear to fall in line with several of the major emphases of his career as a political leader. He faced two serious, related challenges within his community. One was the long-standing effort to promote cohesion among tribal members whose ancestors were from a number of communities within the region, a process that Roberts calls "ethnic fusion" (Roberts 1975:398). Descendants of Samish, Swinomish proper, Kikiallus, Lower and Upper Skagit peoples, and others compose the present-day Swinomish community, although all of the members of these groups did not go to the Swinomish reservation. The Swinomish chief Martin Sampson's comments on the newly formed tribal council of 1928 describe the situation. "Almost everything was in our favor for a successful administration. . . . The only obstacle that had to be hurdled was the fact that these people belonged to four [*sic*] different tribes, and each person and group wanted to be identified with his own tribe" (Sampson 1972:40).

* * *

Wilbur was among the first of a new generation of Swinomish leaders during a transitional period when the demands of governance changed. The federal Indian Reorganization Act was passed in 1934; within two years, the Swinomish had elected a council and adopted a constitution. Wilbur succeeded Martin Sampson as chairman of the Swinomish Tribal Community in 1941, moving up from vice-chairman. He was also the first business manager. Consequently, for Wilbur and others, ethnic fusion was overlaid with the problem of legitimizing the new system of elective officials, government, and community institutions. Wilbur, unlike Sampson, chose to emphasize the economic development of the community rather than the settlement of claims made under the terms of the 1855 Treaty of Point Elliott.[8]

Wilbur's second challenge was creating a viable economy. In the early reservation period, the Swinomish had lost access to gathering, hunting, and fishing locations. In 1892, the commissioner of Indian affairs had prohibited traditional winter spirit dancing and shamanic practices. Meanwhile, Swinomish children were required to attend the Bureau of Indian Affairs Tulalip School, where Indian languages were forbidden and Indian values rejected (Miller 1994). Another bitter blow at the turn of the century was the state of Washington's attempt to hinder Indian fishing by imposing restrictions and licensing requirements, by refusing to recognize treaty rights, and by appropriating the best fishing sites (Sampson 1972:45–47; Boxberger 1989). Wilbur's strategy was to build economic links with the non-Indian community adjacent to the Swinomish reservation, especially after the reorganization permitted the tribe to take corporate action for economic benefit.

One successful tactic was Swinomish promotion of and participation in local events— including county fairs, the La Conner Old Pioneer Days festival, and sidewalk sales—which drew the interest and approval of the white community. The Swinomish used their own special occasions, including elaborate traditional feasts, to commemorate achievements such as the construction of housing. To these celebrations, they invited key people from the white community, treating them to dinner speeches about reservation goals (Roberts 1975:391). Wilbur noted, concerning such occasions, "It is an opportunity we [had] every so often to bring our friends in that are influential in the county…We treated them, made them feel welcome, made them feel that we loved them, and everything like that" (Roberts 1975:392).

Underlying all of Wilbur's work was recognition of his audience; he, and others, had a keen sense of showmanship and publicity. For example, in 1938 the Swinomish erected a totem pole featuring the head of Franklin Roosevelt in a central location on the reservation, an effort that received considerable media attention. The pole "was hewed by Indian Work Progress

Administration workers" and depicted events from Swinomish history.[9] President Roosevelt was invited to attend the totem pole dedication; although he did not, John Collier, the U.S. commissioner of Indian affairs and architect of the Indian Reorganization Act, did attend, a major coup for the tribe in its efforts to attract attention.[10]

A dilemma for Wilbur and the other leaders was how to defend Indian treaty rights (which accrued to the reservation as a whole, as opposed to cash settlements for treaty violations, which accrued to members of the constituent groups within the Swinomish community) and simultaneously maintain good relations with the local white business community. Legal fights in the 1930s with the state over fishing rights made good relations difficult, especially after a 1936 state supreme court ruling (*State of Washington* v. *Edwards et al*) upheld a lower court decision permitting Indians to use fish traps. This ruling was vociferously opposed by state fisheries officials and white fishers, who were prohibited in 1934 from using such devices under the terms of state initiative 77. In 1939, as earlier in the decade, Swinomish fishers were arrested for fishing off the reservation. These circumstances created some volatility in relations between the Indian and mainstream communities. In response, Swinomish leaders focused on efforts to improve the standing of their community as a whole rather than work for constituent individual tribes in claims cases (Roberts 1975:393–394).

In addition, Wilbur wished to increase the autonomy of the Swinomish Business Council, then heavily constrained by the local Indian agent (Roberts 1975:327). Part of Wilbur's task in dealing with the mainstream government and business communities was creating the impression that the Swinomish could manage their own affairs while also supporting, rather than competing with, local non-Indian business people.

*   *   *

By the 1930s the Swinomish had begun to develop and maintain connections to local municipal governments, businesses, and other organizations in the Skagit Valley. Tribal leaders attempted to reduce the Indians' dependence on the mainstream society and reliance on federal loans and grants by emphasizing private enterprise. They encouraged activities like selling fish and promoting employment on the reservation. During this period of adjustment the Swinomish, with great effort, convinced the superintendent of Indian affairs to allow them to use $11,000 to buy the oyster business of a local Japanese-American businessman and to contract to sell the army 80 percent of the oysters produced. The first crop was harvested in 1941, and a profit of $16,000 reported (Sampson 1972:42).

Following this success, the Swinomish hoped to persuade the superintendent to transfer their funds to the local bank, thus giving them full control of their own enterprises. A basic goal, then, was to loosen the close federal supervision. Roberts has claimed that the tribal strategy was to create white demand for fish, labor, and products, as well as for cultural performances, and by so doing gradually move the Swinomish up in the system of ethnic stratification (Sampson 1972:387). Association with a high-visibility mainstream cultural institution like the Washington rowing team fit in well with such a strategy.

In 1941 the region had not yet recovered from the depression, and the UW crew found it difficult to arrange transportation to regattas. In those years the varsity Huskies ordinarily raced twice annually—against the University of California and in the Intercollegiate Rowing Association championship regatta in Poughkeepsie, New York. (The heavyweight crew did not stoop to racing potential rivals such as the University of British Columbia or the Vancouver Boat

Club, although the lightweight crew did.) However, the spring Poughkeepsie trip for 1942 was canceled in 1941. A serious problem facing Coach Ulbrickson, then, was maintaining the visibility of the rowing program during a period without races. One option was competing in novelty races, a strategy that Ulbrickson did not favor.

A related challenge was keeping the rowers mentally sharp, stimulated by competition. Racing against Indian canoes may have held some limited appeal for the coach, a theory supported by the fact that he did nothing to indicate to his rowers that canoes, with short paddles, cannot compete effectively on a straightaway with shells with much longer oars. Bud Rainey, then the UW freshman coach, reported that he did not believe that Ulbrickson was interested in any feature of this race other than stimulating his rowers.[11]

Persuading the Huskies to come to La Conner was a major achievement for Tandy Wilbur, but the timing was only partially in his favor. The end of November was the traditional end of the fall training season for the Huskies (they reassembled in the spring for more training and, ordinarily, the two big races), and the chance to finish fall workouts with a competition may have been irresistible to the coach. Late autumn, however, was the off-season for Indian canoe racers.

*   *   *

On the morning of November 29, Washington coaches and athletes drove in university vehicles the 70 or so miles from Seattle to La Conner. They brought two racing shells with them, lashed to the tops of their vehicles. Transporting the shells was a difficult feat in that era, when no specialized racks yet existed. Crews usually transported their shells by train or borrowed equipment from their hosts.

The Indian pullers assembled along the Swinomish Slough, and a crowd gathered along the La Conner side of the slough. The UW oarsmen spent some time before the race looking at the canoes and canoeing equipment and talking with the paddlers; Al Ulbrickson, Jr., recalled that this was a familiar practice at any competition.[12] Bud Rainey remembered that some betting was going on but noted that the Husky oarsmen were "too poor to be involved."[13]

Tom Taylor, who rowed in the Huskies' number seven seat, recalled, "We went up there and didn't know what the outcome would be."[14] Vic Fomo, the coxswain, was more confident, however. He said, "We really felt we would have to take it easy. We had everyone back from national championships."[15] The UW athletes recalled that they felt the sort of apprehension, the "butterflies," that accompanies any race, except with a twist in this case. They had no idea of the capability of the canoe pullers. The taciturn Ulbrickson—who must have known that the paddlers were no real competition—was not one to explain. The rowers were also somewhat confused about the meaning of Indian canoe racing and who the pullers were. Some believed that the canoes were manned by a random assortment of untrained athletes. Taylor noted, "We were all athletes and the kids in the canoes weren't."[16] But Fomo recalled: "Physically, the Indians were as tough as [we] were, as big, maybe shorter."[17]

In contrast, the canoe pullers were quite aware of the Huskies' elite status as former Olympic champions (although these individuals were not members of the famous 1936 Olympic crew).[18] The young men in the canoes regarded their own racing capacities highly, as did the oarsmen, and the *Lone Eagle* was a canoe of considerable repute in canoe-racing circles. The self-confidence of the pullers was communicated to the oarsmen; Rainey recalled that the "Indians conceived they could beat us."[19]

Newspaper accounts and reports from some of the participants suggest that the race itself was perhaps 1,000 or 1,500 meters, mostly straightaway, an advantage for the oarsmen, who did not race around 180-degree turns. Canoe courses, on the other hand, include several loops, and a premium is placed on the pullers' ability to make tight, fast turns. A common tactic for racing canoes, in fact, is to make a tight turn by steering into the midsection of a rival canoe and rebounding off.

The canoes and shells launched from the sandy banks on the reservation side of the slough, and the athletes must have slowly rowed and pulled up the slough and turned around. The race proceeded down the Swinomish Slough and finished across from La Conner. One photo suggests that the race went in the other direction, but the shot was likely not taken during the race itself. Photos show the Huskies in T-shirts or shirtless, not in their uniforms. The pullers were also predominantly shirtless, a usual practice among Indian canoeists.

All of the athletes, both oarsmen and canoe pullers, recall winning the race. Several Huskies recount that at the start they rowed 100 or so meters and paused, waiting for the much slower canoes to come alongside. This routine, apparently, was repeated several times. One canoe puller remembers taking a huge early lead and holding off the shells at the finish. An oarsman speculated that the Indians may have understood that they won the event as a result of winning a few of the 100-yard sprints. Al Ulbrickson, Jr., recalled that "it became obvious in a hurry that shells were faster."[20] Tom Taylor noted, "We had to change our approach to the race drastically to make it look like something worth watching. We chopped the stroke down to stay even, which is kind of hard in an eight-oared shell."[21]

The *Seattle Times* of November 30, 1941, reported:

> Two boats raced only about 100 yards at a time. The collegians pulled so far ahead of the Indians they had to stop and wait for them to catch up. The Indians, who compete annually in the Coupeville War Canoe races, entered their best boats, the *Susie Q* and *Lone Eagle*. Indians paddled them from a kneeling position and encouraged each other with ear-splitting war cries. Washington's crews settled down to their usual Poughkeepsie championship form and swept to victory easily.

The men who competed in 1941 did not understand the nature of the race at the time, and they remained unsure of what to make of it. The *Seattle Times* account reflects the confusion generated by the race, observing that the race was not a typical competition but earnestly reporting the sweep to victory as if all were ordinary. The Husky oarsmen, the American collegiate champions of the day, had been denied a chance at an Olympic gold medal because the 1940 games were canceled. Nonetheless, they regarded themselves, and were regarded in the press, as the best crew in the world. Some observers have suggested that they were the best crew ever assembled to that time, even regarded by Coach Ulbrickson as superior to the 1936 Olympic championship crew.

* * *

Figure 14. Al Ulbrickson, Sr. (left), the head coach of the University of Washington crew, shown here speaking with Charlie Edwards, a Swinomish leader, did not generally approve of novelty races; nonetheless, he agreed to participate in the Great Race. (Seattle Post-Intelligencer Collection, Museum of History and Industry)

Al Ulbrickson, Jr., who was a young boy at the time, noted that he and his father did not stay after the race for the salmon barbecue and ceremonies hosted by the Swinomish. Coach Ulbrickson went home right away, unamused by the circumstances, and perhaps displeased by the uncompetitive nature of the race. Ulbrickson, Jr., observed that his father did not view the race from a launch, as was customary, and that he was worried about the corrosive effects of saltwater on the shells and fittings.[22] Before he left, however, the coach did participate in a photo session conducted by Seattle newspapermen. Publicity about the race would keep the crew in the public eye, thereby helping to recruit young athletes from Washington high schools and to claim resources and coaching salaries in a period of diminished resources. Officials of the Washington athletics department may have strongly encouraged Ulbrickson to make this trip, recognizing these public relations benefits, a theory that Ulbrickson, Jr., finds plausible. Here Swinomish and University of Washington interests overlapped. Tandy Wilbur, for his part, likely conceived of the event strictly as a media performance, in modern terms, a photo opportunity.

Wilbur desperately needed publicity in order to achieve his political and economic goals, so he refined his approach to the media. A recent Swinomish senate chair, Robert Joe, commented, "He sure was good at the media. When you think back, man alive!"[23]

Wilbur's motivations are clear, but his tactics require clarification. Wilbur generally used the press in two ways: first, he sought out regular coverage of tribal events in order to manage the impression of the Indians formed by outsiders. He and the other leaders "put forth great efforts to improve the Swinomish Reservation's reputation" (Roberts 1975:389). They used a series of advertisements in the *Puget Sound Mail*, published in La Conner, to promote the Swinomish "as modern, progressive, and energetic Indians, concerned with improving their standard of living: they portrayed themselves as honest businessmen, good credit risks, having a democratically elected governing body, and as financial contributors to many public causes" (Roberts 1975:389). This was a successful strategy, and Wilbur noted in his later years:

> I've had more newspapers talking to me about every little thing. I've had more offers for help on the reservation here at Swinomish this last year than I've had in the whole history…I think [that] what's happening is that the governmental agencies are aware of what Swinomish [are] doing, their progress here…what we're attempting to do. And when these information seekers come along, they think of Swinomish and employ them, or send them to us. (Roberts 1975:390)

Wilbur's second tactic was to use the news media to advance Swinomish (or his own) views on pressing issues. For example, during a conflict with the Skagit County Zoning Authority, which wished to rezone reservation lands owned by non-Indians ("alienated lands") for the purpose of attracting an oil refinery, Wilbur went to the press. "We raised so much stink about it that now the people have gone. We did so much yelling that the press took it up" (Roberts 1975:353).

*   *   *

The local media were not used to providing the sort of coverage that Wilbur sought; in fact the newspapers of Skagit County regularly created difficulties for local Indians. A content analysis of coverage by the major papers of Skagit County (the *Concrete Herald* and the Mount Vernon *Herald*, later renamed the *Skagit Valley Herald*) from the second decade of the century to 1987 shows that newspapers failed to report on the routine life of the Indian communities throughout this period. There was very little coverage of intergovernmental cooperation, economic development, or such activities as school events. The news reports largely focused on deviant Indian people and Indian communities dependent on the government. Fifty percent of the reporting about Indians over a 75-year period concerned contentious treaty rights issues, which were represented as opposing white interests. Another 15.8 percent of reports depicted antisocial behavior (Miller 1993).

In addition, the papers responded immediately to the interests of the mainstream society during periods of intense struggle over important resources like salmon. Such reporting, for example, characterized the period immediately after the 1936 court ruling permitting the Swinomish to use fish traps. The volume of reporting on Indian communities increased as much as 500 percent in such periods. Further, the type of reporting changed as well. Over the years the great majority of articles about Indians in these papers can be classified as focusing on lore (precontact lifeways, with an implicit assumption that Indian life as so depicted was gone); Indian antisocial actions, including arrests; politics, including treaty rights; civic affairs, with white intervention on behalf of Indians; and obituaries (Miller 1993:80). During struggles over treaty rights and fisheries, native lore, obituaries, and civic affairs almost disappeared. Instead, Indian crimes and efforts to claim treaty rights dominated the news, and treaty demands were usually depicted as requiring new concessions on the part of the mainstream society rather than as fulfilling legal obligations dating from the nineteenth century.

Tandy Wilbur had to work within this context, and his promotion of a boat race in 1941 acknowledged the newspapers' inclination to run both lore and civic pieces (that is, to describe the contributions of whites to the welfare of Indians). Wilbur apparently recognized that canoe races fit within such existing categories of reportage and could be seen as conforming to white notions of nonthreatening Indian communities, a view that he tried hard to spread. [24] Yet Wilbur wished to present the Swinomish as a sort of model group, deserving of special attention from the mainstream society, from government, and from business investors. There appears to have been no better way to make his point than through an interaction with the Washington crew. The race with the Huskies featured elements of both antiquity and modernity, of passivity and assertiveness. In a period when it was very difficult for Indians to get any media coverage, especially positive coverage, the race was indeed an effective ploy.

*   *   *

Wilbur's use of the media and the Washington rowing program is a dramatic example of the efforts made by Indian leaders to work through internal political disputes and address economic distress on the reservations by contesting the authority and domination of the mainstream society. Wilbur's efforts were to reorient rather than subvert and, in this sense, can be understood as attempts to educate the mainstream society about his own society and its needs and aims. But the story of the race also highlights issues common to Indian and non-Indian peoples of Washington State in the period of the Great Depression, namely, the problems of marginalization (because powerful national and economic centers were located far away), the dilemma of constituting a unified society out of populations with diverse backgrounds, and the common orientation to waterways among societies constructed, at least initially, around boats and water travel.

Considerable scholarly attention has been given to intertribal political efforts to address grievances with the state, including those by the Northwest Federation of American Indians (Bishop and Hansen 1979); intertribal efforts to regain access to the fisheries, culminating in the Boldt decision of 1974;[25] efforts by the Small Tribes of Western Washington to provide social, educational, and health services (Porter 1989); and the development of the intertribal hierarchy of the Shaker church in Washington State in the late nineteenth and early twentieth centuries in response to religious oppression (Amoss 1990). The story of the Great Race documents another sort of leadership strategy, one that is tribal rather than intertribal in nature and, although frequently observed, never adequately described.

Indian community leaders, in fact, have a long history of using powerful cultural settings and symbols in order to engage those from outside the community and to convey Indian views and the associated depth of feeling and significance. This practice formerly took place in winter houses (longhouses) on ceremonial occasions, especially potlatches, when practical issues such as the management of fish, access to resources, and the conveyance of titles and prerogatives were publicly discussed. A similar practice occurs today in winter houses and elsewhere and follows a prescribed sequence. Guests are fed, entertained, and educated (Kew 1990). Special guests are wrapped in blankets and positioned to stand on other blankets. These acts symbolically create a clean ground for change and enclose the wearer within the culture itself. Some of the guests are called as witnesses to the tribe's efforts to educate others and are given a token payment of thanks. The witnesses are told of their obligation to affirm publicly the views that they hear. At this point, orations begin and the honored guests are given a message, which ordinarily contains these elements: who the members of the tribe are, by what right they occupy these grounds (by reason of connection to ancestral events and immortal beings), and how their place in the larger community can be respected. The messages concern topics such as treaty rights, the treatment of Indians in the education system, fisheries, or economic development.[26]

Figure 15. This photograph of the UW athletes and Swinomish canoe paddlers, staged by a Seattle newspaperman, was just the sort of publicity that Tandy Wilbur had hoped to attract when he first conceived of the Great Race. (Seattle P-I Collection, Museum of History and Industry)

Wilbur's effort to host a race between UW athletes in shells and Indians in canoes may be seen as a dramatic example of this political strategy. Entertainment and feasting were used to draw well-known white people to the reservation and to create the context for the delivery of

Swinomish oratory. Further, the Great Race is consistent with Swinomish public relations practices of the 1930s and 1940s, including participation in more prosaic events such as county fairs and sidewalk sales. The special twists in this case are the visitors' contribution to the entertainment, the magnitude of the event, and the media coverage of the powerful images of racing canoes and rowing shells.

Endnotes

[1] Natalie Roberts, "A History of the Swinomish Tribal Community," Ph.D. dissertation (University of Washington, 1975). For another perspective, see Martin J. Sampson, *Indians of Skagit County* (Mount Vernon, WA,1972). Sampson and Wilbur were political rivals.

[2] Oliver (1991). The Coupeville races resumed in 1992.

[3] The Concrete *Herald*, July 10, 1941, ran a front-page photo of Indians dressed in Plains headdresses with this caption: "Indians from 17 tribes of the United States, Canada, and Alaska—once bitter enemies—carry on their intense rivalry in the annual Whidbey Island Indian Water Festival at Coupeville, Washington, July 4, 5, and 6. The event is probably the largest single concentration of Indians in the world." The celebration also included a baseball tournament, a midway, a princess competition, "war dances," and Indian gambling (the bone game), as reported in the July 15 *Herald*.

[4] Telephone interviews, Emmett Oliver, 1993 and 1997. Among the other famous canoes in the area are the *Telegraph, Flying Cloud, Question Mark I, and Question Mark II*. Each boat was carefully constructed to be fast and good at making tight turns. The *Flying Cloud* and other racing canoes are on outdoor display in Coupeville.

[5] Interview, Victor Michalson, Vashon Island, Wash., 1993.

[6] Telephone interview, Vic Fomo, 1993.

[7] Telephone interview, Al Ulbrickson, Jr., 1993.

[8] Martin Sampson later brought suit against the Swinomish community, acting on behalf of the "aboriginal Swinomish," who wished to claim independent tribal status and sue the federal government for failing to fulfill the terms of the Point Elliott treaty.

[9] Mount Vernon *Herald*, Feb. 2, 1938.

[10] Mount Vernon *Herald*, Aug. 22, 1938.

[11] Telephone interview, Bud Rainey, 1993.

[212] Ulbrickson interview.

[13] Rainey interview.

[14] Telephone interview, Tom Taylor, Washington oarsman, 1993.

[15] Fomo interview.

[16] Taylor interview.

[17] Fomo interview.

[18] Interview, Smokey Lyle, Upper Skagit Tribal Center, 1993.

[19] Rainey interview

[20] Ulbrickson interview.

[21] Taylor interview.

[22] Ulbrickson interview.

[23] Personal communication, Robert Joe, 1993.

[24] Roberts (195: 392). Regular front-page coverage of canoe races continued through the 1950s. In 1952 a rivalry between paddlers of the Swinomish *Lone Eagle* and the Upper Skagit *Flying Cloud* was the subject of excited reporting before and after races (Mount Vernon *Herald*, July 3, 7, Aug. 1 2, 22, 1952).

[25] Perhaps the best-known and most influential work on the treaty fisheries is Fay G. Cohen (1986)

[26] I have witnessed a number of such events, as have others working in Coast Salish communities. See Kew (1990:478), and Roberts (1975:391).

References Cited

Amoss, Pamela. 1990. The Indian Shaker Church. In *Handbook of North American Indians*, Vol. 7: *Northwest Coast*, edited by Wayne Suttles, pp 633–639. Washington, D.C.: Smithsonian Institution.

Bishop, Kathleen L., and Kenneth C. Hansen. 1979. The Landless Tribes of Western Washington. *American Indian Quarterly*, 4:20–31.

Boxberger, Daniel L. 1989. *To Fish in Common: The Ethnohistory of Lummi Indian Salmon Fishing.* Lincoln: University of Nebraska Press.

Cohen, Fay G. 1986. *Treaties on Trial: The Continuing Controversy over Northwest Indian Fishing Rights.* Seattle: University of Washington Press.

Kew, J. E. Michael. 1990. Central and Southern Coast Salish Ceremonies since 1900. In *Handbook of North American Indians*, Vol. 7: *Northwest Coast*, edited by Wayne Suttles, pp. 476–80. Washington, D.C.: Smithsonian Institution.

Lincoln, Leslie. 1991. *Coast Salish Canoes.* Seattle, WA: Center for Wooden Boats.

Miller, Bruce G. 1993. The Press, the Boldt Decision, and Indian-White Relations. *American Indian Culture and Research Journal*, 17:75–97.

——— 1994. Swinomish. In *Native America in the Twentieth Century: An Encyclopedia*, edited by Mary B. Davis, pp. 601–602. New York: Garland.

Newell, Gordon R. 1987. *Ready All! George Yeoman Pocock and Crew Racing.* Seattle: University of Washington Press.

Oliver, Emmett. 1991. Reminiscences of a Canoe Puller. In *A Time of Gathering: Native Heritage in Washington State*, edited by Robin K. Wright, pp. 248–253. Seattle: University of Washington Press.

Porter, Frank W. 1989. *The Coast Salish Peoples.* New York: Chelsea House Publishing.

Roberts, Natalie. 1975. A History of the Swinomish Tribal Community. Ph.D. dissertation University of Washington.

Sampson, Martin J. 1972. *Indians of Skagit County.* Mount Vernon, WA: Skagit County Hisotrical Society.

Journal of Northwest Anthropology, Memoir 12:249–259 (2016)

16

Culture as Cultural Defense:
An American Indian Sacred Site in Court*

This essay concerns the latent and implicit ways in which concepts of culture are employed by a set of actors (a panel of judges, expert witnesses of several sorts including myself, and American Indian litigants who appeared in a legal dispute) and what is in part a consequence of these differences in perspective; namely the failure to make a case for the importance of preserving a culturally significant site. I will advance the view that particular constructions of culture employed in the defense and preservation of what are described as American Indian sacred sites are problematic and ineffective and confront the modernist court in precisely the wrong ways. Efforts to construct a notion of sacredness in court as a means of creating legal space appears to be akin to a cultural defense in criminal litigation in that the court must accept premises which are neither shared by the judges' own cultures or the legal sub-culture and thereby stand outside of their values and experiences. U.S. and Canadian judges and judicial bodies face the dilemma of "reckoning culture," or assigning values to conflicting representations about a site. This is paradoxical: simultaneously the claims of epistemological difference are made by litigants while the courts' capacity to understand and the necessity to uphold comparability is upheld. If sacred site discourse is part of the contestation of the landscape by Aboriginal peoples within the nation state (Feld and Basso 1996:4), the issue becomes one of how to do so effectively in a political and legal sense rather than solely an intellectual one.

Some clarification of my position is in order. Political and legal struggles may well succeed in cases in which features of the landscape receive wide recognition and support across cultural groupings and represent national or international Aboriginal aspirations and cultural expressions. The case of Ayers Rock in Australia is such an example (Whittaker 1994; see Barsh 1996 for a consideration of international action to defend sacred sites). Burial sites and reburial issues have attracted much of the current dialogue concerning sacred sites (see Reeves and Kennedy 1993), but sacred sites are more diverse than this single category. However, I do not exclude from consideration sites which appear to have legal protection as cultural properties, including archaeological sites and resources, glyphs, and graves; these may still be vulnerable to destruction or desecration. Indeed, before legal protections can gain force a site must become legally qualified, a dilemma which underlies the issues I address here and which is a cause of consternation to many aboriginal leaders (personal communication, Doreen Maloney, councilor, Upper Skagit Tribe, Sedro-Woolley Washington).

There are many reasons why the discourse of the sacred is problematic in court: the very idea of sacred sites requires judges to endow the landscape with cultural properties beyond the reach and outside the conventional rules of local civil authorities; because of the problems of establishing sacredness as a legal fact; and because of the court's requirement of differentiating between sacred, partially sacred, and non-sacred landscapes. A particular difficulty arises in arguing for the sacredness of sites that are not recognizable as archaeological sites; that is, they do not contain visible or tangible markers as cultural spaces and sounds. One account by a U.S. National Park Service bureaucrat (Rogers 1993:136), for example, noting the obligation of the Parks Service to exercise stewardship over sacred sites as part of the practice of cultural resource

*Authored by Bruce Granville Miller, reproduced with permission and previously published in *American Indian Quarterly*, 22(1):83–97 (1998). University of Nebraska Press.

management, listed museum objects, historic structures, and archaeological sites, leaving out what are perhaps the majority of cultural resources as defined by tribes themselves. Vision quest sites, for example, are said to have left no "footprints"; spiritual beings and Aboriginal supplicants are not well preserved in the archaeological record, often leaving nothing or only small anthropogenic stone structures (Dormaar and Reeves 1993:163).

I examine these issues through the device of a case study of litigation in which I participated in 1993 and 1994. The case, *Citizens to Preserve Nookachamps Valley et al. v. Skagit County, et al.*, (SHB No. 93-14) was heard before the Washington State Shorelines Hearings Board and concerned the disposition of a proposed quarry site. A farm family, the Tewalts, wished to quarry a monolithic feature, a rock some 300' high and 1000' long, in anticipation of a considerable profit. This rock, I later discovered, is glossed "heart" from the Lushootseed (Snyder 1953). A local citizen's group, headed by a tribal attorney for the Upper Skagit tribe and by a council member of that tribe, opposed the quarrying. The tribe itself hoped to stop the issuance of a license through participation as *amicus curie*.

Opposition to the licensure was on several grounds, including the effects on noise, water quality, and aesthetics. These issues were themselves directly linked to the interpretation of sacredness (of what came to be called the Tewalt site in legal proceedings) by senior members of the tribal community. In the legal proceedings noise, water quality and aesthetics were not included among the "cultural, historical, and archaeological resources" in question. The issue of noise in the environment, for example, was treated not as an issue of a particular cultural soundscape, but as sound mitigation in a technical and generic sense, despite current understandings of the relationship of sound to place and, ultimately, culture (see Feld 1996).

The Citizens Committee, via legal intervention, gained two days of site access and asked me, as an ethnographer of the Upper Skagit tribe, to examine the site in preparation for making an expert representation concerning the site in court two weeks later. I arranged to bring six colleagues, all archaeologists or graduate students in archaeology. The archaeologists attempted to find evidence of occupation, use, or short-term residence on the site. I spent part of my time working with an elder concerning the oral traditions about the site. The recently deceased Alice Williams told me a story of Snake and Beaver who wished to marry Frog and Mouse, who refused them. Frog and Mouse, in consequence, were drowned by a flood contrived by Snake and Beaver (an outcome congruent with the long history of a rising and falling watertable in the area). Oral material collected forty years earlier by an ethnographer and the material I collected on this occasion confirmed Tewalt Rock as Snakes' house (Snyder 1953). A quarter mile away is Beaver Lake, the mythological home of the beaver in the story (during our inspection we found several beaver lodges). Beaver Lake was also the site in which an ancestor of the current population was said to have obtained the skedilich power and the rights to employ a spiritually animated board in winter ceremonials. This is one of the most significant of Upper Skagit spirit powers and the site of acquisition is itself a place of spiritual importance. To the other side of the site is the hill that is the location of a starchild myth recorded by deceased elder Martin Sampson (Sampson 1972). From the top of the Tewalt rock one can see both Mt. Baker and Mt. Rainier, sisters in yet another, geographically broader, cycle of myths. In short, this small area was among the most spiritually freighted locations in the Skagit Valley.

On the second day of work a member of the party found what was believed to be a petroglyph of a double-headed snake clearly pecked into the rock. This interpretation was later confirmed by the senior staff archaeologist in the state historic preservation office, Dr. Robert Whitlam, and unanimously by three independent rock art consultants acting on behalf of the Shoreline Hearings Board as authorized by Skagit County (Bard 1994). The site therefore appeared to qualify for protection under Washington state law, Chapter 27.44, Indian Graves and

Records, which protects "glyphic or painted record of any tribe," from disturbance by mining and various other activities, punishable as a class C felony. The Citizens Committee wished to proceed from this legal vantage point.

Ethnographic evidence (Collins 1974) indicates that the double headed snake is associated with an important shamanic power acquired through vision questing. Consequently, for these and other reasons, my own interpretation was that Tewalt Rock was the site of spirit questing by at least one individual who signified this by carving it into a rock. The archeologists also found a hand maul in the area near the petroglyph and, a little farther away, lithic scatter.

The attorneys acting for the Tewalts argued, however, that "the markings [previously described as the double headed snake] were formed when a tool mounted on a bulldozer scraped against the rock" (*Skagit Valley Herald*, August 17, 1995: A5). This opinion was supported by an associate professor of geography brought in as an expert for the farm family, who relied on radiocarbon dating to argue that the "brush rake" hypothesis "is consistent with a number of lines of evidence" (Dorn 1994:13). The three rock art specialists were of the opinion that the markings were not made by "accidental impact of a brush rake," but rather, was a petroglyph made by an "artist" who "undoubtedly used a sharp rock ... to peck out a deep (ca. 2–5 mm) 'channel' into the rock surface" (Bard 1994:2). In addition, an archeologist brought in by the Tewalt family was said to have alleged that the site was either salted or the lithic scatter was caused by preliminary (and illegal) dynamiting of the Tewalt Rock (personal communication, archaeologist Al Reid, November 1994). A member of the Tewalt family told the local newspaper that he had suspicions the maul was not authentic. "We have the evidence but the courts say 'So what? You can't show anyone'" (*Skagit Argus*, January 11, 1995:20).

An astonishing and misleading legal dialogue ensued in which contending experts probed the petroglyph for veracity, submitting it to electron microscope tests in an effort to date the rock art. Efforts to reconstruct the cultural context of the petroglyph divorced it not only from the larger spiritual entity for which it was no doubt produced, but from the context of Coast Salish culture. One archaeological expert contracted by the Tewalt family reported to the court that there were no other cultural materials "in front of the putative rock art panel," even though the lithic scatter and the maul were found in the near vicinity (Whitley 1994:15). Further, arguing from a particularistic geo-political stance, this scholar claimed that there were no similar petroglyphs in western Washington and therefore the double-headed snake was not likely to fall within the legitimate tradition even though less than sixty miles away in Coast Salish territory of British Columbia such art is present (Whitley 1994:15). In addition, the archaeological accounting of the rock art stripped it of its contextualization within the oral traditions of the community, which spoke of Snake, Beaver and other spirit beings.

The panel of judges eventually ruled that:

Skagit County has considered the likelihood that the site contains cultural, historical and archeological resources…It did so by accessing the state computer system known as TRAX [a data base]. The TRAX system yielded a response of no known cultural resources at the Tewalt site.

Although the testimony has been lengthy and passionate on both sides, substantially all of the testimony is grounded upon observation, alone. What is needed, to conclude this issue, is examination of the rock by a trained and neutral expert using a carbon dating or similar process to objectively date the markings on the rock. (Findings of Fact, Conclusions of Law and Order on Remand, SHB No. 93-14)

The judges made no further legal argument concerning cultural issues, moving on in their findings of fact to technical issues of water quality, noise abatement, traffic safety, and aesthetics, but their opinion reinforced the unfortunate notion that culture is discernible primarily by experts and that culture must be uniform (i.e., interpretable by experts in the same manner) and comprehensible to outsiders. The idea of a positivistic, scientific narrative was preferred to oral traditions of the tribe and, by inference, those interested in oral traditions were held to fall outside the bounds of the "trained, neutral discourse" the judges felt was required to decide the case. Physical sciences (such as carbon dating) were preferred to social sciences or to a mixture of approaches. The panel of judges made an effort to protect the petroglyph, but failed, however, to distinguish between what was culturally significant, namely the site where the spirit powers reside, and the secondary representation of the site, namely the petroglyph. The litigants, noting this discrepancy, found this mitigation inadequate.

In order to fulfill the requirement of an outside "trained, neutral expert" to decide between the opinion presented by me and archaeologists in my group and those presented by archaeologists and other scientists contracted by the Tewalts, an M.A. trained archaeologist was subsequently hired. The judges, however, constrained the work of the archaeologist by allowing only three weeks between the Order of Motions calling for a "cultural resources survey" and the date for filing the report, and by limiting the contract to "within the range of $3,500." Further, the judges ordered that "The scope of the "cultural resources survey (i.e., geography and technique) shall be based upon the discretion and professional judgment of the person selected by Skagit County to conduct the same" (Order on Motions, SHB 93-14). The archaeologist made one site visit, during a rain storm. He reported that he found no evidence of occupation or use, but did not report whether he had adequate funding or time to draw a conclusion concerning this issue. He was, however, hired to provide a definitive statement and his report failed to convey the limitations of his investigation (Reid 1994). Subsequently, the panel of judges permitted the issuance of a license for the quarry, and, noting the difficulty of deciding between experts, decided that the rock's markings "are not of archaeological, historical, or cultural value" (*Skagit Valley Herald*, August 17, 1995:A5).

Conceptual Framework

First, a conceptual frame, conjoining approaches to modernity and ethnic competition; in his work on ethnogenesis Sharp (1996) points out that the idea of sacredness is related to the current debate about ethnic group/aboriginal identity positioning. One might note that judges themselves live within the communities in which this debate has currency. Sharp observes that the "sacred" belongs to a primordial discourse which locks local groups into a particular identity construction which itself builds on the idea of critical differences between Indian and dominant societies. Indeed, for American Indians and Canadian First Nations, the issue of presenting themselves as protectors of the sacred earth is emblematic of their "opposition ideology" (Hornborg 1994:253). The problem may be even more fundamental than this, in that some members of aboriginal and mainstream communities hold differing views of culture itself. Whitten (1996:204), in commenting on the significance of confrontational, ethnicbloc nationalist discourse (of which the Tewalt Rock case can be said to be an example), observed that for indigenous people, culture "is that which is worthy of reverential homage." Further, "indigenous culture, as such concepts are manifest in practical and spiritual conflict, [is] characterized by reverential webs of signification..." (Whitten 1996:205). To members of the majority community, culture may remain less problematic, even invisible, except when pushed, for example, to incorporate an Indian understanding of the landscape into the local regulatory regime.

There are several consequences to current differences in perspective and in the salience of ethnic competition. Borrowing from Sharp (1996), I argue that the responses of the dominant society (here embodied by both the attorneys for those proposing to alter the landscape and by the trial judges) to such strategic discourse include these:

1. The cultural grounds on which claims of sacredness are made are taken literally. This strategy produced a dismal outcome in the 1990 British Columbia land claim case *Delgamuukw* v *Regina* (McEachern 1991) in which the judge noted that he could not accept First Nations characterizations of a territory which was said to have been the site of an avalanche caused by a supernatural bear. Literal readings of the sacred simply result in a finding of incompatibility—that is, the court recognizes no concept of land tenure in which land belongs to the supernatural, rather than to Aboriginal people who express their relation to the immortal beings as one of subordination or supplication, as in the Upper Skagit case.

2. A second response is to regard the discourse as part of a "faked culture" asserted by, to use Clifton's (1990) phrase, "invented Indians." This is a view current in right-wing discourse and has culminated in the creation of funds designated to contest Indian efforts to protect cultural sites and protected rights generally (see Ryser 1997). Proponents of this perspective cast doubt on Indian aspirations by attacking their credibility and their authenticity, focusing on variability in Indian phenotype, or on the poverty of documentation of Indian landscape. This issue arose when a Ph.D.-holding archaeologist hired by the Tewalts equated the limited cultural documentation with the absence of cultural practice (Whitely 1994:15), and when the state TRAX computer system failed to show "known cultural resources at the Tewalt site" (Findings of Fact, Conclusions of Law, and Order of Remand, SHB 93-14). Further, discontinuity with ancestors is posited because of the adoption of western technology and material culture. This is referred to by some in British Columbia as the "transistor radio fallacy" because the trial judge in the Delgamuukw case observed that Indians employ modem technology and eat contemporary foods. In this discourse, Indians are culturally contaminated, corrupted descendants of their putatively spiritual ancestors rather than their spiritual heirs.

3. A third response to the "sacred" discourse is one of fear and animosity generated towards those who portray themselves as fundamentally, even absolutely, different while simultaneously asserting a connection to the dominant society through claims on and connections to schooling, treaty fishing, medical care, and so on. This response focuses on the contradiction between claims of sameness and difference and on the position the dominant society assumes as the perpetrators of sacrilege. The imagery of exploding the sacred through literally blowing up a sacred site may well have been too powerful to be palatable for judges whose life experiences did not prepare them to contemplate Indian cosmological concepts, as was the case with the judges on the Shorelines Hearing Panel. I say this because of the nature of the decision rendered by the Panel, but also because of a question put to me by one of the judges during my testimony in this case. He noted that he is a "Catholic boy" and asked me to describe the Tewalt Rock in terms he could understand. In a response reminiscent of a debate in Australia over Ayers Rock (Whittaker 1994), I replied that the rock was something like a significant European cathedral. The Judge's counter, which caused me to have some optimism about the outcome of the case, was to say "no, its more like the holy grail." I didn't immediately think through to the

conclusion he might have drawn, namely, that in accepting my proposition I required him to equate the religious tradition of a subordinated, obscure population with the grandest tradition of authority that he could imagine, surely an equation to be rejected by anyone not a wildly enthusiastic fan of cultural relativism. The holy grail, indeed, is a mythic, unembodied, unobtainable object in the Catholic, Christian tradition, no doubt a suitable analog to the Judge for what appeared to him to be an unembodied site, in fact, a non-site.

4. A fourth response to the discourse of the sacred is to observe whether there is uniformity in the Indian community concerning the interpretations provided the court, to rely on a notion of culture emphasizing shared understandings rather than the current emphasis on diversity and contest (e.g., Comaroff 1996). The legal implication is simply this: a finding of inconsistent interpretation, of diversity of viewpoint, will almost certainly provide grounds on which judges can find there is no relevance in a particular cultural claim of sacredness. It is difficult to demonstrate that an area or an object is sacred in the absence of agreement on this point and in the absence of a legal test of sacredness. Indeed, this occurred in the case in question. One of the judges asked me if all of the landscape was sacred to Indians. I understood this as a potential trap, an obstacle to conveying something meaningful about the site. If all of the landscape was uniformly sacred, then, in practical terms, there were no grounds to preserve any particular part. My response was that the landscape was differentiated; some places are more significant than others, that places differ in their uses and meanings. As a way of undermining the claim of sacredness, of importance of the site, the attorneys for the Tewalts were said to have arranged for a court appearance by a tribal member prepared to testify to a lack of significance of the Tewalt site. As a counter, preparations were made to position a senior tribal elder and historian and senior relatives of the man in the front of the court room in an effort to publicly shame him and to erode his authority to speak. There were differences in how tribal members perceived the issue of the site: some community members saw a potential heavy financial burden in protecting the rock in question; others were disinterested because the rock was located in Nookachamps territory associated with some, but not all, of the constituent families composing the tribe and fell outside of their set of kin connections. Only some of the families knew particulars of the territory, its mythological construction, and cultural uses. Still others were disinterested because they are disinterested generally in what academics might regard as the importance of ethnic identity markers to the community elite. They are confirmed in their identity through the family teachings, the difficulty of life, and the disdain expressed by the surrounding world. They need no further confirmation that they are American Indian.

5. Legal strategies which attempt to inscribe the landscape with Indian sacredness create texts which are written and rewritten by more than one author, and by people other than tribal members. A fifth sort of response to the claims of sacredness, then, is to redefine the claim into a more acceptable form. This, indeed, was the case with the Tewalt Rock, in which the debate about the landscape came to focus exclusively on the tangible and visible petroglyph. One scholar pointed out a difficulty:

> [T]he sites frequently appear to have been…for some sacred purpose, but the Aboriginal traditions themselves may have been lost to the people, and it is often very difficult to accurately reconstruct the sacred significance. Among other things, this inability to clearly understand the ceremonial complex…makes it extremely difficult to determine the limits of the site in

question, for it is impossible to always know what physical features are part of the complex and which are not. (Byrne 1993:103)

Experts thereby created a legal culture of dimunition and containment within the same modernist discourse which is said to be deconstructed by the emphasis on the spiritual. This is a significant weakness of the sacred defense; once opened the discourse is not easily directed and counter discourses come not only from subordinated communities. In the Tewalt case, the spiritual site was legally reduced to the petroglyph, and not the larger cultural context.

Indeed, local non-aboriginal families have their own readings of local history and local landscapes, as Whittaker (1994) noted concerning the Ayers Rock debate. Local commentary emphasized the longevity of the Tewalt families' occupation of the Skagit Valley (of some four generations). The opening statement of the attorney acting for the Tewalt family focused squarely on this issue, characterizing the valley as a long-time farming (read: white) community with an established sense of appropriate land use, itself sensible, quiet, and in tune with rural life generally. Indian people were characterized as interlopers and directly disruptive of the rustic, productive lifeway established by farm families such as the Tewalts. The attorney, in effect, relied on a highly normative, exclusionary accounting of farm culture in setting the stage for advancing his clients' claims. The actions taken to protect the site were described as violating the rights of the clients, and one of the farm-family litigants told a local newspaper that "They've taken our land. They've taken our rights. What else can they do to us?...What they're saying is that they can come in one anyone's private land, find something, then take your land and there's nothing you can do about it" (*Skagit Argus*, January 11, 1995:20).

In contrast, the attorney acting for Upper Skagits emphasized the 9000 years of documented aboriginal occupation. The Upper Skagit narrative, however, did not easily fit within the current dialogue concerning the appropriate uses of the valley, the direct concern of the Shorelines Hearings Board, which had the task of deciding whether quarrying fit into the existing regime of agricultural land-use. In this sense, the Tewalt historical narrative more convincingly addressed the legal question at hand.

Strategies: Site Classification

The issue, then, is what to do in light of these dilemmas in successfully conveying the idea of a culture's sacred site to the courts. One strategy is to present a conceptually more differentiated landscape in legal settings, and to regard the landscape as constituted by various sorts of cultural resources, thereby employing a vocabulary already in use. This strategy may skirt questions such as this: if all the landscape is sacred, how can one differentiate and why should measures be made to protect particular locations? The following system of site classification of sacred sites in the Coast Salish tradition is culturally specific and cannot be generalized to other Indigenous communities, but is suggestive of what might be done elsewhere. This classification system is based primarily on the connection of sites to the role of transformer (a sacred, supernatural creator) in myth times through transformer's connection to the creation of the current features of the landscape. Eight such types of site and a ninth residual category are proposed (abstracted from Mohs 1994):

transformer sites	most are bedrock outcroppings, colders, prominences, caves, river pools; feeling evoked more than physical nature

spirit residences	inhabited by supernatural forces; ghosts, spirits, Thunderbird
ceremonial areas	associated with winter dancing, offerings, observances; longhouses, creeks, sweathouses, lakes, training grounds
traditional landmarks	site of cultural, historical events; pithouses, sites of epidemics
questing/powersites	usually remote areas in mountains, caves, rivers, transformer sites; secret
legendary/ mythological sites	vary in nature; judgment and predicition sites; associated with events/personages
burials	tree, box, funerary, cave, and interment sites; spirits present
other	e.g., astronomical sites, medicinal pools, springs

It is worth noting that individual tribal and band members place greater significance on some categories of sites than on others, although Mohs (1994:198) cautions that "Vested interests aside, each class of sites does incorporate cultural/ethnic significance and each may be considered of equal value within an overall ideological context." Similarly, a Umatilla tribal spokesperson articulated the commonly held view that cultural resources encompass all of creation and consequently the tribe cannot identify and separate all things in nature (Burney 1993:115). While this may be so, efforts at protection may benefit from frank and painful efforts at specification, as noted above, and hierarchilization of cultural resources; surely transformer sites are no doubt more significant than some secondary historical sites. In addition, some sites may be more viable in a legal setting. Such efforts have been made before the fact of legal contestation, for example, in the efforts by Coast Salish to document and preserve sites potentially intruded upon by logging activities within lands administered by the National Park Service in Washington state. In this case, buffer zones of various sizes have been created around spirit questing sites. Spirits, which humans hope to gain as allies, are said to depart an area if it becomes contaminated. Outsiders cannot come close.

Much of the current literature implicitly assumes that sacred landscapes are contested sites in which efforts at conflict resolution and mutual recognition may produce favorable results, even while critiquing the propensity for capitalist society to erode aboriginal rights and cultural resources (see Carmichael et al. 1994; Kelley and Francis 1994). In this view, good will and hard negotiation can result in the preservation of culturally significant landscapes through careful documentation, parcel swaps, government buy-outs of developers, and so on (but see contrary claims in papers delivered to a conference entitled "Sacred Lands: Claims and Conflicts at the University of Manitoba, October 1996). Such swaps do occur, in, for example, the 1994 case of Xá:ytem Rock in the lower mainland of British Columbia, a Stó:lō (Coast Salish) site preserved through government funding and the coordinated activities of a volunteer group and the tribal council. But circumstances are considerably different concerning more localized, less visible cases, where sacred sites are under immediate pressure and where time is often short in finding means to protect them. No doubt the majority of endangered landscapes fall into this latter category.

Feld and Basso (1996:4) noted that social scientists have moved away from theorizing social well-being associated with "rootedness in place" as problematic and perhaps inauthentic to theorizing place largely from the standpoint of contestation and its linkage to local and global power relations. Relatedly, current scholarly argument holds that within the movement to stop the destruction of the landscape "the invocation of spirituality represents...a successful revolt against the language of modernity" (Hornborg 1994:245). In this view, modernity is regarded as a "strategy of conceptual encompassment of local life-worlds" that constitutes a relationship of power and which objectifies, encompasses, and transcends the concrete realities of place (Hornborg 1994:259). Further, the "disembedded language of modernity [it is said] generates ecological destruction" (Hornborg 1994:263). As a consequence, throughout the world environmental and indigenous movements have used the image of the ecological and spiritual aboriginal "to bring their critique of industrial into sharper focus" and to impel the critique of development and of modernist identity construction, discourse, and, ultimately power (Hornborg 1994:246).

Gledhill (1994:197), however, notes that the state's land tenure system constitutes a semiology of domination with implications for development, environmental issues, and conservation. The struggles over indigenous concepts of culture, nature, the sacred, and the land, too, have implications and it is dangerous to be optimistic concerning challenges given the enormous practical implications of the demands for recognition of indigenous views. Gledhill (1994:198) concludes ominously that "the challenge that popular forces have been able to mount to the remorseless progress of the neoliberal, neomodernization agenda, and the continutation of authoritarian patterns of political life, has remained limited."

Mohs (1994:205) discerns four strategies for the protection and conservation of sacred sites: continuing a tradition of silence about the sites, negotiation with government, legal action, and direct action. He argues that in British Columbia (and without doubt some other places) silence is of limited utility at present, that negotiation has yielded limited results within the larger context of tribal legal actions, and that legal protection is limited by the necessity to proceed on a case-by-case basis. But legal protection is also limited by the very way the landscape is conceptualized and described in court and by the "cultural defense" strategy of litigants. Although focusing on "the processes through which local experience is fragmented and absorbed by modernity [constitutes] a step toward the protection and resurrection of place" (Hornborg 1994:264), it is not enough, as Hornborg (1994:263) advocates, to "resist the power of modernity" by refusing to be encompassed. Efforts to produce and emphasize a counter discourse of spirituality radicalizes and limits the grounds on which ethnic expression may be made. While this may be a good strategy concerning well-funded and well-supported national issues, it is a poor stance in addressing what are, at heart, local discourses between Aboriginal peoples and those non-Aboriginals they live within their communities.

The case of the Tewalt rock points to specific problems in making the case for sacredness and in the difficulties of establishing sacredness as a legal fact. It is difficult to perceive directly the grounds on which the panel of judges granted a quarrying permit because the judges themselves asked few questions from the bench and their written statements are short and focused primarily on legal issues other than cultural heritage. However, the questions they posed show the difficulties they faced when asked to "reckon culture," to rule that a site is both outside of their own cultural understanding but within their power to place outside of the local regime of land management and regulation. In this case, complex, obfuscating legal debates made it all too easy for the panel to follow what was no doubt the path of least resistance and issue the quarrying license.

258

References Cited

Bard, James C. 1994. Letter from Cultural Resource Specialist to Mr. David Hough, Skagit County Department of Planning and Community Development. August 8.

Barsh, Russel. 1996. Prospects for International Action to Defend Sacred Lands. Paper presented at the Sacred Lands: Claims and Conflicts Conference, October 24–26, 1996.

Burney, Michael S. 1993. American Indian Consultation Regarding Treaty Rights and Cultural Resources: A Response from the Confederated Tribes of the Umatilla, Cayuse, and Walla Walla of Northeastern Oregon. In *Kunaitupii: Coming Together on Native Sacred Sites*, edited by Brian O. K. Reeves and Margaret A. Kennedy, pp. 111–122. Calgary: The Archaeological Society of Alberta.

Byrne, W. J. 1993. Province of Alberta Perspectives on the Sacredness of Past People and Places. In *Kunaitupii: Coming Together on Native Sacred Sites*, edited by Brian O. K. Reeves and Margaret A. Kennedy, pp.103–110. Calgary: The Archaeological Society of Alberta.

Carmichael, David, Jane Hubert, Brian Reeves, and Audhild Schanche, editors. 1994. *Sacred Sites, Sacred Places*. London: Routledge.

Clifton, James A. 1990. *The Invented Indian: Cultural Fictions and Government Policies.* New Brunswick, NJ: Transaction Publishers.

Collins, June McCormick. 1974. *Valley of Spirits: The Upper Skagit Indians of Western Washington*. Seattle: University of Washington Press.

Comaroff, John L. 1996. Ethnicity, Nationalism, and the Politics of Difference in Age of Revolution. In *The Politics of Difference: Ethnic Premises in a World of Power*, edited by Edwin N. Wilsen and Patrick McAllister, pp. 162–184. Chicago: University of Chicago Press.

Dorn, Ronald I. 1994. Letter to David C. Hough, Director, Department of Planning and Community Development, Skagit County. October 2.

Dormaar, John and Brian O. K. Reeves. 1993. Vision Quest Sites in Southern Alberta and Northern Montana. In *Kunaitupii: Coming Together on Native Sacred Sites*, edited by Brian O.K. Reeves and Margaret A. Kennedy, pp.162–178. Calgary: The Archaeological Society of Alberta.

Feld, Steven. 1996. Waterfalls of Song: An Acoustemology of Place Resounding in Bosavi, Papua New Guinea. In *Senses of Place*, edited by Steven Feld and Steve Basso, pp. 91–136. Santa Fe, NM: School of American Research.

Feld, Steven and Keith H. Basso, editors. 1996. *Senses of Place*. Santa Fe, NM: School of American Research.

Gledhill, John. 1994. *Power and its Disguises: Anthropological Perspectives on Politics.* London: Pluto Press.

Hornborg, Alf. 1994. Environmentalism, Ethnicity, and Sacred Places: Reflections on Modernity, Discourse, and Power. *The Canadian Review of Sociology and Anthropology*, 31(3):245–267.

Kelley, Klara and Harris Francis. 1994. *Navajo Sacred Places*. Bloomington: Indian University Press.

McEachern, Allen. 1991. Reasons for Judgment, *Delgamuukw v. Regina, Smithers*. British Columbia: Supreme Court of British Columbia.

Mohs, Gordon. 1994. Stó:lō Sacred Ground. In *Sacred Sites, Sacred Places*, edited by David L. Carmichael, Jane Jubert, Brian Reeves and Audhild Schanche, pp. 184–208. New York: Routledge Press.

Reeves, Brian O. K. and Margaret A. Kennedy, editors. 1993. *Kunaitupii: Coming Together on Native Sacred Sites*. Calgary: The Archaeological Society of Alberta.

Reid, Alfred. 1994. Letter to Mr. David Hough, Skagit County Department of Planning and Community Development. November 23.

Rogers, Jerry L. 1993. The Perspective of the United States National Park Service. In *Kunaitupii: Coming Together on Native Sacred Sites*, edited by Brian O. K. Reeves and Margaret A. Kennedy, pp.136–139. Calgary: The Archaeological Society of Alberta.

Ryser, Rudolph C. 1997. *The Anti-Indian Movement in the Wise Use Movement: Threatening the Cultural and Biological Diversity in Indian Country*. Olympia, Washington: Center for World Indigenous Studies.

Sampson, Chief Martin J. 1972. *Indians of Skagit County*. Mount Vernon, WA: Skagit County Historical Society.

Sharp, John. 1996. Ethnogenesis and Ethnic Mobilization: A Comparative Perspective on a South African Dilemma. In *The Politics of Difference: Ethnic Premises in a World of Power*, edited by Edwin N. Wilmsen and Patrick McAllister, pp. 85–103. Chicago: University of Chicago Press.

Snyder, Sally. 1953. Unpublished fieldnotes, Melville Jacobs Collection, Suzzallo Library, University of Washington.

Whitley, David S. 1994. Letter to Mr. Merle Ash, "Re: Inspection and Evaluation of Tewalt Quarry Marked Rock."

Whittaker, Elvi. 1994. Public Discourse on Sacredness: the Transfer of Ayers Rock to Aboriginal Ownership. *American Ethnologist*, 21(2):310–334.

Whitten, Norman. 1996. The Ecuadorian Levantamiento Indigena of 1990 and the Epitomizing Symbol of 1992: Reflections on Nationalism, Ethnic-Bloc Formation and Racialist Ideologies. In *History, Power, and Identity: Ethnogenesis in the Americas, 1492–1992*, edited by Jonathon D. Hill, pp. 193–218. Iowa City: University of Iowa Press.

Journal of Northwest Anthropology, Memoir 12:260–262 (2016)

17

The Story of Peter Pan, or Middle Ground Lost*

The historian Richard White elaborated the concept of "middle ground," the contested, transformative space between diverse peoples. He, and others, have pointed out that influence flows in more than one direction in the colonial landscape. Especially in the early days, settler societies were themselves created and changed by the encounter, even as they gradually pushed aside indigenous societies. To this I add that, for the dominant society, memory of these transformations is selective, sometimes strategically so. More is forgotten than remembered about how we got to the present.

In the frantic call to assimilate indigenes, contemporary mainstream discourse overlooks the middle ground and remains oblivious to the long prior history of efforts at assimilation, amalgamation, and even, occasionally, mutual aid. Another voice calls for the mainstream to embrace indigenous viewpoints and practices, also oblivious that this process has been under way long since. There are costs for these acts of forgetting. As Rebecca Bateman recently pointed out in the pages of *BC Studies*, the dominant society continuously recycles the same small set of administrative policies and practices, forgetting earlier failures. Legislators rotate in and out of office, leaving no collective memory of the longevity and nature of the relationship between colonizers and colonized. Public debate on indigenous issues is regularly born anew, always fixated on the exploits of first contact (wherein indigenes encounter sugar that looks like maggots and sailing ships that resemble migratory birds) and on the current moment. This is the Peter Pan Complex—dim, exotic memories of infancy and vivid impressions of the present, with nothing in between.

The version of the Peter Pan story I bring to your attention is not the one from Disney Studios but, rather, the darker book version. In it, Peter can't clearly recall his earlier relationship with Wendy (and her predecessors) or the little brothers, and he takes them on long dangerous flights where, it is intimated, if they fall asleep, they will crash unnoticed into the ocean and drown. He's not interested in Wendy when she grows up. Peter is ageless, yet is interested only in children one could say, his "wards"—as long as they listen to him and do what he wants. He doesn't listen at all. "Girls talk too much," he tells Wendy.

In my story, the Indians (the term of reference in Peter Pan and in the Indian Act) I consider are not the Blackfeet who help Peter attack pirates, but the ones who likely flew with Peter and whose whereabouts were previously unknown. They have now been located. In my telling, there is an adult. He is not Wendy's mother, father, or dog. I found him in the Upper Nicola band Office, near Merritt. He is Scotty Holmes, band land claims negotiator. His office is right in the middle ground Richard White talked about. The land claims building is a small former church, standing almost alone in open rangeland. A few other tribal buildings have been built nearby—a school and a tribal centre among them. The former church is now stripped of liturgical features except a clever, skinny closet where church vestments were once hung, now disguising itself with paint. It's empty and seems useless, but it knows that land claims may be concluded some day, and it can once again have something new to do. It's biding its time; like everything in the middle ground, you don't know where it's been unless you look closely. On the wall is a big, impressive hand-drawn map, framed for safekeeping. Everyone's eyes are drawn to the map. The

---

*Authored by Bruce Granville Miller, reproduced with permission and previously published in *BC Studies*, 131:25–28 (2001).

map is signed by LW. Powell, Okanagan Agency, and it depicts Indian reserves in the late nineteenth century. Indian superintendent Powell is not forgotten by the Upper Nicola band, nor are his words—especially not by Scotty Holmes. Powell was no Peter Pan, but, he, too claimed what he wanted, which was land.

Scotty Holmes has his own story to tell at the moment, and it's just a version of the Peter Pan story (but told from the Indian viewpoint) of promised trips to Neverland led by a boy who promises to forget as quickly as possible in the interest of having fun his way. Peter, recall, pulls his knife on enemies. He's not too kind to the Lost Boys, either. We forgot this part of our own story. We always forget part of the story. In Scotty's story, the federal government negotiated with the Upper Nicola to hold some land on Douglas Lake in "commonage"; however, it quickly forgot about this arrangement and sold off the land to ranching interests when it turned out that ranching would be the best way to have a lot of fun. It was particularly fun for Peter O'Reilly, the Indian reserve commissioner who determined band land allocations, because he is said to have had a financial stake in ranching. The locals remember that part of the story. Scotty adds to it. Later, when the Upper Nicola people working in the former church pointed out that they wanted to have fun, too, the government officials remembered the arrangement but not well enough to know if the commonage was 18,000 or 33,000 acres. They think it's more likely 18,000. They will swap stories with the Upper Nicola band about this—but only "preliminary" stories, not final stories, even though they've had a very long time to prepare their version. The government is distracted by school teachers, buses, and nurses and likes to take its time in the hopes the Upper Nicola will forget or run out of the money needed to gather a crowd and tell the story at the courthouse. They won't, though.

Because Scotty Holmes is a storyteller, with a good story to tell, he can change tone quickly, light-hearted one moment and rather dark the next. It makes for excitement. He knows his audience keeps changing. He says he doesn't care who the B.C. government is, mentioning that "we'll simply have to educate another group." He knows the deep commitment of the government to forgetting and the reverence in which Peter Pan is held. He understands that the government is perplexed because lots of people and cows live in Neverland now. The city folk and the ranchers don't want to give back any land, don't want to turn Neverland back into the middle ground. They've installed electricity. Scotty probably knows that in the old days, when there was a middle ground, people could remember, right in the very church where he is telling his story, that the main character was Moses. Moses' story was about travelling through the desert and taking over land by conquest. The people in the Moses story were very good at remembering but the story is largely forgotten now. The story about forgetting is regarded as more suitable at present, although times change, and one can't always count on this. There is evidence that some courts insist on telling stories about remembering, or at least partly remembering. One court said that the Indians could tell their own story as they remembered it. A new politician, in support of Peter Pan, doesn't like this at all and has promised to get everyone to sign a piece of paper that will ask them if they agree to forget. It will be called a referendum, if it's remembered. Other politicians are suggesting he forget about it.

Scotty Holmes's story is about the future as well as the past. He doesn't know all the details, but he knows the ending, which, oddly, is rather like the past when there was a middle ground. He says that his band will "get the ranch some day. We're working on compensation right now." He wants to keep the negotiations moderate, neighbourly, courteous, "our way." His story can get a bit pointed, though. "You only use your laws to suit your needs; that law doesn't apply when we need it. If you want one law for all, let us make the law! When we follow your law, and it doesn't suit you, you want to change it." He knows the new part of the story about the courts but doesn't choose to emphasize that at the moment. In his story, the Upper Nicola band has "lots of options. It's a new era." The story might not include a stopover at the courts, but, if it does, his relatives are getting prepared. They will know what to say. They've recorded lots and lots of stories, none about Peter Pan, but lots about Coyote and Raven. These are stories all about everywhere in Upper Nicola territory. In my story, these are called "place-names" and "charter myths." But these stories will be told Upper Nicola style. Scotty said: "When it gets back out, it's our world. Not from somebody else's perspective. We will take it from our principles, our beliefs." Both Scotty's and my stories are about middle ground, so these Upper Nicola stories are transformed onto GIS mappings as well as told at home.

I can imagine this telling at the courthouse; it will make a good story, so good I will give it now. The government will tell about Peter Pan, a complicated version in which Peter is a Grown-Up. Even though Peter sometimes fought the pirates, in this version, Peter, the pirates, and the government are friends, or at least allies. They might even be the same person. They all like to capture Indians and they all believe Neverland belonged to them once they showed up there. The Upper Nicola people will tell about 33,000 acres, what the land is called, and what they were doing there when LW. Powell and Peter O'Reilly came around. All the lost Indians will be found now, and they will be seated in the court, listening and telling their story. The Upper Nicola will remember this story, too, and tell it in the future.

Part VI
The Border

The U.S.-Canada border has sliced the Coast Salish world in half. But it is only in the last few decades that the international border has become more directly relevant to Coast Salish people. Previously, even after the establishment of colonial regimes, people travelled freely by canoe and foot between communities, and the Jay Treaty and the subsequent Treaty of Ghent provided guarantees of free movement. This changed after the tragic events of September 11, 2001 in the U.S., and a period of "hardening" of the border has ensued, with serious consequences for the movement of Indigenous peoples. In addition, Coast Salish communities have been under different regimes of state policy, which have led to some distinctive differences between communities to the north and south. I take up these issues in a series of linked publications, starting with Chapter 18, *The "Really Real" Border and the Divided Salish Community*. This essay, written prior to 9/11, points to some forms of cooperation between border services and Coast Salish people living on the border but disputes the postmodern notion of the fluidity of peoples and ideas. I describe how related peoples divided by the border lose track of developments on the other side. In Chapter 19, *Conceptual and Practical Boundaries: Indians/First Nations on the Border of Contagion in the Post-9/11 Era*, I describe changing U.S. perceptions of Canada from a benign neighbor to a country harboring terrorists and contagion and the efforts to pull tribes into the war on terror. This was originally published as a book chapter in *The Borderlands of the American and Canadian Wests: Essays on Regional and Trans-boundary History* edited by Sterling Evans (2006). Chapter 20, *Life on the Hardened Border*, another journal article, follows this theme by theorizing the notion of border, and how it has been reconceptualized and reengineered by the state and the consequences for those living directly on the border.

Figure 16. Sonny McHalsie of the Stó:lō Nation and Bob Mierendorf, National Park Service archaeologist for the North Cascades, at the Hozomeen Gathering in 2009 on the international border.

Journal of Northwest Anthropology, Memoir 12:264–274 (2016)

18

THE "REALLY REAL" BORDER
AND THE DIVIDED SALISH COMMUNITY*

The current academic climate is predisposed to the crossing of intellectual, disciplinary, political, and cultural boundaries.[1] Efforts to connect the global and the local and to transcend boundaries, however, run the risk of becoming institutionalized into newer, non-critical, docile forms of knowledge production that overlook the local concerns of Aboriginal peoples. Scheper-Hughes points ascerbically to this problem:

> In the brave new world of reflexive postmodernists…everything local is said to dissolve into merged media images, transgressed boundaries, [and] promiscuously mobile multinational industries and workers…The flight from the local in hot pursuit of a transnational, borderless anthropology implies a parallel flight from local engagements, local commitments…Once the circuits of power are seen as capillary, diffuse, global, and difficult to trace to their sources, the idea of resistance becomes meaningless. The idea of an anthropology without borders… ignores the reality of the very real borders that confront and oppress "our" anthropological subjects…These borders are as real as the passports and passbooks, the sandbagged bunkers, the armed roadblocks…The anthropology that most Cape Town Xhosa, Venda…and Moslem students want is not the anthropology of deconstruction and the social imaginary, but the anthropology of the really real, in which the stakes are high. (Scheper-Hughes 1995:417)

This essay attempts to address the "really real" of the international boundary dividing Canada from the United States, British Columbia from Washington. My concern is the ways in which the political border creates parallel conceptual and practical boundaries for the First Nations of this region and the ways in which the latter are currently responding to this. Following a widely held First Nations view, I treat the international boundary as an arbitrary but potent fact of life that divides the peoples and communities commonly referred to as Salish. I argue that in the present-day process of rethinking and developing their own community organizations and rearranging their relations to the state (i.e., to the provincial, state, and federal governments) Coast and Interior Salish peoples are, in the pursuit of social justice, intensifying the development of strategies concerning the border.[2] Salish leaders and rank-and-file tribal members acting on their own are now conducting a wide range of strategic activities. The scope and extent of these activities is largely invisible; only a few receive public or academic attention. But it is in their totality that these small-scale efforts become important and reflect the Salish perception that their own identity and intercommunity networks cannot be constructed without their relatives on the other side of the border.

In brief, Salish efforts include: (1) current legal challenges to the state to gain rights of free passage within traditional territories that overlap the international border; (2) initiatives to change the procedures whereby winter Spirit Dancers (who are in a state of extreme spiritual danger) are permitted to cross the border between B.C. and Washington; (3) attempts to promote a form of political unity between Coast Salish bands and tribes; (4) efforts to find medical care within

*Authored by Bruce Granville Miller, reproduced with permission and previously published in *BC Studies,* 112:63–79 (1996–1997).

different regimes of service delivery; and (5) formal recognition of tribal members living on the other side of the boundary.

There is another issue motivating this work: groups living along administrative, state, provincial, and federal borders (as well as along the borders between culture areas as defined in the anthropological tradition) tend to disappear from the landscape, the official record, and the academic imagination. Such groups are frequently amalgamated with others, dispersed, ignored, or treated as participants in another's cultural tradition—a circumstance that complicates the search for legal recognition and social justice.[3]

My examination of these topics rests upon my own fieldwork with the Coast Salish communities of Puget Sound and the Fraser River, interviews with members of these communities (specifically for this project), involvement in on-going litigation, and a reading of the ethnographic and historical materials.

The Background: Salish Affiliative Networks

Those mid-nineteenth century peoples who spoke languages within the Coast Salish family and who lived within Puget Sound, along the Fraser River and its tributaries, and on the southeastern portions of Vancouver Island are the ancestors of the members of some fifty current bands in B.C. and twenty-four tribes in Washington (Miller 1992). Their social organization was made up of fluid local groups composed of one or more households that interacted to form a regional structure (see Miller and Boxberger 1994:270–272). Tribes did not exist prior to interaction with Europeans and state governments but emerged as political entities following treaty negotiations, the establishment of the reserve/reservation systems, and in response to the requirements of subsequent legal actions against the government. Before this, individuals closely identified with the local group within which they were residing and with the larger "speech community." The Coast Salish kinship system emphasized bilaterality and marriage was preferentially exogamous; consequently, individuals had kin in many different villages. Kin ties, then, created a network of relations that extended far beyond one's own river drainage and that, potentially, provided access to the labour and resources of a large population as well as to a rich environment. For these reasons, ethnographers of the Coast Salish have long emphasized the pattern of regional affiliation in their explanations of social organization (Elmendorf 1960; Suttles 1963; Miller 1989).

These affiliative networks have persisted to the present and serve to organize activity in a variety of domains, thereby perpetuating the connectiveness of the larger Coast Salish community (Suttles 1963; Kew and Miller n.d.). Persistent, regular activities bring together peoples from throughout the Coast Salish area for marriage and kinship, commercial fishing, winter ceremonial activity, and summer festivals that emphasize sporting contests and informal mingling. In addition, Salish peoples are drawn together by regularly scheduled events on the Pow-Wow circuit of intertribal festivities.

Among the Aboriginal peoples who occupy a region drained by the Columbia and Fraser Rivers east of the Cascade Mountains in Washington and the Coast Range in B.C. are speakers of seven Interior Salish languages. Members of the constituent communities are referred to here as the Interior Salish peoples, although there was no formal, all-encompassing Interior Salish political organization. As is the case with the Coast Salish, the Interior Salish maintain a vast network of interpersonal ties constructed around kinship, friendship, and trade connections (Hunn 1990). In earlier periods, they created regional task groups for subsistence purposes (Anastasio

1973). The Interior Salish, in common with the Coast Salish, valued exogamous marriage (marriage to people from another village), a circumstance that reinforced the broad network of kin connections. A further factor promoting regional cooperation was the possibility of food shortage due to the thinness and wide dispersal of resources within their region (Richardson 1982).

As is the case with Coast Salish peoples, being a subordinated people and having a common post-contact history of struggling to protect their resources and lifeways has reinforced the connections between Interior Salish peoples. So, too, has placement on reserves and reservations, along with attendance at residential schools (Tennant 1990). In any case, both in the pre-contact period and up to the present day, the broad network of affiliation between Salish peoples and communities has involved those on both sides of the border.

The Dramatic: Aboriginal Challenges to the Boundaries of the State

The case of *Robert Watt v. E. Liebelt and the Minister of Citizenship and Immigration*, on appeal to the Trial Division, Federal Court of Canada, is a case in which, to the Crown, "The issue…is whether an aboriginal person who is neither a Canadian citizen nor a registered Indian has a right to remain in Canada because he belongs to a tribe whose traditional territory straddles the Canada-United States border" (Reed 1994:1). Robert Allen Watt, a forty-one-year-old member of the Arrow Lakes community or tribe, otherwise known as the Sinixt, had been appointed by Arrow Lakes elders to come north into Canada to be "the guardian of a sacred burial site in British Columbia" (Suleman 1994:2) that was then under threat of being turned into a quarry. Watt, born in Washington State and an enrolled member of the Colville Confederated Tribes, lived in the Slocan Valley, B.C., for most of the period between 1986 and 1993 while carrying out his guardian role.

In the nineteenth century the Arrow Lakes people moved from the vicinity of Revelstoke, B.C., in the north to (approximately) Colville, Washington, in the south. Following the establishment of the 49th parallel as the U.S.-Canada boundary in 1846, it became difficult for Arrow Lakes people to continue their traditional patterns of seasonal movement. Many members of the Arrow Lakes community moved to the Washington Territory in 1872 after the establishment of the Colville Reservation, and there, together with the Colville people with whom they had long had marriage ties, they were offered land allotments. In 1902, a small Canadian reserve was created on Lower Arrow Lake and was occupied by twenty-two people. By 1953 the last member of this group, according to Canadian records, was deceased and the reserve reverted to the Crown. The Arrow Lakes people were declared extinct, even though more than 250 were enrolled members of the Colville Confederated Tribes and were continuing to use traditional territories in B.C.

In 1993 an adjudicator of a hearings board within the Ministry of Citizenship and Immigration ruled that, under the terms of the Canadian Immigration Act and because he was not a registered Canadian Indian under the Indian Act, Watt was to leave Canada within thirty days. Of interest here is the fact that the Watt case directly calls into question federal government conventions concerning the definition of "Aboriginal Peoples of Canada." Legal counsel for Watt argued that "the definition of 'aboriginal peoples of Canada' in subsection 35 (2) of the Constitution Act, 1982 is open-ended. The use of the word 'includes'…infers that there may be other peoples who could raise a reasonable claim that they ought to be considered 'aboriginal'" (Suleman 1995:16). The passage in question reads: "In this Act, 'aboriginal peoples of Canada' includes the Indian, Inuit, and Metis peoples of Canada." Furthermore, counsel argued that, given an open-ended definition and the fact that the Supreme Court of Canada has held that section 35 of the Constitution Act is to be interpreted generously and liberally, Aboriginal peoples all along the U.S.-Canada boundary should be included under section 35 as Aboriginal peoples of Canada (see Evans 1995 for a similar argument). In addition, counsel argued that subsection 35 (1) "protects the long-standing aboriginal right to move freely throughout their traditional territories." The Immigration Act, according to this argument, ought not to be interpreted in a manner that "would eliminate the rights of the Arrow Lakes or Sinixt people to freely move throughout their traditional territories."

The Watts case does not stand alone in querying the cross-border rights of First Nations along the international border; indeed, a series of related issues has arisen within the last few years. These issues include the rights of bands and tribes with regards to the management of traditional territories that incorporate watersheds or other natural zones that straddle the border. Recently, the proposal to create an international park in the Skagit Valley of Washington and B.C. has prompted exchanges between Salish political leaders concerning the terms under which this could satisfy mutual Salish interests.[4] In addition, the issue of cross-border participation in negotiating cash settlements for damages to traditional territories has arisen. For example, the creation of Ross Dam on the Skagit River, which damaged thriving salmon runs, led to the negotiation of a settlement in 1994 between Seattle City Light and a coalition of Washington tribes along the Skagit River. This caused the Nlaka'pamux, whose traditional territories extend into the Skagit Valley of Washington, to investigate to what extent they might participate.[5] In this case the issue is that the Nlaka'pamux do not fall under U.S. laws, which define a legal relationship with a named set of tribes. The U.S. trust relationship with Native tribes does not extend to Canadian bands.

In sum, bands and tribes have recently questioned the role of the state in defining Aboriginal communities, in limiting access to territories, and in limiting any liability or trust responsibility to those on only one side of the border. The First Nations claims constitute a proposal for a broader, more inclusive view—a view that would better account for the nature of their own community organization.

The Secret: Aboriginal Challenges to the Intrusiveness of the Border

In common with the religious life of many other indigenous peoples of the Americas, Coast Salish religious life focuses on the relationships between individuals and "immortals," spirit beings who interact with humans as kin and who provide access to powers of various sorts (see Miller 1994 for a vivid description of this relationship). Throughout Coast Salish territory initiates to the society of Spirit Dancers spend an initial winter in the longhouse, receiving training and developing their relationship with their spirit helper. In their first winter as initiates ("babies") they are spiritually reborn and experience a state of ritual instability, at which time they are susceptible to spiritual and physical danger. As the winter progresses, initiates travel to the various longhouses in Washington and British Columbia that, collectively, house the ritual congregation. Initiates travel in ceremonial costumes that provide a measure of spiritual protection; for example, headdresses largely cover their eyes to keep them from danger. In some cases, experienced Spirit Dancers carry masks that are placed in containers that can only be opened in a ceremonial context.

The immediate problem for Spirit Dancers travelling between Coast Salish communities located across the border is the incompatibility of customs regulations and the spiritual state of susceptibility. Initiates may be placed in spiritual danger if, for example, someone looks directly into their faces. Masks and other regalia cannot be handled by non-dancers, and the cedar costumes and headdresses as well as the wooden staffs carried by black-and-red faced dancers sometimes appear bizarre and suspicious to border agents.[6]

A particular difficulty facing the Spirit Dancers is the cultural prohibition on the communication of specific information about winter Spirit Dancing. Dancers do not reveal the nature of their spirit helpers, nor do they ordinarily describe to outsiders the specifics of their regalia or longhouse practices. To reveal specifics could place dancers in physical danger and reduce the efficacy of their relationship with their spirit helpers. This circumstance has made it difficult for Salish peoples to describe their concerns. U.S. officials have recently attempted to educate border personnel concerning these topics, and a member of a Washington tribe has proposed establishing an education module.[7]

Chief Frank Malloway, of the Yakweakwioose Band of the Stó:lō Nation of B.C., noted that border personnel have recently allowed longhouse initiates to pass the border without visual inspection if they are accompanied by longhouse leaders who present identification for each of them.[8] While "oldtimers" (long-time border officials) on the American side merely used to wave Stó:lō Spirit Dancers through the crossing, in more recent years border guards have tightened their scrutiny. However, through a consultative process, many guards have "learned not to look in the mask boxes or at the dancers." As part of this process, longhouse leaders notify border personnel prior to hosting ceremonies requiring the presence of dancers on the other side of the border.

Associate Chief Elva Caulkins of the U.S. Department of the Treasury (Customs Service) reported that, while "Indians" may cross from north to south, this is not unproblematic, and "at times we are going to look."[9] Further, "we don't do an 'attitude check' even if they are lippy. But if they are evasive it can cause problems. Lots of time Indians won't tell us what country they're from. Coast Salish believe both countries are their country. Indians often say they are resident of both. We ask them "where is your longhouse?" [when attempting to determine residency].

In internally circulated professional journals Canadian border officials have published articles that describe ceremonial objects, but these have focused on the material culture of Aboriginal peoples outside of British Columbia (see *The Inspector* 10 [1991], a publication of the Canadian Department of Customs and Immigration). Chief Bernard Charles of the Semiahmoo First Nation, a band whose lands are located directly on the international border, observed in a letter in response to the piece in *The Inspector* that "[we] were disappointed that [your article] contained little or no specific information pertaining to Coast Aboriginal people in Washington state or Southwest British Columbia." Caulkins noted that, due to the failure of Canadian policy to allow largely unrestricted passage, "Indians are angrier at Canadians than the U.S."— a perspective that accurately reflects the view of many Canadian First Nations.[10]

A related problem concerns the movement across the border of goods intended for ceremonies in which members of the wider Coast Salish community are invited to participate. The most notable ceremonies are potlatches, including memorial potlatches, which are held to mark the end of a period of mourning and to acknowledge the rearrangement of the social role of a deceased relative. A potlatch requires the distribution of goods to those in attendance. Senior family members ordinarily spend some years stockpiling blankets, hats, cutlery, plastic domestic items, and many other things for distribution. If these items are taken across the border, then duty must be paid on them—a circumstance that poses a dilemma for Coast Salish peoples. Chief Malloway noted that one man's car was seized following accusations of smuggling when he attempted to bring 200 blankets across the border to contribute to a relative's potlatch. In addition, those bringing home items received at a potlatch may be required to pay duty. The increased cost of potlatching due to the imposition of duties and the threat of legal action over the transport of goods is said to have decreased participation in potlatches across the border.

There are problems concerning the transport across the border of ceremonial or religious items that are not necessarily related to potlatches. The U.S. Fishery and Game Act prohibits the transport of items such as eagle feathers, which First Nations peoples sometimes carry in their vehicles. These feathers are thought by border officials to be associated with the possession and use of drug paraphernalia. Both the duties imposed on goods and the restrictions on eagle feathers constitute a regulatory environment that increases the complexity of Salish life.

The Essential: The Fishery and Problems of Access and Identity

Salish society is fundamentally constructed around the relationship of human beings and non-human beings. Among the most significant of these non-human beings are the Salmon beings, who provide the food that defines Salish culture. In earlier periods, Coast Salish villages were built along rivers or the sea in order to facilitate fishing. The relationship between humans and non-humans has never been solely material, however, and the Salish continue to celebrate their spiritual connection with salmon through First Salmon ceremonies. During these ceremonies, the salmon beings offer themselves to humans as food, and the latter, in turn, demonstrate their understanding and respect for the former. Salish social organization and cultural identity, then, is directly connected to the fishery, a fact acknowledged in the nineteenth century by both Washington and B.C. The treaties of western Washington specified that "Indians" would continue to have access to salmon and other species; in B.C., reserves were established, in part, due to their proximity to fishing stations.

The eventual creation of separate national fishing policies has created significant difficulties for Salish peoples. This is especially so because of the extraordinary richness of the fisheries along the international border (Boxberger 1990). When Aboriginal peoples controlled and regulated their own fisheries, access to resources was determined largely through kinship connections to senior band members, who served as stewards, or managers, of local procurement and processing stations. A structure of use-rights emerged in which patterns of affiliation organized the fisheries through an elaborate protocol. Affiliative patterns spread across what became the international border (see Smith 1950), and people from what is now Washington State fished in the Fraser River and adjoining waters, a circumstance that is now explicitly acknowledged. Ernie Crey, director of Stó:lō Nation fisheries, for example, recently observed that Lummi Nation fishers of Washington traditionally fished salmon stocks that spawned on the Fraser River and its tributaries.[11] In addition, fisheries around the Gulf Islands of B.C. and the San Juan Islands of Washington formerly involved fishers from bands and tribes now located on both sides of the border (Suttles 1990; Boxberger 1994).

But the issue is not a simple one of restoring earlier fisheries management practices. For example, members of one B.C. band have taken the position that they wish to exclude from commercial Native fisheries on the Fraser River any "non-signatory" band members; namely, those who reside in Washington and who are presumed to have access to the Puget Sound Native fishery.[12] Salish fishers of Washington and B.C. remain largely within separate camps, despite the memories of earlier management protocols. Although Native fishers of Washington were excluded from the fishery by the 1950s, today they co-manage the salmon resource with the state Department of Fisheries. Twenty-four tribes have since formed the Northwest Indian Fisheries Commission to facilitate the discussion of the allocation of fish among the various tribes. Similarly, B.C. bands were largely excluded from a fishery that became increasingly more capital-intensive as the century progressed (Newell 1993). The reasons for judgment in the

270

case of *Sparrow v. The Queen,* 1990, interpreted the Constitution Act, 1982, section 35 (1) as protecting the Aboriginal right to fish for social and ceremonial purposes, but they were silent concerning commercial sales. Subsequently, the federal government created a seven-year trial policy, the Aboriginal Fisheries Strategy, to allow limited Aboriginal commercial fishing. In response, Salish First Nations have attempted to create their own commercial fisheries management programs.

As a consequence of these developments, Native peoples and polities have ended up on opposite sides from each other in the international negotiations over fisheries allocations that form the backdrop to the Pacific Salmon Treaty. Distinctive features of Native fisheries management are thereby underplayed and the common interests of Salish peoples are obscured. Some Coast Salish people have responded by attempting to create formalized links across the border through the creation of a Coast Salish "treaty" that recognizes a common heritage and common interests, while others rely on more informal, individual exchanges of information between band and tribal fisheries officers and managers. Nevertheless, the Coast Salish remain partitioned into U.S. and Canadian camps, respectively, concerning the issue of fisheries. The larger problem for the Coast Salish is to articulate a vision of common interests that is compatible with the interests of particular bands and tribes.

The Mundane: Acts of Manipulation and Accommodation

Other responses to the border take the form, not of overt political action but, rather, of mundane, personal acts of manipulation and accommodation. One Coast Salish woman, for example, who was born in a Stó:lō community along the Fraser River in B.C. and who married into a Coast Salish tribe in western Washington, monitors the available health care opportunities for her dependent, a child with a debilitating ailment.[13] She is able to take advantage of the existence of two different national policies concerning public health: as an enrolled tribal member she has access to the services of the United States Public Health Department through a branch known as the Indian Health Service, and as a Canadian citizen she has access to a socialized medical system with a somewhat different array of specialty services for chronic children's diseases. It is significant that she has violated neither the spirit nor the letter of either Canadian or U.S. law in looking after her dependent, nor has she duplicated services. This strategy has required that she maintain active affiliations both with the community of her birth and with the community into which she married.

This care-giving woman is not alone. Other Salish people make use of the differences in the Canadian and American economies and public policies by crossing the border in an effort to improve their circumstances and to find employment. Generally, this requires activating a latent affiliation with a community across the border and relocating there for some months or years. In the case of the members of the Semiahmoo community in B.C., it entails exploiting the job market of Whatcom County, Washington, and daily returning to their reserve. One member of the Semiahmoo Nation noted: "It's easier for the Semiahmoo. So many of us have worked in the U.S. for the past thirty, forty, fifty years. We've been working on and off since teenagers, commuting back and forth. They [government officials] know us at the border."[14]

In common with other Canadian citizens, Aboriginal peoples living on the border make use of differences in pricing. Semiahmoo people shop in Blaine, Washington, bringing home milk, eggs, cheese, and other food products that are ordinarily cheaper in the U.S. Others take advantage of differences in the value of American and Canadian currency by importing goods with Aboriginal content duty-free from the U.S. and selling them on Canadian reserves.[15] This activity, although the product of the differences between the two countries, serves to unite the larger Salish community.

Another distinct pattern involves appropriating and reshaping federal notions of citizenship. This takes two forms. In one form, communities enroll as tribal or band members those people who have ancestral connections to them but who are formally citizens on the other side of the international boundary. Although federally recognized tribes of Washington State do not allow cross-enrollment (enrollment in more than one tribe or band), one non-recognized tribe includes on its roll Aboriginal people who are resident in Canada, who hold Canadian citizenship, and who are eligible for enrollment in a Canadian band.[16] In so doing, this tribe can assert its legitimacy by employing Aboriginal notions of affiliation and membership independent of state-imposed criteria and, simultaneously, fulfill the membership desires of those who claim affiliation and common descent but who live across the international border.

In the other form of reshaping federal notions of citizenship, band members simply claim existing categories of membership and act on them. This is the case for members of the Semiahmoo First Nation, who speak of themselves as "dual citizens" even though they are not formally recognized as such by the U.S. and Canada. They do this for a variety of reasons. Nineteenth-century Semiahmoo territory, like the Arrow Lakes territory, straddles the international boundary, and by claiming dual citizenship band members are able to maintain their connection to place. The Semiahmoo are acting within their perceived rights when they exploit economic and educational opportunities in northern Washington. In addition, the Semiahmoo maintain active connections to the 3,000-member Lummi Nation of Washington and are aware of their presence within that tribe. Finally, the Semiahmoo, who moved north to Canada at the time of the settlement of the international border, have considered legal action to compensate themselves for loss of territory. These are all indications of a continued Semiahmoo presence within Washington.

The Costs

In spite of their relatively successful acts of manipulation and accommodation, the Salish efforts to maintain their communities have a number of costs. There is some truncation of communication between groups despite the efforts to overcome the problems the border poses. It is clear that some ceremonial exchanges are altered or diminished, particularly those requiring the movement of goods across the border. There are also fears of intrusive claims to territory, cash settlements, and legal entitlements by Aboriginal communities across the border. These arise, in part, from the fact that some lands are controlled by bands or tribes other than those that occupied them in the middle of the nineteenth century (when the international border was created). These fears reflect both a misunderstanding of the legal circumstances across the border and a recognition of the capacity of large political entities to extend their reach across the line in order to intervene (for example) in litigation.[17]

In a related matter, some people find themselves, of necessity, residing on the wrong side of the border. This is particularly the case for members of tribes that are not federally recognized, such as the Arrow Lakes in B.C. or the Samish in Washington. In the Arrow Lakes case, there is a recognized tribe in Washington, the Colville Confederated Tribes, with whom they can affiliate, but there are none in B.C. In the case of members of the Samish tribe living on Vancouver Island, the opposite is true.

Finally, there is the sheer difficulty of legal challenges such as that typified by the Watt case. This case failed initially, and although the appeal has not yet been heard, it appears to be an uphill battle.

Conclusion

Salish peoples are currently contesting, inverting, and reconceptualizing the international border in various ways in order to maintain their communities and to preserve their sense of common identity. It is clear that Aboriginal peoples on both its sides persist in thinking of the border as an intrusion and that their responses to it constitute efforts to gain social justice. Although intellectual border crossings may reveal significant features of the current world economic and political systems and the way in which Aboriginal peoples fit into them, the developments considered here are apparent only through an analytic focus on the local and concrete, on the "really real" border rather than on the intellectually transcended border. These local challenges to the American and Canadian states are born of circumstances that long precede current power alignments. However, it is the state itself that has become the power container of modern society, a circumstance that poses a dilemma for Salish peoples inasmuch as the institutional arrangements of the state stop at the border (see Giddens 1987). Consequently, for Aboriginal peoples, the difficulties of carrying out their lives and pressing their claims within two separate national legal systems remains a considerable barrier to the achievement of justice.

Aboriginal efforts are varied, and not all are successful, but they nevertheless point to the fact that academic treatments of the Salish must account for this fundamental feature of identity and community. Furthermore, academic treatments ought to consider the current significance of all of the activity around border issues. It is both this activity and its conceptualizations that are of importance. One might anticipate that border issues will grow in importance to Salish and other Aboriginal peoples as their communities continue the processes of working towards self-government, managing any resources over which they are able to regain control, and challenging the mainstream community to rethink the future of the B.C. Lower Mainland and elsewhere. The results of the 1995 Quebec referendum on secession are widely understood as pushing Canadian society and its governance in new directions, but First Nations are also pushing them in new directions, both forcefully and subtly, as these Salish examples show.

Endnotes

[1] In recent years "cultural borders" has been the theme of academic meetings in many disciplines. The recent interest within anthropology builds on an older tradition of the study of "borderlands" (Alvarez 1995:449). Borderlands are thought to be sites of conflict and contradiction, to generate their own cultures, to be the meeting ground of the First and Third Worlds. See, for example, Fabian 1993.

[2] At present, First Nations in B.C. are negotiating both land claims and treaties with the provincial and federal governments. The First Nations are also creating their own formal systems of governance, social services, education, legal systems, and other programs.

[3] Two such groups are the Inland Tlingit and the Comox. Personal communication, Andy Everson, Comox band member, 1 November 1995; Ingrid Johnson, Inland Tlingit, 6 November 1995.

[4] Personal communication, Doreen Maloney, member of the council of the Upper Skagit Tribe, Washington State.

[5] Personal communication, attorney for the Nlha7kápmx.

[6] Personal communication, Elva Caulkins, Assistant Chief, Department of the Treasury, U.S. Custom Service, Blaine, Washington, 28 February 1995.

[7] Maxine Williams, of the Swinomish Tribe, is currently producing an education module for border officials. Personal communication, Elva Caulkins.

[8] Personal communication, Chief Frank Malloway, 2 June 1995.

[9] Telephone interview, 2 February 1995.

[10] Eleanor Charles of Semiahmoo, for example, is one who holds such an position.

[11] Talk given to UBC Faculty of Law, 25 September 1995.

[12] See *Rebuilding Stó:lō fisheries Law: Report of the Community Consultation Process.* Lower Fraser Fish Authority, 1993.

[13] Notes from interviews with a woman who will remain un-identified.

[14] Personal communication, Eleanor Charles of Semiahmoo.

[15] An example of an import item sold on Canadian reserves is wooden coffins.

[16] This tribe is in the process of obtaining recognition from the U.S. government but currently lacks official status as a tribe. Other Washington tribes may also have enrolled Canadian Aboriginal people.

[17] Some Semiahmoo, for example, have expressed concerns that the Lummi Nation of Washington will make land claims in Semiahmoo territory in B.C., even though the Lummi occupy former Semiahmoo grounds rather than vice versa. In this case the discrepancy in size and resources seems to be at play. The Lummi Nation numbers about 3,000 and is the preeminent fishing tribe in the US. The Semiahmoo number in the sixties.

References Cited

Alvarez, Robert R., Jr. 1995. The Mexican-US Border: the Making of an Anthropology of Borderlands. *Annual Review of Anthropology,* 24:447–470. Palo Alto, CA: Annual Reviews.

Anastasio, Angelo. 1972. The Southern Plateau: An Ecological Analysis of Intergroup Relations. *Northwest Anthropology Research Notes*, 6(2):109–229.

Boxberger, Daniel L. 1990. The Northwest Coast Culture Area. In *Native North Americans: An Ethnohistorical Approach,* edited by Daniel L. Boxberger, pp. 387–410. Dubuque, IA: Kendall/Hunt.

———— 1994. Lightning Bolts and Sparrow Wings: A Comparison of Coast Salish Fishing Rights in British Columbia and Washington State. *Native Studies Review,* 9(1):1–13.

Elmendorf, William W. 1960. The Structure of Twana Culture. *Research Studies*, 28(3):1–565.

Evans, Denise. 1995. Superimposed Nations: The Jay Treaty and Aboriginal Rights. *Dalhousie Journal of Legal Studies*, 4:215–30.

Fabian, Johannes. 1993. Crossing and Patrolling: Thoughts on Anthropology and Boundaries. *Culture*, 13(1):49–54.

Giddens, Anthony. 1989. *The Nation State and Violence.* Berkeley: University of California Press.

Hunn, Eugene S. 1990. The Plateau Culture Area. In *Native North Americans: An Ethnohistorical Approach,* edited by Daniel L. Boxberger, pp. 361–86. Dubuque, IA: Kendall/Hunt.

274

Kew, J. E. Michael and Bruce G. Miller. 1999. Locating Aboriginal Governments in the Political Landscape. In *Seeking Sustainability in the Lower Fraser Basin: Issues and Choices,* edited by Michael Healey, pp. 47–63 Vancouver, BC: Institute for Resources and the Environment/Westwater Research.

Miller, Bruce G. 1992. Women and Politics: Comparative Evidence from the Northwest Coast. *Ethnology*, 3(4):367–385.

Miller, Bruce G., and Daniel L. Boxberger. 1994. Creating Chiefdoms: The Puget Sound Case. *Ethnohistory*, 41(2):267–293.

Miller, Jay. 1993. A Kinship of Spirit. In *American in 1492: The World of the Indian Peoples Before the Arrival of Columbus,* edited by Alvin M. Josephy, Jr., pp. 305–337. New York: Vintage.

Newell, Dianne. 1993. *Tangled Webs of History: Indians and the Law in Canada's Pacific Coast Fisheries.* Toronto: University of Toronto Press.

Reed, B. Justice. 1994. Reasons for Order (lMM-6881-93).

Richardson, Allan. 1982. The Control of Productive Resources on the Northwest Coast of North America. In *Resource Managers: North American and Australian Hunter-Gatherers,* edited by Nancy M. Williams and Eugene S. Hunn, pp. 93–112. Boulder, CO: Westview.

Scheper-Hughes, Nancy. 1995. Propositions for a Militant Anthropology. *Current Anthropology*, 36(3):409–420.

Smith, Marian W. 1950. The Nooksack, the Chilliwack, and the Middle Fraser. *Pacific Northwest Quarterly,* 41(4):330–341.

Suleman, Zool K. B. 1994. Further Memorandum of Argument of the Applicant (IMM-6881-93).

Suttles, Wayne. 1963. The Persistence of Intervillage Ties Among the Coast Salish. *Ethnology,* 2 (4):512–525.

———— 1990. Central Coast Salish. In *Handbook of Native North Americans,* Vol. 7, *Northwest Coast*, edited by Wayne Suttles, pp. 453–475. Washington, D.C.: Smithsonian Institution.

Tennant, Paul. 1990. *Aboriginal Peoples and Politics: The Indian Land Question in British Columbia, 1849–1989.* Vancouver, B.C.: UBC Press.

Journal of Northwest Anthropology, Memoir 12:275–285 (2016)

19

Conceptual and Practical Boundaries: West Coast Indians/First Nations on the Border of Contagion in the Post-9/11 Era*

A few years ago I wrote about the forty-ninth parallel, the international border between the United States and Canada or, more specifically, Washington State and the province of British Columbia, focusing on the largely invisible ways in which the border disrupted and bifurcated the communities of Coast Salish and adjacent Interior Salish peoples. I noted that the climate of the mid-1990s was "predisposed to the crossing of intellectual, disciplinary, political, and cultural boundaries," as part of a response to a modernist theory of society which was said to be a boundary-maintaining system, separating culture from nature, culture from society, culture from the individual, and "traditional" culture from "modern" culture (Miller 1996). Since the 1970s, "Boundary maintaining was out; adventurous, indeed necessary border crossings were advocated between science and literature, ethnography and biography, interpretation and imagination. The greatest challenge became to understand, and thereby overcome, the one border…between Us and the Other, the West and the Rest" (Fabian 1993:52). I observed that these efforts to connect the global and the local and to transcend boundaries posed the risks of becoming institutionalized into noncritical forms of producing knowledge. Nancy Scheper-Hughes put it this way:

> In the brave new world of reflexive postmodernists…everything local is said to dissolve into merged media images, transgressed boundaries, promiscuously mobile multinational industries and workers, and transnational-corporate desires and fetishism. This imagined postmodern, borderless world is, in fact, a Camelot of free trade that echoes the marketplace rhetoric of global capitalism…

> The idea of an anthropology without borders…ignores the reality of the very real borders that confront and oppress "our" anthropological subjects…These borders are as real as the passports and passbooks, the sandbagged bunkers, the armed roadblocks. (Scheper-Hughes 1995:417)

Scheper-Hughes's comments regarding the ease of movement of goods, at least as it relates to the U.S.-Canadian border, now seems dated as the United States continues to pose significant new restrictions on the movement of commercial traffic from its major trading partner, Canada. Her focus on the "really real" borders and ways these oppress local communities, however, remains on target. I could not have imagined in 1996 the ways in which the events of September 11, 2001, and its aftermath would alter the circumstances facing the Salish peoples and disrupt the distinctive ways indigenous peoples manage life in a border zone. The American state, and a circumspect Canadian state, deeply troubled by developments in the United States, particularly the invasion of Iraq and the threats of American reprisals against Canada, have jointly created a new variant of the modernist border zone. This reconfigured zone focuses directly on images of contagion, profanity, danger, and corruption to support public policy. Today those problems faced by indigenous peoples since the mid-nineteenth century persist, but they are now joined with a new set as the government of the United States self-consciously cultivates a perception of a nation under siege and at war with terrorism.

*Authored by Bruce Granville Miller. Reproduced from *The Borderlands of the American and Canadian Wests: Essays on Regional History of the Forty-ninth Parallel* edited by Sterling Evans by permission of the University of Nebraska Press. Copyright 2006 by the Board of Regents of the University of Nebraska.

In some ways the current dilemma is not new, and the British (and the successor Canadian) state and the United States have a long history of dispute and contention along the forty-ninth parallel, but there is a curious reversal. Canadians have long feared and indeed suffered from American intrusion into what is now British Columbia. For example, in 1858 some 30,000 unregulated, armed American and other foreign miners advanced into British Columbia, prompting fears of U.S. annexation of the territory. These miners attacked villages and killed an unknown number of indigenous peoples along the Fraser River in a display of "bold-faced, cross-border American aggression and vigilantism" (Carlson 2003:259). More recently, a member of the Washington State legislature proposed publicly that the U.S. fleet sail up the inside passage between Vancouver Island and the British Columbia mainland to intimidate Canadian negotiators into quickly resolving disputes over the harvest of salmon swimming through international waters. This time it is the Americans' turn to fear the penetration of their soil. The major development has been that in focusing on the twin and conceptually linked threats of terror and epidemic, U.S. policy has forced indigenous interests, particularly for those indigenous communities located directly on the international border, to be set aside once again. The hardening of the international boundary after September 11 poses yet another particularly difficult challenge to communities and continues a long process of making border crossing more difficult. Many Canadian First Nations peoples and American Indians report that ease of movement across the border was the norm until the 1970s. The United States has attempted to create in administrative law the terms of the 1794 Jay Treaty, which allowed for free passage but was voided by the War of 1812; however, Canada has not.

My argument is that the political border creates parallel conceptual and practical boundaries for the indigenous peoples of this region. Following a widely held indigenous perspective, I treat the international boundary as an arbitrary but potent fact of life that divides peoples and communities. I argue that in the present-day process of rearranging their relations to the state (the provincial, state, and federal governments) Salish peoples have intensified the development of strategies concerning the border in the pursuit of social justice. At present, First Nations in British Columbia are negotiating both land claims and treaties with the provincial and federal governments. The First Nations are also creating their own formal systems of governance, social services, education, legal systems, and other programs. Tribes in Puget Sound are considerably ahead in self-governance and institutional growth, a difference which itself puts a wedge between related communities. These activities are largely invisible and receive little public or academic attention, but reflect the perception that Salish identity and community cannot exist without those on the other side of the border.

In brief, these efforts include current legal challenges to the state to regain rights of free passage within traditional territories that overlap the international border. Also, indigenous-driven initiatives are under way to change the procedures whereby winter Spirit Dancers who are in a state of extreme spiritual danger are permitted to cross between British Columbia and Washington. There are attempts to promote a form of political unity between Coast Salish bands and tribes whose interests in the salmon fisher are split by residence within separate nation states and efforts of individuals to find medical care within different regimes of service delivery. In addition, communities seek to control their membership by formally recognizing as tribal members those living on the other side of the boundary. Individual Salish people have exploited the difference in commodity prices and public health to gain personal security in their homeland on both sides of the border.

The Salish peoples are not alone in their responses to the border, and other indigenous peoples (or nations, in current discourse), too, are partitioned into more than one state. The Canadian-American border, for example, separates the Coast Salish and the Interior Salish of

British Columbia from relatives in Washington and Idaho, but also the Nuu-chah-nulth on Vancouver Island and related peoples of the adjacent Olympic Peninsula of Washington, Blackfoot/Blackfeet and Lakota in the Plains, Ojibway/Chippewa in the Great Lakes region, Iroquois in the eastern woodlands, and Mi'qmac on the Atlantic coast are among the many divided peoples. My examination of these topics rests upon my own fieldwork with Coast Salish communities of Puget Sound and the Fraser River since the mid-1970s, interviews with members of these communities and public officials specifically for the study of the border, participation as a participant at various federal government-sponsored events, and a reading of the ethnographic and historical materials.

American Responses to the Events of September 11

The immediate American response along the forty-ninth parallel following the destruction of the twin towers in New York City and related events was to tighten the border, subjecting all traffic into the United States from Canada along the heavily traveled Vancouver to Seattle corridor to search. The PACE lane program, a dedicated, preapproved lane for registered, regular travelers from both countries, was canceled. After several months, security was gradually relaxed and the waiting time for the lines of cars was reduced from several hours, in many cases, to an average of a half-hour, but with episodic longer waits during periods of heightened fear of terrorism known as "Orange Alerts."

As the United States developed its response to what government officials characterized as a war, initially with Osama bin Laden and Afghanistan, and later with Saddam Hussein and Iraq, the domestic focus was on "homeland security" and the attempt to seal the U.S. borders from danger. This effort at preventing intrusions of foreigners into American life took many forms, including the stationing of U.S. officials in the Port of Vancouver to stop the possible movement of weapons of mass destruction through containerized shipping and to catch terrorists hiding among the ships. During a period of intense negotiations over the effective closing of the border to vital Canadian exports, particularly lumber, through the imposition of tariffs, U.S. federal authorities pushed to negotiate the terms on which U.S. military personnel could operate on Canadian soil.

The implications of these policy initiatives for indigenous peoples became clear at a unique Tribal/County Criminal Justice Summit, held at Bow, Washington, on January 8–10, 2003. Here, state and federal officials, including Christine Gregoire, attorney general of the state of Washington, the Hon. Susan Owens of the Washington State Supreme Court, and federal officials representing U.S. Attorney General John Ashcroft, met with tribal and county officials principally to lay out plans for the war on terrorism. In three days of discussions, the argument was made that tribes on the international border were especially vulnerable to intrusion from Canada. According to federal officials, terrorists coming across the border had already established or were likely to establish methamphetamine labs on Indian reservations, and other terrorists were likely to pour in.

In an hour-long presentation, a senior official from the Washington State Department of Health graphically described the possible use of smallpox by terrorists and a new national program to inoculate frontline officials and large segments of the general population. The capturing of public health by political concerns did not go unnoticed, and tribal officials in the packed audience raised several questions. One asked cynically if the terrorists might borrow surplus infected blankets from the U.S. War Department. Another noted that terrorists attempting to use smallpox "would have to be rather dumb." A third asked why the state budget was shifted to combating a hypothetical smallpox outbreak, given that there were health disasters already affecting Indians, including diabetes, AIDS, and TB.

Federal officials described a program for cross-deputizing tribal, county, and state police in order that all could respond immediately to the terrorists who were imagined to be crossing the international border through Indian country or anywhere else. This program held an inherent appeal for tribal police officials, who battle the perception that their officers are inferior to those in the mainstream society. The federal officials proposed a program to provide U.S. Border Patrol high-tech equipment to tribal police helping in the terrorist problem. Efforts were begun to coordinate the goals and objectives of the Border Patrol, the Bureau of Indian Affairs, and the new federal Homeland Security agency. Meanwhile, tribal attorneys noted in private that the FBI, legally responsible for dealing with a set of major crimes committed in Indian country, including murder and rape, had simply stopped doing so in order to concentrate on terrorism. Tribes' legal systems were left with the option of prosecuting murderers on their lands with a maximum sentence of one year or a fine of $5,000. Tribal borderlands became, in a sense, lawless.

Public policy shifts regarding American Indians after September 11 focused on recruiting tribal personnel into the war on terrorism. The long border with British Columbia was described as constituting a serious threat to tribes, and issues of tribal sovereignty were left unconsidered. Justice officials urged tribes, along with all other sectors of American society, to put their own interests aside and to pull together for the common good. In addition, the presentations of federal officials conjoined images of disease, epidemic, and contagion with images of violence, terrorism, disruption, and impurity in the form of alien people and diseases, all coming from Canada.

This effort to link diverse forms of contagion rested, by necessity, on the transformation of the image of British Columbia, and Canada generally. Canada had long been regarded as a docile, bucolic neighbor, as symbolized by the Peace Arch, a structure built directly at the forty-ninth parallel and on the major thoroughfare between the countries, which displays the texts "Children of a Common Mother" and "May these Gates Never be Closed." But stories in the U.S. media suggested that terrorists involved in the September 11 disasters had entered the United States from Canada. Canada was depicted as a haven for terrorists, and British Columbia, in particular, was described on Seattle television and elsewhere in U.S. media as the home of pot growers and drug smugglers. The *Vancouver Sun*, for example, reported the comments of a New York talk radio show host who called Canada a "tin-pot, bankrupt country that has nothing to offer the world but drugs."[1]

Many accounts focused on what was taken to be an inadequate approach by the Canadian government to immigration and border inspection, and the U.S. government pushed negotiations to coordinate services and to coerce Canadian officials into adopting an American approach. Paul Cellucci, American ambassador to Canada, appeared on Canadian television directly to intervene in Canadian domestic policy and later criticized the Canadian prime minister's decision not to send troops to Iraq while intimating coming economic reprisals.[2] Canada's image was transformed to that of a country intent on polluting the United States through its illegal imported goods, its lax policies toward immigrants, especially those from the Middle East, and its ineffective socialist society. U.S. immigration agents began to detain, interrogate, and fingerprint non-white Canadian citizens born abroad who attempted to cross the border. The Canadian minimalist response to the threat of terrorism maddened U.S. officials, but held few implications for indigenes.

Although Salish peoples and communities retain interests in moving back and forth across the border for religious and other purposes, these interests were left unexplored in the rush to plug up the border. However, there remain particular social and cultural issues binding the Salish that have not attenuated with time and that become apparent in examining their patterns of affiliation and systems of meaning. I make a detour from the U.S. war on terrorism into the Salish world to draw out these connections.

Salish Affiliative Networks

The Coast Salish peoples, now grouped into some fifty bands in British Columbia and twenty-four tribes in Washington, are the descendants of speakers of Coast Salish languages who lived within Puget Sound and connecting areas, along the Fraser River and its tributaries, and on the southeastern portions of Vancouver Island and the adjacent mainland (Miller 1992). Other groups are located in Oregon. Their social organization in the early contact period was made up of fluid local groups, composed of one or more households, which interacted to form a regional structure (Miller and Boxberger 1994:270–272) Tribes did not exist prior to interaction with Europeans and state governments, but emerged as political entities following treaty negotiations, the establishment of the reserve/reservation systems, and as a response to the requirements of subsequent legal actions against the government. Before this, individuals closely identified with the local group with whom they were residing and with the larger "speech community" (composed of those who speak a common language). Kin ties created a network of relations that extended far beyond one's own river drainage.

These networks have persisted to the present and serve to organize activity in a variety of domains, thereby perpetuating the connectiveness of the larger Coast Salish community (Kew and Miller 2000) Persistent, regular activities bring together people from throughout the Coast Salish area for marriage and kinship, commercial fishing, winter ceremonial activity, and summer festivals emphasizing sporting contests and informal mingling. In addition there are regularly scheduled events on the Pow-Wow circuit of intertribal festivities that draw Salish peoples together.

The indigenous people who occupy a region drained by the Columbia and Fraser rivers east of the Cascade Mountains in Washington and the Coast Range in British Columbia are the descendents of speakers of seven Interior Salish languages. The Interior Salish peoples maintain a vast network of interpersonal ties constructed around kinship, friendship, and trade connections and, in earlier periods, created regional task groups for subsistence purposes. A further factor that promoted regional cooperation was the possibility of food shortage due to the thinness and wide dispersal of resources within their region.

Existence as a subordinated people and a common postcontact history has reinforced the connections between the various Salish peoples. So, too, has placement on reserves and reservations and attendance in common in government-imposed residential schools. Both in the pre-contact period and up to the present day, the broad network of affiliation between Salish peoples and communities has incorporated those on both sides of the border. Maintaining this system has grown difficult and prompted indigenous responses.

Indigenous Challenges to State-Imposed Borders

The case of *Robert Watt v. E. Liebelt and the Minister of Citizenship and Immigration*, on appeal to the Trial Division, Federal Court of Canada, is a case in which, to the Crown, the issue "is whether an aboriginal person who is neither a Canadian citizen nor a registered Indian has a right to remain in Canada because he belongs to a tribe whose traditional territory straddles the Canada-United States border"(Reed 1994:1). Robert Allen Watt, a member of the Arrow Lakes (Sinixt) Tribe, an Interior Salish people, had been appointed by elders to come north into Canada to be "the guardian of a sacred burial site in British Columba" (Suleman 1994:2). Watt, an enrolled member of the Colville Confederated Tribe, lived in the Slocan Valley, British Columbia, for most of the period between 1986 and 1993 in carrying out his guardian role.

In the nineteenth century the Arrow Lakes peoples moved within a district of lakes from the vicinity of Revelstoke, British Columbia, to Colville, Washington. Following the establishment of the forty-ninth parallel to mark the boundary between the U.S. and British territories west of the Rockies in 1846, it became difficult for the Arrow Lakes people to continue traditional patterns of seasonal movement. Many members of the Arrow Lakes community moved to the Washington Territory in 1872 after the establishment of the Colville Reservation where they were offered land allotments together with other indigenous peoples. In 1953 the Arrow Lakes people were declared extinct by Canada, even though more than 250 were enrolled members of the Colville Confederated Tribes and were continuing to use traditional territories in British Columbia (Pryce 1999).

In 1993 an adjudicator of a hearings board within the Ministry of Citizenship and Immigration ruled that, under the terms of the Canadian Immigration Act and because Watt was not a registered Canadian Indian under the Indian Act, he was to leave Canada within thirty days. The Watt case directly calls into question federal government conventions concerning who and what "aboriginal peoples of Canada" are. Legal counsel for Watt argued, "The definition of 'aboriginal peoples of Canada'...infers that there may be other peoples who could raise a reasonable claim that they ought to be considered 'aboriginal'" (Suleman 1994:16). The passage in question reads, "In this Act, 'aboriginal peoples of Canada' *includes* [emphasis added] the Indian, Inuit, and Métis peoples of Canada." Furthermore, counsel argued that given an open-ended definition and that the Supreme Court of Canada had held that Section 35 of the Constitution Act is to be interpreted generously and liberally, aboriginal peoples all along the U.S.-Canada boundary should be included within Section 35 as being aboriginal peoples of Canada. In addition, counsel argued that Subsection 35 (1) "protects the long-standing aboriginal right to move freely throughout their traditional territories." The Immigration Act, according to this argument, ought not to be interpreted in such a manner that "would eliminate the rights of the Arrow Lake or Sinixt people to move freely throughout their traditional territories."

The Watts case is not alone in querying the cross-border rights of First Nations along the international border; indeed, a series of related issues have arisen in the management of traditional territories that incorporate watersheds or other natural zones that straddle the border. In sum, recent activities by bands and tribes have questioned the role of the state in defining indigenous communities, in limiting access to territories, and in limiting any liability or trust responsibility to those on one side of the border. The First Nations claims constitute a proposal for a broader, more incorporative view that better accounts for the nature of their own community organization. Such claims occur in less conspicuous forms as well.

Indigenous Challenges to the Intrusiveness of the Border

In common with other indigenous peoples of the Americas, Coast Salish religious life focuses on the relationships between individuals and spirit beings who interact with humans and who provide humans access to powers of various sorts. Throughout Coast Salish territory, initiates into the society of Spirit Dancers spend a winter developing their relationship with their spirit helper. As initiates ("babies") they are spiritually reborn and experience a state of ritual liminality in which they are susceptible to spiritual and physical danger. Initiates travel to the several earthen-floor ceremonial longhouses, homes to other groups of babies, in Washington and British Columbia that collectively compose the ritual congregation. Babies travel in ceremonial costumes that provide a measure of spiritual protection; for example, headdresses largely cover their eyes to keep them from danger. In some cases, experienced Spirit Dancers carry masks in containers that cannot be opened except in a ceremonial context.

The immediate problem for Spirit Dancers traveling between Coast Salish communities located across the border is the incompatibility of inspection procedures associated with customs regulations and their own spiritual beliefs. Babies may be placed in spiritual danger if, for example, someone looks directly into their faces. Masks and other regalia cannot be handled by nondancers. The cedar costumes and headdresses and wooden staffs carried by black- and red-faced dancers sometimes appear bizarre and suspicious to border agents.[3] Another difficulty facing the Spirit Dancers is the cultural prohibition on the communication of specific information about Spirit Dancing. To reveal specifics could potentially place a dancer in spiritual danger and reduce the efficacy of their relationship with their spiritual helper.

Associate Chief Elva Caulkins, of what was then the U.S. Department of Treasury (Custom Service), told this author in 1995 that while Indian people may cross from north to south, this is not unproblematic and "at times we are going to look." Further, "we don't do an 'attitude check' even if they are lippy. But if they are *evasive* [emphasis mine], it can cause problems. Lots of time Indians won't tell us what country they're from. Coast Salish believe both countries are their country. Indians often say they are resident of both. We ask them, 'Where is your longhouse?' [in the attempt to determine residency]."[4] The new U.S. efforts at patrolling the border complicate the efforts to establish working agreements between the congregation of Spirit dancers and border officials. The border staff is larger, and many officers, new to the area, are unaware of the practices of the local indigenous peoples. Detailed inspections heighten the risk of difficulty.

Canadian border officials have published articles describing ceremonial objects in internally circulated professional journals, but these have focused on the material culture of Native people outside of British Columbia. Caulkins noted to this author that "Indians are angrier at Canadians than the United States, due to the failure of Canadian policy to allow largely unrestricted passage," a perspective that accurately reflected the view of many Canadian First Nations until September 11.

A related problem concerns the movement of goods intended for potlatches, ritual events that require the distribution of goods to people in attendance. Potlatch goods taken across the border are subject to duty. In one incident, a man's car was seized by U.S. officials following accusations of smuggling as he attempted to bring two hundred blankets across the border to a relative's potlatch. In addition, there are problems concerning the transport of other ceremonial or religious items across the border. The U.S. Fishery and Game Act prohibits transporting items such as eagle feathers, which indigenous peoples sometimes carry in their vehicles. These feathers are thought by border officials to be associated with the possession and use of drug paraphernalia. Both the duties imposed on goods and the restrictions on eagle feathers constitute a regulatory environment that increases the complexity of the regular conduct of Salish life.

The Salmon Fishery and Problems of Access and Identity

Among the most significant relationships of traditional Salish peoples are with the salmon beings that provide the food that defines Salish culture. In earlier periods, Salish villages were built along rivers or on the saltwater to facilitate salmon fishing. The relationship has never been solely material, however, and Salish maintain their spiritual connection with salmon through the conduct of First Salmon ceremonies in which salmon beings make themselves known and humans demonstrate their respect for the salmon. Salish social organization and cultural identity, then, are directly connected to the fishery, acknowledged in the nineteenth century by both Washington

State and British Columbia. The treaties of western Washington specified that Indians would continue to have access to salmon and other species; in British Columbia, reserves were established in particular locations in part because of the proximity to fishing stations.

The eventual creation of separate national fishing policies has created significant difficulties for Salish people, especially given the extraordinary richness of the resources in the area along the international border. Previously, access to resources was determined largely through kinship connection. Affiliative patterns were spread across what became the international border, and people from what is now Washington fished in the Fraser River and adjoining British Columbia waters, a circumstance which is explicitly acknowledged today. Ernie Crey, former director of Stó:lō Nation fisheries, for example, observed that Lummi Nation fishers of Washington traditionally fished salmon stocks that spawned on the Fraser River and its tributaries. In addition, fisheries around the Gulf Islands of British Columbia and the San Juan Islands of Washington formerly incorporated fishers from bands and tribes located now on both sides of the border.

However, contemporary Salish Indian fishers of Washington and British Columbia remain largely within separate camps, despite the memories of earlier management protocols. Although Indian fishers of Washington were excluded from the fishery by the 1950s, today they co-manage the salmon resource with the State Department of Fisheries. British Columbia bands were similarly excluded from a fishery that became progressively more capital-intensive through the twentieth century (Newell 1999). The Reasons for Judgment in the case of *Sparrow v. The Queen,* 1990, interpreted the Canadian Constitution Act of 1982, Section 35 (1) as protecting the aboriginal rights to fish for social and ceremonial purposes, but was silent concerning commercial sales. Subsequently, the federal government created a trial policy, the Aboriginal Fisheries Strategy, to allow limited indigenous commercial fishing. In response, Salish First Nations have attempted to create their own commercial fisheries management programs.

As a consequence of these developments, Indian people and polities have ended up on opposite sides in the international negotiations over fisheries allocations that form the backdrop to the Pacific Salmon Treaty. Distinctive features of Indian fisheries management are thereby underplayed, and commonalities of interest between Salish peoples are obstructed. Some Coast Salish peoples have responded by attempting to create formalized links across the border through the creation of a Coast Salish "Treaty" recognizing a common heritage and interests, and other rely on more informal, individual exchanges of information between band and tribal fisheries officers and managers. The larger problem for the Coast Salish remains in articulating a common vision that is compatible with the circumstances of particular bands and tribes.

Personal Accommodations to the Border

Other responses to the border do not take the form of overt political action. Rather, they can be seen as personal acts of accommodation to the partitioning of the community by the international boundary. One Coast Salish woman, for example, who was born in a Stó:lō community along the Fraser River in British Columbia and who married into a Coast Salish tribe of western Washington, monitors the available health care opportunities for her dependent with a debilitating ailment.[5] She uses the existence of two national policies concerning public health as an asset; as an enrolled tribal member she has available the services of the Indian Health Service, and as a Canadian citizen she is eligible for the provisions of a socialized medical system with a somewhat different array of specialty services for chronic children's diseases. It is significant that she has not violated the spirit or the letter of either Canadian or U.S. law in looking after her dependent, nor has she duplicated services. This strategy has required that the caregiver maintain active affiliations with the community of her birth and the community into which she married.

Other Salish people make use of the differences in the Canadian and American economies by movement across the border in an effort to find employment. Generally this requires activating a latent affiliation with a community across the border and relocating for some months or years. In other cases, for example, with members of the Semiahmoo (Canada) community, this entails exploiting the job market of Whatcom County, Washington, and a daily return to their reserve. One member of the Semiahmoo Nation noted, "it's easier for the Semiahmoo. So many of us have worked in the United States for the past thirty, forty, fifty years. We've been working on and off since teenagers, commuting back and forth. They [government officials] know us at the border."[6] Since September 11 it has been uncertain whether crossing the border to work will remain a possibility.

In common with other Canadian citizens, indigenous people living on the border have previously made use of differences in pricing. Semiahmoo people shop in Blaine, Washington, bringing home milk, eggs, cheese, and other food products that are ordinarily cheaper in Washington. Others have taken advantage of differences in the value of American and Canadian currency through importing goods with Native content duty-free from the United States for sale on Canadian reserves. This circumstance, although the product of the differences between the two countries, has served to unite the larger Salish community. New restrictions impede this movement.

Indigenous Citizenship and the Border

Another distinct pattern is the appropriation and reshaping of federal notions of membership and citizenship. This takes two forms. In one, communities enroll as tribal or band members those people who maintain ancestral connections but who are formally citizens across the international boundary. Although federally recognized tribes of Washington State do not allow cross-enrollment (enrollment in more than one tribe or band), one tribe included on their roll Native people residing in Canada, holding Canadian citizenship, and eligible for enrollment with a Canadian band. Other Washington tribes may also have enrolled Canadian Native people. By doing this, the tribe can assert its existence as a legitimate tribe by employing aboriginal notions of affiliation and membership independent of criteria imposed by the state and, simultaneously, fulfill the desires for membership of those who claim affiliation and common descent but live across the international border.

A second means of reshaping federal notions of citizenship is by simply claiming existing categories of membership and acting on them. This is the case for members of the Semiahmoo First Nation who speak of themselves as "dual citizens," although they are not formally recognized by both the United States and Canada as such. They do this for a variety of reasons. Nineteenth-century Semiahmoo territory, as is the case with the Arrow Lakes, straddles the international boundary, and band members maintain their connection to place. Semiahmoo people act on their perceived rights by exploiting economic and educational opportunities in northern Washington. In addition, Semiahmoo maintain active connections to the 3,000-member Lummi Nation of Washington and are aware of the Semiahmoo presence within that tribe. Finally, Semiahmoo, who moved north away from a portion of their territories at the time of the settlement of the international border, have considered legal action for compensation for territory. These are all indications of a continued Semiahmoo presence within Washington.

Conclusions

Despite efforts at resistance and accommodation, the border imposes consequences on the Salish communities. There is some truncation of communication between groups despite the efforts to overcome the problems the border poses. Groups are not fully aware of the political circumstances and governmental forms of those on the other side (Miller 2001). It is clear that some ceremonial exchanges are altered or diminished, particularly those requiring the movement of goods across the border. These arise in part from the control of lands by bands or tribes other than those who occupied them in the middle of the nineteenth century when the international border was created. These fears reflect both a misunderstanding of the legal circumstances across the border and recognition of the capacity of large political entities to extend their reach across the line, to intervene, for example, in litigation. Some Semiahmoo, for example, have expressed concerns that the Lummi Nation of Washington will make land claims in Semiahmoo territory in British Columbia even though Lummi occupy former Semiahmoo grounds rather than vice versa. In this case the discrepancy in size and resources seems to be at play. The Lummi Nation numbers about 3,000 and is the preeminent fishing tribe in the United States. The Semiahmoo number in the sixties.

On a related note, some people find themselves of necessity residing on the wrong side of the border. This is particularly the case for members of tribes that are not federally recognized, such as the Arrow Lakes in British Columbia or previously the Samish in Washington (although the Samish were newly recognized by the federal government as an "official tribe" in 1996). In the Arrow Lakes case, there is a recognized tribe in Washington, the Colville Confederated Tribes, with whom they can affiliate, but none in British Columbia. In the case of members of the Samish Tribe living on Vancouver Island, the opposite is true. Finally, there is the sheer difficulty of legal challenges such as the Watt case. This case failed initially, and although the appeal has not yet been heard, it appears to be an uphill battle.

Nevertheless, Salish people are currently contesting and accommodating the international border in various ways in order to maintain their communities and to preserve their sense of common identity. Indigenous people on both sides of the border persist in thinking of the border as an intrusion and think of their responses to the border as efforts to gain social justice within the Canadian and American states. The difficulties of carrying out their lives and pressing their claims within two separate national legal systems remain a considerable barrier to the maintenance of community and the achievement of justice.

Both the activity and the conceptualizations are of importance. One might anticipate that border issues will grow in importance to Salish and other indigenous communities as they continue the processes of building their own governance and managing any resources over which they are able to regain control. This is especially so given the current policy initiatives linked to the U.S. war on terrorism that further bifurcate the Salish world and make passage considerably more difficult, time-consuming, fraught with the possibility of detention and arrest, and subject to increased surveillance. As is often the case, the fates of indigenous peoples and communities are determined by events and circumstances far away from their homes. U.S. policy makers, in their fixation on terrorism and the Middle East, are largely unconcerned with indigenous issues. To the U.S. government especially, the border zone, including the Indian reservations, is now characterized as a region of contagion and danger rather than as a region occupied by the descendents of the earliest inhabitants who still form a distinct, connected community lapping across the border.

Endnotes

This essay is an expanded and updated version of a paper presented at the conference of the American Historical Association-Pacific Coast Branch, Vancouver B.C., August 2001.

[1] *Vancouver Sun*, March 26, 2003, A6.

[2] *Vancouver Sun*, March 26, 2003, A1; *Toronto Globe and Mail*, March 26, 2003, 1.

[3] Personal communication, Doreen Maloney, member of the Council of the Upper Skagit Tribe, Washington State, February 1995.

[4] Personal communication, Elva Caulkins, assistant chief, Department of the Treasury, U.S. Custom Service, Blaine WA, February 28, 1995.

[5] Notes from interviews with a woman who will remain unidentified here.

[6] Personal communication, Eleanor Charles of Semiahmoo, January 1995.

References Cited

Carlson, Keith Thor. 2003. The Power of Place, the Problem of Time: A Study of History and Aboriginal Collective Identity. Ph.D. dissertation, Department of History, University of British Columbia.

Fabian, Johannes. 1993. Crossing and Patrolling: Thoughts on Anthropology and Boundaries. *Culture*, 13(1):49–54.

Kew, J. E. Michael and Bruce G. Miller. 1999. Locating Aboriginal Governments in the Political Landscape. In *Seeking Sustainability in the Lower Fraser Basin: Issues and Choices*, edited by Michael Healey, pp. 47–63. Vancouver, BC: Institute for Resources and the Environment/Westwater Research.

Miller, Bruce G. 1996. The "Really Real" Border and the Divided Salish Community. *BC Studies*, 112:63–79.

———— 1992. Women and Politics: Comparative Evidence from the Northwest Coast. *Ethnology*, 31:367–84.

———— 2001. *The Problem of Justice: Tradition and Law in the Coast Salish World.* Lincoln: University of Nebraska Press.

Miller, Bruce G., and Daniel L. Boxberger. 1994. Creating Chiefdoms: The Puget Sound Case. *Ethnohistory*, 41(2):270–72.

Newell, Dianne. 1999. *Tangled Web of History: Indians and the Law in Canada's Pacific Coast Fisheries.* Toronto: University of Toronto Press.

Pryce, Paula. 1999. *Keeping the Lakes' Way: Reburial and Re-creation of a Moral World among an Invisible People.* Toronto: University of Toronto Press.

Reed, B. Justice. 1994. *Reasons for Order*. IMM-6881–93.

Scheper-Hughes, Nancy. 1995. Propositions for a Militant Anthropology. *Current Anthropology*, 36(3):409–420.

Suleman, Zool K. B. 1994. *Further Memorandum of Argument of the Applicant* (IMM-681–93).

Journal of Northwest Anthropology, Memoir 12:286–302 (2016)

20

Life on the Hardened Border*

The many Coast Salish groups distributed on both sides of the U.S.-Canada border on the Pacific coast today face significant obstacles to travel across the international border, and in some cases are denied passage or intimidated into not attempting to cross. Historically, the Coast Salish peoples of the Salish Sea—including Puget Sound in what is now the United States, southeastern Vancouver Island in Canada, the adjacent mainland, and the lower Fraser River and other nearby areas—were mutually connected in large-scale social networks of marriage and kinship. People traveled through the region to participate in the ritual lives of neighbors, including winter and summer ceremonials, and for mutual defense against outsiders (Miller 2007a). During the early contact period, Hudson's Bay Company factors at the new trading forts remarked on the hundreds of freight canoes traveling the Salish Sea to sell goods (Maclachlan 1998). The present-day Coast Salish people continue to travel, now largely on land, between communities.

The current situation regarding travel by Aboriginal people reflects the hardening of the border by U.S. officials following the events of what has become known as 9/11. After extremists launched an assault on the World Trade Center towers in New York City a bureaucratic environment emerged that was increasingly hostile to the interests of these Aboriginal groups because of demands for security. In addition, the problems encountered by individual Aboriginal travelers at the border reflect a transformed American impression of Canada, now commonly treated politically and administratively as a state from which enemies of America are positioned to harm American interests.

These new perceptions create an environment that enables Homeland Security officers to regard Aboriginal peoples seeking to cross the border (under legal conventions that allow the passage of Aboriginal peoples) as suspect. Officers then act on their own received, stereotypical notions of what a "real Indian" looks like and deny passage to those they consider to be fakes. The cooperation between American border personnel and Aboriginal people, based on personal relations, which until recently characterized the Peace Arch border crossing at the Washington State–British Columbia border, has now disappeared.

These border issues reflect a larger pattern of the denial of Aboriginal rights and challenges to tribal sovereignty by the American state and its citizenry. Kevin Bruyneel, for example, writes that in response to litigation involving the Mille Lacs Band of Ojibwe, former Minnesota governor Jesse Ventura believed that if the tribe held treaty rights established during the nineteenth century, they should use birch bark canoes (Bruyneel 2007). Bruyneel's analysis points to the spatialization of the discourse reflected in Ventura's comments: if tribes are part of and within the United States and its political system, they are not sovereign and cannot make demands on the state; if they are sovereign, they are outside of the United States and also cannot make demands. Further, Bruyneel points to a temporal dimension to Ventura's public comments, in that Aboriginal or treaty rights are thought to be from an archaic time and without application to the modern world. In brief, Bruyneel argues that, although Ventura's views do not create policy, the United States seeks to bind tribes narrowly in space and time in order to limit political and economic self-expression, and, more broadly, self-identity. Others have pointed in the same direction, including Gayla Frank and Carole Goldberg's recent work on the U.S. federal government's efforts to erode the sovereignty of the Tule River tribe of California through the diminution of its territory and efforts

*Authored by Bruce Granville Miller. Reprinted from the *American Indian Culture and Research Journal*, Volume 36, Issue 2, by permission of the American Indians Studies Center, UCLA. © 2012 Regents of the University of California.

to erode historical systems of leadership (Frank and Goldberg 2010). My analysis is consistent with Bruyneel's approach, but includes the additional twist that U.S. law provides rights, in theory, to Aboriginal people who are spatially distinct in quite a different way, anomalous in that they are not resident in, or citizens of, the United States. This anomaly has become intolerable to some officials in a time of suspicion and fear.

The border problems addressed here are not unique to the Salish Sea or the Coast Salish people. They reflect dilemmas faced by the many Aboriginal communities all along the 49th parallel dividing the United States and Canada, and for Aboriginal peoples moving within their own homelands overlapping the U.S.-Mexico border. To some extent, the borderlands have local features, and some regions are more isolated and less amenable to careful control by border officials. The Salish Sea region is one of the most densely populated and is carefully regulated by border officials; the desert region along the Arizona-Sonora state border, for example, is the opposite, although here, too, surveillance has increased. I leave it to others to detail just how the current regimes of control are manifested in other regions, however, and give my attention to the Coast Salish world, with particular focus on the issues facing Aboriginal peoples of Canada who attempt to enter the United States.

The circumstances for those Coast Salish resident in the United States who hope to enter Canada are quite different. Canadian law has not embedded legal rights for Aboriginal movement across the border in the same way as the United States, and Canadian courts have denied the applicability of an eighteenth-century agreement known as the Jay Treaty. Canada remains less openly concerned with the movement of terrorists into Canada, a circumstance that appears to frustrate U.S. officials. American border practice is constructed on a quasi-military model, and the Canadian counterpart is constructed on a civilian model, although Canadian Border Service personnel will soon be outfitted with guns for the first time. The United States has recently attempted to push Canada into a uniform border policy, which would entail the elaboration of the so-called continental security perimeter.

In making these arguments, I rely on my own previous border studies, current interviews with Coast Salish people about their experiences at the border, and the case of a Coast Salish man, Dr. Peter Roberts, a dentist, who was detained for attempting to cross the border in 2008 by virtue of his status as Aboriginal and his green card (permanent residency card) (Miller 1996, 2007b). In addition, a justice summit held in 2003 provides direct insight into American approaches to the border as they concern Aboriginal people; and because Washington State is a border state, with Seattle a short drive from the forty-ninth parallel, coverage of border issues by the *Seattle Times* gives a useful indication of American attitudes and approaches.

The Years Prior to 2001

There have not always been difficulties in border transit. In 1794, the predecessor government to Canada, Great Britain, signed the Treaty of Amity, Commerce, and Navigation (commonly known as the Jay Treaty) with the newly formed United States, which recognized the right of free travel of Aboriginal peoples across the international border. Soon afterward the War of 1812 abrogated this treaty, but in 1814 its terms were reestablished in the Treaty of Peace and Amity (otherwise known as the Treaty of Ghent).

In more recent years the terms of the Jay Treaty have largely been integrated into U.S. administrative law and practice. The website of the U.S. Embassy, Consular Services Canada puts it this way: "The Jay Treaty, signed in 1794 between Great Britain and the United States, provided that American Indians could travel freely across the international boundary. The United States has codified this obligation in the provisions of Section 289 of the Immigration and Nationality Act (INA) as amended. Native Indians born in Canada are therefore entitled to enter the United States for the purpose of employment, study, retirement, investing, and/or immigration."[1]

By the 1990s, U.S. officials attempted to facilitate the movement of Coast Salish winter spirit dancers across the border. As I previously have written:

> The immediate problem for Spirit Dancers travelling between Coast Salish communities located across the border is the incompatibility of customs regulations and the spiritual state of susceptibility. Initiates may be placed in spiritual danger if, for example, someone looks directly into their faces. Masks and other regalia cannot be handled by non-dancers, and the cedar costumes and headdresses as well as the wooden staffs carried by black- and red-faced dancers sometimes appear bizarre and suspicious to border agents.

> A particular difficulty facing the Spirit Dancers is the cultural prohibition on the communication of specific information about winter Spirit Dancing. Dancers do not reveal the nature of their spirit helpers, nor do they ordinarily describe to outsiders the specifics of their regalia or longhouse practices. To reveal specifics could place dancers in physical danger and reduce the efficacy of their relationship with their spirit helper. This circumstance has made it difficult for Salish people to describe their concerns. U.S. officials have recently attempted to educate border personnel about these topics, and a member of a Washington state tribe has proposed establishing an education module.

> Chief Frank Malloway, of the Yakweakwioose Band of the Stó:lō Nation of B.C., noted that border personnel have recently allowed longhouse initiates to pass the border without visual inspection if they are accompanied by longhouse leaders who present identification for each of them. While "oldtimers" (long-time border officials) on the American side merely used to wave Stó:lō Spirit Dancers through the crossing, in more recent years border guards have tightened their scrutiny. However, through a consultative process, many guards have "learned not to look in the mask boxes or at the dancers." As part of this process, longhouse leaders notify border personnel prior to hosting ceremonies requiring the presence of dancers on the other side of the border. (Miller 1997:69–70, 2007b)

Coast Salish people living on the border, and known to border guards, previously moved easily and "[exploited] the job market of Whatcom County, Washington [with] a daily return to their reserve [in Canada]. One member of the Semiahmoo Nation noted 'It's easier for the Semiahmoo. So many of us have worked in the U.S. for the past thirty, forty, fifty years. We've been working on and off since teenagers, commuting back and forth. They [government officials] know us at the border (Miller 1997:74).'"

The United States has imposed particular rules for identifying those Aboriginal people born in Canada who qualified for inclusion under the terms of section 289 of the Immigration and Naturalization Act. Eligible people must provide evidence to Homeland Security showing at least 50 percent blood quantum (although in some U.S. federal documents the figure is given as 51 percent). The documentation could be an identification card from the Canadian Bureau of Indian and Northern Affairs (sometimes called INAC) or a written statement from a band official regarding ancestral origins on band letterhead, together with documentary evidence (including birth certificates or other records). The specific blood quantum and photographic identification must be provided.

The United States does not consider some factors that are regarded as relevant in Canada, such as whether an individual holds federal status or whether that individual is a member of a treaty band. Significantly, Métis association identification cards are generally not accepted.[2] However, Canadian Métis have recently gained new forms of official recognition, in the Charter of Rights and Freedoms contained within the Constitution Act of 1982. Section 35(2) acknowledges their status as, in the language of the document, "Aboriginal people." In addition, Métis resource rights have been established in Canada through litigation, notably the 2003 *Powley* case. Still, the Métis have not gained traction with U.S. officials as legally recognizable indigenes. This is another case in which internal attributions of identity and those of the Canadian state are ignored by the United States in favor of blood quantum criteria. The term *Métis* is sometimes used to refer to people of mixed Aboriginal and European descent. However, Métis academic Chris Andersen and Métis lawyer Jean Teillet observe that *Métis* refers to a nation with its own membership codes and not simply to those of mixed ancestry.[3]

"Border Hardening" Post-9/11

The events following the terrorist attacks on the World Trade Center buildings in New York City and elsewhere have largely eliminated all of this local cooperation based upon personal relations. During previous years, in many cases border officials knew Coast Salish people by sight and officials cooperated in the movement of spiritually vulnerable longhouse initiates. The *Seattle Times* reported that since September 11, 2001, some two thousand officers have been added to border services in the north.[4] The border is no longer as quiet as it once was, and now the main north-south passage between Washington State and British Columbia, the Peach Arch crossing, is bristling with dozens of Homeland Security personnel. New security devices have been emplaced and upgraded cameras have been installed. A U.S. government report notes the administrative changes following the creation of the Department of Homeland Security: "The United States now has a unified inspections operation at the borders; one inspector is charged with examining people, animals, plants, goods, and cargo upon entry to the country…The transfer of these functions to the Department of Homeland Security (DHS) marks a significant policy shift concerning all of these functions, clarifying that—although there are important commercial, economic, health, humanitarian, and immigration responsibilities—*ensuring the security of our borders is the top priority*."[5]

Ruth Ellen Wasem and colleagues write, "After the September 11, 2001 terrorist attacks, Congress enacted further measures aimed at improving immigration inspectors' terrorist detection capabilities [through the 2002 Enhanced Border Security and Visa Reform Act (PL 107-173)]. Congress also included antiterrorism provisions in legislation reauthorizing the U.S. Customs Service in 2002. CBP [Customs and Border Protection] inspectors now are tasked with more effectively accomplishing the laws and policies of the legacy agencies."[6]

As these reports indicate, the terrorist events of 9/11 led to new U.S. policies that have had the indirect outcome of *hardening* the border (a term that entered the lexicon by 2004 and implies enhanced security) for those Aboriginal peoples moving about in their historic homelands. The war on terror has stimulated the routinization and diffusion of American exceptionality, the implicit notion that normal due process and human rights might be appropriately eroded or suspended. However, U.S. officials have responded minimally to requests to negotiate these differences from Aboriginal tribes located along the northern border in the United States and from bands in Canada and have treated these Aboriginal entities as if they were the equivalent of local governments, with little voice and no leverage (Luna-Firebaugh 2002).

I argue that these adverse effects on Coast Salish peoples are not primarily the direct results of policy but rather are unintended consequences. They are examples of the tendency in U.S. policy to fail to consider the implications for the Aboriginal peoples of North America in the pursuit of issues that register as more important. The U.S. emphasis post-9/11 has been on what is viewed as security over any other issue, a position that has resulted in the slowing down of the massive economic activity that moves across the international border and the movement of private citizens and of Aboriginal peoples with particular rights to cross the border.

My argument, further, is that the present U.S. emphasis on security, or hardening, allows individual Homeland Security officers to exercise their own idiosyncratic opinions regarding the Coast Salish peoples of Canada (and their entry into the United States) in ways that had the result of denying them admission. These idiosyncratic views, however, are shaped in particular ways. Notably, phenotype—the observable traits of a person—comes to stand in metonymically for race and political affiliation with Coast Salish historic communities. Now Homeland Security officers sometimes exercise their own stereotypic views of what Coast Salish, or any Aboriginal person, should look like. These views influence their decisions regarding whether these people can be allowed to enter or whether they should be excluded from the United States. This is not new in American policy and practice, and the allotment of lands to individuals based on readings of Native American bodily characteristics (for example, hair and feet) is one such earlier iteration (Simpson 2008).

Relatedly, outsiders' emphasis on phenotype as a measure of Aboriginal identity is associated with a widespread disbelief in "Indians" as a legitimate category with legal standing and the related idea that many or all Indians are "fakes" who have been assimilated culturally and amalgamated biologically. Elizabeth Furniss, for example, described the non-Aboriginal dismissal of those who, as a result of intermarriage, are regarded as "not-real" Indians (to use the local terminology) in British Columbia and hence are the recipients of undeserved wealth and special status (Furniss 1999). These fake Indians are thought to undermine the values of mainstream society and to be responsible for criminal behavior (Furniss 1999:113). This is a particular problem for many Coast Salish people who frequently do not look like the well-known stereotype of Plains or prairie people.

In public discourse and policy, Aboriginal people are thought to constitute a race and, hence, are subject to particular forms of regimentation. Renisa Mawani documented the historical use in British Columbia of regulatory regimes based on race and the "prevailing anxieties of racial contamination" that would result from the mixing of Indian, white, and black populations (Mawani 2009). Notably, these regimes included restrictions on travel. She writes further, "For the colonial regime, fears of contamination, immorality, and criminality underpinned cross-racial encounters between aboriginal and mixed-race peoples, rendering these proximities to be dangerous and in need of spatial and legal governance while also creating new markers of racial differentiation in the process" (Mawani 2009:42). These spatial practices of governance have continued and are manifested today in the regulation of Aboriginal people at the border.

Although this appears paradoxical, evidence suggests that a mainstream response to a contemporary increase in claims of treaty rights and sovereignty is a denial that Aboriginal peoples are even present. This is one means of denying treaty rights to people who previously had been unable to exercise them and appear to the mainstream population as threats to local resources and livelihoods. Jean O'Brien, for example, noted the "myth of extinction" employed in local histories in New England states as a means of erasing Indians and undermining their claims to land and rights (O'Brien 2010). In an earlier study, I argued that following the judgment in what became known as the Boldt Decision (*U.S. v. Washington*), which found for the right of Coast Salish peoples of Puget Sound to receive half of the regional salmon catch, local non-Indian residents of the Skagit River valley reported being unaware of any local Indian people or tribes (Miller 1993). This is despite their considerable numbers and, in many cases, their common attendance in the school system. Aboriginal people can be simultaneously regarded as lawless, fake, and not present at all. Furniss reported that all of this commonsense racism coexists with an ideology of ethnic tolerance, equality, and a multiculturalism that condemns racism (Furniss 1999:120).

These developments, meanwhile, take on additional salience with the widely reported increased aggressiveness of Homeland Security personnel toward those presenting themselves for entry. On May 25, 2008, for instance, the *Seattle Times* reported the revocation of NEXUS passes, the "trusted traveler" program that facilitates movement through the border for program members.[7] Some NEXUS program members lost their passes for criminal actions or minor violations of border rules (such as possession of an apple), even for violations by family members or co-residents of their homes. One might speculate that the increase in revocations allows Homeland Security to provide Congress with statistical evidence of vigilance against terrorists or other wrongdoers, an important issue in elections. In another instance, on March 5, 2010, the *Montreal Gazette* reported the story of a Canadian woman interrogated at the U.S. border based on an arrest in 1991 by Toronto police, with no subsequent charge.[8] First Nations people are not alone in experiencing difficulties at the border, yet the results are distinctive and more onerous for them in that, as Coast Salish people, along with other Aboriginal peoples of North America whose historic territories have been on both sides of what is now an international border, they frequently press for the right to move freely across this imposed boundary.

Changing Perceptions of Canada

Another line of argument is that the current treatment of Coast Salish peoples at the border reflects a transformed American notion of Canada in the post-9/11 world. Prior to 9/11, American images of Canada were benign and reflected American and Canadian cooperation on a variety of security projects, including the Distant Early Warning Line (DEW Line) defense system and the construction of the American highway through the Yukon to Alaska during World War II. Long-term cooperation at the many border stations across the northern border of the continent allowed for decades of easy movement for Aboriginal and other peoples, and only in recent years has this been constrained (Luna-Firebaugh 2002:160). American public imagery has reflected this cooperation and images of frozen Canadian ponds, beavers, and genial, polite, and ineffectual neighbors have long been paramount. These are the very images deployed in the 2010 Vancouver Olympic closing ceremonies (including giant figures of beavers, ice skaters, and men in plaid), in what was reported to be an effort to overcome growing American antipathy, appeal to American sensibilities, and promote American tourism to Canada by showing Canada's ability to be self-deferential.

The fear of the outside world resulting from the unprovoked attack on the United States has pushed policy makers to create the appearance of an impenetrable border able to block the entry of foreign terrorists. As late as 2009, prominent American public figures, including Secretary of Homeland Security Janet Napolitano, continued to articulate the incorrect view that some of the 9/11 terrorists entered the U.S. from Canada. U.S. media emphasize the movement of potential terrorists and illicit drugs pouring down from Canada. Meanwhile, on the U.S.-Mexico border, new laws in the U.S and hysteria around the "drug war" and illegal immigration have increased the danger for Aboriginal people crossing north, who risk being shot by the U.S. Border Patrol or vigilantes.[9] The same outcome, increased danger, has arisen on the U.S.-Canada border.

These new images of Canada have been conflated into a picture of contagion and threat, pushing Americans to rethink their previous good relations with Canada, and more recently, pushing Canadian authorities to create a joint border policy. Although the circumstances on the northern and southern U.S. borders are quite distinct, Canada now is the object of American fear, as has been the case for Mexico for some time. Politicians have been unwilling to separate the quite different issues regarding the U.S.-Mexico border from those regarding the U.S.–Canada border. There are, for example, far fewer residents of Canada attempting to enter the U.S. illegally in search of employment, and there is no large-scale war between groups involved in the drug trade, which is reported to take the lives of several thousand Mexicans annually. Further, while American fears of Hispanic migration escalates and efforts are undertaken to restrict the legal rights of migrants, the population of Canada is predominantly white and non-Hispanic. Unlike Mexico, Canada remains a wealthy first-world nation with an intact public health system.

In recent American public articulations, however, Canada is a country that facilitates the movement of international terrorists through a lax immigration policy and a purported overreliance on American vigilance toward terrorists. This notion of Canadian moral laxness and permissiveness, which must be overcome by rough American vigilance, is reflected directly in the behavior of Homeland Security agents at the border. Further, American agents appear to have internalized the notion of Canadian category confusion—that Canadians allow the illegitimate slippage of people into existing legal categories, including immigrant, refugee, and Aboriginal, which give them special rights. Prior to 9/11, U.S. authorities complained of undocumented aliens passing into the United States from Canada. The *Seattle Times* coverage shows that concern on the U.S.-Canada border in particular was with economic immigrants and refugees from Asia.[10]

This perspective suddenly changed and the *Seattle Times* quickly sounded the battle cry, reporting just two weeks after the 9/11 attack: "While thousands of U.S. soldiers are being shipped halfway across the globe to fight terrorism, little manpower has been focused on a problem much closer to home: Canada. Experts on both sides of the 4,000-mile border say the nation to the north is a haven for terrorists, and that the U.S.-Canada line is little more barrier than ink on a map."[11] An otherwise liberal Washington State senator made an early articulation of assigning blame to Canada for the event: "Sen. Patty Murray, D-Wash., expressed dismay that some of the terrorists involved in the Sept. 11 attacks entered the United States from Canada. 'The fact that some of these terrorists were known by our intelligence community and were not caught at our northern border is even more disturbing," Murray told colleagues at a recent hearing of the Senate Appropriations Subcommittee on Treasury and General Government. 'They saw this weakness in our security system and exploited it for a deadly end.'" [12] The same day, the *Seattle Times* reported, "The White House has asked the U.S. Customs Service, the Immigration and Naturalization Service (INS) and the Border Patrol to devise a comprehensive counter-terrorism plan for the U.S.-Canada border. In response, Customs has requested 490 new Customs agents, 90 special agents and a significant increase in funding for bomb-detection devices, according to a congressional source. If the White House doesn't take action, Congress might move first. Efforts are under way to produce additional funding for more Customs and Border Patrol agents along the border."[13]

The *Seattle Times* noted on December 11, 2001, "There is a national consensus on the need to enhance security across the United States. Although Attorney General John Ashcroft has clearly stated that none of the Sept. 11 terrorists came across the Canada-U.S. border, there have been calls to increase security at the border—with National Guard troops, helicopters, additional INS staff and closer inspections of people and vehicular traffic."[14] Ashcroft's understanding of the absence of any Canadian role in the movement of the 9/11 terrorists was quickly forgotten in transforming the image of Canada for American political purposes. But the *Seattle Times* also took note of the economic traffic across the border, "It may surprise some to learn that Canada is our most important trading partner, accounting for 25 percent of U.S. exports—more than Japan or Mexico. Trucks cross the border every 2.5 seconds (45,000 trucks a day), 200 million people cross every year, and that cross-border trade totals $475 billion a year—$1.3 billion per day."[15]

The new U.S. border initiatives caught Canadian authorities off guard. The *Seattle Times* reported on December 25, 2002, "According to Canadian officials, the CIA and FBI have swamped Canadian intelligence and law enforcement authorities with requests to conduct surveillance and investigations into suspected terrorists on Canadian soil. Both U.S. agencies believe the threats are directed at the United States."[16] A *Seattle Times* piece on January 20, 2005, showed the effects of the new practices on the ground: "Dozens of people from Canada have been turned back at the U.S. border or prevented from boarding U.S.-bound airplanes in recent months because of suspected links to terrorism, sensitive U.S. government documents show."[17] These fears were not only held by the government. On October 4, 2005, the *Seattle Times* reported the creation of a vigilante squad, the Minutemen, who vowed to patrol the U.S.-Canada border as similar groups have done on the U.S.-Mexico border.[18] They created a center near Blaine, Washington, in historic Coast Salish territory on the saltwater.

The Summit

American fears about the border were made clear in a unique meeting entitled the "Federal, Washington State, County and Tribal Justice Summit," held January 8, 2003, at Bow, Washington (which I attended and at which I gave a keynote speech).[19] In this meeting, federal officials hoped to convince Coast Salish tribal authorities to cross-deputize their tribal police with state police so that they could respond quickly to episodes of terrorists crossing through tribal territories located on the international border into the United States. Offers of high-tech equipment to tribal police were met with interest from the tribal police chief but not from tribal chiefs and chairs, who sensed an infringement on their lands. (On August 8, 2006, the *Seattle Times* noted the continued emphasis on high-tech equipment in plans to deter terrorists during hearings held with local authorities.)[20]

A federal health official outlined a plan to inoculate all frontline health officials along the length of the northern border against smallpox brought by terrorists into the United States. This prompted one tribal chairman to ask if the smallpox would be supplied "by the U.S. War Department," a reference to the idea that contaminated blankets were once given to Indians by soldiers.[21] (This inoculation plan was put into effect but eventually was halted by criticism from the community of health professionals.) When a member of the audience noted that American Indian communities were already suffering from epidemics of diabetes, arthritis, obesity, and other diseases, and that the diversion of funds to a hypothetical and entirely far-fetched episode of contagion overlooked these real problems, the official hung her head in apparent shame at being the bearer of such an inept message.

As I have noted, and as Mawani and Furniss have previously shown, there has long been fear of Aboriginal space going back to the early period of colonization, which in the case of the Coast Salish region was the mid-nineteenth century (Furniss 1999; Mawani 2009). Initially, this was linked to fears of military opposition to colonialism and later to the creation of a "frontier myth" that opposed the values of the self-made white man to that of indolent, oversexualized Indian people. In the post-9/11 world, the mainstream imagery of Aboriginal people additionally includes a focus on the difficulties in controlling the production, distribution, and use of illegal drugs, untaxed cigarettes, and other contraband. Because to mainstream views tribal land appears to be uncontrolled and, perhaps, uncontrollable under tribal leadership, new fears emerged of the use of these lands by terrorists intent on using germ warfare.

An anomalous policy that permitted free passage of a relatively small category (Aboriginal people), combined with the notion that, as reported in the summit, terrorists were crossing the international border through Indian country, and terrorists and drug dealers were using borderland reserves and reservations to concoct and store illicit drugs and contagions that could cause epidemic disease pushed border officials to question the entry of Coast Salish and other Aboriginal people. Similar problems have arisen in other areas along the U.S.-Canada border. Audra Simpson, writing about Mohawk territory, notes "the way in which indigeneity and sovereignty have been conflated with savagery, lawlessness, and 'smuggling' in recent history (Simpson 2008:191)."

The efforts by First Nations of Canada to obtain unobstructed passage into the United States and the efforts of American Indian tribes to do the same for passage into Canada are far from new and have emerged episodically throughout the last several decades (Luna-Firebaugh 2002:168). U.S. tribes and Canadian bands have asked for an exemption from the requirement of showing a passport for their members and have been opposed by state officials on both sides of the border. National Aboriginal organizations in both countries, including the National Congress of American Indians (NCAI) and the Assembly of First Nations (AFN), continue to keep border issues on their agendas.[22] In 2001, the AFN, for example, passed Resolution 28, the Aboriginal and Treaty Border Crossing Rights Resolution, which noted Canada's refusal to recognize border rights, in particular the failure to enact Section III of the Jay Treaty legislatively, which contains provisions for crossing the border. The AFN called on Canada to recognize these rights. In 2006, the First International Aboriginal Cross Border Summit, with representatives of the federal governments, the AFN, and the NCAI was held to consider border issues.

The Case of Dr. Roberts

This was the overheated political environment when Dr. Peter Roberts, a Coast Salish man living in Tsawwassen, British Columbia, and a member of the Campbell River Band, attempted to cross into the United States in 2007. His green card was a particular sort that is issued to document that the bearer is a Status Indian of Canada with a minimum of 50 percent blood quantum (half descent from Indian people). These are the grounds on which Aboriginal people can pass freely into the United States without further documentation. According to his attorney, the card was an obscure, now obsolete type (SA-1), originally issued to Roberts in 1966, as opposed to the Jay Treaty green card (S-13).[23] *Seattle Times* reporter Lornet Turnbull, who covered the case of Roberts, reported to anxious Seattle residents in an article titled "Rights by blood" that "if you are a Canadian with at least 50 percent aboriginal blood" you have the right to:[24]

- Cross the U.S./Canadian border freely
- Live and work in the United States and be eligible for public benefits such as Medicaid and Supplemental Security Income
- Register for college or a university in the United States as a domestic rather than foreign student.

You do not have to:

- Obtain a work permit to hold a job in the United States
- Register for the military
- The U.S. government cannot keep you out of the United States or deport you.

This discourse, in this instance articulated by a reporter, transformed membership in an Aboriginal polity (or community) into an issue of commonality based on descent and referenced by the metonym *blood*. Blood quantum officially entered into U.S. political practice during the late nineteenth century and now serves to bifurcate members of American Indian tribes into those with rights to federally funded services and those without such rights (Sturm 2002; Miller 2006). In addition, tribes that rely on blood quantum in determining membership also, in effect, differentiate access to tribal services. American federal policy further entrenched blood as a determinant of membership with the passage of the Indian Reorganization Act of 1934, which required the creation of tribal membership rolls. Since then, blood quantum has been determined from the information recorded on these rolls. Further, INS determined that 50 percent blood quantum was necessary for passage of Aboriginal peoples of Canada into the United States. The Revised Citizenship Act of 1952 further imposed the use of the idea of blood quantum. This, says Mohawk scholar Simpson, created a racialization of identity in which descent is equated with race and means that blood quantum, thought to indicate race, takes precedence over other forms of recognition (Simpson 2008:200).

The federally unrecognized Coast Salish Hwlitsum Band of British Columbia, for example, is composed of those acknowledged by the Crown as Status Indians and those who are not. The differences are measured by quanta of descent rather than by participation in and acceptance by the community. In any case, in effect the United States imposes its own criteria on Coast Salish communities whose membership spans the international border. Meanwhile, ideas of blood are sometimes conflated with phenotype in the practice of Homeland Security, as occurred with Dr. Roberts.

The *Seattle Times* reported on January 15, 2008, that Dr. Roberts's green treaty card was seized as he attempted to cross the border: "Peter Roberts is a Canadian citizen and a member of the Campbell River Indian Band who, until two months ago, enjoyed unrestricted access to the United States—the right to work and live here if he wanted to. The 54-year-old never has. A dentist with the fair complexion of his Ukrainian mother and the facial features of his full-blooded native dad, Roberts lives on the Tsawwassen Indian Reserve in British Columbia, just up the road from the U.S. border."[25]

Homeland Security officials, noted the *Seattle Times*, questioned Roberts's lineage and whether he had sufficient blood to qualify for passage. "I guess in their eyes I don't have status, based on how I look," Roberts said.[26] But a complicating factor is that the United States was then working on a plan to further "harden" the border by requiring everyone crossing the border to show a passport. This became policy by 2008, under the Western Hemisphere Travel Initiative, the travel implementation of Section 7209 of the Intelligence Reform and Terrorist Protection Act of 2004.

A hearing regarding Roberts's case was held in an obscure federal immigration court, known colloquially as the "Port Court," at the point of entry on the border at the Peace Arch. I attended this hearing and here will detail it, and the events around it, to indicate the ways in which the legal processes following the determination of frontline Homeland Security officers regarding admissibility have the effect of intimidating Coast Salish people crossing the border, even those with legal counsel, education, and social standing in the mainstream society. The *Seattle Times* noted, "At Roberts' hearing this Friday, attorneys for the government will ask an immigration judge to revoke all his Aboriginal rights to the U.S. An unfavorable ruling could make it difficult—if not impossible—for him to obtain permanent residence here if he ever sought it."[27]

There were unusual characteristics to this court and the proceedings. First, Homeland Security officials attempted to bar some observers from entry to the court, an effort circumvented by telephone communication with a national official of the Department of Justice in Washington, DC, who gave instructions that the court was open to the public.[28] Second, the attorney acting for Homeland Security informed the judge that he would check through border records to see what charges could be brought against Roberts in a subsequent hearing, a practice sometimes referred to as "fishing." Questions were raised about the accuracy of Robert's and his daughter's cards issued by the Campbell River [Coast Salish] Band.

The *Seattle Times* reported on January 15, 2008, that

> By law, Canada's native people—even those with a criminal record—cannot be denied entry to the U.S., and they cannot be deported. To invoke their treaty rights at the border, they must present what's called a "blood quantum" letter from their bands detailing their lineage. The letter is often presented along with a status card, a standard, federally recognized photo ID that Canadian bands issue to their members. To document their treaty status, simplify border crossings and avoid the need to always carry blood documents, families sometimes ask the U.S. government for special treaty-linked green cards—like Roberts' family did when he was a child. But government lawyers say they have the right to revoke these cards, just as they do with regular green cards, if they believe the cards were improperly granted in the first place. "Just because you've been given one doesn't mean you were given it correctly," said Dorothy Stefan, chief counsel for U.S. Immigration and Customs Enforcement. "You need to show that you're 50 percent—and that's where it becomes tricky. If you can't prove it . . . you get a chance to go to court and prove you have status." Saunders [lawyer for the defendant] said the burden is on the government to prove Roberts is not what his blood documents show him to be—the grandson of full-blooded Campbell River Indians. "We have letters from his band detailing my client's status going back to the 1800s," Saunders said.[29]

And further,

> Roberts doesn't have a criminal record and said he never experienced border problems until last fall, when a guard at Point Roberts lectured him about the need to always show his green card when seeking entry. He challenged the guard, invoking his treaty rights—and was denied entry. After that, Roberts said, he was hassled each time—stopped, questioned at length, at times fingerprinted and at times turned away—always at Point Roberts, but never anywhere else. In November, guards finally seized the card, granting him a temporary document to travel to Hawaii for the holidays. "I guess it's a kind of reversed prejudice," Roberts said. "In our family, we don't go out of our way to say we're Indian. We just live our lives."[30]

Then, the *Seattle Times* reported,

> In November, U.S. Customs and Border officials, apparently not believing Roberts had enough Indian blood to qualify for it, seized his green card. Roberts said he

believes the border agents were responding to the way he looks; his fair complexion comes from his mother, he said.[31]

Port Court at the Peace Arch crossing was then a second-story room immediately above the large area in which interviews are conducted with the few people who cross the border on foot and with selected travelers in cars and buses (the entire border facility is now reconstructed for greater security). The room was distinct from conventional American courtrooms; it was small, some twenty-five by forty feet, and plain, with four rows of double tables. On January 18, 2008, the immigration judge, attired in a blue sports jacket and tie, a recorder, two bailiffs, a senior attorney acting for Homeland Security, a *Seattle Times* reporter, and an attorney acting for Dr. Roberts were among those in attendance. All told, fifteen people came to participate or watch, which is a small number given the potential implications of the proceedings for Aboriginal people. Officials initially skirmished around the receipt of notice and the filing of an exhibit.[32]

Len Saunders, an immigration lawyer practicing in Blaine, Washington, a small town located directly on the border, told the court that he was not sure if pleading to the allegations brought by Homeland Security on behalf of his client was appropriate because Roberts was considered a Native of North America and not a citizen of the United States or of Canada. However, the judge's questions clarified that Roberts was born in Canada and, in the eyes of Canada, was a citizen there. No final designation regarding citizenship was made at this point. Homeland Security argued that they had evidence that Roberts did not have the minimum 50 percent blood quantum and noted that Roberts has multiple immigration files and may seek permanent residence in the United States. They will, the attorney added, search Roberts's files further to determine if he is eligible under the Immigration and Naturalization Act, Section 289. In response the judge noted that the factual issues needed an evidentiary hearing and that Homeland Security would conduct further investigations. He added that under Immigration Court procedures there is no requirement to produce documents, that is, hand copies over to the other side (the process known as discovery). At this point, Saunders had not seen the government evidence against his client. An evidentiary hearing was set for a later date. Discussion among the judge, the attorney acting for Homeland Security, and Saunders made it clear that the government had not prepared for the hearing. Although Saunders had dropped off his sixty-three-page filing on behalf of his client with the government offices in Seattle, some ninety miles to the south of his office in Blaine, the attorney for Homeland Security had not read it.

The government however, produced a March 3, 1966, affidavit by Roberts's grandmother, which they claimed showed Roberts's blood quantum to be less than 50 percent. In response, Saunders requested an estoppel argument, which would have prevented Homeland Security from making its allegation contradicting the evidence that Roberts's blood quantum was sufficient, previously accepted as factual. The judge ruled that case law gave him limited authority to make an estoppel argument under the ruling in *Hernandez-Puente*.[53] That ruling had held that "the Board of Immigration Appeals and the Immigration judges are without authority to apply the doctrine of equitable estoppel against the Immigration and Naturalization Service so as to preclude it from undertaking a lawful course of action that it is empowered to pursue by statute and regulation."[33]

Further, the judge noted that "admission to the U.S. is each time an individual evaluation," and that despite having been admitted in the past, and having been given the form I-551 showing him to be an American Indian born in Canada, and being in a category with rights to pass the border (a form issued to Roberts on June 9, 1995), these were not sufficient for Roberts to now be admitted to the United States.[34] Homeland Security was free to question his admissibility on any occasion, despite previous admissibility. As an intended immigrant (Roberts was considering this possibility at retirement) he came under additional scrutiny. The judge stated that if he did not find him to be 50 percent blood, as a Canadian, his immigration might be blocked. In addition, he observed, "The respondent has the burden to show his admissibility to the United States." Saunders took a different view and responded that "He [Roberts] has overcome this—the burden is on the federal government." To this, the judge observed, "this [form] 551 is different" and concluded, "It is not the case where to lose status the government has to show convincing evidence." All evidence, he said, will be in writing pending an upcoming hearing. The judge did, however, note that he was relying on hearsay evidence regarding the genealogy of Roberts's grandmother (hearsay refers to evidence given by nonexpert parties and is restricted to what one has heard and seen personally). He observed that her declaration was important, stating, "I don't know if she is alive. The parties need to address this."[35]

A legal assistant working for Saunders told me optimistically that he believed the judge's comment on "hearsay" evidence meant that he would not accept a document by the grandmother showing blood quantum. Saunders observed that once a right such as border crossing is established it cannot be revisited, added "it's a fishing expedition," and provided his opinion that at the border Homeland Security thought Roberts was white and then dug around in his file to come up with a charge.[36] He observed that Aboriginal people of an earlier period sometimes obscured their own Aboriginal status because of the difficulties they faced from Indian agents and other government authorities, and that this may have influenced the information on the affidavit of Roberts's grandmother. In any case, Homeland Security information did not agree with that held by the Campbell River Band, a federally recognized Canadian First Nation.

At this point, Roberts's position was entirely precarious. He had been detained and denied entry originally on the basis of biased perception about phenotype and its relationship with indigeneity. Now the court had ruled that the burden of proof was on the defense and that the government's case could be minimal. In addition, Homeland Security was free to rummage through the files to find any other issue that might derail Roberts' case, or that of anyone else in his family. Ultimately, Roberts decided not to run the risk of the court refusing him his rights to cross the border—as an Aboriginal person with 50 percent blood quantum—and thereby possibly jeopardize a later move to the United States.

The issues regarding the case of Roberts can be understood in light of the experiences of other Coast Salish people. One Canadian Status Coast Salish man recently noted that, in his effort to present his band [identity] card and pass through the border under the rights granted Aboriginal people, the Homeland Security officer at the Peace Arch border patted his handgun in its holster on his hip and told him, "Canada gives out band cards like popcorn. Do you get my message?" This man observed that he felt that he was singled out because of his appearance. He didn't appear dark enough or have other phenotypical characteristics that non-Aboriginal people conventionally ascribe to Aboriginals. These might include long black hair, particular facial characteristics, and short limbs. This man's observations are far from unusual among those Aboriginal peoples living along the international border. The explicit threat made by the act of patting a handgun was sufficiently intimidating to the elderly Coast Salish man that he observed, "He didn't need to tell me twice. I got out of there."[37]

All of this places Coast Salish peoples in a conflicted position. The U.S. Department of Homeland Security, an agency created in the aftermath of the events of September 11, 2001, wants U.S. tribes to facilitate the entry of nontribal personnel onto tribal lands along the border. Further, Homeland Security hopes to equip and arm the tribal police heavily, describing the Coast Salish lands as the site of drugs and terrorists. Homeland Security places U.S. interests above those of Aboriginal peoples; the claim made at the summit was that it must do so and tribal leaders must comply. At the same time as it demands cooperation, Homeland Security reinscribes Aboriginal peoples and lands with new and demeaning imagery.

Discussion and Conclusion

The hardening of the international border dividing the United States and Canada and, more specifically, Washington state and British Columbia is, at first blush, puzzling, in light of the larger processes of globalization, which have tended to deemphasize borders in favor of newer arrangements of free-trade zones.[38] It is more in line with developments in air travel worldwide, which now make extreme demands on passengers, requiring such measures as the examination of shoes and, even more onerous, the use of full-body scanning devices.

The hardening of the border should also be considered in light of international agreements, which grant rights to full contact among fellow members of an Aboriginal group across the border. The 1989 International Labor Organization, convention 169, part VII, calls for governments to facilitate contacts and cooperation between Aboriginal and tribal peoples across borders, including economic, social, cultural, spiritual, and environmental activities. In addition, Article 32 of the 2007 UN Declaration on the Rights of Aboriginal Peoples, now signed by Canada and the United States, maintains that Aboriginal people divided by international borders have the right to maintain and develop contacts with their own members across the borders, and that states, in consultation with the Aboriginal people, will take effective measures to ensure the implementation of this right. The draft Organization of American States Declaration on the Rights of Aboriginal Peoples similarly calls for the rights of mobility and full contact with those with whom ethnic, religious, or ethnic ties are shared.[39]

Sondra Wentzel notes the role of border guards in the management of Aboriginal peoples at remote borders: "As a consequence of the processes sketched…, which together lead to more presence of the state in formerly remote areas, indigenous peoples in 'borderlands' all over the world increasingly face very practical problems. These range from difficulties in maintaining social and cultural relationships with relatives and community members to serious limitations to traditional trade and newly developing opportunities for labor migration to violent harassment by border guards."[40] However, one might note that new practical problems have arisen for Aboriginal peoples on far-from-remote borders.

Further, even if U.S. policy may appear to conform to international agreements, in practice, the intimidation and personal biases of individual border guards who may believe that they are acting in support of American policy and interests obstructs many Aboriginal people.

I have written previously of Coast Salish efforts to manage the international boundary that divides their member communities:

> Salish people are currently contesting, inverting, and reconstructing the international border in various ways in order to maintain their communities and to preserve their sense of common identity. It is clear that Native people on both sides of the border persist in thinking of the border as an intrusion and that they think of their responses to the border as efforts to gain social justice within the Canadian and American states. The difficulties of carrying out their lives and pressing their claims within two separate national legal systems remains a considerable barrier to the achievement of justice. (Miller 1997:76)

But the current practice of Homeland Security seems to reflect efforts to manage Aboriginal people that conform to Foucauldian notions of disciplinary control. Coast Salish people who violate mainstream notions of phenotype are managed and regulated not by federal regulations that explicitly exclude them but rather by local authorities, who act to implement more localized ideas of identity. The salient question is how Coast Salish individuals and groups negotiate their own circumstances, particularly in light of inconsistencies in the state records, and the suspicion toward Aboriginal people exhibited by frontline security personnel.

In the case of Roberts, there are both too many records (including those that appear to be poorly understood by Homeland Security and court officials) and too few. In particular, the use by the Port Court of decontextualized hearsay evidence that was given a half-century ago, during a period when many Aboriginal people felt they must obscure their own identity as a matter of safety and in order to obtain employment and housing, suggests that the management and availability of archival material is a serious issue. Here, the archival materials don't appear to be available to the Coast Salish people—the records are decontextualized and unavailable. The Homeland Security department appears to have no burden of duty to share documents in order that a hearing be equitable. Meanwhile, Roberts's archival record is insufficiently complete to allow a fully contextualized understanding of his circumstances.

In the end, the cases of Roberts and the other Coast Salish people, including the elder intimidated at the border, are determined not by public policy but rather by the perceptions of the gatekeepers, who act on internalized and unexamined notions of indigeneity. In the current context of fear of contagion and of terrorism, American exceptionalism, or the willingness to act outside of the spirit of the law, allows a hardened border to deter those Coast Salish and other Aboriginal people who ought to be allowed to cross under both national law and international agreements.

Endnotes

[1] U.S. Embassy, Consular Services Canada, http://www.consular.canada.usembassy.gov/first_nations_canada.asp (accessed March 6, 2010).

[2] U.S. Embassy, Consular Services Canada.

[3] Chris Andersen, "I'm Métis: What's Your Excuse? On the Optics and Misrecognition of Métis in Canada," Canadian Association for the Humanities and Social Sciences, Fedcanblog, 2011, http://blog.fedcan.ca/2011/02/22/%E2%80%98i%E2%80%99m-metis-what%E2%80%99s-your-excuse%E2%80%99-on-the-optics-and-misrecognition-of-metis-in-canada/ (accessed April 23, 2009); Jean Teillet, personal communication, Louis Riel opera opening-gala roundtable discussion, Chan Centre, University of British Columbia, Vancouver, January 3, 2010.

[4] Rob Hotakainen and Adam Sege, "Northern Border Staffing Levels Draw Scrutiny," Seattle Times, September 11, 2011, http://seattletimes.nwsource.com/html/localnews/2016179990_border12.html (accessed December 4, 2011).

[5] Ruth Ellen Wasem, Jennifer Lake, and Lisa Seghetti, Domestic Social Policy Division; James Monke, Resources, Sciences, and Industry Division; and Stephen Viña, American Law Division, CRS [Congressional Research Services] Report for Congress: Border Security: Inspections Practices, Policies, and Issues, May 26, 2004; emphasis added.

[6] see note 5, see page 9.

[7] Lornet Turnbull, "Past Trips Up Some Canada Border-Crossers Previously Cleared for the Fast Lane," Seattle Times, May 25, 2008, http://seattletimes.nwsource.com/html/localnews/2004437253_nexus25m.html (accessed December 3, 2011).

[8] Kevin Dougherty, "U.S. Security Makes Some Insecure; Will the Introduction of Secure Flight Make Air Travel More Complicated for Canadians?," Gazette (Montreal) March 5, 2010, final ed. Date Accessed: 2012/03/28. http://www.lexisnexis.com/hottopics/lnacademic.

[9] Lornet Turnbull and Janet I. Tu, "Minutemen Watch U.S.-Canada Border," Seattle Times, October 4, 2005, http://seattletimes.nwsource.com/html/localnews/2002538196_borderpatrol04m .html (accessed December 4, 2011).

[10] James L. Eng, "More Koreans Illegally Enter U.S. Via Canada—Problem Has 'Gotten Out of Hand,' Say Border Patrol Officials," Seattle Times, February 4, 1996, http://community.seattletimes .nwsource.com/archive/?date=19960204&slug=2312344 (accessed December 4, 2011).

[11] James Neff, Duff Wilson, and Hal Benton, "Few Resources Spent Guarding Canada Border," *Seattle Times,* September 23, 2001, http://community.seattletimes.nwsource.com/archive/?date=200 10923&slug=border23m0 (accessed December 4, 2011).

[12] Kevin Galvin and John Hendren, "Bills Would Tighten U.S.-Canada Border," *Seattle Times*, October 10, 2001, http://community.seattletimes.nwsource.com/archive/?date=20011010&slug =border10m (accessed January 13, 2012).

[13] See note 12.

[14] Jeff Morris and Barry Penner, "Guarantee Security and Jobs along U.S.-Canada Border," *Seattle Times*, December 11, 2001, http://community.seattletimes.nwsource.com/archive/?date=2001 1211&slug=perimeter11 (accessed December 4, 2011).

[15] See note 14.

[16] Dana Priest and DeNeen L. Brown, "Calls across Canada-U.S. Border Traced to al-Qaida Suspects," *Seattle Times*, December 25, 2002, http://community.seattletimes.nwsource.com/archive/ ?date=20021225&slug=canada2 (accessed December 4, 2011).

[17] "Dozens Rejected at Canada-U.S. Borders, Airports for Suspected Links to Terrorism," *Seattle Times*, January 20, 2005, http://seattletimes.nwsource.com/html/nationworld/2002156368 _webcanada20.html (accessed December 4, 2011).

[18] "Minutemen Watch," *Seattle Times*, October 4, 2005.

[19] Bruce G. Miller, Keynote Address: "Tribal Culture and Tribal Law," Federal, Washington State, County and Tribal Justice Summit, Bow, WA, January, 8, 2003.

[20] Lornet Turnbull, "Border Security Focus of Hearings," *Seattle Times*, August 8, 2006, http://community.seattletimes.nwsource.com/archive/?date=20060808&slug=border08m (accessed December 4, 2011).

[21] Field notes, Justice Summit, January 8, 2003.

[22] Assembly of First Nations, http://www.afn.ca/index.php/en/policy-areas/nation-building -and-re-building-supporting-first-nation-governments (accessed April 22, 2011).

[23] Lornet Turnbull, "Canadian Indian Wonders Why U.S. Yanking Back Welcome Mat," Seattle Times, January 15, 2008, http://seattletimes.nwsource.com/html/localnews/2004125576_jaytreaty15.html (accessed December 4, 2011).

[24] See note 23.

[25] See note 23.

[26] See note 23.

[27] See note 23.

[28] Field notes, January 18, 2008, concerning all descriptions of Dr. Roberts's hearing in the Port Court.

[29] See note 23.

[30] See note 23.

[31] See note 23.

[32] Board of Immigration Appeals, Rescission Proceedings under Section 246 of the Immigration and Nationality Act, A-22918876, Interim Decision, #3153, decided June 20, 1991.

[33] See note 28.

[34] See note 28.

[35] See note 28.

[36] Interview with attorney Len Saunders, April 14, 2008.

[37] Field notes, February 9, 2010.

[38] Sondra Wentzel, "Akwesasne Revisited: The Relevance of Mohawk Experiences for Aboriginal Peoples in Border Areas in the Amazon." Paper given to Brazilian Anthropology Association Annual Meeting, Porto Seguro, Brazil, May 2008.

[39] See note 38.

302

40 See note 38.

References Cited

Andersen, Chris. 2011. I'm Métis: What's Your Excuse? On the Optics and Misrecognition of Métis in Canada. Canadian Association for the Humanities and Social Sciences, Fedcanblog, 2011, http://blog.fedcan.ca/2011/02/22/%E2%80%98i%E2%80%99m-metis-what%E2%80%99s-your-excuse%E2%80%99-on-the-optics-and-misrecognition-of-metis-in-canada/ (accessed April 23, 2009).

Bruyneel, Kevin. 2007. *The Third Space of Sovereignty: The Postcolonial Politics of U.S.-Aboriginal Relations.* Minneapolis: University of Minnesota Press.

Frank, Gayla and Carole Goldberg. 2010. *Defying the Odds: The Tule River Tribe's Struggle for Sovereignty in Three Centuries.* New Haven, CT: Yale University Press.

Furniss, Elizabeth. 1999. *The Burden of History: Colonialism and the Frontier Myth in a Rural Canadian Community.* Vancouver: University of British Columbia Press.

Luna-Firebaugh, Eileen M. 2002. The Border Crossed Us: Border Crossing Issues of the Aboriginal Peoples of the America. *Wicazo Sa Review,* 17(1):159–81.

Maclachlan, Morag, editor. 1998. *The Fort Langley Journals, 1827–30.* Vancouver: University of British Columbia Press.

Mawani, Renisa. 2009. *Colonial Proximities: Crossracial Encounters and Juridical Truths in British Columbia, 1871–1921.* Vancouver: University of British Columbia Press.

Miller, Bruce G. 1993. The Press, the Boldt Decision, and Indian-White Relations. *American Indian Culture and Research Journal,* 17(2): 75–97.

———— 1996. The 'Really Real' Border and the Divided Salish Community. *BC Studies,* 112: 63–79.

———— 2006. Who Are Indigenes? A Comparative Study of Canadian and American Practices. *American Behavioral Scientist,* 50(4):1–16.

———— 2007a. *"Be of Good Mind": Essays on the Coast Salish.* Vancouver: University of British Columbia Press.

———— 2007b. Conceptual and Practical Boundaries: Indians/First Nations on the Border of Contagion in the Post- 9/11 Era. In *The Borderlands of the American and Canadian Wests: Essays on Regional and Trans-Boundary History,* edited by Sterling Evans, pp. 49–66. Lincoln: University of Nebraska Press.

O'Brien, Jean M. 2010. *Firstly and Lastly: Writing Indians out of Existence in New England* Minneapolis: University of Minnesota Press.

Simpson, Audra. 2008. Subjects of Sovereignty: Indigeneity, the Revenue Rule, and Juridics of Failed Consent. *Law and Contemporary Problems,* 191(71):191–213.

Sturm, Circe. 2002. *Blood Politics: Race, Culture, and Identity in the Cherokee Nation of Oklahoma.* Berkeley: University of California Press.

Part VII

Political Recognition

In both the United States and Canada there a number of Indigenous communities, including Coast Salish peoples, without recognition by the federal government. The absence of recognition strips these communities of those rights and programs available to them through federal and provincial authorities and from international protocols aimed at protecting the sovereignty and cultures of Indigenous peoples. The absence of recognition for groups such as the Duwamish and previously the Samish in the United States and the Hwlitsum in Canada has pushed leaders to honor their ancestors, in their terms, by demanding recognition. The issue of non-recognition, the topic of my book, *Invisible Indigenes* (2004), raises interesting and continuing questions for Coast Salish peoples concerning what groups should have direct relations with the state. Chapter 21, *Who Are Indigenes? A Comparative Study of Canadian and American Practices,* published in *American Behavioral Scientist*, looks at issues of legal definitions of indigeneity. Chapter 22, *After the F.A.P.: Tribal Reorganization after Federal Acknowledgment*, provides a description of a Coast Salish community, Upper Skagit, immediately after renewed federal recognition and the consequences of this change in status. I should point out that this community is dramatically changed from the one I described twenty-five years ago, and has now more than doubled in population and owns profitable hotels, a casino and other business. The reservation has a number of new facilities and the tribe has become a major employer in the region.

Figure 17. Upper Skagit children touring ancestral archaeological sites at Ross Lake in 2015.

Journal of Northwest Anthropology, Memoir 12: 304–316 (2016)

21

Who Are Indigenes?
A Comparative Study of Canadian and American Practices*

The U.S. and Canadian governments have long diverged in the ways in which they identify the Indigenous peoples and communities within their borders. These differences, and their implications, have perhaps never been so great as they have been since the late 1970s and the development of a U.S. program intended to provide a process whereby nonrecognized Indigenous communities could, in principle, gain or regain federal recognition. Although Canada, too, has a process, it remains poorly developed, almost an afterthought. Seen from the perspective of the members of these communities unable to obtain federal recognition, however, these differences are insignificant. Analytically, American and Canadian policies produce the same result; namely, it is hard to gain recognition, although this does happen in rare cases. This is not unimportant. Recognition by the federal government holds significance for Indigenous people because it creates eligibility for various federal programs and, in some cases, entitles communities to whatever rights their ancestors reserved for themselves in signing treaties with the federal entity. Equally important, however, is the emotive component. Recognition serves as a form of validation of claims to Aboriginal identity that puts previously nonrecognized communities on the same footing as other Aboriginal communities.

Here, I set the comparative study of American and Canadian policy and practice in a historical perspective. American and Canadian policies toward nonrecognized communities do not arise out of thin air; rather, they reflect the histories of interaction between Euroamericans and Indigenous peoples, particularly emergent conceptualizations of the other and subsequent legislation, administrative policy, and legal judgments. My argument, therefore, is that differences in these policies arise from divergences in national understandings regarding who Indigenous peoples are and how they can be administered and costs suppressed. I give particular attention to the conceptual problems inherent in both American and Canadian approaches to granting recognition to nonrecognized communities.

The United States today explicitly accepts the existence of such communities but continues to rely on the case law and other precedents in American history and the outdated social science concepts that produced the problem of nonrecognition of legitimate communities in the first place. The Canadian approach seems to be based on the hope that such communities will simply go away. The American approach is detailed and doctrinaire, biased toward European-derived concepts of community, political practice, and knowledge, and has established a standard of evidence required for recognition that cannot be met by many legitimate groups. On the other hand, the Canadian approach is hardly tied to any rigorous legal tests or social science at all. The Canadian government is aware that there are Indigenous groups that wish to amalgamate, thereby creating a new group, and that there are Indigenous groups that wish to fission, a process that also creates new entities. However, there is limited recognition that there are freestanding groups that wish to obtain recognition without amalgamating with existing recognized groups. The primary hurdle for such Canadian groups, therefore, is not meticulously proving that they are a political community in a Euroamerican sense but rather getting neighboring recognized bands to divide existing federal funding.

*Authored by Bruce Granville Miller, reproduced with permission and previously published in *American Behavioral Scientist*, 50(4):462–477 (2006).

There are complex backgrounds to the current-day problems of determining which groups ought to have direct political relations with mainstream federal government, and I address this only briefly here (however, for more detail, see Miller 2003). When Europeans encountered Indigenous peoples of North America after 1492, there were initially no difficulties in understanding who was Indigenous and who was European, although Europeans frequently misunderstood Indigenous social organization and the patterns of individual affiliation with groups and for centuries produced garbled accounts of Indian tribes. The issue quickly became even less clear as biological amalgamation occurred; as people of mixed ancestry came to form new, distinct (métis or mestizo) communities; and as people of European descent came to occupy the landscape and displace Indigenous settlements.

The British government, parent to both the United States and Canada, sought to establish political relationships with Indigenous societies to advance its own economic, religious, and political goals and to gain allies in the competition with French, Spanish, and Russian colonizers. This effort was articulated in the Royal Proclamation of 1763, which attempted to systematize political relations. In the colonial period, British policy treated Indigenous societies as parallel states and arranged bilateral agreements and treaties. But following the triumph of Britain over rival colonizers in North America north of Mexico, and especially after the successful independence movement of the American colonies, Indigenous peoples' roles as political, economic, and military allies declined and there was little inclination to continue to treat Indigenous communities as worthy of state-to-state negotiations. Indigenous communities became redefined in various ways, and simultaneously, Indigenous peoples reorganized themselves in response to their new circumstances and to resist domination by the state. Sider (1993) identified several patterns, including amalgamation into larger political and military units, such as the Nuu-chah-nulth Confederacy on the West Coast and the enlarged Iroquoian Confederacy in the East. Others adapted American-style political and legal systems, notably the Cherokee, in the vain hope that this would enable them to continue as freestanding peoples. Still others moved away from contact with the mainstream, often moving into progressively more marginal territories. Many of the descendants of peoples who chose this latter strategy are today members of unrecognized tribes officially unknown to the state.

Indigenous peoples became the objects of federal manipulation in new ways in the late eighteenth and early nineteenth centuries as policy makers and courts struggled to unilaterally define the now confused relationship with Indigenous peoples. These new definitions and policies in turn created new understandings of who Indigenes were and how they could be recognized. Indians, to use the language of everyday life, were believed to be in need of missionizing and could be known as those who were pagan. In addition, Indians were the people who were premodern in their economic practices, had not yet embraced industrial life, and were believed not to engage in market systems of exchange, production, and distribution. Indians came to be defined as wards of the state, in conformity with a growing perception that Indigenous peoples were behind Europeans in social evolution and, hence, were childlike. Or Indigenous communities were "domestic dependent nations" in the words of U.S. Chief Justice Marshall, who attempted to account for the underlying problem of the earlier history of state-to-state relations and the apparent success of American domination in his time (see *Cherokee Nation v. Georgia* 1831).

By the late nineteenth century, the conceptions of Indians had changed considerably, and simple binary oppositions between Indian behavior and beliefs and those of Euroamericans were no longer applicable. Indians could not be simply identified through their practice of pagan religion because many attended Christian churches. In a similar manner, many were successful entrepreneurs in the new economy or agriculturalists, as in the Jeffersonian ideal. Neither were Euroamericans and Indigenes distinct biological populations and, thus, it became difficult or impossible to identify Indigenes by phenotype, clothing, or other visible criteria. In response, new concepts were developed to fill the void. In the United States, the abstract concept of "blood" became an important signifier. Federal policy came to rely on blood quantum, or degree of "Indian blood," begun in the 1880s, as a means of limiting services to some members of Indigenous communities and potentially, eventually eliminating entire communities from the trust relationship. In Canada, the federal Indian Act pulled together previous legislation in the attempt to clearly identify Indians and create the conditions for political control by Ottawa.

The attempts to provide definitions of who Indigenes were progressively removed self-identification from the communities themselves and imposed yet again new conditions to be worked out. In Puget Sound, Washington State, for example, dense networks of social affiliation through marriage, mutual participation in ceremonial life, common efforts at defense, and other forms of social life were overlaid with new, federally imposed notions of "tribes." These federally recognized tribes, because they were the political unit that held sanctioned relations with the U.S. government, influenced the perceptions of community members who came to emphasize their commonalities with fellow members of their recognized tribe at the expense of their broader kin affiliations (Harmon 1998).

By the early years of the twentieth century, although there was considerable confusion regarding the identity of Indigenes, this was not yet a critical issue from the viewpoint of state managers because Indian populations were at or near the historical nadirs. Into the middle of the past century, Indians were still generally thought of as remnants, and communities were believed to be undergoing amalgamation into the mainstream. Public policy, violent predation of Indians, and disease processes contributed to this state of affairs. U.S. federal policy in the late nineteenth century, under the so-called Dawes Act (the General Allotment Act of 1887), was built on the idea of enfranchisement and of converting the remnant tribal people to citizens and individual landholders. Recognizing the failure of assimilationist policy under the Dawes Act and other legislation, the Wheeler-Howard Act of 1934 (informally called the Indian Reorganization Act, or IRA) provided legislation to establish formal tribal self-government.

This recognition of sovereignty, however, was paired with the assimilationist practice of pushing communities to organize into European-like polities in the 1930s. Furthermore, the Indian Reorganization Act made special problems for tribes without a land base, as the government sought to decide which tribes might qualify for self-government and economic development. After interviewing Indian people and visiting communities, government representatives added 21 communities to the list of recognized tribes (Miller 1991). The remaining unrecognized tribes became all the more invisible, however, and the lines between recognized and unrecognized gradually became more distinct and rigid.

In the years 1954 to 1962, the state emphasized termination of tribes, the revocation of state–tribal status, and the sale of communal lands. More than 100 tribes were terminated in this period, although some have since been restored. Efforts were made to sever individuals from their home communities, assimilating them into mainstream life by a program of relocating men to urban centers and the mainstream job market.

Formal Efforts at Recognition in the United States

This background brings us to the 1970s, a period in which congressional hearings led to the public acknowledgement of the circumstances of the many unrecognized Indigenous peoples. The United States has formally recognized Indigenous peoples and groups in several ways during the past 200 years. Until 1871, some tribes were recognized by treaty, a nation-to-nation relationship, but without establishing a clear definition of *Indian* or *Indigene*. Governmental relations have also been established through statutes, contracts, or appropriations. Other tribes have been recognized by presidential (executive) order that established reservations in some cases, until Congress barred such measures by statute in 1919 (Quinn 1992). Congress now relies on the recommendation of the Secretary of the Interior in acknowledging tribes, employing an agency established in 1978, now known as the Branch of Acknowledgement and Research (BAR), to help in determining eligibility (Quinn 1992).

Congress has never defined the term *tribe* or proscribed the rules governing federal recognition (Slagle 1994:195), although the BAR has attempted this. In fact, the government first created a comprehensive list of tribes in 1979, 157 years after the establishment of the Bureau of Indian Affairs (BIA). The idea of recognizing a tribe initially referred to "knowing" or realizing a tribe's existence; later, it referred to the creation of a jurisdiction and formal, legal recognition (Quinn 1992:38–39). As far back as the nineteenth century, particular tribes were designated as such for particular purposes, leading to the awkward circumstances in which groups were tribes for some purposes but not others (Quinn 1992:43). Meanwhile, some federal statutes apply to tribes with federal recognition only, whereas others apply to Indian persons (Ruby and Brown 2001:176).

However, the U.S. Supreme Court has ruled that the federal government has a trust responsibility to federal tribes and that once recognized as a tribe by treating it as sovereign, a presumption arises that the federal recognition continues, despite any changes in the nature of the tribe. Congress, however, can and has decided to remove tribes from the trust relationship and federal recognition (Slagle 1994:196). Although the federal government espouses a policy of recognition of sovereignty, this is tied to the repudiation of recognition of small, obscure tribes whose land and other claims are thought finalized and whose population is thought to be extinct or too small for viability.

Morris (1988) concluded that after several unsuccessful efforts to reduce the budget for federal programs, the Reagan administration attempted to reduce the number of Indian people who might qualify for programs. Morris wrote, "To date, every conceivable criteria—blood quantum, tribal enrollment, personal and family income, employment, even education—has been used by the [U.S.] Administration to deny Indians access to federal programs" (Morris 1988:734). These methods became ways of terminating the content of the federal trust relationship, if not the relationship itself. All of these forms of governance by the state pit group against group and reduce the number of claimant groups and claimant individuals thought to be encumbering the federal system.

Federal Recognition and the Lost Tribes

In September of 1978, the BIA created the Federal Acknowledgement Project within the Division of Tribal Government Services for the purpose of evaluating petitions for recognition. In 1981, the project became a branch within the division and was renamed the Branch of Federal Acknowledgement. The project was merged in 1984 with the Branch of Tribal Services and renamed yet again, this time as the BAR, its current name (Quinn 1992:58). Today, those tribes engaging in the effort to become federally recognized must enter an "unforgiving and Byzantine acknowledgement process" (Field 1999:195) run by a team of BAR anthropologists, historians, and genealogists.

The success of the civil rights movement of the 1960s and the heightened politicization of Indigenous communities in the 1970s contributed to a reopening of the issue of the treatment of both minorities and Indigenous peoples in the United States. A 1975 federal court ruling in the case of *United States v. Washington* held that treaty language entitled the Indigenous peoples of Washington to half of the salmon catch in Puget Sound and adjacent waters. The decision held in favor of the rights of unrecognized groups with respect to provisions in treaties. As a consequence, the landless, unrecognized tribes in the state of Washington acted to be included in the landmark decision and a quick process permitted the inclusion of a few tribes onto the federal rolls. Other tribes were not able to establish eligibility and became more effectively excluded from a relationship with the federal government.

There were many other developments for unrecognized peoples in the period. In 1975, the Passamaquoddy and Penobscot peoples of Maine successfully claimed wrongful termination of recognition as tribes and seizure of their lands by the government of the state. The tribes argued that under the federal Trade and Intercourse Acts of 1790 and 1793, lands could not be alienated from Indigenous peoples by any entity other than the federal government. The Mashpee Wampanoags of Massachusetts, however, were unsuccessful in their suit filed in 1975, although their case, too, argued for a new means to proceed (see *Mashpee Tribe v. New Seabury Corp.*, 1979). Eventually, tribes throughout the country, but especially in the Southeast and Northwest, sought recognition.

By the mid-1970s, then, pressure mounted on the BIA to establish a clear, unified process for evaluating tribes' demands for recognition in the absence of any single definition. The American Indian Policy Review Commission (1977), established by Congress, observed in its report that

> inconsistencies and oversights in the Indian policy of the United States are exposed by one stark statistic: There are more than 400 tribes within the Nation's boundaries and the Bureau of Indian Affairs services only 289. In excess of 100,000 Indians, members of "unrecognized" tribes, are excluded from the protection and privileges of the Federal-Indian relationship…There is no legal basis for withholding general services from Indians, with the sole exception of specific termination acts. (1977:461)

This report provides statistics that show approximately 133 unrecognized Indian communities, of which 76 provided population figures showing a figure in excess of 111,728. At least 23 of the communities held land, although the federal government did not provide protections under Indian law; 37 of the communities had formal treaty relations with governments predating the creation of the United States; at least 29 had U.S. treaty rights derived from obligations the United States assumed from the colonial period or from treaties signed by the United States; at least 25 had been mentioned in BIA records and "are familiar to the United States as tribes of Indians" (American Indian Policy Review Commission 1976:467).

The policy of explicitly and publicly, as opposed to tacitly, refusing to recognize particular tribes, the American Indian Policy Review Commission's (1977) report notes, is recent and gained support during the period of congressional termination (1954 to 1962): "The BIA appears to have believed that since termination was the new policy Congress would not want to acknowledge the special relationship to other tribes" (1976:463).

The new recognition process was established in 1978 under Part 83 of Title 25 of the Code of Federal Regulations (Slagle 1989:325). In effect, the practices are administrative rather than the result of legislation. The conceptual foundation was derived from the landmark legal text, the *Handbook of Federal Indian Law*, by Felix Cohen (1942). BAR criteria consequently reflects what tribes have come to be thought to be during the long history of relations with the federal government and its predecessors. The BAR criteria conform to the idea that tribes must fit within an administrative framework and consequently must be geographically bounded and politically centralized to be easily serviced and regulated. The BAR (1988) put it in these terms:

> Early Supreme Court decisions determining whether a tribe was recognized or not said that Indian tribes were recognized because of actions of Congress or the executive department, actions which were based on how an Indian group was dealt with by individuals, or agencies outside of the group. These actions included the existence of a treaty between the group and the Federal Government, the existence of a reservation, the existence of congressional legislation dealing with the group, and the establishment of an Indian agency for the group.

> Court decisions also considered tribal recognition in terms of the internal character of an Indian group. The most important of these decisions was <u>Montoya v U.S.</u> (1901) [180 U.S. 261, 268] that stated a working definition of an Indian tribe as:

> - composed of Native Americans of common ancestry
> - united in a community with a single leadership or government
> - presently inhabiting or having historically inhabited a particular territory.

The 1913 case of *United States v. Sandoval* provided that the community must be identified as such (BAR 1988:7). The regulations were revised in 1994 but have not gone beyond this ethnocentric 1901 *Montoya* interpretation of how to determine who Native Americans are.

Government Criteria for Recognition

The BIA (1978) regulations established seven tests for achieving recognition:

1. establish that they have been identified from historical times to the present on a substantially continuous basis as "American Indian" or "aboriginal"
2. establish that a substantial portion of the group inhabits a specific area or lives in a community viewed as American Indian and distinct from other populations in the area, and that its members are descendants of an Indian tribe that historically inhabited a specific area
3. furnish a statement of fact which establishes that the group has maintained political influence or other authority over its members as an autonomous entity throughout history until the present
4. furnish a copy of the group's present governing document, or in the absence of such a written document, a statement describing in full the membership criteria and the procedures through which the group currently governs its affairs and its members
5. furnish a list of all known current members of the group and a copy of each available former list of members based on the group's own defined membership criteria. The membership must consist of individuals who have established, using evidence acceptable to the Secretary of the Interior, descendancy from a tribe which existed historically or from historical tribes which combined and functioned as a single autonomous entity
6. establish that the membership of the group is composed principally of persons who are not members of any other North American Indian tribe
7. establish that neither the group nor its members are the subject of

congressional legislation which has expressly terminated or forbidden the Federal relationship.

As soon as these regulations were established, several problems became obvious to concerned parties. A significant problem was the applicability of the legal tests given the nature of Indigenous social organization. In effect, standards were created that cannot necessarily be met if a tribe was, in fact, Indigenous. Anthropologist Wayne Suttles addressed this issue in testimony before the Senate Select Committee on Indian Affairs in 1988; he observed that "agents of the government seem to be requiring western Washington Indians who seek recognition to produce evidence that the government's false assumptions about them are true" (*Federal Acknowledgement Process* 1988:1). These two false assumptions regarding western Washington Indigenous peoples are the image of chiefly authority and the image of the self-sufficient "little" society. Suttles noted, "Initially, agents of the United States government itself, in order to facilitate the transfer of title and establish legitimate relations with the Indians, helped create these false images" (1988:1), which they now use to undermine efforts at federal recognition.

Suttles (*Federal Acknowledgement Process* 1988) argued further that the Indigenes of western Washington were not organized into tribes ruled by a powerful chief prior to the treaty period. Leaders did not hold offices that gave them authority over anyone beyond their households or their villages prior to the 1840s and 1850s. The other false image is "that of a region peopled by wholly autonomous villages or tribes, each a self-contained, homogenous 'little community' or independent society" (*Federal Acknowledgement Process* 1988:4). Suttles observed that these ideas seem to be the image of the tribe employed by the Federal Acknowledgement Program (later, the BAR), a view later confirmed in print by a BAR anthropologist, who noted, "The definition of tribe in the regulations …is derived from the case law…As such it reflects non-Indian concepts about 'tribe' which tend to imply a coherent, stable, solitary society with distinct political institutions and more or less uniform ancestry" (Roth 1988:21).

Requirements that an Indigenous group (which is the successor to nineteenth-century peoples) demonstrate the prior existence of a clearly bounded community with formal political leadership suitable to showing the "maintenance of political influence or other authority" reflects a Euroamerican view of political organization. And Indigenous peoples did not necessarily record evidence of their political processes in the middle of the nineteenth century.

But furthermore, Suttles (*Federal Acknowledgement Process* 1988) wrote that these images of tribes "also appeals to some anthropologists who like to pigeonhole peoples into categories like 'bands,' 'tribes,' and 'chiefdoms'"(p. 2). This description reveals yet another problem that has come to plague the BAR acknowledgement process. As tribes have attempted to move through the process of acknowledgement, most unsuccessfully, the stakes have gradually risen and the amount of evidence required has increased. Slagle, for example, noted the "peculiar difficulties" with the present tests and the increased evidentiary burden (Slagle 1989:327). The Federal Register (1994), in fact, indicates that some petitions are more than 20,000 pages long. As the standards of evidence become more and more daunting, Indigenous groups are forced further and further into the documentation of a past that never existed, as Suttles observed in his discussion of myths of chiefly and bounded societies. The very success of some communities in forcing its documentation of ancestral social organization into preestablished, Western-derived, ethnocentric concepts of prior Indigenous life pushes other communities to attempt to do this as well because they understand implicitly this will be required.

Miller and Boxberger (1994) drew attention to this dilemma in the mid-1990s, advancing Suttles's (*Federal Acknowledgement Process* 1988) argument that the social organizations of western Washington Indigenes in the early contact period were not chiefdoms. Daniel Boxberger and I attempted to dislodge misleading efforts to fit ethnohistorical materials into older, now-dated anthropological categories of bands, tribes, and chiefdoms, categories once developed to advance debates about understanding the relationships between environment and society and other intellectual problems of the 1950s and 1960s. We pointed to the problem for tribes trying to make the case that they were once bounded chiefdoms with centralized authority, not only for tribes making this argument in their submissions to the BAR but also for those following after whose documentation could be easily refuted. We drew the connections between the nature of BAR guidelines, the problem of escalating demands, and the heartfelt efforts made to try to fulfill BAR requirements by twisting the data. We believed, with Suttles, that BAR legal tests ought to recognize western Washington tribes, and tribes from other regions, in their own terms.

Other academics have pointed to the fundamental, albeit unwitting, appearance of ethnocentrism in the BAR process; scholars have pointed out that criteria overlook the fact that informal, as opposed to formal, leadership is rarely documented and that the BAR gives little weight to oral history not based on firsthand experience (see Miller 2003:80–84). Consequently, written documents, primarily produced by government officials, become the de facto means to prove political influence or authority in the obscure past. Notions of social control other than through hierarchical means, as Miller and Boxberger (1994) pointed out concerning Puget Sound, are overlooked. Those tribes that avoided contact with Whites, understanding the damage this would bring, by moving to swamps, hollows, or other inaccessible locations, were now put in a position of having to show evidence of formal, documented political authority (Beinart 1999:37).

Furthermore, the BAR process is tinged with an underlying ethnocentrism through its reliance on written documents that themselves rely on racist perspectives and racialized criteria. Anthropologist Jack Campisi noted, for example, that nineteenth-century censuses used in Louisiana recognition cases include racial categories that sometimes exclude Indigenous peoples as a separate entity by including them with "colored" (Beinart 1999:38). Furthermore, Greenbaum (1985, n.d.) wrote that because unrecognized tribes rarely have reservation land, they have intermingled with non-Indigenous peoples more than members of recognized tribes and, hence, the distinctiveness of their communities may be less apparent to outsiders. In addition, although the BAR tests do not consider blood quantum directly, the provision for being identified as Indian by the surrounding community is an obstacle for groups that do not appear to be phenotypically Indian, especially in southern states if they appear to be partially African American (Greenbaum 1985, n.d.:18). McCulloch and Wilkins (1995:370) observed that tribes' demands for recognition are more likely to succeed if they are considered legitimate by the general public as well as other tribes; this includes appearing in a way that the mainstream expects Indians to appear.

Developments in Canada

As I have suggested, the issues have developed rather differently in Canada during the past few decades. In 1830, the official British–Canadian policy was to encourage civilization and save Indians from a state of perceived barbarism. This effort met with resistance from Indians and Whites alike because the policy required the creation of reserves, where instructors (missionaries, teachers, and others) could work with Indian people. By 1850, legislators acted to protect Indians from intrusion by Whites and seizure of lands for nonpayment of debt. In Lower Canada, now known as Quebec, an early legislative effort was made to define Indians (Surtees 1988:89). There were four provisions in early legislation defining Indians:

First, All persons of Indian blood, reputed to belong to the particular Body or Tribe of Indians interested in such lands, and their descendants; Secondly, All persons intermarried with any such Indians and residing amongst them, and the descendants of all such persons; Thirdly, All persons residing among such Indians, whose parents on either side were or are Indians of such Body or Tribe, or entitled to be considered as such; Fourthly, All persons adopted in infancy by any such Indian, and residing in the Village or upon the lands of such Tribe or Body, and their descendants. (Frideres 1989:22)

In 1851, an amendment to this precedent-setting legislation provided that marriage to Indian men conferred status to nonstatus women, but marriage to Indian women did not provide status to in-marrying men. The British–Canadian approach in the middle of the nineteenth century, thus, favored a concept of Indian based on a mixture of biology (blood quantum), culture (Frideres 1989:3), gender, and residence. The legal categories of people were binary; one was assigned to either Indian or White society, including those of mixed ancestry. The situation on the ground was more complex, however.

By 1857, Canadian policy favored assimilation, in addition to the contradictory policy of isolation, to remove all distinctions between Indians and other Canadians. Assimilation was to be achieved by enfranchisement. After the creation of the Dominion of Canada in 1867, a new Indian Act of 1868 confirmed the principles of civilization and enfranchisement; changes to the definition of Indian omitted the blood quantum factor, which has become a hallmark of American policy (Frideres 1989:23), although the blood quantum criteria has not altogether disappeared. Instead, cultural and linguistic attributes and gender became associated with Indianness and Whiteness. Frideres (1989) noted that

if a person evidenced a certain way of life, he or she was designated Indian or white, although in everyday life having evidence of visible phenotypical traits of an Indian made it difficult to pass oneself off as a non-Indian. (Frideres 1989:23)

As western treaties were established in the late nineteenth century, people of mixed ancestry often "took treaty" and became Indians under the Indian Act of 1876, rather than declaring themselves non-Indian.

Since the late nineteenth century, there have been four Indigenous legal categories: status Indians, nonstatus Indians, Inuit, and Métis. With time, the category of status Indian has come to have the most attention, with others diminishing in importance (Frideres 1989:24). The Indian Act of 1876, which consolidated earlier legislation, together with the establishment of official rolls of legally recognized (status) Indians, made it possible to clearly identify who was legally an Indian. In addition, any new criteria for establishing legal status could be applied to all those on the roll. Those who met the criteria could be retained and others dropped from the roll, and parents and offspring could be evaluated separately. Those struck from the roll were classified as nonstatus Indians, and they were neither Indians, Métis, nor White (Frideres 1989:23–24).

The concept of Indian became highly gendered and problematic for women, as in the earlier Lower Canada legislation. The Indian Act of 1876 specified in Section 12 (1)(b) that "a woman who married a person who is not an Indian" is therefore not entitled to registration. Nor would her children have status. However, children of White women who married status Indian men were eligible for status. In addition, on marriage, a woman lost her band status and became a member of her husband's band. A consequence of this provision was the administrative alienation of generations of women and their children from status as recognition.

Enfranchisement itself was also based on a gendered concept and a male ideal. Legislators perceived that men, rather than women, could lead the way to assimilation. The enfranchisement program was a failure and as a consequence, the federal government undertook a number of new attempts to erode Indian society and promote enfranchisement and assimilation. These included efforts to replace traditional leaders with elected tribal councils, the banning of religious ceremonies, the allocation of enfranchisement without consent (legislated in 1920, repealed in 1922), and the creation of a system of "location tickets." Men were granted deeds to portions of reserve land as private property, which then became alienated from collective holdings, as a way of eventually ending reserves altogether. After three years and the proper use of his land, a holder of a location ticket became enfranchised. Furthermore, Indigenous peoples from the 1920s to 1940s gave up their status to receive the right to go to school, vote, or drink. In addition, men who served in the armed forces in the two World Wars and other conflicts were enfranchised without consent and in some cases, land holdings removed from them (Steckley & Cummings 2001:123–125). The policy of enfranchisement was ended in 1985 with the passage of Bill C-31. The Indian Act was amended so that those who had given up status could regain it and so that it became impossible to give up status. In addition, provisions for the removal of Indian status of women marrying non-Indians were removed.

Today, culture, race, language, and gender are no longer the basis of definitions of *Indian*; it is now a legal category, and those who are culturally or ancestrally Indian but do not fall under the Indian Act are not legally Indians, even if accepted as such by Indigenous communities. The Canadian Constitution Act, passed in 1982, affirms existing Aboriginal and treaty rights and Section 32 states that all laws and policies in Canada must be consistent with these rights. Canadian policy and programming, however, runs counter to the constitutional requirements (Frideres 1989:367). The vague language of the Constitution Act does not easily clarify the circumstances of those whose rights are not clearly in existence, particularly those of nonrecognized bands.

There are now more than 600,000 registered Indians, although many more have Indian ancestry. Most of those registered are attached to a band in addition to being on the roll of Indians held in Ottawa, the national capital. There are some 27,000 who are registered Indians but have no band membership, and this figure gives some sense of the large but unknown number of still-unrecognized tribes. There are also some 10,000 who have band membership but are not registered (Frideres 1989:27). Definitions of *Indian, nonstatus, Métis,* and *Inuit* remain contested categories. The Canadian construction of Indian has also provided the means for aggregating diverse groups into a common category of Indian and thereby loosing groups and individuals, pruning the rolls of recognized Indigenous people, and reducing costs.

Meanwhile, unlike the United States, Canada has no explicit legal tests for the recognition of new Indigenous bands, although the Indian Act allows federal officials to amalgamate or divide already existing bands. Section 2 (1) of the Indian Act definitions specifies that bands can be declared into existence by government action. The real issue for Canadian officials is cost, rather than the ability to demonstrate continuity, authority over members, or the other tests of authenticity as in the U.S. case. The provisions for recognition for new bands remain directed at the fissioning of existing recognized bands, not the recognition of those previously unknown to the state. A special advisor (British Columbia) to the Minister of Indian Affairs and Northern Development put it this way:

> Under this policy, a group must essentially reach an agreement with an existing First Nation on the sharing of assets and liabilities…Any creation of a new First Nation should result in no additional funding requirements…I should explain that the policy on First Nation creation was formulated in response to the reality that

INAC [Indian and Northern Affairs Canada] does not receive additional funding from Parliament when it recognizes a new group as a "Band" within the meaning of the Indian Act. (K. Langlands, personal communication, June 22, 2001)

The Indian and Northern Affairs Canada (n.d.) policy chapter "Newly Constituted Bands," specifies that

the department may recommend for ministerial approval a request to form a newly constituted band (other than a band division) where the following criteria can be met: The members of the group requesting the formation of the new band are mainly status Indians comprising an existing, viable and ongoing community located at the site of the proposed reserve. (chap. 11.2.1.2)

In addition, the criteria include the acquisition of a land base, an environmental review, the identification of funding from within existing sources (with some exceptions "resourced on a case-by-case basis"), and assurances from territorial governments to cover service costs from the creation of a new base. Also, there must be consultation with either federal officials overseeing "specific claims" or "comprehensive claims" if a land claim is involved, an assessment of the impact on other federal government departments addressing third-party interests. Finally, there is a requirement to advise proposed new band members that they must sign statements of intent to become members.

The procedures for seeking recognition take six steps (Indian and Northern Affairs Canada, n.d., chap. 11.3); Step 1 is a formal request for recognition as a new band and Step 2 is a "regional analysis and recommendation." The third step is a "headquarters review," a review conducted in light of the criteria described above. This leads to the rejection or approval by the deputy minister, which is not in itself a binding commitment on the part of the government. Step 5, a "consultation with electorates," is a phase in which "relevant electorates must confirm agreement with the terms of the proposal." There is no requirement under the Indian Act for consultation, but a plebiscite may be conducted within the region. A membership list for the proposed new band is created prior to the vote. Alternatively, consultation with the relevant electorate may be carried out. The results of either a plebiscite or a consultation is conveyed to the headquarters. The final, sixth, step occurs once a land base is secured, approval of the affected electorate obtained, and other conditions met. Then, a ministerial order under Section 17 of the Indian Act creates the new band.

A policy issues analyst at the Department of Indian Affairs in Vancouver, D. Denomy, observed that he and others he had consulted knew of no cases of bands becoming recognized if not already part of an existing band (personal communication, May 8, 2001). Denomy noted that Indigenous groups such as the Hwlitsum of British Columbia might seek to use political processes outside of the Indian Act; although the federal government is developing new policy, this will not likely contain provisions for the process of recognition.

Conclusion

The argument is commonly made that public policy regarding Indians in Canada lags behind that of the United States by a decade or two, but this may not be the case regarding nonrecognized communities. In this instance, although both federal governments act to reduce expenses for Aboriginal affairs by limiting the number of tribes/bands and recognized individuals, U.S. policy has more forthrightly accepted the fact that many groups have been wrongly denied status as Indigenous nations or communities. However, the U.S. response has been to create an agency that operates within a rigid set of regulations based on bad case law and ethnocentric understandings of the Aboriginal social organization and transmission of knowledge. Furthermore, the U.S. practice obscures the concern for federal expenditures. The Canadian side, for its part, openly acknowledges its concern for costs and has created a vague and frankly political procedure for recognition. As is so often the case with U.S. and Canadian policies and practices that appear quite different, the outcome is largely the same for Aboriginal people stuck without recognition. They face a long and difficult road to recognition, and the odds remain against them.

References Cited

American Indian Policy Review Commission. 1976. *Report on Terminated and Nonfederally Recognized Indians* (Task Force Ten: Final Report to the American Indian Policy Review Commission). Washington, D.C.: Government Printing Office.

———— 1977. *Final Report* (Vols. I & II). Washington, D.C.: Government Printing Office.

Beinart, P. 1999. Lost Tribes. *Lingua Franca*, 9(4):32–41.

Bill C-31. 1985. Act to Amend the Indian Act. R.S.C. c.32 (1st Supp.).

Branch of Acknowledgement and Research. 1988. *Overview of the Federal Acknowledgement Process* [Pamphlet]. Washington, D.C.: Bureau of Indian Affairs.

Bureau of Indian Affairs. 1978. *Guidelines for Preparing a Petition for Federal Acknowledgement as an Indian Tribe*. Washington, D.C.: Bureau of Indian Affairs.

Canadian Constitution Act. 1982. Schedule B (U.K.). Cherokee Nation v. Georgia, 30 U.S.C. 1 (1831).

Cohen, Felix. 1942. *Handbook of Federal Indian Law*. Albuquerque: University of New Mexico Press.

Federal Acknowledgement Process: Hearings before the Select Committee on Indian Affairs, Senate Oversight Hearing on Federal Acknowledgement Process, 100th Cong., 2nd Session (1988) (testimony of Wayne Suttles).

Federal Register. 1994. Volume 59, No. 38, 9291.

Field, L. 1999. Anthropologists and the "Unacknowledged Tribes" of California. *Current Anthropology*, 40(2):193–201

Frideres, J. 1989. *Aboriginal Peoples in Canada: Contemporary Conflicts*. Scarborough, ON: Prentice Hall.

General Allotment Act of 1887, 24 Stat. 338.

Greenbaum, S. 1985. In Search of Lost Tribes: Anthropology and the Federal Acknowledgement Process. *Human Organization*, 44(4):361–367.

Greenbaum, S. n.d. *In Search of Lost Tribes: Anthropology and the Federal Acknowledgement Process*. Unpublished manuscript.

Harmon, Alexandra. 1998. *Indians in the Making: Ethnic Relations and Indian Identities Around Puget Sound*. Berkeley: University of California Press.

Indian Act of 1868, 31 Vic. cap. 2.

Indian Act of 1876, 39 Vic. cap. 18.

Indian and Northern Affairs Canada. n.d. Newly Constituted Bands. In *New Bands/Band Amalgamation (NBBA), Lands Manual.* Available from http://www.anc-inac.gc.ca

Mashpee Tribe v. New Seabury Corp., 592 F.2d 575 (1979).

McCulloch, A. M., and Wilkins, D. 1995. Constructing Nations within States: The Quest for Federal Recognition by the Catawba and Lumbee Tribes. *American Indian Quarterly,* 19(3):361–390.

Miller, Bruce G. 1991. The Forgotten Indians and Federal Recognition. *Friends Journal,* 37(9): 22–24.

———— 2003. *Invisible Indigenes: The Politics of Nonrecognition.* Lincoln: University of Nebraska Press.

Miller, Bruce G., and Daniel L. Boxberger. 1994. Creating Chiefdoms: The Puget Sound Case. *Ethnohistory,* 41(2):267–293.

Morris, C. 1988. Termination by Accountants: The Reagan Indian Policy. *Policy Studies Journal,* 16(4):731–750.

Quinn, W., Jr. 1992. Federal Acknowledgement of American Indian Tribes: Authority, Judicial Interposition, and 25 C.F.R. 83. *American Indian Law Review,* 17(1):37–69.

Roth, G. 1988. Comment in Reply: Dialogue on Federal Acknowledgment of Indian Tribes. *Practicing Anthropologist,* 10(2):21–22.

Ruby, Robert H., and John A. Brown. 2001. *Esther Ross: Stillaguamish Champion.* Norman: University of Oklahoma Press.

Sider, Gerald. 1993. *Lumbee Indian Histories: Race, Ethnicity, and Indian Identity in the Southern United States.* Cambridge, UK: Cambridge University Press.

Slagle, A. 1989. Unfinished Justice: Completing the Restoration and Acknowledgement of California Indian Tribes. *American Indian Quarterly,* 13(4):325–346.

———— 1994. Branch of Acknowledgement and Research. In *Native America in the Twentieth Century: An Encyclopedia,* edited by M. B. Davis, pp. 195–196. New York: Garland.

Steckley, J., and B. Cummings. 2001. *Full Circle: Canada's First Nations.* Toronto, ON: Prentice Hall.

Surtees, R. 1988. Canadian Indian Policies. In *Handbook of North American Indians,* Vol. 4: *History of Indian-White Relations,* edited by W. E. Washburn, pp. 81–95. Washington, D.C.: Smithsonian Institution.

United States v. Sandoval, 231 U.S. 28 (1913).

United States v. Washington, 520 F.2d 676 (9th Cir. 1975). Wheeler-Howard Act of 1934, 48 Stat. 984-986.

Journal of Northwest Anthropology, Memoir 12:317–324 (2016)

22

After the F.A.P.: Tribal Reorganization after Federal Recognition[*]

In an article appearing in the late 1970s, Nancy Lurie wrote of the difficulties facing contemporary Indian tribes in maintaining political unity:

> Informed observers of the American Indian scene…are aware of an apparently irresistible urge of Indian groups to defeat themselves just at the point when unified efforts have brought desired goals within their grasp. Once the outside opposition to Indian objectives is on the run, unity begins to crumble… Perhaps there are more communities than we know which are quietly and peacefully managing their affairs… Unfortunately we do not hear about them. (Lurie 1979:325)

For a number of Indian tribes, the most important goal in the 1970s and 1980s has been the achievement of official status as a tribe in the eyes of the federal government. In 1978 a specific program was developed (the Federal Acknowledgement Project or FAP) to rule on the petitions of Indian communities seeking to be recognized. The Bureau of Indian Affairs reported that 100 groups had petitioned for acknowledgement as of August, 1985, and that as many as 150 petitions may be filed eventually (BIA Publications n.d.). Barsh (1988:20) reported that as of mid-1988, eight petitions have been approved from over 100 applicants. In addition to these tribes, several others obtained recognition in the early 1970s as part of the landmark Washington State "Boldt" fishing decision (Cohen 1986).

In light of the considerable interest in the controversial FAP process (see for example Hajda and Roth, letters to the *Anthropology Newsletter*, 10 (2) 1988: Suttles, testimony before the Senate Select Subcommittee on Indian Affairs, March 26, 1988, or the associated issue of ethnic identity and tribal recognition, Clifford 1988), and in light of Luries's comments on the difficulties Indian communities face when outside obstacles have been overcome, I ask: what happens to Indian tribes that succeed in achieving recognition? Are they subject to "apparently irresistible urges" to defeat themselves just as they have achieved their goal of self-government and have become eligible for benefits such as health care within the Indian Health Service? Or, are there examples of successful adaptations to the new circumstances brought by acknowledgement? Just what does acknowledgement bring to a tribe?

To answer these questions I use data obtained during two years of field work, 1986–1988, with the Upper Skagit Indian Tribe, Sedro-Woolley, in western Washington. The Upper Skagits were among the tribes recognized in 1973, and for fifteen years their community has been adjusting to the resultant changes. While the period since 1973 has been difficult, Upper Skagit is indeed a post-FAP success story. Today this Coast Salish tribe has about 515 enrolled members, and the Upper Skagits have developed resources and an infrastructure of agencies to meet community needs. There is a council with fairly broad representation, a 74-acre reservation with 50 HUD homes, health and social services, and a tribal enterprise system that employs a number of tribal members and is likely to employ more in the future. These positive developments are supported by community values which have largely held factionalism in check. Cultural practices have been restored which had lapsed or had been practiced only in association with other tribes.

[*]Authored by Bruce Granville Miller and previously published in *Journal of Ethnic Studies*, 17(2):89–100 (1989).

Upper Skagits Before Acknowledgement

Upper Skagits have traditionally lived all along a hundred mile stretch of the banks of the Skagit Riber and in adjacent areas. Although the Upper Skagits were party to a treaty with the U.S. in 1855, an impassable two mile-long bog boom delayed White settlement in most of the Upper Skagit territory until the 1880s (Collins 1974). Few of the Upper Skagits moved to the several nearby reservations in western Washington; instead many preferred to avoid White contact and moved up the Skagit Valley to take allotments under the terms of the federal Homestead and Allotment Act of 1862 and the Indian Homestead Act of 1884 (Roblin 1916:3). By 1917 most of the allotments had been cancelled (Boxberger 1987:14) and shortly thereafter Upper Skagits moved into White areas. Gradually the tribal members dispersed after it became hard to make a living in the Skagit Valley largely because of State regulation of fishing on the Skagit River. Consequently, by the 1950s the frequent contact between tribal members living along the river, which characterized the nineteenth and early twentieth centuries, had disappeared. With the exception of the several small pockets of tribal members who still remained in the valley, contact between tribal members was sporadic. The remaining tribal activities included annual gatherings and religious services at the Shaker Church located in the town of Concrete. The tribal government was left with little authority over members, had few resources, and narrowly focused on the issues of the restoration of treaty fishing rights and on obtaining compensation for lands taken by the federal government under the terms of the treaty. Nevertheless, resistance to state fishing regulations and the issue of treaty rights gave Upper Skagits a common bond.

Postacknowledgement

After acknowledgement, the tribe obtained funds to rent headquarters in Burlington, Washington. While they sought land for new quarters, tribal members developed the apparatus of government. A council was established in 1974, with 7 members, each elected for staggered 3-year terms. A tribal court system was established, and the tribe entered in 1976 into a joint fisheries management and enhancement program (The Skagit System Cooperative) with two other tribes, the Swinomish and the Sauk-Suiattle. The tribe joined the Northwest Washington service unit of the Indian Health Service, and eventually a nurse-practitioner and other staff provided services on the reservation. Land was found for the reservation in Sedro-Woolley, and the houses were constructed there in 1982 with HUD money. These houses came under the direction of a newly created housing administration, CITHA (Cascade Inter-tribal Housing Authority), established along with the Sauk-Suiattle and Stillaguamish tribes.

These developments were on the surface, however, and deeper changes took place within the social system itself. The loosely affiliated families that compose the Upper Skagit Tribe were brought face-to-face in a manner unprecedented in their history. Never before had so many tribal members lived in such close proximity, nor had so many been directly involved in tribal affairs for several decades. The heightened contact created tension and antagonism between the constituent families as the ground rules were hammered out for the competition over the resources newly made available to the tribe.

Many of the struggles between Upper Skagit people after acknowledgement can be characterized as competition between universalistic (tribal-wide) and particularistic (family) interests. Upper Skagit society is bilateral and families are multi-household networks of kind who coalesce around those with leadership ability. Family members assist each other in daily life and form fishing cooperatives. Families range from almost 100 members and three generations of adult members living in a dozen or more households to twenty members of two generations living in four houses. For most, primary loyalty lay with the family, and only secondarily with the tribe. The development of the tribe, and access to the subsequent benefits available to the families, depended on some measure of tribal cohesion.

Initially, in the middle 1970s, families residing outside of the Skagit Valley prior to acknowledgement were opposed in their attempts to obtain treaty fishing rights by families that had remained in the valley. The returning families succeeded in gaining fishing rights, but in 1981 long-term residents of the Skagit Valley brought a petition demanding the recall of three tribal councilors who also held positions in the tribal administration. The charge was conflict of interest. Underlying the recall attempt was the competition between those families that had remained in the valley and newcomers who had gained political and administrative control of the tribe. The newcomers' attempts at establishing universally-applied standards for tribal employment and operations in order to meet federal regulations were misunderstood by those who thereby felt excluded from full participation in tribal decisions (and also felt unrecognized for their courageous efforts in the 1960s to protest state restraints on tribal fishing). Many perceived a threat to the old political system, under which an informal council largely composed of elders, and solely of men, operated on a consensual basis.

The recall petition failed to remove any of the three councilors, but the effort did produce a council resolution prohibiting simultaneously sitting on the council and serving as general manager. Moreover, the hiring authority was taken from the Council, and a separate committee was established for this purpose. These two actions served to redistribute authority within the community.

The initial effect of this recall election was divisive. Voting in the annual tribal elections diminished from 124 in 1981 to 56 in 1983. Many Upper Skagits report that they experienced a sense of disillusionment with their own new government. Simultaneously, one of the largest and most important families split apart as a corporate group following the death of the second of their two outstanding leaders. Many members of this family dropped out of active participation in tribal affairs and some left the area.

Over time, the wounds from the struggle have healed and a positive benefit has accrued. The failure of the recall established that universal standards of performance would prevail over strictly family interests in the administration of the tribe. Also, the separation created between the council and administration convinced many tribal members that a few people would not dominate the tribe. In effect, both sides gave ground for the common good. Gradually, participation in tribal affairs increased. In 1987, for example, 102 tribal members cast votes in the tribal election.

This competition between the families has helped create new community political values. Perhaps the most important of these is the emphasis on *balance* in office holding in several ways. Tribal members in 1988 nearly universally reported that they cast votes to avoid domination of the council by either or both of the two largest families. A balance has arisen between the sexes as well. While the earliest post-acknowledgement councils were predominately male, more recently women have been in the majority. The councils of 1975–1977 were composed of five men and two women. Since 1979 women have been in the majority, generally holding four seats to three male. The experience of 1984, in which women held six of the seven seats, has not been repeated.

While many tribal members report that they intentionally vote to create a balance, in part balance is the unintended outcome of the struggle between emphasis on tribal affairs (universalism) and family life (particularism). One simple way for tribal members to support tribal interests without hindering their own family interests is to vote for "neutral" candidates. Neutral candidates are those who are not members of a large family and frequently are people with technical skills useful in governance and administration. Tribal members, therefore, by voting for these neutral "technocrats" can, at one stroke: (1) diminish the control exercised by other families over the tribal council and resources, and (2) support someone with technical skills that are important to tribal operations.

The 1987 election illustrates the importance of balance and the nature of voting tactics. This election was unusual in that a coalition was temporarily created between families as the result of a struggle over fundamental community values. One of the large families split over the issue of support for a family member dismissed from his post in a multi-tribal operation. The performance of the family member is unclear, and in any case is not the issue. As Cohen (1981) demonstrated in his work on Sierra Leone, groups (in the Upper Skagit case, these constituent groups are families) must defend their own interests, but in such a way that it does not appear to other groups to be openly particularistic. Several members of the large Upper Skagit family accepted the dismissal of their family member, asserted the primacy of universalism and its critical importance to tribal unity (although not in those terms), and failed to help protect their family member's job. Other members supported this man, and were perceived by many community members as particularistic in doing so.

Subsequently the two segments of the family opposed each other in the tribal election, resulting in the defeat of a family member. Another eventually withdrew. The removal of these two avoided a majority of their family on the council. Later, a neutral candidate was appointed to fill a vacancy on the council, and the balance on the council was maintained both in sex and family composition.

The new political system has so far largely avoided the over-representation of any single family, of either sex, of fishermen, reservation residents, or any age group (Miller 1988). Councilors who are primarily supported by family members and who are expected to represent the families' interests on the council are balanced in numbers on the council by the technocrats. The primary characteristic of technocrats is post-high school education and experience in tribal administration. The Council of 1987, as an example, was composed of three technocrats, three traditional family leaders, and a neutral. In 1988, there were three traditional family leaders, two technocrats, and two neutrals. Such a council composition includes both those whose focus is on off-reservation concerns and who are effective in representing the tribe in dealing with regional and national bureaucracies (such as the BIA, IHS, various fishing agencies, police forces and social service agencies) and those who are less instrumental in orientation, who participate routinely in tribal ceremonial life and day-to-day reciprocity, and who are effective in directing and helping coalesce tribal opinion.

The council can also be characterized as relatively stable, especially through a useful defacto division of interests. A small set of councilors has been repeatedly elected and has developed special expertise or interests. In addition, although they are members of several families, these long-term councilors have learned to work together despite earlier bitter rivalries. The 1987 council, for example, contained five members who had served at least three terms. One had a special interest in social services, another was an expert in fisheries management, a third was a voice of the long time valley residents and of traditional cultural practice, a fourth was a fisherman who operated the tribal wood shop, and a fifth was an advocate of education.

Cultural Life

So far, my focus has been on the evolution of tribal leadership and the tribal council since federal acknowledgement in 1973. The changes in the lives of average Upper Skagits have been equally significant. Perhaps the most important of these changes have been in the cultural domain.

Collins (1974) provides the most comprehensive report of Upper Skagit culture in the period immediately before acknowledgement. A comparison of her work and the present-day accounts of tribal members illustrates the degree to which common residence on the reservation after acknowledgement has influenced cultural life. The creation of the reservation is not the only force acting on Upper Skagit cultural life, and there have been restorations of traditional practice at other Puget Sound tribes in the last several decades. In the Upper Skagit case, however, for the first time in many years there has been the critical mass necessary to hold cultural events which had waned during the years of dispersal.

Collins noted (1974:240): "In 1969, when I last visited the Upper Skagit, there had been a steady movement toward integration into White culture." This included assimilation through marriage, which broke down the traditional kinship practices (Collins 1974:241). Robbins' study (1980:21) of 44 Upper Skagit tribal members found "…of the 38 marriages…18 are matches between Indian people." Six of these were Upper Skagit couples. Robbins does not specify that these marriages occurred after the creation of the reservation, and likely most were not. By the 1986–1988 period, all the marriages of reservation members which came to my attention were exclusively with Indians, although not necessarily Upper Skagits. Partnerships were created with Navajos in two instances, with members of other Puget Sound tribes and with Upper Skagits.

While it is true that present-day kinship practices are not strictly traditional, the new proximity between tribal members allows tribal elders to advise reservation residents to avoid marriage to those who traditionally would have been ineligible. It is my impression that this practice of the discussion of kinship is considerably more frequent in the later 1980s than in the preceding decade. There are now ample opportunities for the public airing of the importance of kinship: elders and others bring up kinship and genealogy at the sporadic tribal dinners at the tribal center, and at the many ceremonial events that now occur on the reservation. In addition, the traditional emphasis on family has been reinforced through the new importance of families in the contemporary political process.

Collins noted by 1969 the diminishment of the practice of the potlatch, the taking of Indian names, and the disappearance of "power houses" where guardian spirit dances occur (1974:242). All three of these important cultural practices have received new life on the reservation. In 1985 a "smokehouse" ("power house" in Collins' term) was constructed and by the following year there was a great deal of participation by Upper Skagits in the winter ceremonials held inside. The 80' x 30' Smokehouse attracts large crowds, and for the first time since the 1940s, Upper Skagits are being taken into the *seowin* society at Upper Skagit. Loud drumming at the Smokehouse is a near nightly occurrence during the winter season, and the drumming is audible over the whole of the reservation. The actual practice of the winter ceremonials varies somewhat from tribe to tribe, and the gradual emergence of a distinctive Upper Skagit form makes the winter ceremonial an ethnic boundary marker. This clarification of boundaries is part of the development of cohesion within the tribe, and the Smokehouse draws participants and visitors from most Upper Skagit families. (See Amoss 1978 for a discussion of a similar circumstance at the nearby Nooksack Tribe.)

Potlatching too, is now more frequent. The distribution of gifts at funerals and memorials for family ancestors was common practice in the period from 1986–1988. Potlatching (or, as it is sometimes called, the "give-away") is now significant enough that in some cases the expenses have been several thousands for gifts alone. In other cases, funeral potlatching is less extravagant, but nevertheless, still present. Collins noted (1974:242) that "...the accumulation of property of a proper type for gift-giving had disappeared from many homes." By 1988, people once again actively planned for the staging of events which required gift-giving.

The naming ceremonies that Collins described (1974:243) as having completely disappeared by 1969, were restored by the late 1980s. Namings were still quite unusual in the early 1980s, with only one reported, but by the end of the decade several were planned each year. In several instances, families staged multiple namings, with names "brought out" for adults and children.

Other traditional aspects of cultural life were restored after acknowledgement. The practice of giving away or destroying the personal and many of the household effects of a deceased tribal member was restored on the reservation. At least one family has staged annual "first salmon" ceremonies, formerly an important element of ceremonial life. "Burnings," the practice of annual feasts for the spirits of the dead, were common in the late 1980s, apparently through the influence of reservation residents from neighboring tribes.

In 1988, tribal members began the construction of a massive canoe shed and of canoes for participation in the inter-tribal canoe races. Upper Skagit participation in these races had not occurred since a few races in the early 1950s. Regular participation of Upper Skagit canoes in races had not occurred since the 1930s.

In addition to reviving old activities, acknowledgement has also brought new social activities for Upper Skagits. Group events are frequently held at the tribal center, including religious events, seasonal dinners, and meetings of veterans. Baseball, softball, and basketball teams are now sponsored by the tribe.

Problems Facing the Tribe

Political and cultural successes are not the whole story. Robbins (1986) documented the difficulties facing the Upper Skagit government as an IRA (Indian Reorganization Act) government; that is since their federal acknowledgement. He wrote:

> The Upper Skagit tribal government is experiencing great difficulties. Much of the time spent by elected leaders and tribal employees (often the same people) is used to seek grants and contracts...The Tribe badly needs expertise, consistent long-term planning, and more control over funds and policies and there does not seem to be a solution to this problem. (Robbins 1986:64)

> The Upper Skagit tribe has been bewildered by contradictory guidelines that rain down on them from above; they simply cannot keep up with sudden changes in directions and policies from federal offices. They much prefer funding allotments that would allow them to sustain a staff that could count on funds and that would have essential control over those monies. (Robbins 1986:65)

The problems Robbins mentions had not disappeared by 1988. Problems in obtaining reliable and adequate funding for tribal programs have made it difficult to find and retain employees. For example, the position of tribal early childhood education teacher went unfilled for several months in 1987 pending the outcome of grant applications. Low salaries have contributed to a rapid turn-over in the tribal police force and made staffing the tribal health facility a cause of concern for tribal leadership. The turnovers in staff, inadequate staffing, and vacancies which leave programs out of operation for a time, slow the growth of trust in individual staff members and inhibit confidence in the ability of the tribal administration to provide useful services. Tribal members have not yet overcome the attitudes produced by years of powerless and the attacks on their livelihood (especially fishing) by the state. Such attitudes are now directed towards their own government, a point noted by Robbins (1986). This feeling of detachment from government is not yet overcome. For these reasons many tribal members remain frustrated by the difficulties in obtaining services. Other programs appear out of sync with the interests of tribal members, are poorly explained to the community, or are operated by non-tribal staff who have not achieved community trust. Programs such as the 1988 Displaced Homemakers Program and the high school equivalency training (GED) have drawn few interested participants.

In 1988 the staff was chronically short of personnel, and this has made it difficult for the tribal management to communicate adequately with the tribal community. The tribal newsletter was an early casualty of understaffing (the last edition was June 1987), and no other vehicle for spreading news remains other than special mailings to tribal members, leafletting the 50 HUD homes on the reservation, and the informal grapevine. Difficulties in communication exacerbated existing frustrations and unhappiness over the poor salmon catch. For example, in the summer of 1988, tribal members brought a petition calling for the removal of the tribal Fisheries Manager and the Fisheries Committee.

Conclusion

As Robbins has pointed out, the problems facing the tribal government will not be easily overcome. However, the Upper Skagits have achieved notable successes. The new organization of the tribe has allowed the representation of tribal interests in several important issues. In the early 1970s a nuclear power plant was proposed for the Skagit Valley (the Skagit Plant). Although the tribe was initially disallowed as an independent intervenor, tribal resistance to the project was an important force in successfully resisting the project. The Upper Skagit Tribe, along with other members of the multi-tribal Skagit Systems Cooperative, contracted for an independent assessment of the plants' potential impact on their lives (Robbins 1979).

Acknowledgement of the tribe has also allowed the Upper Skagit to protect their own interests in the treaty salmon fishery of Western Washington, and in off-reservation treaty hunting. Non-acknowledged tribes, such as the nearby Samish, are left out of this process.

A former Upper Skagit Chairman described the effects that acknowledgement, and the accompanying restoration of treaty fishing rights under the Boldt decision, has had:

> Decades of decay in many Indian communities have given succeeding generations fewer reasons to follow the traditions and to remain active in tribal society…In years past, most talented Indian people left the reservations. Driven away by the lack of jobs or a future, they fled to opportunities in the cities. Their exodus sapped strength from the reservations…Following the 1974 decision, many young Indian people returned to their tribes at first only to fish. But now they stay on because they see renewed activity in their tribal communities ….Those willing to learn have found new opportunities, training, and employment…. (Fernando 1986:xxiv)

The Upper Skagit case is one in which divisive factionalism has not torn apart the community after success in reaching the goal of federal recognition (and the subsequent attainment of restored fishing rights and the establishment of a reservation). To the contrary, community norms have developed which facilitate tribal cohesion and which hold the centrifugal force of the family system in check. The Upper Skagit people are now in a position to respond to challenges to their livelihood and way of life in a way that was impossible before the acknowledgement process.

References Cited

Amoss, Pamela. 1978. *Coast Salish Spirit Dancing: The Survival of an Ancestral Religion.* Seattle: University of Washington Press.

Barsh, Russel Lawrence. 1988. A Challenge for Anthropologists. PA Comment. Dialogue on Federal Acknowledgement of Indian Tribes. *Practicing Anthropologist*, 10(2):20–21.

Bureau of Indian Affairs. n.d. Information About Acknowledgement. Pamphlet.

Clifford, James. 1988. *The Predicament of Culture.* Cambridge: Harvard University Press.

Cohen, Abner. 1981. *The Politics of Elite Culture: Explorations in the Dramaturgy of Power in an African Society.* Berkeley: University of California Press.

Cohen, Fay G. 1986. *Treaties on Trial: The Continuing Controversy Over Northwest Indian Fishing Rights.* Seattle: University of Washington Press.

Collins, June McCormick. 1974. *Valley of the Spirits: The Upper Skagit Indians of Western Washington.* Seattle: University of Washington Press.

Fernando, Andres. 1986. Introduction. In *Treaties on Trial*, edited by Fay G. Cohen, pp. xv–xxvi. Seattle: University of Washington Press.

Hajda, Yvonne and Russel L. Barsh. 1988. Correspondence. *Anthropology Newsletter*, 29(3):2.

Lurie, Nancy Oestreich. 1979. The Will-o'-the Wisp of Indian Unity. In *Currents in Anthropology: Essays in Honor of Sol Tax*, edited by Robert Hinshaw, pp. 325–35. The Hague: Mouton Publishers.

Miller, Bruce G. 1988. A Sociological Explanation of the Election of Women to Formal Office: The Upper Skagit Case. (Ms.).

Robbins, Lynn Arnold. 1979. Cultural Impact Assessment. Ms. in possession of Upper Skagit Tribe.

——— 1980. Upper Skagit Fishing Households: Location, Composition and Multiple- Family Cooperation. (Ms.).

——— 1986. Upper Skagit (Washington) and Gambell (Alaska) Indian Reorganization Act Government: Struggles with Constraints, Restraints and Power. *American Indian Culture and Research Journal*, 10(2):61–73.

Roth, George. 1988. Correspondence. *Anthropology Newsletter*, 29(3):2.

——— 1988. PA Comments. Dialogue on Federal Acknowledgement of Indian Tribes. *Practicing Anthropologist*, 10(2):21–22.

Suttles, Wayne. 1988. Testimony of Wayne Suttles, Ph.D., Professor Emeritus, Portland State University, Before the Senate Select Committee on Indian Affairs. May 26.

Part VIII
Evidence Rules and Oral History

A landmark Canadian Supreme Court decision, *Delgamuukw*, 1997, held that oral histories should have the same footing in law as written histories. But how can this be done? This was the topic of my 2011 book, *Oral History on Trial: Recognizing Aboriginal Narratives in the Courts*. In Chapter 23, *The Oral and the Written in Understanding Treaties,* I use examples from among Coast Salish oral historians, and building on my own work as an expert witness on oral materials in Canadian courts, show the grounds on which oral traditions/histories can fit within the Common Law system. In addition, I argue that the so-called Douglas Treaties with Coast Salish of Vancouver Island should be considered oral rather than primarily written treaties.

Figure 18. Upper Skagit Blessing of the Fleet on the Skagit River in 2014.

Journal of Northwest Anthropology, Memoir 12:326–337 (2016)

23

The Oral and the Written in Understanding Treaties*

The Vancouver Island treaties are often referred to as the "Douglas" treaties, named for Governor James Douglas who negotiated fourteen treaties with First Nations leaders on Vancouver Island from 1850 to 1854. These treaties were the subject of the Vancouver Islands Treaties Conference held at Vancouver Island University in 2012. Panelists were asked to address several questions, including how to honour the spirit and intent of the Pre-Confederation Treaties of Vancouver Island and address the challenges of treaty interpretation. I concern myself here with the issue of how to determine the spirit of the treaties and to implement them.

The case has been made that thinking transnationally is important to understanding how people move through time and space, challenging and transforming the claims of the nation-state in various ways. Historian Alexandra Harmon (2008:12) advises that the study of the treaties negotiated with Coast Salish peoples on both sides of the international border should be undertaken with this in mind. She writes, "Histories illuminating the nature and origins of such things as ethnic groups, technologies of power, and subaltern responses to colonialism testify to the value of looking across international borders." Further, she notes that some contemporary American and Canadian tribes "dealt with more than one government" and that well into the nineteen century, the British continued their colonial activities in places, including Washington Territory, that would become part of the United States (Harmon 2008:11). And Harmon draws on unpublished work of Canadian legal historian John Borrows, who, she writes, cites "numerous reasons to consider Canadian and U.S treaty making in tandem—reasons beyond the fact that the two nations share some historical roots, a language, and an English legal heritage" (Harmon 2008:15). These reasons include the fact that the treaties in the two countries served the same purposes of enabling settlers to colonize and develop large areas of land while assuring Aboriginal people of home sites and access to resources. But further, information and relations crossed the international border. Harmon writes,

> The first governor of the colonies that became British Columbia negotiated fourteen recorded treaties with Aboriginal inhabitants beginning in 1850 and ending in December 1854, the same month that Isaac Stevens called his first treaty council. Like Stevens, Governor James Douglas was dealing with people from whom his compatriots and fur-trader colleagues in the area obtained food, labor, and other vital services. Because the international boundary bisected indigenous homelands and extensive kinship networks, the two men even treated with some of the same tribal groups and individuals. (Harmon 2008:15)

In addition to these arguments, I add that all of the Coast Salish peoples faced the same predicament at the time of the nineteenth century treaties with the colonizers. The world of the Coast Salish people, those whose homelands are in what is now British Columbia and western Washington State, was thrown into desperate turmoil by the middle of the nineteenth century. Repeated epidemic reduced the population and violent conflict threatened their security. In the midst of these changes, Coast Salish communities of Vancouver Island participated in the creation

*Authored by Bruce Granville Miller in 2015.

of a series of agreements with a representative of the British Crown that have come to have the status of treaties.

These agreements are unusual in that they were not written at the time of the meetings, and hence have both oral and, later, written versions. These oral versions have not been given their due and in the honorable implementation of these treaties the oral traditions must, arguably, be given far more consideration. To make sense of the treaties, and the oral histories associated with them, as Harmon and Borrows suggest, I set them in an historic and comparative frame, looking at treaty making in the adjacent Washington territory. In arguing that the oral and the written evolve together through the courts, I examine recent developments in the Canadian legal system regarding how oral histories might be understood. Finally, in the interest of creating space for these oral materials, and in showing that there is a long tradition of doing so, I point to earlier traditions of interplay between the oral and written.

For Coast Salish peoples, the mid-nineteenth century was far more violent and disruptive than is commonly perceived. Schaepe (n.d.) found warfare to be underrepresented in the anthropological literature for the region overall, but especially so for the south coast. He explicitly discussed this passive representation of Coast Salish as a reflecting "lingering colonial and anthropological misrepresentation of these societies, Coast Salish particularly, as passive peoples who 'fight with food' rather than weapons." (Angelbeck n.d.:1). Jay Miller writes,

> Military aspects of the Coast Salish have long been disparaged and are currently being suppressed in public contexts. Often viewed as marginal victims and unprepared fighters, Coast Salish instead relied on famous warriors (war lords) and their forts to provide safety from raids and slaving. (2011:71)

But a string of disastrous epidemics of smallpox, measles, and other diseases, beginning in the late eighteenth century had reduced the population dramatically, leaving some regions vacant and thereby encouraging the movement of groups to new territories (see Sampson 1972; Boyd 1994). Anthropologist Robert Boyd (1994:16) noted the observations of Peter Puget, a lieutenant-in-command of *Chatham*, of the British Navy expedition sent in the 1790s to create a detailed survey of the Pacific North American coast from the Columbia River to Alaska: In a summary statement on the Indians of Puget Sound and the Strait of Georgia, Peter Puget stated: "the Small pox most have had and most terribly pitted they are; indeed, many have lost their eyes . . ."

Boyd (1999:166) gives an example of devastation from disease, in this case the significant presence of smallpox, likely in 1853, among the aboriginal Swinomish of northern Puget Sound. He cites field notes from anthropologist Wayne Suttles (1948) with his informant Peter Charles, who said that the village at Swinomish Slough was wiped out except for a Swinomish prophet (Indian doctor) and his extended family. Anthropologist June Collins (1980:7) writes "all or nearly all of the Upper Skagit villages (except those on the Sauk) were burned deliberately by their Indian owners during the smallpox epidemic in the last century and were permanently abandoned." Swinomish leader Martin Sampson (1972:25) mentions the deliberate abandonment of a village in Jarman's Pairie in Nuwhaha territory in the 1830s. Collins gave a graphic report of disease via her informant, Peter Fornsby. Fornsby told Collins:

> The Indians got smallpox from Nooksack. They had to look out. They got Nooksack sickness, smallpox. One old man went to Nooksack, helped a woman sick with smallpox. He got the sickness. They left him on a little island below

Mount Vernon. They left him there. He stayed there. My father used to hunt there. He used to go and talk to his relation. He used to holler, 'You alive yet?'

The old man hollered back, 'Yes, yes!'

When the first settler came into Utsaladdy, a doctor came in. My father and the rest of us were moving down to Camano. A White doctor called us into shore. I got vaccinated; all the kids got it. They vaccinated my right shoulder. I never got smallpox.

They got killed from smallpox at Skagit City. Lots of Indians got killed. At kikiálos, at Fir—they got killed there. Mr. Ball brought smallpox. He was a logger. He married an Indian woman, Mrs. Joe Lish; he stayed with the Indians. That is the way the Indians died. We traveled around in canoe, but we never got out. We were scared to get out and look. [Collins 1949:307]

The consequences of disease left groups vulnerable to attack by neighboring groups and by Aboriginal peoples from farther away. Anglebeck and McClain's (2011) research on the battle of Maple Bay in 1830s, a Vancouver Island location, between allied Coast Salish bands and northern Lekwiltok raiders, gives a good picture of the militarization and violence of the times. They write that the battle was a conflict involving "scores to hundreds of war canoes" (Angelbeck and McLay 2011:360).

In addition, their work shows the continuing presence of oral histories reaching back to the period before the establishment of the international border in 1846 and before the 1850s Vancouver Island treaties in Coast Salish communities. Many stories of the battle demonstrate remarkable consistency over generations (Angelbeck and McLay 2011:360), although the many accounts are each distinctive. In the Island Hul'qumi'num Coast Salish traditions, the oral traditions of the Battle at Maple Bay are known as *syuth*, or "true history," which Anglebeck and McLay note are distinguished from fables and moral tales or *sxwi'em* (Angelbeck and McLay 2011:367). Citing Bierwert's seminal 1999 work, Anglebeck and McLay emphasize that Coast Salish oral literature is decentralized and contains multiple versions. The multiple versions provide details of which other tellers were unaware and indicate "the way different individuals, families, and communities perceive, apply meaning, and retell the event in their own local history"(Angelbeck and McLay 2011:368).

Both Roberts (1975), writing about Puget Sound and Arnett (1999, 2007), describing the Gulf of Georgia, show another side of the disruption, namely the use of Indian doctors to defend corporate family units against outsiders, including other Coast Salish families. But in addition, armed violence between U.S. forces and tribes over the mountains from the Coast Salish, and briefly in the fledgling city of Seattle, was underway. Coast Salish people of both Washington state and British Columbia were well aware of these conflicts (Foster and Grove 2008:94) and, for the most part, chose not to participate, even though many had relatives over the mountains and in the interior, areas engaged in fighting between settlers and Indigenous groups. There were exceptions, however, and some Coast Salish warriors, intent on directly resisting colonization, may have been pushed out of their home communities and aggregated in the few communities which wished to stand in opposition. Anthropologist Jay Miller (2011:77) notes that historically, "Coast Salish combat relied not on soldiers nor armies but rather on champions who took on war lord status when they mobilized labor to build and maintain fortified locations or fort to protect their community." It is these warriors who worried colonial authorities and who were pushed out of their communities by village headmen. Examples of communities which aggregated such powerful men include the Lamalchi people of Kuper Island, who repulsed the British Navy in 1863 with gun fire, killing a crew member, some days before being were shelled (Miller et al. 2013), and Leschi and his allies in southern Puget Sound (Blee 2014).

Yet still other communities did not engage in military opposition, particularly away from their territories, but did so sporadically in repulsing surveyors (an example is the Upper Skagit; Collins 1974). Some of these groups avoided contact with newcomers, moving into the mountains—including some bands of Skagit and Sauk-Suiattle. These groups either did not sign treaties or sent only secondary men to the treaty meetings. In short, Coast Salish communities faced the choice of military engagement with the colonizers in various ways, or negotiating the terms of their mutual residence in the Coast Salish territories.

Throughout all of this, officials of Great Britain, and after 1867, Canada, and the United States were in close contact, both as representatives of their governments and as individuals (Foster and Grove 2008:104, 111; Harmon 2008:16). British Columbia Governor Douglas, who had once lived in Oregon Territory and served as a judge there, made a personal loan to Isaac Stevens, the governor of Washington Territory, during the so-called Indian Wars. A letter of January 29, 1859 from the President of the United States, James Buchanan, to U.S. federal politicians shows the intimacy of this arrangement, and the considerable fear of violent retaliation by Aboriginal people opposed to the official and unofficial forces of colonization:

> To the Senate and House of Representatives:
>
> I transmit a report from the Secretary of War, with the accompanying documents, recommending the repayment to Governor Douglas, of Vancouver's Island, of the sum of $7,000 advanced by him to Governor Steven of Washington Territory, which was applied to the purchase of ammunition and subsistence stores for the forces of the United State in time of need and at a critical period of the late Indian war in that Territory. As this advance was made by Governor Douglas out of his own private means, and from friendly motives towards the United States, I recommend that an appropriation may be made for its immediate payment, with interest.
>
> Washington, January 29, 1859 (Buchanan 1859).

The report Buchanan refers to contains ominous language and reveals why Governor Douglas was relied on: "Early in the year 1856 the available supplies near the scene of hostilities, on Puget's Sound, being nearly exhausted; the Territory being without funds, and all endeavors to obtain advances of money or goods from private sources having failed" (Buchanan 1859:2).

Duff's Analysis of Treaty: the Written and the Oral

The Douglas Treaties of 1850 to 1854 were created in this atmosphere of fear and disease, which culminated in some of the violence I have mentioned, and disorder on the edge of empire, and they are remarkable in the process by which they were created. The late University of British Columbia anthropologist Wilson Duff provides considerable insight into this process in his publication, *The Fort Victoria Treaties*, which appeared in *BC Studies* (1969). Duff's work reveals that what is most distinctive about the treaties is that the signatories, various Aboriginal leaders and community members, do not, collectively, appear to have signed documents with the text of the treaty written on them. The details vary by treaty, however, but the implications are the same. These treaties have both written forms and oral versions in the oral traditions held in the communities. For many reasons, some of which I consider here, both versions should be given weight in any legal or other proceeding.

It is not entirely novel that there be slippage in text between the time of the treaty meetings and the treaties themselves negotiated by agents of the colonial regimes and Aboriginal peoples. The Treaty of Point Elliott signed in 1855 between the United States and northern Puget Sound tribes, for example, may not have been well understood by signatories. There are in effect two oral versions: English and Chinook Jargon (a trade jargon), which was translated into the local Coast Salish languages. However, in this case, the leaders signed a document that actually contained the written English text of the treaty. (To be clear, there is some dispute concerning whether some leaders actually signed or had the document signed for them). Hence, in litigation arising from claims of treaty rights (or, more exactly, rights retained by tribes under the treaty) the written treaty can be understood as being the most significant legal article and considerable debate takes place around how this was understood by Indians at the time. There is no consideration of a separate, oral treaty, however. But I suggest that this is the case regarding the Douglas treaties, and that consideration be given to the nature of oral treaties.

To get at this point, I first consider a sampling of the evidence for the claim of an oral treaty by examining Duff's work. I want to be clear that I reject Duff's view that the hand-written documents he describes are, in his words, "*the* legal versions" (emphasis mine; Duff 1969:8–9). They are not the sole legal versions, but, rather, one legal version. Because the idea of an oral treaty appears novel, I point to another historical example of complementary written and oral documents and the ways the interplay between them can be understood as to not be merely an anomaly, but, rather, leave open the possibility of productive interplay.

The Douglas treaties by their very nature take us far afield and I understand that it was not until the Vancouver Islands Treaties Conference held at Vancouver Island University in 2012, and organized in part by a descendant of one the principals involved in these treaties, then Snuneymuxw Chief Douglas White III, Kwulasultun, that all of the signatory bands had in their possession written copies of the treaty. This is both shocking and revealing. This circumstance creates a rift big enough to allow movement in new directions and I wish to move far away in time and space to make my point. And, since the canon in common law countries supposes that treaties and other agreements should be understood in light of how the weaker party understands them, it is my premise here that a focus on oral histories regarding the Douglas treaties might move both closer to the nineteenth century Indigenous understanding and conform to best practices in the common law.

James Douglas, then Chief Factor of the Hudson's Bay Company, wrote a letter of May 16, 1850 to Archibald Barclay, secretary of the Company and located in London, "I attached the signatures of the native Chiefs and others who subscribed the deed the purchase to a **blank sheet** on which will be copied the contractor Deed of conveyance, as soon as we receive a proper form, which I beg may be sent out by return Post . . . ." (quoted in Duff 1969:7–8; emphasis mine). Wilson Duff, writing about the so-called Douglas treaties:

The treaties themselves, somewhat edited to tidy them up, were published by the provincial government in 1875 and have attained a certain historical stature in that form. **It is the original hand-written documents, however, that are the legal versions.** These are found in the Provincial Archives in a large, hardcover notebook, inscribed "Register of Land Purchases from Indians . . . The treaty book was evidently made up by Douglas himself, since most of it, including the title on the front cover, is in his distinctive hand. Sections of the texts of the treaties, as will be explained later, are in another hand and a few scribbled notations have been added at a later time, but **by and large the treaties may be said to have been penned by James Douglas himself** (emphasis added, Duff 1969:8–9).

Duff notes further that treaties were penned in more than one hand (Duff 1969:11). And, concerning the second set of treaties, dated April 30, 1850, Duff writes that Douglas wrote in pencil a memorandum or prologue describing the territory of the groups involved in the treaty-making, "likely done in the presence of the Indians and served as the basis for the description to be written later into the body of the text. These prologues were not included in the published version of the treaties, **and in some cases their wording is somewhat different than in the text. . . .**" (emphasis added, Duff 1969:11–12).

There is some question regarding the "signatures" of the participants, and Duff notes, regarding the Chilcowitch treaty that "Twelve men headed by "Quasun' made their marks and received in payment thirty pounds. **Their X's seem remarkably uniform, as is the case on all the other treaties; perhaps they did not actually take the pen in hand as their marks were made**" (emphasis added, Duff 1969:13).

Duff provides considerable evidence of the existence of oral histories relevant to treaty held by Coast Salish people at the time of the writing of his *BC Studies* journal article in 1969 (Duff 1969). In addition, he provides evidence of many errors in the writing of the treaties. Most notably Duff writes, "The Nanaimo [know now as the Snuneymuxw First Nation] treaty, strangely, has no text whatever, although it is obvious (and the courts so ruled in the White and Bob case) that Douglas intended that it have the same text as the rest" (Duff 1969:22). And, Duff writes that in the case of the North Saanich treaty of February 11, 1852, boundaries of the tribal lands were "settled on the basis of verbal descriptions. It is doubtful that Douglas had an accurate map to work with, and even if he did, it is more doubtful that the Indians could read it. Their mental maps and his had to be reconciled, as did any confusions which arose over landmarks, descriptions, and distances. Such confusions are apparent in several of the descriptions of the treaties…" (Duff 1969:24).

Duff concludes that Douglas reinterpreted British legal conceptions underlying the treaties, including the very idea of purchase, into aboriginal concepts, as he understood them. The signatory groups assisted this by acting as corporate groups which "owned" the land, thereby distorting ethnographic fact (Duff 1969:52).

My own understanding of the question of interpretations of treaties is informed by my work over the last three decades with Puget Salish peoples—the immediate relatives of those Georgia Straits Salish we are considering here, and, further by work with Fraser Salish and Coast Salish on Vancouver Island and the Gulf Islands. The changes in Puget Salish communities since I began to work with them in the 1970s are dramatic. Some are now major economic engines, employers of people from throughout their region and beyond their reservation borders. They have control over health, child welfare, law enforcement, and they have codified their own visions of justice for their own courts. Significantly, much of this progress has resulted from litigation which has relied on Indigenous interpretations of treaty.

The Nature of Treaties

There are several characteristics of treaties that have bearing on how they ought to be treated. First, they are **frameworks of agreements**; they do not provide definitive answers to many questions, nor ought they. They must be living documents and to do this must establish something of the direction of relations among interpenetrating jurisdictions. Historian Chris Friday (2008:177) got at this issue in his analysis of the performative aspects of the late nineteenth century and early twentieth century Treaty Day events in Puget Sound. By "performative" he refers to events in which included speakers gave formal orations about treaty and also winter or spirit dances. These dancers were officially banned, but were deployed during Treaty Days celebrations, an event itself sponsored by white government authorities. Friday observes that there are changes in these performances: "Such transformations of the performance of treaties reveals how orality and the written word have evolved together, making treaties living documents." To Friday, performances of treaty are "transcripts of resistance" (Friday 2008:177). He observes that contemporary speeches about treaty by Coast Salish leaders "fit well into the long lineage of public performances of the treaty" (Friday 2008).

Friday's observation fits well with Cruikshank's (1994) concept that oral history, instead of being merely primordial articulations from the past, enable communities to address contemporary issues. In effect, they connect the past and the present. Friday notes, further, that the variation over time in performance of the Stevens treaties by Coast Salish of Puget Sound "came about because Indians mobilized the treaties and their understandings of them for the purposes of the day" (Cruikshank 1994). These Indians did not invent new interpretations, Friday concludes, but "**elaborated creatively on the original promises**..." (Cruikshank's 1994; emphasis mine). I return to this point in a discussion of the idea of midrash.

There is no reason to think that treaty interpretation won't bring dispute. Perhaps it should in order for change to arise, a point recognized by Max Gluckman (1955) in his work on the role of conflict in creating peace, or, in his phrase, the "peace in the feud."

Second, treaties are **relational**—they begin by recognizing the other as an equal in their ability to negotiate, even if the reality on the ground is or was of unequal power. The search for **common intention** is not only possible or plausible, it is the experience for the Puget Salish relatives of the Coast Salish of B.C. The fear and loathing associated by the public with the negotiation of contemporary treaties in British Columbia under the present B.C. Treaty Commission established in 1993, for example, is unwarranted and unnecessary.

In Puget Sound, treaty interpretation has included the **dramatic**—including *U.S. v Washington*, a 1974 treaty rights case which established tribal rights to half the salmon harvest, a subsequent 1995 case which clarified and established rights to shellfish, and, currently, efforts to establish treaty off-reservation hunting. But more often it concerns the **mundane**—agreements between neighboring jurisdictions on jail space, zoning, water, and so on. Sometimes it involves the extension of jurisdiction by Indigenous authority, as in the case of a local municipal government recognizing tribal code which forbids cutting the hair of tribal youth (including those incarcerated by the municipality) or the requirement that incarcerated tribal members be allowed to attend funerals (Miller 1997). In these cases, I think, it was simply easier for municipal governments to cooperate with treaty tribes with recognized sovereignty over their membership. Treaty, then, involves agreements at multiple levels—federal, provincial, local, and with First Nations governments. These relationships are apparent in the text of the recent Tsawwassen First Nation treaty on the B.C. lower mainland.

Treaty interpretation in Puget Sound, Washington state has involved complex wrangling over the meaning of the mid-nineteenth century treaty writers as well as the understandings of the Aboriginal people gathered to hear. In *U.S. v Washington* 9213, Subproceeding 89-3 (the shellfish phase off the Boldt Decision) much of the trial turned on historian Richard White's evidence regarding whether the term **fish** in the 1850s included shellfish to the American Indians and to the white treaty negotiators. White clearly established that it did. In this case the written word, the black letter law, was contextualized historically and by what the tribes understood at the treaty meetings at Point Elliott.

Often inspiration for local problems comes from afar. It should—that is the Judeo-Christian tradition of the bringing of the law by outsiders, including Moses (raised in Pharoah's household, but the lawgiver to Israelites) and Ezra (who led a group of Jews from Babylonian exile to Jerusalem where he proclaimed the law). This practice of inspiration from afar is evident in Coast Salish notions of the coming of new powers from other dimensions—under water, from the sky, and even in the creation of Coast Salish societies by people who come from the sky. Coast Salish oral traditions speak of the movement of Transformers, who traveled through river valleys setting the landscape right, safe for humans, and establishing the law (Miller 2001).

In this spirit, consider the manner in which ancient Israelites and their successor Jewish communities engaged with the interplay between the oral and the written. In the discussion of Vancouver Island treaties and of the Puget Salish performance of treaty described by Friday, I am reminded of the Jewish practice of midrash—the finding of meaning in text through new, unexpected insights. Midrash is a way of interpreting Biblical stories that goes beyond simple distillation of religious, legal or moral teachings. It fills in many gaps left in the biblical narrative regarding events and personalities that are only hinted at. It might be thought of as openness to possibility.

For Jews of the ancient and medieval world, both oral and written versions of the Talmud—there were two—were in play. Neither were superordinate; both were relevant, but, if anything, the oral took precedent (Armstrong 2006). This practice closely resembles current efforts by Aboriginal peoples to find ancestral legal practices in their own oral traditions, looking at Transformer stories, stories of culture heroes, for example, most notably by John Borrows (2010) and Val Napoleon (2014). The overlap between conceptions of the mainstream society and First Nations in understanding the relationship between the written and the oral provides common ground in considering the future of the Vancouver Island treaties.

In the Puget Sound treaties we can find treaty references to the provision of a physician. Article 14 of the 1855 Treaty of Point Elliott, for example, says "And the United States finally agree to employ a physician to reside at the said central agency, who shall furnish medicine and advice to their sick, and shall vaccinate them; the expenses of said school, shops, persons employed, and medical attendance to be defrayed by the United States, and not deducted from the annuities." These references are taken to mean today the right to the full provisioning of health services. Over time, these phrases have been translated into the creation of on-reservation tribal health services through the U.S. Indian Health Service, and, more recently, health services administered by the tribes themselves.

A second example is the court's determination in *United States v Washington* that the treaty phrase "to fish in common with citizens" means that Aboriginal people have rights to harvest half of the salmon catch. These kinds of decision, one might say, come out of a very old tradition of adjudication, of consideration of what the Coast Salish people understood by these terms in their day. The decision also reflects an openness to emergent mutual understandings.

Although the oral remains among First Nations and within the mainstream population, the displacement of the oral by the written comes at a cost. This is an old theme. The historian of religion Karen Armstrong wrote, describing the work of the prophet Jeremiah's reservations about the written Torah, "How dare you say: 'We are wise, and we possess the law of Yahweh?' he asked his opponents. 'See how it has been falsified by the lying pen of the scribes!' The written text could subvert orthodoxy by a mere sleight of the pen, and distort tradition by imparting information rather than wisdom" (2006:114). The former librarian of the U.S. Congress, Daniel

Boorstin, captured the sense of this passage in the other great predecessor society to the contemporary Western world, classical Greece:

> Plato lived in an age of transition in Athens when the written word was invading the world of learning. And this seems to confirm the warnings (reported by Plato) of the Egyptian god-king Thamus to Toth, the [legendary] inventor of writing. "This discovery of yours will create forgetfulness in the learners' soul, because they will not use their memories; they will trust to the external written characters and not remember of themselves. The specific which you have discovered is an aid not to memory, but to reminiscence, and you give your disciples not truth, but only the semblance of truth" (*Phaedrus*). (Boorstin 1999:40)

Our ancient world ancestors were concerned about an over-emphasis on writing. They understood that it allowed facts to displace wisdom and for individuals, without tutelage and outside of a relational view of the world, to make claims to truth. A recent example of this failure to recognize the relational lies in federal guidelines that have emerged after legal rulings by the Supreme Court of Canada in *Haida*, and other decisions that underline the obligation of government to consult meaningfully with First Nations in resource development. Despite these decisions, the 2011 *Aboriginal Consultation and Accommodation: Updated Guidelines for Federal Officials to Fulfill the Legal Duty to Consult*, instead of aiming for reconciliation, although this is claimed in the document (page 10), perpetuate Canada's historic colonial practices. They are developed in reaction to court decisions and litigation but are narrowly legalistic in their approach. The authors appear to have ignored Jeremiah's warning.

What Have We Done in Canada Courts Recently about Aboriginal Oral Knowledge?

Oral History on Trial (2011) describes the response of the Crown to what must have been perceived by their representatives as a crisis following *Delgamuukw*, 1997. The Supreme Court of Canada held in this title case that oral histories would have the same footing as written history in Aboriginal cases. The Crown response was to create several hostile and erroneous ways of understanding the oral traditions and oral historians of Aboriginal communities (Miller 2011). These tactics included an emphasis on **contagion**—of two sorts; one, the idea that oral historians who had read the published anthropology and histories of their communities were no longer independent sources of knowledge and could be disqualified. Second, the oral histories which incorporate **world motifs** are contaminated—and are therefore not real histories. Stó:lō oral historian Sonny McHalsie responded to these misunderstandings of oral history and oral historians by noting "When I read [anthropologists] Wilson Duff or Hill-Tout, I'm not reading what he wrote, but what the person [oral historian] who told him said. I'm not in Duff's mind, but that of the person who told him. I look at the filters" (quoted in Miller 2011:97). Further, the existence of world motifs does not eliminate local referents.

The court, at the urging of the Crown, has stumbled on the idea that oral histories can perform more than one task simultaneously. Oral histories, Cruikshank (1997) tells us, contain both commentary on issues of the day and embed direct insights into the past. And the Crown has argued that oral histories fail on the grounds of **chronology**—unaware of Aboriginal use of markers of time and context. Further, the Crown argues that history must be of a particular sort—

and the ideas present in oral histories must conform to western historiography. And, that once put on paper, oral histories can simply be analyzed by practices and concepts of outsiders. In effect, contextualization—the usual work of historians, the Crown has argued, should be dispensed with.

I don't wish to dwell any further on this; I've detailed this in print and to the court. I've suggested that both European-derived white people and Aboriginal people have histories of engaging nuance, of incorporating change; of seeing common good. Treaties, of all of the legal documents, are inherently about interpretation in light of new understandings and changed circumstances.

There is a written history of a Coast Salish community, by a white historian, which I do not wish to name here, in which community oral histories are featured until the moment that the settler population arrives and asserts itself. Then, the oral drops out and documents are the source of information. That's the wrong approach here. It's a kind of a trap. Coast Salish communities do retain oral histories. In fact, a relative of Chief White, Clifford White and his friend David Bob, arrested for hunting deer out of season, told the surprised court that they claimed a treaty right to hunt based on the Douglas Treaty for the region of Nanaimo signed by Douglas with "The Nanaimo Tribe" in 1854. This agreement, understood to be a treaty, held that tribal members were "at liberty to hunt over the unoccupied lands as formerly." Long out of the memory of the Crown, the agreement had persisted in the minds of the First Nations.

References Cited

Angelbeck, Bill. n.d. *Conceptions of Coast Salish Warfare: The Phantoms of Pacifism and Victimhood.* Document in possession of author.

Angelbeck, Bill and Eric McLay. 2011. The Battle at Maple Bay: The Dynamics of Coast Salish Political Organization through Oral Histories. *Ethnohistory,* 58(3):359–392.

Armstrong, Karen. 2006. *The Great Transformation: the Beginnings of Our Religious Traditions.* Toronto: Vintage Canada.

Arnett, Chris. 1999. *The Terror of the Coast: Land Alienation and Colonial War on Vancouver Island and the Gulf Islands, 1849–1863.* Vancouver: Talonbooks.

———— editor. 2007. *Two Houses Half-Buried in Sand: Oral Traditions of the Hul'qumi'num' Coast Salish of Kuper Island and Vancouver Island by Beryl Mildred Cryer.* Vancouver: Talonbooks.

Blee, Lisa. 2014. *Framing Chief Leschi: Narratives and the Politics of Historical Justice.* Chapel Hill: University of North Carolina Press.

Boorstin, Daniel J. 1999. *The Seekers: The Story of Man's Continuing Quest to Understand His World.* New York: Vintage Books.

Borrows, John. 2010. *Drawing Out Law: A Spirit's Guide.* Toronto: University of Toronto Press.

Boyd, Robert. 1994. Smallpox in the Pacific Northwest: The First Epidemics. *BC Studies,* 101 (Spring), The First Nations in British Columbia: 5–40.

———— 1999. *The Coming of the Spirit of Pestilence: Introduced Infectious Diseases and Population Decline among Northwest Coast Indians, 1774–1874.* Seattle: University of Washington Press, 1999.

Buchanan, James. 1859. Letter to U.S. Senate and House of Representatives, 35th Congress, 2d session, House of Representatives, Ex Doc No. 72.

Collins, June McCormick. 1949. John Fornsby: The Personal Document of a Coast Salish Indian. In Indians in the Urban Northwest, edited by Marian W. Smith, pp. 285–341. *Columbia University Contributions in Anthropology*, 36. New York.

———— 1974. *Valley of the Spirits*. Seattle: University of Washington Press.

Cruikshank, Julie. 1994. Oral Tradition and Oral History: Reviewing Some Issues. *Canadian Historical Review*, 75(3):404–18.

———— 1997. Negotiating with Narrative: Establishing Cultural Identity at the Yukon International Storytelling Festival. *American Anthropologist*, 99(1):56–69.

Duff, Wilson. 1969. The Fort Victoria Treaties. *B.C. Studies*, 3:3–57.

Friday, Chris. 2008. Performing Treaties: The Culture and Politics of Treaty Remembrance and Celebration. In *The Power of Promises: Rethinking Indian Treaties in the Pacific Northwest*, edited by Alexandra Harmon, pp. 157–185. Seattle: University of Washington Press.

Foster, Hamar and Alan Grove. 2008. 'Trespassers on the Soil': *United States v. Tom* and a New Perspective on the Short History of Treaty Making in Nineteenth-Century British Columbia. In *The Power of Promises: Rethinking Indian Treaties in the Pacific Northwest*, edited by Alexandra Harmon, pp. 89–127. Seattle: University of Washington Press.

Gluckman, Max. 1955. The Peace in the Feud. In *Custom and Conflict in Africa*, edited by *Max Gluckman*, pp. 1–26. Glencoe, IL: The Free Press.

Harmon, Alexandra. 2008. Introduction: Pacific Northwest Indian Treaties in National and International Historical Perspective. In *The Power of Promises: Rethinking Indian Treaties in the Pacific Northwest*, edited by Alexandra Harmon, pp. 3–32. Seattle: University of Washington Press.

Miller, Bruce Granville. 1997. The Individual, the Collective and Tribal Code. *American Indian Culture and Research Journal*, 21(1):107–130.

———— 2001. *The Problem of Justice: Tradition and Law in the Coast Salish World*. Lincoln: University of Nebraska Press.

———— 2011. *Oral History on Trial: Recognizing Aboriginal Narratives in the Courts*. Vancouver: UBC Press.

Miller, Bruce Granville, Bill Angelbeck, Al Grove, Raymond Wilson. 2013. The Hwlitsum First Nation Traditional Use and Occupation of the Area now Known as British Columbia. Volume 2: Hwlitsum Marine Traditional Use Study.

Miller, Jay. 2011. First Nations Forts, Refuges, and War Lord Champions Around the Salish Sea. *Journal of Northwest Anthropology*, 45(1):71–87.

Napoleon, Val. 2014. *Mikomosis and the Wetiko*. Indigenous Law Research Unit, University of Victoria.

Roberts, Natalie A. 1975. A History of the Swinomish Tribal Community. Ph.D. dissertation, Department of Anthropology, University of Washington.

Sampson, Martin J. 1972. *Indians of Skagit County*. Mt. Vernon, WA: Skagit County Historical Society.

Schaepe, David. n.d. Paper in possession of author.

Cases Cited

Haida Nation v. British Columbia (Minister of Forests), [2004] 3 S.C.R. 511, 2004 SCC 73.

United States v. Washington, 443 U.S. 658 (1979) decision 9213, Subproceedings 89-3.
R. v. White and Bob (1965), 52 D.L.R. (2d) 48.

Sample Text of Douglas Treaty

Swengwhung Tribe – Victoria Peninsula, South of Colquitz.

Know all men, we, the chiefs and people of the family of Swengwhung, who have signed our names and made our marks to this deed on the thirtieth day of April, one thousand eight hundred and fifty, do consent to surrender, entirely and forever, to James Douglas, the agent of the Hudson's Bay Company in Vancouver Island, that is to say, for the Governor, Deputy Governor, and Committee of the same, the whole of the lands situate and lying between the Island of the Dead, in the Arm or Inlet of Camoson, where the Kosampsom lands terminate, extending east to the Fountain Ridge, and following it to its termination on the Straits of De Fuca, in the Bay immediately east of Clover Point, including all the country between that line and the Inlet of Camoson.

; and the land shall be properly surveyed, hereafter. It is udnerstood, however, that the land itself, with these small exceptions, becomes the entire propery of the white people for ever; it is also understood that we are at liberty to hunt over the unoccupied lands, and to carry on our fisheries as formerly.

We have received, as payment, <u>Seventy-five pounds sterling</u>.

In token whereof, we have signed our names and made our marks, at Fort Victoria, on the thirtieth day of April, one thousand eight hundred and fifty.

(Signed) Snaw-nuck his X mark and 29 others

Done before us,

(Signed) Alfred Robson Benson, M.R.C.S.L.

Joseph William McKay.

Journal of Northwest Anthropology, Memoir 12:338–339 (2016)

Postscript

In these essays I have advocated for an anthropology that concerns itself with the interactive space between the dominant society and the contemporary Coast Salish peoples and communities. However, we also need to learn about Coast Salish epistemology and ontology because this inevitably informs our understanding of their current world. We can continue to foreground culture, both as a concept and a practice, because it leads us to consider both similarities and dissimilarities and the ways, such as creating court systems, that the Coast Salish seek to protect themselves from further malign surveillance and exclusion. We can find value and new questions and approaches in integrating time scales from archaeology into ethnographic and ethnohistorical studies. Further, we can usefully engage new social theory regarding topics such as the state, border societies, the individual, the law, and gender.

We can also usefully write in several voices—employing data-driven research that identifies salient variables and also experience-near work that uses the totality of human sensory abilities and enables us to work more fully and cooperatively with Coast Salish peoples. This is not to suggest that the Coast Salish are not sometimes themselves the anthropologists (including archeologists); we are now well into an age in which research agendas and the subsequent writing are established both by the Coast Salish and in collaboration with outsider academics and applied researchers.

Disciplinary lines are now breached and historians engage social theory generated by anthropology, and anthropologists use historical methods and materials. Archaeologists of today, including Michael Blake, Dana Lepofsky, Bill Angelbeck and others, cross over into what was once the domain of sociocultural anthropology. I find it continually interesting and helpful to walk the landscape with archaeology colleagues (as well as First Nations and American Indian people such as Sonny McHalsie and Scott Schuyler). We frequently ask the same research questions but on different time scales, and with the same communities and community members, cultural advisors, and leaders. The meeting ground for scholars of these disciplines is sometimes ethnohistory but need not be limited to that. Historians such as Keith Carlson work with living communities, which informs their historical studies, in part because the Coast Salish of today remain bearers of their own historical practices and oral traditions. I have learned, as have many others, that they have a lot to say about the lives of their forbearers and they, after all, continue to live in the same locations that their ancestors have occupied for millennia. In fact, we are now past the time in which armchair historians or anthropologists can write about the Coast Salish from a distance; relying on written texts only. Coast Salish people want to know what academics and others are saying about them and they want to engage in writing themselves.

We live in a period in which good relations have been established between academics and communities. Suttles and his generation, and Erna Gunther and her generation, slightly earlier, were generally deeply involved with and concerned for the communities they wrote about. Still, this relationship has been enhanced and transformed. Today, instead of carrying out salvage anthropology and writing descriptive work of single communities following a formulistic set of topics we continue on the path Suttles established of using new research concepts (in his case ecological anthropology) to address particular topics and questions of interest and value to

*Authored by Bruce Granville Miller in 2015.

communities. These include medical anthropology, literary studies, legal studies, landscape studies and more.

The Coast Salish are thought to be one of the "Northwest Coast" peoples. That culture area has been said to define, to some extent, their historic way of life. Joe Jorgensen (1980) did the greatest work in testing this point in his monograph *Western Indians*, an underused classic. And Suttles and others have used the culture area device to explain variation in forms of social organization. But we are not stuck with this concept and we can examine the Coast Salish in broader frames of reference, just as we are not stuck with the concepts of seasonal rounds, watersheds, or the notion of the historically passive Coast Salish, the objects of assault by northern raiders (although we downplay the assault by the Americans, British and Canadians). We can embrace these concepts for what they can tell us while encompassing them within their field of utility.

Finally, we can use ideas and data generated in working with Coast Salish peoples to contribute to the growing anthropology of the contemporary world. This is already underway, with Boxberger's work and, I hope, with my own work on the mechanisms of state disavowal of and failure to recognize the Indigenous peoples within their borders and with transformations within the Coast Salish communities, such as gender roles and attributions.

I look forward to the work of a younger generation of scholars, such as Bill Angelbeck's publications on anarchist theory. These people are integrating ideas from a range of scholarly disciplines and developing new ones, in working together with the Coast Salish to help them continue to reconfigure their place in contemporary society. Maybe the tracks I've laid down here will provide some inspiration to them. I've got more work to do myself.

Reference Cited

Jorgensen, Joseph G. 1980. *Western Indians: Comparative Environments, Languages and Cultures of 172 Western American Indian Tribes*. San Francisco: W.H. Freeman & Co.

Appendix

Professional Publications and Presentations by Bruce Granville Miller

Refereed Books (Sole Author)

2011   *Oral History on Trial: Recognizing Aboriginal Narratives in the Courts.* Vancouver: UBC Press. (winner of K.D. Srivastiva Prize for Excellence in Academic Publishing, 2012; Listed in Hill Times, "Canada's Politics and Government Newsweekly" as one of the best 100 books in 2011 in Canada on Political, Government, Public Policy, and Canadian History).

2004   *Invisible Indigenes: The Politics of Non-Recognition.* Lincoln: University of Nebraska Press.

2001   *The Problem of Justice: Tradition and Law in the Coast Salish World.* Lincoln: U of Nebraska Press.

Refereed Books (Edited)

2016   *Upper Skagit Historic Atlas*, edited by Bruce Granville Miller, Bill Angelbeck, Molly Malone, and Jan Perrier. Upper Skagit Tribal Community, Sedro-Woolley, Washington.

2007   *Extraordinary Anthropology: Transformations in the Field*, edited by Jean-Guy Goulet and Bruce Granville Miller. Lincoln: University of Nebraska Press.

2007   *"Be of Good Mind": Essays on the Coast Salish.* Vancouver: UBC Press.

1992   *Anthropology and History in the Courts.* Special Issue, *BC Studies*, 95 (two reprintings)

Refereed Journal Articles

2016   *Coast Salish Borderlands and the Erosion of Sovereignty.* Special issue on law and cultures (revue Anthropologie et sociétés) (French), 40(2)

2015   Anthropological Experts and the Legal System: Brazil and Canada, *American Indian Quarterly*, 39(4): 391–430. Gustavo Menezes and Bruce Miller

2014   An Ethnographic view of Legal Entanglements on the Salish Sea Borderlands, *UBC Law Review*, 47(3):991–1024.

2012   Life on the Hardened Border. *American Indian Culture and Research Journal,* 36(2):23–45.

2006   Who Are Indigenes? A Comparative Study of Canadian and American Practices. *American Behavioral Scientist*, 50 (4): 462–477. (Thematic Issue)

2006   Bringing Culture In: Community Responses to Apology, Reconciliation, and Reparations. *American Indian Culture and Research Journal*, 30(4):1–17.

2003   Justice, Law, and the Lens of Culture. *Wicazo Sa Review*, 18 (2):135–149.

2001   The Story of Peter Pan: or Middle Ground Lost. *BC Studies*, 131:25–28.

1998   Culture as Cultural Defense: A Sacred Site in Court. *American Indian Quarterly*, 22(1):83–97.

1998   The Great Race of 1941: A Coast Salish Public Relations Coup. *Pacific Northwest Quarterly*, 89(3):127–135.

1997   Evolution or History: A Response to Tollefson. *Ethnohistory*, 44(1):135–137. (Daniel L. Boxberger and Bruce G. Miller)

1997   The Individual, the Collective and Tribal Code. *American Indian Culture and Research Journal*, 21(1):107–130.

1996-97 The "Really Real" Border and the Divided Salish Community. *BC Studies*, 112:63–79.

1995   The Dilemma of Mental Health Paraprofessionals at Home. *American Indian and Alaska Native Mental Health: The Journal of the National Center*, 6(2):13-33. (Miller, Bruce G. and Jen Pylypa)

1995   Folk Law and Contemporary Coast Salish Tribal Code. *American Indian Culture and Research Journal*, 19 (3):141–164.

1994   Creating Chiefdoms: The Puget Sound Case. *Ethnohistory*, 41(2):267–293. (Miller, Bruce G. and Daniel L. Boxberger)

1994   Women and Tribal Politics: Is There a Gender Gap in Tribal Elections? *American Indian Quarterly*, 18(1):25–41.

1994   Contemporary Tribal Codes and Gender Issues. *American Indian Culture and Research Journal*, 18(2):43-74.

1994   Contemporary Native Women: Role Flexibility and Politics. *Anthropologica*, 35(1):57–72.

1993   The Press, the Boldt Decision, and Indian-White Relations. *American Indian Culture and Research Journal*, 17(2):75–97.

1992   Women and Politics: Comparative Evidence from the Northwest Coast. *Ethnology*, 31(4): 367–383.

1992   Common Sense and Plain Language. Special Issue, Anthropology and History in the Courts, *BC Studies*, 95:55–65.

1992   Introduction. Special Issue, Anthropology and History in the Courts, *BC Studies*, 95:3-6.

1990   An Ethnographic View: Positive Consequences of the War on Poverty. *American Indian and Alaska Native Mental Health: The Journal of the National Center*, 4(2):55–71.

1991   Review Essay: Handbook of North American Indians. Volume 7, Indians of the Northwest Coast. *BC Studies*, 1991–92:173–184.

1989   Centrality and Measures of Regional Structure in Aboriginal Western Washington. *Ethnology*, 28(3):265–276.

1989   After the FAP: Tribal Reorganization after Federal Acknowledgment. *Journal of Ethnic Studies*, 17(2):89–100.

Refereed Book Chapters

2013   Anthropology of Art; Shifting Paradigms and Practices, 1870s–1950. In *Native Art of the Northwest Coast: A History of Changing Ideas*, edited by Charlotte Townsend-Gault, Jennifer Kramer, and Ke-ki, pp. 203–233. Vancouver: UBC Press.

2007   The Politics of Ecstatic Research. In *Extraordinary Anthropology: Transformations in the Field*, edited by Jean-Guy Goulet and Bruce Granville Miller, pp. 1–14. Lincoln: U of Nebraska Press.

2007   Introduction. In *Extraordinary Anthropology: Transformations in the Field*, edited by Jean-Guy Goulet and Bruce Granville Miller, pp. 186–207. Lincoln: University of Nebraska Press.

2007   Introduction. In *"Be of Good Mind": Essays on the Coast Salish*, edited by Bruce Granville Miller, p. 1–29. Vancouver: UBC Press.

2006   Conceptual and Practical Boundaries: West Coast Indians/First Nations on the Border of Contagion in the Post-9/11 Era. In *The Borderlands of the American and Canadian Wests: Essays on Regional and Trans-boundary History*, edited by Sterling Evans, pp. 49–66. Lincoln: University of Nebraska Press.

2004   Salish. In *Aboriginal Peoples of Canada: A Short Introduction*, edited by Paul Magocsi, pp. 237–250. University of Toronto Press.

2004   Rereading the Ethnographic Record: The Problem of Justice in the Coast Salish World. In *Coming Ashore: Northwest Coast Ethnology, Traditions and Visions*, edited by Marie Mauze, Michael Harkin, and Sergei Kan, pp. 309–322. Lincoln: University of Nebraska Press.

2004   Tribal or Native Law. In *A Companion to the Anthropology of American Indians.*, edited by Thomas Biolsi, pp. 95–111 London: Blackwell. (Blackwell Companion to the Anthropology of American Indians Series.

1999   Contemporary Tribal Codes and Gender Issues. In *Contemporary Native American Cultural Issues*, edited by Duane Champagne, pp. 103–112. AltaMira Press.

1999   Discontinuities in the Statuses of Puget Sound Indian Grandmothers. In *American Indian Grandmothers: Traditions and Transitions*, edited by Marjorie Schweitzer, pp. 103–124. Norman: University of Oklahoma Press.

1999   Salishan. In *An Encyclopedia of Canada's Peoples*, edited by Paul Magocsi, pp. 88–93. Toronto: Multicultural History Society of Ontario.

1999   Locating Aboriginal Governments in the Political Landscape. In *Seeking Sustainability in the Lower Fraser Basin: Issues and Choices*, edited by Michael Healey, pp. 47–63. Vancouver: Institute for Resources and the Enivronment/Westwater Research. (J.E. Michael Kew and Bruce G. Miller)

Invited Review Essays

1995   North Out of Focus. In *The Literary Review of Canada*, 4 (3):22–23.

1994   Who's Looking After The Fish? In *The Literary Review of Canada*, 3(7):14–16.

1993   Unconquered British Columbia. In *The Literary Review of Canada*, 2(3):18–19.

Other Invited Contributions

(in press) Political Mobilization through Repatriation, "Revista Perfiles de la Cultura Cubana" (Spanish)

2012 Reponse to Angelbeck, Bill and Colin Grier, Anarchism and the Archaeology of Anarchic Societies: Resistance to Centralization in the Coast Salish Region of the Pacific Northwest Coast (with CA Comments and Reply). *Current Anthropology,* 53 (5): 576-77.

2012 Foreword to Building Bridges to Justice: Realizing Contemporary Indigenous Visions of Justice in Canada Through the Culturally Sensitive Interpretations of Legal Rights. By David Leo Milward. Vancouver: UBC Press. ix–xviii.

2011 Consultant to and author of excerpts on Aboriginal people and communities in The Chuck Davis History of Metropolitan Vancouver (Harbour Press, 2011, 574 pp.)

2011 "Central Coast Salish" and "Native People of the Northwest Coast." Entries in the Canadian Encyclopedia.

2007 Response to Nesper, Larry, Negotiating jurisprudence in tribal court and the emergence of a tribal state: the Ojibwe in Wisconsin" (with CA Comments and Reply). *Current Anthropology*, 48(5):692–693.

2005 Response to Alexander Dawson's Review of Invisible Indigenes. *BC Studies*, 145:135–137.

2004 Salish. World Book Publishing, Chicago. World Book Encyclopedia/World Book Online. Vol. 17:6.

1994 Swinomish. In *Native America in the Twentieth Century: An Encyclopedia*, edited by Mary Davis, pp. 620–621. New York: Garland.

1994 Snohomish. In *Native America in the Twentieth Century: An Encyclopedia*, edited by Mary Davis, pp. 601–602. New York: Garland.

1994 Samish. In *Native America in the Twentieth Century: An Encyclopedia*, edited by Mary Davis, pp. 567–568. New York: Garland.

1994 Upper Skagit. In *Native America in the Twentieth Century: An Encyclopedia*, edited by Mary Davis, pp. 668–669. New York: Garland.

1993 Letter to Editor (Response to J.K. Krueger). *BC Studies*, 98:108–109.

1991 The Forgotten Indians and Federal Recognition. *Friends Journal*, 37(9): 22–24.

Conference Proceedings

2007 A Brief Consideration of the Politics of Ecstatic Research. *Quaderni di Tule IV: Proceedings of the XXVI International Congress of Americanists*, pp. 405–411.

Invited Presentations

2015 Invited Keynote: Repatriations: Working with Museums. Ontario Chiefs Heritage and Burials Policy Forum, November 4.

2015 Invited Panelist, Repatriations. Ontario Chiefs Heritage and Burials Policy Forum, Nov 4-6.

2015   Invited Talk, Oral History and Litigation. National Land Claims Research Workshop, Six Nations of the Grand River, October 5.

2015   Invited Keynote: What's Changed in the Coast Salish World Over 40 Years? One Person's View. Kwikwetlem: A Celebration of Coast Salish History, Culture and Identity. All Nations Festival, Coquitlam, B.C. July 23.

2015   Invited Discussant: Roundtable on Cultural Translation, thought leaders and practitioners, Morris J. Wosk Centre for Dialogue and SFU Centre for Dialogue, June 17.

2015   Invited Talk: Indigenous Peoples of Canada in the Contemporary World. Colloquium 6, Tourism in Traditional and Indigenous Communities. State University of the Amazonas, Manaus, Brazil. May 8.

2015   Invited Speaker: Canadian Indians at the US-Canada Borderlands. Studies in Interethnic Relations Symposium (Lageri), Department of Anthropology, U of Brasilia. April 24.

2015   Invited Talk: An Ethnographic Perspective on Coast Salish on the International Border. Department of Anthropology, University of Sao Paulo, Brazil. April 27.

2015   Invited Talk: Indigenous Mobilizations for Repatriation of Ancestors from Civic Institutions. Seminario Internacional: Identitdades y Movilizaciones Colectivas. Instituto Cubano de Investigacion Cultural Juan Marinello. Habana, Cuba, April 14.

2015   Invited Talk: First Nations/Pueblos Indigenous en la Universidade de la Columbia Britanica. Seminario Internacional: Identitdades y Movilizaciones Colectivas. Instituto Cubano de Investigacion Cultural Juan Marinello. Habana, Cuba, April 15.

2015   Invited Talk: Indigenes at the Contested Border. Seminario Internacional: Identitdades y Movilizaciones Colectivas. Instituto Cubano de Investigacion Cultural Juan Marinello. Habana, Cuba, April 15.

2015   Invited Speaker: Canadian Indians at the US-Canada Borderlands. Studies in Interethnic Relations Symposium (Lageri), Department of Anthropology, U of Brasilia. April 24.

2013   Invited speaker, "Oral History on Trial," Sponsored by School of Community and Public Affairs, Centre for Oral and Digital Story Telling and First People's Studies Program, Concordia University, Montreal, October 24.

2013   Invited speaker, Missing Women Commission of Inquiry: Unpacked and Revisited. Centre for Policy Research on Culture and Community, Simon Fraser University, First Nations Studies, SFU, and the Social Justice Centre, Kwantlen Polytechnic University, Harbour Centre, Vancouver. July 9, 2013.

2013   Invited Plenary speaker, "Life on the Hardened Border," Law on the Edge Conference, jointly presented by the Canadian Law and Society Association and the Law and Society Association of Australia and New Zealand. Vancouver, July 1.

2013   Invited talk given at Concordia University, Montreal, "Naxaxalhts'i's: An Oral Historian Answers the Crown" First People's Studies and Centre for Oral and Digital Storytelling. October 25, 2013 (two hours).

2012   Invited talk to Bamfield Marine Sciences Centre archaeology field school, Archaeology, Law and Oral History, August 17, 2012.

2012   Invited Speaker, Conference on Pre-Confederation Vancouver Island Treaties, Vancouver Island University and Sneymuxw First Nation, May 10-11.

2012   Invited Panelist, Aboriginal Oral Histories in the Courtroom: More than a matter of evidence. UBC Press Forum, Liu Centre, UBC, February 8, 2012, 2.5 hours.

2012   Invited Speaker and Workshop presenter on global indigenous issues, Building Bridges Conference on Native American History, Gustavus Adolphus College, St. Peter, Minnesota, March 10.

2011   Invited Speaker, Oral History and Evidence Law. National Claims Research Workshop. Quebec City, September 27.

2011   Invited Discussant, UBC Law and Society "Author Meets Readers" Series, Green College, UBC, September 29.

2011   Oral History as Evidence. Talk given to National Tsing Hua University, Hsinchu, Taiwan, Anthropology Department. May 9.

2011   Oral History. Invited presentation to Symposium on Indigenous Legal Traditions Conference, Justice Canada, Indian Affairs, Ottawa, March 9.

2010   A Glimpse Into a Possible Future, Indigenous Law in Coast Salish Traditions. Sponsored by U Victoria Faculty of Law, the Cowichan First Nation, et al. Cowichan First Nation. B.C., Oct 15.

2010   Indigenous Politics on the Northwest Coast. Talk given to National Endowment for the Humanities Summer Institute—Peoples of the Northwest Coast. Vancouver, July 7.

2010   Invited Discussant, Law and Society Speakers Series, Author Meets Critics. Green College. April 7.

2010   Invited speaker, IBA (Indigenous Bar Association) Elders' Gathering on Oral History Evidence, March 29-31, 2010 at Turtle Lodge, Manitoba.

2010   Panelist, Louis Riel opera opening gala roundtable discussion moderated by UBC President Stephen Toope, with Jean Teillet, Aboriginal lawyer and Louis Riel's great grand niece, Bruce Dumont, President of Métis Nation B.C., Chan Centre, UBC. January 3.

2009   Invited presentation to "The promotion and application of sociocultural rights in Brazil and Canada" sponsored by the Canadian Embassy, the Brazilian federal Ministério Público, and the University of Brasilia. Brasilia, Brazil, November 27.

2009   Talk to Hozomeen Mountain Gathering, "Sharing What We Know," on Coast Salish social networks, Skagit Environmental Endowment Commission, September 13. 2009.

2009   Lecture to Quest University; "Coast Salish Ideas of Nature," September, 2009.

2008   Invited Opening convocation lecture, "Indigenous Tribunals in the Contemporary Period," for The Laboratory of Dynamic Territories, Institute of Social-Environmental Studies, Federal University of Goias, Brazil, November 10.

2008   Invited Talk Given to Federal University of Goias, Orality and Indigenous Societies in Canada. IV Intercultural and Transdisciplinary Seminar, Science and Language, Nov. 10.

2008   Oral Histories in Canadian Tribunals. Talk Given to Department of Anthropology Colloquiam Series, University of Brasilia, Brazil, October 8.

2008   Three Legal Issues for Canadian First Nations, talk Given to Department of Anthropology, Federal University of Curitiba, Brazil, October 21.

2008   Indigenous Ideas of Justice in the Contemporary World. Talk Given to GERI, University of Brasilia, October 3.

2008   Aboriginal Space and Contested Human Rights Talk, Given to GERI, University of Brasilia, Brazil, September 12, 2008.

2008   Invited lecture, Narrativity and Canadian-First Nations Relations, Given to Canada Seminar, Harvard University, December 1.

2008   Invited lecture, The Only Good Indian is a Capitalist and Other Dilemmas in a Resource Extraction Province, given to Red Cents Conference, Borrego Springs California, November 24.

2007   What Do We Know About Sacred Sites in the Coast Salish World? Invited talk given to the Archaeological Association of British Columbia. Vancouver, September 20.

2007   Invited Panel Discussant, Federal Department of Justice, British Columbia Regional Office, Conference entitled "Sui Generis Litigation: Reconciling History and Law?"

2007   Panel, New Research Directions in the Academy. First Nations House of Learning, University of British Columbia, February 22–23.

2006   Aboriginal Space in the Tribunal, talk given to Faculty of Law colloquium series. October 21.

2006   Indigenous Human Rights, Talk to Indigenous Rights, Vancouver branch (Amnesty International), May 6.

2004   Where Does Ecstatic Research Take Us? XXVI International Congress of Americanists, Perugia, Italy, May 9.

2004   Invited speaker, Expert Witnessing. Talk given to National Aboriginal Law Litigation Conference, Canada, Vancouver, February 3.

2003   Invited speaker, A Short Commentary on the Land Issue in BC. Address to National Land Claim Meetings, hosted by Union of BC Indian Chiefs, Vancouver. October 18.

2003   Invited speaker, Anthropologists, Lawyers, and Tribes: Implications for Knowledge Production. Native Studies Colloquium, Dartmouth College, Hanover, New Hampshire, May 23.

2003   Invited speaker, Invisible Indigenes. Anthropology Department Colloquium, Dartmouth College, Hanover, New Hampshire. May 22.

2003   Anthropologists, Lawyers, and Tribes. People of the River Conference, Mission, BC, April 1.

2003   Community, Wellness, and the View from Below. Peter Wall Institute Conference, Re-Imaging Community: Decolonizing, Postnationalism, Healing, and Well-Being. May 22.

2003   The Kitchen Decision. Law and Society, Green College, November 3.

2003   Keynote Address: Tribal Culture and Tribal Law. Federal, Washington State, County and Tribal Justice Summit, Jan 8, 2003. Bow, Washington.

2002   Invited speaker, Invisible Indigenes. University of Washington Department of Anthropology Lecture Series, Indigenous Rights, Indigenous Resources, Indigenous Futures. Seattle. October 14.

2002   The Dilemma of Alternative Dispute Resolution in First Nations. Green College Thematic Lecture Series, The Shifting Culture of Conflict. February 25.

2001   Indigenous Law and Intellectual Property. Innovation, Creation, and New Economic Forms Conference. Corpus Christi College, University of Cambridge, UK. December 13.

2001   Invited speaker, Indigenous Responses to Historical Grievances. Adam Institute International Conference: Attitudes Towards the Past in Conflict Resolution. Jerusalem, Israel. November 29.

2001   Invited panelist, Thinking Through Treaties Seminar, Lower Mainland Treaty Advisory Council, Halfmoon Bay, B.C. September 22-23.

2001   Invited speaker, Nuu-chah-nulth Whaling and the Treaty of Neah Bay, Whaling and the Nuu-chah-nulth People Seminar, Autry Museum, Los Angeles, March 22.

2000   Invited speaker, History and Tradition: Three Coast Salish Representations of Justice. Northwest Coast Conference in Honor of Claude Levi-Strauss, Paris, College de France, June 21.

2000   Invited speaker, Simon Fraser University Department of Archaeology Graduate Colloquium Series. A Sacred Site In Court. February 5.

1999   Invited speaker, B.C. Archaeological Society Lecture Series, Vancouver Museum. The Nookachamps Site: A Sacred Site in Court. November 18.

1999   A Sacred Rock in Court. Paper presented to Sto:lo People of the River 11 Conference. Chilliwack, BC, October 23, 1999.

1997   Green College Speakers Series. Tribal Justice: Remembering the Past, Envisioning the Future. October 9.

1996   Second Annual Sto:lo Nation Justice Conference, Chilliwack, B.C. Keynote talk. Tribal Justice: What is it? October 31.

1995   Talk given to the UBC Faculty of Law Colloquium Series, Puget Sound Indian Court System. A Model for B.C.? October 16.

1993   Simon Fraser University, Department of Sociology and Anthropology Colloquium Series. Tribal Councils and Tribal Law: Where Headed? February 22.

1992   Anthropology Symposium Series, University of Victoria. A Model of Coast Salish Family Network Cycling and Health Services Delivery. February 28.

Journal of Northwest Anthropology, Memoir No. 11

An Ethnographic Assessment of Some Cultural Landscapes in Southern Wyoming and Idaho

by

Deward E. Walker, Jr., Pamela Graves, Joe Ben Walker, and Dan Hutchison

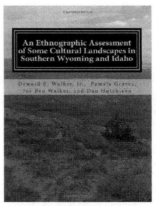

This two-part report focuses on one of the most pressing issues in federal land management today: how to address the effects of major energy projects on large land masses that are sacred to American Indians. Despite decades of assessments conducted under the National Environmental Policy Act and the National Historic Preservation Act, the importance of cultural landscapes to tribes continues to be overlooked. The situation is dire.

The report is an assessment of various tribal cultural landscapes in southern Wyoming and Idaho and their place in Shoshone-Paiute-Bannock culture. The report responds to a request by the Shoshone-Paiute Tribes of the Duck Valley Indian Reservation for ethnographic research concerning identification and function of cultural landscapes in the vicinity of the Gateway West Transmission Line right-of-way in southern Wyoming and Idaho. Part I is an assessment of published literature concerning cultural landscapes previously recorded by anthropologists and other scholars. Part II has been prepared from ethnographic information secured from tribal elders and cultural experts, some of which is included with the 35 cultural landscape descriptions. Interviews focused on both the past and present uses of these cultural landscapes by tribal members, including their locations, histories of use, purposes, and various cultural resources each may contain. Included is an ethnographic photo log of 269 photographs of 35 cultural landscapes

March 2015 • 325 pages • 300 color photographs
available through Amazon.com $49.95

Journal of Northwest Anthropology, Memoir No. 10

Tribal Trio of the Northwest Coast

by Kenneth D. Tollefson
edited by Jay Miller and Darby C. Stapp

The *Journal of Northwest Anthropology* is pleased to present this life-long collection of work from anthropologist Kenneth D. Tollefson, who came to the Pacific Northwest in 1965 to teach at Seattle Pacific University. Over the years, Dr. Tollefson found time to assist several Pacific Northwest tribes in their struggles to perpetuate and retain tribal autonomy. In this Memoir, Dr. Tollefson presents his work with three Northwest groups: the Tlingit on the coast of present-day Alaska; the Snoqualmie, who live on the western slope of the Cascades east of Seattle; and the Duwamish, who live at and around Seattle on the western shores of Puget sound in the south Salish Sea.

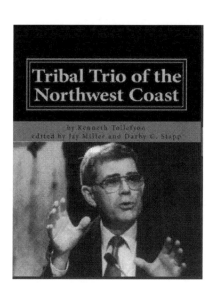

Dr. Tollefson's generosity, skill, substantial, and most useful testimony are a tribute to the wonderful traditions of university scholarship.
Durwood Zaelke, DC Staff Attorney, Sierra Club, Wilderness Society

Ken's work is engaging reading, and a big help to our cause. Bravo!
Cecile Hansen, Chair, Duwamish Tribe

Ken's work is like listening to our elders, with added graphic illustrations to help us appreciate what is culturally important.
Thomas Dalton, Tlingit, Hoonah Raven, son of George, head Eagle Chief

Ken has been an academic fighter for the Snoqualmi, through right, wrong, and justice.
Harriet Turner, Snoqualmi researcher and elder

February 2015 • 226 pages
available through Amazon.com $14.99

Journal of Northwest Anthropology
Memoir Series[1]

Memoir 6 (2002)
It's About Time (híiwes wiyéewts'etki) It's About Them (paamiláyk'ay) It's About Us (naamiláyk'ay): A Decade of Papers, 1988–1998 .... Michael S. Burney and Jeff Van Pelt, editors

Memoir 7 (2012)
Festschrift in Honor of Max G. Pavesic ....Kenneth C. Reid and Jerry R. Galm, editors
$19.99

Memoir 8 (2012)
Action Anthropology and Sol Tax in 2012: The Final Word? .... Darby C. Stapp, editor
$10.99

Memoir 9 (2014)
Rescues, Rants, and Researches: A Re-View of Jay Miller's Writings on Northwest Coast Indien Cultures ....Darby C. Stapp and Kara N. Powers, editors
$12.00

Memoir 10 (2015)
Tribal Trio of the Northwest Coast ....Kenneth D. Tollefson
$14.95

Memoir 11 (2015)
An Ethnographic Assessment of Some Cultural Landscapes in Southern Wyoming and Idaho ....Deward E. Walker Jr., Pamela Graves, Joe Ben Walker, and Dan Hutchison
$49.95

Memoir 12 (2016)
The Contemporary Coast Salish: Essays by Bruce Granville Miller .... Bruce Granville Miller and Darby C. Stapp, editors
$19.95

---

[1] The *Journal of Northwest Anthropology* publishes occasional monographs and collections under the *Memoir* series. *Memoirs* 7 through 12 are available through Amazon.com. *Memoirs* 1 through 6 appear as *Northwest Anthropological Research Notes Memoirs*; available through Coyote Press, PO Box 3377, Salinas, CA 93912. <http://www.californiaprehistory.com>

Printed in Poland
by Amazon Fulfillment
Poland Sp. z o.o., Wrocław

31103752R00201